Chapels of England

Chapels of England

Buildings of Protestant Nonconformity

Christopher Wakeling

Historic England

Published by Historic England, The Engine House, Fire Fly Avenue, Swindon SN2 2EH
www.HistoricEngland.org.uk
Historic England is a Government service championing England's heritage and giving expert, constructive advice.

First published 2017

ISBN 978-1-84802-032-0

© Christopher Wakeling 2017

The views expressed in this book are those of the author and not necessarily those of Historic England.

The right of Christopher Wakeling to be identified as author of this work has been asserted by him in accordance with the Copyright, Designs and Patents Act 1988.

Figs 3.2, 3.26, 4.3, 4.25, 4.30, 5.32, 6.7, 6.12, 6.13, 6.14, 7.4, 8.1, 8.23, 8.28, 8.32, 8.33, 8.37 and 8.39 are © of the author and Figs 3.25, 6.46 and 7.18 are from the author's collection;
Figs 2.1, 2.19, 3.20, 4.13, 4.20, 5.3, 5.4, 5.30, 5.31, 6.32, 6.41 and 8.17 are © Crown Copyright. Historic England Archive;
Figs 5.8, 6.5 and 6.6 are sourced from the Historic England Archive;
Figs 2.33, 3.16, 5.25 and 6.17 are sourced from the Historic England Archive (Christopher Stell Collection);
All other images are © Historic England Archive (unless credited otherwise in the caption).

Application for the reproduction of the Historic England Archive images should be made to Archives Services Team, Historic England, The Engine House, Fire Fly Avenue, Swindon SN2 2EH; telephone (01793) 414600.

Every effort has been made to trace the copyright holders and we apologise in advance for any unintentional omissions, which we would be pleased to correct in any subsequent edition of this book.

British Library Cataloguing in Publication data
A CIP catalogue record for this book is available from the British Library.

Brought to publication by Rachel Howard, Robin Taylor and Sarah Enticknap, Publishing, Historic England.

Typeset in Georgia Pro Light 9.5/11.75pt
Edited by Catherine Bradley
Indexed by Caroline Jones, Osprey Indexing
Page layout by Pauline Hull
Printed in the UK by Gomer Press

Frontispiece: Primitive Methodist chapel, Englesea Brook, Cheshire, as enlarged in 1832. [DP166366]

Contents

Preface

Nowadays someone wanting to illustrate the religious diversity of Britain might well choose a photograph that juxtaposes a spire and a minaret. But religious diversity is not a creation of recent times. Among the neighbours of Wren's London churches, for instance, there were places of worship for such incomers as Huguenots, Dutch Calvinists, Jews and Lutherans, and also for a range of native groups including Baptists, Independents, Presbyterians and Quakers. There was even a time, during James II's reign, when Roman Catholics erected 'mass houses'. Subsequent generations added greatly to the mix, and since the early 19th century Anglican churches in England have always been outnumbered by other places of worship. Not that the literature on our religious buildings has reflected this diversity. The present book tries to move a step closer to the time when a comprehensive history of English religious architecture can be written. It deals with the buildings of the various Protestant denominations other than the Church of England, and covers the period from the 17th century to the present. As a shorthand, these denominations are here referred to as Nonconformist.

The book aims to provide a history of Nonconformist architecture, using existing buildings wherever possible. Its examples are drawn from almost every part of England, and include some of the smallest wayside chapels as well as grand urban structures. A good deal of attention is paid to the interiors of buildings that many people know – if at all – only from the outside. In all this, photographs play an essential role, revealing places in a way that prose cannot. Despite the loss of very large numbers of chapels in the past half-century, there are still around 20,000 Nonconformist congregations in England, and so the sample of buildings included in this book is inevitably not perfectly representative.[1] An effort has been made to mention the most influential Nonconformist buildings and to give examples of the most common types. There is no implication that the chosen chapels are the best of their kind, however, and many personal favourites have had to be omitted. The chronological structure should allow the reader to follow the main architectural developments in the Nonconformist world, chapter by chapter. Plan-forms, architectural styles and internal arrangements are analysed at each stage. Denominational changes sometimes come to the fore (as with the emergence of Methodism in Chapter 3), and at other times play a secondary role. Several of the boxed essays trace aspects of worship that cut across the chronological divisions of the main text.

The early chapters of the book have to depend on the often rather limited records of lost buildings, combined with the evidence from surviving (and usually much-altered) chapels and meeting houses. Even for the first half of the 19th century it is rare to find unaltered examples, although contemporary plans and illustrations exist of some larger buildings. From around 1850 architectural records are fuller, and the later chapters of the book can draw on a greater range of source material, including architectural and denominational journals, as well as being able to illustrate a higher proportion of less-altered buildings. The long bibliography and regular footnotes hint at the debt that is owed to a yet wider range of publications.

Readers will note that two works are cited quite frequently. Christopher Stell's definitive inventories of chapels and meeting houses provide comprehensive coverage of surviving 17th- and 18th-century examples in England, as well as many later buildings.[2] *The Quaker Meeting Houses of Britain*, David Butler's catalogue of Quaker meeting houses for the Friends' Historical Society, documents all the surviving Quaker buildings and many long-lost examples.[3] Both works are indispensable, and provide a selection of plans and references. Despite such scholarship, there is still a great deal to learn and it is hoped that other researchers will be stimulated to pursue many of the topics that are only touched on in this book.

Future research

There is still much potential work to be done on the buildings of the various denominations and sects. The Unitarians and Quakers have been well treated, as has to some extent the Salvation Army, but there is no general account of Methodist buildings since 1840 nor any systematic history of the buildings of three of the oldest denominations – the Baptists, Congregationalists and Presbyterians – let alone the many younger religious movements. Recent years have seen a welcome interest in the careers of specialist Nonconformist architects (including T L Banks, James Cubitt, Thomas Howdill, James Simpson, Thomas Thomas and John Wills), and there is scope for more. A number of good local studies of chapel building have been published (Cornwall, East Yorkshire, Essex, Islington and Norfolk come to mind), while Sussex and Kent have valuable inventories of their Victorian places of worship; all of these help to inform the picture of national developments. Essential material is to be found in the countless histories of individual chapels that are based on often unique archive material. This may be the primary tier of Nonconformist history, but it is potentially the richest. Surprisingly, only a tiny number of Nonconformist buildings have been thoroughly investigated archaeologically – most notably, Goodshaw chapel, Rawtenstall – the results of which suggest that the methodology has much to teach us, especially for the oldest structures.

No less important is the story of how chapels were financed, from the guinea bricks of Sunday-school children, via the denominational chapel-building funds, to the Nonconformist squires and industrialists who paid for their local chapels. Chapel fittings are also a deserving area of study, especially as the pressure grows to remove organs, pulpits and pews. And – despite the pioneering work of Christopher Stell, John Harvey, Peter Forsaith and others – there is much more to be said about the visual and material culture of Nonconformity: chapel decoration, communion ware, ministerial portraits, libraries, Sunday-school banners and commemorative crockery. The special events of Nonconformist life (including foundation-stone ceremonies, anniversary gatherings, Sunday-school parades and outings, weddings, harvest festivals, bazaars, concerts, pantomimes, lectures, social clubs and sporting activities), at least since the advent of photography, are reflected in many pictorial histories of chapels. Ned Williams has served the Black Country especially well in this respect. Almost every one of these topics would merit a systematic study, and it is beyond the scope of the present work to attempt to cover all aspects of such a rich history.

A note on the terms used in this book

As with Protestantism as a whole, the denominations covered in this book are multifarious; no umbrella term can cover them adequately. At first they were labelled collectively as Dissenters or Nonconformists.[4] Towards the end of the 19th century the more positive concept of the Free Churches gained currency. None of these entirely fits the bill, however. Methodists especially resisted the earlier names, and the Free Church movement ultimately excluded Unitarians and other non-Trinitarian denominations. For the purposes of this book *Dissent* is generally used when referring to the late 17th and early 18th centuries, while *Free Church* is used for certain developments after about 1890. For want of any better label – and in spite of its many shortcomings – *Nonconformist* is otherwise used generically throughout.

A similar difficulty applies to the categorisation of buildings. Initially, virtually all purpose-built places of Nonconformist worship were referred to either as chapels or meeting houses. Quakers and many Puritans avoided using the word *church* for a building rather than a body of Christians. During the later 19th century, however, a small number of Nonconformist congregations began to call their buildings churches, and this became more general in the 20th century. Other names were used from time to time, among them tabernacles, citadels and central halls. Sometimes this book uses the word *chapel* as a generic term, referring to all types of Nonconformist buildings.

Another potential area of confusion concerns local groups of worshippers. In this book they are invariably referred to as congregations, although some denominations do not use the term. The Quaker equivalent, for instance, is meetings, and Wesley referred to Methodist societies. Baptists, Congregationalists and some others have always spoken of a formally constituted body of worshippers as a church – a usage which has a long pedigree, but which appears only sparingly in this book so as to avoid confusion.

In general the book uses terms that are likely to be clear to the general reader, even if they do not always correspond with usage in particular denominations or places. Nonconformists exhibit no more uniformity in their language than in their theology or forms of worship.

Acknowledgements

This book would not have come into being without the support, inspiration and stimulation of innumerable people. Long ago, Professor Stefan Muthesius encouraged my interest in Victorian chapels, and Marianne, my wife, helped me realise that Nonconformist architecture could only be understood in an international context. Then the University of East Anglia generously allowed me to spend three years researching a far-from-fashionable topic. Over subsequent decades I occasionally returned to write or speak on the subject, thanks to the invitations of such friends and colleagues as Dr Paul Barnwell, the late Professor Chris Brooks, Sarah Brown, Neil Burton, Bridget Cherry, the late Dr Colin Cunningham, Dr Jenny Freeman, the late Professor Andor Gomme, Roland Jeffery, Dr John Maddison, Dr Adam Menuge, Dr Philip Morgan, Dr Chris Skidmore and Dr Kate Tiller. Meanwhile, by fostering an interest in myriad other topics, the adult students of Keele University have done their best to keep me intellectually alert and open to fresh ways of thinking.

An essential expression of thanks must go to the people who have opened their chapels to show me around. They are the successors to generations of chapel-goers who have shaped, cared for and cherished these buildings. Another debt is to my fellow members of the Chapels Society and the Society of Architectural Historians of Great Britain, from whom I have learned so much. The same can be said of those with whom I have worked in the Methodist Church, the Baptist Union and other denominations. Of the many institutions whose staff have been at pains to help I should mention the university libraries of East Anglia, Cambridge and Keele; the British Library, the RIBA Library and Dr Williams's Library; and local libraries in Bristol, Ipswich, Leeds, Manchester, Norwich and Stoke-on-Trent.

The long list of people who have regularly shared ideas with me includes John Anderson, Professor Clyde Binfield, John H Y Briggs, the late David Barton, David Butler, Dr Sandy Calder, Dr Angela Connelly, Dr Peter Forsaith, Andy Foster, Rosalind Kaye, Stuart Leadley, Professor Ted Royle, Ian Serjeant, the late Christopher Stell and Dr David Wykes. Among the many people who have helped with particular points during the writing of this book, I must thank Dr Rod Ambler (on Lincolnshire topics), Anne Anderson (in Cheshire), John Booth (of Stoke-on-Trent), Dr Charles Brown (on Denys Hinton), Mr J Butcher (of Birmingham), the Revd Stephen Copson (on Baptist matters), Peter C Davis (Taunton), Colin Dews (on Leeds topics), John Ellis (on Kent), Dr Tim Grass (on the Strict and Particular Baptists), Chris and Lillian Harris (of Gloucestershire), Donna Cothliff (of Haslingden), Colin and Michael Howard (on Sutton), Steve Irish (of Bristol), Dr David Knight (on Blackheath), Jeremy Milln (of Stafford), Andrew J Morgan (on Jehovah's Witnesses), the Revd Tony Parkinson (on modern octagons), the late E Alan Rose (Manchester Methodism), Andrew Shepherd (of Sheffield), Roger Thorne (Exeter), Hilary Smith (on Fulneck) and Dave Watts (on Pentecostal churches). A special word of thanks must go to Trevor Cooper, whose reading of the draft text stimulated many a good idea and saved the book from several potential minefields. All the errors are my own, however.

To Sarah Brown (then of English Heritage, now at the University of York) I owe the invitation to write this book, and for supporting the project through subsequent changes at what has become Historic England I am grateful to Dr Linda Monckton. From start to finish, it has been a pleasure to work with Dr Robin Taylor and his successor Rachel Howard as editors. Likewise, I have been fortunate to work with Catherine Bradley, whose deft copy-editing has much improved the text. Finally my thanks must go to the photographers. They have regularly opened my eyes to buildings which I thought I knew, and it is their work that makes the book so special.

This book is dedicated to Marianne, without whose encouragement it would never have been begun, and without whose help it might never have been completed.

Dissenters and places of worship before 1689

In August 1657 Exeter's great cathedral was divided in two by the construction of a partition wall. Few deeds can better illustrate the contested nature of religious life in 17th-century Britain. The wall was erected because of tensions between two different Puritan groups, both of whom laid claim to the cathedral, which under the Commonwealth had lost all the trappings of ecclesiastical and royal authority. After the removal of the bishop's seat and choir stalls, the eastern part of the building had been fitted up for worship by a Presbyterian congregation, while the former nave was adapted for use by a group of Independents (or Congregationalists) as early as 1650.[1] After some years of cohabitation, the Independents insisted on the wall, which cost the considerable sum of £800. Such arrangements were not unique to Exeter. The large parish church in Great Yarmouth (Fig 1.1) was similarly divided – an Independent congregation meeting in the chancel and Presbyterian services being held in the nave – and two congregations shared the biggest church in Hull, separated by a brick wall.[2] Generally the arrangements were quickly undone after the Restoration of 1660, but sometimes the physical changes remained for many years, to be obliterated only by 19th-century restorers.

Fig 1.1
St Nicholas, Great Yarmouth, Norfolk. This vast medieval building – at about 23,000 sq ft reputedly the largest parish church in England – accommodated both Presbyterian and Independent congregations during the 1650s. [DP160150]

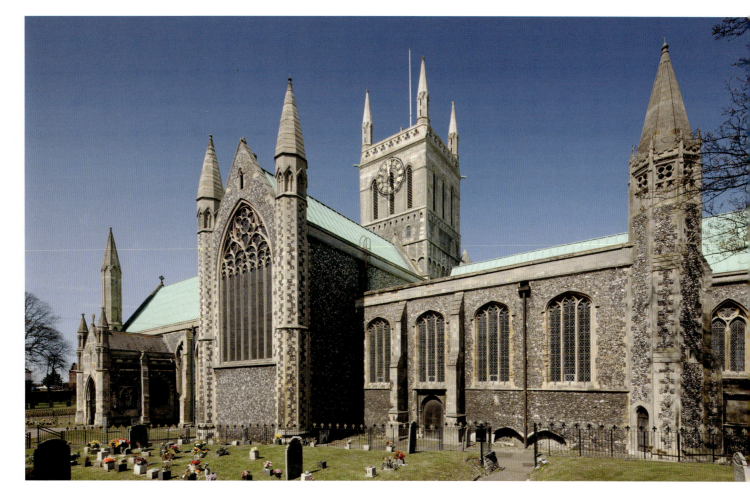

Such examples, almost always overlooked by guidebooks and mentioned with embarrassment even by some academic historians, are nonetheless illuminating. One obvious lesson to draw is that religion in Britain after the Reformation was remarkably unstable. Famously there was a continual tension between those on the one side who hoped for a return to the Church of Rome and papal authority, and those on the other who conformed to the Church of England with the monarch at its head. At any time a change of monarch could have wholly reversed the situation, as it did when Mary came to the throne and leading Protestants were burned at the stake. More commonly there were shifts of emphasis within the spectrum of Protestantism, the most radical change being the ascendancy of Presbyterianism and Independency during the Commonwealth. Some people of almost all religious persuasions spent years in self-imposed exile to avoid persecution, and there were periods when places of worship became the focus of dispute and change.

A second thing to note is that the religious spectrum in post-Reformation Britain was fairly wide. The majority of the population usually conformed to the Church of England, of course, though this ranged from people suspected of having 'popish' sympathies to those of Puritan inclination. Those who failed to conform included stalwarts who sustained their Catholic allegiance through thick and thin, and a long list of Protestant groups. As we have seen, the most conspicuous of the Protestant Dissenters in the middle years of the 17th century were Presbyterians and Independents, but Baptists and – newest of all – Quakers were also strong in places. From 1662 these four groups formed the core of Dissent or Nonconformity. (A summary account of each group is contained in the Appendix.) In addition to such native bodies there were congregations of refugees and expatriates from the Low Countries, France, Germany and Scandinavia, and after 1656 there were Jewish as well as Christian settlers. In due course all of these movements, and many that appeared only in later centuries, were to build their own places of worship.

The final point to draw from the examples of Exeter, Hull and Yarmouth is less obvious. It is that British Christians, like their continental counterparts, generally wanted to worship in existing church buildings. Not only Anglicans and Catholics assumed this attitude, but large numbers of Dissenters did too. Reformers in Britain were no less likely than their Dutch cousins – or their Lutheran contemporaries – to lay claim to medieval church buildings. For such people there was no aesthetic objection to the often splendid religious architecture of the Middle Ages. The argument was clearly expressed by a Presbyterian minister in Suffolk in 1700:

> Let none think that I have spoken a word to the derogation of the honour of those stately, magnificent and sumptuous structures, our public churches, which the Christian piety and liberality of former ages erected for the convenient assembling of particular congregations in their parochial districts every Sabbath day, together with their indowments. ... Had we the liberty of those places, we should seek no other.[3]

These views, though not universal (as we shall see), were very widely held by the groups who came to be called Nonconformists.

The years after 1689 witnessed the Nonconformists' first great campaign of building, and are the subject of Chapter 2. However, the buildings of that campaign did not emerge in a vacuum. This chapter therefore focuses on the historic roots of Nonconformist architecture.

Luther's act of nailing 95 theses to the door of the Schlosskirche in Wittenberg in 1517 is the one event that British schoolchildren might remember from the story of the Reformation. Though it was not quite so decisive an affair as, say, the Battle of Hastings, its use in our schoolbooks is telling. It shows us that the story of the Reformation cannot be understood without recourse to continental events. Luther, Calvin and Zwingli are essential figures, even if Knox, Browne and Fox have significant roles as well. As in theology, so in architecture: the British Reformers were conscious of international developments. In the 16th century the arrival of Protestant refugees provided some English cities with the first demonstration of fully reformed practice. In London, for instance, Edward VI gave the nave of the former Augustinian church in Austin Friars to a congregation of Protestant refugees, predominantly Dutch and Flemish, who fitted it out for their needs.[4] The preaching of the word was central, and so a pulpit was attached to one of the nave piers, with pews set out around it for the congregation. If it followed Dutch precedent we can imagine that women sat closest to the preacher, with men sitting or standing around the perimeter of the seated area. There was a raised place – *'opt hoighte'* – on which anyone accused of breaking church rules would stand while their offences and their penances were announced from the pulpit. It was at Austin Friars that the Dutch Calvinist practice of sitting around a table to receive communion was introduced into England. While the building was being prepared, the Dutch worshipped in the chapel of the former hospital of St Anthony, Threadneedle Street, which subsequently became the home of a French Calvinist congregation.

Another example of this process was to be found in Norwich, which experienced a huge influx of refugees fleeing religious persecution in the Low Countries, especially after the 1560s. As in London, an old monastery provided a convenient place in which the Dutch could worship; in Norwich it was the former church of the Blackfriars or Dominicans (Fig 1.2).[5] Thus the preaching-centred services of the Dutch Calvinists were housed in a building designed for the needs of the oldest of the preaching orders. Before 1625 Norwich's Dutch seem to have worshipped in the former nave, using only 'their own chairs, which they caused to be removed every time, the same day or next'.[6] This brings to mind Bruegel's painting of the *Battle Between Carnival and Lent* (of 1559), which portrays a throng of faithful citizens leaving church, several of them bearing aloft chairs that they have taken to church to avoid having to stand during long sermons. The acoustics and sightlines of large churches of the late Middle Ages may have been good for preachers, but congregational seating had not always been so great a priority. After 1625 Norwich's Dutch moved into the former chancel of the Blackfriars' church, which they fitted up with seats. Disappointingly, no early illustrations seem to have survived of the ways in which these communities of 'strangers' adapted their late medieval surroundings for Reformed worship. Yet there are numerous reminders of their presence, such as the memorial to the Dutch pastor Joannis Elison and to the son who succeeded him in Norwich.

The exchange of ideas with the continent was not dependent on these incomers, however. Many British churchmen went abroad, often when changes of regime left them vulnerable to persecution at home. To take one example, John Knox, chaplain to Edward VI, went overseas at the accession of Mary I in 1553. In Geneva he met Calvin and in 1556 became minister to an

Fig 1.2
The great preaching church of the former Blackfriars or Dominican monastery in Norwich. In 1540 it was sold to the city, which allowed a congregation of Dutch Calvinists to worship here – first in the nave and after 1625 in the chancel (just visible on the right). [DP160402]

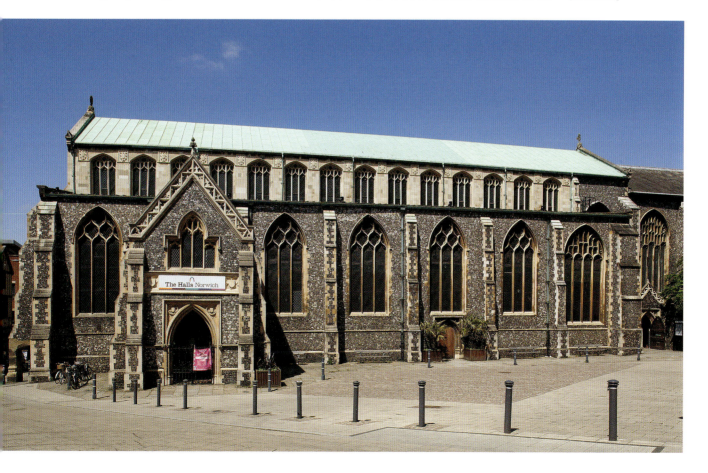

English congregation in the 13th-century church of Notre-Dame-la-Neuve, where he entered into the busy round of preaching-centred worship entailing three or more sermons each week.[7] Three years later Knox returned from exile and helped to compose a handbook for the new Scottish church. That handbook, the *First Book of Discipline* (1560), describes Reformed worship as requiring 'a bell to convocate the people together, a pulpit, a basin for baptising, and tables for ministration of the Lord's Supper'.[8] This prescription sets the scene for many places of Protestant worship: a single space in which the congregation can conveniently gather to hear the preaching of the word, witness baptisms and share communion.

A different example of exile is offered by Robert Browne, an English reformer who is generally seen as one of the founders of Independency or Congregationalism. Browne was powerfully affected by the idea that churches should be free from any kind of state control, and that each congregation should determine its own life and order. Following imprisonment for setting up a separatist church in Norwich in 1581, Browne sought refuge in the Dutch town of Middelburg, just when the 1579 Union of Utrecht had established freedom of worship across the United Provinces of the Netherlands. Browne's followers in Middelburg met for worship in his own house rather than a borrowed church building, but were able to do so openly, free from the persecution that caused many separatists in Britain to gather only with great secrecy.[9] Moreover, Browne's congregations would have had the chance to see some of the many kinds of worship that were to be found in various architectural settings in the liberal Netherlands.

After the succession of James VI of Scotland to the English throne as James I in 1603, the momentum of Puritan emigration gathered pace. In Amsterdam in 1607 an English Reformed congregation was established in the brick-built chapel of the former Béguine (a semi-monastic sisterhood), which had been closed for some 30 years, and a little later an English Reformed congregation was granted use of the former St Peter's church in Rotterdam.[10] These congregations were in many ways an English-speaking counterpart of the Dutch Reformed Church, and their access to redundant medieval church buildings was sometimes officially sanctioned – rather like the granting of former monastic buildings to Dutch refugees in London and Norwich. At the same time, however, there were groups reflecting

a wider spectrum of British religion in the Netherlands. English separatist congregations, followers of Robert Browne, were particularly evident in Amsterdam. In 1608 members of a church from the Nottinghamshire village of Scrooby briefly joined the Amsterdam Brownists, before moving to Leiden a year later. These Scrooby exiles, led by John Robinson, produced the core of the Pilgrim Fathers, who sailed from Europe in 1620 to establish a new society and ultimately to build new places of worship.

Back in Jacobean Britain religion continued to be a deeply contentious area of public life. Catholic hopes of advance were badly served by the Gunpowder Plot of 1605. Conversely the Scottish church – Presbyterian since Knox's day – had episcopacy imposed upon it in 1612. South of the border, despite the harrying of Dissenters, there were many strongholds where the Church of England was of strict Calvinistic character. Sheffield was one such town. For some 65 years between 1597 and 1662, all of Sheffield's clergy were Puritans (interrupted only when Royalist forces briefly held the town in 1643–4).[11] One vicar was thought to have been a follower of Robert Browne's separatist ideas, and another espoused the Presbyterian cause. In Sheffield, as in most places, shifts of theological emphasis were literally accommodated within the walls of the medieval parish church. This was not an era when many people ventured to build churches.

Among the relatively few new places of worship from the Jacobean period is a chapel a few miles from Liverpool. It was built for the people of an isolated hamlet that was created when new farmland was set out. Toxteth Park chapel – now known as the Ancient Chapel of Toxteth (Figs 1.3 and 1.4) – was built by 1618. Its minister was Richard Mather, a convinced Puritan, who migrated to Massachusetts in 1635 and took a leading part in shaping Congregationalism in New England. The Toxteth chapel continued to foster reforming views and, after maintaining its uncertain ecclesiastical status for some time, was licensed as a Presbyterian meeting house in 1672. Because the building was extensively rebuilt in the 1770s, we have frustratingly slight evidence of its original appearance. It seems to have been constructed of stone, and comprised a rectangular space, large enough for the local community to gather conveniently around the pulpit. We can only guess at the layout of pulpit and seats, though there might have been a gallery from quite early.

This was not all, however, for, as Christopher Stell has noted, the chapel seems to have had a

Fig 1.3
Ancient Chapel of Toxteth, Liverpool. Built in the reign of James I (1603–1625), this may be the oldest surviving English chapel to have been erected by forerunners of the Nonconformists.
[DP166652]

Fig 1.4
Interior of the Ancient Chapel of Toxteth, Liverpool. Although the Jacobean chapel was substantially rebuilt in the 18th century, the 'chancel' arch is apparently original and the foreground pew door is dated 1650.
[DP166656]

chancel-like projection, presumably for the communion table.[12] If so, it can be inferred that the chapel had permanent provision for communion, rather than the temporary setting up of a table in the nave as was then common in Britain. The boldly pointed 'chancel' arch is apparently the one original feature in what is now a round-arched building, so quite possibly the chapel's architectural details were originally Gothic. All in all, Jacobean Toxteth seems to suggest that Puritans strove for decorous architecture, even in out-of-the-way locations, and that they had no special reason to dissociate themselves from the Gothic habits of medieval church building.

During the 1630s life in England became increasingly difficult for those on the Puritan wing of the church. Charles I and Archbishop Laud promoted High Churchmen, and more strictly Calvinist clergy either managed to conform or else resigned. The diaspora of British Protestants grew, especially in the Netherlands and New England. It was in the 1630s in Massachusetts that the term 'meeting house' entered the English language. In early Puritan settlements in America the communal building usually served as a place for secular meetings as well as worship (some, indeed, also acted as forts or garrisons). The name thus naturally expresses the idea of a multipurpose place for gatherings, and avoids any hint of being consecrated or, even worse, dedicated to a saint. Like the settlers' other buildings in New England, these meeting houses were invariably of timber, since wood was conveniently to hand and the skills of carpentry were more commonly found than those of the mason. Meeting houses were generally fitted out with fixed benches and sometimes galleries, as appropriate for a town meeting as for a sermon-centred congregational service. None of the earliest examples has survived, but their widespread presence in the 1630s is well attested. By happy coincidence the first known reference, dating from 1631/2, is to a 'new meeting house' at Dorchester, MA, the very town in which Richard Mather of Toxteth was to settle in 1635.[13]

Most accounts of English places of worship during the 1640s and 1650s emphasise destruction. Bombardment in the Civil War left a few places half ruined, and some parliamentary soldiers ransacked cathedrals where they were stationed. In an attempt to cleanse churches of idolatrous images, many remaining carvings of saints were toppled and countless stained-glass windows smashed. And from a desire to undo the High Church transformations of Archbishop Laud's reign, altar rails were stripped away in parish churches across the land. This, understandably, was a time that High Churchmen loathed. Yet for the many Protestants who had suffered under the former regime, it was a period of hope and even liberation. A good number of Baptist congregations (perhaps two hundred by 1660) emerged from the shadows, and George Fox embarked on the path that was to lead to the foundation of Quakerism.[14]

For the Presbyterians and Independents, however, there was the possibility of yet greater prominence. A clear example is provided by William Bridge, who had been removed from his post as a curate in Norwich by Matthew Wren in 1636 and in the same year sailed to Rotterdam, where he became pastor of the English church. He returned to England in 1641, becoming town preacher in Great Yarmouth, where he organised an Independent church with a congregation largely composed of others who had returned from the Netherlands.[15] This congregation was one of the two for whom Yarmouth's parish church was fitted up for worship (*see* p 1). Bridge also served an Independent congregation gathered in the Norwich church of St George, Tombland (Fig 1.5). St George's church proved inadequate for the large number of Norwich people wishing to hear Bridge's preaching, and so a gallery was constructed across the chancel, close to the centrally sited pulpit.[16] No picture of this arrangement is known, but an approximation of it may be gained from the interior of Whitby parish church, where a probably grander gallery cuts across the chancel arch, allowing its occupants a clear view of the pulpit (and the *back* of the preacher's head).

William Bridge was an influential figure in Cromwell's England, often preaching in London and taking a strong role in national negotiations over religious affairs. Among much else, he had a hand in the decision to allow Jews to settle in Britain in 1656. He was one of the most prominent of the Independents, whose cause was well supported in many parts of Britain. But generally at this time the Presbyterians were dominant (some hoped for a unified church north and south of the Scottish border) and more often occupied the pulpits of Commonwealth Britain. Bury St Edmunds illustrates one effect of this: the town had two parish churches, by then referred to as 'parish meeting-houses', and both were used by Presbyterian congregations. The Independents complained to Cromwell and the

Fig 1.5
St George, Tombland,
Norwich. Strikingly close to
the cathedral, this medieval
church was a stronghold of
William Bridge, a leading
Independent minister of the
mid-17th century.
[DP168485]

Council of State of the unfairness of this, as they had to pay rent to hold their services in the shire hall. They asked permission to use one of the two church buildings, or at least 'the chancel of Mary's parish' which might be partitioned off 'from the body of the meeting-house'.[17] This concession, had it been offered, would have resulted in an arrangement like those in Yarmouth, Hull and Exeter. Thus Bury offers further evidence for these two main groups competing to use the traditional places of worship, albeit ones newly named in the American way.

To find new places of worship that reflected the Puritan spirit of the day, we can turn to Yorkshire, where two chapels were erected around 1650 for squires of apparently Presbyterian inclination. The chapel at Bramhope, called by Pevsner 'one of the most valuable of *incunabula* of Protestant or Puritan ecclesiastical planning in England', has claimed an important place in the history of Nonconformist architecture, even though its ecclesiastical status was ambiguous.[18] It was built in 1649 as a type of private chapel for Robert Dyneley of Bramhope Hall, in whose grounds it stood. Even in its present surroundings, by the entrance to a hotel 4 miles from Otley, it retains a special charm (Fig 1.6). Bramhope chapel is a long, low building, neatly constructed of local stone and – at least now – with a shallow, stone-flagged roof. John Knox would be pleased to see a bellcote on the west gable. There are no Gothic features, but nor is there evidence of Renaissance classicism: the two doors have gently curved heads and a rhythm of similar curves links the stone mullions within the rectangular windows. The long south front is approximately symmetrical, implying a desire for visual effect as well as practicality. On entering one immediately senses that this was a place in which to sit listening to sermons (Fig 1.7). Each side of a central gangway is a range of seating, the oldest of which includes some stout benches, a box pew with ball finials and another with carved decoration. Otherwise the pews are largely 18th century. Perhaps at first the congregation mostly had benches, with enclosed pews for the more important members of the community. The one square pew that seems to be original is directly opposite the pulpit, which stands not quite halfway along the north wall, flanked by two windows to help light the preacher's texts and with a canopy to assist the acoustics, as well as to dignify the preacher's role.

All this attests to the central part played by sermons. Yet communion was also important, even if – as was then usual among Protestants – it was celebrated less frequently. The central gangway leads eastwards to a special space, lit by the chapel's largest window, where a wooden communion table must originally have stood. In its place now is a stone altar with railings, dating from the 19th century when the chapel was in Anglican use.[19] A similar, though architecturally more showy, chapel was built near Barnsley, for Sir Edward Rodes of Great Houghton Hall. The original plan of Great Houghton chapel, said to have been built in 1650, closely resembled that of Bramhope, but there were significant changes in 1957–64.[20]

The Bramhope and Great Houghton plans – thin rectangles, with no structural separation into nave and chancel, and with the pulpit against a long wall amid the congregation – are not the most obvious shape for auditory places of worship. Compact plans, such as the squarish one at Burntisland church in Fife, seem better calculated to accommodate a congregation gathered around a pulpit. A possible source for the Bramhope type lies in the ways that long, sometimes narrow, medieval churches were adapted after the Reformation. Making the pulpit a focal point of such long buildings logically led to a position almost halfway along, and the eastern space could still be used for communion without the need for a chancel. In the Netherlands such layouts were created by the Dutch Reformers in relatively small medieval churches (for example at Tinallinge, Oudega and Niebert).[21] Newly built Dutch churches of the 17th century normally avoided the biaxial layout, however, preferring a closer coupling of pulpit and communion area, often within a less elongated plan-form. And in that respect, most Dissenters – and some Anglicans – in England and Wales were to do the same. Bramhope's plan is rooted in the Middle Ages while bearing the germ of some later developments, a point which can also be made of its exterior. Southern doors had ample precedent in Britain, where the south porch was generally the chief entrance to a church, and many churches had a secondary (priest's) door in the south wall of the chancel. But there is greater visual balance between the pair of entry points at Bramhope, and in effect the long wall is a regular façade, anticipating what was to become a leitmotif of much chapel architecture.

When Charles II took the throne in 1660 he did so with a promise of religious toleration, but within two years the situation was wholly transformed. The 1662 Act of Uniformity, which

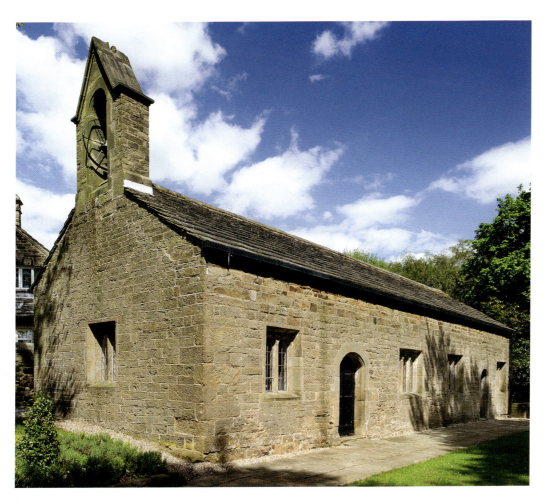

Fig 1.6
Although the walls and
roof were raised slightly
in the 19th century,
Bramhope remains one
of the key buildings for
our understanding of
Puritan chapel architecture
around 1650.
[DP16626]

Fig 1.7
The central position of
the pulpit at Bramhope
underlines the vital
importance that Puritans
attached to preaching,
while the elongated
east–west plan provided
a seemly, and separate,
focal point for communion
services.
[DP166265]

insisted on episcopal ordination and compelled clergy to assent to everything in the revised Book of Common Prayer, led to the resignation or removal of more than 2,000 ministers from parish churches.[22] Around 200 of these men were Independents, and some 20 were Baptists. A great many of the others were Presbyterians, but probably the largest number were 'mere Puritans who had hitherto eschewed sectarian labels'.[23] Even in Scotland, episcopacy was imposed. From this point, with most Presbyterians and Independents – as well as Baptists and Quakers – outside the walls of the Church of England, it is possible to identify all four of these broad groups as Dissenters or Nonconformists. Many determined congregations endeavoured to gather privately in houses or hired halls. The minister ejected from St Stephen's Walbrook, London, for instance, was able to worship with his flock in the great hall of Crosby Place, thanks to a Presbyterian patron.[24] In 1664, however, the screw was tightened by the first Conventicle Act, which prohibited more than four people from worshipping together except for Anglican services. Though the Act lapsed in 1669, a second Act was passed into law a year later and new means of enforcing the law were introduced. Ironically, persecution probably increased a congregation's sense of itself as a gathered community of believers, a concept which (in contrast to the idea of a parish) underpinned the thinking of Independents, Baptists and Quakers.

Despite enduring the lion's share of suffering, it was the newly founded Quakers who proved the most resolute of builders in these penal times. Perhaps this was partly because they, unlike many other Dissenters, had no strong ambition to return to worship in the great parish churches. The history of their first premises in London is one of unusual determination.[25] From 1655 Quakers leased a large medieval hall behind the Bull and Mouth Inn near Aldersgate, reportedly capable of holding 1,000 people – presumably standing. As well as meetings for worship, it also accommodated what in effect were the central offices of Quakerism. When this was destroyed in the Great Fire of 1666, a lease was taken on rooms in Devonshire House, an Elizabethan mansion just outside the city wall in Bishopsgate. Because these rooms were of limited size, Quakers also built a new meeting house in 1668 off Gracechurch Street in the heart of the city, where the White Hart Inn had stood until the Fire. Gracechurch Street meeting house was quite large, some 40 feet by 50 feet (12.2m by

15.2m), and the city authorities unsuccessfully attempted to have it demolished. It survived, however, and Quakers continued to worship on the site until the 1860s.[26] Meanwhile, building plots became available at Devonshire House in 1677, and one was acquired for a substantial new Quaker meeting house (of 1678). This building was roughly the same size as that in Gracechurch Street, although – out of a determination to provide better ventilated premises – its main chamber was an impressive 19 feet (5.8m) high, and even its first-floor meeting room was 13 feet (4m) high.

In Bristol the Quakers used two or three premises before 1670, when they embarked on a purpose-built place of worship, apparently twice as large as either of the London examples.[27] Its site was part of a former Dominican monastery, and James Millerd's 1673 plan of Bristol depicts one end of the new meeting house: a two-storey building, three-bays wide, with corner pilasters and a parapet or cornice, all topped by a steep hipped roof with a large lantern. The drawing hints at a design ultimately derived from recent French – or maybe Dutch – architecture, even if only as interpreted by an artisan builder. It was the enterprise of a substantial and socially significant congregation: the approach to the meeting house was sometimes blocked by the coaches of well-heeled Quakers.[28] Congestion must also have occurred inside the building, for the original gallery on the north side was supplemented by another on the west in 1676, a third on the south in 1688 and the fourth in 1693. Quakers, having no paid ministers and no sacraments, had no need for pulpit, communion table or font. The original seating in Bristol seems to have been of movable benches which were probably set out to face the stand – a raised platform the width of one wall on which sat Quakers with a recognised aptitude for ministry. By the end of the century some of the benches were provided with backs. The building was fully used, with a partitioned space for weekday worship as well as a schoolroom, meeting rooms and the caretaker's flat. It was demolished and a larger successor was erected on the same site in 1749. An interesting comparison can be made with the Quakers' oldest surviving purpose-built meeting house, that at Hertford (Fig 1.8), which opened in 1670 – the same year as the Bristol example.[29] It was soundly built of red brick, but its twin-gabled façade shows no hint of classicism. The suggestion has been made that it was designed so as to be capable of conversion into houses, if necessary.

Fig 1.8
This Quaker meeting house in Hertford, 1670, is the Quakers' oldest surviving purpose-built meeting house. Originally the façade – with twin doors and deeper ground-floor windows – would have been a little more imposing.
[DP160135]

That the Quakers were exceptional in building during the often bitter years of the Restoration has to be reiterated. Matters eased in 1672, however, when a Declaration of Indulgence allowed Dissenters to worship without interference, provided that the minister and the meeting place were licensed. The opportunity was brief, for the Declaration was withdrawn in 1673, but more than 1,600 ministers were registered and more than twice that number of buildings.[30] The halls of the guilds and the London companies were often identified in this way, as were numerous private houses. Some Presbyterians opposed participation, arguing that the process consolidated their separation from the national church, while some other groups refused to co-operate on the grounds that the state had no right to control religion. But most denominations took advantage of the Act to worship more openly, and a good few congregations built. The Independents of Great Yarmouth, one of the two congregations that had worshipped in the parish church until 1661, collected £800 for a new meeting house in 1673. It was a large place, 50 feet by 60 feet (15.2m by 18.3m), with a gallery around, six seats deep.[31]

Meanwhile in Leeds a stately chapel had been erected by the Presbyterians in 1672. Ralph Thoresby, a distinguished member of the congregation, described it as having 'a row of pillars and arches, *more ecclesiarum*'.[32] This emphasis on churchiness perhaps reflects the Presbyterians' reluctant Nonconformity (Thoresby was in fact later to join the Church of England). Whether or not this is the case, the two-storey chapel built for the Presbyterians of Leeds was a prepossessing piece of architecture, almost certainly more elaborate even than the Quaker meeting house in Bristol. As Richard Hewlings has observed, 'Presbyterian godliness and sobriety did not preclude architectural display'.[33] Giant Tuscan pilasters gave a bold classical rhythm to its elevations, and from the centre of its broad, seven-bay front projected a tower-like entrance block topped by a lantern (or possibly small belfry?) stage.[34] The design may have been informed by recent Dutch architecture, and made a significant contribution to the townscape of Leeds, as William Lodge's sketch of *c* 1680 records. An even larger meeting house was constructed for the Presbyterians in Taunton in 1672, notable for its plan which resembled a capital T, the pulpit being at the junction.[35] T-plans for places of worship possibly came from the Netherlands, but are more strongly associated with Scotland.[36] The most prominent example must have been Edinburgh's Tron church, built in 1636–47 for a congregation ejected from St Giles when it became a cathedral. That the Dissenters of Taunton employed such a plan is evidence that at least some English chapel builders were open to new plan-forms as early as the 1670s.

It is worth dwelling on the examples from Bristol, Leeds and Taunton, even though all three buildings have long since been replaced, because they show that urban congregations often had architectural expectations as well as practical needs. Indeed, the fact that each building was superseded by more up-to-date designs in later centuries rather underlines the point. But the loss of these and so many other important urban meeting houses of early date has sometimes skewed the history of Nonconformist architecture, emphasising the charming and the

vernacular at the expense of the stately and the architecturally polite. In a mirror image of this process, the Anglican legacy of vernacular church buildings was almost written out of history by the end of the 19th century. So far as Nonconformity is concerned, Quakers seem to have been responsible for a high proportion of the newly built rural meeting houses before 1689. And such a country place of worship, designed without reference to the latest architectural fashions, provides the final example of this chapter.

One of the most famous of the early Quaker meeting houses is at Brigflatts, near Sedbergh, nowadays in Cumbria (Figs 1.9 and 1.10). The rugged landscape between the Yorkshire Dales and the Lake District was fruitful territory for George Fox's itinerant preaching in the 1650s. His followers there at first met privately, but in 1674 they determined to build a meeting house at Brigflatts, a small hamlet of flax weavers in the bottom of the valley.[37] The process was very much a community effort: local Quakers donated and transported building materials, and helped

Fig 1.9
Quaker meeting house at Brigflatts, near Sedbergh, 1675. A robustly vernacular building of local stone, it is quite different from the Quakers' (slightly earlier) grand meeting house in Bristol.
[DP143728]

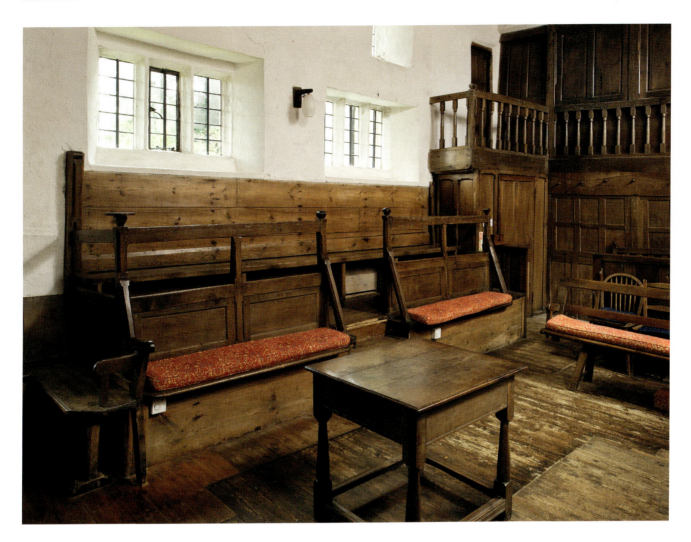

Fig 1.10
Interior of the Quaker meeting house, Brigflatts. The two-tiered stand of oak was for those Quakers who would play a leading role in the worship.
[DP143725]

with the construction. And at first sight it might be taken for one of the area's whitewashed farmhouses: sturdily built of stone and with small, mullioned, south-facing windows under dripmoulds.[38] Such features reflect an intimate understanding of the local climate and the possibilities of local materials. But the meeting house was far from being the humblest of local buildings. The two-storey porch lends it a little status, as well as giving protection from the weather, and the stone-flagged roof is said to have been one of the first local instances where thatch was not used. When the meeting house opened in 1675 there was a wooden gallery only on the west side, but the window rhythm suggests that a larger gallery was anticipated, and indeed in 1714 galleries were added to the east and north, along with a staircase. Under the two middle windows is the stand, facing a range of benches, the backs of which were added in 1720. In the 20th century Brigflatts came to represent a certain ideal of early Quakerism,

inspiring the meeting house at Letchworth Garden City and giving the title to two poems by Basil Bunting, whose gravestone is in the burial ground at Brigflatts.[39]

Looking back

Since the late 17th century, generations of Nonconformists have been brought up with stories of their predecessors' struggles. Accounts of Elizabethan Dissenters suffering years of harsh imprisonment without trial, or of the brutal breaking up of worship during Charles II's reign, have become part of the narrative by which Baptists, Independents, Presbyterians and Quakers define themselves. Knowledge of those sufferings has also coloured many interpretations of the Nonconformists' architectural legacy. R W Dale claimed that early chapels and meeting houses were 'mean buildings in obscure places', and that this was partly through fear of

Graveyards and memorials

Even before the 1689 Act of Toleration, many Nonconformist congregations had created their own graveyards. At Brigflatts in Cumbria, for instance, Quaker burials began in 1656, 18 years before construction of the meeting house, while in Tewkesbury, Gloucestershire the Dissenters' burial ground was in use by about 1680 (so probably predating the creation of the adjacent Baptist chapel). Securing decent burial places and avoiding the interference of hostile parish clergy in funerals continued to be a priority for most Nonconformists until well after 1689. Only in 1880 did non-Anglicans gain the right to conduct burial services in parish churchyards. In London, Bunhill Fields had been available for Nonconformist burials since the late 17th century, but it was not until the 19th century – when private and municipal cemeteries became common, at least in large urban areas – that the situation eased more generally, and many chapel graveyards were closed or fell out of use.

In general, there is nothing distinctive about Nonconformist burial grounds. For instance, at Cote Baptist chapel, Oxfordshire, a range of 18th-century headstones and table tombs can be seen, very much as in a parish churchyard. Some are relatively plain, but others are carved with lively motifs. By the late Georgian years a wider repertoire of monuments began to appear, and the burial grounds of some 19th-century chapels bear ample witness to the monumental mason's art. Obelisks, crosses, pedestals and urns are often found, and more complicated designs are not unknown. Two denominations deliberately broke with such habits, however: the Quakers and Moravians.

The graves of many early Quakers were marked by table tombs or headstones, sometimes inscribed with elaborate epitaphs. Though a few such examples survive (for example at Scotton, near Knaresborough in Yorkshire) the majority were removed after 1717, when the movement's Yearly Meeting described the erection of memorials as a vain custom. For long after, Quaker burial plots were recognisable only by a mound of soil. In the 1850s, however, it was thought best to avoid future confusion by marking the site of each burial with a small headstone of a standard shape, bearing only the deceased's name, age and date of death. Thereafter such headstones were widely employed for new Quaker burials, and in some places were also introduced over previously unmarked plots, including that of William Penn at Jordans, Buckinghamshire.

The gravestones of William Penn, Isaac Penington and other early Quakers at Jordans, Buckinghamshire. [DP160115]

Grave markers at the Moravian settlement at Ockbrook, Derbyshire, where the burial ground was consecrated in 1752.
[DP160636]

Moravians have a much longer tradition of understated, egalitarian, gravestones, and those at Ockbrook, Derbyshire are characteristic. Small, rectangular slabs lie flat in the turf, each inscribed with the name and dates of the deceased. They are arranged not in family groups, but according to the community's categories: married women in one area and married men in another, with further sections for children and unmarried adults of either sex.

Until the Cemeteries Clauses Act of 1847 intramural burials were permitted, and many old chapels and meeting houses have wall monuments that record such interments. Ministers were often honoured in this way, as were other influential or wealthy members of the congregation. By way of example, Norwich's Octagon chapel (*see* pp 55–6) has several notable instances, including a charming memorial to Sarah Petty, carved by Thomas Rawlins and dated 1751. The desire for commemorative tablets in chapels did not entirely end with the 1847 ban on intramural burials, however. Some interesting late Victorian memorials can be found (for example at Wesley's chapel in City Road, London), and very many chapels have memorials to the First World War.†

The ornate memorial to Sarah Petty in the Octagon chapel, Norwich, sculpted by Thomas Rawlins.
[DP160146]

magistrates and the mob, and partly because of the apprehension – long after 1662 – that 'new political convulsions' might deprive congregations of their buildings.[40] Dale's views, which have been shared by other commentators, are plausible, yet they should be treated with care. Some of the places of worship erected for Dissenters after 1662 probably *were* mean, but others were impressive enough, as we have seen. And, while some were located in what Dale called 'obscure places' (a characteristic also of some Wren churches, it might be noted), others were certainly prominent.

Giving a rounded account of the Nonconformists' pre-toleration-era buildings is not easy, however. Of the buildings that have gone, there are precious few depictions and virtually no interior views. A tiny number of surviving buildings from the first half of the 17th century can claim to have been built for Puritan worship, and each has been sufficiently altered to pose questions of interpretation. From the period between 1662 and 1687, at least a dozen purpose-built Quaker meeting houses (besides a few early adaptations of secular buildings) remain in some form, but none of the major urban examples – such as in London or Bristol – is among them. For the Baptists, Independents and Presbyterians, no surviving purpose-built places of worship seem to date from the reigns of Charles or James II, and only one or two adapted premises.

Some general points can be made, however. First, it seems that there was no flight from Gothic architecture. Toxteth hints at the continued use of pointed arches in the Jacobean period, and Puritans vied with each other to use medieval cathedrals and churches during the Commonwealth. By the 1670s – if not before – classical elements were employed for major chapels and meeting houses, though many smaller buildings were vernacular. So far as plan-types were concerned, the nave-and-chancel pattern generally gave way to rectangular, single-chamber buildings. The elements emerged of what was to become a familiar format: one long wall treated as the façade with a symmetrical arrangement of windows and entrances, and the interior dominated by a pulpit that stood (perhaps between a pair of windows) against the far wall. Other types existed, of course, and it is possible that Taunton's T-shaped meeting house was not the sole instance of more novel plans. Quaker interiors had ranks of benches facing a stand, and all denominations used galleries wherever required. It was not merely a matter of bringing people within sight and sound of the pulpit, but also of shaping a gathered community of worshippers. The idea of a gathered church, theologically fundamental for the Independents, was increasingly the reality for all Nonconformist congregations after the 1662 ejection and the persecution that ensued.

2

The age of toleration

In the late 1680s the seesaw of British religious history tilted first one way, as James II inclined the state towards Roman Catholicism, and then another, as the combined weight of William and Mary returned the balance firmly in favour of Protestantism. When James II's 1687 Declaration of Indulgence extended rights of worship to everyone, some Nonconformists took the opportunity to build new premises, but most were suspicious of James's Catholic motives. William and Mary posed no such threat, however: he was rooted in Dutch Calvinism and she was firmly Anglican. In the spring of 1689 their Act of Toleration was passed, preventing Roman Catholics from worshipping freely, but confirming the rights of all other Nonconformists – except Unitarians – to worship without penalty or disturbance. In England and Wales it came to be recognised that the Church of England would retain its bishops, as a result of which most Presbyterians resigned themselves to the status of Nonconformists. In Scotland, however, where the established church became Presbyterian once more in 1690, it was the Episcopalians who were to feel excluded. Protestant Dissenters (that is, Nonconformists) in England soon registered thousands of buildings for worship. Mostly these were houses or hired accommodation, but gradually, once congregations had gained confidence in the efficacy of the Act, a new generation of purpose-built chapels and meeting houses began to appear.

Manchester provides a good illustration of these times. In the 1650s the pulpit of what is now Manchester Cathedral had been occupied by Henry Newcome, a gifted and much-respected Presbyterian minister who continued ministering to groups of followers through the subsequent decades of hardships and penal persecution.[1] Once James II's Declaration of Indulgence had been published in 1687 Newcome grasped the opportunity to preach openly, and attracted a large congregation at a friend's barn. This makeshift arrangement continued for a few years after the accession of William and Mary. The barn's inadequacies eventually became acute, however, and in 1693 Newcome's followers decided to erect a new place of worship. The foundations were laid on 18 July 1693 amid 'many curses and reproaches': as Newcome's diary records, there was no shortage of 'ill-willers and ill-wishers'.[2]

It was to be a large building – so much so that Newcome worried about safety as the massive roof took shape – and appears to have had some fine classical detailing, including a Venetian window. It was not cheap: after a Jacobite mob ripped out the seats in 1715, £1,500 was awarded as compensation for the damage. For the opening service on 24 June 1694 Newcome preached on 'Holiness to the Lord', from Exodus 28: 36. This choice of text suggests an emphasis on the architectural propriety of the new chapel, while also implying that the Dissenters were still like God's people in the wilderness. The chapel was in fact erected on part of a meadow, but it was precisely the area in which fashionable Manchester was to build during the next few decades. The building was certainly not hidden away; within 15 years St Anne's church was built for Anglican use just a hundred yards away. Cross Street chapel, as it became known, prospered and was a landmark for Manchester's liberal Nonconformists until its reconstruction after severe bomb damage in the Second World War.

Urban buildings to c 1711

In the decades after 1689 purpose-built Nonconformist buildings became a significant feature of virtually every major town and city in England. As in Manchester, many of these were conspicuous. Urban sites of sufficient size were often most readily obtainable away from the medieval core, and it was a common occurrence for new meeting houses to be erected in what soon became smart residential quarters. In Birmingham, for instance, John Pemberton, the Quaker ironmaster who developed the town's fashionable Old Square from 1697, sold a nearby site to the Quakers for their new meeting house. This building, opened in 1703, fronted directly on to Bull Street and was later described as 'a large convenient place, and notwithstanding the plainness of the [Quaker] profession,

rather elegant'.[3] It no longer survives, but both York and Norwich do still have early Nonconformist buildings in streets of high-quality early Georgian houses.

The Presbyterian (now Unitarian) meeting house (1692–3) in St Saviourgate, York (Figs 2.1 and 2.2), stands out for its compact cruciform shape.[4] Four neat arms extend from a low, square crossing-tower capped by a pyramid roof, the effect being heightened by the absence of external

Fig 2.1
Presbyterian (now Unitarian) meeting house, St Saviourgate, York, built in 1692–3. It was designed for a distinguished congregation in what was to become one of the handsomest streets in early Georgian York.
[YC03605]

ornament. Its plan clearly expresses the idea of a Christian church, without evoking the religion of the Gothic era. Nothing quite like it is known to have been built in England at the time, although many Dutch, Scandinavian and Scottish churches were built on cruciform plans in the 17th century.[5] Thomas Colton, the Presbyterian minister in York, had recently graduated in Leiden, and inspiration for the Greek-cross plan probably came from the Netherlands.[6] As in most of the other early Protestant examples of such a Greek-cross plan, the pulpit was set at one angle of the crossing; this placed the minister in clear view of the congregation, and thereby reconciled the symbolism of the cross with the practical needs of preaching-centred worship. Box pews filled the ground floor, with a small gallery above the entrance. Communion services focused on the north-west arm of the meeting house, where there seems originally to have been a table. Worshippers perhaps sat around this to receive communion, or the bread and wine may have been taken to communicants in their seats. The building was the creation of an influential congregation, including several distinguished families who had guarded the flame of Presbyterianism

in York since the 1660s. Lady Hewley occupied a prominent pew near the pulpit, and many succeeding worshippers are commemorated around the building. The monument to Rachel Sandercock (of 1790), with its classical figure of a widow reading beside a funerary urn, aptly represents the learned tradition associated with York's now-Unitarian meeting house (Fig 2.3).

Fig 2.2
The much-altered interior of St Saviourgate meeting house, York, which dates from the late 17th century. It would have seemed loftier originally: until 1859 the four arms had barrel vaults and the ceiling of the tower was higher.
[DP181117]

Fig 2.3
Among the many memorials in St Saviourgate meeting house, York is this impressive monument to Rachel Sandercock (who died in 1790), by Philip or Charles Regnart.
[DP181114]

Fig 2.4
The imposing façade of Old Meeting, Norwich, 1693. Built in a quarter favoured by rich merchants for their own houses, it provides a bold architectural expression of Nonconformists' hard-won right to worship without persecution. [DP173927]

Fig 2.5
Old Meeting, Norwich. Carved and moulded details, especially in the capitals of the pilasters and the eaves cornice, reflect the attention given to the design of the building. [DP160221]

A quite different example of assured urban building, also completed in 1693, is the Independent meeting house (now called Old Meeting) in Colegate, Norwich (Figs 2.4 and 2.5).[7] Its plan is more characteristic of this first wave of Nonconformist buildings: a straightforward rectangle, with entrances in one of the long walls and the pulpit in the middle of the opposite wall. What is so striking here, though, is the confident way in which the broad, red-brick façade is decorated with giant Corinthian pilasters, almost as if calculated to dispel the idea that Nonconform-

ists liked nothing so much as a bare wall. Now rather hemmed in by later buildings, its composition can no longer be properly appreciated. The strong horizontal lines of the five-bay façade are emphasised by the cornice and string course (which at first sight resembles a series of drip moulds) and are continued by the flat-canopied doorways, whose position in the outer bays draws the eye to each end.[8] Robustly balancing this are the vertical elements, especially the pilasters and windows, while the central sundial squarely epitomises the rectilinear theme. There is a rewarding interplay of flat wall plane and moulded relief, and the warmth of the red brick is held in check by crisp white details. Initially the roof was steeper, probably clad in imported Dutch pantiles, and there were mullion-and-transom windows rather than the present sashes (and so originally less opportunity for white in the red-and-white mix).

The meeting house must have been one of the grandest pieces of architecture of its date in Norwich – a kind of artisan baroque that was rooted in the Netherlands. Dutch classicism had much affected English architecture since the 1660s, but Old Meeting's special affection for the Netherlands went back to William Bridge's ministry in exile, and the connection was maintained long into the 18th century. There are many Dutch precedents for a two-storey façade of red brick with giant pilasters, yet it seems that a new creative eye was at work in Norwich.[9] The Old Meeting produced an architectural offspring almost immediately: Norwich's second Quaker meeting house (of 1694–9) in nearby Gildencroft had a steep roof and a wide, many-windowed façade with pilasters and string course, clearly derived from Old Meeting.[10] Quakers were evidently not impervious to architectural fashion.

It has been claimed that Norwich's Old Meeting house is an unassuming, modest affair, marked by an austerity that is the product of a supposed Puritan inheritance.[11] This seems unconvincing, however, for the design looks more like the statement of a group that was keen to make its mark. Whether the interior was equally ambitious cannot be determined with certainty. It now has a venerable atmosphere, with memorials to many generations of worshippers, but most of its original fittings, including a 'handsome brass' chandelier, have been lost – possibly when the roof had to be rebuilt.[12] What has survived, however, is the

wooden gallery on three sides of the building. With Doric columns below and Ionic above, the gallery is consciously classical – perhaps ultimately indebted to the 'Ionica super Dorica' gallery in de Vries's design for a Protestant church.[13] Its purpose, of course, was to allow large congregations to be seated within easy sight and sound of the preacher, and to this end the tiered seating is angled towards the pulpit (Fig 2.6). Perhaps the ground-floor pews were also raised in tiers, as happened elsewhere. A pair of tall north-facing windows (originally square-headed) flanks the pulpit, giving natural light to the preacher. Furthermore, unlike the York example, the communion service must always have centred on a table close to the pulpit, emphasising again how the building was designed around a single focal point.

As was noted in Chapter 1, the Presbyterians of Bury St Edmunds conspicuously occupied the town's two parish churches during the Commonwealth. In 1690, the year after the Act of Toleration, they acquired a house in Churchgate Street in which to worship, and in 1711 erected a striking new meeting house on the site.[14] It makes a stunning contribution to the town, with a façade

Fig 2.6
Interior of Old Meeting, Norwich. Although the fittings are mostly of the later 19th century, the gallery is original and the seating may approximate to the layout of 1693. [DP160225]

Meeting houses, temples, tabernacles and synagogues

In the wake of the Reformation, Christians of all kinds became involved in a search for the founding principles of church practice. Theologians of the 17th century went back to biblical first principles and early Christian practice to find guidance for the design of places of worship. Because medieval church buildings were the result of centuries of cultural accretion, the early history of Christianity and its Judaic roots became essential topics. The Old Testament was combed for evidence, and sites in the Middle East assumed seminal importance. Many attempts were made to visualise the lost Temple of Solomon in Jerusalem, and French Calvinists generally referred to their buildings as Protestant *temples*. British Nonconformists, however, although interested in Solomon's Temple, were inclined to refer to their buildings in other terms. For instance, at the opening services of the Presbyterian meeting house in Bury St Edmunds in 1711 (*see* pp 21–4) the minister preached on a text from Exodus (40: 34): 'Then a Cloud covered the Tent of the Congregation and the Glory of the Lord filled the Tabernacle.' The imagery of tents and tabernacles was more than a reminder of the transience of life on earth. It was widely employed by Nonconformists who might hope for a return to the parish church, and for whom the analogy with the exiled Israelites was potent.

The word 'tabernacle' was also used by Anglicans as a name for the temporary churches erected in London following the Great Fire in 1666, while Roman Catholics continued the late medieval habit of applying the term to a container for the consecrated host. In the 18th century the name was used for George Whitefield's great chapels (*see* Chapter 3). A century later it was revived by Charles Haddon Spurgeon, whose Metropolitan Tabernacle inspired a network of Baptist buildings (*see* pp 142–5).

Though tabernacles were inherently associated with transience, and temples were associated with sacrificial worship, there was a third type of Jewish building – the synagogue – which Nonconformists were not slow to invoke. In 1705, for example, the text from Luke 7: 5, 'He loveth our nation, and he hath built us a synagogue' was inscribed over the door of the Independent chapel at Chipping, Lancashire. In 1689 the same words were used during the funeral sermon for Robert Dyneley to praise his initiative in building the chapel at Bramhope (*see* pp 8–9). Synagogues provided a good model for Nonconformists, having no altars and being designed for the reading of God's word, with preaching, prayer and singing. Furthermore the word *synagogue*, deriving from the Greek *synagein*, 'to bring together', might well be rendered into English as *meeting house*. This analogy was reinforced by experience in 17th-century Amsterdam, where galleried interiors seem to have developed in parallel for Jewish and Protestant worship.

In 1656 Jews began to return to Britain, many of them Sephardic migrants from the Netherlands, and the chief inspiration for Britain's oldest surviving synagogue, that in Bevis Marks, London, was Amsterdam's great Spanish and Portuguese synagogue of 1671–5. With its galleried interior, gleaming brass candelabra and close-packed congregational seating, Bevis Marks Synagogue (1699–1701) seems strangely familiar to Protestant visitors. Its builder, perhaps not coincidentally, is reported to have been a Quaker, Joseph Avis.[†]

carefully fashioned of red and brown brick (Fig 2.7). Slender pilasters and a moulded cornice provide the rectilinear motifs, but the real energy of the composition comes from curves. An outer pair of great, round-headed windows flanks a central door, above which are a segmental pediment, an oval window and a circular sundial. Carved keystones, elaborate rainwater heads and moulded brick panels complete the effect. It is a masterpiece of artisan baroque. The galleried interior is of matching quality (Fig 2.8); its centrepiece is a graceful canopied pulpit, reached by a spiral stair and served by a pair of oval windows. A wooden urn atop the canopy echoes one in brick outside, above the door. Most of the components of the interior were of a kind familiar to any visitor to Wren's city churches, yet Wren generally set pulpits against columns or had them stand alone. The composition of a wall-mounted pulpit, framed between high,

Fig 2.7 (above)
Presbyterian (now Unitarian) meeting house, Bury St Edmunds, 1711. Though lacking its central pediment, the façade is otherwise remarkably complete and impressive. [DP165331]

Fig 2.8 (left)
Interior of the Presbyterian (now Unitarian) meeting house, Bury St Edmunds. A fine ensemble of pulpit, desk and (later) communion rail, with very generous north-facing windows. [DP152869]

round-headed windows was becoming a distinctly Nonconformist feature.

Very little is known with certainty about the process of designing Nonconformist buildings at this time. There is no evidence for the systematic use of professional designers, although the sculptor Caius Cibber acted as architect for the Danish Lutheran church of 1694–6 in Well Close Square, part of London's bustling East End.[15] That building, clearly indebted to Wren's city churches, was the stately centrepiece of a new residential square. Yet such use of an architect was extraordinary. Colvin said of this period that 'most people, indeed, still thought it unnecessary to involve anyone but a master workman when undertaking building operations', and in this respect Nonconformists seem not to have been exceptional.[16] There were many resourceful Nonconformists – both ministers and laypeople – with the vision and means to direct the design of a place of worship. Close contact with continental Protestants provided Nonconformists with ideas for a great variety of plans and architectural treatment. Prints of Dutch buildings (such as those of the 1650s by Veenhuijzen) were widely available, and views of the demolished Protestant temple at Charenton seem to have been well known. Some congregations

presumably had access to architectural pattern books, and most parts of England could boast a few up-to-date buildings from which new ideas and builders' skills might be assessed. Nor was it unknown for a congregation to model its chapel on a nearby example, as happened in the case of Norwich's Gildencroft Quakers (*see* p 21). Another instance is in Cheshire, where, between about 1690 and 1694, meeting houses were built in Macclesfield, Knutsford and Dean Row. Unusually the broad façade of each has twin external staircases incorporated into the end porches, thereby minimising the loss of internal space for stairs.[17]

Masonry construction was not the inevitable choice, even for well-connected congregations. In Ipswich the large Presbyterian (now Unitarian) meeting house of 1699–1700 was constructed of timber by Joseph Clarke, a local 'house-carpenter'.[18] The idea of a timber-framed meeting house prompts thoughts of New England, and there is a hint in the building contract that weather-boarding might indeed have been intended. In fact the walls are plastered externally and have a prominent cornice (Fig 2.9), suggesting a masonry structure but without the panache of the giant pilasters of the Norwich design. The rectangular, cross-framed windows

Fig 2.9
The north front of the timber-framed Presbyterian (now Unitarian) meeting house, Ipswich, 1699–1700. Gallery staircases are at each end, close to the doorways.
[DP165344]

give an underlying rhythm to each elevation, enlivened by pedimented doors and – quite unexpectedly – oval windows. As has been seen from the later chapel at Bury St Edmunds, these windows, properly called *oeils de boeuf*, were a sophisticated choice, derived ultimately from baroque architecture. There is nothing remotely baroque about the resolutely oblong plan of the meeting house, however. The five-bay façade towards Friars Street has doors in the outer bays, as at Norwich, and the pulpit likewise stands in the middle of the opposite long wall, with a gallery of tiered seats on the other three sides. Daniel Defoe, visiting Ipswich in 1720, judged the inside of the meeting house to be 'the best finished of any I have seen, London not excepted'.

Much has survived of the ensemble that Defoe so admired (Fig 2.10). Four tall timber columns support the cross-roof beam, from which hangs a splendid three-tiered brass chandelier, more elaborate than almost any other example of its date. The pulpit, approached by a stair with spiral-turned balusters, is enriched with naturalistic carving (Fig 2.11), and around the building other carved details repay attention: a winged cherub over the clock, and plant forms,

Fig 2.10 (above)
Interior of the Presbyterian (now Unitarian) meeting house, Ipswich. Although altered in R P Jones's restoration of 1900, much of its original character has been retained.
[DP152863]

Fig 2.11 (left)
The luxuriant carving on the pulpit of the Presbyterian (now Unitarian) meeting house in Ipswich, evidence that early Nonconformists were not necessarily averse to decoration.
[DP152867]

doves and cherubs on the doorway brackets. These things, although less extensively deployed than in the major London churches, might plausibly be the work of someone trained in Grinling Gibbons's circle. That Gibbons was Dutch born reminds us also that many Dutch Calvinist churches had richly carved fittings. Nevertheless, at the opening service in 1700 the Ipswich minister, John Fairfax, felt it necessary to defend the high quality of the building by arguing that 'it is but reasonable that an house for God and his solemn service should equal, if not exceed our own habitation'.[19] This was the same sermon, quoted early in Chapter 1, in which Fairfax pointed out that Presbyterians were having to build only because they had been denied use of the parish churches.

A few Nonconformist congregations were indeed able to worship in old church buildings.

In Morley, West Yorkshire, for instance, Dissenters used the medieval church from at least 1700 until 1874, when they built a new Congregational chapel – called St Mary's in the Wood – on the same site.[20] Another example is in Colchester, where a 13th-century building known as St Helen's chapel was fitted out by Quakers in 1700–1 as an ancillary to their chief meeting house (Fig 2.12).[21] Generally, however, Nonconformists adapted secular premises if they lacked the means to build from scratch. Tewkesbury's Old Baptist Chapel is a rare and interesting illustration of this (Fig 2.13). Built in the 14th century as a timber-framed house in an alleyway near Tewkesbury's abbey church, it was converted for the local Baptist congregation, probably around 1700 and certainly by 1711.[22] Its present form is the result of a serious attempt in the 1970s to recreate its 18th-century appearance, following a long period of subdivision and disrepair (Fig 2.14). The modest dimensions give an intimate drama to the place. The pulpit, framed by two tall windows, is barely 10 feet (3m) from the gallery opposite, and a single-tier chandelier sheds sufficient light for worship in winter evenings. As in the Independent and Presbyterian buildings, services would have centred on the pulpit, and the oak table before it would have been the focus for communion. However, the chapel's extra dimension was only apparent when baptisms took place. On such days, benches were moved back and heavy floor-panels lifted to reveal a brick-lined baptistery, large enough for total immersion. If Tewkesbury's Baptists at first used the river for baptismal services, they clearly valued the opportunity to accommodate the rite more decorously in the heart of their chapel.

As with almost all other early Nonconformist chapels, those in York, Norwich, Ipswich, Bury St Edmunds and Tewkesbury are no longer in their original form. Internal changes have been most radical. At all five the initial pattern of ground-floor seating and communion arrangements has been lost. A seating plan does survive, however, from the meeting house in Abingdon, built, like that in Ipswich, for Presbyterian worship in 1700.[23] It shows a somewhat smaller timber building of similar proportions, with twin entrances in one long wall and the pulpit against the far wall. Box pews, mostly about 6 feet by 6 feet (1.8m by 1.8m), occupied the periphery of the ground floor, reached from a gangway – generally then called an alley – which encircled the central block of pews. Immediately across

Fig 2.12
The medieval St Helen's chapel, Colchester was built on Roman foundations and is now used as a Greek Orthodox church. The chapel was adapted as a Quaker meeting house in 1700–1.
[DP160392]

from the pulpit was the table pew, not set apart but placed amid the other pews. Perhaps worshippers received communion sitting (in successive groups) around the table, so as to emphasise the association with the Last Supper; or perhaps the bread and wine were taken to people in their seats. Similar layouts existed elsewhere, and until recently a fairly complete version was retained at the meeting house in Ringwood, Hampshire (*see* p 40).

Before leaving the Abingdon plan, however, it is worth noting the allocation of most pews to named people. This system, by which individuals or families rented pews, had become a common means of generating income and raising funds in Anglican churches, as Wren reluctantly acknowledged.[24] It was taken up by most Nonconformist groups, apart from Quakers, as the necessary way of paying for a building's upkeep and often also for the minister's salary. Self-reliance was the maxim of chapel finance, in contrast to the state church's dependence on church rates and tithes – to which Nonconformists were forced to contribute, as they wryly observed. Much could be written about the social significance of pew rents, but all denominations recognised a need to provide for visitors and the poor. In this respect it is interesting to observe that in Abingdon the free seats (generally in long rather than square pews) were in the centre of the building, whereas in some other cases free seats occupied out-of-the-way corners.

Fig 2.13 (above)
The Old Baptist Chapel, Tewkesbury was adapted as a place of worship in about 1700, in an alley where the Baptists already had a burial ground.
[DP081201]

Fig 2.14 (left)
Old Baptist Chapel, Tewkesbury, as restored in the 1970s (but before the recent painting of the woodwork). The baptistery, which is covered by heavy boards when not in use, takes its place along with the pulpit and communion table at the heart of this venerable chapel.
[DP081204]

Rural buildings to c 1711

Country chapels were mostly smaller than their urban counterparts. Naturally the majority reflect the building traditions of their districts, and some – as we shall see – were adapted farm buildings. However, it is quite misleading to characterise rural chapels as merely barns. A good case in point is the Quaker meeting house at Jordans, Buckinghamshire (Fig 2.15). From at least the 1660s Quakers in this part of the Chilterns had gathered for worship at Jordan's Farm, and it was on part of the farm's land that their meeting house was built in 1688, following James II's Declaration of Indulgence.[25] With its tall, hipped roof it reflects the Dutch taste of the times, and the two most prominent sides of the building have a fashionable chequerboard pattern of dark-glazed headers and red stretcher bricks. The high windows indicate the hall-like character of the main space while the two-storey bay suggests the gallery at one end of the meeting house. The brick-floored interior, with whitewashed walls, dark dado and open-backed benches, is the outcome of at least one 18th-century refit (Fig 2.16). As in many other early Quaker buildings, even small ones, there is a small gallery that would have been partitioned off when women met separately for business meetings (Fig 2.17). The space below was used as a dwelling for many years.

In the 20th century Jordans gained a special place in Quaker iconography, partly because of its inherent charm – white-painted shutters, diamond-paned windows and wisteria-clad façade – and partly because of its associations with William Penn, the founder of Pennsylvania

Fig 2.15 (above) Quaker meeting house, Jordans, Buckinghamshire, 1688. An almost stately example of rural Quaker architecture, celebrated internationally for its associations with William Penn and other eminent figures from the early years of Quakerism. [DP160127]

Fig 2.16 (right) Interior of the Quaker meeting house, Jordans. The stand and raised panelling across the end wall probably date from 1733. [DP160119]

and one of Quakerism's early heroes. Penn worshipped here and was buried in the grounds, and visits by American pilgrims helped to sustain interest in the building from its closure in 1798 to the resumption of weekly worship in 1910. After a devastating fire in 2005 that destroyed the roof and much of the interior, a detailed restoration project has recreated virtually all that had been lost.

A contrasting architectural example is Bullhouse chapel, built in 1692 on the hills beyond the small Yorkshire town of Penistone.[26] Solidly constructed of millstone grit, with curved heads to the mullion-and-transom windows, kneeler stones to the gable ends and ball finials, it is a characteristic piece of 17th-century Pennine architecture (Fig 2.18). Like the chapel at Bramhope (*see* pp 8–9), it was very much an offshoot of a big house: in this case Bullhouse Hall, which stands close by and which had been registered for Presbyterian worship during the short-lived Declaration of Indulgence in 1672. It was for Elkanah Rich of Bullhouse Hall that the purpose-built chapel was erected in 1692, and its Presbyterian minister served also as chaplain to Elkanah (the name means 'possessed by God'). The single-storey chapel is entered in one of the long sides, via a porch set centrally between two pairs of windows. If not a place of worship, it might be taken for a school. Inside, what must be the original pulpit survives, unusually placed on an end

wall and flanked by windows carved with the arms of the Rich family. In such a relatively small chapel this layout would not have left any worshipper too far from the preacher, but whether it was an innately conservative or a rather progressive choice is a matter for conjecture.

Many chapels of similar size to Bullhouse were designed with the pulpit in the centre of

Fig 2.17
The gallery of the Quaker meeting house, Jordans. Quaker women also conducted their business meetings there, at which times it would have been enclosed by shutters.
[DP160121]

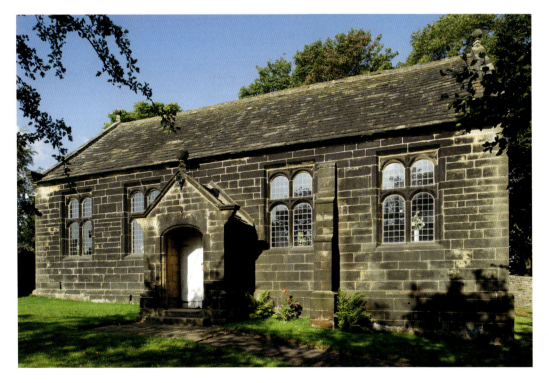

Fig 2.18
Bullhouse chapel, near Penistone, South Yorkshire, 1692, was originally Presbyterian, and is now undenominational. It is a solid and carefully built chapel of local millstone grit. Bullhouse chapel's minister was also chaplain to the Puritan owners of the nearby hall.
[DP143293]

one of the long walls. A good example survives in the small village of Rivington (Fig 2.19), one of several Lancashire places in which Nonconformists had maintained control of the old church building (a chapel-of-ease rather than a full parish church) through much of the later 17th century. In 1703, however, after the Bishop of Chester asserted his right to impose a minister on Rivington, the Presbyterians arranged to build a new 'chapel or oratory', which has survived with relatively few alterations.[27] Most of the panelled box-pews remain, almost filling the ungalleried building. An unusual feature is the canopied pew of the Lords Willoughby of Parham, one of the leading families to patronise the cause. Its canopy projects only a short distance, but its status is unmistakable. Rather like the magistrates' pew in many Dutch churches, it faces the pulpit across the full width of the chapel. Architecturally Rivington chapel is not of the highest status, but it was a good deal more

decorous than some of the county's Anglican chapels-of-ease.[28] The wide façade is a neat rectilinear composition. Its two cross-windows have oblong glazing (rather than the diamond panes of the side windows) and their flat lintels coincide with a high string course echoed by plain dripstones over the doors. All is symmetrical save for the bellcote above and the slight distinction between the two door-lintels.

There were many small rural congregations whose limited funds constrained any architectural ambitions, yet whose buildings have gained a strong place in the affections of modern visitors. The Quaker meeting house of 1710 at Come-to-Good, south of Truro, is a case in point (Figs 2.20 and 2.21).[29] Though it cost only £53, there was great difficulty in finding the money. The walls of the meeting house were made of cob (essentially a mixture of local soil and straw), and it has been suggested that both the roof frame and the windows were reclaimed

Fig 2.19
Rivington chapel (now Unitarian), Lancashire, 1703. This little-altered chapel was built close to the Anglican church in which the Nonconformist congregation had worshipped until the end of the 17th century.
[BB92/09476]

Fig 2.20 (left)
The Quaker meeting house at Come-to-Good, Cornwall, 1710, is perhaps the most rustic of Quaker buildings. Originally its entrance was in the centre of the south front shown here.
[DP160685]

Fig 2.21 (below)
Interior of the Quaker meeting house at Come-to-Good. The gallery, added in 1717, also served as a room for women's business meetings.
[DP160692]

from other sites. The roof is thatched, and the thatch extends over the open linney or stable at one side. Thatched churches were common in other parts of England (Norfolk had about 270 in the early 19th century), yet in Cornwall cob and thatch seem not have been employed for churches.[30] Perhaps, then, Come-to-Good seemed inferior, or merely quaint, to polite Cornish society, but its battered whitewashed walls and deep thatched roof are now the essence of the Picturesque.

Rural Nonconformists, just as much as their urban counterparts, most often made use of existing premises in the early years of toleration. Barns were a common choice, often being capable of rudimentary adaptation without great cost. For instance, at Great Warford in Cheshire, a 16th-century barn was acquired by a Baptist church in 1712 and fitted up with galleries and benches to serve as a meeting house.[31] Because of subsequent subdivision, it is not easy now to imagine the building as it was when first used for worship. One of the oldest surviving Nonconformist buildings in Wales, Maesyronnen Independent chapel (of 1696–7) is thought to have begun life as a barn or cow-house.[32] Such structures were not necessarily easy to acquire, however: it was one thing for a farmer to allow meetings in a barn at certain times of year, and another for him to sell such a building. Since many Dissenters met in each other's homes during the years of persecution, it was also natural to consider converting domestic premises for worship. So, for example, Quakers who had been meeting at a farmhouse in Shipley, West

Fig 2.22
Blue Idol Quaker meeting house, near Coolham, West Sussex. The box-framed 16th-century house was adapted for Quaker worship in 1692.
[DP160410]

Fig 2.23
Independent chapel at Walpole, Suffolk. It was created in about 1689, when a 16th-century timber-framed house was extended (gaining the second ridge of its double-gabled roof) and fitted out for worship.
[DP152843]

Sussex, acquired and altered another near Coolham for use as a place of worship in 1692 (Fig 2.22). The timber-framed, partly weatherboarded building was adapted at a cost of £53 (the same sum as was spent on building Come-to-Good) and, under the romantic name of Blue Idol meeting house was restored by young Quaker volunteers after the First World War.[33]

Another example, involving a much more extensive process of adaptation, is at Walpole in Suffolk (Fig 2.23). In 1689 an Independent congregation who had gathered in various homes obtained a lease on a large house at the edge of the village.[34] The wooden framework of the house was largely retained, but extended at the rear to make a sizeable tall space that could be fitted out for worship. Two great wooden posts (and later a third) were introduced to support the widened roof and to help carry the weight of galleries. As the set piece of the meeting house a pair of big, round-headed windows was installed in the new back wall, with the pulpit and elegant tester between: a hallmark of respectable chapels for decades to come. Though the basic arrangement of Walpole Independent meeting house has survived, much of the furniture, fittings and decoration is of later date (Fig 2.24). The result is a kind of hallowed liveliness which is now carefully conserved by the Historic Chapels Trust.

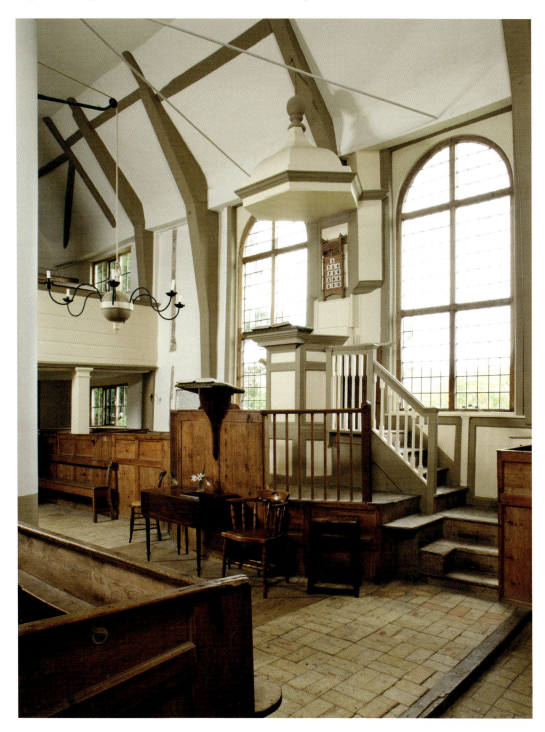

Fig 2.24
Independent chapel at Walpole. Despite the horizontal lines and limited fenestration of the façade, the interior is surprisingly lofty and well lit. [DP152846]

Under attack, 1710–15

After the accession of Queen Anne in 1702 events had gradually begun to move in favour of the High Church; with the Tory ascendancy of 1710 it looked as though the British seesaw was pivoting once more and that toleration was imperilled. Indeed, the fall of the Whigs was preceded in the spring of 1710 by an outbreak of mob violence directed at Nonconformist places of worship in several parts of England.[35] Buildings were wrecked, pews were hauled out and burned in the street. By then purpose-built chapels and meeting houses had become a significant feature of virtually every major place in England, and it was not only drunken rioters who resented this. It was quite common for a growing town or suburb to have two or three such buildings, and perhaps only one Anglican church. Such was the case in Deptford, where the vicar complained that because the population of 12,000 could not possibly be accommodated in his parish church, many people went to the meeting houses of the 'Quakers, Presbyterians and Anabaptists' (each of which had been built since 1700).[36] His complaint was made to Parliament on 6 April 1711, the very day on which legislation was enacted to build 50 new Anglican churches around London. The government accepted the vicar's argument that something had to be done to counter the culture of Dissent. What were these 50 new churches to be like? Christopher Wren's often-quoted advice on the design of these churches emphasises their Protestant character:

> in our reformed Religion, it should seem vain to make a Parish-church larger, than that all who are present can both hear & see. The Romanists, indeed, may build larger Churches, it is enough if they hear the Murmur of the Mass, and see the Elevation of the Host, but ours are to be fitted for Auditories.

The aim was for 'all to hear the Service, and both to hear distinctly, and see the Preacher'.[37]

Wren's views here would have been as acceptable to a Presbyterian or Independent as to an Anglican. The establishment's determination was not merely to provide accommodation for worship, however, but to meet the threat of Dissent and irreligion by building churches 'of stone and other proper Materials, with Towers or Steeples to each of them', as the 1711 Act spelled out.[38] It is interesting to reflect on the novelty of the Act's prescription. While the preference for stone was partly a matter of architectural fashion, of Dutch brickwork giving way to Italian-inspired masonry, the question of towers and spires was purely ecclesiastical. Wren's success in contriving varied towers and spires for the post-Fire churches had shown a way of distinguishing church buildings from, say, schools or town halls. Of course, many Anglican churches of the 17th and 18th centuries had no more than a bellcote, and for Nonconformists even that was not the rule. Spires were hardly cheap: Wren's at St Mary-le-Bow had cost £7,388 out of a total for the church of £15,645.[39] The Act of 1711 resulted in some spectacular buildings by Hawksmoor, Gibbs and Archer (including that of St Paul, Deptford), but at a monumental cost; only a fraction of the envisaged 50 were actually built.[40] Nonconformists, unaided by government grants or local taxes, were unable to match such expenditure or such bravura design.

During the final months of Anne's reign, the government passed the Schism Act to prevent Nonconformists from teaching or from running any kind of educational establishment. Its aim was to throttle Dissent, in particular by closing the academies in which future ministers were taught.[41] The succession of George I in 1714 therefore came as a relief to Nonconformists, but raised opposition elsewhere; the following year witnessed a Jacobite rebellion in which some 30 chapels and meeting houses were damaged or destroyed by rioters. The case in Manchester has already been mentioned.[42] Another example occurred at Newcastle-under-Lyme, Staffordshire, where in 1694 the Presbyterians had built a meeting house almost literally in the shadow of the Anglican church, from which they and their minister had been ejected in 1662. In 1715 the meeting house was burned down by a mob, and it was claimed that one of the churchwardens played a key part in the destruction by delivering 'a great hammer out of the steeple to knock down the meeting house door'.[43] A national scheme of compensation paid for all this damage, however, and the buildings were soon restored or enhanced. In retrospect it is not so much the attacks of 1715 as the responses to them that demonstrate the underlying stability of the 'age of toleration'.[44]

Dissent sustained, 1715–1740

The new chapels and meeting houses erected in the 20 years or so after the death of Queen Anne in 1714 were mostly built by a younger generation than that which experienced the heady atmosphere of William and Mary's glorious revolution. There was a reduction in the overall number of new Nonconformist places of worship being opened, partly because many well-established congregations had already provided for themselves. By now – perhaps reassured by the settlement after the 1715 riots – even cautious Nonconformists were inclined to accept the desirability of purpose-built accommodation. In Evesham, for example, a Presbyterian congregation had begun in 1696 by renting a barn, which they purchased five years later and only in 1737, under a scholarly new minister, was a site purchased to erect a chapel.[45] The new building is an attractive composition, with a façade of honey-coloured stone beneath a long hipped roof. The interior, although much altered, has reminders from each stage of the chapel's history, including a pair of oil paintings of Paul Cardale (the minister for whom the building was erected) and his wife, Sarah.

Like many others of that generation, the chapel in Evesham (Fig 2.25) seems to be the product not of architectural adventure so much as an evaluation of the first meeting houses and chapels constructed in the wake of 1689. The long-wall type of entrance façade was evidently felt to have served Nonconformists well, since it had become almost standard for larger chapels by the 1720s, and even small chapels were generally designed in this way. Anglicans occasionally took up the theme, but chiefly in buildings with a long internal axis.[46] Nonconformists at this time tended still to feel that the natural place for a pulpit was as the centrepiece of a wide wall, not at one end of a long space; but there was no consensus on the matter. As might be expected, account was taken of the shift in architectural fashion. Gradually the taste for Dutch motifs declined, although the basic outline of a steep hipped roof was to remain part of the repertoire of Nonconformist architecture for decades to come. In places an appetite remained for motifs of an ultimately baroque kind, but more usually the architectural character settled into something that might be called early Georgian.

A selection of three double-storey chapels from different parts of the country suggests the

Fig 2.25
The Presbyterian (now Unitarian) chapel, Evesham, Worcestershire, 1737. Separated from the bustle of the town in its own walled graveyard, the chapel has a broad front, attractively faced in Cotswold stone. [DP081210]

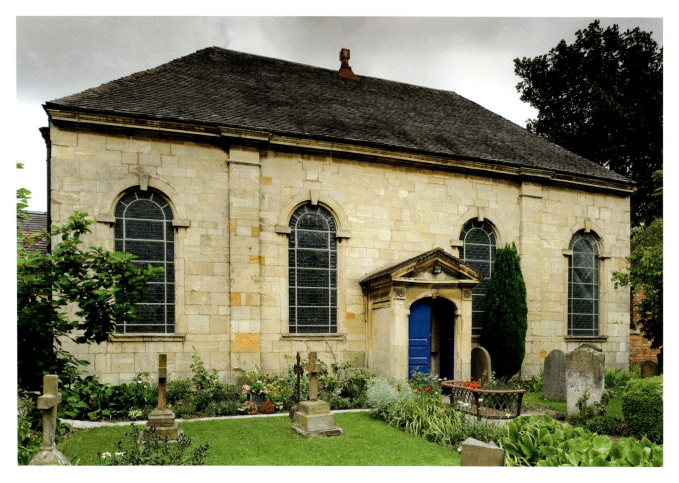

range of architectural treatment that could be given at this time to buildings of similar plan. Each has its entrances in one long wall, with the pulpit in pride of place on the opposite wall, and is – or was – fitted up with galleries on three sides. The small Norfolk village of Oulton is the first example (Figs 2.26 and 2.27), built in 1731

for an Independent congregation that had been formally constituted only in 1724.[47] Its symmetrical four-bay façade has doors in bays one and four, giving convenient access to the corner stairs as well as to the ground-floor seats, by now a well-tested scheme. The red-brick walls and pantile roof were part of the stock-in-trade

Fig 2.26
Independent chapel, Oulton, Norfolk, 1731 (the '1728' irons are of the late 20th century). Restored and conserved by the Norfolk Historic Buildings Trust, the chapel has those touches of Dutch architecture that were once common in East Anglia.
[DP152872]

Fig 2.27
Independent chapel, Oulton. Its atmospheric interior includes many late 19th-century fittings. Perhaps the ground floor was originally filled with box pews, similar to those which survive in the galleries.
[DP152875]

of Norfolk building, as were the shaped gables that grace each of the side walls. Yet Dutch gables were already falling out of fashion and a less conservative builder might also have introduced sash windows from the start.

If Oulton's meeting house speaks an East Anglian vernacular, there is virtually no regional accent in the design of the chapel built in 1721–2 for a Presbyterian congregation at Chowbent (Figs 2.28 and 2.29) in Lancashire. The stone details, especially the quoins and window surrounds, help to animate the brown-brick exterior, but the design was hardly calculated to compete with St Martin-in-the-Fields. In fact

Fig 2.28
Chowbent Presbyterian (now Unitarian) chapel, Atherton, Lancashire, 1721–2. The main entrance has always been in the long north front, which is not shown in this photograph, rather than one of the gable-end walls. The small vestry extension shown here is a later addition.
[DP143733]

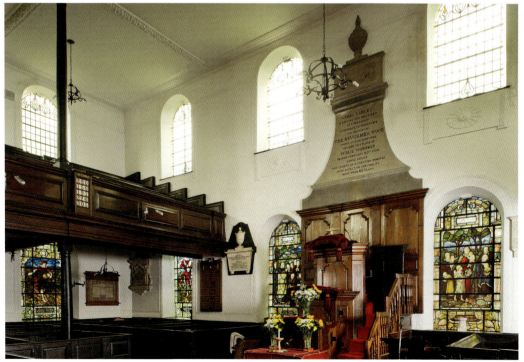

Fig 2.29
Interior of Chowbent chapel. Above the fine three-decker pulpit is a memorial to James Wood (1672–1759), the chapel's minister who helped to stem the Jacobite rebellion in 1715.
[DP143739]

Chowbent chapel must have been designed to outdo the 'small brick edifice' from which its congregation had been expelled in 1721, a chapel-of-ease to the parish church of Leigh.[48] This might not have been a major architectural challenge, but its prominent location and the approach through a pair of decidedly baroque gatepiers show that the new Chowbent chapel did not lack in confidence. And it is interesting to note that many of the building's features (including the round-headed openings, gable-end pediments and bellcote) were to appear in later chapels-of-ease, as Anglican patrons tried locally to raise their game.[49]

The concluding example from this Nonconformist trio was erected, probably in 1721, for a Baptist congregation in Taunton (Figs 2.30 and 2.31). Mary Street Unitarian chapel, as it has become, has a similar layout to those at Chowbent and Oulton, although now (at least) with a central doorway rather than a pair of entrances in the outer bays.[50] Its façade was originally of brick and had three oval windows to the first floor. Something of that quite generous architectural effect can be imagined from the chapel's surviving rear elevation, which was not embellished in the 19th century, and where a single oval window is supported by a pair of round-headed ones.

Internally, these three chapels offer no less of a contrast. Oulton is the least elaborate, its apparent simplicity enhanced by a cool palette. Yet this was no Puritan barn: the gallery front has fluted pilasters and the pulpit's backboard and canopy were inlaid with a pattern of stars and linear decoration. The interior of Chowbent chapel is much richer, with dark woodwork and a sense that succeeding generations have added to its atmosphere. There is a complete three-decker pulpit (though a memorial to the building's first minister rises where a canopy must have been) and a virtually full set of box pews with panelled doors; the stairs also have turned balusters. Some of the ceiling's decorative plasterwork must be original, although one cannot easily tell how extensively it was augmented in 1901, when the chapel was restored.

Taunton has one of the most handsome interiors of any early Georgian chapel. The pair of square, fluted wooden pillars that support the roof is especially grand: they stand on high plinths to display their moulded bases and rise to Corinthian capitals which bear elaborate block entablatures. Between them, hanging from a virtuoso piece of wrought ironwork, is a three-tiered brass chandelier topped by a dove. The carving on the pulpit and its backboard is of matching quality, and it might be assumed that

Fig 2.30
Mary Street Baptist chapel (now Unitarian), Taunton, dating from c 1721. The façade gained many of its present features in the 19th century. The upper windows were originally oval (see the Ipswich meeting house in Fig 2.9). [DP166305]

any canopy would have been similarly decorated. If the pillars obscured the view from a few places, the seating arrangement was intended to improve the situation. Each pew was deep enough to allow for seats on one side only, 'which at once preserves a beautiful uniformity, and secures the people from the unpleasant and unbecoming situation, to which double pews expose part of an auditory, that of staring in each others faces, and sitting with their backs to the preacher'.[51] The present layout more or less fulfils this description, but the pews are not in their original form, and it is not known whether the chapel had an internal baptistery.

There were always a few Nonconformist buildings in which the chief entrance was at one end. The Danish and Swedish Lutherans had each built a church of this form in the east of London, although such plans were by no means the rule for Lutherans in any country. In due course native English Nonconformists (and their American cousins) were to follow this habit, and a straw in the wind of change is offered by the Old Meeting House (as it came to be called) at Ringwood in Hampshire (Figs 2.32 and 2.33), which was built in 1727–8 for a congregation of about 500.[52] This was laid out with the entrance in one of the short walls, aligned with the pulpit at the far end, and with a full set of galleries and box pews. Structurally it is quite ambitious, with a vaulted ceiling running the length of the building and subsidiary vaults on the cross-axis between the wooden columns that support the roof and galleries. As Godwin Arnold

Fig 2.31
The magnificent interior of Mary Street chapel, Taunton. Its imposing tone is set by the giant Corinthian pillars and the central chandelier.
[DP166307]

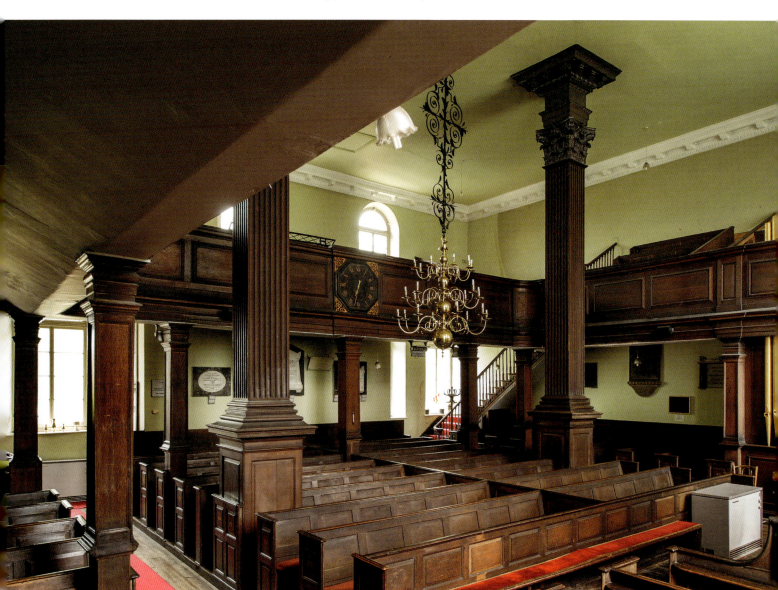

Fig 2.32 (right)
Interior of Old Meeting House, Ringwood, Hampshire, 1727–8; a 19th-century pulpit has replaced the presumably taller original, which would have helped the preacher to command the attention of those in the gallery as well as the length of the chapel. Closed for worship in the 1970s, the meeting house is now run by a local charity. [DP166276]

Fig 2.33 (below)
Plan of Old Meeting House, Ringwood showing the arrangement of the table-pew, placed lengthwise facing the pulpit. Marking a turn away from the broad-fronted chapels that were still most usual, Ringwood nonetheless retained a central block of pews. [RCH01/118/01/02/046]

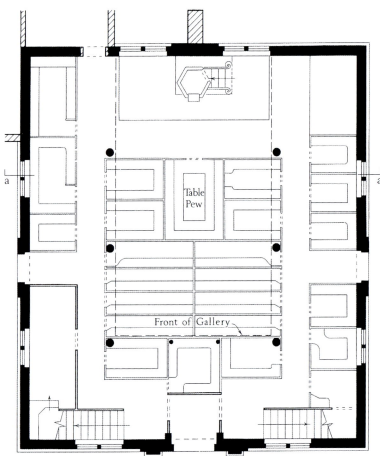

observed, the inspiration seems to come from Wren's church of St James in Piccadilly, which Wren cautiously offered as a model auditory church.[53] The differences are also instructive, for at St James's it was the altar that stood against the east wall; the pulpit stood before it, in the middle of the central gangway. At Ringwood the positions were reversed, with the table-pew for communion services set 'tablewise' (that is, with one end towards the pulpit) amid the central block of pews. Liturgically, the building embodies at its heart Calvin's concept of the communion as a shared meal, while also giving due prominence to the preaching of God's word. It must have been acceptable for the pulpit to be marginally further from some hearers than would have been the case had the plan been turned through 90 degrees.

In other respects this fascinating building was not ideal. The main entrance has to serve both sets of gallery stairs as well as the ground-floor pews, and the low subsidiary doors, part way along each of the long side walls, cannot have helped substantially. Wren's St James's had no such problems, possessing a multiplicity of entrances – three via the west tower alone – in addition to dedicated gallery doors. Visually the main entrance at Ringwood does have some authority; it is not only larger than the others, but is also accompanied by a stone pediment and well-made brick pilasters. Yet the façade in which it sits is of strangely ambivalent design, the half-hipped roof being neither a confident statement of arrival nor an acknowledgement that this is a secondary aspect. In an apparent attempt to resolve the matter, a small gable affirms the central axis. Yet despite these short-comings Ringwood is important, not least because it shows that preachers could command a long as well as a broad audience.

Each of the post-1715 chapels mentioned so far is of some size. But what of the smaller chapels in this period? A few were of the type that David Butler has called 'gable entry' meeting houses, but these were greatly outnumbered by those with a long-wall façade (Butler's 'side entry' buildings). Two examples of the latter give a flavour of the range of architectural treatment that was achieved by smaller Quaker congregations. The meeting house in Stafford bears the date 1730 and was built to supersede a presumably smaller one of 1680 (Fig 2.34).[54] Though far from lavish – the site cost £12 and a further

£144 was spent on construction – it has a neat, four-bay façade of brick, with a pedimented canopy above the door. It is emphatically upright, and even the small oval window is vertically aligned. As in a school, the high windows supply daylight without the distraction of looking out on the passing world. The meeting room extends the full width of the front, with the stand (for those with a recognised gift for ministry) at the north end, on the left. At the south end is a small gallery, reached by stairs immediately to the right of the door. In some ways it is a miniature version of Jordans (*see* p 28), albeit less rustic in character.

The second example was built in 1729 for Quakers near the village of Claverham (in northern Somerset.[55] As with the Stafford building, this replaced an earlier meeting house (of 1674) on a nearby site. Its rubble walls, for long limewashed but now flat-rendered, must have enhanced its rustic character, but the design was far from vernacular. The centrepiece of the façade is a lively composition of round-headed windows and doorway, plus a small oblong

Fig 2.34
Quaker meeting house, Stafford, 1730. Although the fenestration of this small building reflects the fact that the main space is to the left of the door, it does not reveal the presence of a gallery and attic room on the right.
[DP160657]

Fig 2.35
Quaker meeting house, Claverham, Somerset, 1729. The centrepiece of the impressive façade is topped by an unusual sundial (with three dials) and an urn. [DP166204]

window, all with proud keystones. Standing on a pedestal above all this is a sundial in the form of a square stone urn, with carved flames permanently flickering from it (Fig 2.35). Nothing here quite conforms to the archetype of Quaker quietism. The building has two wings, making a kind of E-plan, with an upswept parapet at each outer corner, rising to a chimneystack. Each wing had a gallery looking into the meeting room. And on the ground floor each wing provided almshouse accommodation (hence the chimneystacks) for a poor Quaker, an early instance of the way in which Nonconformists sought to accommodate the social as well as the spiritual needs of their communities.

Conclusion

The relative confidence with which some Nonconformists built after 1689 is evident in the striking exterior design of such surviving examples as in Norwich, York, Bury St Edmunds and Claverham. None could hope to compete with the Anglicans' most expensive churches, though doubtless some Nonconformists wondered about what architectural heights they might reach if allowed just part of the public money that had financed, say, Hawksmoor's London churches. For their part, many Anglicans resented the impunity with which Nonconformists were able to build opportunistically, wherever a congregation could be gathered. The vicar of Deptford was not alone in complaining about the competition offered by the stream of new chapels and meeting houses in growing urban areas.

Although the 1689 Act of Toleration finally extended freedom of worship to so many of those who had been forced to gather covertly, it had the effect of consolidating a division. It suited many people – then and subsequently – to see the nation in binary terms, with the establishment and its church buildings on one side and Nonconformists with their meeting houses on the other. But it is much more accurate to speak of a continuum than of a binary system. Low Churchmen and Presbyterians often had more in common than they shared with High Churchmen on the one hand or with Quakers on the other. Architecturally, too, one should think of a continuum. Across the board in England, Christians were erecting auditory places of worship, in which – as the Victorians came to think – the denominational distinctions were at times less marked than the similarities. Externally as well as internally it must have been difficult to distinguish some chapels or meeting houses from some Church of England places. Most Nonconformist buildings of the period certainly had long-wall façades, but Anglicans were sometimes happy to use the same feature. Nor was architectural quality a firm dividing line, since even the relatively plain exterior of Chowbent chapel compared favourably with many Anglican chapels-of-ease. It is easy now to forget that some fairly simple buildings were erected for the Church of England as well as for Nonconformists.

3

Enthusiasm and enlightenment

Around the middle of the 18th century the pace of Nonconformist building activity quickened. This was partly a natural process of renewal, as some existing buildings became too small or dilapidated, and partly a response to the increase in population. The main Dissenting groups (Presbyterian, Independent, Quaker and Baptist) were far from moribund, but ultimately more significant was the emergence of new religious movements – essentially from within the Established Church, though with an infusion of ideas from continental Protestantism.

Among the new European arrivals were the Moravian Brethren (*Unitas Fratrum*), a body whose origins lay in the Czech Reformation led by Jan Hus. After the Thirty Years' War the movement was suppressed and its celebrated bishop, the educational pioneer Jan Comenius, died in exile in 1670. Groups of followers survived, however, and in the early 1720s some sought refuge in Saxony, where they established a settlement they named Herrnhut (the Lord's keeping). Revitalised through contact with German Pietism, the Brethren became enterprising missioners to many parts of the world. In Britain they not only opened places of worship, but also developed whole settlements, rather as at Herrnhut. The oldest of these is near Pudsey in West Yorkshire, where a hillside site was purchased and called Fulneck (Fig 3.1) – after the Moravian town of Fulnek, where Comenius had been minister until 1621.

Fig 3.1
Moravian settlement, Fulneck, West Yorkshire, begun in 1744. Unlike the more commanding south front, the north side (shown here) is not seen to advantage because of the lie of the land. Yet the chapel, which dates from 1746–8 and gained its bellcote-topped entrance block in 1770, has a strong and characterful presence. [DP033591]

Like a miniature Versailles, Fulneck grew laterally into a long frontage that can only be properly appreciated from the air. The central bays of its *piano nobile* (where Versailles has its gallery of mirrors) contain the chapel of 1746–8, which drew admiring visitors even before it was finished: 'It stands on the side of a hill, commanding all the vale beneath, and the opposite hill. The front is exceeding grand, though plain, being faced with fine, smooth, white stone.'[1] This grandness is partly to do with height, because the sloping site allows for a full storey of rooms beneath the chapel itself. But it is no less to do with architectural treatment, as can still be appreciated on the south side: beneath a balustraded parapet the great windows are punctuated by emphatic keystones, and at the centre is a pedimented aedicule, corresponding with the position of the pulpit inside.[2] Though evidently not the work of a mere builder, the

design is not exactly scholarly; its author is said to have been Edward Graves of Newark – to whom no other buildings have been attributed.[3] The main access to the chapel has always been from the north side, where an entrance block, topped by a bellcote, was added in 1770.

The chapel's interior (Fig 3.2), with galleries on three sides and pulpit centrally set against a long wall, has been significantly altered, but its quality can be judged from the architraves of the doors and windows, the moulded cornice and the rococo organ case. The organ, evidence of the Moravians' great love of hymns, was made for Fulneck by the distinguished Swiss organ builder John Snetzler/Johannes Schnetzler, and installed by 1750 (though since rebuilt and re-located from the east gallery). None of this came cheaply, even without the expense of construction on such a steeply sloping site. In 1747 the expected cost of the chapel was around

Fig 3.2
Interior of the Moravian chapel, Fulneck, West Yorkshire, 1746–8. The Snetzler organ, though later enlarged, had first occupied the side gallery (facing the camera). The present pews replaced the original seating in 1888.

£3,000, perhaps excluding the timber, which was a gift from Moravians in Norway.

Fulneck embodies many of the changes that were to affect Nonconformist buildings. By mid-century the more important chapels incorporated features from the palette of Palladian rather than generically baroque architecture, and the names of architects or designers began to occur a little more frequently in the context of chapel building. In this respect Nonconformists were part of a process that was common in secular as well as religious architecture. The organ was indicative of a general change in worship, but one that especially affected Nonconformists. From their Bohemian predecessors the Moravian Brethren had inherited a very strong tradition of hymnody, and congregational hymn singing had become quite widespread among English Nonconformists (Quakers excepted) since Isaac Watts, the eminent Independent pastor, began to publish collections of hymns in the first years of the century.[4] For the time being, however, organs were still exceptional in chapels. Moravians were also exceptional and forward looking in their provision of accommodation beyond the needs of worship. The Quakers had made some moves in this direction (as we saw at Claverham, *see* pp 41–2), but nowhere as extensively as at Fulneck.[5]

Any visitor to Fulneck is bound to be struck by the sheer extent of the buildings, housing the social as well as the spiritual needs of the congregation.[6] Cottages that pre-dated the Moravians' arrival provided the first family homes, but the visual emphasis was to be on new communal premises, with the chapel at the heart of things. An early drawing shows a proposal to have residential accommodation in pavilions, linked to the chapel on each side by lower blocks. This design was abandoned, perhaps through difficulty with the architect, or simply the offer of bricks. Within a year of the chapel opening, however, the Moravians embarked on the construction of a detached brick house to its west for single men and another to the east for single women, both three-storey buildings of rather Palladian proportions. The rooms below the chapel were soon given over to boarding schools for boys and girls, reflecting the Moravians' special interest in education, and the roof was heightened to provide attic dormitories. By stages the long terrace was filled with buildings, including a house for widows, a minister's house, a shop and inn, workshops (some for weavers) and a new block for the boys' school.

Fulneck belongs in part to the long tradition of ideal communities, but from the Nonconformist perspective it is important too for demonstrating the principle that a chapel can have rooms for a range of social purposes.

John Wesley and George Whitefield

The most significant of the new religious movements in mid-18th-century Britain was Methodism. John Wesley, the founder of Methodism, was profoundly influenced by the Moravian Brethren, whom he first met in 1735, and it is interesting to consider his first buildings in this context. Wesley visited their settlement at Herrnhut in 1738 and immediately noted 'the orphan-house; in the lower part of which is the apothecary's shop, in the upper, the chapel, capable of containing six or seven hundred people'.[7] In the chapel the use of an organ and other instruments caught his attention, and later he recorded the Moravians' extensive educational curriculum. Understandably it was the spiritual life of the Brethren that most concerned him, but their organisational habits and social instincts were also to leave a lasting impression.

As an ordained Anglican minister, Wesley did not wish his campaign of spiritual renewal to break from the Church of England. On his return to Britain he preached wherever he could: in parish churches if possible, in other buildings or in the open air if necessary. He first resorted to dedicated premises in 1739, building a room in Bristol and adapting a derelict ordnance foundry in London's Moorfields. Both buildings were needed as places in which Wesley's followers could gather for prayer and preaching (though not for communion, which they were expected to receive at their parish churches), but each place served the movement's wider needs as well. The Foundery contained – besides a galleried preaching-space for up to 1,500 hearers and a room in which 300 could gather for weekday services or meetings – a schoolroom, a room for the sale of Methodist publications, a preachers' house and an apartment for Wesley himself.[8] In due course, with echoes of Herrnhut, an almshouse was created and a free dispensary for the poor established, as well as a lending society (a kind of credit union). The Foundery was at once a headquarters for Methodism, a place of worship and a welfare centre.

Communion

In the 16th century Protestants were almost universally critical of the Catholic Church's practices regarding communion. Most reverted to the early Christian practice in which worshippers received both bread and wine, while tables were often preferred to altars. Perhaps representative of many of the first Nonconformist places of worship was the Congregationalists' adapted meeting house in Cockermouth, where from the 1680s 'the church sat down together at the Lord's table' each month. This possibly involved the use of temporary trestle tables, but some Nonconformists certainly had long table-pews permanently in place; in the 18th century one at Linton in Cambridgeshire could accommodate 'thirty persons or more'. An alternative tradition, in which the bread and wine were taken to people in their pews, was also common in the 17th century, and is still usual in many Nonconformist denominations. Although the practice may be less immediately redolent of the Last Supper, it requires only a small table.

By the 18th century Anglican clergy expected worshippers to receive the consecrated bread and wine kneeling at the communion rail, and this habit was generally followed by Methodists, for whom it remains usual. Around the start of the 20th century questions of hygiene led to the widespread adoption of individual communion glasses among Nonconformist denominations. In many chapels one can find slots or holes for the used glasses, either in the pews or else behind the communion rail.

Among the denominations who have always placed special emphasis on weekly communion are the Brethren, who refer to the service as the breaking of bread and typically pass a loaf around the congregation, with each person breaking off a piece. A communion cup is likewise passed from person to person, so that each may drink a little of the wine. By contrast, Jehovah's Witnesses celebrate a memorial meal only once a year, on the eve of Passover. Unleavened bread and wine are passed from hand to hand, but only those Witnesses who are 'convinced of a heavenly hope' actually take the elements.

One unusual outcome of Protestant interest in early Christian customs was the love feast, based on the agape meal held in New Testament times in connection with communion. Many early Baptist congregations celebrated the love feast as a preparation for communion, as did the Moravians. Inspired by the Moravians, John Wesley introduced the practice of love feasts into Methodism: after sharing a token meal (typically of water and plain cake), Methodists would testify to Christ's influence. It was an important part of Methodism at a time when the movement was converting large numbers of people, but thereafter its use greatly declined. In the 18th century Moravians also practised foot-washing as part of the preparation for communion, a custom which later became a feature of Seventh-day Adventist services.

Communion is not celebrated by Quakers or the Salvation Army, although both bodies respect the serious purpose which underpins other denominations' practice.†

The communion table at Abbey Congregational church, Romsey, forms part of a characteristic late 19th-centry ensemble with the pulpit and organ. [DP166284]

The Methodists' first purpose-built chapel was begun in May 1739 in the Horsefair, Bristol (Fig 3.3).[9] The building was much smaller than the Foundery, though it must have fulfilled many of the same functions. It became not only the Methodists' chief building in what was for them a very fruitful district, but also a staging post from which ministers could reach the growing networks of followers in the west of England and south Wales. For a while the chapel seems also to have accommodated a school and in 1745, as Methodism became more organised, the conference of Methodist ministers met here. Having steadily outgrown its capacity, John Wesley's New Room was enlarged to its present size and orientation in 1748. Extending the building on its squeezed site was hardly easy, as the irregularities of the plan reveal. Quite how it looked externally will probably never be known: the main round-headed window might be of this date, but little else survives, and unlovely roughcast conceals the masonry.

Once inside, however, it is possible to appreciate the essence of the mid-Georgian building (Fig 3.4). Six giant columns stretch before one, and the perspective is emphasised

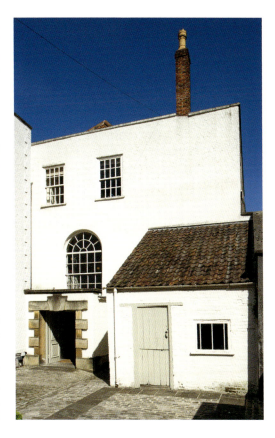

Fig 3.3
John Wesley's New Room, Bristol, dating from 1739 and 1748, was the Methodists' first purpose-built place of worship. Beside the main entrance is a stable for ministers' horses.
[DP166234]

Fig 3.4
Interior of John Wesley's New Room, Bristol. The glazed lantern helps to illuminate the hemmed-in chapel, and also allows proceedings to be overseen from the preachers' rooms on the first floor.
[DP166243]

by the long side galleries. Whether because of liturgical preference or the limitations of the site, the chapel is laid out lengthwise and one's eyes are drawn irresistibly to the delightful, two-storey pulpit at the far end. This is not a narrow piece of furniture from which a scholarly sermon might be delivered to a dispassionate congregation, but a pair of spacious boxes, from which the preacher would urge every hearer to be saved by faith. Only the lower element (the reading desk) is original; its upper partner (mounted over the north entrance) replaces one that was removed in the 19th century. Most unusually the pulpit is reached from the galleries via generous stairs picked out by white-painted balusters, an arrangement created in 1929–30 as part of a serious re-Georgianising of the chapel by the architect George Oatley. Other introductions from that time are the railed communion area and the chamber organ by Snetzler – neither of which would have been thought necessary in 1748, though hymns were already a popular element of Methodist worship and Charles Wesley's first selection had appeared as early as 1739.[10] Little, perhaps none, of the original seating survives, but the retention of elements from three different centuries means that – as Ison said – 'the tactfully restored interior makes an immediate and lasting impression of refined simplicity'.[11] As with many of the earlier meeting houses, the interior today owes as much to an early 20th-century expectation of Nonconformity as it does to the original aesthetic.

John Wesley's New Room was a headquarters as well as a place of worship. A small stable was built in the chapel forecourt for the ministers, and the nearby sculpture of John Wesley on horseback (by A G Walker, 1932) is a memorial to the thousands of miles he travelled from this site. Above the chapel is a whole floor of bedrooms, studies and meeting rooms for Wesley and other itinerant preachers (Fig 3.5). Through the heart of that upper floor is a glazed octagonal lantern, which gains extra light for both the chapel and the preachers' rooms and ingeniously allows a watchful eye to be kept on the pulpit from above. If the critics of Methodism were apt to view it as hysterical and disorderly, the New Room's unobtrusive vantage point is witness to John Wesley's determination to oversee a well-regulated movement. Though his journal gives no hint as to how the New Room was designed, he surely took as much care in commissioning the building as he did in supervising ministers. A plausible suggestion is that Wesley employed George Tully, an accomplished local builder-architect. Tully designed several prominent buildings during the 1740s and, together with his son William, built the nearby Quaker meeting house of 1747–9.[12] This shares several features with the New Room, not

Fig 3.5
The first-floor common room of John Wesley's New Room, Bristol. This room was used by Wesley and his fellow itinerant ministers when they were based in Bristol. Much of the room's present character and furnishing dates from George Oatley's restoration of 1929–30.
[DP166251]

least a central lantern for top light and ventilation (but not in this case for surveillance). The Quakers' building was better finished than Wesley's, but Tully, himself a Quaker, was no doubt able to work – as Wesley would have required – within a constrained budget as well as a constricted site.

London and Bristol were the first two bases for Wesley's evangelising campaign, and in 1743 they were joined by a third: the Orphan House in Newcastle.[13] Though this building seems never to have served the function implied by its name, it became a thriving place of worship and an important centre for the Methodists' work in the north of England and in Scotland. In these early decades building was not a priority for Wesley, however: Methodism in his eyes was still a network of activists within the Church of England.

The most newsworthy of Wesley's Methodist associates was George Whitefield, whose phenomenal success in preaching to the coal miners of Kingswood had led Wesley to Bristol in particular and to open-air preaching in general. In 1741, however, the two men fell out theologically. Whitefield became convinced of the Calvinistic view of predestination (hence the characterisation of Calvinistic Methodism), while Wesley proclaimed that Christ had died for all men, not merely the elect. In that year Whitefield's London followers built a chapel, close to the Foundery in Moorfields. Whitefield called his great wooden edifice the Tabernacle after the Israelites' tabernacles in the wilderness (see box, p 22), 'because, perhaps, we may be called to move our tents'.[14] There was a Moravian-influenced pattern of activities beyond the round of services: weekday meetings, a school, an employment exchange and, for a while, a workshop. In 1752–3 the timber structure was replaced by a brick building, 80 feet (24.4m) square, with galleries on each side, and reputedly capable of holding 4,000 hearers. With its square, pyramidal roof topped by a broad lantern, the Tabernacle bore a certain resemblance to some of the big early meeting houses familiar to Whitefield from his recent, four-year preaching tour of America. It quite upstaged the makeshift premises of Wesley's Foundery.

By this time, through contact with Selina, Countess of Huntingdon, Whitefield had begun to relish the challenge of converting more sophisticated individuals. In 1756 another square chapel (reportedly 70 feet (21.3m) square) was erected for him in Tottenham Court Road (Fig 3.6), intended to appeal to the population of London's West End.[15] If its design was basically

that of the Moorfields building, the details were more striking. The central three bays of the façade were picked out with pilasters and carried a mannered pediment with what might have been a bellcote. Each corner of the building carried a ball finial, while atop the steep, pyramidal roof was a wide lantern, inspired by the Halicarnassus mausoleum, with an ogee dome. The building's bricklayer-architect, Matthew Pearce, was hardly a scholarly practitioner, but he was evidently capable of adopting decorative elements from architects of Hawksmoor's generation, as well as being quite up to the demands of constructing one of the country's largest Nonconformist chapels.

An engraving shows this landmark building in 1764, by which time its emphatic squareness had been compromised by a 'semi-octagonal' extension towards the road of 1759–60.[16] A pair of carriage entrances led to the forecourt (the Prince of Wales and his sisters are said to have attended several times), and at the rear were two sets of almshouses which the well-heeled congregation was expected to support. The galleried interior, as shown in an early 19th-century engraving, had a sequence of square columns bearing an entablature and thence a high-coved ceiling. In pride of place was the three-decker pulpit, from which Whitefield and his fellow preachers were able to command some 3,000–4,000 hearers. There had been celebrity

*Fig 3.6
Whitefield's Tabernacle, Tottenham Court Road, London, 1756 by Matthew Pearce (demolished). This was the smartest of the big chapels erected for George Whitefield, the leading Calvinistic Methodist preacher. Only three years after opening, extensions were begun.
[Redrawn by Bradley in 1889 from a 1756 original, from Phillips 1964, fig 304]*

preachers long before this era of evangelism, but the creation of a series of super-chapels, based on one man's power in the pulpit, was something quite new. Neither of the London tabernacles survives, though successor buildings stand on each site, and only the forlorn shell remains of the large tabernacle at Kingswood, Bristol that was built for Whitefield in 1741 after his split from Wesley.[17]

The buildings of Old Dissent at mid-century

Long-wall façades

Before looking at the subsequent architecture of these newer religious movements, it is important to consider the chapels and meeting houses built in the meantime for the long-established Dissenting groups and their continental cousins. During the 1750s and 1760s all four of the by now familiar denominations (Presbyterians, Independents, Quakers and Baptists) erected a growing number of new places of worship, sometimes benefiting from the spiritual resurgence kindled by Methodism.[18] In rural areas these new buildings mostly employed the tried and tested pattern of a symmetrical

long-wall façade. One such is the sturdy stone Baptist chapel built in 1760 (at a cost of £192) on an exposed hillside site at Goodshaw, north of Rawtenstall, Lancashire, and enlarged in stages over the next 50 years.[19] The present façade (of 1809?) has generous sash windows rather than the mullioned openings that survive in older parts of the chapel, but otherwise it illustrates the continuing strength of architectural habits established in the 'age of toleration'. Goodshaw's atmospheric interior seems to encapsulate those habits. There is a complete set of box pews, raked galleries on three sides, a double-tiered brass chandelier with dove finial and a high-canopied pulpit that overlooks a wide communion pew (Fig 3.7). Close inspection shows that many of these fittings, like the building itself, were altered during the late 18th or early 19th century to meet the needs of the growing congregation, but the effect is still essentially Georgian.

The same cannot be said, however, of Underbank chapel (opened in 1743), whose interior has sadly few reminders of its mid-18th-century appearance.[20] The exterior is of such quality (Fig 3.8) as to make the loss of the interior especially regrettable. Underbank chapel (now Unitarian) stands on a once isolated hillside at Stannington, 4 miles west of Sheffield, and must always have been a landmark. Its broad façade has many of the same elements as at Goodshaw. Each is symmetrically composed with two storeys of windows in the outer bays, doorways in the second and fifth bays and a pair of taller windows at the centre. Yet the character of Underbank is quite different. Bold keystones and quoins richly punctuate the facade, and the rectilinear rhythm gives way to curves for the central windows and the *oeils-de-boeuf* above the doors. These features, drawn from the repertoire of English baroque, were hardly the latest fashion in 1743, but they were brought together with such brio that Underbank has deservedly figured in almost every account of early Nonconformist architecture.

In 1743, the same year in which Underbank chapel opened, a substantial Huguenot chapel was built in Fournier Street, Spitalfields (Fig 3.9).[21] Large numbers of the French Protestants who had fled Louis XIV's persecution in the 1680s settled in the East End of London (many of them working in the silk trade), and by 1700 they had nine places of worship in Spitalfields. The new chapel in Fournier Street was the product of prosperity. Its broad, six-bay façade is an expanded variant of a Nonconformist type –

Fig 3.7
Interior of Goodshaw Baptist chapel, near Rawtenstall, Lancashire, 1760 and later. The communion table in the foreground stands below the pulpit, in a pew which seems usually to have been occupied by singers. [K860001]

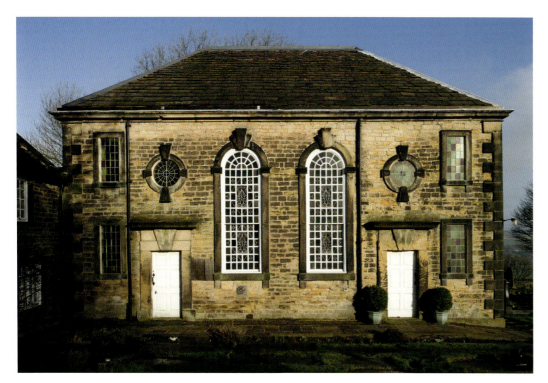

*Fig 3.8 (left)
Underbank chapel (now
Unitarian), Stannington,
South Yorkshire, 1743. The
boldly composed façade has
been admired by
generations of
commentators and is the
subject of one of John
Piper's spirited drawings.
[DP157020]*

*Fig 3.9 (below)
Huguenot chapel (now a
mosque), Fournier Street,
London, 1743. The long-
wall façade fits well into the
Georgian streetscape while
emphasising the public
character of the building in
contrast to its largely
domestic neighbours.
[K040854]*

the type indeed represented at Goodshaw and Underbank – but tailored to fit the horizontal lines of the adjacent London terraces. Uniformly fenestrated, with segment-headed windows below and round-headed ones above, the neat brick façade is capped by a cornice at much the same height as the parapets of the street's houses. The middle four bays project a little and are given added importance by a triangular pediment, within which is a sundial, inscribed *umbra sumus* ('we are a shadow'). As the chapel occupies a corner site, its east face, on to Brick Lane, is also emphasised, with a pediment extending its full width. This unusual pairing of pediments has been described as suggesting 'a Greek cross of which the arms have been pushed in'.[22] The centrepiece of the side elevation is a Venetian window, a fashionably Palladian motif, quietly heralding one end of Fournier Street, while the monumental Serliana of Hawksmoor's Christ Church trumpets the other.

Immediately next to the chapel in Fournier Street was the minister's house, and adjacent in Brick Lane was the vestry and school – an arrangement of which Wesley would surely have approved. The surveyor responsible for building (and probably designing) all this for the French was Thomas Stibbs, a carpenter whose skills were put to good use here. Photographs show that the wide interior was cleanly spanned, giving uninterrupted sightlines from the galleries

which ranged around three sides (west, south and east) of the chapel. With a capacity of almost 2,000, the chapel was fitted with box pews and its pulpit presumably stood on the north side, facing the entrances: an essentially conventional plan, even if the architectural details were relatively up to date.

It is worth outlining the history of the Fournier Street chapel since the decline of its French congregation.[23] In 1809 it became the headquarters for the London Society for Promoting Christianity among the Jews, and from 1819 it was leased by the Wesleyan Methodists. In 1897 it became Spitalfields Great Synagogue, serving some of the many Ashkenazi refugees from Eastern Europe who by then populated the area. The well-lit, galleried interior nicely suited the needs of a Jewish congregation, and Stibbs's Venetian window provided a more than adequate setting for the necessarily east-facing Torah Ark, though part of the gallery had to be dismantled to make way for the Ark and some pews were removed for the bema (or reading platform). In the late 20th century Spitalfields became home to many Bangladeshi Muslims, and in 1975 the building was converted into a mosque (Brick Lane Jamme Masjid), for which

purpose many of the remaining fittings were stripped out in 1986. Few buildings encompass the religious history of British immigration quite so vividly.

Short-wall façades

The long-wall façade type of plan had extraordinary staying power and was to be used by chapel-builders for many decades more. Yet from the middle of the 18th century onwards new urban chapels were increasingly often designed to present a short, rather than a broad, face to the world. A clear illustration of this is the former George's meeting house, Exeter (Fig 3.10), which was built in 1760 (the start of George III's reign, hence the name) to supersede two older Presbyterian meeting houses.[24] Its handsome façade is wide enough at 50 feet (15.2m), but the building stretches back almost half as far again. Although the site was relatively narrow, it was long enough to allow the façade to be set back from the street, with space for a pedimented Tuscan porch in what was originally a forecourt. Stylistically George's meeting house was conservative for its date, and at least part of the magnificently canopied

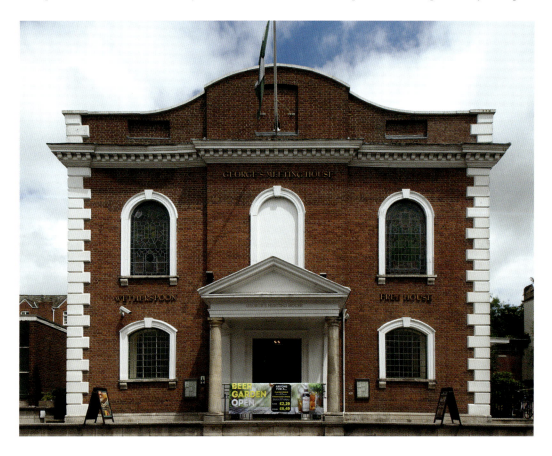

Fig 3.10
The former George's meeting house, Exeter, 1760. Facing on to a busy main street, this was built for one of Exeter's foremost Nonconformist congregations. The three-bay façade reflects the turn to a long internal axis. [DP160672]

pulpit came from the previous James's meeting (named for James II, under whose Declaration of Indulgence it was erected in 1687). The plan is thus more likely to have been part of a gradual shift in Nonconformist attitudes rather than a radical rejection of earlier habits. Another sign of this is the unresolved relationship between the gently curved parapet of the façade and the great hipped roof that rises beyond.

No such duality exists at the Presbyterian (now Unitarian) Westgate chapel (Fig 3.11) of 1751–2 in Wakefield, however.[25] Here the gabled roof structure is directly expressed in the pedimented façade, and for good measure a domed bellcote emphasises the point. The Gibbs surrounds of the windows are essentially baroque motifs, their white masonry crisply emphasised against the red brickwork, but otherwise the design shows more signs of Palladian taste – an appropriately sophisticated note in this part of Wakefield, where the houses of leading merchants were soon to be built. On the side elevations are tall recessed windows, almost mannerist variations of the Venetian window theme. It is tempting to seek a designer for this, and John Carr, the pragmatic Palladian architect who grew up in nearby Horbury, has

sometimes been proposed. However, many of the details could have been derived from one of the numerous new pattern books by such men as William Halfpenny or Batty Langley.

As Britain became more urban, competition for good sites accelerated. No doubt the change to short-wall façades was affected by Nonconformists' desire to have an architectural presence in towns where street frontages were at a premium, but there is no doubt either that the move away from long-wall façades was accompanied by internal changes. Where the main entrance was in a short wall, it came to seem natural for the chief internal focus – the pulpit, and usually also the communion table – to lie straight ahead. A parallel can be made with the Anglican church of St George, Bloomsbury (of 1716–31), designed by Hawksmoor to have an eastward altar, despite the north–south alignment of the site. Parishioners seem never to have been comfortable with this liturgical nicety, and in 1781 the altar was placed at the north end, facing the main entrance on the building's long axis.[26]

Nonconformist Protestants, seeing no need to face east, were unlikely to risk such problems: for them a short-wall façade was generally

Fig 3.11
Presbyterian (now Unitarian) chapel, Wakefield, 1751–2. With its stylish punctuation, this is one of the most emphatic mid-Georgian examples of a gable-end façade. [DP143341]

associated with a long internal axis. Such was the case in both Exeter and Wakefield, though neither retains its original fittings. A little-altered example survives, however, in London's Whitechapel: the chapel of St George, built in 1762–4 for a German Lutheran congregation.[27] Squeezed on to a narrow site in Alie Street, the chapel has a three-bay façade with doorways in the outer bays. Inside there is no middle gangway such as could be found in most Anglican – and indeed most Lutheran – buildings; instead lateral gangways separate the central block of pews from those along each side. This pattern, so favoured by Nonconformists, reflected the importance of seeing and hearing, rather as in

Fig 3.12
Interior of St George's Lutheran chapel, Alie Street, London, 1762–4. In the confined space of this narrow building, the pulpit and communion table compete for attention with Decalogue panels and royal arms.
[DP155964]

the theatre. Since square pews were coming to seem old-fashioned, almost all the pews are long, with a seat on only one side so as to face the pulpit (a tendency noted earlier at Mary Street Baptist chapel, Taunton). Galleries extend the full length of the building, supported by eight Tuscan columns, and across the entrance end. The organ which now occupies the end gallery dates from 1885–6, but its predecessor was probably in place by the 1780s. Music played an important role in services from the outset.

Two aspects of the chapel show how Nonconformists might need to adjust to worship in a long, rather than a broad, building. Extra stairs lead down directly from each gallery to the communion area, avoiding an otherwise lengthy route, and hymn boards hang along the gallery fronts – conveniently for those whose eyesight is not sharp over a distance. Even the short-sighted will sense something of the splendour that surrounds the pulpit, however. Flanking the pulpit is a very grand pair of Decalogue panels (once a prominent feature of many places of worship, Christian and Jewish), with fine gilt lettering in German and elaborately carved frames.[28] Unmissably placed above the pulpit are the Royal Arms of George III, a large and gilded wooden carving attesting to the Lutherans' support for the Hanoverian dynasty.[29] Close in front of the pulpit is the communion table, its position like that in many English chapels, but also thoroughly Lutheran (Fig 3.12). Its immediate setting was altered by the introduction of a most unusual canvas reredos, perhaps from the 1780s. Records show that German craftsmen were responsible for many of these special fittings, but the building is likely to have been designed by Joel Johnson, the London carpenter–builder whose firm erected the chapel. The façade, with its Venetian window and lunette, is more readily understood in the context of English, rather than German, architecture of the 1760s. Moreover, its present plain pediment originally carried a clock and a three-tier bell turret similar to that which Johnson had previously built at St John's, Wapping.[30]

Other plans

It is always dangerous to generalise about so varied a phenomenon as Nonconformity, and this is especially true in architectural matters. Chapels and meeting houses of the 18th century came in many shapes, not just the convenient typology of long-wall and short-wall façades.

In this context the (now Unitarian) Octagon chapel in Colegate, Norwich is of exceptional importance (Fig 3.13). It was built in 1754–6 for a congregation of well-connected Presbyterians, replacing their first purpose-built place of worship in Norwich, which had been completed by 1689.[31] Initially it was thought that the new chapel would have a rectangular plan, its entrance front being in the short side facing the street, like many other urban chapels of the time. In the event an octagonal plan was adopted, however, and this has attracted attention ever since. The allure of its neat geometry is captured in John Wesley's oft-quoted description of the exterior: 'It is eight square, built of the finest brick, with sixteen sash-windows below, as many above, and eight skylights'.[32] Even more remarkable is the interior of the chapel (Fig 3.14), where the domed central space is bounded by eight giant, fluted Corinthian columns; each bears a deep

entablature block and round arches, an idea possibly adapted from James Gibbs's circular design for St Martins-in-the-Fields. Behind the columns a raked gallery runs around the chapel, so that its pews, like those underneath, could follow the octagonal lines of the wall. The pulpit is set in front of the gallery, facing the entrance (and a well-placed clock) across a block of pews. Since 1802 an organ has occupied the gallery space behind the pulpit. Except for the columns interrupting certain sightlines, the plan of the building enables the preacher to be clearly seen and heard, and also shapes the congregation's sense of itself as a body of worshippers.

Octagons had been employed for secular auditories, such as Inigo Jones's Cockpit Theatre, Whitehall and the Dublin House of Commons, and there were also many ecclesiastical precedents, from the Calvinistic Netherlands to Counter-Reformation Italy.[33] The almost exactly

Fig 3.13
Octagon chapel (now Unitarian), Norwich, 1754–6. As Wesley implied, this important chapel is to be understood in a European – not merely a British – context. [DP160398]

contemporary Lutheran church in Rellingen, near Hamburg (1754–6 by Cay Dose) was just the latest German example. However, Norwich's was the first major instance of an octagonal place of worship in modern England. At least one London architect (Robert Morris) supplied designs for the building, without success. It has long been assumed that the chapel's architect was the local builder Thomas Ivory, one of the chief contractors, but Vic Nierop-Reading has recently suggested that the basic scheme came from the chapel's highly capable minister, John Taylor.[34]

Fig 3.14
Interior of the Octagon chapel, Norwich. Although the seating has been altered and space created in front of the pulpit, the fine interior remains one of the most impressive of its age. [DP160139]

What is beyond doubt is the quality of work in the building. It made a real impression on Wesley, who visited in 1757, the year after its opening:

> I was shown Dr. Taylor's new meeting-house, perhaps the most elegant one in Europe. … The inside is finished in the highest taste and is as clean as any nobleman's saloon. The communion table is fine mahogany; the very latches of the pew-doors are polished brass.[35]

None of this came cheaply (at a reported total of more than £5,000 the chapel cost as much as many fashionable Anglican churches of the time), but the chapel was the religious home for many of Norwich's most influential families. Among the first subscribers to the building fund were a Martineau and two Mottrams; some of their illustrious descendants are among those named either on the numerous wall tablets or on the sword- and mace-rests that are witness to the generations of civic leaders who have worshipped here (Fig 3.15). The chapel had many architectural offspring, as we shall see, and helped to broaden the repertoire of English religious architecture for the Established Church as well as Nonconformists.

Norwich's Octagon chapel became a benchmark for Wesley. In 1772, for instance, while on a preaching tour of Yorkshire, he had cause to recall it:

> on Wednesday, the 8th, I went to Halifax. My old friend, Titus Knight, offered me the use of his new meeting, larger than Dr. Taylor's, at Norwich, full as superb (so he terms it in his poem,) and finished with the utmost elegance.[36]

Titus Knight had been a Methodist, but in 1762–3 he became an Independent minister in Halifax with a congregation that outgrew its first home in ten years, and for whom the new chapel had been completed a few weeks before Wesley's visit. Knight's building (which had opened in May 1772) was not octagonal but square, and indeed it subsequently came to be known as Square chapel (Fig 3.16).[37] (Even if, as seems possible, it was named for a nearby square of superior houses, the sobriquet was more accurately applied to the chapel than to the irregularly shaped residential development.) Its proportions are systematically Palladian, the gallery level being treated externally as the *piano nobile* below a blind attic storey with short rectangular recesses.

For its use as a place of worship, the square plan offered none of the disadvantages of a long-axis building and provided a space in which most seats could be within relatively close range of the pulpit. It was effectively a central plan, like an octagon (if structurally more straightforward). Yet the squareness was more than practical: each of the four elevations had a central Venetian window, as if to highlight the biaxial symmetry. It seems likely that the inspiration came from Whitefield's unambiguously square London tabernacles (in which Titus Knight had preached), and beyond them perhaps to descriptions of the Holy of Holies in Solomon's Temple. Wesley, it might be noted, was more taken with the size and splendour than the shape, and Knight's ambitious poem (*Hhadash Hamishcan: or, the New Chapel, at Halifax*) was in part a defence of those qualities:

> But since you deem this House too large, and fine,
> I'll lead your envious Thoughts to Palestine.
> View foolish Solomon, at vast Expence,
> Erect a House, which for Magnificence,
> For Elegance, and Ornament, as far
> Excell'd this House, as doth the Sun, a Star.[38]

Fig 3.15
Octagon chapel, Norwich. The sword and mace rests record the names of various mayors of the city who have been members of the distinguished congregations here. [DP160147]

Fig 3.16
Square chapel (Independent), Halifax, 1772. Converted for use as an arts centre since 1988, Square chapel is still one of the town's landmark buildings. [RCH01/118/01/03/066]

There is an echo here of John Fairfax's justification of the scale and adornment of the Ipswich meeting house in 1700 (*see* p 26). Nonconformist splendour was not an invention of the later 18th century, still less of the 19th. As for the size of Square chapel, Wesley rejected Knight's invitation to preach there; he calculated that more people would attend in the open air, and so 'preached in the cow-market, to a huge multitude'.[39] Square chapel flourished nonetheless, but in the late 20th century it suffered subdivision and the almost total loss of fittings. Recently reborn as the centrepiece of a new arts complex, its celebrated shape remains: conceived in a Palladian tradition and born at a time when neo-classicism was beginning to give new value to pure geometry.

Mention must also be made of the interest in curved plans. Possibly the oldest Nonconformist example is the Presbyterian meeting house (now Roman Catholic) at Bewdley, Worcestershire (Fig 3.17), erected in about 1778.[40] Its side walls are essentially straight, but the end walls are gently curved, their rounded form emphasised by the sweep of the shallow slate roof. Inside, a curved gallery occupies the entrance end of the chapel, and the pulpit had a commanding place between a pair of round-headed windows in the centre of the curved wall opposite. The box pews, now replaced by benches, were similarly curved, thereby angling worshippers naturally towards the pulpit. Was the plan conceived as a means of focusing attention on the pulpit, or in order that a curved wall behind the pulpit might amplify the speaker's voice? Or even for the external novelty? Perhaps all three.

It is difficult to find a precise precedent for the plan, although a few larger churches of similar shape had been built in Germany.[41] Fully elliptical churches were certainly known in 18th-century Germany, and perhaps the oldest major example in Britain is the First Presbyterian church, Rosemary Street, Belfast (1781–3).[42] Roger Mulholland, its architect, followed Catholic baroque precedent in organising the building around the long axis, with the pulpit at one of the narrow ends and an organ in the gallery opposite. Some of the ground-floor seating, and all of that in the gallery, follows the curved lines of the building. Wesley preached here in 1789 and was smitten by its design:

It is the completest place of public worship I have ever seen. It is of an oval form; as I judge by my eye, a hundred feet long, and seventy or eighty broad. It is very lofty, and has two rows of large windows, so that it is as light as our new chapel in London; and the rows of pillars, with every other part, are so finely proportioned, that it is beautiful in the highest degree.[43]

Fig 3.17
Interior of the Presbyterian meeting house (now Roman Catholic), Bewdley, Worcestershire, about 1778. In the space now occupied by the reredos, a pulpit originally stood against the wall, its tester level with the window tops. [DP164587]

Wesley's admiration for the building seems not to have had any repercussions in Methodism, but several other elliptical places of worship were designed in the 1780s, including St Andrew's church, George Street, Edinburgh (1781–4; Presbyterian), the Pauluskirche, Frankfurt (begun 1789; Lutheran) and All Saints' church, Newcastle upon Tyne (1786–96; Anglican). However, each was laid out around the short axis. It was to be several decades before English Nonconformists fully embraced the idea of an elliptical auditory church.

The buildings of the evangelical revival after 1750

As has already been noted, George Whitefield (whose Methodism had become Calvinistic and thus separated from Wesley's movement) grasped the opportunity to create a chain of great tabernacle chapels during the 1750s. His building campaign was not sustained, however, partly because of his absence on missionary work in America. At this stage attention turns to the maverick figure of Selina Hastings, Countess of Huntingdon. One of Wesley's earliest followers, she had embraced Calvinism in the 1740s and fostered many of Whitefield's efforts. While retaining her allegiance to the Church of England, in the 1760s she opened what were technically private chapels at fashionable resorts, supplied by men who were nominally her personal chaplains.

The most talked-about of her early chapels was built in The Vineyards, Bath in 1765.[44] What faces the street is the house in which she stayed when in Bath, and which provided lodgings for ministers (Fig 3.18). Attached to its rear is the large chapel, stretching away from the street (Fig 3.19). Such an arrangement justified the legal status of the chapel, but despite this description there was no attempt to disguise the enterprise by blending in with the city's renowned terraces.

Fig 3.18
Countess of Huntingdon's chapel, Bath, 1765. With its array of ogee windows, the Countess's own villa is most visible from the street.
[DP166256]

The Countess had a visual flair – once attending a royal birthday party dressed in a fashion 'more properer for a stucco staircase than the apparel of a lady' – and her house and chapel immediately attracted attention as one of Bath's first examples of the new fashion for Gothic.[45]

For such an independent woman, the appeal of Gothic surely lay in its association with ideals of liberty. The diminutive castellated house has ogee-headed windows, some with clustered columns and some grouped in threes, with a happy disregard for classical proportions. All of this engaging display sets the tone for the chapel beyond, which was visited in 1766 by no less an arbiter than Horace Walpole of Strawberry Hill. He reported it to be 'very neat, with <u>true</u> Gothic windows' and admired the mahogany light-stands and brackets in the same taste.[46]

In attending to the novel architecture, some commentators – though not Walpole – have overlooked the chapel's unusual layout. Because it had no show front, visitors (except for Lady Huntingdon's guests, who used an internal route from the house) entered the chapel from the side, at right angles to the long internal axis. At the west end, furthest from the street, a dais extended the full width of the chapel; a broad-winged eagle lectern stood on each side, one for the minister and the other for the clerk. Walpole noted that each of the lecterns had a red cushion and a scarlet armchair. Here was the stage on which the minister played the leading role, and from which he ascended the pulpit – set, with a third eagle, in the middle of the end wall (Fig 3.20). Despite the ample space afforded by this platform, the railed communion table was given its own place in an apse at the opposite end of the chapel.

Such polarisation of word and sacrament was unusual, to say the least. A later Anglican example (of 1782) is known, at Teigh in Rutland, although there the church is seated like a college chapel, allowing its congregation to turn either way. This might have worked for those Walpole described as the 'elect ladies' in the side galleries at Bath, but not for those sitting in the body of the chapel, with the communion apse behind them. Wesley, who administered communion here (and later the same day preached, in Walpole's presence), says nothing about the liturgical arrangements. Whoever the architect was, it seems most probable that the determined Countess had more than a hand in the planning, and also in the choice of style. One of her next projects was the transformation of a farmhouse into her own ministerial training college at Trefecca in mid-Wales, a task for which she introduced a quite accomplished repertoire of Gothic motifs.[47] Relations with Wesley at first remained cordial, and in 1769 he preached on her birthday in Trefecca, but within a year the Countess began to remove his supporters from the college. Almost inevitably she broke from the Church of England too, and in 1783 the creation of the Countess of Huntingdon's Connexion, unequivocally Calvinistic, was marked by the ordination of some of the Trefecca students in her London chapel.

It will be clear by this point that Wesley maintained an extraordinary network of contacts with Anglicans and Nonconformists alike. Few of his contemporaries can have visited so many places of worship. During the first decades of his ministry he built little, however, remaining highly reluctant to provoke a separation from the Established Church. Only in the 1760s did the pace of building quicken for his followers, and at that stage Wesley frequently recommended the octagon, undoubtedly as a result of his visit to Norwich in 1757. Between 1761 and 1776 at least 14 octagonal Methodist chapels were built, in locations ranging from Cornwall to Aberdeen.[48] Part of the attraction must have been their distinctive external form – an eye-catcher in both urban and rural settings – which served the growing movement well. In Taunton, for instance, the octagonal chapel (Fig 3.21) opened by Wesley in 1776 would have contrasted boldly with the town's four meeting houses built by Dissenters more than half a century before.[49] It was a trim

Fig 3.21
(Wesleyan) Methodist chapel, Taunton, opened in 1776. Now restored for office use, this was one of the last of the octagonal chapels to be built for Wesley.
[DP166297]

building of red brick, with circular windows at gallery level and round-headed windows below, seen to advantage across a spacious forecourt. The proportions of its tiled, pyramidal roof were influenced by Wesley's preference for shallow-pitched structures, perhaps again a desire to distance his movement from the architectural fashions associated with the 'age of toleration'.[50]

External appearances were only part of the reason for Wesley's advocacy of octagons, of course. The shape was, he argued, 'best for the voice, and on many accounts more commodious than any other'.[51] Naturally he must have believed that octagons were well-suited for preaching, but perhaps he also felt

Fig 3.22
Wesley's chapel, City Road, London, 1777–8. Built to replace Wesley's first London premises (a former foundry), the new chapel was soon seen as the headquarters of what was becoming an international movement.
[DP155970]

that his beloved congregational hymn singing was nurtured in such spaces: the psychology of eye contact as well as the physics of acoustics. The nature of services in such a building can be imagined. All eyes would turn to the pulpit for the sermon, with the focus shifting as the congregation rose to join together in heartfelt Methodist song. All the better if the place were packed. So far as is known none of Wesley's octagonal chapels had its sightlines impaired by roof-bearing columns, such as those in Taylor's Norwich chapel, and as a rule galleries did not extend behind the pulpit. In these respects the Taunton example was characteristic. But it was the last such building to be erected for Wesley. Within a year he was to embark on a landmark chapel of quite different character.

In 1776, worried about the continuing lease of the Foundery, Wesley and his local committee began to plan for a successor building to act as the Methodists' chief place of worship and headquarters in London. The site, only yards away from the Foundery, was in the new City Road, and offered a more auspicious setting (Fig 3.22). Wesley's journal for 29 November refers to 'the several plans which were offered for the new chapel', but does not say whether there was an octagonal scheme among them. Perhaps the need for a large building on a relatively narrow site determined the outcome: a rectangular chapel, whose façade was in one end of the building, facing City Road.[52] Not only was this type of plan becoming the norm for chapels such as those in Exeter and Wakefield, but also Wesley was used to such a layout at his Bristol New Room. The wide-spanned interior of the City Road chapel (Fig 3.23) – its sightlines uninterrupted by giant columns – was dominated by a sumptuously classical three-decker pulpit, which stood on the building's long central axis, facing the entrance.

By now Wesley had come to accept that provision should be made for the communion service in certain of his chapels, and at City Road it was part of every Sunday's morning service.[53] In contrast to the Puritan tradition there was a communion rail, at which people would usually kneel. More unexpectedly the communion area was placed behind the pulpit (a position then much more familiar in Anglican than Nonconformist buildings) in a shallow apse, with a reredos of Decalogue, creed and Lord's Prayer panels. This arrangement cannot have been agreed without Wesley's approval, and it was to influence Methodist builders for some time. Did it reflect a desire for a more seemly setting, or did it allow communion to be administered more efficiently to very large congregations? The chapel will have been alarmingly full on occasion, and circulation could have been a problem. In addition to the block of pews which seems always to have filled the centre, as well as others below the gallery, there was standing room inside the entrance and also behind the two rows of gallery pews. Wesley's egalitarian policy of denying pew-renters the right to claim pews as their own (explicitly reinforced here in 1787) would have facilitated the efficient filling of seats on busy occasions.[54] In an attempt to avoid crushes at the main west door, there were supplementary entrances in the long south wall.

Since November 1778, when the unfinished chapel was first used for worship, there have been so many changes that its original appearance cannot easily be imagined. Wesley's description of the building on its opening day as 'perfectly neat but not fine' might be as much a reflection of financial caution as an aesthetic principle, for even seven years later he spent a week 'in the unpleasing but necessary work of going through the town, and begging for the poor men who had been employed in finishing the new chapel'.[55] The brick exterior was virtually unadorned, and its rhythm of round-headed windows, the lower ones in arched recesses (now best appreciated at the rear elevation), resembles some of the minimally neo-classical schemes of George Dance junior – who, as Clerk of the City Works, drew up plans for this area. The interior was far from lavishly decorated, but it does seem to have been more than 'perfectly neat'. To take one example, the ceiling combines winged cherubs in sunbursts with more classical motifs in a spare version of Robert Adam's style. Who designed

Fig 3.23
Interior of Wesley's chapel, City Road, London. It has been greatly embellished since the 18th century (eg the 1890s stained glass in the apse and the jasper columns below the gallery), and the pulpit was reduced in height in 1864.
[DP155975]

all this is still a matter for speculation, although the identity of its builder has long been known: Samuel Tooth, a Methodist local preacher.

Long after the opening service, building work continued at Wesley's City Road chapel. It was not only a matter of furnishing and decorating the chapel, but also of providing for the other functions of the Foundery. For small weekday services a morning chapel was erected on the north side of the main building, and in August 1779 the premises were sufficiently well equipped to host the annual conference of Methodist preachers. On the south side of the chapel a house was built for Wesley (to the designs of George Dance) and to the north two houses were constructed, one of which acted as the office for Methodist publications. The movement steadily outgrew this promising location, but worship has always continued on the site. Today the much-embellished chapel is also a place of pilgrimage as a sort of cathedral of world Methodism.

The building of Wesley's new London chapel did not transform Methodist architecture, but it did exert an influence. An early instance of this was the chapel in New King Street, Bath, for which Wesley laid the foundation stone on 17 December 1777 (that is to say, while the City Road chapel was under construction), and which he described as 'about half as large as that at London, and built nearly upon the same model'.[56] Many in Methodism must have felt that they had here a template, for in 1790 the governing conference resolved that 'all preaching-houses are to be built in future upon the same plan as the London or Bath chapel'.[57] Another interesting instance of the City Road plan, with the communion table behind the pulpit, and a separate morning chapel, was the chapel built for Manchester's flourishing Methodists in 1779–80 (Fig 3.24); Wesley opened the building in 1781, describing it as being 'about the size of that in London'.[58] The plan and dimensions might have resembled the London original, but the appearance did not, for the Manchester chapel was Gothic. It had a dramatic silhouette, thanks to a battlemented parapet with crocketed pinnacles, and the façade to Oldham Street bore a Gothic paraphrase of a Venetian window and a prominent ogee dripmould in the gable end. It was not Manchester's first taste of the Gothic Revival, but the town had seen nothing quite like it before. Inside the chapel the gallery fronts had elaborately carved Gothic panels, and in 1871 it reminded a visitor 'of some of those large old-English churches which we occasionally see in remote country parishes'.[59]

This was probably not the first occasion when Gothic features were used in one of Wesley's chapels, and it was certainly not the last. Another instance occurred in Whitby, where in 1788 a new chapel was built in Church Street to replace an octagonal building lost to coastal erosion. The new chapel, though it was planned with a broad façade, had pointed windows and doors, and was considered by Wesley to be 'one of the most beautiful chapels in Great Britain'.[60]

Fig 3.24
(Wesleyan) Methodist chapel, Oldham Street, Manchester, 1779–80 (demolished). It was built on the lines of the City Road chapel, but with fashionably Gothic details.
[Courtesy of Manchester Libraries, Information and Archives, Manchester City Council, M68528]

By this date Wesley was in his late eighties, and the movement of which he remained the central figure was preparing for a future as a body fully independent of the Church of England. Its buildings were to be increasingly significant, and from 1784 they were legally controlled by the annual conference of 100 Methodist preachers.

The final example in this chapter returns to the Moravians, with whom it began. Fulneck remained their chief settlement in England, although settlements in Bedford and at Ockbrook, Derbyshire, are evidence of their strength in the years around 1750.[61] A new phase of development occurred in the 1780s, for instance with new building work at East Tytherton, Wiltshire, which the Moravians had inherited from an originally Calvinistic Methodist group.[62] Yet by far the most impressive of their late 18th-century developments was the new settlement of Fairfield, at Droylsden (Fig 3.25), some four miles east of Manchester, which was opened in 1785.[63]

Unlike the predominantly linear plan of Fulneck, Fairfield was laid out with one square of buildings within another. Its streets are lined mostly by family houses, along with former workshops and smaller social premises, while the largest buildings are spread in a line along the southern boundary of the village, facing out (originally across fields) to the Ashton-under-Lyne turnpike road. The centrepiece of this south-facing range is the chapel (of 1784–5), marked out not only by its great width and pediment but also by a belfry atop its broad-hipped roof (Fig 3.26). Its internal arrangements were akin to those at Fulneck, with the pulpit on the north wall and an organ gallery over the centre door opposite. Flanking the chapel

is a pair of houses, those of the minister and steward, and beyond are the large buildings which originally accommodated single women and single men, and later served as schools. The village is still able to convey the sense of a community, ordered but far from regimented, with the chapel as its communal centre.

While the social pattern is that which the Moravians had established in Germany, the

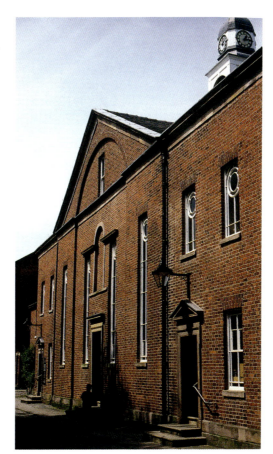

Fig 3.25
Fairfield Moravian settlement, Greater Manchester, 1784–5. The chapel is in the centre, with the three-storey houses for single women and single men to left and right respectively.
[View of Fairfield, engraving after Johannes Swertner, 1794]

Fig 3.26
Fairfield Moravian chapel. The windows were lengthened in 1908 when the chapel was changed internally; the pulpit was moved at this time from the north to the east wall.

understated architecture of Fairfield is British. Basic plans and elevations for Fairfield were drawn by the young Benjamin La Trobe, a future star of American architecture. He had been born at Fulneck and attended school there, taking the opportunity to draw various Yorkshire buildings; his teenage years were spent as a student at the Moravians' elite institutions in Germany, incidentally broadening his experience of Moravian planned settlements.[64] By 1784, when Fairfield's foundations were laid, the 20-year-old La Trobe was in London, from where his father led the Moravian Church in Britain. Although Fairfield was the last such Moravian settlement to be built in this country, it was to inspire Nonconformist builders long into the 19th century, and even beyond.

Conclusion

In the half-century after 1740, the pattern of chapel building in England was changed. Unsurprisingly the architectural styles of Wren's time had given way to the tastes of pattern-book Palladianism, fancy Gothic and early neo-classicism. More notable are the changes in plan-form. Some well-heeled urban Nonconformists began to prefer chapels laid out on the long axis, while others adopted octagonal and other central plans. More subtly, the layout of chapels was affected by Nonconformists' early enthusiasm for congregational hymn singing. The Moravians represented a renewal of the fertile relationship between British Nonconformity and continental Protestant movements, profoundly influencing the character of Methodism at its embryonic stage and giving architectural expression to the concept that social provision was a natural extension of worship.

Architecturally the older Dissenting denominations were still of consequence in the middle years of the 18th century (witness the Norwich Octagon), while Whitefield's great tabernacles were powerful expressions of the evangelical revival. During the 1770s and 1780s Wesley's Methodists were of rising importance. This did not in itself lead to significant architectural change, since Methodists' needs for worship did not differ radically from those of many Dissenting (or, indeed, Anglican) congregations. The difference is best explained as one of *process* rather than product. A meeting house of the earlier period is likely to have been shaped by the resources, skills and contacts of the local congregation. Methodism also drew on these things, but Wesley's personal authority was such that he influenced most decisions about whether or what his followers should build. The idea that one building could become a model, to be adapted for use in many other parts of the country – as happened first with Wesley's octagons and then with the City Road plan – might be compared to the dissemination of Cistercian monastery plans or of Jesuit churches, but it was something new in post-Reformation England.

In his assessment of church building in late 18th-century London, John Summerson acknowledged the role of the newer Nonconformists:

> John Wesley had raised a great porticoed hall in the City Road in 1777–8; Whitefield another, as conspicuous, in Tottenham Court Road in 1756; and Rowland Hill his octagonal auditorium in the Blackfriars Road in 1783. People flocked to these places and others like them. The Church of England on the other hand had nothing new to show but a few proprietary chapels and chapels-of-ease, served from the mother churches and regarded without loyalty or affection by perfunctory suburban congregations.[65]

This judgement is rather hard on suburban Anglicans, and perhaps understates the role of the Church of England's new buildings, but it does convey an important notion. The Nonconformists seemed to be building in cities, towns and villages across the country, while so often the Anglicans were not. Many in the establishment will have felt with some anxiety that Nonconformists were benefiting from the Church of England's apparent lethargy.

4

The age of Methodism

A century on from the golden 'age of toleration', the late 18th century witnessed a fresh burgeoning of Nonconformist building activity.[1] The best indicator of this phenomenal growth is the record of new chapels and meeting houses certified by the Registrars-General. In each decade between 1691 and 1750 Dissenters made fewer than 50 new registrations for permanent places of worship. What happened in succeeding decades is remarkable:

1751–1760	55
1761–1770	85
1771–1780	158
1781–1790	251
1791–1800	832
1801–1810	1,470
1811–1820	2,645

Before reflecting on the impact of chapel building on this scale, two qualifications must be made about the figures. First, not quite all of these registrations were for purpose-built premises, since a proportion would have been for buildings adapted from other purposes, but the statistics specifically exclude temporary places (such as houses or rented property), which were recorded separately. Second, the figures are imperfect because the incidence of registration was affected by the magistrates' more rigorous enforcement of the law after 1790. Yet even if the figures for the 1790s are misleadingly high as compared with the preceding decades, nothing can conceal the underlying trend. New chapels and meeting houses were opening in unprecedented numbers.

The simplest explanation for this increase is to be found in the advance of Methodism, as the title of this chapter suggests. In the 20 years between 1776 and 1796, membership of Wesley's movement in England swelled from 30,875 to 77,402, and the need for permanent buildings grew as Methodism finally separated from the Church of England: Methodist chapels seemed to spring up everywhere. But the simple expla-

nation – though valid – is insufficient, because the Congregationalists and Baptists enjoyed similar growth rates, chiefly through an evangelical impetus which paralleled that of Methodism, and they built accordingly. Paradoxically, even the less evangelical groups (Presbyterians and Quakers) opened many more new buildings in the decades around 1800 than they had half a century earlier, although the absolute numbers were still small. In short, almost all Nonconformist denominations contributed in some degree to the Methodist-led surge of building activity.

An alternative perspective is demographic, focusing on the Nonconformists' ability to build opportunistically wherever fast-growing populations were underserved by the pattern of Anglican parishes. There is some truth in this, for the Church of England spread its resources most thinly in many of the most rapidly developing industrial areas, such as Lancashire. But evangelical initiatives led to the building of new chapels even in some well-churched country districts, and it seems that Nonconformists were little more successful than Anglicans in London and other major areas of urban expansion.[2] The fact is that almost every part of the country was affected by the late-Georgian rise of Nonconformist building activity: elegant spa towns as well as raw industrial hamlets, and scattered agricultural communities as well as the teeming metropolis.

The great increase in chapel building during these years was achieved in challenging circumstances. That the population was expanding rapidly made the task of winning souls more daunting.[3] That lives were increasingly dislocated – by migration from rural to urban areas and from agriculture to industry – further complicated the task of spiritual and pastoral outreach. Furthermore, the fact that Britain was at war with France for long periods between 1793 and 1815 put new difficulties in the way of anyone wishing to build. Moreover, in the midst of these problems, many Nonconformist congregations shouldered a new responsibility: Sunday schools. The Sunday-school movement (popularly supposed to have been started by Robert Raikes in 1780) was directed not at the more or less respectable children of existing church- and chapel-goers, but rather at the vast number of poor children for whom there was no other educational provision.[4] Sundays were the only day available, at least for children who worked in factories. There was invariably a moral – indeed, generally a religious – aspect to the curriculum, and from the outset people of many religious persuasions were actively involved. All kinds of premises were hired or erected for the schools, but Nonconformists became much more inclined than Anglicans to conceive of the school as part of the same premises as the chapel. The architectural results of that commitment are a thread that runs through this and subsequent chapters.

In the decades around 1800 Nonconformists showed a growing propensity to think strategically about their congregations and their chapels – sometimes nationally, but more often at a county or regional level. On the one hand, where Old Dissent was in decline, resources might be consolidated. So it was in Nottinghamshire, where in 1800 the Quakers sold eight of the county's rural meeting houses to finance the enlargement of the meeting house in Mansfield, an enlargement apparently required in order to make the building 'more commodious for the Quarterly Meeting' rather than with a view to growth in membership.[5] By contrast, where Old Dissent had been reinvigorated by the spiritual revival that Methodism had inspired, there were concerted efforts to expand. In Norfolk, for instance, the 12 separate Baptist congregations which existed in 1790 gained a sense of corporate unity under the de facto leadership of Joseph Kinghorn (who became a Norwich minister in that year) and established a dozen more congregations by 1822.[6] At the same time, more than half of the existing Baptist congregations in Norfolk built or rebuilt their chapels and new places of worship were erected for at least three-quarters of the new congregations.[7]

North-west England was one of very many areas in which Congregationalists – conscious of the Methodists' success 'in the most unpromising places' – banded together to support itinerant preachers, each of whom would systematically take the gospel into a circuit of neglected towns and villages.[8] Not all of those preaching stations were ultimately successful, but a good proportion recruited sufficient followers to form an independent congregation and to erect a chapel. It was a process that contributed materially to the spread of evangelical Nonconformity.

Late 18th-century chapels

A selection of five chapels illustrates the range of circumstances that led Nonconformists to build in the last years of the 18th century, as well as the variety of architectural outcomes. The first example is the distinguished meeting house built in 1788–9 for a wealthy congregation (originally Presbyterian, but by then increasingly of Unitarian persuasion) in Lewin's Mead, Bristol (Figs 4.1 and 4.2).[9] At that time the booming city of Bristol was studded with places of worship. In addition to Wesley's New Room and one of Whitefield's tabernacles, there were substantial buildings for the Quakers, Baptists, Presbyterians, Independents and Moravians, while the Anglicans had recently rebuilt several of the city's medieval churches. The existing meeting house in Lewin's Mead had been built after the Act of Toleration and, although – or perhaps because – its centenary was approaching, the congregation decided to have something larger and better appointed, albeit with a traditional long-wall façade to the street. Extra land was bought, and the local architects were passed over in favour of William Blackburn, the reforming prison architect (and Presbyterian) who was then building a handful of gaols in Gloucestershire and the County Bridewell in Bristol.[10] Externally the new meeting house was as assured as its congregation, the Palladian proportions of its ashlar façade giving way to neo-classical details at the centre. Internally the galleried main space is coolly understated, lit by great lunette-headed windows on every side. No columns are needed to support the 70-foot (21.3m) span of the coffered ceiling, thanks to Blackburn's scheme of suspending it on chains from the roof trusses. Ground-floor sightlines also benefit by the use of slender cast-iron posts beneath the galleries.

Here was a space not for evangelical passions, but for rational exposition, commissioned by a congregation that was moving from orthodox Christianity to Unitarianism. It is a sign of the congregation's social status that stables and coach houses for worshippers were provided behind the meeting house, and its commitment

Fig 4.1 (far left) Lewin's Mead meeting house, Bristol, 1788–9 by William Blackburn. This assured building was designed for a Presbyterian congregation that was becoming Unitarian. [DP166260]

Fig 4.2 (left) Interior of Lewin's Mead meeting house. The mahogany pulpit, retained when the building was converted for offices in 1987, overlooks a railed space for the communion table. [DP166257]

to learning can be gauged from the building of a lecture room – where younger members of the congregation were taught and the chapel library was kept – in 1818; additional schoolrooms were added in 1826.[11] Despite conversion to office use in 1987, the meeting house retains much of its dignity and a surprising number of original fittings.

From an example of Old Dissent reasserting itself in the competitive religious environment of a prosperous city, we turn to a case in which one of the newer Nonconformist groups was quick to establish itself in a fledgling industrial community. At the heart of the small Lancashire town of Tyldesley is a chapel built for the Countess of Huntingdon's Connexion in 1789–90.[12] If one thinks of the Countess's chapels as being fancy Gothic creations in such fashionable resorts as Bath, Tyldesley chapel (Fig 4.3) is a useful corrective. Its two-storey brick façade has rudimentary Venetian windows beneath a (now rebuilt) bellcote, and it stands among streets of workers' houses. A local textile manufacturer, Thomas Johnson, gave the land and building materials. The interior has been greatly changed, but local evidence suggests that the Countess's preference for bifocal worship was followed originally, with the pulpit (unexpectedly, in view of the gable-end entrances) on one long wall and the communion table opposite.

The chapel's raised site allows for an undercroft of schoolrooms, roughly on a level with the adjacent street – an early occurrence of what was to become a favoured way for Nonconformists to provide social and educational accommodation in urban situations. By 1790 Sunday

Fig 4.3 Tyldesley chapel, Tyldesley, Lancashire, 1789–90. Built for the Countess of Huntingdon's Connexion, and most recently used by a Pentecostalist church.

Fig 4.4 (right)
Wesleyan Methodist
chapel, Little Walsingham,
Norfolk, 1792–4. This is
a well-composed example
of the chapels built in the
years after Wesley's death,
as Methodism became a
denomination in its own
right.
[DP152853]

Fig 4.5 (below)
Interior of Wesleyan
Methodist chapel, Little
Walsingham. The gallery
is largely unchanged,
but the wide pulpit and
ground-floor seating date
from the late 19th century.
[DP152858]

schools were making a mark across the country, and such new industrial townships were prime candidates for them. Incidentally, it was in the main schoolroom here that John Grundy, one of the chapel's wardens, installed a stove to heat the chapel, and on this basis in 1864 patented a system of heating that had been fitted in more than 1,000 places of worship by the time of his death in 1879.[13] As Tyldesley's first religious building, the chapel must have played a dominant role in the town's formative years. The first Anglican building (a chapel-of-ease to the parish of Leigh) was opened as late as 1824, and the diocesan history laconically remarks that the town 'was spared the surfeit of Anglican churches which afflicted many other places'.[14]

Lancashire's notoriously stretched parochial system naturally provided opportunities for enterprising Nonconformists, but in the 1790s rural chapel building also became a marked feature in eastern counties, a region where the Church of England's network of parishes was relatively strong.[15] In 1792–4, for instance, the

Wesleyan Methodists erected an attractive chapel at Little Walsingham (Figs 4.4 and 4.5), a village-sized Norfolk town.[16] The chapel occupies a site close to a ruined Franciscan friary, one relic of Walsingham's medieval role as a place of pilgrimage with a shrine of the Virgin Mary. Wesley, visiting the town to preach in 1781, had greatly regretted the loss of such noble monastic buildings, but whether he contemplated adapting the remaining fragments for Methodist use is not known.[17]

The new chapel which his followers began just over a decade later was deemed large enough in 1851 to hold over 400, almost half of Walsingham's population, although it is to be imagined that at least some chapel-goers came from surrounding villages. It is almost a model version of the square, two-storeyed pattern that had become familiar for medium-sized chapels in the later 18th century; scaled-down descendants of Whitefield's tabernacles, perhaps? Norfolk has a number of examples of the kind, generally built of red brick and with roofs of dark pantiles. The Walsingham chapel stands out for the consistency of its well-proportioned design, with uniform round-headed openings on each elevation, and a neat pyramid roof. A pair of Tuscan columns frames the central entrance, and a jaunty weather vane graces the apex of the roof. It is not the work of a professional architect, but presumably that of a conscientious local contractor, aided no doubt by the 'book of architecture' that was purchased at a cost of 16 shillings.[18] Such striving after decorousness would surely have pleased Wesley; the appearance of respectability must have been particularly desirable at a time when some Dissenters were openly sympathetic to the revolutionary cause in France. Financially the congregation must have been stretched, however, for the building cost about £750 (roughly one-third of the cost of the Lewin's Mead meeting house), and a debt of £630 remained in 1809, 15 years after the chapel opened. The chapel's interior is notable for original box pews in the steep gallery, which extends around three sides of the building, while the open benches below and the rostrum pulpit appear to date from the late 19th century.

Methodism and its offshoots were not the only challenge to the Anglican Church in rural England in the late 18th century. In some places the older Dissenting denominations were strong enough to build afresh – often reinvigorated by the evangelical spirit of the age. In 1785, for instance a new Baptist chapel was opened in the east Devon hamlet of Prescott (Fig 4.6), superseding the first meeting house which had stood on the site for some 70 years.[19] The new chapel was about the same size as that built by the Methodists in Walsingham and, like it, had a gallery on three sides. Its plan is a long one,

Fig 4.6
Prescott Baptist chapel, near Culmstock, Devon, 1785. Even in rural locations, chapel builders were beginning to use gable-end façades by the 1780s.
[DP160667]

however, with a gable-end façade and the pulpit at the far end. Such plans, which appear to have been more favoured by urban congregations a few decades earlier, were becoming more common in rural situations by this time.

The interior offers a case study in conservative renewal. The communion table is probably that of the early 18th-century building, along with re-used parts of the pulpit and gallery seating ('NI' and 'WM' inscribed their initials in 1719 and 1721 respectively). Understated craftsmanship is the hallmark of what was built in 1785: octagonal posts of oak support long cornice-beams and thence a vaulted ceiling, and the galleries have neatly panelled fronts. One touch of artistry is the swan-necked pediment above the pulpit, a reminder of the age of Chippendale. It was retained in the renovations of 1892, when the ground-floor seating was altered and the main part of the pulpit was replaced by a broad rostrum. The rostrum's charming balustrade of pierced rails provides a backdrop for the communion table – and on occasion for baptismal services, since beneath the boards on which the table stands is a full-size baptistery: in full view at the heart of the congregation when in use, but not occupying crucial space at other times.

Having looked at examples from city, town, village and hamlet, the final building in this selection of chapels from the end of the 18th century is a small wayside structure. Such chapels will be familiar to any traveller, beside a West Country lane or on a Pennine moor, perhaps, with no obvious source of worshippers. Sometimes their purpose was to serve people who lived on scattered farms and hamlets across a thinly settled landscape; sometimes they were built for small congregations who gathered from several villages or towns. An attractively restored wayside chapel of 1798 in east Wales can be taken as a representative of the era. Known as Pentre Llifior Methodist chapel (Figs 4.7 and 4.8), it stands between the villages of Berriew and Bettws Cedewain in Powys, on what is now a minor road but which then was the highway between the busy textile centres of Newtown and Welshpool. It was built for a group of Wesley's followers who had first met for worship in a nearby farm in 1778, but perhaps also attracted attenders from further afield.[20] Across the road is a stable for the preacher – and presumably for the congregation's use also. The chapel itself is a neat brick building, with round-headed windows and intersecting glazing bars. As at Prescott the chapel is entered at one end, but the gabled façade is set unusually at right angles to the road, with the result that a side wall abuts the highway, its wooden shutters offering protection against casual damage. It is a small building, having cost less than £212, and the two-row gallery over the entrance seems to have been squeezed in.

Fig 4.7
Pentre Llifior Wesleyan Methodist chapel, near Bettws Cedewain, Powys, 1798. Small wayside chapels such as this were as much a part of the Methodist repertoire as large urban chapels. Its design is of a kind that became ever more familiar during the 19th century. [DP166358]

Fig 4.8
Interior of Pentre Llifior
Wesleyan Methodist chapel.
Even so small a chapel has
room for a gallery. The
building was charmingly
restored after its
bicentenary in 1998.
[DP166363]

Many of the chapel's internal details are original, though the light fittings and the delicious colour scheme – crème de menthe and white – are part of a campaign of restoration since 1998. The pulpit and the space before it were perhaps altered in the 19th century, creating what looks like an oversized communion pew but effectively acted as that Welsh phenomenon, a big seat (or *sêt-fawr*) in which chapel officials would sit, rather like the elders in certain synagogues or deacons in some Calvinistic traditions. As with most historic places of worship, the Methodist chapel at Pentre Llifior has accrued layers of meaning with every generation of worshippers, and so (as with Wesley's New Room) no attempt to recreate its original appearance can be completely authentic. Yet its very survival reminds us that Nonconformists have always been flexible enough to respond to local needs, building where they might have a congregation and building as large or small as the circumstances allowed.

Chapel building, c 1800–20

The statistics cited at the start of this chapter show that chapel building accelerated through the decades from 1750 to 1820, and that in the decade to 1820 an average of five new chapels or meeting houses was opened each week. Nonconformist chapels became as characteristic a part of the Regency scene as cinemas were of the 1930s or supermarkets have become today. Building on such a scale called for exceptional resources – a matter exacerbated by the inflationary effects of the wars with France – and some degree of coordination.[21] If denominational planning came instinctively to Methodists, whose governing conference regulated all the movement's affairs, it was a more novel experience for other Nonconformists, particularly the Independents, who prized the autonomy of each congregation. Yet even the Independents were to become more organised. In Thomas Wilson they found a supporter adroit enough to act as an unofficial strategist for the denomination's building programme while also being wealthy enough after his retirement (as a textile manufacturer) in 1798 to finance a great many chapels.[22] And even as the major Nonconformist denominations sharpened their organisational skills, so the wave of chapel building was further swollen by the new religious groups, including three secessions from the main Wesleyan body (the Methodist New Connexion, the Primitive Methodists and the Bible Christians) and the New Jerusalem – or Swedenborgian – Church.[23]

Although the different strands of Nonconformity were often rivals, they continued to have much in common architecturally. Plan-forms remained those that were current at the end of the 18th century: although gable-end façade chapels were predominant, long-wall façades were not entirely abandoned, and octagons were sometimes favoured – as can be gauged from W F Pocock's *Designs for Churches and Chapels* (first published in 1819).[24] Signs of the Greek or Roman Revivals might be introduced into the late Georgian architectural repertoire, but such stylistic details were more often an indicator of a congregation's social status than its denominational affiliation. Simplified classical or Gothic motifs would appear where the details of a design were left to a contractor, and more competent motifs suggest the involvement of a professional. The marked growth in the number of practising architects is clearly reflected in their use for Nonconformist places of worship in these years. Like John Dobson of Newcastle, many architects worked impartially for any religious body, and the example of Thomas Rickman, who worked on scores of Anglican commissions despite his Quaker costume and habits of speech, shows that there was no necessary connection between an architect's faith and his work.[25] Naturally some chapel-going architects, such as William Jay, gained Nonconformist chapel commissions through their social contacts, but one exceptional case deserves special attention, that of William Jenkins.

William Jenkins and larger chapels, c 1800–20

The first building known to have been designed by William Jenkins is the Wesleyan Methodist chapel of 1804 in Carver Street, Sheffield – built to supplement, not to supersede, the town's first Methodist chapel.[26] Its imposing five-bay façade is derived from that of Wesley's City Road chapel in London, with the difference that *both* tiers of round-headed windows are recessed in blank surrounds, and there is a full-width gable-end pediment, in addition to that over the three middle bays. Other refinements include the introduction of string courses and a central Venetian window. We might also note the inclusion of a tablet in the pediment, announcing this to be a Methodist chapel. Distinguishing a place of worship in this way was becoming necessary, as the religious field became more crowded. It suggests too that there was nothing distinctively Methodist about this kind of architecture, or at least nothing that the general public would identify as Methodist.

The grand interior – now altered for adaptation as a pub – was also modelled on Wesley's chapel, except that the communion table stood in front of the pulpit. It was 'elegantly fitted up' with deep galleries on cast-iron columns, and provided a place of worship that attracted the elite of Sheffield as well as the poor. Besides the chapel itself there were ministers' houses, rooms for schools and meetings, and the caretaker's residence. William Jenkins, had good reason to understand the practical needs of the commission since he was at that time the superintendent minister of the local Wesleyan circuit.[27] His close understanding of Wesley's chapel may have been derived from the changes made to that building in 1800, with which Jenkins's name is associated. Of the architectural training he is said to have had before entering the ministry in 1788, unfortunately nothing is known.

After the opening of Carver Street chapel, Jenkins continued as a minister, moving to other circuits as is expected in the Methodist system. Meanwhile other Wesleyan chapels were built to a variety of designs. For instance, the large chapel in New Street, York (erected in 1805, demolished in 1966), was built on the plan of a square 'with the front corners cut off', presenting to the street a quasi-octagonal appearance.[28] It was an ambitious scheme, and the showpiece façade was proudly recorded in a contemporary engraving. The architect, a former pupil of James Wyatt, was John Rawstorne, who was then based in York. Another instance of a local architect being employed is in Chester, where Wesleyans turned to the renowned Thomas Harrison to design a successor for their octagonal chapel. The resulting building (of 1811, in St John Street) originally had a curved façade and, despite subsequent changes, still bears touches of Harrison's noble neo-classicism in its lunette windows.[29] This habit of employing local architects has continued in Methodism ever since, contributing a good deal of variety to the church's building stock.

By 1810, however, William Jenkins was back at the drawing board. He became a supernumerary minister in that year, and seems to have spent much of the following decade in designing chapels for his fellow Wesleyans around the country. At a time of Methodism's constant expansion, his role apparently was that of a reliable insider, efficiently providing shapely, practical buildings. Many of Jenkins's designs were variations on the pattern of Carver Street, Sheffield – and thus ultimately indebted to Wesley's City Road building. Two surviving examples

Fig 4.9
Wesleyan Methodist chapel,
St Peter's Street,
Canterbury, 1811 by
William Jenkins. Both
externally and internally
the design had echoes of
Wesley's City Road chapel
in London (see Fig 3.22).
[DP160393]

are in St Peter's Street, Canterbury (dated 1811) (Fig 4.9) and Bondgate, Darlington (dated 1812), both with two-storeyed brick façades, five bays wide.[30] In each case the middle three bays break forward slightly under a pediment and the windows are uniformly round-headed. The differences are slight: at Canterbury only the centre three bays of windows are recessed, and an open porch was provided. And at Darlington the inscribed tablet in the pediment specifically announces the building to be a 'Wesleyan chapel' rather than the more generic 'Methodist chapel'. Only eight years on from Carver Street, the senior branch of Methodism was having to distinguish itself from its own seceding groups. Thanks to wartime inflation these buildings were far from cheap, and in 1830

the trustees of the Canterbury chapel bore a debt of £6,721 (the original cost of the building having been £8,287). Both the Darlington chapel and that at Canterbury have been extensively altered internally, but records show that Canterbury had the City Road arrangement of a tall central pulpit, behind which was an apsidal recess for the communion. Jenkins's knowledge of Wesley's chapel served him – and Methodism – well. Yet it is misleading to think of him as a kind of licensed operator, reproducing versions of the movement's shrine for faithful congregations across the land.

When the Methodists of Bath approached Jenkins they already had a version of Wesley's City Road chapel, one built in 1777–8 (*see* p 64). Jenkins's task was to design a further

Fig 4.10 (right)
Walcot Wesleyan Methodist chapel, Bath, 1815–16 by William Jenkins. This is one of the grandest and most explicitly classical of the many chapels that Jenkins designed for the Wesleyans. [DP166345]

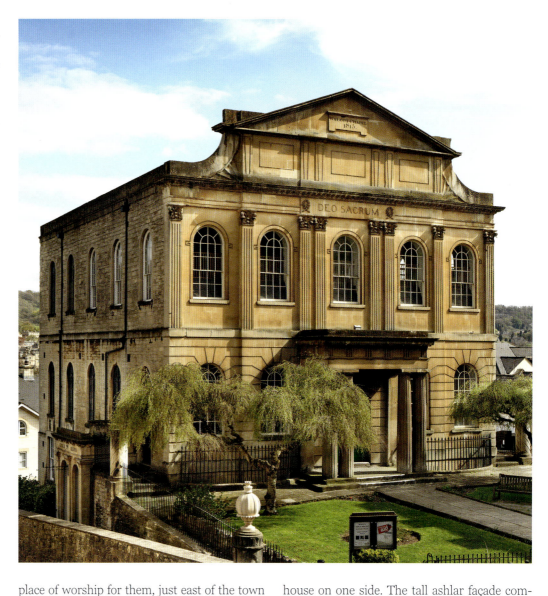

Fig 4.11 (opposite)
The elegant interior of Walcot Wesleyan Methodist chapel, Bath. The communion table was probably originally in a recess below the organ loft, as at City Road, with a two- or three-deck pulpit in front. [DP166335]

place of worship for them, just east of the town centre. The resulting Walcot chapel (now known as Nexus) (Fig 4.10), of 1815–16, is a more elaborate type of building than those at Darlington or Canterbury.[31] Compositionally it is like several others in which Jenkins gave extra height to the five-bay façade by inserting a blind attic between the cornice and the three-bay pediment. The Mint Wesleyan chapel, Exeter and Lambeth Road chapel, London (of 1813 and c 1817, respectively; both demolished) were of this group.[32] Two local factors distinguish Walcot chapel from its architectural siblings: it is of Bath stone rather than brick, and it gains a certain grandeur from its steeply sloping site, amid a streetscape of late 18th-century terraces. Jenkins fully realised the opportunities of the situation, placing the chapel back from the street with an enclosed garden in front and the minister's

house on one side. The tall ashlar façade commands this space, and for it Jenkins produced what was surely his most explicitly classical design: banded ground-floor rustication, a monumental Greek Doric porch and fluted Corinthian pilasters at first-floor level. If the classicism is not altogether scholarly it nonetheless has gravitas, and the main entablature carries the bold legend *Deo Sacrum* ('dedicated to God'), as if to rise above sectarian concerns.

Internally, Walcot chapel is fascinating (Fig 4.11). It was probably laid out with the communion table in a tall recess behind the pulpit, as at City Road, but must soon have been altered to produce one of the archetypal 19th-century interiors. In 1818, within a couple of years of opening, the chapel acquired its organ, reportedly from Bath's Assembly Rooms.[33] In chapels where the pulpit stood against a flat wall, an

organ might best be placed in the gallery opposite or a side gallery (as at Fulneck, *see* p 44). But where there was a large recess – as in chapels with the City Road arrangement – a natural expedient was to install the organ there, in a gallery behind the pulpit. So it was at Walcot, where the organ is shown off to advantage by a classical frame that acts rather like a proscenium arch.

Here were the ingredients for a new departure in chapel design. As Lutherans had long realised, an organ case can provide a splendid backdrop for the pulpit, and acoustically such a position allows the organ to have maximum effect. Several British examples are known from years around 1800. For instance, at Norwich's Octagon chapel (of 1754–6) an organ was installed in the gallery behind the pulpit in 1802, and the octagonal Anglican church of St John, Chichester (1812–13, by James Elmes) similarly had its organ in the east gallery, behind a wineglass pulpit.[34] What was notable about the scheme at Walcot, however, was that the upper part of the communion recess provided an almost ideal organ chamber, decorous and practical. Similar

arrangements were adopted in a number of Jenkins's other chapels, including those in Sheffield and Canterbury. And Brunswick Wesleyan chapel, Newcastle upon Tyne (1820–1) (Figs 4.12 and 4.13), which was based on Jenkins's scheme for Kingston chapel, Hull, was apparently designed from the outset to have an organ chamber behind the pulpit.[35] Within a few decades the organ backdrop had become one of the most widespread features of grand chapel interiors.

The introduction of organs into large chapels became less unusual in the early 19th century. Although Methodists had always made great play of congregational singing, hitherto organs had rarely featured in their chapels. Until this time – and indeed for decades more in some places – there would have been a group of amateur musicians whose playing was often more enthusiastic than refined. Typically there was a bass viol (forerunner of the modern cello), a flute and perhaps a horn. Ousting them in favour of organs has been seen as 'a token of the Wesleyan leaders' struggle to secure order and respectability'.[36] In this light, having an organist almost literally back-to-back with a minister marked a

Fig 4.12 (below) Brunswick Wesleyan Methodist chapel, Newcastle upon Tyne, 1820–1. Modelled on a design by William Jenkins, Brunswick chapel was later to have its façade partly obscured by the hall (built in 1884 and enlarged in 1956).
[DP156989]

Fig 4.13 (below right) Interior of Brunswick Wesleyan Methodist chapel, Newcastle upon Tyne. This watercolour by T M Richardson shows the original galleried interior, with box pews, organ loft, communion alcove and tall pulpit.
[BB77/07414]

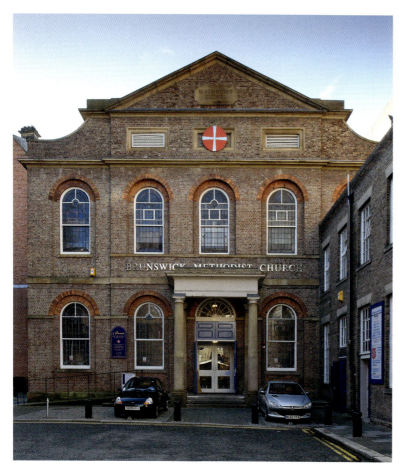

Music

Singing has had a place in the worship of virtually all Nonconformist denominations, although some Baptists initially opposed the practice and it has not had a central role in British Quaker worship. In the 17th and 18th centuries unaccompanied psalm-singing was a standard element of most Nonconformist services. In 1763, for instance, James Boswell described a London congregation of 'Dissenters roaring out the Psalms sitting on their backsides'. In addition to the metrical psalms, however, hymns became a feature of worship for a growing number of Nonconformists. The hymns of Isaac Watts (first published 1707) were particularly influential, being taken up by the new Methodist movement as well as by many Dissenters. Yet while Watts set his hymns to a few standard metres, the Methodists employed a variety of lively tunes, some adopted from secular music. Congregational hymn singing was a key characteristic of evangelical Nonconformity, long before Anglicans generally adopted the habit.

At first the singing of psalms and hymns was led by a precentor (sometimes a deacon, elder or steward) who might use a tuning fork or pitchpipe to start the tune. During the second half of the 18th century new approaches were introduced, later becoming widespread. In some chapels a group of singers led the singing, and a particular pew or bench was allocated to them: at Goodshaw Baptist chapel, Lancashire, for instance, it seems that they sat in the (communion-) table pew. Musical instruments also began to make an appearance, most commonly a bass viol and sometimes a flute, clarinet or bassoon.

A more lasting change was the introduction of organs, which appeared in some large chapels during the 1790s (having been championed by Moravians several decades earlier) and generally replaced the other instruments. At Stourbridge Presbyterian chapel (of 1787), for instance, an organ and singers' gallery was erected in 1794, facing the pulpit. Very soon Nonconformists realised that by putting an organ gallery behind the pulpit one could achieve good acoustic results without occupying prime seating space, and so was born a classic 19th-century chapel ensemble of organ, pulpit and communion area – often with the singers in the organ gallery. In smaller chapels musical bands generally gave way to pianos or harmoniums in the later 19th century. Musical instruments were still not welcomed in all Nonconformist chapels, however. The famous Baptist preacher Charles Spurgeon insisted on unaccompanied singing at his great Metropolitan Tabernacle, for example, and in the 18th century a bass viol was ejected from a Suffolk chapel on the grounds that it had no soul and therefore could not worship God.

The spread of so-called gospel hymns and songs in this country has often been traced to 1874–5 when the American evangelists Dwight Moody and Ira Sankey made an extended visit to Britain. Coinciding with this, in 1875, William Booth published *Revival Music* for what was soon to be called the Salvation Army. The Salvation Army quickly became associated with religious songs set to popular, often secular tunes, usually led by brass bands and 'songster brigades'. The effectiveness of this approach resulted in the development of tiered platforms, large enough for sizeable bands and choirs – not only in Salvation Army citadels, but also in the missions and central halls of other evangelical denominations. In more traditional kinds of chapel, organs remained the usual instrument until late in the 20th century, although pianos were sometimes introduced for smaller congregations or less formal types of worship. Over the past 40 years, however, guitars, drum kits and electronic keyboards have become a common feature of many chapels; pipe organs have fallen out of use in many places. Black majority churches have helped to popularise gospel music, with spirited choirs and instrumentalists, while the wider spectrum of charismatic and Pentecostal congregations has adopted similar kinds of praise-singing, often influenced by pop music. Increasingly often desks or booths have been installed, from which sound and projection systems can be controlled.[†]

'Musick alone with sudden charmes can bind/ The wand'ring heart or calm ye troubled mind.' This Congreve-derived motto graces the hymn board in the (originally Presbyterian) chapel of 1711 at Chinley, Derbyshire.
[© James O Davies]

step towards the professionalisation of worship. Jenkins, as a minister-architect, must have been aware of this, and perhaps grasped the attendant danger of depriving congregations of their sense of involvement in worship. So it is interesting to note that he generally broke with the conventional arrangement of straight-fronted galleries. At Walcot the gallery is U-shaped, and in other instances he created a continuous gallery, sweeping around behind the pulpit as well as at the entrance end.

It was a pattern that became common in the Nonconformist world as the century went on. The change enabled Jenkins marginally to increase the seating capacity and, by angling the gallery pews around the curve, to focus attention on the pulpit. Yet paradoxically the layout also makes those in the gallery more aware of one another. So was this 'part of the struggle to secure order', or was the intention to give gallery users a yet greater sense of belonging to a united body of worshippers – rather as had been possible in the

octagonal chapels of the previous century? These curved galleries come to life most fully when a packed congregation joins together in full voice to sing a popular hymn. Chapels such as Walcot, so often dismissed as preaching boxes, might be better described as hymn halls, given their emphatically communal purpose.

Before leaving Walcot, we should also note its extensive range of subsidiary accommodation, behind and below the chapel itself. Jenkins exploited the possibilities of the hillside site to provide a school hall and meeting rooms at a lower level – rather as at Tyldesley, discussed earlier in this chapter, but with even more space to exploit. Walcot evidently ran a big Sunday school, and may have had day schools as well. And because the chapel's elaborately fitted-out auditorium was hardly suitable for the needs of such schools, Jenkins devised extensive suites of ancillary rooms. Early in 1819 more than 70 of Bath's Sunday-school teachers had an opportunity to inspect the new teaching accommodation at Walcot chapel, and also to appreciate its suitability for other functions, as the whole company 'sat down to a handsome supper provided for them in the schoolroom' below the chapel.[37] In the Anglican world the tendency was for school buildings to be detached from the church premises, signalling a firm distinction between secular and religious architecture. For most Nonconformists, however, the chapel-and-school-hall complex expressed the close link between social and spiritual ministry.

Jenkins's designs inspired many imitations, such as the Wesleyan chapels in Tiverton (1814), Shepton Mallet (1819) (Fig 4.14), Stockton-on-Tees (1823) and Newcastle upon Tyne (1820–1, already mentioned) – all of which had tall, five-bay façades such as that at Walcot.[38] Other denominations shared a taste for the attic-less version. One that pre-dates Jenkins's first known work is the Unitarian new meeting house (now Roman Catholic) in Moor Street, Birmingham, which was built in 1802 with a three-bay loggia and paired Ionic pilasters. St Mary's Baptist chapel, Norwich (1811–12, by Francis Stone; demolished 1942) had a façade a little more like those by Jenkins in Canterbury and Darlington, though with deeply projecting eaves – inspired by Inigo Jones's Covent Garden church, perhaps – and a wide Doric portico.[39] Its vaulted interior was fine enough, but, with straight galleries confined by a double tier of columns and a blind wall behind the pulpit, it was decidedly more staid than the chapels designed by Jenkins.

Fig 4.14
Wesleyan Methodist chapel (now in secular use), Shepton Mallet, Somerset, 1819. It is one of the many chapels to have been influenced by William Jenkins's designs, both externally – as this impressive façade suggests – and in the internal arrangement. [DP166289]

Altogether closer to Jenkins in spirit was the long-demolished Ranelagh chapel, Chelsea (of 1818), which W F Pocock designed for a Calvinistic Methodist minister.[40] Its frontage, with minor variations on the five-bay formula, was flanked by steps to the basement Sunday school, while – in line with Pocock's background – the interior had a Wesleyan pedigree: there was a deep horseshoe gallery, and the axial three-tiered pulpit was backed by an organ above and a communion recess below. Lendal Independent chapel, York (1816, by J P Pritchett and Charles Watson; now in secular use) had an elegant version of the by-now standard frontage. Yet its nearly square interior was fitted out almost like a theatre, with a steep U-shaped gallery occupying more than half the space at first-floor level and a smaller straight-fronted upper gallery squeezed in above.[41] The horseshoe shape of the main gallery even determined the ground-floor pattern of seating and gangways. Here was a space for dynamic ministry.

Similarly the recently created Methodist New Connexion could enthusiastically embrace what might be called the Jenkinsian interior, sometimes with real ambition. The New Connexion's Bethesda chapel, in Hanley, Staffordshire (as rebuilt in 1819 to the designs of J H Perkins) (Fig 4.15), was claimed to be England's largest chapel, with a comfortable capacity of almost 2,000, but capable of squeezing in 3,000 people on special occasions by the use of flap-seats and other expedients.[42] Its great interior was audaciously spanned by means of exceptionally long beams, specially imported from Canada, so that the gallery could be unconfined by roof supports. Even in the chapel's previous incarnation (from 1811) its gallery's rounded shape was adventurously echoed in the building's external form, and in 1819 that plan was realised on a yet grander scale, resulting in a gently curved rear wall of chequerboard brickwork that still dominates the chapel's graveyard.[43]

As a showpiece for the emerging New Connexion, Hanley's Bethesda chapel was later embellished several times, but the sweeping curve of its deep gallery has always been retained. Even when the chapel was only comfortably full, its preachers will have faced something like a wall of worshippers in the gallery, a sight by turns daunting and inspiring. Paradoxically one of the earliest Nonconformist uses of an almost horseshoe-shaped building, with a matching gallery, is not from an evangelical context but the Quakers' Devonshire House meeting houses,

London (by John Bevans), which were constructed in 1793–4 after a review of various public buildings and a consideration of the 'effects of a design somewhat novel'.[44]

Medium-sized chapels, c 1800–20

Such large buildings are not the whole story, of course, and very large numbers of medium-sized chapels were erected. William Jenkins designed at least two examples, the earlier of which was for the Wesleyan chapel of 1811 in Stafford.[45] Jenkins's drawings show a neat, square building, its three-bay façade bearing a hint of Soane's minimalist manner, although the repertoire of motifs is familiar from Jenkins's work at Canterbury and elsewhere. The scheme for the Stafford chapel resembled that at Little Walsingham rather than the City Road type: the pulpit stood against the windowless end wall, with the railed communion area in front of it, facing a central block of pews and – below the galleries – rows of forms. In the event, however, the contractor had to omit most of the nice details. Round-headed windows were sacrificed in favour of flat lintels, and the recessed wall

Fig 4.15
Bethesda Methodist New Connexion chapel, Hanley, Stoke-on-Trent, enlarged 1819 by J H Perkins. Now in the care of the Historic Chapels Trust, Bethesda by its size and well-ordered design demonstrated the strength of the young Methodist New Connexion. [DP160661]

planes abandoned, perhaps in an effort to curtail costs in such an inflationary period. Even so the building debt was only extinguished in 1841, after which the body of the chapel was finally fitted out with pews and a schoolroom was also built. If Jenkins's design for Stafford was an abbreviated paraphrase of his chapels at Canterbury or Darlington, that for the Wesleyan chapel in New Inn Hall Street, Oxford (of 1817–18; demolished 1969) was a reduced version of his Walcot chapel, Bath (*see* p 76). Like Walcot, it presented a classical face to the world, what Pevsner called 'a heavily Grecian façade without any strictly archaeological motifs'.[46] Such elaboration was easier to afford after Waterloo, when the inflation of the war years abated. The chapel seated perhaps 800 to 1,000, and beyond were rooms for the Sunday school and the weekday charity school.

These medium-sized chapels by Jenkins were not fundamentally different from a great many places of worship built at the time. The three-bay façade with a central door and two storeys of windows under a pedimented gable was not an invention of the early 19th century, and it continued for decades after. The essential ingredients can be seen, for instance, in the red-brick Wesleyan chapel of 1815 in Newport Pagnell, Buckinghamshire (Fig 4.16), which has neatly sashed, round-headed windows and an oval plaque with the name and date.[47] Local resources and preferences led to countless variations on this theme. The repertoire included square-headed or pointed windows, eccentric doorways and hipped roofs or parapets. At the Congregationalists' former Claremont chapel, Pentonville Road, London (1818–19; now used by the Crafts Council) (Fig 4.17), the pediment is limited to the centre bay,

Fig 4.16
Wesleyan Methodist chapel, Newport Pagnell, Buckinghamshire, 1815. The essential components of many late Georgian chapel façades can be seen here: three bays of round-headed openings in two tiers, under a gable-end pediment. [DP157549]

which projects slightly and bears an Ionic portico: a pattern not unlike Jenkins's design for Oxford.[48]

More abstract effects could be achieved by contrary means, for instance at Sandhutton Wesleyan chapel, North Yorkshire (of 1815), where a relatively broad arch encloses the recessed central bay of an unpedimented brick façade.[49] A rather refined composition is to be found at the former Wesleyan chapel in Newport, Isle of Wight (of 1804; now a theatre) (Fig 4.18), in which the recessed brickwork of the arched centre bay rises with a lunette window into the gable-end pediment.[50] It was perhaps calculated to compete with the Roman Catholic chapel (of 1792) in the same street, whose three-bay gable-end façade belongs to what Bryan Little has called the 'Methodist' idiom of Catholic building that followed the 1791 Catholic Relief Act,[51] so firmly had 20th-century commentators come to associate such designs with Nonconformity.

Internally, these medium-sized chapels were generally less innovative than their larger cousins. In the Oxford example the gallery appears to have been limited to the entrance end, but in the Newport chapel the gallery continues along each side wall. Both buildings had a shallow apse for the pulpit as the focal point. Encircling galleries seem not to have been so common, but they existed – for instance at the Wesleyan chapel

of 1812 in Uttoxeter, Staffordshire (which externally resembles the Newport building), although this has been refitted.[52] A special case is the chapel of the Countess of Huntingdon's Connexion in Worcester (Fig 4.19), where in 1815 a relatively conventional building was transformed into something of much greater capacity.[53] The original chapel, built in 1771–3 and almost entirely rebuilt in 1804, was as nearly rectangular as the awkward, city centre site would allow. In 1815 it was extended eastwards, bursting the previous confines of its site with a round-ended transept, and so creating a kind of squashed-keyhole plan. Sweeping around the new east end were concentric lines of pews, on the ground floor and in the swerving gallery, all focused on the pulpit that stood above twin lecterns and table in the oval communion area (Fig 4.20).

Any lingering desire by the Countess's followers for bipolar buildings was abandoned in this companionable relationship between the word and the sacrament. Almost every succeeding generation enriched the unique interior of the Worcester building, and the east end provided a magnificent subject for one of John Piper's lively collages. Since 1987 the chapel has served as a concert hall, sensibly exploiting the auditory nature of its original role and retaining most of its fixtures and fittings.

Fig 4.17 (above left) Claremont chapel (Congregational), Pentonville Road, London, 1818–19 (now Crafts Council). Originally the façade was of bare brick, with few mouldings. The stucco, cornices and so forth date from about 1860. [DP150849]

Fig 4.18 (above) Wesleyan Methodist chapel, Newport, Isle of Wight, 1804 (now a theatre). An otherwise conventional three-bay façade is here enlivened by a recessed giant arch that rises into the pediment. [DP164001]

Fig 4.19
Countess of Huntingdon's
Connexion chapel,
Worcester (now a concert
hall). To the right is the
main arm of the chapel,
essentially of 1804, while
the stuccoed bow belongs to
the transept-like
enlargement of 1815.
[DP164582]

Fig 4.20
Interior of Countess of
Huntingdon's Connexion
chapel, Worcester.
Photographed before the
chapel's sympathetic
adaptation as a concert
hall from 1978–87, the 1815
extension provided a rich
setting for the pulpit and
communion table.
[FF80/00095]

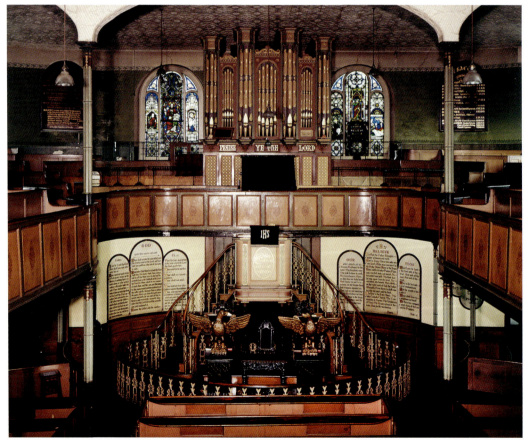

Almost in a category of its own, Jireh chapel, Lewes (Fig 4.21) deserves attention at this point. It was built (at a cost of about £1,755) in 1805 for a congregation of radical Calvinists whose views were no longer welcome at the local Countess of Huntingdon's Connexion chapel.[54] Perhaps the urgency of the situation led to the choice of timber construction. The cause prospered, and in 1826 the chapel was lengthened at what is now the entrance end and its fittings were much altered. First impressions, hardly enhanced by the present road system, are of a brick chapel with a three-bay front. But the structure is timber-framed and the bricks of the façade are in fact mathematical tiles, the local speciality. Rectangular windows and doorways (the neatest shape in such circumstances) are accordingly dominant, with a single round window in the gable end for variety.

The interior seems hardly to have been altered since 1826, and plainly encapsulates a spirit very different from that of the great Methodist chapels of the era (Fig 4.22). This is partly structural, for the lines of timber columns which support the roof and galleries seem to impose a discipline inimical to the open spaces and encircling galleries of Jenkins's chapels. More profoundly, however, the difference is to do with worship. At Jireh singing would have been unaccompanied by instruments, and so the

Fig 4.21
Jireh chapel, Lewes, 1805 and 1826. Slate covers the south wall and mathematical tiles line the façade of this timber-framed chapel.
[DP165336]

narrow pulpit dominates the space, with no display of organ pipes to distract the eye. Indeed, all that one sees behind the pulpit is the first-floor vestry door from which the preacher emerges. The worshippers would have been pressed together on the open forms (now given backs or adapted as box pews) in the centre of the chapel, or else seated in the full set of box pews which occupy each side of the ground floor

Fig 4.22
Interior of Jireh chapel, Lewes. From the hat pegs to the pulpit, Jireh preserves the spirit of its founders. The absence of an organ – following Calvin's disapproval of musical instruments – only enhances the importance of the pulpit.
[DP165338]

Fig 4.23
The pulpit, clerk's desk and communion table at Jireh chapel, Lewes, virtually untouched by later fashions in chapel furnishings. [DP165339]

and the gallery above. The unvarnished woodwork lends an almost Shaker consistency to the interior, and neat rows of hat pegs line the whitewashed walls. Hymns would have been announced by the clerk, whose desk stands below the pulpit (Fig 4.23). Perhaps one of the deacons would have used the pitchpipe and led

the congregational singing from the unusually large communion area, which seems to have served a purpose similar to the *sêt-fawr* ('big seat') in Welsh chapels (for example Pentre Llifior, *see* pp 72–3). As at St George's Lutheran church (*see* p 54), stairs lead down to the communion area directly from the galleries. There is an almost Cistercian lack of imagery, but in the vestry are portraits of the first two charismatic ministers who occupied the pulpit here. The first, Jenkin Jenkins, had been a student at the Countess of Huntingdon's college at Trefecca, and the second was his mentor William Huntington (not to be confused with Huntingdon). Huntington was a former coal-heaver whose eloquence had been praised by the poet Robert Southey, and whose funeral cortège from Tunbridge Wells to Lewes is said to have had 2,000 followers.

There were alternatives to the gable-end-entry type of chapel. A small number of medium-sized chapels were still being designed with their entrances in one of the long walls. One such is the tabernacle at Dursley, Gloucestershire, a prepossessing chapel of 1808, whose main door was originally in the pedimented centre bay of the south-west wall.[55] If this was innately conservative, the choice of uniformly pointed Gothic windows suggests a less cautious attitude. The short side elevation was treated with equal architectural display, however, and has served as the entrance (with the addition of a buttressed porch) since the later 19th century.

Fig 4.24
Adrian Street chapel (Unitarian), Dover, 1819–20 by Thomas Read. This octagonal chapel was built for a formerly Baptist congregation, following the 1813 Act which extended freedom of worship to Unitarians. [DP160395]

In the late Georgian period the interest in centrally planned buildings was sustained by Nonconformists and Anglicans alike. Octagonal chapels continued to be built, though several were of elongated rather than regular shape – a pattern familiar in the Reformed Netherlands.[56] One such elongated octagon was Zion chapel, Leeds, built in 1793–4 for the Countess of Huntingdon's Connexion and reopened as a consecrated Church of England place of worship in 1801.[57] Another was the New Jerusalem (or Swedenborgian) temple in King Street, Derby, which was built in 1820 and had a two-storey entrance block with a Venetian window.[58]

Neither building has survived, but there is still a striking example in Dover: Adrian Street chapel (Fig 4.24), built in 1819–20 for a formerly Baptist congregation then turning to Unitarianism.[59] Its architect, Thomas Read (sometimes spelt Reed), was at the time working on St Leonard's church in Deal, but because of his commitment to Unitarian principles he 'kindly and gratuitously' designed the chapel in Dover and supervised its construction. One of the long walls of the extended octagon provides the main front, with a deeply projecting pediment on two pairs of elementary pilasters, all framing a large, quasi-Venetian window. Architecturally the Adrian Street chapel is more heterodox than rational. The building's novel external form may have been what justified the choice of an octagonal plan, for the internal arrangements do not wholly exploit the shape's potential. Most of the box pews are laid out in straight rows and a curved gallery occupies the south end of the chapel, facing a segmental apse which originally contained the pulpit below a sunburst motif, but is now filled by an organ.

Smaller chapels, c 1800–20

There is little evidence for the involvement of architects in the design of small chapels in the years before 1820, and there is sometimes a vernacular flavour to their design. A good example is in the Wallingfen area of East Yorkshire (Fig 4.25), where a new settlement grew up in the late 18th century at a point where a causeway through the fen crossed a new canal. From the 1790s Wesleyan Methodists met for worship here in a large room over four cottages, and in 1812 they built a chapel behind the cottages in what is now the village of Newport.[60] Some materials were reused from the previous house

on the site, but even so the cost of construction (about £782) proved to be a great burden.

The brick chapel is almost square, 13 yards by 12 yards (12m by 11m), with a hipped pantile roof, and its entrances are in one of the slightly longer walls – a slightly old-fashioned touch. An unusual feature of the façade is its combination of round-headed windows on the upper floor with pointed arches for the doorways and lower window. Perhaps the idea came from the older Wesleyan chapel in nearby Market Weighton, which had similar Gothic openings below and square windows above. If the visual inconsistency has a practical justification (insufficient height for taller windows at gallery level, perhaps) it must be inferred that the pointed style was the more desirable so far as the chapel's builders were concerned. The same preference can be noted inside, where the pulpit stands on the back wall between a pair of tall Gothic windows. Around three sides of the chapel there is a gallery, its corners canted rather than round, and the gallery pews give an impression of the kind of seating that is likely to have filled at least part of the ground floor. The chapel had seating for about 400 people, and was the village's chief place of worship for some time (a Primitive Methodist chapel opened in 1827, but the Anglican church began a mission here only in 1854).[61] Some idea of the chapel's social role is gleaned from the fact that it ran a day school

Fig 4.25
Wallingfen Wesleyan Methodist chapel, Newport, East Yorkshire, 1812. A naïve mixture of pointed and round-headed windows adds to the charm of Wallingfen chapel.

from the 1820s until a board school opened in the village in 1880. The day school and the chapel's Sunday school used the large upper room in which the Methodists previously met for worship.

Providence chapel, Chichester was built in 1809 for an independent Calvinistic congregation that was related to the one at Jireh in Lewes.[62] Like that, it was founded by seceders from the Countess of Huntingdon's Connexion. Externally Providence is an almost archetypal small chapel (Fig 4.26), with tall, round-headed windows and a three-bay gable-end façade. In the pediment is a circular plaque inscribed with the building's name and date. Providence is a slightly grander version of the wayside chapel at Pentre Llifior (*see* p 72), and all of its architectural elements can be found in 18th-century places of worship. Around the turn of the century the pattern became a common one for small chapels, capable of being varied according to local materials, tastes and needs.

Few examples of the period are as well preserved internally as Providence (Fig 4.27), however. Ian Nairn called it 'poor but honest', as the Victorian song has it, and referred specially to the original fittings.[63] The wineglass pulpit is entered, rather like Jireh's, directly from an upper vestry door, although at Providence the drama of the preacher's elevation is accentuated by the absence of galleries near to the pulpit. The clerk's desk again stands below the pulpit in a generously sized communion area, and evidence survives

*Fig 4.26 (above)
Providence chapel,
Chichester, West Sussex,
1809. With its two tall
windows and materials
of contrasting colour, the
gable-end façade is an
almost archetypal
composition for small
chapels of the 19th century.
[DP160437]*

*Fig 4.27 (right)
Interior of Providence
chapel, Chichester. As with
Quakers, the independent
Calvinist congregation here
opted for open benches
rather than box pews.
[DP160441]*

Fig 4.28 (left)
Quaker meeting house,
Spiceland, near Uffculme,
Devon, 1815. To the left of
the door is the gallery and
to the right is the main
worship space.
[DP158323]

Fig 4.29 (below)
Interior of Quaker meeting
house, Spiceland. The finely
detailed pine stand and
wooden chandelier convey
a mood of elegant rusticity.
[DP158325]

here for the way in which hymn singing was led: the narrow communion table has two sloping-sided fittings which allowed it to serve as a stand for singers' books, when not in use for communion services. Despite the fact that the chapel is entered by a central door, the Nonconformist preference for a central block of seating is followed, allowing the preacher to face a mass of hearers rather than a gangway. Further seats are set out in rows along each side of the chapel, with more in the gallery above the entrance. These are not box pews, but fixed benches, with back-rails and arm-rests. Such seats are normally associated with Quakers, whose principled opposition to pew rents – and thus the apparatus of box pews and appropriated places – might possibly have been shared by Providence.

An especially complete example of a small Quaker meeting house from these years is found in a picturesque rural setting near the Devon village of Uffculme. Spiceland meeting house, as it is known (Fig 4.28), was built in 1815 on the site of its 17th-century predecessor, and its basic form had a long pedigree in Quaker architecture.[64] The four-bay façade and hipped roof recall the pattern of Jordans meeting house (of 1688, *see* p 28), rather than the gable-end façades of later years, but the round-headed sash windows are more of their time, and their refined glazing bars hint at the quality of the joinery within. Meetings for worship are held in the main room, on the right of the building, lit by the two easternmost windows (Fig 4.29). Across its end wall is the raised stand for recognised speakers and elders, and the remainder of the space is occupied by long benches of spare design, with plain back-rails and curved arm-rests. Illumination came from a chandelier of rustic elegance, its turned wooden stem sprouting slender metal branches. Opposite the stand is a gallery, its woodwork all of a piece with that of the panelled internal porch and incorporating neat shutters to create a room below the gallery, thereby enabling women and men to hold their business meetings separately. The quality of the building must have been at least partly due to Daniel Henson, named as the builder by an inscription discreetly placed on the outside of the rear wall.[65] Spiceland is not altogether typical of its time, since even Quakers had begun to build gable-end-entry meeting houses (for example Winchmore Hill, London, of 1791) and were devoting much energy to the rebuilding of urban meeting houses (such as at York in 1817).[66] However, it is evidence of the movement's sustained concern for architectural propriety in the country as well as the town.

Membership of Quakerism at this time was comparatively middle class, and therefore better able to afford building projects despite a marked decline in numbers. At the other end of the Nonconformist spectrum were such new Methodist groups as the Bible Christians and Primitive Methodists, both of which were established as separate from the Wesleyan body in the first two decades of the 19th century and attracted growing numbers of members among such groups as farm labourers and miners. The roots of Primitive Methodism are generally traced to a revivalist camp meeting held in 1807 – much to the distaste of the Wesleyan authorities – at Mow Cop on the Cheshire–Staffordshire border. Four years later the Primitive Methodists built their first chapel in the nearby town of Tunstall, designed so that it could be made into four houses if the new organisation proved to be short lived.[67] The cause prospered and in 1822 that first building was superseded, but the precautionary principle was justified as the initial chapel was indeed adapted to create a short terrace of cottages.

A few miles north, on a hillside above Congleton, stands Cloud chapel (of 1815), the oldest surviving Primitive Methodist place of worship still in regular use (Fig 4.30).[68] Despite stories of its having been erected in three weeks at a cost of only £26, Cloud chapel was built to last, and was constructed with obvious care. Any suggestion of cheap or hurried work is countered by the evidence of the masonry, for instance in the symmetrical pattern of the large stone dressings around the windows facing east across the Dane Valley. Showing a more up-to-date attitude than at Spiceland, the small, ungalleried chapel is laid out on its long axis, entered through one of the short walls (though an extension partly covers this façade). At the far end stands a square

Fig 4.30
Cloud Primitive Methodist chapel, on the Staffordshire border near Congleton, 1815. A small chapel, but one of substance and decorousness, it was built for the newly established Primitive Methodists.

pulpit, below a round-headed window, with memorials to 19th-century worshippers on the wall alongside. Even if the Primitive Methodists in this upland district were of limited means, Cloud chapel suggests that the fledgling movement devoted a good deal of attention to the quality of its buildings. Architectural decorum was not confined to large chapels nor to Old Dissent.

What provision was made for ancillary activities in smaller chapels at this time? Newport in Wallingfen was exceptional in having a separate room in which schools and social gatherings could be held. Adjacent vestries or minister's houses (as at Providence, Chichester) must often have been used for small gatherings, but few small chapels had such facilities. Thus, by default, the main worship space in many chapels will have been used for teaching children and for meetings. Even at Spiceland, where a partition allowed the creation of a subsidiary room, extra accommodation was required, as a result of which a lean-to extension was erected in the 19th century and a freestanding schoolroom in 1985.[69] Cloud chapel continued as a single-cell space, housing the range of chapel-related activities, until 1958, when extra land was given so that a small extension could be built as a meeting hall and Sunday school.[70]

The establishment response

Throughout the period covered in this chapter Anglicans and Nonconformists continued to build within the auditory tradition that Wren would have recognised, accommodating congregations within convenient sight and sound of the pulpit. Buildings for large congregations naturally had galleries. In some ways this common heritage had been strengthened as Methodists introduced more Anglican habits – including prayer-book services and the practice of taking communion at the rail – into Nonconformity. And there was sufficient collaboration in Islington in 1806 for a chapel to be built where evangelical Anglicans and Congregationalists worshipped together.[71]

Yet within this shared tradition, differences of emphasis were apparent. The design of larger chapels was ever more likely to reflect the dynamics of congregational worship: not only a middle block of seats, but curving galleries, wide-span roofs and central organs as well as pulpits. Each of these features could be found –

if rarely together – in Anglican churches, but the reaction against what Nigel Yates saw as chapel-style interiors was already afoot in the Church of England. In places Anglicans were breaking up their three-decker pulpits, so that pulpit and reading-desk could be located on either side of the chancel, giving a clear view of the altar.[72] This move, pushing the pulpit to one side, was certainly not intended to win friends in the Nonconformist world, but it was gaining ascendancy and was incidentally to be boosted by the Church Building Act of 1818, which tried to impose the arrangement.[73]

The 1818 Church Building Act, by which parliament agreed to provide a million pounds for a coordinated campaign of Anglican church building in expanding centres of population, resulted from establishment fears that whole communities were effectively beyond the reach of the Church of England. In some ways the initiative recalls that of just over a century before, the 1711 Act by which the government of the day had planned to finance the building of 50 new churches in urban centres as a reaction to demographic change and the Dissenters' first great burst of building activity. In both cases there was an associated fear of irreligion and social disorder, but the establishment had been stung on both occasions by the success of what might be called the religious opposition. The explicit intention of the 1818 'Million Pound' Act, therefore, was that the new churches should be different from Methodist chapels.[74]

This was at once flattering to Nonconformists and a great challenge to them. Lord Liverpool, who introduced the bill in the House of Lords, explicitly said that its purpose was 'to remove Dissent'.[75] Rather as in 1711, the government was seeking to out-build Nonconformists by throwing the weight of state finance into the battle. Unlike 1711, however, the money was quite effectively deployed, especially after 1824, when a further half-million pounds was added to the cause. In contrast to the 50 new churches planned in 1711, more than 500 new churches were built with the aid of government grants between 1818 and 1852. When compared with the figures cited at the start of this chapter (over 2,500 Nonconformist places of worship opened in the ten years to 1820) these numbers seem insignificant, but the new churches were large and prominent. The relationship between those churches and the Nonconformists' new buildings is one of the threads running through the next chapter.

One effect of the 'Million Pound' Act was to highlight the difference between the Church of England and other denominations in the financing of places of worship. Because Nonconformists normally had to find the money for chapel building within their own resources (even if this involved decades-long mortgages or loans), it was galling to see the government's willingness to pay for new Anglican churches being justified as an attempt – as supporters said – to place 'Churchmen and Dissenters on an equal footing'.[76] It did not escape attention that Anglicans and non-Anglicans alike had contributed the revenue from which government funds were dispensed. Rubbing salt into the wound, many Anglican parish churches had their running costs and repairs met by ratepayers, a practice that was increasingly challenged from 1818. In Sheffield that year the parish church's pew-owners were reminded that other local people 'maintain their own religious establishments, without having or seeking any assistance whatever for them'.[77] This warning shot was evidently not heeded, with the result that in 1819 a proposed church rate of two pence in the pound was rejected in Sheffield, and in 1820 Manchester's ratepayers likewise voted against the imposition of a church rate for their town's new churches.[78] All this merely stiffened the resolve of Nonconformists to increase their congregations and to build accordingly.

5

Growth and renewal, 1820–50

There was no slackening in the pace of chapel building after the boom years of the Regency. If anything, there was a slight increase in tempo. For the next 30 years new chapels were to open at a rate that consistently exceeded even the remarkable level achieved in the decade to 1820. The sustained building campaign was prompted essentially by the need to accommodate ever larger numbers of followers. This was especially true of the Methodists, Baptists and Congregationalists, whose membership growth in the period to 1850 outpaced even the exceptional rate of population increase. The stream of chapel building was also quickened by such recently established groups as the Methodist New Connexion, Primitive Methodists and Swedenborgians, and a small contribution was made by other emerging Nonconformist bodies, including the Brethren (sometimes known as the Plymouth Brethren), the Catholic Apostolic Church and the Free Church of England.

A special case is that of the Unitarians, who had been specifically denied the toleration which other Protestants had enjoyed since 1689, but who finally gained freedom to worship in 1813. Many Presbyterians – and some Baptists – had adopted Unitarianism, and they were to build a number of very distinguished chapels, especially once their legal rights were clarified in 1844.[1] Whether these buildings were warranted by an expansion in Unitarian numbers or by a desire to give architectural expression to the movement's new-won liberty is not clear. The old Presbyterian cause, much weakened by the coming out of Unitarianism, undertook very little new building, but several notable Presbyterian chapels were built as a result of Scottish migration into England. Even the Quakers, whose numbers declined very markedly during this period, erected some substantial buildings in these years, especially around London and certain other cities.[2]

An interesting change seems to have affected the design of Nonconformist places of worship in the decades after the battle of Waterloo. The chapels that had been built during the first 20 years of the 19th century were more uniform in character than their earlier counterparts had been. This was partly a response to the scale of the demand: it had often been expedient for Jenkins and other architects or builders to adapt a plan that had been proved elsewhere, rather than to start from scratch with each commission. But it was also an outcome of the prevailing aesthetic conventions: late Georgian architecture allowed decent elevations to be designed without recourse to the full apparatus of either classical or Gothic design. This proved especially convenient during the inflationary war years. If money allowed, a Greek porch might be added or Gothic windows included, but for the moment more elaborate effects were unusual.[3] By about 1820, however, a change was discernible, with many new chapels presenting a grander face to the world. Such effects were, of course, different from the artisan baroque of the 'age of toleration' or the pattern-book Palladianism of the mid-Georgian years. This was the era in which the first cohort of professional architects emerged – men anxious to distinguish themselves from the grubby world of the builder. They designed many of the larger chapels of the time. During the war years most had been deprived of the opportunity for overseas travel, but there were numerous source books of classical architecture, not least Stuart and Revett's multivolume *The Antiquities of Athens*.[4] In parallel with this, the serious study of indigenous medieval buildings was stimulated by a variety of publications, including *An Attempt to Discriminate the Styles of English Architecture* by the Quaker, Thomas Rickman.[5]

The 1820s

In 1820 an impressive chapel was built in New Road, Brighton (Fig 5.1) for a congregation whose theological development had led them from a Calvinistic Baptist background to a more liberal position, and then to Unitarianism.[6] The

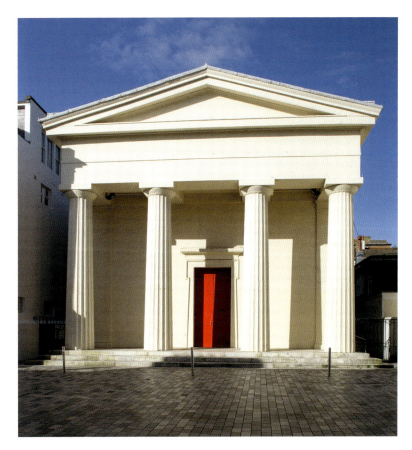

new chapel was unequivocally Greek. In contrast to the many-windowed façades that characterise chapels of the previous 20 years, it has a full-height portico with four fluted Doric columns and a mighty pediment, while its entrance wall is blind, save for a Vitruvian doorway. The accomplished design was by the local architect A H Wilds, perhaps following a suggestion by the Unitarians' minister Dr John Morell, a classical scholar and enlightened teacher.[7] Evidently the design of the portico was inspired by published drawings of such Athenian monuments as the Temple of Hephaistos (the Theseion), but it is not a replica of any building, and the Greek inscription which initially graced its frieze was a quotation from the New Testament.[8] Brighton's first Greek Revival place of worship – Trinity chapel in Ship Street, also by A H Wilds – had been erected three years earlier for another Nonconformist preacher, Thomas Read Kemp.[9] However, the Unitarian chapel made a more uncompromisingly Greek contribution to the townscape, as befitted the scholarly character of its minister, and is almost an admonishment to the resort's prettier buildings. Meanwhile in London, Stamford Street (Fig 5.2) is graced by another noble Greek

Fig 5.1 (above)
Unitarian chapel, Brighton, 1820 by A H Wilds. This is a striking Greek design for the congregation of a scholarly minister.
[DP165334]

Fig 5.2 (right)
Blackfriars Unitarian chapel, Stamford Street, London, 1823 possibly by John Rennie. Resembling an ancient Athenian fragment, this portico is all that remains following the demolition of the chapel in the 1960s.
[DP150867]

portico, the only surviving part of Blackfriars Unitarian chapel of 1823.[10] Here the portico is even closer in scale to the main elevation of the Theseion, with six fluted Doric columns supporting a deep entablature and full-width pediment.

Publications such as *The Antiquities of Athens* could supply architects with precise measurements of ancient porticoes, but were of scant use when it came to designing the interior of a 19th-century chapel. At Stamford Street the Greek spirit was sustained internally by a pair of detached Doric columns, between which the pulpit stood in a recess, with a glimpse beyond of a further top-lit chamber – perhaps intended as the equivalent of the adytum in a Greek temple. At first the chapel had no gallery, but one was later erected, its balustrade being described as 'the kind of thing which an Athenian would have produced if he had thought of using cast-iron for such a purpose'.[11] Elsewhere some chapels were fitted out like a semicircular classical theatre, with concentric rows of seats rising in tiers and the pulpit centre stage – on the principle that the chapel-goers of 19th-century Britain shared similar auditory needs with the theatre-goers of Hellenistic Athens.[12]

One of Brighton's Doric chapels, the then Congregationalists' building in Union Street, was rebuilt in 1825 on such lines, although its steep bank of seats was altered in 1863.[13] As with the curved galleries noted in Chapter 4, the classically inspired, theatre-like arrangement of the Union Street chapel was evidence of the Nonconformists' propensity to borrow ideas from secular architecture. C A Busby, probably one of the architects of the Union Street scheme, had not only designed a theatre (in 1817, for St Petersburg, Virginia), but had also drawn a plan of the American Capitol, including the semicircular chambers of the Senate and the (recently rebuilt) House of Representatives during a visit to Washington in 1819.[14] Meanwhile, the leading protagonist of the Greek Revival, William Wilkins, was advising the Archbishop of Canterbury that 'the most perfect form' for new churches would be 'that of the ancient theatres', but feared that the concept would raise 'an unsuitable association of ideas'.[15] Some Nonconformists, at least, were not afraid to go where Anglicans feared to tread.

During the 1820s the British taste for things Greek, further stimulated by the Greek War of Independence and the display of the Parthenon Marbles in a temporary Elgin Room at the British Museum, influenced much new architecture.

Nonconformists could not compete with the Anglicans' most lavish buildings in the Greek style, such as the spectacular new St Pancras church in London (of 1819–22), which cost over £82,000 and was assisted by the imposition of a parish rate.[16] Yet Nonconformists did enjoy one natural advantage. Like the temple builders of ancient Athens, they were happy with the logic of gable-end pediments, whereas Anglicans were likely to compromise classical aesthetics by the incorporation of towers above porticoes – as at St Pancras. The point can be illustrated in Truro, where two places of worship were built in the late 1820s to the designs of a local architect, Philip Sambell. St John's church came first (in 1827–8), at a cost of £1,842 – most of it (£1,407) supplied from the second parliamentary grant. A sum of £200 was added by the Commissioners so that Sambell could add a belfry to his Greek design 'with a view to giving the building a more church-like appearance'.[17] The establishment's determination that its new churches 'should be different from Methodist chapels' did not always lead to better architecture.[18] Truro's Wesleyan chapel (Fig 5.3) followed in 1829–30. It had a more generous budget (of £2,500), which Sambell spent on a

Fig 5.3
Wesleyan Methodist chapel, Union Street, Truro, 1829–30 by Philip Sambell. Even without recourse to a full portico, Sambell here used giant pilasters to achieve a more monumental effect than William Jenkins created elsewhere for the Wesleyans.
[BB72/04184]

Fig 5.4
St Andrew's Presbyterian
chapel, Rodney Street,
Liverpool, 1823–4,
photographed before the
fire of 1983. The imposing
frontage, by John Foster
junior, caught the attention
of Schinkel in 1826.
[BB75/05593]

good granite façade with Greek Doric pilasters, but no tower or belfry.[19] Writers have generally been impressed by the chapel's fine frontage, despite – or perhaps because of – the fact that the budget did not allow for a giant portico. It deserves mention here that Sambell (a practising Baptist) was later to advocate the classical theatre principle of chapel seating, but for the time being he employed relatively conventional layouts: straight-fronted galleries at the Anglican church, and for the Wesleyans a more dynamic, encircling gallery, combined with a City Road arrangement such as William Jenkins (see pp 62–3) had used.[20]

Fully developed Doric chapels were not common, even where funds were generous. Other classical orders could be called into play if greater elaboration or taller proportions were desired. An interesting example is St Andrew's Presbyterian chapel, erected for a Scottish congregation in Rodney Street, Liverpool (Fig 5.4), in 1823–4.[21] The body of this building was planned by the church's management committee, assisted by their Scots-born surveyor Daniel Stewart, but for the façade they depended on John Foster junior, who was soon to succeed his father as the corporation architect and surveyor.[22] Young Foster had first-hand experience

of Doric architecture, having assisted in excavations at Aegina, but for his Scottish clients he opted for richer effects and greater height. Two fluted Ionic columns graced the entrance to a recessed porch, its void contained by a pair of solid corner-blocks, each of which continued upwards with a square lantern tower. Of course, Foster was hardly the first person to give vertical emphasis to a temple front without perching a spire astride a pediment. Yet his composition, generally similar to one of Robert Smirke's designs for the Commissioners in 1818, compares favourably with the frontage of St George, Regent Street, London (the one church designed for the Commissioners by Foster's colleague, C R Cockerell), which was under construction in 1823–4.[23] Set in its spacious graveyard in one of Liverpool's smartest streets, St Andrew's had a commanding presence; it was striking enough to merit a sketch by Schinkel in 1826.[24] At the time of writing the building is being rescued for secular use after years of dereliction, following a fire in 1983.

More straightforward variations on the Ionic temple theme appeared in a number of new chapels at this time. In 1824, for instance, a chapel was erected in South Place, Finsbury for one of London's Unitarian congregations. Alongside a terrace of routine late Georgian houses, the giant Ionic columns and wide pediment of the chapel's façade had a substantial presence, even though space did not allow for a prostyle portico.[25] The situation contrasts with the spacious site in Mount Street, Manchester (Fig 5.5), where a new meeting house was built for a prosperous Quaker congregation in 1828–30 to the designs of Richard Lane.[26] Despite the generous scale of the site, enabling the meeting house to be set well back from the street, there is no real portico. Instead the centre three bays of the five-bay façade have a pediment and attached Ionic columns. The Ionic order, which lends a certain grace to the large building, appears to have been derived from the Temple of the Illisus (measured drawings of which had appeared in Stuart and Revett's *The Antiquities of Athens*), though without the fluting of the Athenian original. Even Cecil Stewart, writing without much sympathy in 1956, thought the frontage 'as fine as anything of similar size by Sir Robert Smirke'.[27] The Greek theme continued inside, with fluted Doric columns below the galleries and an extended cornice above the stand to act as a sounding board.

More notable, however, was the plan. As in several larger Quaker meeting houses of the time, there was no stinting on circulation space. From a deep internal porch one passed to a broad lobby, off which lay the gallery stairs and from which two wide corridors led along the sides of the building to the main space for worship. When not being used for worship, this 'principal apartment' – described as being 'particularly handsome, reaching indeed to elegance in its dimensions and finish' – could be subdivided to allow men's and women's business meetings to be held separately.[28] The partition was 'effected so quietly and speedily as almost to appear the effect of magic' by means of sliding shutters (weighing nearly 10 tons), half of which rose from below the floor while the rest descended from the roof space.[29] Modern technical ingenuity was also brought to bear on the problem of heating and ventilation. A warm-air system was provided by a stove on an improved principle (perhaps one with ducts to various parts of the meeting house?), and stale air was drawn out via ceiling grilles.[30] Such attention to the control of temperature and the circulation of

Fig 5.5
Quaker meeting house, Mount Street, Manchester, 1828–30 by Richard Lane. The building is notable externally for its imposing Greek details, and internally for its innovative technology and spacious circulation areas. [FF000158]

fresh air was found in other innovative buildings of the time, and by the 1820s often coincided with the introduction of gas lighting.

Among those Quakers who knew the building well was one of Richard Lane's pupils, Alfred Waterhouse, whose subsequent reputation for well-functioning buildings might have been rooted in his time in Lane's office. In the early 1860s Waterhouse's own draughtsmen occupied the basement of the meeting house, from where the plans were drawn for Manchester's Assize Courts, Strangeways Prison and a trio of Congregational chapels.[31] Since that time the meeting house has been greatly altered by the insertion of further accommodation, chiefly in 1923 and 1961–3, and most traces of Lane's great interior design have been lost. Externally, however, the building still embodies something

of Lane's ambition, to bring to Manchester 'the refinement and beauty of the Greeks, in the golden age of Pericles'.[32]

Many urban chapels built at this time were dignified by the inclusion of a giant order of columns, but an even larger number made use of single-storey porches with classical columns and an entablature. In this way Regency patterns of chapel design were affected by the Greek Revival, without the full apparatus of a temple front. A case in point is the meeting house erected in 1825–6 for Norwich's Quakers (Fig 5.6), on the site of their 17th-century building in Upper Goat Lane.[33] With its two-storey, three-bay façade and single-storey porch, the meeting house resembles certain medium-sized chapels of the previous decade (for example the Wesleyan chapel in New Inn Hall Street, Oxford, see p 82), but its classical details are more powerful. Two pairs of unfluted, stocky Doric columns carry the central porch, and matching pilasters continue the sober theme across the façade, one storey above another. There are no windows to the ground floor, just three round-headed windows above. It is not so much an attempt to recreate the beauty of Periclean Athens – more an attempt to marry the noble simplicity of early Greek architecture to a contemporary type of chapel frontage.

The architect was J T Patience, and when he came to design the nearby Catholic chapel (in Willow Lane, Norwich, 1828–9) he employed the same basic composition, making it a little less chaste by the use of Ionic columns, Corinthian pilasters and a small pediment.[34] That the Catholic building has been described as 'an established Nonconformist design' is another acknowledgment of the shared architectural values that were to be found across the religious spectrum.[35] Internally, of course, the differences were more apparent. The Jesuits of Norwich might not have been able to rival the splendours of the Gesù in Rome, but Patience was able to provide them with a fine classical setting for the altar.[36] The Quakers' meeting house, with no need for a pulpit – let alone an altar – is necessarily less elaborate, but the main space for worship gains a certain refinement from the line of Ionic columns (and its matching entablature) below the east gallery.

Norwich, with its two meeting houses, had a very distinguished tradition of Quaker worship. Elizabeth Fry had been a member of the congregation until her marriage in 1800. Her brother, Joseph John Gurney, was a leading advocate of

Fig 5.6
Quaker meeting house, Upper Goat Lane, Norwich, 1825–6 by J T Patience. The Doric porch overlooks a courtyard flanked by subsidiary blocks. An arched overthrow and its lamp mark the entrance. [DP160447]

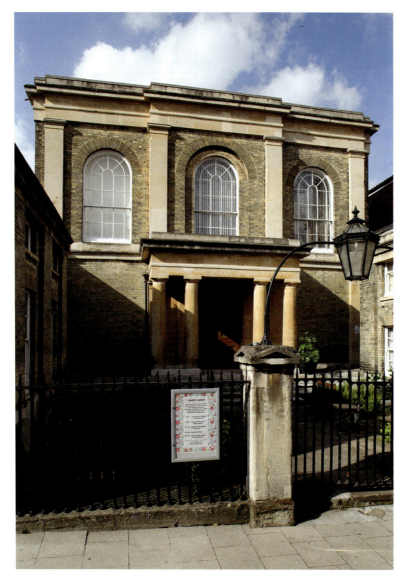

the new building of 1825–6, but more in the hope of increasing numbers than because of an existing demand for further seats. Consequently the ground plan of the main chamber was only a little larger than its 17th-century predecessor, but the building's overall footprint was greatly increased. As with the Manchester meeting house, a surprising amount of space was given over to circulation and ancillary accommodation: the porch gives way to a lobby and thence an inner vestibule with a cloakroom and a library, while lateral corridors lead to the women's meeting room at the rear.

One effect of the Quakers' retention of the term 'meeting house' is to underline the long-held conviction that their buildings are not exclusively places of worship. In Norwich (and some other urban meeting houses of the time) this idea is expressed externally by the provision of wings, flanking the entrance and identifiably subordinate to the central part of the building.[37] It is a device which emphasises the change from wide to long plan-forms, and also makes a significant contribution to the townscape.

Stylistically the wings can be rewardingly compared with those of the now-demolished Elmham Hall, Norfolk (of *c* 1825–30) by D J Donthorn.[38] Patience's design is less radically stripped of detail than Donthorn's, but the simplification of Greek forms seems to have been shared.

Long before the Greek Revival affected chapel building some Nonconformists had taken up Gothic, and this tradition continued in every decade of the 19th century. In the 1820s a new spirit was discernible. Widcombe Baptist chapel, Bath (built for an Independent congregation in 1820–1), can be taken as a starting point (Fig 5.7).[39] Its broad, north-facing frontage has a naive directness, as if its author has welded two identical chapels together. The pointed sash windows have intersecting glazing bars, and the medieval mood continues with a battlemented parapet. Inside, the gallery stands on slender clusters of wooden columns reminiscent of 18th-century Gothic. Something of the newer spirit of the 1820s can be gleaned from what remains of the former Ebenezer Wesleyan chapel

Fig 5.7
Widcombe Baptist chapel, Bath, 1820–1. Built for an Independent congregation, the chapel, with its simply pointed windows, exemplifies an unsophisticated approach to Gothic. [DP166354]

(of 1823, by Joseph Botham) in Green Lane, Sheffield.[40] Despite the similarities with Widcombe – a crenellated façade with two tiers of pointed windows – the three-light Gothic windows here are complete with hood moulds and, enterprisingly enough, neat curvilinear tracery. And in contrast to the Widcombe frontage, which is weakly articulated by pilasters, the Sheffield façade had octagonal buttresses with unusual turrets and as its centrepiece a pinnacled tower, for which 'an open-work corona' had been initially planned.[41] Even without that crown, Ebenezer was a landmark in Sheffield's expanding northern quarter.

The most discussed Gothic chapel of these years, however, was the 'National Scotch' (that is, Presbyterian) church,, in Regent Square, London, of 1824–7 (Fig 5.8).[42] Its fame came partly by association with its celebrity minister Edward Irving and partly from its architectural presence, for the twin-towered front of the building was based on no less a monument than York Minster. A Strawberry Hill designer might have

turned to the Minster's west front for its wealth of carved detail, but at Regent Square there was almost no surface ornament, as if the architect (William Tite) was intent on demonstrating the structural purpose of buttresses and pinnacles.[43] The result was substantial and yet – in contrast to the screen-like façades of such English cathedrals as Wells and Lincoln – also emphasised the vertical effect of Gothic. Not that the building was bare: the tracery was quite elaborate, and there was no shortage of crocketing.

When it came to the interior, rather than imitate stone vaulting, Tite employed a shallow pitched ceiling, like that of a 15th-century church, as a means of spanning the entire width of the church without columns.[44] Galleries ran the full length of the building, and an early illustration shows that the ground floor was at first occupied by two blocks of box pews with (unusually) a broad central gangway.[45] Facing along the gangway was Edward Irving's narrow pulpit with its pinnacled canopy, framed by a tall Gothic arch in the centre of the end wall. Apparently communion was celebrated, not from a railed area below the pulpit, but from table-pews of a kind familiar in older meeting houses.[46] It was in these surroundings that something approaching scandal occurred in 1831, when members of the congregation began speaking in tongues. Irving's gradual willingness to condone these 'gifts of the Spirit' led to his expulsion from the Church of Scotland, and the creation in 1833 of the Catholic Apostolic Church, popularly known as the Irvingites. Ever since that time the Regent Square building has been associated with this new development in British church history, but it also merits a place in the polite history of religious architecture.

During the 1820s there seems to have been a change too in the range of Gothic employed by the builders of small rural chapels. Rudimentarily pointed windows continued to appear in some otherwise plain wayside chapels, but more developed medieval effects were beginning to be seen. A remarkable instance is the former Congregational chapel of 1820 in Armitage, Staffordshire (Fig 5.9), whose plan seems to have been partly inspired by that of the nearby parish church, complete with north aisle, chancel and diagonal buttresses.[47] In place of the medieval church's west tower, Armitage chapel has a two-storey porch with a Tudor-arched doorway and traceried wheel window, while the chancel-like eastern arm is a vestry rather than a communion sanctuary. Nonetheless this small village chapel shows that Gothic was increasingly recognised as more than a mere style. The gallery is confined to the west end of the building, facing what might be taken for a chancel arch, beside which stands the pulpit. Evidently the driving force behind the chapel was Thomas Birch, a local solicitor. Like a village squire he had a family vault below the chapel, and he and his wife are commemorated by a pair of matching memorials on the wall of the north aisle. Perhaps this aisle acted as a kind of family pew (paralleling its counterpart in the parish church, which was assumed to have been built by the Lords of Handsacre), or perhaps it was used for the Sunday scholars. Either way Mr Birch kept a proprietorial eye on things, and any disputes about the punctuality of Sunday-school teachers were resolved by reference to the clock in his servants' hall.[48]

Fig 5.9
Congregational chapel, Armitage, Staffordshire, 1820. This small village chapel was built to a medieval plan-type as well as having pointed arches. [DP160655]

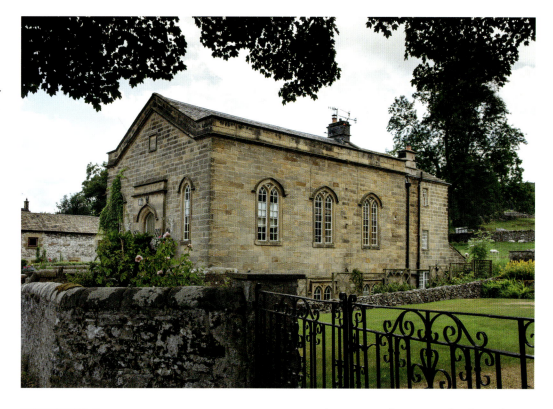

Another case of squirearchical Gothic is the former Congregational chapel of 1826–7 in Middleton by Youlgreave, Derbyshire (Fig 5.10).[49] Its plan is a conventional rectangle, with a gable-end façade, and there are no buttresses or other signs of a Gothic structure. The tracery is more consistently treated than that at Armitage, however: there are arched heads and shaped drip-moulds throughout, and stone mullions for the two-light side windows. The patron was Thomas Bateman of Middleton Hall, and Christopher Stell has attributed the chapel's Gothic details to Bateman's son William, an amateur archaeologist.[50] Antiquarian interests, so often associated with the early Gothic Revival, were certainly not confined to Anglicans. Indeed the most famous person connected with the Middleton chapel was a scholarly investigator of ancient burial sites in the Peak District, another Thomas Bateman. His grave lies behind the chapel (Fig 5.11), and his marble memorial – along with that of his wife – occupied a prominent place on the wall above the pulpit.[51]

Not everyone who commissioned a chapel building during the 1820s was committed to the taste for Greek or Gothic forms. Perhaps the most unlikely demonstration of this was Mount Zion chapel, Devonport (of 1823–4, by John Foulston) (Fig 5.12), which was built in 'a variety of oriental architecture', a hybrid style that was often known as Hindoo.[52] Nash's Brighton Pavilion must have been the source of many details, which included Mughal pinnacles, diamond-pattern parapet and 'Indian' windows. The chapel was part of a Picturesque assembly of buildings by the same architect, among such neighbours as a Doric town hall, Egyptian library and Ionic town house. Modern observers might cavil at the potential association of minarets (or, more personally, the lifestyle of the Prince Regent) with what Foulston called 'Calvinistic worship', but so far as is known this seems not have worried the congregation. The design certainly provided them with a distinctive presence in a town that had many places of worship, and is a corrective to many assumptions about the plainness of Protestant architecture.[53]

However, Foulston's description of the chapel pays more attention to the practical arrangements than to the style. His published plans show that the building was laid out like some of the newest Methodist chapels, incorporating a wide central block (and two side blocks) of forward-facing pews on the ground floor, and a deep U-shaped gallery with a bank of curved seating at the entrance end. Pulpit and reading desk were set in a shallow apse, designed both to give resonance to the preacher's voice and also to allow a comfortable distance between the pulpit and the nearest pews. Foulston favourably compared this scheme with the Commissioners' preferred location of pulpit and desk either side of a central gangway, but also complained that he had been made to squeeze as many sittings as possible into the chapel, allowing a knee-scraping 2 feet 4 inches (0.7m) between rows, and 'probably in no chapel has less room been occupied by the staircases to the galleries'.[54] This was a world away from the lavish provision in the Quakers' large new meeting houses.

Fig 5.12
Mount Zion chapel, Devonport, 1823–4 by John Foulston. Even theologically conservative congregations – here a Calvinistic body – might venture on unusual architectural forms, although this oriental essay was exceptional as far as chapels were concerned.
[RIBA Collections 22730, from Foulston 1838, plate 96]

What's in a name?

Nowadays it is customary for a place of worship in Britain to have its identity proclaimed by means of a notice board, inscription or banner, but this was not always so. Until the early 19th century, such signs seem to have been quite exceptional. Local people would have known the identity of a building, and visitors had only to ask. Early Nonconformist buildings were often referred to simply as 'the chapel' or 'the meeting house', sometimes qualified denominationally or by street name (for example the Quaker meeting house or Gravel Lane chapel). Occasionally a minister's name might be the distinguishing factor, as with Whitefield's Tabernacle. By the later Georgian period, however, there was need for greater differentiation, as the pace of Nonconformist building quickened and the risk grew of confusion with the increasingly numerous Anglican chapels-of-ease.

In the years around 1800, two changes occurred. One was the growing use of external inscriptions. New chapels might have a prominent stone tablet bearing the denomination's name, and perhaps also the date. Among Wesleyans, William Jenkins was particularly associated with this development. The second change was the increased use of nondenominational names. The wars with France stimulated a vogue for patriotic or royalist names, and quite a number of Brunswick chapels appeared. More widespread was the choice of biblical names. The Methodist New Connexion (founded in 1797) was especially inclined to choose such names as Bethesda or Mount Zion, in an attempt to distinguish itself from the Wesleyan connexion of Methodists. Most of the Strict Baptist chapels were similarly given a biblical name, perhaps in order to mark their separation from more liberal Baptist causes: Ebenezer, Bethel and Salem were among the most popular choices. The use of biblical and more generic names (such as Hope and Providence) was by no means restricted to these newer groups, however, and may be found in many denominations.

A few names whose meaning or association may not be clear to modern visitors are:

Aenon (or Enon) – fountain. The place where John the Baptist baptised (John 3: 23).
Bethel – house of God.
Bethesda – house of mercy, or healing pool.
Bethlehem – house of bread.
Cave Adullam – the resting place. David's place of refuge when fleeing from Saul (I Samuel 22: 1).
Ebenezer – stone of help. Samuel commemorated a victory over the Philistines by erecting a stone which he called Ebenezer, saying, 'hitherto hath the Lord helped us' (I Samuel 7: 12).

Fig 5.13
Independent chapel, Roxton, Bedfordshire. The chapel began as a barn, which by 1825 was adapted in delightful rustic fashion for worship. It was subsequently extended with two wings. [DP155986]

A much smaller chapel, also connected with the Picturesque aesthetic, can usefully conclude this section. In the small Bedfordshire village of Roxton, a Nonconformist landowner, Charles James Metcalfe, had made a barn available for occasional services since 1808 and an Independent congregation was constituted there in 1822 (Figs 5.13 and 5.14).[55] Barns had been a common recourse for rural Dissenters during times of persecution and sometimes after. During the early 19th century, however, this fact came to be used as a means of denigrating Nonconformists and their architectural achievements. As one critic wrote, 'Popery is the religion of cathedrals, Protestantism of houses, Dissenterism of barns'.[56] Against this background, when the Roxton barn was first adapted and then enlarged to create a permanent place of worship, it was decided to flaunt rather than disguise the building's rustic character.[57] Around the outside of the

Elim – a place with many wells, where the Hebrews camped after crossing the Red Sea (Exodus 15: 27).
Emmanuel – God with us (Matthew 1: 23).
Galeed – a heap of stones which was a witness to the covenant between Jacob and Laban (Genesis 31: 47–8).
Jireh – from Jehovah-Jireh, the Lord will provide (Genesis 22: 14).
Rehoboth – ample room. Isaac dug a well, which he called Rehoboth, saying 'the Lord hath made room for us' (Genesis 26: 22).
Salem – peace. 'In Salem also is his tabernacle, and his dwelling place in Zion' (Psalm 76: 2).
Zion (or Sion) – sunny. One of the hills of Jerusalem, and thence the city as a whole; the Holy Land, or allegorically, heaven.
Zoar – small.

Some other names may seem less immediately redolent of chapel culture. When many older chapels were becoming Unitarian, a few congregations reacted by choosing to call their buildings Trinity. Partly for the same reason, traditional Presbyterian congregations with a largely Scottish membership often adopted the patronal name of St Andrew. Later in the 19th century Christ Church began to appear as a name for some Nonconformist places of worship, occasionally with the desire to avoid sectarianism. Gradually, as denominational consolidation gathered pace, the name Trinity commonly came to signify the coming together of three congregations – a tendency that became very widespread with late 20th-century ecumenical partnerships.†

Bethesda Methodist New Connexion chapel, Hanley, Stoke-on-Trent. [DP160666]

Fig 5.14
Independent chapel, Roxton. The Metcalfe family presumably occupied the family pew (here seen with a stained-glass window) on the left. [DP156067]

chapel are tree trunk columns, which support the thatched roof and bear 'branches' that frame views of ogee-headed windows and white-washed walls. It is a rare instance of a religious building in the *cottage orné* fashion, at once a charming place of public worship and a romantic feature in the prospect from the big house.

The 1830s and 1840s

Accounts of early Victorian religious architecture are generally dominated by an assessment of Pugin's contribution and the impact of Ecclesiology. The idea spread that Gothic was the only acceptable style for new church buildings, and that there should be a separate chancel in which the sacrament of the communion could be celebrated. Despite the resistance of evangelical Anglicans, the Church of England began to turn away from its Protestant history, and to reject much of its architectural legacy too. Many Nonconformists responded with deep distrust to these developments, or at least to the theological implications, but others were at least cautiously interested. Overall for the Nonconformist world, however, the effect was to increase the range of architectural options. The entire repertoire of classical forms (which continued to shape so much secular architecture) remained available to chapel builders, and the repertoire of medieval forms grew. It was partly a matter of styles, but more radically of structure and of plan-types. In short, Nonconformity retained the heterogeneous, and sometimes adventurous, characteristics which are the hallmarks of Victorian architecture.

Like all categories of building in the Victorian era, chapels acquired a national as well as a local audience. From the early 1840s the illustrated magazines (*The Illustrated London News* began publication in 1842 and *The Builder* in 1843) featured a selection of the latest chapels alongside engravings of new Anglican churches, railway stations, town halls and other secular buildings from around the country. As a rule the best buildings were generously described, and the Nonconformists, or their architects, provided good copy. Even *The Ecclesiologist* (established 1841), which famously led the Anglicans' abandonment of post-Reformation architecture, sometimes found it necessary to pay attention to Nonconformist buildings. For some congregations this publicity may have further increased the range of architectural options, but for others chapel design was still rooted in local or denominational traditions.

Although far from novel by the 1830s, the type of large urban chapel with a curved gallery, which William Jenkins had helped to develop for Methodist congregations, retained its popularity. A successful designer in this tradition was James Simpson, a West Yorkshire joiner-turned-architect, who worked for most denominations, but especially for his fellow Wesleyans.[58] The largest of his early commissions was Oxford Place Wesleyan chapel, Leeds (1835). Its well-fitted interior had a deep encircling gallery with a prominent organ rising above a pulpit apparently inspired by the Choragic Monument of Lysicrates.[59] Externally Simpson's design was relatively conservative: the unpedimented five-bay façade with entrances in the end bays looked like a continuation of a late 17th-century meeting-house format, albeit applied to a long rather than a wide chapel.[60] Within a few years Simpson had gained the confidence to introduce more monumental elements in his architecture, as can be seen at the Centenary Wesleyan Methodist chapel, York (1839–40) (Figs 5.15 and 5.16).[61] Through its name, Centenary chapel was a reminder that Methodism (begun 100 years earlier by John Wesley) was here to stay, and the chapel's giant portico of unfluted Ionic columns nobly reinforces the message. If this was Simpson's first foray into fully fledged classicism, it was nicely calculated as a piece of townscape. The building created a strong feature at the newly widened southern end of St Saviourgate and upstaged the just-opened Salem Congregational chapel (1838–9, by J P Pritchett), whose Ionic portico closed the northward vista.[62]

Beyond the façade, the Centenary chapel demonstrated Simpson's confidence in many other ways. The plan is not rectangular, but U-shaped, a pattern which – as described in Chapter 4 – had been adopted for a few chapels in earlier decades; Simpson himself had encountered it at Brunswick Wesleyan chapel, Leeds (of 1824–5 by Joseph Botham), where he had supplied the joinery.[63] At Centenary the pulpit and organ are placed at the entrance end (as a consequence of which the preacher's back is turned to the street), facing the chapel's curved far wall and the array of handsome box pews that follow the sweep of the building. By that date the construction of deep galleries on a minimum number of cast-iron columns was hardly innovative, but the imposing scale of Centenary's gallery – 11 rows deep around the curved end of the chapel – still makes a thrilling sight. The building's height, emphasised externally by the proportions of the portico, is generous internally, and the classical theme is continued by the coffered ceiling and its moulded frieze of running foliate motifs. Although Simpson was to design many more chapels, as we shall see, giant porticoes do not seem to have been a common feature of his work.[64] Perhaps expense was a factor. The Centenary chapel cost £7,785, as compared to c £5,000 for the only fractionally smaller Wesleyan chapel in King Street, Derby (of 1841), which Simpson designed with a single-storey Doric portico in antis.[65]

Some of Nonconformity's greatest contributions to neo-classicism were created in the first five years of Victoria's reign, just as the Church of England was abandoning the style in the wake of Pugin's assault on classicism as a pagan culture. Ionic designs, externally similar to Simpson's, were not uncommon.[66] Doric chapels were less usual, but two mighty examples were built for Congregationalists in Yorkshire at this time. Although neither has survived, they deserve mention here in order that the full range of chapel architecture can be understood. East Parade chapel, Leeds (1839–41, by Moffat and

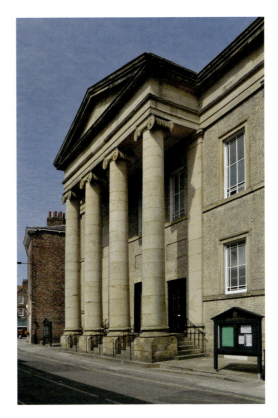

Fig 5.15 (right)
Centenary Wesleyan (now Central) Methodist chapel, York, 1839–40 by James Simpson. Commemorating a hundred years of Methodism, the chapel is one of the more monumental of Simpson's designs.
[DP181103]

Fig 5.16 (below)
Interior of Centenary Wesleyan (now Central) Methodist chapel, York. The gallery and its seating are virtually unchanged, but the rostrum-pulpit is not original and some ground-floor seating has been removed.
[DP181099]

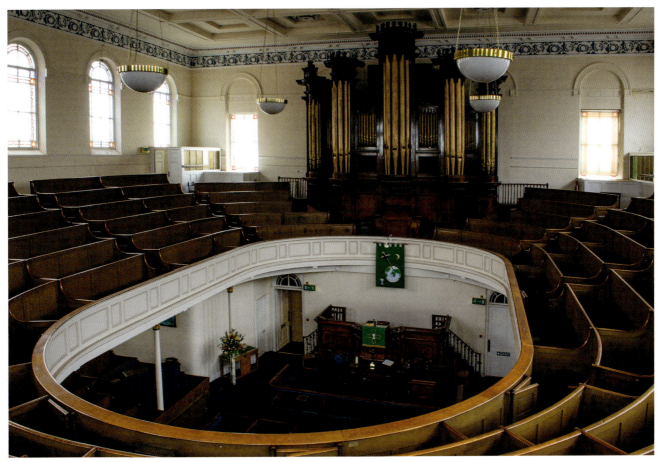

Fig 5.17
Former Catholic Apostolic church (now St Mary on the Quay), Bristol, 1839–40 by R S Pope. In erecting this impressive Corinthian chapel, the young Catholic Apostolic Church over-stretched its resources, and so sold the building to the Roman Catholics. [DP166290]

Hurst) and Albion Street chapel, Hull (by H F Lockwood, completed in 1842) each had a portico of six fluted columns, approached by a broad flight of steps.[67] In each case the podium gave a classical dignity to the chapel, and served the practical need of allowing schoolrooms or meeting rooms to be created below the main worship space. The Hull chapel, built at a cost of about £8,000, had a more consistently temple-like form and Schinkelesque clarity. Even after half a century of industrial pollution, it had the power to inspire the viewer:

> The whole is raised on a bold flight of steps and when seen with a bright sun falling on it slantwise and throwing strong sharp shadows over the capitals and across the cella wall behind, really gives an impression such as is seldom met with in England of some of the beauties of Greek architecture.[68]

More evidence of Greek influence in these years can be found in Bristol, in what is now the Roman Catholic church of St Mary on the Quay (Fig 5.17). The chapel was built in 1839–40 to the designs of R S Pope for the followers of Edward Irving, properly called the Catholic

Apostolic Church.[69] Pope's dignified temple stands on a high plinth above what was indeed originally a quayside, its portico of six fluted Corinthian columns bearing richly carved capitals modelled on those of the Choragic Monument of Lysicrates. Set back from the portico is a somewhat lower screen wall, giving the building a greater lateral presence and providing a seemly backdrop for the perron steps. The Irvingites expected an elaborate liturgy, and their building was provided with shallow transepts and a distinct chancel, heralded by a pair of Corinthian columns. A financial crisis, however, forced the sale of the premises three years after its construction in 1839 to 1840. It finally opened in 1843 under the auspices of the Roman Catholic Church, for whom the layout was quite acceptable and whose local bishop had a passion for classical churches.[70]

At this stage another long-lost chapel has to be included, the stupendous building of 1841–3 erected for the Wesleyans in Great Thornton Street, Hull (to the designs of H F Lockwood and Thomas Allom).[71] Even in a town with a fair number of major neo-classical buildings – including Albion Street Independent chapel and Kingston Wesleyan chapel (*see* note 5:64) – the chapel in Great Thornton Street stood out. H-R Hitchcock, the American architectural historian, described it as 'perhaps the handsomest church begun in the year 1841 by any other architect than Pugin', and thought that it put almost all Anglican churches of the period to shame.[72] The subject of Hitchcock's appreciation had a frontage of 160 feet (49m), and was raised, Propylaea-like, about 10 feet (3m) above the street. At its centre was a Corinthian portico of eight columns, linked by Greek Doric stoas to outer temple-pavilions. Perhaps, as Derek Linstrum has suggested, the composition was influenced by contemporary French architecture, or perhaps inspiration came from Thomas Hamilton's well-known design for the Royal High School in Edinburgh.[73]

What then was the purpose of the Great Thornton Street chapel's unusual length and elevation? The classically detailed chapel itself, 60 feet (18.3m) wide and 90 feet (27.4m) long, was represented by the main temple portico. Behind the main, galleried worship space was an assembly hall, below which were five classrooms. The right-hand pavilion served as a sacristy (one imagines that the Methodists preferred to call it a vestry), while that on the left was the caretaker's house. Almost all of the extensive ground level seems to have been given over to catacombs,

however, which could be entered directly from the street via one of the massive pedimented gateways.[74] Like many Nonconformists, it seems that Hull's Wesleyans were responding to the current crisis of graveyard provision, which led locally to the opening of Hull's General Cemetery in 1847, and it may not be coincidental that funerary provision was still often associated with classical architecture.[75] The chapel-plus-catacombs formula was soon outlawed, and so Great Thornton Street chapel proved not to be a model for further places of worship.[76] Stylistically, too, it had no immediate progeny. Hitchcock felt that it belonged to the brief heyday of the temple church, its classicism being of 'such distinction [as] was rarely achieved after this date'.[77] Yet, as a confident affirmation of the belief that classicism could play a central role in 19th-century architecture, Lockwood and Allom's design was to remain a potent force.

Enterprising chapel architects were quite capable of varying the rectangular format, either for townscape reasons or for internal convenience. A good example of the former is the Great George Street Congregational chapel, Liverpool (of 1840–1, by Joseph Franklin; in secular use since 1967), which sits near the intersection of five major streets (Fig 5.18).[78] Franklin responded to this challenge superbly, fronting

Fig 5.18
Congregational chapel, Great George Street, Liverpool, 1840–1 by Joseph Franklin. This landmark chapel with monolithic Corinthian columns was built at considerable expense for the congregation of a leading minister. It is now in secular use. [AA040498]

the rectangular chapel with a portico of fluted Corinthian columns that almost encircle a cylindrical, domed porch. Nash's church of All Souls church in London's Langham Place might have been the precedent, but the Great George Street chapel is much more richly detailed, and – along with St George's Hall – helps to mark Liverpool's turn to Roman rather than Greek sources.

A more extensive departure from the rectangular plan can be found in what was nicknamed the 'Pork Pie chapel' (in secular use since 1946), in Belvoir Street, Leicester (Fig 5.19), built in 1845 for an important Baptist congregation to the designs of Joseph Hansom.[79] Hansom had already designed one strongly classical building for Leicester's Nonconformists, the Proprietary School in New Walk (of 1836–7), to which he gave a massive Tuscan portico: never mind that the mayor approvingly called it a Grecian building.[80] When it came to the Belvoir Street commission, Hansom employed a stubby variant of the U-shaped plan which, as we have seen in discussion of the Centenary Wesleyan chapel, York (*see* pp 106–7), had been enjoying a minor success among some chapel builders for its internal practicality. His bold stroke was to treat the rounded part of the building as the façade, endowing it with a giant order of engaged

Tuscan columns, which carry a deep entablature. The curve, continued above with a recessed Doric clerestory, was emphasised by a pair of cylindrical entrance- and stair-towers (another homage to the Choragic Monument of Lysicrates) squeezed into the corners of the street frontage. All this shows to effect in the relatively narrow street, and from the approach in Bowling Green Street. Hansom also appears to have exploited the practical advantages of the plan, for praise was given to the chapel's acoustic properties and effective lighting, and there was a lecture hall and schoolroom.[81] More recently Hitchcock admired the ingenuity of Hansom's plan, but judged the design to be 'essentially secular in character', presumably because it resembles neither a medieval church nor a classical temple.[82] Yet much of the vitality of Nonconformist architecture during the 19th century arises from precisely such freedom to disregard ecclesiastical convention.

Both Liverpool's Great George Street chapel and Leicester's Belvoir Street chapel were very much in the public eye, not least because of their conspicuous locations. For less prominent buildings, however, many congregations opted for more limited touches of classicism. In 1834–5 the Quakers of Gloucester had a new meeting

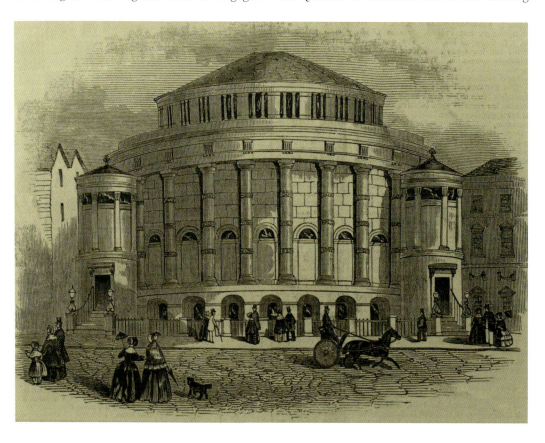

Fig 5.19
Baptist chapel, Belvoir Street, Leicester, 1845 by Joseph Hansom. Though Hansom is more famous for Gothic churches for Roman Catholics, this unusual Nonconformist chapel is characteristic of his earlier reputation for classical designs. It has been in secular use since 1946. [Engraving from The Illustrated London News, 25 Oct 1845, 268]

house built in a quiet city lane, to the designs of S W Daukes (sometimes spelt Dawkes).[83] It was entered in one of the long sides, and the high brick frontage bore a range of round-headed windows, those at each end framed in arched recesses: a restrained Soanean motif that was hardly innovative by this date. Perhaps such conservatism suited both the client and (for the moment) the architect. Daukes can only just have been establishing himself in the city, after training as assistant to J P Pritchett in York.[84] Gloucester's meeting house (Figs 5.20 and 5.21) has retained most of its internal fittings, among them the main stand and wall benches, as well as the sash shutter which subdivides (or opens up) the lofty – but ungalleried – space.

Fig 5.20
Quaker meeting house, Gloucester, 1834–5 by S W Daukes. Largely hidden by the entrance block (of 1879), this meeting house of the 1830s is a wide building with windows in arched recesses.
[DP166230]

Fig 5.21
Interior of Quaker meeting house, Gloucester. Among the features to survive from the 1830s are the stand and wall benches, as well as the heating and ventilating grilles.
[DP166229]

Fig 5.22
The Room, Stafford,
1839–40 is one of the oldest
buildings erected for the
Brethren, and its entrances
were initially in the long
side elevation. It is now an
Evangelical church.
[DP160659]

Fig 5.23
Primitive Methodist chapel,
Englesea Brook, Cheshire,
1828 and 1832. The school-
room was added in 1914.
Even the least sophisticated
of chapels is likely to reveal
a concern for architectural
propriety, as the neat
façade here shows.
[DP168480]

A few discreetly classical details distinguish the joinery.

When the Quakers in nearby Cheltenham built their new meeting house a year later, in 1835–6, a similar scheme was adopted, but (with an eye to the town's more fashionable reputation?) the architectural treatment was a little more classical: the square lines of its ashlar façade were accentuated by a neat cornice, architraves framed the outer windows and a rudimentarily Greek doorway marked the entrance.[85] Neither of these Gloucestershire meeting houses had the short-

wall façades or generous circulation space that we have seen being taken up by Quakers in Manchester and Norwich, nor was the developed classicism of those larger meeting houses apparent. Quakers were more varied than is often supposed and their buildings reflect this, in the 19th century as in the 17th.

Another kind of understated classicism is to be found in a building first known simply as The Room, in Stafford (Fig 5.22). It dates from 1839–40, and is one of the first purpose-built places of worship of the Brethren (or Plymouth Brethren), a movement then barely a decade old and which established itself in Stafford only in 1838.[86] Given the Brethren's reluctance to draw attention to themselves, the absence of a grandly columned portico is no surprise. Yet the Stafford building is much more substantial than its name suggests. It is a two-storey brick building, initially with entrances occupying (in the old-fashioned way) the terminal bays of the long east wall. The northern gable end, however, carries a full-width pediment with broad eaves. Thus the idea of a temple front was evident from the start, and the architectural logic was subsequently accepted when the entrance was transferred to this façade.[87] In a piquant cultural clash, the Room's crisp pediment faced the churchyard of St Mary's, the medieval parish church of Stafford. It is difficult to imagine that the Anglicans felt embarrassed by the presence of the Brethren's new building, but its trim appearance must have helped to highlight the dilapidated condition of the old church. Within a handful of years George Gilbert Scott undertook a major restoration of St Mary's, not merely putting it in good repair, but also removing most traces of the previous three centuries of worship.[88]

Small rural chapels of this time rarely exhibited even such classicism as is seen at The Room. A case in point can be found in Englesea Brook (Fig 5.23), a south Cheshire hamlet where a Primitive Methodist chapel is the sole place of worship.[89] The small chapel was built in 1828, reportedly for only £113, on land given by a local farmer. It was a time when the Primitive Methodists were recruiting new members at a prodigious rate and in 1832, just four years after the opening, the chapel was enlarged. Although bearing a date stone of 1828, the façade is in fact from 1832, the result of extending the building some 7 feet (2.1m) towards the road. Explicitly classical details are absent, but the brick front is of neat design using Flemish bond, and consists of a round-arched doorway between flat-headed sash windows (two below and two above). Its vertical presence is emphasised by the gable end, and one can almost sense an implied rhythm of pilasters and pediment. Internally the chief survivor from the 1832 alterations is the gallery, which was built above the entrance and provided about 60 seats in three tiers of box pews (*see* Frontispiece). Like many small chapels on the threshold of polite architecture, Englesea Brook must have been erected without the involvement of a professional designer, yet care was evidently taken to create something that was more than merely pleasant in appearance. There is a sense of decorum here that belies the idea of Primitive Methodism as a rough and ready religion, spiritually enthusiastic but careless about its appearance. Hugh Bourne, one of the founders of the movement, was buried at

Englesea Brook in 1852, and since 1986 the chapel has served not only as a place of worship, but also as a museum of Primitive Methodism.

Although the great majority of country chapels were rectangular (either of the more traditional, wide-fronted plan-type or the increasingly common format with a gable-end façade), more enterprising patterns were occasionally ventured. The tradition of central plans was not entirely confined to urban Nonconformity. Two good examples are to be seen in the Suffolk villages of Fressingfield (Figs 5.24 and 5.25) and Friston where, in 1835 and 1834 respectively, hexagonal red-brick chapels were built for Strict Baptist congregations.[90] The plans of these elongated hexagons are attractive, almost crystalline; from a practical perspective they seem to combine some of the virtues of the octagon with the

Fig 5.24
Strict Baptist chapel, Fressingfield, Suffolk, 1835. Like another Baptist chapel – not far away at Friston in Suffolk – Fressingfield has a very unusual shape. Its similarly shaped extension (on the left) was rebuilt in the 1980s.
[DP160148]

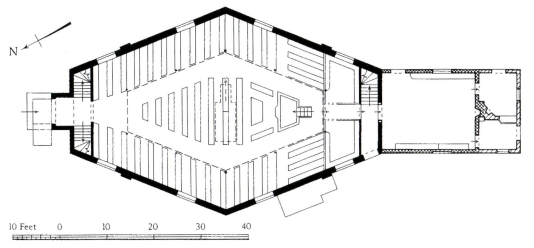

10 Feet 0   10   20   30   40

Fig 5.25
Strict Baptist chapel, Fressingfield. The plan – drawn before the rebuilding of the extension and loss of ground-floor pews – shows the neat geometry of the 19th-century design.
[RCH01/118/01/04/059]

growing preference for long-axis chapels. There was a central diamond of seating, complete with a tapering table-pew and trapezoidal communion table, on to which the pulpit looked down.[91] Echoing this shape, the gallery is of the same elongated hexagonal form. It provides a dramatic vantage point from which to witness baptisms, as the baptistery is beneath the boards at the centre of each chapel. The external appearance is less elegant, partly because the hipped roofs have a visual logic at odds with the proportions of the fenestration, as if there were a struggle to translate the plans into three dimensions.

All this, and the absence of such motifs as pediments or columns, fits the suggestion that the designs were not the work of a professional architect, but perhaps of William Brown, pastor of the Friston chapel, or George Denny Spratt, who ministered at Fressingfield. Brown is believed to have gained some knowledge of surveying and architecture and to have 'superintended several large buildings in London, among them two chapels', while Spratt was a builder.[92] It has been inferred that these extraordinary buildings were intentionally coffin-shaped 'as an object lesson in the mortality of life'.[93] Faced with so beguiling a theory, there is little point in complaining that coffins never are quite this shape. In any case, since both chapels stand in a drift of gravestones, they have become memento mori, even if that was not the purpose of their shape.

If Friston and Fressingfield evoke comparisons with the central plans of continental Protestantism, a chapel in Dorset prompts thoughts of America. The building in question is the Congregational (now United Reformed) chapel of 1841 at Longham (Fig 5.26), near Poole.[94] Above its gable-end façade rises a white-painted octagonal bell turret (complete with clock and bell) which terminates in a slim spire and weather vane – suggesting a closer affinity with the New England meeting house tradition than with recent British neo-classicism.[95] The chapel was the brainchild of Joseph Notting, a boot manufacturer and tanner who had successfully evangelised Longham's scattered rural population during the later 1830s. In a village without its own church he doubtless saw the chapel as the community's natural place of worship, and the new building was thought to be 'quite a village cathedral'.[96] The phrase overstates the case, but it seems that Longham was being considered for development as a model village: Notting was perhaps anxious to assert the central status of the chapel in contrast to the church-dominated

pattern of other nearby estates and model villages in what is now Bournemouth.[97] Spires were a novelty for Nonconformists, and were hardly common even among the new Anglican churches of the district.[98]

The plans for Longham's chapel were drawn up by a local builder, William Gollop, and it can be guessed that he was the author of the classical details. On the front a sturdy Tuscan porch is set below tall pilaster-arches, with an open pediment above and neatly capped Ionic pilasters at each end. The result is not in the least colonial; more likely an elaboration of the pattern seen at, for instance, Newport Wesleyan chapel, Isle of Wight (see p 83). The chapel is constructed in yellow-grey brick, with brighter yellow brick dressings on the façade and terracotta-coloured trim to the side elevations. Such polychromy, predating Ruskin's *Stones of Venice* by a decade, perhaps reflects the builder–architect's instinctive delight in his work. By the 1840s the design of new Anglican churches was almost exclusively in the hands of the emerging architectural profession, but there were still some opportunities for artisan designers in the Nonconformist world.

An interesting urban comparison with the Longham chapel is offered by the former Presbyterian chapel in Broad Street, Birmingham, (of 1848–9, by J R Botham; now in secular use).[99] Both have clock towers as a central feature, and both demonstrate a somewhat eclectic approach to the classical tradition. Birmingham's Presbyterians had, as recently as 1824, opened an octagonal chapel with a giant Doric portico.[100] It quickly proved to be beyond their means, however, and it may be that their Broad Street chapel represents not only a downsizing, but also a deliberate avoidance of monumentality – or rather of the kind of monumentality associated with stricter neo-classicism. There is thus no portico, but an elaborate 110-foot (35m) tower, which begins classically enough but has a pagoda-like roof. This was very far from being the first Nonconformist bell tower, but its inclusion here was part of a growing use of towers and spires in the 1840s, accompanied by an increasing expectation that chapels should have a bell.[101] Did chapel committees follow the 1818 Church Building Commission in feeling the need to make a mark in crowded towns?

One motif of the Broad Street tower seems to have been borrowed from the local Commissioners' church of St Thomas (1827–9, by Rickman and Hutchinson), although the overall effect is much more eclectic.[102] The happy mix of

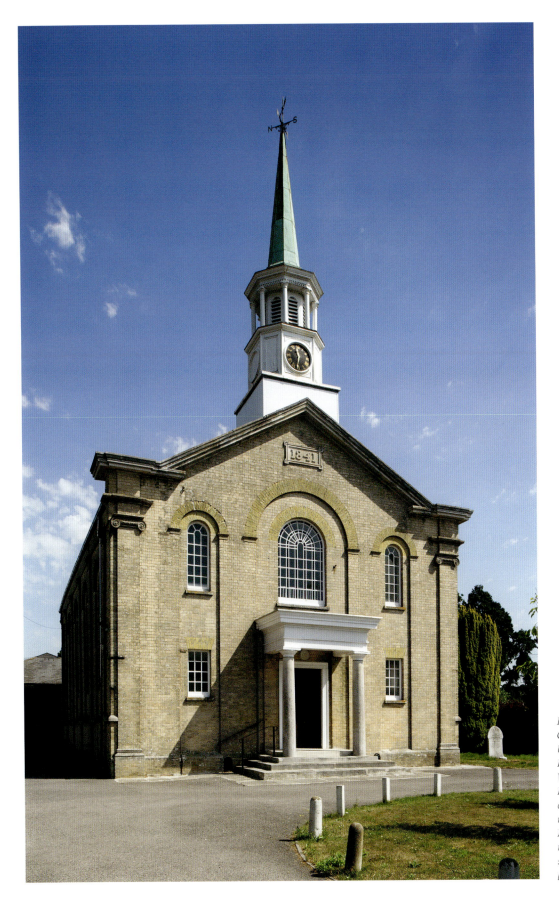

Fig 5.26
Congregational (now
United Reformed) chapel,
Longham, Dorset, 1841.
With its echo of New
England, the Longham
chapel was part of a
wider tendency among
Nonconformists to increase
the use of towers and
spires.
[DP166272]

motifs seen in the tower of the Broad Street chapel continues below, where Renaissance motifs are combined with older forms, and the robust, blue-brick masonry is heightened by dressings of grey brick and stone. A remarkable feature of Botham's design was that all the windows along the nine-bay side wall are blind; the chapel building was entirely top-lit, with a ceiling of obscured glass panels below a series of skylights.[103] Here, some two years before Street's letter on town churches, was recognition of the special needs of places of worship in industrial cities.[104] The interior, approached via a domed vestibule, was a galleried rectangle, with an arched recess for the minister's platform at the far end. The chapel was fitted, not with box pews, but with open-ended pews (described as 'benches, having enclosed backs and ornamental ends') of a kind that was gaining favour with many denominations.[105] From its stand-out tower to its top-lit space for worship, the Broad Street chapel provides evidence of the Nonconformists' propensity for change in the 1840s – a propensity that was not the preserve of Gothicists.

These examples from Longham and Birmingham give a flavour of the range of ways in which Nonconformists responded to the challenges of rural and urban England in the 1840s. To understand the full range, however, one has to consider the growing influence of Gothic and other medieval forms on Nonconformist architecture.

Gothic chapels of the 1830s and 1840s

Nonconformists, as previous chapters show, had been creating Gothic chapels of increasingly sophisticated kinds for more than half a century. This seems never to have been a problem, and indeed rarely caused comment. Walpole had remarked on the Countess of Huntingdon's use of Gothic in Bath, but his was a special interest. Perhaps more characteristic of the period is John Wesley's failure to mention the matter of architectural styles, even when praising the design of the new chapel at Whitby, which had pointed windows.[106] By the time that Victoria came to the throne, however, things had begun to change, at least for the most culturally alert congregations. The critical point was Pugin's assertion that Gothic was the only true Christian style. After the publication of his *Contrasts* in 1836, anyone building a classical church or chapel was open to criticism for having adopted what Pugin had stigmatised as pagan architecture. Undeterred by this, many Nonconformists continued to build classically, as we have seen and shall see again in future chapters. But in what circumstances was Gothic now preferred?

The small independent chapel at Binfield Heath, in the south-east corner of Oxfordshire (Fig 5.27) was opened in 1835, the year before *Contrasts* appeared. It was one of the last in a series of similar-looking chapels to be erected in the district for James Sherman, an Independent minister from Reading.[107] Eschewing the most familiar types of small chapel building, Sherman favoured what looks like the archetypal church from a set of toy buildings, consisting of a rectangular block under a pitched roof, with an entrance tower at the gable end and Gothic windows throughout. Most of these chapels were the first purpose-built places of worship in their localities, and their physical presence – rather as in the case of the chapel at Longham – reflects an intention to help create a place rather than find a corner in an existing one.

Binfield Heath chapel is a particularly satisfying example, standing back from the road with sufficient green space of its own to show the diminutive building off to advantage. It is well built of ashlar masonry, with neat stepped buttresses and plain lancet windows along each flank. The battlemented bell tower is what catches the eye, however, and it has more elaborate Gothic details: paired louvred openings with hood-moulds in the belfry stage, two-light windows with cusped tracery below and, squeezed between a pair of diagonal buttresses, the hollow-chamfered doorway under an ogee hood with foliate motifs and headstops. Internally the chapel has lost some original features, but the scissor-brace roof with tracery motifs continues to set a Gothic character, and ranks of benches quite probably reflect the original seating pattern. Above a modern pulpit, the painted motto *Praise Ye the Lord* may be late 19th century, but is nonetheless a reminder of the continuity of worship in this building since before Victoria's reign. At the rear of the chapel is a schoolroom, built as early as 1836, and indicating an unusual determination to provide dedicated teaching accommodation, even in such rural locations.

James Sherman did not pay for this series of chapels (a plaque at Binfield Heath records that the funds for its construction came chiefly from Sarah Adams, a wealthy member of Sherman's congregation at Castle Street in Reading), but his must have been the architectural vision as well as the missionary enterprise.[108] Sherman's evident resolve to build in the Gothic style was surely affected by his background in the Countess of Huntingdon's Connexion. He had been trained at the Countess's college in Cheshunt and spent his formative first years of ministry at her famously Gothic chapels in Bath and Bristol before moving to Reading in 1820/1.[109] If Sherman's promotion of Gothic architecture was rooted in an 18th-century attitude, his chapels were shaped by a more recent sensibility, and their counterparts (albeit much larger, and urban) are the plainest of the Gothic churches that resulted from the 1818 Church Building Act.

While the Sherman chapels were a recognised brand in the countryside around Reading, the Gothic chapels designed by James Fenton are a recognisable type in towns across a swath of eastern and southern England. Fenton was another man whose tastes were formed before Pugin's *Contrasts* was published, and he produced classical and Gothic designs with apparent equanimity for Independent (or Congregational) and Baptist chapels throughout the 1830s and 1840s. Perhaps, as Colvin implied, Fenton's aptitude was for classical composition, in which he employed 'modest but effective' features 'without the use of an order.'[110] Yet either he or his clients often wanted something different, and perhaps as many as half his Nonconformist

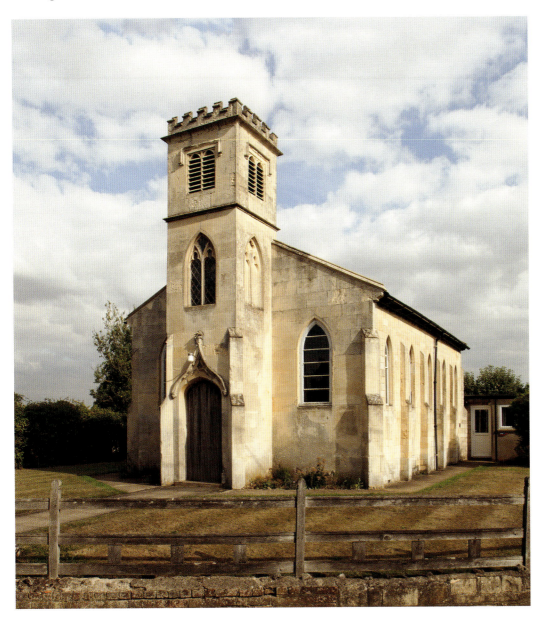

Fig 5.27
Independent chapel,
Binfield Heath, Oxfordshire,
1835. This is one of a series
of such small chapels
planted in the country
around Reading with the
encouragement of James
Sherman, a local
Independent minister.
[DP160414]

Fig 5.28
Baptist chapel, Boston,
Lincolnshire, 1837. Its
broad frontage was
designed in the manner
of James Fenton, and has
a pleasing variety of
Gothic incident.
[DP160407]

commissions were Gothic, of a kind that Colvin thought 'less sophisticated', but which other writers have found quite pretty.[111] What is clear is that Fenton, despite a reputation as 'an architect of great respectability and celebrity in chapel building', was not in the forefront of the Gothic Revival, and the windows of his Gothic chapels had intersecting glazing bars (in the Georgian tradition) rather than fully developed tracery.[112]

This can be seen at the Baptist chapel of 1837 in Boston, Lincolnshire, a building that can be attributed to Fenton on stylistic grounds with some confidence (Fig 5.28).[113] As with Fenton's documented Gothic chapels, its façade is essentially of pale brick with stone details, and there is no tower. It also has another Fenton characteristic, a pair of gabled porches, not in the centre, but in the flanking bays: a direct expression of the Nonconformist layout with two gangways leading to one central block and two side ranks of seating. At first sight the frontage, divided into bays by buttresses, might be taken to represent a nave and lower, double, side aisles. But a second glance shows that outermost bays give access to the rear of the site (including the Sunday-school building) and behind the façade the main body of the chapel turns out to be roofed as a conven-

tional single space. Internally the medieval theme is continued by the side windows and the tracery decoration of the roof beams, but the gallery, which occupies all four sides of the chamber, rests on slender classical columns. The General Baptist congregation for whom the chapel was built traced its origins to 1651, and in the early days had met for worship in a medieval church.[114] For Dissenters such as these, Gothic architecture may have been an active choice, at once fashionable and traditional. If James Fenton was indeed the architect here, the design marks a transition. His earlier Gothic chapels treat the three-bay gable end more straightforwardly, while at Billericay in 1838 and at Lincoln in 1840 he heightened the contrast between the centrepiece and end bays, and abandoned intersecting glazing bars in favour of lancet windows.[115]

It seems possible that the Methodists, who had built their fair share of Gothic chapels in the later Georgian period, became rather less keen on the idea for a few years following Pugin's rise to prominence. The Gothic strain did continue, however, as is shown by the Wesleyan chapel of 1837–8 (architect unknown) in Newbury, Berkshire (Fig 5.29).[116] As compared with the Baptist chapel in Boston, this is less pretty and more serious in appearance: externally of stone (from Bath?) rather than brick, tall rather than wide and with plain lancets throughout. On the main front two pierced octagonal turrets frame the projecting centrepiece, which includes a stone-vaulted porch beneath a triple lancet window. An ogee canopy embellishes the entrance, its pattern echoed in the two small porches of the outer bays, which were added in 1898.[117]

Beyond the entrance, the plan is of the kind created by William Jenkins a quarter of a century before, which in turn depended on the City Road arrangement of the 1770s (*see* pp 62–3). A gallery occupies all four sides of the main space, and behind the pulpit is a communion recess with an organ above. Furthermore, in a refinement of what might be called the Jenkinsian sense of openness, the front of the gallery is

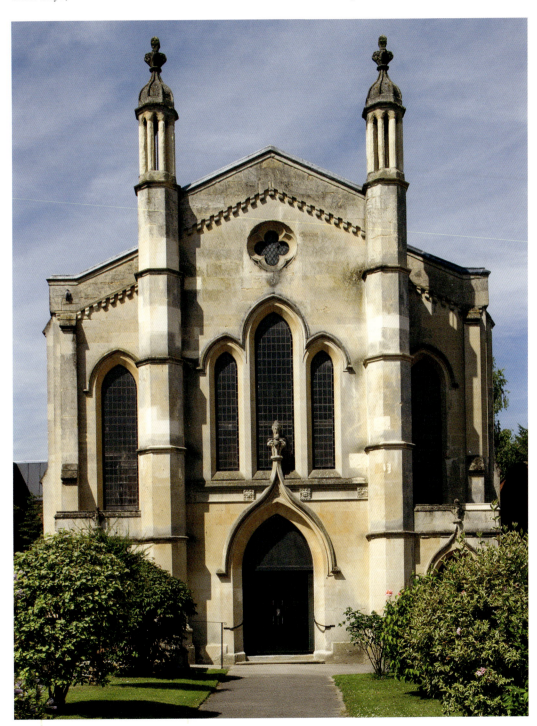

Fig 5.29
Wesleyan Methodist chapel, Newbury, Berkshire, 1837–8. Conveying a sense that Gothic was not merely a matter of pretty tracery, Newbury's Wesleyan chapel even has a stone-vaulted porch.
[DP166273]

Fig 5.30
The Apostles' chapel,
Albury, Surrey, 1837–40
by William Wilkins and
William McIntosh Brookes.
Tall but without aisles,
the chapel reflects the
Catholic Apostolic Church's
growing taste for a
panoply of medieval
features, including a
chapter house (left).
[BB70/07522]

cantilevered several feet forward of the slim columns. This auditory space is not fitted out with Jenkins's classical motifs, however. Just a hint of a Tudor arch can be detected in the ceiling, and Gothic elements are more explicit elsewhere. The octagonal stone pulpit sets the mood with cusped panelling, a theme which continues around the gallery front, and the organ case (albeit later) might have been modelled on a medieval altarpiece. By the time that the chapel was built, Tractarianism was in full flow (*Tracts for the Times* having been begun in 1833 to propagate Church principles 'against Popery and Dissent'), and a Tractarian clergyman claimed to have been alarmed by mistaking Newbury Wesleyan chapel for an Anglican chapel-of-ease.[118]

Since any number of earlier chapels-of-ease might have been mistaken for Nonconformist places of worship, this story reveals more about the current state of affairs in the Church of England than about Nonconformist architecture.

For activists in the Oxford Movement it became increasingly desirable, as Simon Bradley has observed, for Anglican buildings to be visually distinct from those of the Nonconformists.[119] In 1840 the Tractarian critic of Newbury's Wesleyan chapel pinned his hopes on ecclesiology:

> Dissenters will copy the modern cheap church, but ... they will not copy lofty clerestories, long and ungalleried aisles, churches twice as high as they are wide, and four times as long, elaborately worked altars, carved oak ceilings, and such proprieties.[120]

The expectation was not entirely justified, however. Among the Nonconformists there were indeed congregations and individuals with the ability and will to commission Gothic buildings of a kind that even ecclesiologists could praise. It is a story that unfolded fully in the 1840s, but that was already embodied in a few chapels of the 1830s.

The Apostles' chapel at Albury in Surrey is the most important place of worship to survive from the early years of the Catholic Apostolic – or Irvingite – Church (Fig 5.30). It was begun in 1837 for Henry Drummond, sometime banker and politician, who had become patron of the parish church on buying Albury Park as his family home in 1819.[121] From 1826 he organised a series of annual religious conferences at Albury, involving the local rector, and during the early 1830s adopted a prophetic ministry which took him firmly away from the Church of England, into fellowship with the followers of Edward Irving. Drummond continued as patron of the parish living (later paying for the building of a new Anglican church in the village, and creating a mortuary chapel for his family in the old church), but he also set about the construction of a sanctuary for the newly established Catholic Apostolic Church, just north of Albury Park. The architects on whom Drummond called were William Wilkins, star of the Greek Revival, and William McIntosh Brookes.[122] Thirty years earlier Wilkins had worked for Drummond at Grange Park, Hampshire, creating one of the key monuments of English neo-classicism. He could also turn his hand to Gothic, however, and it must be inferred that he was asked to do so here.

The Apostles' chapel, which opened for worship in 1840, is unequivocally Gothic, with crocketed pinnacles, battlemented parapets, stepped buttresses and large windows with Perpendicular tracery. Yet more notable is its cruciform plan, comprising not only a west tower, nave, transepts and east-facing chancel, but also an octagonal chapter house. It is easy to understand why some of the final drawings referred to this as a cathedral church. The building had to serve the needs of a college of 12 apostles (for whom the chapter house was presumably intended, and whose stalls line the chancel), as well as the local congregation.[123] Although Drummond was vehemently opposed to Roman Catholicism, the building bears witness to the new movement's declining adherence to Calvinistic practice and the growing influence of Catholic liturgy. A stone altar beneath a carved wooden canopy occupies the central position against the east wall, and the pulpit is on the north wall of the nave, west of the north transept. The nave seating consists not of box pews, but of open benches, their poppy-head finials lining the central processional gangway. There is a wealth of further detail, and it is not impossible that Pugin designed some of the later items while creating the Drummonds' mortuary chapel in the old parish church (1843–7) and remodelling the family house (from 1846).[124]

In the year that Albury opened, the Catholic Apostolic Church began construction of a yet more ambitious building on Catharine Street in Liverpool. Featuring a stone-vaulted ambulatory, flying buttresses and tall clerestory, it promised to be Liverpool's most complex Gothic structure.[125] As with the French cathedrals which were its inspiration, work began at the east end, but the planned crossing tower and spire were beyond the congregation's resources, and the nave was erected during the 1850s to a simplified pattern.[126]

With its increasing emphasis on ritual (derived from both Roman and Orthodox traditions), the Catholic Apostolic Church was hardly at the core of Nonconformity, and there is a temptation to exclude its buildings from the scope of this book. But the followers of Irving and Drummond were not the only Nonconformists to adopt more devotional forms of worship and more consistently Gothic architecture in these years. In this context it is the Unitarians who deserve attention. An instructive starting point is the Unitarian chapel of 1837–9 in Upper Brook Street, Manchester (Fig 5.31), shamefully derelict at the time of writing. Its architect was no less a figure than Charles Barry; he had won the competition for the vast new Palace of Westminster in 1836, but nonetheless found time in 1837 to prepare three Grecian and two Gothic

Fig 5.31
Unitarian chapel, Upper Brook Street, Manchester, 1837–9 by Charles Barry, photographed before it became derelict in the late 20th centuy. Barry's chapel was an influential design for Unitarians.
[BB72/00038]

designs for the chapel, and subsequently further designs in Norman and Early English styles.[127] The last of these options was finally adopted instead of the trustees' initial preference for Doric, partly for the sake of economy, but perhaps also on aesthetic grounds. The minister, J J Tayler, was later to write:

I find the ecclesiastical architecture of Amiens, Beauvais and Rouen rich to an extent which cloys; and much prefer the greater simplicity of our own, especially our Early English (the Ionic of Christian art), which I dearly love.[128]

While the new chapel was hardly daring either in style or structure, it showed a more scholarly approach to Gothic than Barry's earlier commissions. Plain lancet windows and sturdy gabled buttresses are closely spaced along each side elevation, and the roof is steeply pitched, very much as a serious student of 13th-century architecture would have expected. Pyramid-capped pinnacles stand sentinel at each end, but there is no tower.[129] Greatest elaboration is reserved for the giant recess, with banded shafts, which embraces the entrance (an idea used by Barry at St Peter's, Brighton, of 1824–8) and the end window, in which plate tracery appears. All this was well within Barry's ability, although the entrance front may perhaps have been designed for him by Pugin.[130] Inside, the full width of the chapel was spanned by a tunnel vault (of plaster

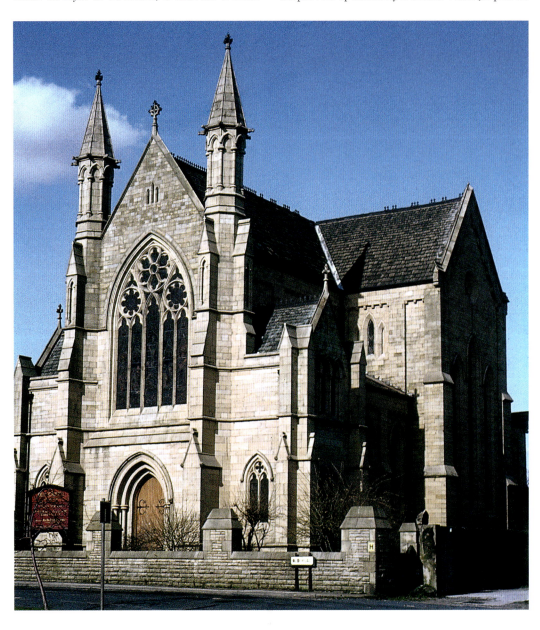

Fig 5.32
Unitarian chapel, Dukinfield, Cheshire, 1839–40 by Richard Tattersall. The present front is of 1893 by Thomas Worthington, adding staircase wings to Tattersall's planned façade.

rather than stone), and the wall behind the pulpit is embellished by a rose window. This relatively severe Gothic building provided a setting for the decorous services that Tayler and his circle of Unitarian ministers favoured. At first there were no side galleries (and only a small gallery above the entrance) so that the long vista emphasised the hierarchical arrangement. Tayler introduced a more sophisticated liturgy, with a paid choir to lead the congregation's responses.[131] When side galleries were introduced, in 1849, they were shallow projections from the wall, intended to improve the building's poor acoustics and subdue its draughts rather than to alter its congregational dynamics.[132]

In several respects the chapel in Upper Brook Street and its counterpart at Dukinfield, some six miles away in Cheshire (Figs 5.32 and 5.33), represented different strands of Unitarianism. In contrast to the well-heeled suburban congregation and more innovative ministry of Upper Brook Street, Dukinfield's worshippers were from a growing industrial community and its minister inclined to a more conservative position.[133] Yet both buildings, which opened within 12 months of each other, were unequivocally Gothic. Dukinfield Old Chapel – the very name speaking of tradition – was built in 1839–40 on the hilltop site where its predecessor had stood since the time of Queen Anne, and the 1707 date stone is preserved over the vestry door of the present chapel. Dukinfield had long been a hamlet in the parish of Stockport, and the chapel was its chief place of worship and the natural burial place for many generations of local people. By 1830 the hamlet had a population well above 14,000, and the rebuilding of Old Chapel, perhaps influenced by the construction of Dukinfield's first Commissioners' church in 1838–40, was finally precipitated by a storm which damaged the 18th-century building in January 1839.[134]

A young Manchester architect, Richard Tattersall, gained the commission with an enterprising design that reworked the pulpit-focused tradition of Protestant worship in a Gothic framework. The tall, steep-roofed chapel is cruciform, with transepts, side aisles and clerestory. Internally, however, rather than the long nave-and-chancel arrangement that one might expect we find a relatively short space, culminating in a great vertical set piece, like the organ-topped pulpitum of a medieval cathedral, aligned with the east wall of the transepts. This screen provides a backdrop for the communion area, and

carries an expanse of carved wooden panelling from which the canopied pulpit stands out as the heart of the building. Completing the ensemble is the organ gallery, with space for singers. Behind all this, occupying the expected chancel space, are the organ chamber and vestry. From the vestry a set of steps provides the only access to the pulpit. Front of house, an exhilarating

Fig 5.33
Interior of Unitarian chapel, Dukinfield, Cheshire. The splendid design successfully adapts Gothic architecture to the needs of pulpit-centred services. [DP143748]

space is provided for the congregation, with high galleries on three sides and arcades of slim (iron-cored) compound columns below the quadripartite rib vault of the nave. The lancet windows, often in groups of three as if to forestall any accusation of crude anti-Trinitarianism, have in places gained stained glass (the earliest from the 1870s and 1880s). By way of emphasising the chapel's long history and its aesthetic credentials, the walls display several memorials from the previous building, including one to the portrait painter John Astley (1724–1787).

Alan Petford has noted that the opening service in 1840 'was the occasion for the introduction of a new liturgy based, significantly, on that produced for Upper Brook Street Chapel by

J. J. Tayler', and that the choir chanted a psalm 'very beautifully'.[135] On the following day a wedding service was held in the chapel, taking advantage of the Marriage Act of 1836 and helping to reinforce the chapel's public role.[136] At the time of its opening, however, the chapel was not complete. Tattersall's spirited design for the west front – complete with a clock that would have made yet more of the chapel's public role – was omitted for want of funds, and it was only in 1893 that the present elevation and staircase wings were erected.[137] As Tattersall had intended, Decorated tracery was used here, rather than Early English lancets, making a fine show across the town.[138]

The challenge of deploying Gothic forms for the auditory needs of Protestant worship was approached in varied ways during the 1840s. When James Simpson turned his hand to the task for the Wesleyan chapel at Headingley, Leeds (of 1844–5) (Fig 5.34), he abandoned his familiar patterns in favour of something a little more like Tattersall's at Dukinfield.[139] That is to say that the main space of worship consists of a nave, galleried side aisles and transepts, with the pulpit on the building's central axis.[140] The aisle roofs slope more gently, however, and proportions are likely always to have been a little broader than those at Dukinfield, even before the transepts were brought into the main space of the chapel. Most strikingly the interior does not give the impression of a web of masonry. It is rather a frank construction of iron and timber: cast-iron columns (not concealed in stonework) carry the galleries and continue up to support an arcade of arched wooden braces and a series of hammerbeams.

This paraphrase of medieval design, perhaps anticipating both the French rationalist architect Viollet-le-Duc and and the 'rogue' Anglican architect E B Lamb, enabled the wide space to be spanned with minimal interruptions to the congregation's sightlines. Exposed iron columns had been used in two or three Commissioners' churches, but these would have aroused ecclesiological scorn by the 1840s.[141] At Headingley the well-tried seating pattern of box pews was maintained, with the largest block filling the centre of the chapel and further rows below the gallery: going Gothic did not in itself require central gangways or open-ended benches. Simpson's work here is an early instance of the iron-columns-and-open-timber-roof formula, which was to be used with variations by quite a number of chapel architects over the next 20 years or so.

Fig 5.34
Interior of Headingley Wesleyan Methodist chapel, Leeds, 1844–5 by James Simpson. Iron columns enabled Simpson to create a nave and galleried side aisles without significantly impeding the sightlines. [DP168477]

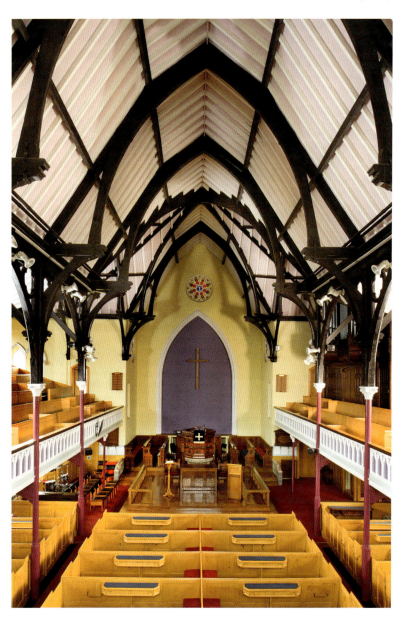

Although the Headingley chapel reveals a desire to acknowledge the structural distinctiveness of Gothic, Simpson did not always do so; his more famous Gothic work, the (now demolished) Wesleyan chapel of 1844–7 at Summerseat, Lancashire, was entirely spanned by a level ceiling on the same principle as his classical chapels.[142] Another example of this approach is to be found in Buckingham Baptist chapel, Queen's Road, Bristol, of 1842–7 (Fig 5.35).[143] The architect here was R S Pope, whose Corinthian temple for the Catholic Apostolic Church in Bristol we have seen earlier in this chapter.[144] Pope followed no party lines on style, and for the Baptists he disregarded the current preference for English Gothic in favour of continental architecture of the 13th century. In contrast to the stately classical terraces of Clifton, Buckingham chapel has a vertiginous roofline, accompanied by an (originally more extensive) set of pinnacles, and carries a wealth of carved details derived from Rayonnant architecture, such as the west front of Strasbourg Cathedral. It is said that Pope offered to work without payment on condition that his fee be devoted to ornamental work on the chapel, which if true suggests a strong commitment to the details of the design as well as a sympathy for the Baptists' cause.[145]

Whether the interior lived up to the external architecture is difficult to say. There were galleries along each side as well as above the entrance, and an organ was quickly added to the plans. Stone for the building was quarried on site, and in 1865 a schoolroom was created below the chapel, an arrangement which – as we have seen – nicely suited Nonconformist needs.[146] The proportions and disparities of Buckingham chapel have drawn understandable criticism, but at its opening 'the richness of the front excited much admiration', and more recently it

Fig 5.35
Buckingham Baptist chapel, Bristol, 1842–7 by R S Pope. Despite the loss of some pinnacles, the chapel still offers a marked contrast to the horizontal lines of the neighbouring terraces.
[DP166209]

has been called 'a magnificent essay in the high Gothic of the late 13th century'.[147] It certainly helps to illustrate the increasing range of approaches which could be found in the Nonconformist world, at the very time when the repertoire of Anglican church architecture was being narrowed.

Just 10 minutes' walk from Buckingham Baptist chapel is a building that takes us to a different part of the spectrum of Nonconformists' Gothic. Highbury Congregational chapel was built at the top of St Michael's Hill, Bristol, in 1842–3 (Fig 5.36). One of the chief benefactors was W D Wills, a member of the tobacco family, and the job of designing Highbury chapel fell to his nephew, a young architect with no significant previous commissions to his name. The man in question was William Butterfield, later to become the most fastidious of High Church architects, but who for the moment benefited from his own Nonconformist upbringing.[148] What Butterfield provided for the Congregationalists drew on English rather than continental sources and was as sturdy as Pope's design was spiky: unpinnacled buttresses, roofs of gentle pitch and rubble walling.[149] As Paul Thompson has observed, the irregular quoins and rubble masonry suggest the influence of Pugin's *True Principles*, published only months earlier.[150] Highbury chapel was also asymmetrical, not only in the Picturesque placing of the stair turret and porch, but also in the wilfully uncoordinated rhythms of the clerestory and main arcade. The arch-braced collarbeam roof idiosyncratically ignores the structural logic of the piers below.

Here in embryo were many characteristics of Butterfield's contribution to High Victorian Gothic. Yet the chapel was not an ecclesiological blueprint. In good Protestant tradition the pulpit was the focal point, standing in the centre of the east wall and facing an undivided central block of pews. There was no organ or other musical instrument. For Butterfield, the lack of chancel or apse might even have been welcome, insofar as it gave full scope for what was to become his preferred continuous roof ridge. By restricting the gallery to the west end, a compromise was reached between the Congregationalists' needs and the architect's knowledge of medieval precedents. The inclusion of a west gallery, which of course justified the Picturesque stair turret, perhaps also determined the relatively tall proportions of the arcade. Even so, however, the stone columns reduced visibility from some

Fig 5.36
Highbury Congregational chapel, Bristol, 1842–3 by William Butterfield. Its square, turreted tower was part of E W Godwin's extensions of 1863. The building is now used by the Church of England.
[DP166294]

positions – in both the gallery and the side aisles. Fittings were of a high quality: the pews and other woodwork were of oak, and the window above the stone pulpit had stained glass by Thomas Willement, an established designer who in the 1840s was employed by Pugin and the Ecclesiologists. Gas lighting was supplied from the outset, as was becoming more common in urban chapels, although it seems that the workmen were not all experienced in the new technology, because some five holes were made in the pipework by a scaffolding bar.[151] For the large Sunday school, Butterfield created a room alongside the main building.

Almost from the outset, Highbury chapel and its school prospered. The first extensions were undertaken in 1863 (by E W Godwin, the gifted architect who as a schoolboy had watched the building take shape), followed by a second gallery in 1865 and further enlargement in 1893.[152] In 1972, however, the chapel closed and was subsequently bought by the Church of England, which undertook a liturgical reordering of the space. Although the quality of Butterfield's earliest architecture can still be seen, the original purpose and layout has been effectively lost from view. Early Protestant traditions are still represented, however, both in the figures of Isaac Watts and Martin Luther in the west window (of 1950, replacing one lost in a bomb blast, *see* p 211) and in the memorials to five local men martyred on this site in the reign of Mary Tudor.[153]

By the later 1840s all of the major Nonconformist denominations, except the Quakers, had built places of worship that reflected something of the seriousness of early Victorian Gothic. At Wantage, Berkshire a relatively small Wesleyan chapel (perhaps of as late as 1847, by F W Ordish) seems to have been the town's first example of the new architectural mood.[154] This steep-roofed rectangular building, without pinnacles or tower, and built with rubble masonry, is resolutely understated. At first sight the entrance front is notable only for its Decorated window and doorway, with a string course between, but then one notices the subtle asymmetry of a small lancet window, which lights the gallery stairs. To the rear of the chapel, separated by a traceried screen, were a vestry and schoolroom, overtaken in 1857 by a larger suite of school and classrooms 'in harmonising style' (by Poulton and Woodman).[155] *The Illustrated London News* thought that the chapel represented 'the growing disposition' of communities to build places of worship in 'our own sadly-neglected but peculiar English style'.[156] Within a few years the Established Church in Wantage was to join this movement wholeheartedly, although the parish's next new Anglican building (at Charlton, of 1847–8, and coincidentally by Butterfield) was a cheap brick structure, barely Gothic.[157]

An equally interesting case study is to be seen 10 miles away at Bourton, near Shrivenham. The Baptist chapel (now village hall) that was opened in Bourton in 1851 was an elaborated version of Wantage's Wesleyan chapel and was also designed by Ordish, using Decorated Gothic.[158] In this instance, however, the chapel occupies a focal position in the village, and a prominent bellcote emphasises the building's status in the community. The chapel was paid for by a local Baptist, Henry Tucker, whose nearby seat, Bourton House, had been built to Ordish's designs a few years earlier.[159] The Anglican church, erected nine years later, had to settle for a site on the edge of the village.

At Darwen, Lancashire the Church of England had grasped the opportunity to build in the 1820s, thanks to the million pound grant of 1818 (*see* p 91), and the resulting St Peter's (formerly Holy Trinity) is a fine design of 1827–8 by Rickman and Hutchinson in Perpendicular Gothic. But Darwen was a Nonconformist stronghold, and in 1847 one of the town's two long-established Independent congregations erected what Pevsner called 'the most rewarding bit of ecclesiastical architecture at Darwen', just across the valley from St Peter's.[160] The new meeting house in Belgrave Square was a spirited Early English design by Edward Walters, featuring a tall nave, separately ridged side aisles and transept, and a huge open porch topped by a fantastic westwork screen.[161] Its powerful role in the townscape of Darwen continues to the present day, although the building was declared redundant many years ago.

The most notable of the dozen or more chapels designed by Edward Walters was the Cavendish Street Independent chapel, Manchester (of 1847–8, now demolished). The building commanded its quarter of the city with a broach spire 166 feet (50.6m) tall, and had a full complement of clerestoried nave, side aisles and transepts.[162] Within this plan the auditory nature of congregational worship was maintained, however; steep galleries looked down on the elaborate pulpit, while a choir gallery and organ filled the apse. Even the *Ecclesiologist* devoted a long article and a shorter notice to the chapel. If only the pulpit and organ were pushed aside

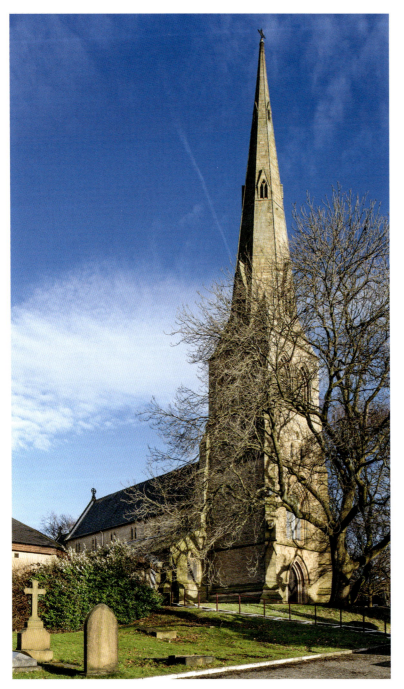

in favour of a proper chancel, the *Ecclesiologist* mused, the chapel could easily be used for Anglo-Catholic worship.[163] Such comments undoubtedly boosted the suspicions of many Nonconformists who since Pugin's *Contrasts* had come to see Gothic architecture as a fifth column for the Church of Rome. Other Nonconformists, however, were not in the least deterred.

Of all the Protestant denominations, it was the Unitarians who challenged the *Ecclesiologist*'s assumptions most comprehensively, with a series of major Gothic chapels from the late 1840s onwards. As we have seen (at Upper Brook Street, Manchester and at Dukinfield), Unitarians were often able to commission serious designs from influential architects; their leading ministers meanwhile developed more liturgical forms of worship, as if to demonstrate that their faith was not an arid rationalism. Invigorated by the Dissenters' Chapels Act of 1844 to rebuild some of their older – originally Presbyterian – chapels and meeting houses, several Unitarian congregations embarked on conspicuous new buildings. A good example is the chapel erected at Gee Cross (part of Hyde, Cheshire) in 1846–8, replacing one from the 18th century (Fig 5.37).[164]

Gee Cross was a place that the Unitarians could regard as theirs, and accordingly the new chapel has a commanding presence, set back from the road in a large and leafy graveyard, with a 145-foot (44.2m) spire. With its clerestoried nave, low side aisles, south porch and distinct, east-facing chancel, the chapel looks for all the world like a medieval parish church – or, more precisely, the kind of medieval church which ecclesiological architects then admired. (The important school premises have always been physically separate.) Pugin declined the invitation to supply a design, but there is an uncanny resemblance to his St Oswald's, Liverpool (of 1839–42), both in the general massing and the broach spire – which had its prototype in Newark's 14th-century example.[165] In the event, the task of designing the chapel went to the local firm of Bowman and Crowther, who had absorbed the lessons of Pugin's *True Principles* and also had impeccable Unitarian credentials.[166] Bowman and Crowther drew inspiration from a number of sources, perhaps looking to Howden, North Yorkshire (which the Manchester architect Edmund Sharpe was to illustrate in his *Architectural Parallels* of 1848) for the unusual feature of paired clerestory windows at Gee Cross. However, the underlying character of the building is one which Pugin could have admired.

The visiting Unitarian minister who spoke after the opening service at Gee Cross in August 1848 described Bowman and Crowther's design as 'asserting the right of a Dissenting Chapel to look like a parish church, and to be used as a parish church without the least danger of our worship being interrupted'.[167] The echo here is of John Fairfax in 1700, explaining that Ipswich's Dissenters had built a new meeting house only because their preferred place of worship, the parish church, had been denied them. Yet there was a new dimension too. In the summer of 1848, with continental Europe in the throes of revolution, the image of what Pugin called 'the complete English parish church of the time of Edward I' must have seemed essentially conservative, reassuringly so to those who feared that Dissenters were too easily stigmatised as unpatriotic. Though leading Unitarians might spend months abroad to keep abreast of the latest German theology and philosophy, their architecture for the moment was insular.[168]

Internally the chapel at Gee Cross is a fascinating balancing act between ecclesiology and the auditory tradition (Fig 5.38). The chancel was set aside for 'the administration of the Lord's Supper and the celebration of marriages' and the communion table (made of stone and gilded) commands the space, alongside an octagonal stone font with a spire-like hanging cover.[169] There is, of course, nothing un-Protestant about having a separate area for communion, and a serious ecclesiologist might be disappointed to find no rood screen or other indication that the chancel is a holier place than anywhere else in the chapel. As if in deference to the campaign being waged by the *Ecclesiologist*, the long nave and aisles are without galleries, while the pulpit stands not on the main axis, but on the north side of the chancel arch. Conversely the full width of the nave is occupied by oak pews (with doors), in reassertion of the Nonconformist habit. The arcades of stone columns inevitably interfere with sightlines from the side aisles (as at Butterfield's Highbury chapel), however, and the space cannot pretend to be the single congregational chamber which characterised so many earlier chapels. At the back of the chapel, below the west tower, is a set of canopied choir-stalls, along with a Gothic-fronted organ. Stained glass – originally by William Warrington – fills the Geometric tracery of the east and west windows, and glass by Morris and others has further enhanced the devotional atmosphere which the chapel's creators sought.[170]

Architectural historians can recognise Gee Cross as the first of a line of Unitarian chapels, but at the time of its construction its significance was as much political as aesthetic. As the inscription above the north door proudly records, Gee Cross represented a new freedom for Nonconformist congregations to build 'Under the Protection of that Act of Public Justice ... Which secures to Nonsubscribing Dissenters peaceful Possession Of the Chapels and Endowments of their pious Forefathers'.[171]

The architecture of the earlier Middle Ages appealed in certain situations to Nonconformists, just as it did to Anglicans. For instance, the Cornish-based architect Philip Sambell, whose classical buildings have already been mentioned, produced Romanesque designs for two Baptist chapels: Clarence Street, Penzance, of 1835–6 (Fig 5.39) and Wendron Street, Helston, of 1836–7.[172] The former retains much of its original detail, including a generous use of round-headed arches and chevron mouldings,

Fig 5.38
Interior of Gee Cross Unitarian chapel, Hyde, Cheshire. Bowman and Crowther were able to bring an impressive understanding of medieval architecture to the task of creating this powerful chapel.
[DP166650]

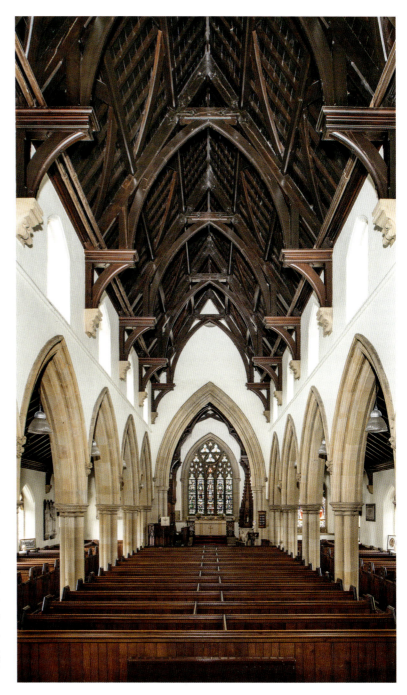

internally as well externally. Most likely, Sambell's use of Romanesque was affected by Thomas Hope's illustrated *Historical Essay on Architecture,* which was published in 1835 and helped to stimulate interest in pre-Gothic buildings, especially those of Italy and Germany.[173] Perhaps men rooted in the classical tradition – as were both Sambell and Hope – felt more affinity for a style that was essentially a continuation of classical forms than they did for Gothic. However, Sambell's championing of the auditory nature of worship (*see* note 5:20) could also have made him wary of Gothic. Certainly, a decade later in Devon, George Wightwick ceased to design Anglican churches because of his commitment to 'the principle of a peculiar form for the *auditorium* of a Protestant church'; his final ecclesiastical commission was an Anglo-Norman

façade for Courtenay Street Congregational chapel, Plymouth, of 1847–8.[174]

Beyond its intrinsic qualities, Romanesque architecture provided church builders and chapel builders with another option in the catalogue of styles, an increased opportunity to distinguish one new place of worship from the others. Cavendish Baptist chapel, Ramsgate (1840, by James Wilson) illustrates the point (Fig 5.40). Ramsgate had relatively recently seen the building of a Perpendicular Gothic Commissioners' church (St George's, 1824–7), a stuccoed neo-classical synagogue (for Moses Montefiore, 1831–3) and an Early English chapel for the Congregationalists (Ebenezer, 1838–9).[175] And so, when the Baptists came to erect their new chapel in Cavendish Street, either they or their architect chose a vigorous Romanesque scheme that was designed

Fig 5.39
Baptist chapel, Penzance, 1835–6 by Philip Sambell. Romanesque architecture became a fruitful model for congregations or architects who wanted medieval effects, but were cautious about the associations of Gothic. [DP160697]

to be different and believed to be progressive.[176] Not only was the style distinctive, but – unusually for a large chapel of this date – the frontage is one of the building's long walls, with entrances in bays one and seven. The façade is quite deeply modelled, relying for its effect on stout polygonal buttresses, splayed openings with shafts and a remarkable skyline of pierced turrets. Originally the pulpit occupied the centre of the far wall, but the layout was later turned through 90 degrees; the pulpit now sits below the gallery before one of the short walls, surrounded by a handsome ensemble of round-arched features.

By 1842 the Romanesque revival was sufficiently strong to provoke a broadside from *The Ecclesiologist*, followed two years later by the journal's emphatic proclamation that 'Gothick is the only Christian architecture'.[177] The criticism of round arches was not wholly effective in the Church of England, and less so beyond. One of London's most prominent examples of the revived Romanesque is Bloomsbury Central Baptist chapel (of 1845–8) (Fig 5.41), by John Gibson, who set up in practice only in 1844.[178] Even more obviously than in Ramsgate, the local context was significant. Bloomsbury Baptist chapel faces on to what was to become the north end of Shaftesbury Avenue and, as *The Illustrated London News* reported, took its place

between the 'neat Gothic' church of the French Protestants and the 'tasteless pile' of the (Anglican) Bedford chapel. This latter, it continued, acted 'as a good foil to set off the elegant character and design of the new [Baptist] Chapel, which is in the Lombardic style of architecture'.[179] 'Lombardic' here was presumably being used as generic term for Romanesque, in the way that Thomas Hope had recommended, but some features of Gibson's design do indeed seem to have their origins in north Italian buildings: thin stone strips and corbel tables articulate the brick masonry, and the twin towers originally culminated in attractively tiled spires with corner pinnacles – an echo of the famous campanile at San Zeno Maggiore, Verona.[180]

Legend has it that Bloomsbury chapel's two spires were suggested by Morton Peto, who largely financed the building and may have chosen its architect as well as its first minister.[181] Whatever the truth of this, Gibson's creditable design outdid not only its immediate neighbours but also the then uncompleted Roman Catholic church of St John, Islington (begun 1842 by J J Scoles) – which was similarly intended to have a symmetrical pair of spires to its Romanesque façade – and is also said to have inspired a number of American churches, including the Central Congregational church, Providence, Rhode

Fig 5.40
Cavendish Baptist chapel, Ramsgate, 1840 by James Wilson. This extraordinary façade – Romanesque in detail, but surely not modelled on any medieval composition – has lost its formidable array of turrets. [DP160397]

Island (by Thomas Tefft).[182] Having lost its spires after the Second World War, the chapel no longer rises above its neighbours; its appearance had already been compromised in 1913 by the insertion of an extra floor in place of the original large central gable above the rose window.[183]

The interior has likewise seen extensive changes. It appears that Gibson's almost square auditorium was initially fitted out with two tiers of galleries and had a system of gas lighting and ventilation on Faraday's principle (Faraday having advised on the same matter at the Palace of Westminster). The chapel's location, halfway between the notorious Seven Dials district and the salubrious Bedford Square, inspired a ministry with an active social purpose, involving a local refuge, ragged school and mission, and a 'veritable crusade of preaching in theatres and music halls'.[184] An institute was opened in Oxford Street, and it was the expiry of the lease on those premises that prompted the construction of an additional floor and the reordering of the basement schoolrooms at Bloomsbury chapel in 1913.[185]

The choice of Romanesque for the (long demolished) Independent chapel of 1850 in Red Lion Street, Boston, Lincolnshire was probably another case of helping to distinguish one place

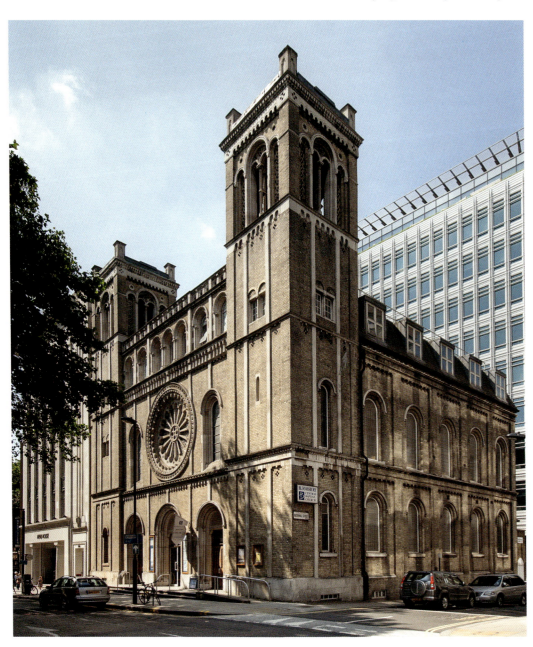

Fig 5.41
Bloomsbury Central Baptist chapel, London, 1845–8 by John Gibson. This very creditable piece of Romanesque design was originally completed by a pair of spires.
[DP150839]

of worship from what might be called its competitors.[186] Unlike the town's other churches and chapels at that time, the new building even boasted a spire, risking comparison with the prodigious – but spireless – Stump of St Botolph's church.[187] The architect of the new Independent chapel was Stephen Lewin; he normally worked in Gothic, and one storey of the tower bore intersecting semicircular arches as if to demonstrate the origin of pointed architecture.[188] Lewin's response to the Independents' need for school accommodation was to provide room for 400 pupils at ground level and to set the chapel itself on the first floor, approached by a long flight of broad steps. This all helped to give the building greater prominence.[189] Internally the Romanesque idiom continued. There was a semicircular apse with seats in an arc behind the pulpit – akin to the clergy seats of an early Christian basilica – and the roof was supported by a sequence of semicircular ribs, employing the innovative technique of laminated timber.[190]

An altogether more rustic use of pre-Gothic forms is to be seen in the formerly Congregational chapel (of about 1844) at Little Longstone in the Derbyshire Peak District (Fig 5.42). This small chapel sits on the edge of the hamlet, its graveyard setting surrounded by a characteristic dry-stone wall, and might at first glance be taken for a Saxon survival. Coursed limestone is used for the walls of the building, but rough-hewn sandstone blocks are used as dressings, giving a calculatedly primitive character to the place and anticipating the work of the American architect H H Richardson. The porch, rising the full height of the gable end and topped by a very sturdy ashlar bellcote, has a round-arched entrance and a circular window; each is framed by the rusticated blocks that, at a lower level, merge with the quoins. In the flanking walls are loophole openings, thoughtfully glazed so as to dispel any hint of defensive archery being deployed on unwelcome visitors, and each of the chapel's side walls has three round-headed windows. Clare Hartwell has recently discovered that Thomas Haigh of Liverpool designed the chapel, although it would also be satisfying to discover some link with Thomas Bateman. The author of *Ten Years' Diggings in Celtic and Saxon Grave Hills*, he was buried in 1861 at the Congregational chapel at Middleton by Youlgreave (*see* p 102), six miles away.

The appeal of the Romanesque style lay partly in its being medieval without being Gothic. Something similar could be said of late Tudor and Jacobean architecture, whose forms often

Fig 5.42
Congregational chapel, Little Longstone, Derbyshire, 1844 by Thomas Haigh. Outside the standard models of medieval architecture, Little Longstone has an attractive air of rough-hewn solidity.
[DP160628]

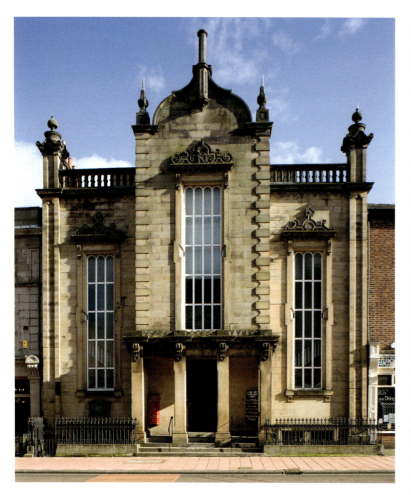

*Fig 5.43
Congregational chapel,
Carlisle, 1842–3 by John
Nichol. The tall windows
of this Jacobean mannerist
façade help to illuminate
the galleried interior.
[DP066714]*

incorporated Renaissance motifs yet were not fully classical. A rare example of this in the Nonconformist world is the Congregational chapel in Lowther Street, Carlisle (1842–3, by Mr Nichol of Edinburgh), a building whose upright façade carries spiked finials, a curved gable and three tall, rectangular windows with strapwork ornament above (Fig 5.43).[191] This display of early 17th-century mannerism gives way inside the building to a quieter range of submedieval forms, but the lofty interior is spatially impressive. Slender quatrefoil columns carry both the U-shaped gallery and (presumably) the wall plate, from which a barrel-vaulted ceiling gives extra height to the central space and echoes the round-headed window of the central organ recess. Designed to shape the congregation into an active body of worshippers, all with a clear view

of the preacher, it is a compactly Protestant interior, comparable to such overtly Gothic chapels as that of the Unitarians in Dukinfield or the United Presbyterian church, Renfield Street, Glasgow (now demolished).[192]

Approaching 1850

By the late 1840s the range of architectural options had greatly increased for Nonconformists, as it had for those commissioning secular buildings. In some cases this resulted in more varied plan-forms as well as different styles. Historians have tended to emphasise the growing influence of scholarly Gothic in these years, for which there is ample evidence, as this chapter has shown. But it is important to underline the limits of this interpretation. The *Congregational Year Book*, which began publication in 1846, was illustrated with engravings of recent buildings, and so became the denomination's chief organ for the transmission of architectural ideas. In 1847 it carried a substantial article on the topic of chapel architecture.[193] The anonymous author considered the virtues of both the 'Grecian and English styles' before finally opting for the latter, with 'the Roman or Basilic' [that is, Romanesque] style as an acceptable alternative. Highbury chapel, Bristol was referred to as 'one of the most complete edifices we have seen' in the 'English style', but it was not illustrated, and one suspects that the six depictions of grandly classical chapels might have outweighed the author's understated preference for Gothic.

Another notable publication from these years is Andrew Trimen's book, *Church and Chapel Architecture*, which appeared in 1849. Its ambitious scope – a section each for churches, chapels and Jewish buildings – was matched by the author's relatively broad-minded approach to architectural styles, a factor which must have recommended the book to many outside the Church of England. Among the examples are chapels in Early English, Tudor, Italian and Corinthian styles, and a range of denominations is mentioned. Overall, such diversity gives a representative picture of Nonconformist practice in these years.

6

The age of pluralism, 1850–90

Nonconformists continued to devote great resources to chapel building in the decades after 1850 and erected significantly more places of worship than the Church of England.[1] The major denominations – Methodist, Baptist and Congregational – continued to grow in absolute numbers, roughly in line with the rise in population, although the prodigious recruitment of new members (so marked a feature of early 19th-century Nonconformity) became a rarer phenomenon.[2] As congregations increased, and in the expectation of further increases, great numbers of existing chapels were rebuilt and many new ones were erected. This was most noticeable in major urban areas, where Nonconformists became more versatile builders. They redeveloped their landmark chapels in busy locations, planted new chapels in the affluent suburbs and determinedly opened chapels in the closely packed streets of poorer quarters. Some town chapels were rebuilt principally in order to accommodate Sunday schools.[3] Nor was chapel building neglected in small towns and villages. The Primitive Methodists, for example, especially strong in rural districts, embarked on such a wholesale campaign of construction that this came to be known as the connexion's Chapel Building Era.[4] The flow of chapel building was augmented too by new bodies, from the Wesleyan Reformers (mostly United Methodist Free Churches after 1857) to the Salvation Army, and by a marked increase in the number of Presbyterians in England.[5] Essentially this was a period when the Nonconformists, whether long established or more recent, deployed architecture as a means of consolidating their work. New chapels were an expression of enduring vitality.

Local conditions and national patterns

There is no doubt that denominational rivalry occurred – within Nonconformity itself as well as between Nonconformists and Anglicans.

The official census of attendance at places of worship in 1851 almost inevitably sharpened this competitive instinct; local religious leaders often vied with each other, hoping that a more conveniently located, more attractive building would help to maintain or improve a chapel's fortunes.[6] (Not that *financial* profit was likely, however: most chapels were heavily indebted for years after opening.) Newcastle-under-Lyme, Staffordshire provides a case study and hints at the growing importance of Sunday-school work.[7] In 1853 the town's chief Primitive Methodist chapel – bursting at the seams, according to the 1851 census – was rebuilt, and behind it a Sunday school was erected in 1856.[8] Then in quick succession Newcastle's three late 18th-century chapels were superseded. First in 1857–8 the Methodist New Connexion built a smart new Ebenezer chapel in leafy surroundings and used its existing building, just 100 yards away, as its school and lecture hall.[9] Next the Congregationalists opened their new chapel in 1859 – apparently no more capacious than its predecessor, but with a large school hall below the main worship space and built in an up-to-date Gothic style with polychrome brickwork.[10] Finally the Wesleyans moved across town, near to the New Connexion and Congregationalists, where in 1860–1 they optimistically erected Newcastle's largest chapel (with French High Gothic details) and a new school close at hand.[11] Within 10 years of the census, therefore, Newcastle-under-Lyme had a set of new Nonconformist places of worship, each of them architecturally distinct. More than a decade was to pass before the town's Georgian parish church was rebuilt in line with new Anglican practice.[12]

Similar denominational rivalry was to be seen in the countryside. Take, for instance, the small Lincolnshire village of West Torrington, which appears barely large enough to sustain a single place of worship, but which in 1851 had a small Wesleyan chapel (of 1843) and a medieval parish church, seating 80 and 85 respectively.[13] In 1859 a neat, new, yellow-brick chapel was built for the Wesleyans, with perhaps just a few more seats than either its predecessor or the parish church.[14] It is tempting to see this as a reproach to the parish church, across the road, where an unequivocal ritualist had been installed as vicar in that same year.[15] However, the real rivals may have been the Free Methodists, very active in this part of Lincolnshire, who built a chapel in West Torrington which looks like the cheerful twin of the Wesleyan chapel.[16] Religious politics were complicated, even in small communities.

Inexorably these fascinating local relationships formed part of a wider pattern. Somewhere around the century's mid-point there was a shift in the balance between chapel building as a local initiative and as a nationally coordinated movement. By 1850 most denominations had national committees to guide – and often to help finance – the construction of new places of worship. Methodism, with its strongly centralised governance, had been first to act in this way, but by 1853 even the old Independents accepted the need for strategic organisation, with the creation of the English Congregational Chapel-Building Society.[17] Alongside these developments there were denominational publications that began to include engravings of recent chapels: among them were the *Congregational Year Book*, the *Wesleyan Chapel Committee Report* and the *Baptist Handbook*.[18] Such central guidance disseminated good practice and architectural design, and also helped the spread of professional reputations.

There was nothing new about architects specialising in work for Nonconformists, as we have seen in Chapters 4 and 5 with William Jenkins, James Simpson and James Fenton, but a much larger number emerged in the second half of the century. The habit was certainly strengthened by the new atmosphere in the Church of England, then becoming more exclusive in its choice of architects, and in places excluding non-Anglicans on principle. For buildings of moderate size or larger, Nonconformists steadily came to depend either on architects who worked chiefly with secular commissions or on those who specialised in chapel work. It is also clear that the Nonconformist specialists were to be found across the country, and that they were less concentrated in London than the big names of the Anglican world.

A good place in which to see this specialisation in action is Shrewsbury – a town in which anyone searching for architecture from the 40 years after 1850 might still be advised to start with the chapels. Between 1850 and 1890 the town's stock of Nonconformist places of worship was transformed. Most of the existing chapels and meeting houses were superseded by larger buildings, and a handful of new ones was erected. Of the seven major chapels to be built or rebuilt in that time, all but one were by specialist architects. In 1862 the Welsh Congregationalists' tabernacle was built as a replacement for their small chapel of 1845. The new building was Italianate, to a design by Thomas Thomas, an Independent minister from Swansea who is known to have been the architect of at least 189 (and possibly over 800) chapels.[19] The English Congregationalists quickly followed, erecting a landmark Gothic chapel in Abbey Foregate in 1863, and rebuilding their 18th-century meeting house in Swan Hill in 1868; both of these schemes were chiefly the work of George Bidlake of Wolverhampton.[20] He worked for Nonconformist clients in many parts of the country, and a version of the Abbey Foregate design appeared in 1865 in his book *Sketches of Churches Designed for the Use of Nonconformists*.

In the 1860s a new Presbyterian congregation was established in Shrewsbury, and for them an unusual neo-Norman chapel was constructed in Castle Street in 1870. It was designed by R C Bennett, a Weymouth architect with a handful of Nonconformist commissions to his name.[21] Later it was the turn of the Baptists, whose chapel in Claremont was replaced by a new classical building in 1877–8. For this they turned to Richard Owen, a Liverpool architect who worked very extensively for Nonconformists in Wales and north-west England.[22] Soon the Wesleyans decided to rebuild their St John's Hill chapel, employing a busy Methodist specialist, G B Ford of Burslem, for the handsome Italianate building, which opened in 1879.[23] Ford's design was publicised nationally by means of an engraving in the *Wesleyan Chapel Committee Report* for 1878. However, out-of-town architects did not have a monopoly of chapel work in Shrewsbury. A B Deakin, who had begun to make his mark with commercial and domestic buildings in the town, designed extensions and a new façade for the Unitarian chapel in High Street in 1885, while the borough surveyor, T Tisdale, designed the Calvinistic Methodist chapel (of 1863) in Frankwell Quay.[24] In some other places such general practitioners undertook a larger proportion of the Nonconformist work, but Shrewsbury is otherwise characteristic in pointing to the divide that grew up between the chief Anglican practitioners and their Nonconformist counterparts.

The increasing availability of specialist architects and of denominational guidance did not diminish the diversity of chapel architecture, certainly in the matter of styles. Shrewsbury, with its range of classical, Italianate, Gothic and Norman chapels, is again representative. On the whole, this pluralism served Nonconformists well. In general it kept the design of chapels within the broad stream of contemporary architecture, while also reflecting the diversity of religious practice in England. In particular it allowed congregations to select designs which could be distinctive in any local pattern of religious buildings, and so gave variety to the appearance of a town or city.

Small chapels

Much of this chapter deals with chapels in broad stylistic categories. These categories are most useful for the major buildings, but can also be seen to include some of the smallest examples: diminutive temples and Gothic wayside chapels were not uncommon through the 19th century. However, even in the age of specialist architects, many small chapels were designed without much reference to the great historic styles. Two examples from West Torrington have already been mentioned, and a closer study of three further cases can suggest the variety of circumstances that shaped some of these smaller chapels.

The hamlet of Wath, in Yorkshire's Nidderdale, has a chapel that was erected for the local Wesleyans in 1859–60.[25] Its sundial is a reminder of the different pace of life in upland farming settlements, something that continued long into Victoria's reign. The chapel is an appendage to a pair of stone-built cottages, constructed of the same sandstone and matching them in height and width. Although it is not exactly vernacular, neither is it quite classical: its round-headed doorway and tall windows with their keystones speak a different language from the architectural rhythms of the locality, yet it lacks the syntax of classicism. Much of the chapel's distinctiveness comes from its shape. Squeezed into the small and awkwardly angled piece of ground between the end of the cottages and the roadside, the irregular, five-sided chapel conforms to no model. The interior, with a gallery and staircase ingeniously fitted across the widest wall and a pulpit in the opposite angle, has many of its original fittings as well as the evidence of successive generations who have worshipped here. Below the pulpit is a harmonium, while above the preacher's head hang a decorated hymn board and an attractive panel urging everyone to 'Rejoice in the Lord always'.

Another lively interior is to be found in the Bible Christian chapel of 1863 at Wheal Busy (Fig 6.1), one of the mining communities near Chacewater in Cornwall.[26] Wheal Busy's chapel

Fig 6.1
Wheal Busy Bible Christian (now Methodist) chapel, near Chacewater, Cornwall, 1863. This sturdy stone chapel was built for one of the liveliest branches of Methodism. The gallery is to the right of the entrance, the pulpit to the left. [DP160702]

is conventionally rectangular, with its entrance in one of the long sides and the pulpit on one of the short walls, an increasingly common arrangement for those small chapels in which the tradition of a long-wall façade was continued into the later 19th century. Punctuating the rubble masonry at the building's corners and around the windows are neat granite blocks, alternately long and short, but there is no hint of classical detail, and the window openings have segmental heads of red brick. It all seems more like the aesthetic pragmatism of a mining engineer than the example of a Gibbsian pattern-book. A Gothic inflection can be seen in the later porch, but not on a scale to compromise the building's robust character. The interior is special, not so much because of its end gallery, added in 1882 and little altered, but because of the survival of its ground-floor fittings. In the centre is a block of box pews, their outer panels pierced by a run of turned balusters – a feature not common in Britain, but more familiar in New England meeting houses, where they are known as spindle-topped pews.[27] Along the side walls, where chairs now stand, there were presumably benches or forms initially. Matching the central block of pews is a set piece arrangement of leaders' pew, pulpit and flanking box pews – an ensemble once characteristic of small Cornish chapels.[28] The pulpit, perhaps later extended into its present rostrum shape with standard lamps, is the focal point of

the interior, and above it in modern lettering on the deep red wall is the motto 'Jesus is Lord'. From its colour scheme to its electronic organ, almost everything in the Wheal Busy chapel has changed in some way in the past century and a half. Yet one can still sense the original layout, and also the evangelical purpose which has continued here since 1863.

Small chapels were not confined to rural districts, of course. In 1886 a congregation of Strict and Particular Baptists opened its first purpose-built chapel, called Zoar, on St Mary's Plain, Norwich (Fig 6.2).[29] Zoar is not as tall as the adjoining two-storey house and, with accommodation for only 100, it was a minnow compared to the large Regency building, just yards away, which was home to the city's most substantial Baptist congregation.[30] The chapel's architecture is calculatedly undemonstrative. The neat grey-brick elevation to the street has two round-headed windows, a matching doorway and the entry to a low covered passage which gives access to the back of the building (where cheaper red bricks were employed). There are rudimentary pilasters, but none of the decorative touches that might have enlivened, say, a contemporary terrace house. The interior was similarly understated, with bare walls, a boarded dado and a plain, old-fashioned wooden pulpit raised on a 'wine-glass' stem. It appears that there was no organ, harmonium or piano. The pews were

Fig 6.2
Zoar Baptist chapel, Norwich, 1886. Small chapels such as this continued to be built, almost regardless of architectural fashions, at least until the end of the 19th century.
[DP160464]

relatively up-to-date, having sloping backs and open ends, but were otherwise unremarkable.

Such asceticism was not merely the outcome of restricted finances, but also reflected a desire to avoid worldliness. Zoar's was one of that small group of Baptist congregations (associated with the *Gospel Standard* magazine) not allied with the region's association of Strict and Particular Baptists – let alone the more open Particular Baptists, who tended to belong to the Baptist Union. Zoar's demure decor contrasted with that of the nearby St Mary's Baptist chapel, which in the same year, 1886, was refurnished with 'woodwork of the highest quality and wood carving by the noted Norwich artist James Minns'.[31] At a time when the Baptist world was rife with talk of latitudinarianism and even heresy among its clergy (talk which led Charles Haddon Spurgeon to withdraw from the Baptist Union in 1887), it is easy to imagine that the worshippers at Zoar felt that they were holding fast to principles that their more worldly neighbours had abandoned.[32]

Zoar, and chapels such as those at Wath, Wheal Busy and West Torrington, are likely to have been designed by a process of negotiation between a local builder and a representative of the congregation. In some places members of the congregation will have helped with the construction. Many of the smallest chapels were built without even a vestry space, let alone a schoolroom, and so the one chamber often accommodated all kinds of meetings and events, as well as Sunday schools and services. As early as 1847 the *Congregational Year Book* had ridiculed such small country chapels, calling them 'non-descript structures' which would not have been erected 'had some competent persons been consulted'.[33] However, the *Year Book*'s supporting illustrations are a caricature, depicting an architectural carelessness (such as round-headed openings without voussoirs or keystones) that is at odds with the reality. It is a credit to their builders that small Victorian chapels have come to be prized by the wider world in recent years as attractive and solid creations, studied by historians and architects, and often adapted for new uses in the case of redundancy. Small chapels constitute an important part of the total stock of Nonconformist buildings, and continued to be built in very significant numbers throughout the years covered by this chapter.[34] There was a gradual rise in the proportion of those that firmly crossed the threshold into polite – as opposed to vernacular – architecture, and a few examples will feature in remaining sections of this chapter.

Classical chapels

Classical architecture remained in the repertoire of virtually every Nonconformist denomination after 1850, albeit with less emphasis on purely Greek forms and more of a turn (as in the secular world) to a range of Roman, Italianate and Renaissance sources. Very commonly the designs were provided by architects who were equally adept at classical or medieval modes. It is interesting in this respect to look at the work of Andrew Trimen, a stylistically versatile specialist whose *Church and Chapel Architecture* (of 1849) was mentioned in Chapter 5. In 1853 the English Congregational Chapel-Building Society commended two sets of his designs, one Gothic and one classical.[35] Trimen was far from being a full-blooded Goth, but nor was he a neo-Athenian. His classical chapels from the 1850s are recognisably variations on a single theme, each with a pedimented portico at the centre of its façade, but pragmatically adapted to the needs and budget of its congregation. At the start of the decade Trimen created the Caledonian Road Congregational chapel (of 1850–1; demolished) in a newly built part of Islington.[36] He employed a relatively grand portico with a pair of fluted Tower-of-the-Winds columns between square piers, reached by an imposing flight of steps, since the chapel was raised over a semi-basement Sunday school – an increasingly common expedient for urban chapels. Although the design was understandably described as Grecian, it was largely built of white brick, and provided seats for 1,000 at a total cost of around £3,000.[37]

For an established group in the smarter surroundings of Kensington, Trimen designed Allen Street Congregational (now United Reformed) chapel (of 1854–5), extensively faced in Bath stone, and providing 1,200 seats at more than double the cost of the Islington example.[38] The budget could surely have permitted a full-width colonnade, but the architect nonetheless retained a narrower portico – about half the width of the façade – on this occasion with two pairs of unfluted Corinthian columns. A couple of handsome standard lamps still herald this main approach to the chapel, but there are also subsidiary entrances (perhaps to avoid congestion?) in the first bay of each side elevation. Corinthian pilasters are wrapped around those bays, with an associated parapet to emphasise the treatment of the entrance block as a unit. The classical theme continues inside, where two Corinthian pilasters provide a backdrop to the communion area. This

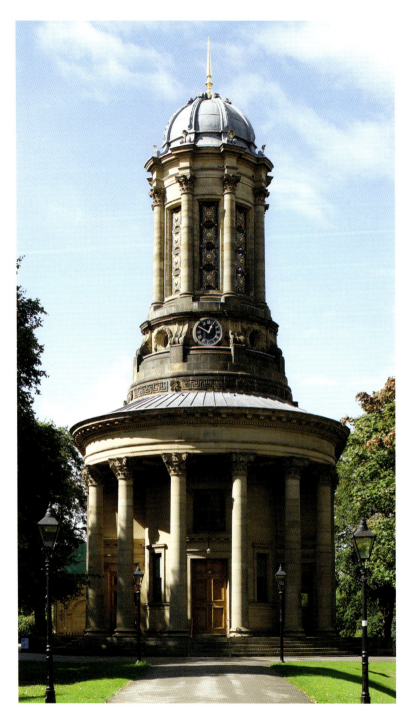

(for weekday as well as Sunday-school purposes) was erected alongside.[39]

In contrast to this metropolitan affluence is the comparatively small Congregational chapel (now in secular use) of 1859 in Shaftesbury.[40] The building was designed by Trimen as a reduced variant of the two earlier schemes, using Bath stone for the frontage. Again there is a central pediment, borne on two pairs of Corinthian columns, but projecting only marginally from the face of the building and matched by a single Corinthian pilaster at each end of the façade. This was regarded as an exemplary design for a small town chapel: in 1862–3 it was included in the illustrated appendix to the Congregationalists' *Practical Hints on Chapel-Building,* and a later article on the denomination's Gothic chapels praised it as being 'far superior to a number of Gothic churches'.[41] Emphasis was laid on the fact that an architecturally respectable chapel for almost 500 worshippers had been built at a cost of less than £1,500. Such essentially classical architecture continued to appeal to many Nonconformists, from the humble to the grand.

There was something of a resurgence in the use of classical styles among Nonconformists in the late 1850s. One of the most impressive examples of the period is the Congregational (now United Reformed) chapel built in 1856–9 as the chief place of worship in Titus Salt's model town of Saltaire, West Yorkshire (Fig 6.3).[42] It was proudly illustrated as the frontispiece to the *Congregational Year Book* in 1860, and even a century later was mildly praised by a fastidious Pevsner.[43] The architects, Lockwoood and Mawson, could certainly have supplied a Gothic design if required, but Lockwood's classical predilection perhaps coincided with a desire on Salt's part for a kind of opulence that could not easily have been achieved with medieval styles.[44]

Internally the chapel is indeed sumptuous (Fig 6.4), replete with scagliola columns, ormolu chandeliers, coffered barrel-vault and – as a climax to the long vista – a magnificent organ. All this recalls the neo-Roman splendours of St George's Hall in Liverpool or Leeds Town Hall, a comparison that reinforces the unbroken connection between secular architecture and the Nonconformist world. As Derek Linstrum has observed, the first great civic building by Lockwood and Mawson (St George's Hall in Bradford, of 1851–3) was internally similar to Lockwood's major chapels of the 1840s in Hull, with its wide, flat ceiling and galleries on cast-iron columns.[45]

area was originally dominated by a tall mahogany pulpit (first occupied by the cultured minister John Stoughton), centrally placed before a Father Willis organ. In other details, however, not least the wide ceiling with pendant bosses and a shallow lantern light, Trimen freely departed from ancient precedent. Although this grand chapel was initially without major ancillary accommodation, a lecture hall was very soon added (in 1856), and in 1869 a separate school building

Now Lockwood and Mawson turned the tables by designing a chapel interior that resembled the latest town halls, and the virtual absence of galleries at Saltaire makes the comparison more compelling.[46] Without galleries the lavish decorative scheme can be more readily appreciated, and the original pulpit was a little lower than in many large chapels.[47] These departures, along with the introduction of a central gangway, may appear to be concessions to ecclesiology, a suspicion strengthened by the fact that the building was known as a Congregational church (rather than chapel). Ecclesiologists would have baulked at the idea, not only because of the classical architecture, but because there is no attempt to create a chancel: the pulpit stands in an axial position before the organ, with the communion table in front, a clearly Protestant arrangement. Furthermore the handsome oak pews, specially designed by Lockwood and Mawson, are incrementally higher towards the back of the building, to ensure that everyone should have a clear view of the preacher.

Externally the Saltaire building is of equally high quality. The semicircular Corinthian portico, from which a round tower rises, and the side elevations with giant pilasters have something of the Roman spirit of Great George Street Congregational chapel, Liverpool (of 1840–1), although the domed tower, tall enough to have held a set of six bells, is more of a baroque *tempietto*. Rather like a rural parish church, the chapel stands alone in a leafy, landscaped setting, but the sloping site allows for an undercroft of rooms

Fig 6.4
Interior of Congregational chapel, Saltaire. One of the most sumptuous chapels of its day, it was quite comparable to the most splendid civic architecture.
[DP143300]

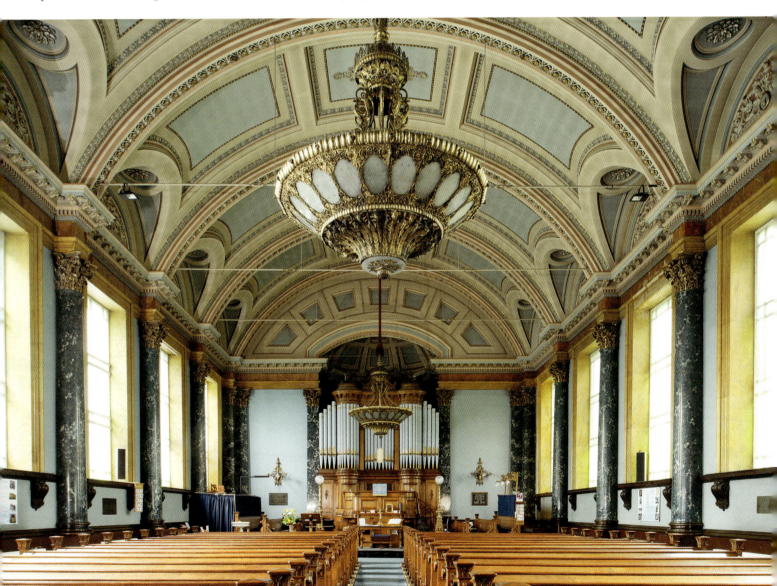

on the north side. These rooms were either inappropriate or ultimately inadequate for the Sunday school, as a large Sunday school (Italianate, but with 'little embellishment') was built on a nearby street in 1875–6 at a cost of nearly £10,000.[48] It is notable that the school was laid out on the new American system, with 22 classrooms opening off the main hall.[49]

Titus Salt paid for both the Saltaire chapel and its school, and it is easy to see the chapel as his shrine: his monogram appears above the windows, his body rests in the family mausoleum, erected on the south side of the chapel, and his sculpted bust now stands in the vestibule. None of this should mislead one into thinking that this was Salt's usual place of worship. He normally attended services at Lightcliffe Congregational chapel, near his home. Yet his lifelong commitment to Congregationalism ensured that Saltaire's Congregationalists had a

magnificent building which easily eclipsed the township's two (later) Methodist chapels. Now that Saltaire has become a world heritage site, the chapel is an international reminder of the progressive contribution made by Nonconformists to Britain's industrial culture.

An even more emphatic endorsement of classical architecture for Nonconformist purposes came with the building of the Metropolitan Tabernacle at Newington Butts, South London (Figs 6.5 and 6.6). This mammoth chapel was created specifically for the charismatic Baptist preacher Charles Haddon Spurgeon, who was just 25 when the foundation stone was laid on 16 August 1859.[50] Spurgeon's ability to gather vast audiences was already almost legendary and, having outgrown the usual Nonconformist places, he had taken to preaching in less conventional locations: first Exeter Hall in the Strand and then the new Surrey Gardens Music Hall

Fig 6.5
Metropolitan Tabernacle, Newington Butts, London, 1859–60 by W W Pocock, photographed probably c 1911–19. The Metropolitan Tabernacle remains forever associated with C H Spurgeon, the great Baptist preacher for whom it was built.
[CC73/01939]

became his regular venues. By 1857, when he preached to almost 24,000 hearers in the Crystal Palace, the idea of a super-chapel was already taking shape. A site was chosen, at a major road junction near the Elephant and Castle, and an architectural competition was announced. The rules stipulated that 'Gothic designs will not be accepted', and at the stone-laying ceremony Spurgeon argued that Greek, the language of the New Testament, was the true Christian tongue; every Baptist place of worship 'should be Grecian – never Gothic'.[51] This direct challenge to Puginian orthodoxy was associated with an unequivocally Protestant agenda, and Spurgeon was also forthright in his rejection of the new tendency (as at Saltaire) to call a Nonconformist building a church. His new chapel was to be known as a tabernacle, professedly invoking the Old Testament account of God's people in the wilderness, but doubtless also inviting compari-

son with the great preaching centres erected for George Whitefield in the 18th century (*see* p 49).

When Spurgeon's Metropolitan Tabernacle (by W W Pocock) opened in 1861, it had 4,600 seats and standing room for perhaps another 1,000 hearers, all focused on the broad rostrum from which its founder spoke.[52] His props were extraordinarily informal. There was no pulpit or lectern, but a table with reading lamp, an upholstered chair and sofa. The baptistery and the communion table were prominent enough, but occupied a lower level of the rostrum, with the school and lecture hall tucked away below the main auditorium. The interior was hardly classical at all; it owed more to the cast-iron structure of Surrey Gardens Music Hall (as encouraged by the competition conditions) than to any ancient prototype, and although the exterior made a bold show of pilasters, pediments and balustrades, only the great Corinthian portico could – to

Fig 6.6
The dramatic interior of the Metropolitan Tabernacle, London. This photograph, apparently predating the fire of 1898, captures the theatre-like layout of the enormous venue.
[DD97/00051]

stretch a point – be called Greek.[53] In the event the portico is the only part of the building to have survived both the fire of 1898 and bombing in the Second World War; consequently Spurgeon's Graecophile rhetoric retains more force than if we were still able to inspect the heterogeneous architecture of the Tabernacle as completed in 1861.[54]

Before long, versions of the Metropolitan Tabernacle began to appear. In 1864 the Congregationalists employed John Tarring to rebuild Whitefield's great chapel in Tottenham Court Road, with a mighty Doric (or was it Tuscan?) portico and twin towers in a paraphrase of Pocock's design, and in 1865 the Strict Baptists of Walworth built their Surrey tabernacle, 'a very successful imitation – in miniature, of course – of the great Tabernacle', fronted by a portico of six Ionic columns.[55] Versions continued to be built for at least 20 years, including, for instance, the Tuscan-porticoed Baptist tabernacle in Swindon (of 1886, by W H Read; demolished 1977–8).[56]

One of the surviving late offspring is Zion Baptist tabernacle in Newtown, Powys (of 1881,

by George Morgan of Carmarthen) (Fig 6.7).[57] The building resembles the Metropolitan Tabernacle in having balustraded staircase bays and a proud Corinthian portico (not exactly Greek in its proportions) which is approached by a broad flight of steps because the chapel is raised over a semi-basement school. Amidst the predominantly Gothic character of Newtown's other chapels, including those for Welsh-language congregations, Zion's classicism stands out; it was a departure (though not the first) from George Morgan's usual Romanesque mode.[58] The attractive combination of red brick and freestone seems to anticipate Edwardian baroque architecture, but the genes of Spurgeon's building can still be traced. Like many of the other examples, Zion has internal features which put one in mind of the Metropolitan Tabernacle, including a generous preacher's rostrum (Spurgeon's departure from a narrow pulpit was exemplary), bow-fronted galleries, slender iron columns and a high arcade of semicircular arches. On the other hand the centrepiece of the chapel is a magnificent proscenium arch of

Fig 6.7
Zion Baptist tabernacle, Newtown, Powys, 1881 by George Morgan. The building is clearly indebted to Spurgeon's great tabernacle, though it also anticipates Edwardian tastes in architecture.

marble columns, like a huge Serliana or Venetian window. It houses an organ that serves as a backdrop to the preacher – a far cry from Spurgeon's chapel, where instrumental music had no place and the pastor stood with little more than a cliff of listeners behind and around him.

It is in some ways surprising that any classical chapels were built for Wesleyan congregations after 1850. In that year, with the encouragement of the Wesleyan conference, the Reverend Frederick Jobson published *Chapel and School Architecture*, a book which gave short shrift to ancient architecture as a model for chapel builders:

> Lyceums, Museums, and Athenæums, may be built after Roman and Grecian models, and will then best accord with the names they bear; but let us not dishonour the religion we profess, by imitating Pagan temples in the erection of buildings where "the blood of bulls and goats" is not to be shed, – but where is to be worshipped, in faith and love, the Divine Saviour of Mankind.[59]

Many Wesleyan congregations followed this advice, but many others spurned it. For some, surely, the taint of Puseyism still clung to Gothic. And though a classical chapel might (as Jobson argued) be mistaken for a concert room, theatre or town hall, it became ever less likely to be mistaken for an Anglican church as the Church of England became exclusively a builder of Gothic places of worship.[60] For some Wesleyans, the choice of a classical style was more pragmatic, affected by the local context or the strengths of a favoured architect.

James Simpson of Leeds, the Wesleyan architect whose earlier work was noted in Chapter 5, was still very active in the second half of the century; he continued to design variations on the well-made classical designs which were his forte. A little-altered example which opened in 1861 (Simpson's 71st year) is to be seen at Morley, West Yorkshire.[61] Simpson was known to the congregation here, having enlarged their 18th-century premises in 1837, and the replacement chapel he now designed for them was a kind of temple in Renaissance dress; its four-bay gable-end façade had no portico, but instead paired central doorways in a sturdy Tuscan surround. The windows throughout have vigorously modelled surrounds, and the full-width pediment is enriched by carving around a central oculus. Is there just a hint here of the richer

classicism associated with Cuthbert Brodrick, the Leeds architect with whom Simpson's son John worked as an assistant in the 1850s?[62]

Internally the chapel is an almost complete example of Simpson's well-practised approach: encircling gallery, box pews and full-span coffered ceiling (Fig 6.8). Even the mahogany pulpit has survived, not overtaken by the change to rostrum pulpits, together with its matching railed communion area. Behind is the classical organ case of 1863. This fine interior embodies some arrangements that would have been familiar to Methodists of the Regency years, and which William Jenkins in turn had based on 18th-century patterns. It would certainly have seemed old-fashioned to Jobson and the Wesleyan Gothicists, but one must assume that the Wesleyans of Morley were more concerned to have an updated version of a tried-and-tested

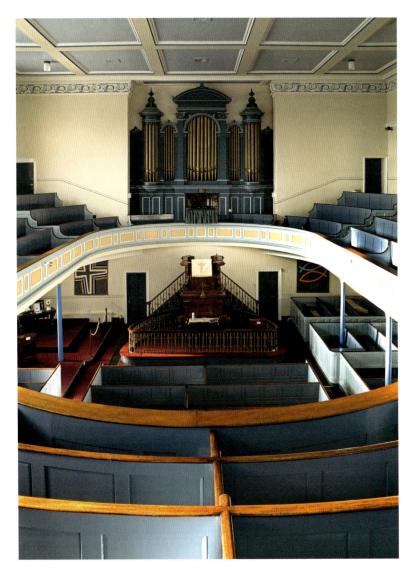

Fig 6.8
Interior of Wesleyan Methodist chapel, Morley, West Yorkshire, 1861 by James Simpson. The little-altered chapel, complete with its original pulpit, represents the survival of early 19th-century arrangements.
[DP056614]

design, one that could be relied on to meet their needs. Simpson had turned his hand to Gothic designs before; he surely would have done so again in this case had his clients required it.

An interesting instance of competitive classicism among Methodists is to be found in the Lincolnshire town of Market Rasen. In the years around 1850 the Wesleyan cause in this area had lost perhaps 45 per cent of its members as a result of the national disruption associated with the Fly-Sheet controversy. This led to the formation of a Free Methodist congregation which built its first chapel in 1852, replacing it in 1861 by a large new building with a powerful Corinthian temple front.[63] The town's Wesleyans were not crushed, however, and on the site of their existing building

they opened a major new chapel in 1863 (Fig 6.9). Its massive Ionic portico outdid that of the Free Methodists' building (which had only attached, not freestanding columns) and dominated the streetscape.[64] The architect, William Botterill of Hull, was quite capable of supplying a Gothic design, but in this case his Wesleyan clients were perhaps keener to demonstrate that they could beat the usurping body at its own game than they were to risk having a building like the medieval parish church, coincidentally rebuilt in 1862. Internally the chapel is recognisably from the same stock as James Simpson's work in Morley, with a broad-span ceiling, a gallery curved at both ends and a fine set of box pews (Fig 6.10). Nice details include glazed screens for

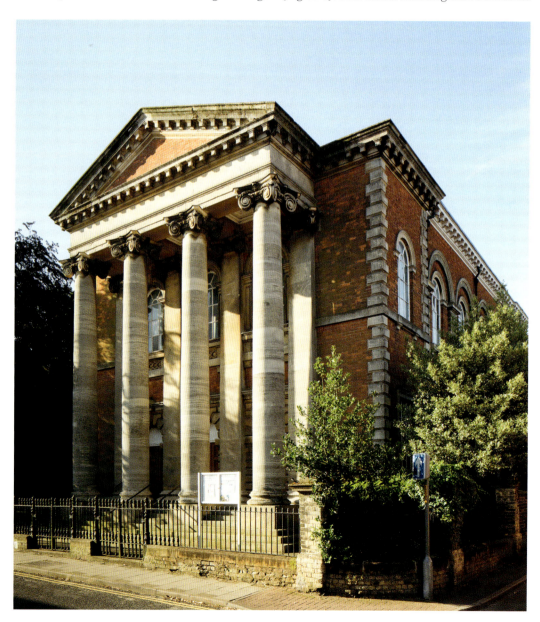

Fig 6.9
Wesleyan Methodist chapel, Market Rasen, Lincolnshire, 1863 by William Botterill. The mighty portico was designed at least in part as a riposte to the town's Free Methodists, who had so recently built a new chapel nearby.
[DP165319]

the backmost ground-floor pews (Fig 6.11) and one-seat stewards' pews in the gallery. Decorum was evidently important for the Wesleyans here. One would be hard pressed to describe the interior decoration as consistently classical, however – neither in the original pulpit (elements of which form the centre of the present rostrum) and railed communion area, nor in the organ case above.

Several variations on the temple theme were developed by the Bradford architects Lockwood and Mawson, who were accomplished classicists – as Saltaire attests. One of their confident designs can be seen in the stone-built Wesleyan chapel of 1861–2 in Oxford Street, Harrogate (Fig 6.12).[65] The five-bay, pedimented front is strongly composed, with a sequence of giant, engaged, Corinthian columns and angle pilasters, which extend to the first bay of each side elevation. Ten years before, Lockwood and Mawson had explored this idea at St George's Hall, Bradford, but the result here in Harrogate is more fully orchestrated, for instance in having pediments above the staircase windows and by filling the main pediment with a garlanded roundel. It is all of a piece with the spa town's public buildings, and in marked contrast to the new Congregational chapel in Victoria Avenue (of 1860–2), a

Decorated Gothic building for which Lockwood and Mawson were also the architects.[66] In this case it seems likely that Harrogate's Wesleyans wanted to avoid comparisons with the local Congregationalists; they perhaps opted to play to the architects' classical strengths rather than risk further stretching their more limited abilities in Gothic. Lockwood and Mawson managed to turn received wisdom – that Gothic was cheaper – on its head, by providing accommodation for more

Fig 6.10
Interior of Wesleyan Methodist chapel, Market Rasen. The finely finished design includes a deep encircling gallery, with stands for the singers' music at the front of the gallery behind the pulpit. [DP165324]

Fig 6.11
Wesleyan Methodist chapel, Market Rasen. Among many refinements, the chapel has these apparently original glazed screens to protect the rear pews from draughts. [DP165327]

Fig 6.12
Wesleyan Methodist chapel,
Oxford Street, Harrogate,
Yorkshire, 1861–2 by
Lockwood and Mawson.
The rich classical façade
was evidently intended to
contrast with the local
Congregational chapel, a
Gothic design then being
built by the same architects.

*Fig 6.12
Weslyan Methodist chapel,
Oxford Street, Harrogate,
Yorkshire, 1861–2 by
Lockwood and Mawson.
The rich classical façade
was evidently intended to
contrast with the local
Congregational chapel, a
Gothic design then being
built by the same architects.*

than 1,000 in the classical chapel at a cost of about £4,000, as against 700 seats in the Gothic chapel at a cost of about £5,000.[67] Not that the Wesleyan chapel has the atmosphere of a cheap building. Its well-lit interior has two rows of tall cast-iron columns; between these is a coffered vault, whose segmental curve is echoed in the organ case above the pulpit (Fig 6.13). Because the columns are slender and set well back from the front of the (originally U-shaped) gallery, they seem not to enclose but to open up the space, drawing everyone into the act of worship. Below the chapel itself are the schoolrooms, taking full advantage of the sloping site.

*Fig 6.13
Interior of Wesleyan
chapel, Oxford Street,
Harrogate. The vaulted
ceiling adds to the height
of the gallery space and
provides a graceful setting
for the organ.*

Seating

It is almost impossible to think of Nonconformist interiors without thinking of seating. From the outset the exposition of scripture played a central part in Protestant worship, and long sermons required attentive listeners. As an expedient after the Reformation (and perhaps before), many worshippers took chairs or stools into church to avoid standing for long periods. This presumably also happened in some purpose-built chapels and meeting houses, although Nonconformists provided more extensive kinds of seating wherever possible. Loose forms – the simplest and cheapest option – were often supplied, but came to seem too rudimentary for long-term use by adults in all but the poorest situations. Benches with a railed back offered more support and appealed especially to Quakers, for whom they remained the norm until the 20th century. However, box pews (that is, with doors) are the most widespread kind of seating to survive from the Georgian period. Their high sides provided some protection from draughts in what were usually unheated buildings. Squarish pews – with seats on more than one side – were common in early chapels and meeting houses, although linear pews were always more convenient in galleries.

John Wesley, and some other Nonconformists, wanted men and women to sit separately for worship, but it is not clear whether this was generally observed. Quakers did follow such a pattern until late in the 19th century, however, generally with women on one side of the room and men on the other; they were consciously following a practice common in 17th-century Anglican churches. (Note, however, that women could play a leading role in Quaker worship, as caricaturists sometimes observed. Quaker women met separately from men not for worship, but to conduct their business meetings.)

Seating arrangements from before about 1850 do not often survive intact. Although some new chapels were fitted out with linear box pews even in the 1860s, open-ended pews were more usual from mid-century. Over the following decades many older seats were replaced or adapted. Sometimes tall-sided pews were reduced in height and doors were removed. Even more common was the adaptation of upright-backed pews to give the sloping backs which were being advocated from the 1840s. Pre-1850 seating in galleries is less likely to have been altered, not least because the prestige associated with the front-of-gallery seats declined when three-decker pulpits fell out of fashion in the later 19th century.

Many chapels have numbered pews, a reminder of the system of pew rents which was once common also in English churches; dating from the 17th century, the practice came under attack in the mid-19th century, but still lasted in many places until after the First World War. In a few places (Union Chapel, Islington, for instance), there survive wooden seating-plans with peg-holes, which could show the available pews at a glance. Pew rental was never universal, however, and it was abandoned by both Nonconformists and Anglicans during the later 19th and early 20th centuries.

The later Victorian period saw the refinement of pew design – often incorporating metal umbrella holders into the pew ends – and by the Edwardian period chapel architects such as George Baines were creating high-quality bespoke pews, sometimes in curved layouts. Meanwhile the reaction against pews was becoming evident. Tip-up seats helped to foster an unecclesiastical atmosphere in the Methodists' central halls, and individual chairs were preferred in some mission halls to allow flexible use of the space. For much of the 20th century, however, fixed seating continued to be the most usual choice in Nonconformist places of worship. In recent decades the desire for movable chairs has come to the fore, partly because of more dynamic styles of worship and partly because of the growing expectation that a chapel can also be used for other purposes, such as playgroups, lunch clubs or dance classes.†

Union Chapel, Islington, London. The peg-board plan enabled the renting of seats to be monitored at a glance. [DP151748]

Fig 6.14 (right)
Wesleyan Methodist chapel,
Snaith, near Goole, 1861–2
by Lockwood and Mawson.
This variant on the
architects' design for
Harrogate achieves a quite
different effect through the
use of red brick and stone.

Fig 6.15 (below)
Unitarian Free Christian
Church chapel, Hastings,
1867 by George Beck.
Even among Unitarians,
classical designs were still
preferred in some places
during the later 19th
century.
[DP165335]

Within weeks of designing this building, Lockwood and Mawson used it as the basis of their proposal for another Wesleyan chapel, that (of 1861–2) at Snaith, a small town near Goole (Fig 6.14).[68] Such recycling of ideas was obviously an efficient use of a busy architect's time, but perhaps the second client benefited from the opportunity to revise the earlier design. The Snaith version is of red brick, with ashlar for the columns and decorative details; the rich colour is complemented by the greenery of what must have been a rather elegant drive. Furthermore, because the schoolrooms (of 1848) lay at the back of the site, there was no need to incorporate such facilities in the chapel. In other respects the differences are less obvious, but sufficient to allay any suspicion that Snaith's Wesleyans were getting a mere copy of the Harrogate design: the columns and pilasters are Ionic rather than Corinthian, for instance, and there are keystones to the lower windows. The pediment retains its anthemion motifs at the ridge and each end, and internally too there have been few changes. The columns, ceiling and gallery structure repeat the format from Harrogate, including the U-shaped gallery, its straight end matching the classical proscenium arch that squarely frames the (later enlarged) organ. A fortunate survival is the original pulpit, set above a wide, wooden screen that acts as a backdrop to the communion area.

Surprisingly the pews – which retain their numbered doors and acorn hinges – are more sophisticated than the Harrogate examples; those on the ground floor are gently curved (turning worshippers to the preacher) and most have a central shelf and lockable drawer for family hymn books or bibles. As in many larger chapels of the period – especially, but not exclusively, those of classical design – the floor slopes towards the pulpit, so as to enhance the sightlines. While the Anglican world turned away from box pews and favoured raised chancels rather than sloped naves, in Nonconformity there were many opportunities to continue refining what might be called the Protestant auditorium.

Where budgets did not run to a grand portico, many chapel builders employed the simpler and trusted pattern of a gable-end façade endowed with pediment and pilasters. One example is the Unitarian Free Christian Church chapel in South Terrace, Hastings (Fig 6.15), designed by architect George Beck and built in 1867 at a cost of £710.[69] Its rendered Doric frontage nestles into a terrace of three-storey houses, rather as a pedimented house is *primus inter pares* in a Georgian square. Even cheaper than this, at £395, was the Primitive Methodist chapel (of 1866, by Thomas T Allen) in Great William Street, Stratford-on-Avon.[70] Despite the very modest budget, the chapel introduced a colourful note into a narrow street of modest terrace houses. Entirely outlined in blue brick, its red-brick façade is enlivened by pilasters of blue, and yellow-brick details underline the full-width pediment, which rises above the ridge line of the neighbouring homes. Over succeeding decades the elements of these three-bay, pedimented frontages continued to provide a template for chapel builders of limited means, and constitute one of the archetypal images of Nonconformity.

There were more innovative approaches to the classical tradition. Among the chapel designs to attract wide interest was that for Albion Congregational chapel in Sneinton, Nottingham (of 1855–6) by the young Tyneside architect, Thomas Oliver junior (Fig 6.16).[71] Oliver's Nonconformist work was more often Gothic. In this case, however, he seems to have found inspiration in the type of chapel façade which is represented by the Baptist chapel in Truro (of 1848–9, by Philip Sambell; now in secular use), and which in turn can be seen as a grander version of such designs as the 1804 Wesleyan chapel in Newport, Isle of Wight (*see* p 83): the central bay is arched and rises into the pediment

to echo the round-headed window below.[72] Oliver injected some brio into the pattern, with fluted Roman Ionic pilasters and a satisfyingly deep entablature that curves generously up into the pediment. This centrepiece of the façade encloses a tall, round-headed window carefully aligned with the middle pilasters of the recessed Doric porch, while on each side the two storeys of windows are subsumed within a Roman pillar-and-arch rhythm that continues along the sides of the building. A planned campanile was not built, but even so the building was a striking addition to the thriving district.

From the outset the design had the blessing of the English Congregational Chapel-Building Society and it was selected as the Society's model

Fig 6.16
Albion Congregational chapel, Sneinton, Nottingham, 1855–6 by Thomas Oliver junior. One of the Congregationalists' model designs, it helped to enliven the classical repertoire of chapel architecture. It is now subdivided for residential use.
[© Elain Harwood]

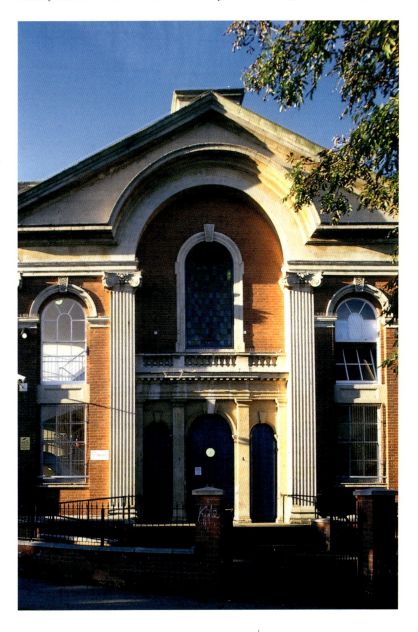

chapel, in the expectation that 50 versions of it would be erected in five years.[73] It is not clear that this materialised, however, at least not in England. Thomas Oliver himself employed virtually the same design for an Independent chapel in East Street, Middlesbrough (of 1856–7), which was illustrated – along with the Nottingham chapel – in the *Congregational Year Book* for 1857.[74] One person who does seem to have studied these engravings is the Reverend Thomas Thomas, a Welsh minister-architect who adopted the motif of a giant arch rising into a gable-end pediment for very many of his chapels.[75] Salem Independent chapel, Porthmadog (of 1860) is an early example of this so-called halo arch in Thomas's work, and is closely derived from Oliver's model design.[76]

It has been suggested that the giant-arch-and-pediment feature had its source in Alberti's important church of Sant' Andrea, Mantua.[77] The parallel is not close enough to be convincing, but the Italian Renaissance was certainly of growing interest to architects in the middle years of the 19th century.[78] For example, the Newcastle architect John Dobson – with whom Thomas Oliver's father is said to have worked – turned to Renaissance ideas when he designed

St Columba's Presbyterian chapel in North Shields (of 1856–7) (Fig 6.17).[79] St Columba's is in a square with many Regency houses, from which it stands out by the quality of its architecture rather than as an obvious place of worship. Dobson here modelled the building not on a Greek temple nor a medieval church, but on Italian town houses of the kind designed by Sanmicheli in the early 16th century. The five-bay façade has a rusticated ground floor with square-headed openings; on the upper floor is an order of engaged Doric columns framing round-headed windows. Dobson adapted the idea of a palazzo to the needs of a chapel by equating the gallery (then still the location of the premier seats in many Nonconformist places of worship) to the *piano nobile*, and providing vestries and stairs on each side of the entrance.[80] Almost 20 years later, in 1875, the Primitive Methodists built a similar chapel (now a Roman Catholic church) in Wilton, Wiltshire, albeit with pedimented upper windows and pilasters rather than columns.[81] The first floor in this case is relatively tall, expressing the fact that the main worship space is entirely at that level and subsidiary rooms occupy the ground floor.

Such direct indebtedness to Renaissance prototypes was not common. Shrewsbury's chapels, mentioned above, may provide a more representative picture. In three of them (the Welsh Congregational tabernacle of 1862, Claremont Baptist of 1877–8 and the new Unitarian frontage of 1885) one finds a common architectural vocabulary of pilasters and pediments, round-headed windows and balustraded parapets. Yet none of the elevations – to say nothing of the interiors – is purely derived from Italian pattern books. During the High Victorian years the description of a building as being in the Italian style might be taken to cover a very wide range of designs, from Romanesque to baroque. Shrewsbury's Wesleyan chapel of 1879 exemplifies an eclectic attitude to Italian sources, its pediment crowning a lively display of moulded brick and carved stone details that owes as much to medieval architecture as to the classical tradition.

As if in response to Jobson's criticism that a classical chapel risked confusion with secular buildings, a small number of architects began to consider the use of towers and spires for classical places of worship. A fragmentary reminder of this is to be seen in north London, where the façade remains of the United Presbyterians' ambitious chapel (of 1862–3 by Edward Habershon) in Highbury Park. The body of the chapel, which was described as being 'in the Italian style', was demolished after closure in 1942.[82] Park Church, as it was known, was a landmark in the leafy new suburb, elevated above street level and made even more conspicuous by a steeple to one side of the entrance. Pevsner saw something of Hawksmoor in the design, although the spire is perhaps closer to Wren.[83] Certainly the concept of a single steeple, classically detailed but Gothic in silhouette, puts one in mind of Wren's city churches. Nonconformists were now happy to reclaim such a feature – and its associations with a thoroughly Protestant period of English religion – not merely because of the Anglicans' current retreat from Protestantism, but more specifically because an Act had just been passed which was to lead to the demolition of a dozen of Wren's churches before the end of the century.[84]

During the 1870s, a decade when no fewer than six of the Wren churches were destroyed, a Congregational group moved from its early 19th-century Poultry chapel in the heart of London to a major new building, the City Temple, on the recently completed Holborn Viaduct. The City Temple (of 1872–4, by H F Lockwood of Lockwood and Mawson) was created for a gifted preacher, Joseph Parker, and to some extent served as a Congregational response to Spurgeon's Metropolitan Tabernacle.[85] Contemporary reports described the huge City Temple as being in the Italian – or even the light Italian – style, but its two-storey porch and tower (virtually the only parts not to have needed rebuilding after bomb damage in the Second World War) suggest at least a nod in Wren's direction.[86] The portico might be seen as a 16th-century Italian precursor of the west front of St Paul's Cathedral, and the domed lantern similarly could be a proto-baroque version of the cathedral's celebrated west towers. Joseph Parker's success at the City Temple was audacious. He filled the 2,500-seat building with attentive congregations in the very years when historic Anglican churches were being demolished wholesale for want of worshippers in the increasingly uninhabited City, and the architecture of his new building underlined the paradox of his achievement.[87]

The best preserved of the Nonconformist examples of this general style is the Wesleyans' Hinde Street chapel (Fig 6.18) in the West End of London, built in 1886–7 and designed by James Weir as the successor to a Regency chapel on the same site.[88] As with the City Temple, Hinde Street chapel has a two-storey portico, but the

comparison with St Paul's is even closer since there are coupled columns (Doric below, Corinthian above). Again it has a single tower, which in this case rises through octagonal stages to a spire – an idea possibly derived from the much taller steeple at St Bride's, Fleet Street. By taking inspiration from Wren, was James Weir trying to show up the starved spire of Nash's nearby All Souls, as well as associating Methodism with the architecture of the threatened City churches?

For the side elevation, Weir adopted a restrained Palladianism, a simplified version of the Whitehall Banqueting House, which looked well in this smart quarter of Georgian London. After the rectilinear spirit of the exterior, one enters the chapel via a curved vestibule to see a giant arch – supported by two pairs of Corinthian columns – with a richly detailed, domed, semicircular apse in which there are round-headed windows and matching arcaded panels.

A bow-fronted rostrum pulpit projects into the main worship space from the centre of this set piece, facing the U-shaped gallery, and the curved theme is continued by the deeply coved ceiling (with cross-curves between its ribs) and coving to the underside of the gallery. Acoustics and sightlines were certainly assisted by this layout, and Weir clearly had an eye for practical details as well as aesthetics. Classically patterned panels of etched glass allow light in without causing distraction from the street, and stained glass was only allowed in the windows (now artificially illuminated) behind the pulpit. School facilities were provided in a large space below the chapel, and there were classrooms, a church parlour and caretaker's flat in the adjacent house, which formed part of the original scheme.

Although Wren's work provided an occasional theme for Nonconformist (and secular) architects into the 20th century, it was hardly

Fig 6.19
Congregational chapel, Upper Street, Islington, London, 1887–8 by Bonella and Paull. Among the abundance of Queen Anne features, note the generous windows of the semi-basement school. The building is now used for offices.
[DP150856]

the only strand of classicism to command attention. For the Primitive Methodists, James Weir designed the handsome New Surrey chapel (of 1886–8) in Blackfriars Road, London, with an almost fully glazed façade that had a hint of Dutch Renaissance design about it.[89] The Queen Anne Revival affected Nonconformist buildings rather less than might have been expected, but at least one prominent example must be mentioned in its scope: the Congregationalists' former chapel in Upper Street, Islington, of 1887–8, by Bonella and Paull (Fig 6.19).[90] Characteristically for the style, the red bricks and tiles are the foil for white-painted glazing bars and Portland stone dressings, accompanied by plenty of attractive moulded brickwork and robust ironwork. A large Ipswich window almost fills the Dutch gable, while a pretty cupola gives the building a distinctive silhouette. From a planning perspective the chapel was most notable for its semi-basement school hall (lit by very generously sized windows), off which more than 20 classrooms could be created by a system of low partitions. This was indeed an embodiment of sweetness and light.[91]

'Blood and fire', by contrast, is the motto inscribed on the keystone above the gates to the Salvation Army barracks of 1882–3 (by E J Sherwood) in Gillygate, York (Fig 6.20). William Booth's great evangelical movement had been named the Salvation Army in 1878, and within a year began to refer to its halls as barracks.[92] This was a period of very rapid expansion. As in many other towns, York's Salvationists first worshipped in adapted premises – from 1881 a redundant skating rink in Gillygate – yet within two years were able to move into their first purpose-built accommodation, designed by Edmund James Sherwood, appointed as in-house architect by Booth in 1880.[93] Like a large Methodist chapel of the Regency, the frontage has a five-bay gable for the main hall, but the projecting centrepiece contains a wide gateway rather than doors, while battlemented parapets give further expression to the Army's military metaphor. Funds did not permit much decoration, but the wings carry large roundels with the Salvation Army's 'blood and fire' crest (Fig 6.21).[94] Architecture and imagery were intentionally direct – all part of Booth's distinctive mission to the unconverted masses. The same spirit was evident in Sherwood's designs for the Army's medium-sized premises, such as the example of 1885–6 at Beverley in East Yorkshire (now demolished).[95] A battlemented gable end

Fig 6.20 (above)
Salvation Army barracks, York, 1882–3 by E J Sherwood. This early example of the Army's purpose-built premises helped set the tone for the movement's distinctive architecture.
[DP181110]

Fig 6.21 (left)
Salvation Army barracks, York. While generally avoiding expensive decoration, the Army's architects often made a show of the 'blood and fire' crest.
[DP181109]

Fig 6.22
Welsh Baptist chapel,
Eastcastle Street, London,
1889 by Owen Lewis. By
using external stairs and
breaking the rules of polite
architecture, Lewis found
a new way to express the
characteristically multi-
layered nature of such
an urban chapel.
[DP151003]

and porch supplied the fortress imagery. The interior consisted of an open hall, economically spanned by a lightweight curved roof, with a tiered platform filling the far end, below the Army's crest. Movable benches and chairs presumably enabled the hall to be used for a variety of events.

While it is hardly fair to locate the Salvation Army's buildings in either of the stylistic camps that had marked the mid-Victorian era, there is no mistaking the classical theme in the Welsh Baptist chapel (of 1889) in Eastcastle Street,

just north of Oxford Street, London.[96] The design was by Owen Lewis, a commercial specialist whose previous work included the building that became the London Palladium, and he filled the narrow frontage on Eastcastle Street with a suitably unconventional composition (Fig 6.22). Four widely spaced Corinthian columns front a tall, open portico, and support a full-width entablature, above which two tiers of crazily detailed windows vie for attention. Within the great void of the portico a flight of steps leads to the main door; a pair of boldly balustraded external stairs give access to the gallery and lesser stairs unobtrusively descend to the basement hall, resulting in an almost Piranesian inventiveness of routes and levels. Ian Nairn has said of the building that 'it does to the fussy metropolitan *hôtel* of the 1880s what the best Welsh chapels did for the pedimented Nonconformist box'.[97]

Owen Lewis's wayward attitude to the proportions and architectonic qualities of classical architecture was shared by many architects of the era, but the outcome in this case is compelling. Having to shoehorn a chapel and its ancillary accommodation into a narrow site, tight against the neighbouring premises, caused significant problems, but the main chamber actually gains from such limitations (Fig 6.23). With only a long clerestory lantern for daylight, the large space seems almost intimate, like the top-lit synagogues of the East End. The side pews are angled slightly towards the front, and a bow-fronted gallery encircles the auditorium beneath a deeply coved ceiling, further directing attention on to the ensemble of pulpit, baptistery and communion area. Music has played an essential role in the worship here – Welsh chapels can hardly be imagined without it – and the chapel is barely big enough to contain the organ pipes that rise behind the pulpit.[98] It seems somehow appropriate that this vibrant building was the place where Lloyd George chose to worship when in London, and that his larger than life personality occasionally occupied the pulpit.

The Welsh Baptist chapel is just a stone's throw from the Ecclesiologists' model church of All Saints in Margaret Street (begun in 1849 by Butterfield), and it is fascinating to visit the one building after the other. Although both were creative solutions to the problem of constricted urban sites, the one celebrated the long Reformed tradition of congregational worship, with the pulpit and sacraments physically central, while the other embodied a return to a high medieval

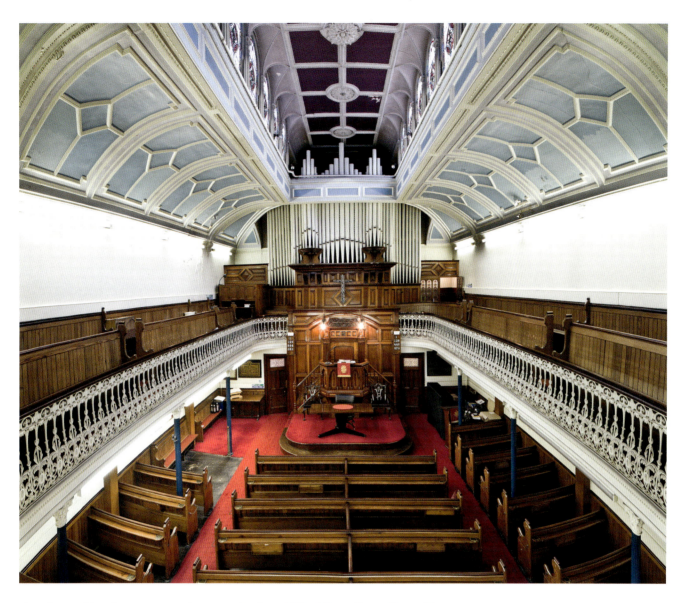

churchmanship, the sacramental spaces clearly separated from the congregational area. It might be said that these different approaches to worship, and such consequential matters as the inclusion or omission of galleries, are more fundamental than the question of style. Many fully Protestant places of worship were built to Gothic designs, and fully Catholic ones could be built on classical lines. Yet although classical architecture could be used for quite a variety of plan-forms, most classical chapels of the High Victorian years were in fact built with rectangular plans, generally with wide-spanned roofs and, in the case of larger chapels, with surrounding galleries. In turning now to the Nonconformists' adaptation of medieval styles in these years, we shall also encounter some more varied approaches to planning.

Medieval styles: Romanesque

Romanesque architecture continued to find a place in the repertoire of many chapel architects after 1850. As an example of the initial tendency to draw on Anglo-Norman sources, the example of the Congregational (now joint Methodist and United Reformed) chapel in High Street, Ware can be cited (Fig 6.24). It was built in 1858–9 to the designs of a local builder, John Brown, who punctuated the gable-end façade with round-arched and circular openings that are variously enriched with billet, lozenge, chevron or reel mouldings as if to demonstrate the range of late Norman ornament.[99] Another didactic touch is found in the central triple window, whose middle arch is pointed so as to suggest the transition to Gothic. The sides of the building have more

Fig 6.23
Interior of Welsh Baptist chapel, Eastcastle Street, London. The extraordinary top-lit space is a triumph over the limitations of the hemmed-in site.
[DP150196]

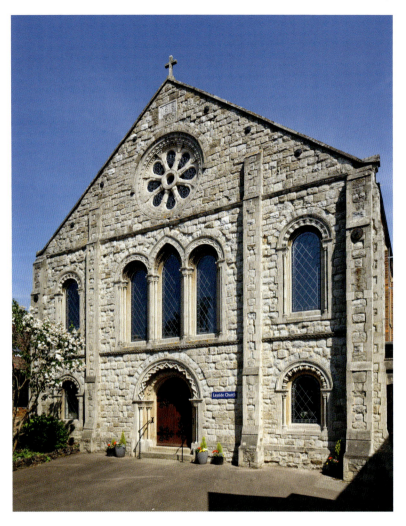

Fig 6.24
Congregational (now joint
Methodist and United
Reformed) chapel, Ware,
Hertfordshire, 1858–9 by
John Brown. Romanesque
architecture retained its
appeal for chapel builders
into the 1850s.
[DP161383]

regular, round-headed windows, but are filled with contemporary patterned glass – not a common survival. Unusually for a Nonconformist chapel, a stone cross (originally in the form of a Celtic cross) was placed at each end of the roof ridge, in what looks like an insistence that the symbol was not the prerogative of High Churchmen and Catholics. The Norman theme was continued in the more interestingly detailed Sunday-school building (also by Brown, and built at the same time, though later extended) which stands to one side of the chapel forecourt.

By the late 1850s, however, the Norman revival was past its peak, perhaps tainted by accusations of its primitive nature, and a wider range of sources is evident in most chapels of Romanesque or *Rundbogen* (round-arched) character. The Baptist chapel in City Road, Bristol (of 1859–61, by Medland and Maberly of Gloucester), for instance, was described as being in a modified Byzantine style, although the 'crude and stiff' forms associated with Byzantine

decoration were avoided.[100] In contrast to the wide-roofed frontage of the Ware chapel, the Bristol example is crisply basilican, with a deep clerestory, and aisles set back from the façade, on the general lines of the renowned Anglican church of 1841–5 in Wilton. The two tiers of aisle windows (round-headed below, circular above) reveal that there are galleries, despite the stone columns of the nave arcades. Such an arrangement hardly creates a perfect space for congregational worship, but it affords the gallery users a better opportunity of inspecting the capitals of the columns – each carved with a different kind of naturalistic foliage – as well as some view of the pulpit and the baptistery.

It is interesting to turn from the chapels in Ware and Bristol to a slightly later work by an architectural practice more experienced in Nonconformist commissions. The Wesleyan chapel in Maiden Street, Weymouth (of 1866–7, by Foster and Wood of Bristol; gutted by a fire in 2002) had a wheel window in each gable end and otherwise a pattern of round-headed openings, like the previous pair of examples.[101] Characteristically for its date, however, the architectural treatment was freely based on Italian Romanesque sources, both in the extensive use of brick and the arcaded loggia. It had an air of cheerful vitality, not archaeological scholarship. The resourceful plan was also a pragmatic response to the congregation's needs rather than a model layout. Given the constrained, street-corner site, Foster and Wood chose to set the necessary schoolrooms on the ground floor, with the galleried chapel immediately above, producing a sheer three-storey side elevation. From each corner of the façade stepped entrances led (via the first-floor loggia) to the chapel, in which relatively slender cast-iron columns provided an almost unobstructed space for Methodist worship.

Although an organ was not installed (in the rear gallery) until a few months after the opening, music played a central role in the services, and the legend 'Gloria in excelsis Deo' was emblazoned on the spandrels of the roof. Similar texts in English from the Book of Psalms were painted on the end walls – perhaps during the 1878 redecoration – and the gallery front was picked out in purple and gold.[102] Behind the pulpit, commandment panels were installed: a tradition which had lapsed in many places, but which was here incorporated into a suitably Romanesque blind arcade. Round-arched styles, ranging from explicitly Norman to Renaissance, continued to appear in the repertoire of

Nonconformist architecture throughout these decades and beyond, and were to be taken up by several architects whose roots were more firmly in the Gothic Revival.

Medieval styles: Gothic

In the decades after 1850 there was a steady and sustained increase in the number of Gothic chapels. Of the major Nonconformist denominations, it was among the Unitarians, Congregationalists and Wesleyans that the keenest advocates of medieval styles could be found, but almost all denominations – even Quakers and Primitive Methodists – were to erect Gothic buildings in these years. Gothic was seen least often in small rural chapels and most often featured in large urban chapels.[103] Among the architects who specialised in Nonconformist work, a few were committed Goths, but even architects who inclined to classicism (such as James Simpson or Lockwood and Mawson) were happy to produce a Gothic design if the client wished for one. Because there were stylistic options, the design of places of worship was hardly ever as acrimonious for Nonconformists as it could be for Anglicans. In the case of one north London Wesleyan chapel, for instance, it was reported that, 'after vacillating for a short time between the classical and Gothic styles, the trustees chose the latter, and the plans were accordingly prepared and adopted'.[104]

The publication of Frederick Jobson's *Chapel and School Architecture* in 1850 marks a convenient starting point for this period, although much of the book had already appeared in weekly articles in *The Watchman* newspaper.[105] Jobson was a talented Wesleyan minister who was to serve the connexion at the highest level. Before entering the ministry he had studied architecture with E J Willson of Lincoln (a friend of the young A W N Pugin), and so became a key adviser on architectural matters in Wesleyanism.[106] His purpose in *Chapel and School Architecture* was to persuade his readers of the suitability of Gothic architecture for Nonconformist needs, in which cause he deployed many of Pugin's arguments. However, he also sought to purge the style of its association with modern Catholicism:

Truth in Architecture is appearing; and the modern successors of the Puritans work not a little Gothic into *their* houses of worship, and thus give increasing practical proof that they perceive Truth in Architecture is not necessarily connected with Error in Religion.[107]

Jobson's book went on to illustrate a number of exemplary designs for Nonconformist use, ranging from a village chapel to large metropolitan buildings. Four of the chapels in question had been designed by James Wilson of Bath (whose Ramsgate Baptist chapel featured in Chapter 5, *see* pp 130–1), the prizewinning entrant in the Wesleyans' competition to design a Gothic chapel to accommodate 750 people.[108] There is no doubt that *Chapel and School Architecture* helped give wide currency to Jobson's ideas and to Wilson's designs, but the book appeared at a bad time. As a result of the Fly-Sheet controversy, which focused on the autocratic governance of the Wesleyan connexion, Wesleyanism was at a low ebb, and thus not building so many chapels.[109] Meanwhile the seceding Reformers were unlikely to adopt Jobson's preferred type of architecture because the book was fulsomely dedicated to Jabez Bunting, their arch-opponent.

By the mid-1850s Wilson's Methodist commissions began to pick up again, and the Wesleyan chapel (of 1855–7) in Manchester Road, Haslingden is an enlarged and elaborated version of his prizewinning model design.[110] As originally built it was rectangular, with a small extension behind the pulpit wall for the organ loft and vestries. Tall, traceried windows, their transoms coinciding with the galleries, mark the side elevations, alternating with stepped pinnacles that rise to a pierced parapet. The entrance front is grander than the model design, being divided into three bays by a pair of octagonal turrets that frame a large Perpendicular window – a faint echo of the versions of King's College, Cambridge which appeared on some of the Commissioners' churches. Internally, though the roof was steeper and the details medieval, the arrangements were like those in a contemporary chapel of classical guise. There was a gallery on three sides, and the broad central block of pews faced a handsome Gothic pulpit and matching communion rail, behind which a 'chancel' arch enclosed the organ gallery.[111]

Haslingden was one of Wilson's larger chapels, seating more than 1,000, but he also designed very small buildings for the Wesleyans, such as the 100-seat chapel (of 1857) in the Staffordshire village of Alton.[112] This diminutive sandstone chapel, with attractively cusped heads to its small windows, has none of Wilson's

Fig 6.25
Lavington Independent (now United Reformed) chapel, Bideford, Devon, 1856–9 by E M White. Nonconformists were generally unconcerned about the orientation of their chapels, and so could exploit valuable street frontages (here south-facing) regardless of direction.
[DP166197]

Architects working for other denominations also produced wide-spanned and galleried Gothic chapels. The Independents of Bideford, for instance, replaced their late 17th-century meeting house with a new building named Lavington chapel (in memory of a long-serving minister) in 1856–9 (Fig 6.25).[113] The new chapel, designed by E M White, has a gabled façade between twin staircase-towers with needle spires. As a Baptist contribution one might choose Heath Street chapel, Hampstead (of 1860–1, by C G Searle); it employs a similar arrangement, though its turreted staircase towers are busily buttressed and the windows have Decorated rather than Perpendicular tracery.[114] Each chapel has an attractive interior, retaining galleries on cast-iron columns, and an open timber roof (that in Hampstead having hammerbeams); although each has gained a new pulpit and organ ensemble, the spirit of the mid-Victorian buildings has survived.

These chapels, like the Wesleyans' model design, could be described as a translation of the Jenkinsian chapel into Gothic form. Many architects, however, saw this approach as half-hearted, certainly when it came to larger Nonconformist commissions. Some acknowledgement was needed of the fact that aisled structures were an almost universal feature of all but the smallest medieval churches. J P Pritchett and Son of Darlington were among the architects to find a solution, as can be seen in the Baptist chapel they designed for Sansome Walk, Worcester (of 1863–4) (Figs 6.26 and 6.27).[115] Its main roof is steeply pitched, but shallower roofs cover the side aisles. Along the line where the change occurs, the quasi-hammerbeam roof is supported by a row of slender cast-iron columns, very similar to the arrangement at James Simpson's Headingley chapel (*see* Fig 5.34).

In addition to this, the Pritchetts provided transepts – not merely because of the medieval precedent, but also because they afforded an opportunity for more seats near to the pulpit. The principles of a Protestant auditorium were scrupulously observed, since the axially placed pulpit and communion area (with baptistery below) are in full view, and the organ gallery and vestries occupy what might otherwise be called a short chancel. A broad block of open-ended pews fills the centre of the chapel, and there are further pews in the aisles and the west and transept galleries (the planned aisle galleries having not been required). School accommodation was added four years later.[116] With its high roof

elaborate trimmings; the sturdy masonry, plain coping stones and kneelers were designed to withstand the moorland weather. Perhaps Alton's Wesleyans ventured on this replacement for their former chapel, having been emboldened (or shamed?) by the presence of Pugin's showcase buildings elsewhere in the village. The nearer neighbour, however, is the Independents' red-brick Providence chapel of 1845, which sits on the hillside just above, and the juxtaposed examples of classical and Gothic architecture look like an illustration from Pugin's own *Contrasts*.

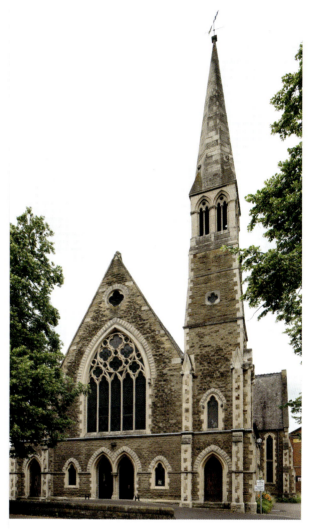

the most of its site. The St Ives chapel sits in a row of buildings, and so its impact is concentrated on the 'west' (actually north-east) front: a large single doorway is placed between a pair of steeply gabled bays with tall windows that have roundels of curvilinear tracery. Over the central bay rises a 150-foot (46m) broach spire with four clock faces. The spire dominates the town's market place and now looks down on a statue of Oliver Cromwell, erected in 1901.

Tarring's north London chapel stands at a crossroads. Its pinnacled tower and spire are set over a side bay by the street junction – thereby giving secondary emphasis to the traceried west window – and provides a more varied side elevation onto Falkland Road, where its school building is also located. The internal treatment also differed from the St Ives Free Church, in particular because the London chapel has a gallery on three sides; it rests on foliated spandrel-brackets and has decoratively panelled timber fronts. Neither building retains all its original fittings, since the St Ives chapel was subdivided around 1980 and the building in Lady Margaret Road has been a Roman Catholic church since 1969.

For Nonconformists the primary advantage of iron columns was that they offered only minimal interference to a chapel's sightlines. A further advantage was that they could be used

Fig 6.26 (left)
Baptist chapel, Worcester, 1863–4 by J P Pritchett and Son. Elaborately Gothic chapels – often with spires – became established in the repertoire of almost all denominations.
[DP164578]

Fig 6.27 (below)
Interior of Baptist chapel, Worcester. With its axial pulpit, central block of pews and provision for galleries, the Pritchetts' design was unequivocally a Protestant auditorium.
[DP164581]

and large west window with Decorated tracery, the chapel is airy and well lit, and the same features – assisted by a small spire – give the building a strong presence in the street.

John Tarring, active in London, was another of the architects who sometimes retained the auditory spirit of Nonconformist worship in Gothic buildings by the use of cast-iron columns in place of bulkier stone arcades. Two of his chapels from the 1860s can illustrate this point: the Free Church (of 1863–4), commissioned by a congregation of Independents and Baptists in St Ives, Huntingdonshire and the formerly Wesleyan chapel (of 1863–7) in Lady Margaret Road, north London.[117] Both are steeply roofed, without transepts or discrete aisle roofs, but with cross-gables to gain height for the side windows. Internally each roof is supported by arch-braced timbers on a series of barley-sugar, cast-iron columns that were strong enough also to support galleries. Externally each was designed to make

had influenced church architects from Pugin to Tarring, nor yet to the patterned Italian brick-work that had inspired Street and Cranston, but rather to plainer forms. Paired and tripled lancet windows, augmented by a few small, round-headed openings, take us back to the earliest stages of pointed architecture, while the coni-cally roofed turret explicitly connects the design with early French Gothic, a taste first champi-oned by William Burges a decade earlier.

There were some Nonconformists who whole-heartedly embraced the architectural programme of the ecclesiologists, including chancels, central gangways and off-centre pulpits, and for whom the use of galleries and cast-iron columns was unacceptable. Easily the most ambitious instance is the church of Christ the King in Gordon Square, Holborn, now partly used by the University of London's chaplaincy, but built for the Catholic Apostolic Church – which, although Noncon-formist, had come a very long way from its Presbyterian roots. Even without the full length of its planned nave or 300-foot (91m) spire, this slumbering giant of a building (of 1851–3, by Raphael Brandon) is of cathedral size, and has a complete sequence of side aisles, crossing and transepts, with a further chapel – currently the Lady Chapel – beyond the chancel.[129] Without the need for galleries, the high arcades carry a tri-forium tier below the clerestories and, while the nave has a hammerbeam roof with carved angels, the chancel has a full stone vault. The Catholic Apostolic Church, whose rituals were alien to Protestants and whose theology was heretical to Catholics, was by this date far from the main-stream of Nonconformity, and the building in Gordon Square represents one end of the spec-trum of English religious architecture in the 19th century.[130] Unitarians also continued to erect Gothic buildings for worship of a liturgical char-acter, however, following the example of their Gee Cross chapel (see pp 128–9).

Todmorden, a town that once straddled the Yorkshire–Lancashire boundary, has one un-missable place of worship, the Unitarian chapel of 1865–9 by John Gibson (Figs 6.30 and 6.31).[131] From the first glimpse of its fine spire, half way up the hillside, one's interest is whetted. Unlike Gibson's Romanesque design for the Bloomsbury Baptists, this is Gothic in full flower, combining something of the solidity of his Anglican church at Shenstone, Stafford-shire (of 1852–3) with a touch of the fragile beauty of his renowned 'Marble Church' at Bodelwyddan (of 1856–60). Like each of those other churches, this has separately ridged side aisles, a rose window above the entrance and Decorated Gothic tracery. Its crocketed spire – as at Bodelwyddan – seems to derive from Northamptonshire's medieval examples. Tod-morden's Anglican churches cannot compete with this landmark of a building and, to under-line its claim to supremacy, the chapel tower has an illuminated clock and a peal of eight bells. All told it cost almost £30,000 (roughly seven times

the cost of the nearby Commissioners' church), funded by the Unitarian sons of John Fielden – the reforming MP and mill-owner who had been a leading member of the congregation and had helped to finance its previous building.[132]

The new building, commissioned because the Sunday school had grown to fill the old one, is part of a chain of scholarly Gothic chapels built by the Unitarians from Liverpool to Leeds. Internally it slightly resembles the 1846–8 example at Gee Cross (see Fig 5.38), but the vista is longer – aided by a central gangway along the nave and leading between choir stalls into the chancel to culminate in a large, stained-glass window above the communion table. The transepts, so prominent externally, play no part in the congregational space: one was intended as a mortuary chapel and the other houses the organ and vestry. From the nave most worshippers could see the minister at the reading desk or in the pulpit (which stand either side of the chancel arch), but sturdy marble columns block the view from many parts of the side aisles, while the choir might be heard but was hardly seen by any of the congregation. At the front of the left-hand aisle, where an Anglo-Catholic church might have set up a side altar, is a generous space for the gem-like font. The timber roof of the nave gives way to lierne vaulting in the chancel. Despite the clerestory windows – externally unseen – and tiny openings higher in the roof, the light levels foster a sense of religious mystery, augmented by the stained and coloured glass. Materials were of the best: oak, stone and marble, each carved with a high degree of craftsmanship.[133] An account of the opening service records that 'the scholars and teachers assembled in the old *Chapel* and marched across to the *Church*' [my italics], where the eminent visiting preacher William Gaskell reassured his audience that it was valid for art to be used to enhance religion so long as one's inner sincerity had not been compromised.[134]

During the second half of the 19th century it almost came to be expected that a new Unitarian chapel (in England, at least) would be Gothic, and often that meant having a nave, chancel and side aisles. A more liturgical form of worship and an openness to the role of art were perhaps a reaction to the criticism that theirs was an arid, rational faith. The Manchester architect Thomas Worthington, himself a Unitarian, rebuilt a number of significant chapels for the denomination, including among them Brookfield church (of 1869–71) at Gorton in east Manchester.[135] Its benefactor was Richard Peacock, who wished to provide a Nonconformist place of worship for the workers at his Gorton foundry, just as his partner Charles Beyer was doing for Anglican worship.[136] The interior is more open than that at Todmorden; above its large chancel arch is a mural of angels, while the whitewashed walls of the nave have medallion portraits of Wycliffe, Erasmus, Priestley and King Arthur, among others.[137] Rather as at Todmorden there is a commanding spire to one side, with a peal of eight bells, while in the burial ground is an impressive shrine of white limestone to Richard Peacock.

Another notable example of Unitarian Gothic from these years is the former chapel in High Pavement, Nottingham (of 1874–6, by Stuart Colman of Bristol).[138] In this tall and airy building

Fig 6.31
Interior of Unitarian chapel, Todmorden. The rich architectural effects may have been intended, at least in part, to counter accusations that Unitarianism was aridly rational.
[DP169329]

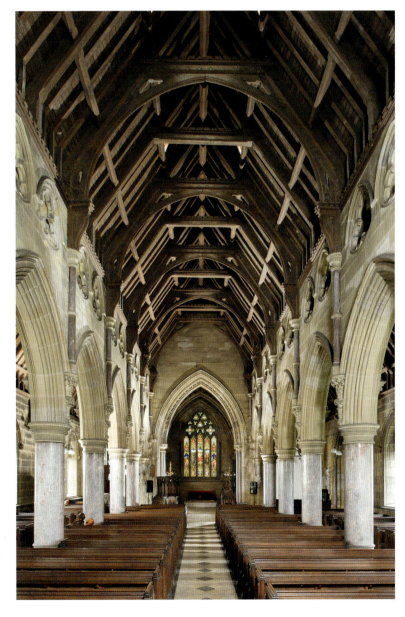

the spirit of corporate worship was facilitated by using the short chancel only for communion, keeping the choir as well as the pulpit in the nave and setting the transept pews at right angles to the building's main axis. Colman's Gothic is less orthodox than Worthington's or Gibson's, as can be seen from the muscular tower that faces High Pavement, but he is rather more representative of the propensity of later Victorian architects to adapt medieval prototypes to Nonconformist needs. The chapel's major treasure is the great chancel window, splendidly filled with Morris & Co glass in 1904, most of the 21 figures being designed by Burne-Jones. It is tempting to describe it as the east window, but it actually faces south-west. Even those Nonconformists who were committed to Gothic principles tended to be pragmatic on the question of orientation.

Medieval styles: innovative plan-forms

In most places chapel-goers were less willing than their Anglican counterparts to sit behind large columns in side aisles. As early as the 1850s some chapels were built with narrow side aisles that were merely passageways, giving access to the main body of pews. Such a scheme, for a now demolished Presbyterian church in London, attracted the attention of *The Builder* when the drawings were exhibited at the Royal Academy.[139] A similar arrangement was employed a little earlier at the Congregationalists' new Square chapel, Halifax (of 1855–7, by Joseph James), a spectacular piece of architecture that was damaged by fire in 1970 and largely demolished.[140] What caught the eye of most commentators about the Halifax building was its exterior – Rodney Hubbuck described it as 'an astonishing swashbuckling pastiche' of the east end of Selby Abbey and Pugin's spire at Cheadle – but its plan was no less remarkable.[141] Here was a broad, high nave with transepts and, in lieu of a chancel, an organ recess behind the central pulpit: in effect, a T-shaped layout. With raked galleries in the transepts and another across the entrance end, the chapel was kept virtually free of columns, ensuring that everyone could see the pulpit. A broad body of pews (with doors) and two side blocks occupied the ground floor, and gangways were arranged to provide access to the pews rather than to create processional routes to the communion area. Both the quality of the Gothic work and the practical provision for a congrega-

tion of up to 1,300 were admired, and it was reported that the architect's aim had been 'so to adapt the forms and details of Gothic architecture as to make them conform to the requirements of the form of worship used by the Congregationalists'.[142] Since the fire that gutted the building in 1970, the astounding tower and spire have been retained as a landmark, and with them part of one transept and a fragment of the nave wall and side aisle – sufficient to remind the world of the chapel's innovative plan-form.

During the second half of the 19th century an increasing number of architects adapted medieval architectural forms to the needs of their Nonconformist clients. Sometimes the restrictions of an urban site were the trigger for inventive solutions, as in the case of the relatively narrow plot of land in Jewry Street, Winchester, on which a 1,000-seat Independent (now joint Methodist and United Reformed) chapel and large school opened in 1853.[143] Deprived of the opportunity of side lighting, the architect (W F Poulton of Reading) was unable to consider creating a basement schoolroom, and he thus placed the two facilities in tandem, with the chapel fronting the street. The tall, gabled façade, its height originally matched by four pinnacles, distinguishes the place of worship from its classical neighbours, and a pair of canted bays hints at the unusual shape of the chapel: an elongated octagon. Grasping the long-acknowledged advantages of octagons for congregational worship, Poulton provided an unusually tall variant (Fig 6.32). This allowed room for two tiers of gallery (though only one was constructed) and made the most of Gothic's verticality with an arcade of lancet arches on compound piers, above which a forest of timbers rose to support a boarded ceiling and a central lantern.

Despite a modern subdivision of the chapel, involving a new floor at gallery level and the creation of a dais on one of the long sides, there is still something uplifting about the space.[144] The architecture is strong enough, and the proportions tall enough, to withstand a little of such treatment. Beneath the galleries on the longest sides ran two corridors, which gave direct access to the rear schools from side doors on the street front. The schoolroom was another largely toplit hall, with classrooms, vestry and apartments for the master and caretaker above. Poulton was a capable planner of Nonconformist buildings, and the Winchester scheme was soon taken up, almost in its entirety, for a French Congregational church in St Helier, Jersey.[145]

The shape of the Jewry Street chapel was partly a pragmatic response to constraints of the site and partly a return to the ideal centralised plans which had a noble pedigree in religious architecture. Each of these impulses can be traced in Nonconformist buildings over the following decades, almost invariably in Gothic or Romanesque designs. Fan-shaped chapels were sometimes suggested by tapering sites, an early instance being Percy chapel, Bath (now Elim Pentecostal), built in 1854–5 to the designs of H E and A Goodridge, with a long Lombardic façade that gives no clue as to the building's irregular hexagonal layout.[146] More externally expressive was the short-lived Ancoats Congregational chapel, Manchester (1861–5, by Alfred Waterhouse).[147] The building filled the wedge of land in the acute angle between two streets and had a prominent tower and broach spire at the street junction. In both Bath and Ancoats the

Fig 6.32
Interior of Jewry Street Independent (now joint Methodist and United Reformed) chapel, Winchester, 1853 by W F Poulton. The chapel was designed with room for a second tier of galleries, which were never needed. Since this photograph was taken, however, the interior has been divided horizontally.
[BB77/00305]

Fig 6.33 (right)
St George, Tufnell Park,
London, 1865–8 by George
Truefitt. Recently rescued
from dereliction, the
building now houses the
House on the Rock church
(see Fig 8.42), for whom
additional rooms have been
erected alongside.
[DP151598]

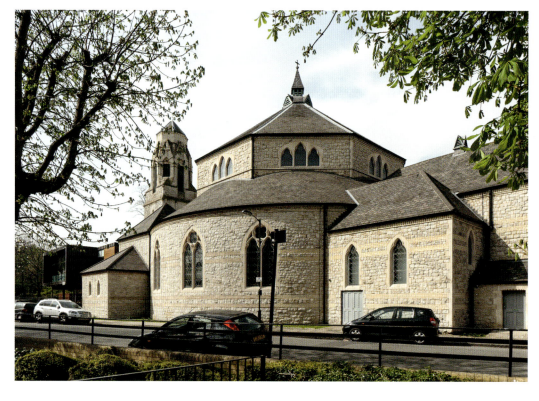

Fig 6.34 (below)
St George, Tufnell Park,
London. Designed by
Truefitt in his capacity as
surveyor to the Tufnell Park
estate, and built for a
congregation that seceded
from the Anglican Church.
[DP151593]

pulpit and communion table stood at the narrow end of the site, with an angled arrangement of pews and gallery filling the splayed auditorium. This eminently practical design was not unlike one created when the Diorama in Park Square, Regent's Park was converted into a Baptist chapel by John Thomas in 1854–5.[148]

Meanwhile other architects devised variations on the octagon, understating the Gothic ornament in order to emphasise the shape. Harecourt Congregational chapel, Islington (of 1855–6, by W G and E Habershon) combined elements of a Greek cross with an essentially octagonal plan, and the formerly Congregational chapel in Charlotte Street, Carlisle (of 1860 by Ralph Nicolson) has a bold octagonal core, from which subsidiary blocks extend along the narrow site.[149] In 1865–8 in Tufnell Park, north London a congregation which hovered between Anglicanism and the Free Church of England built an octagonal preaching church (architect George Truefitt).[150] The building was ringed by a circular ambulatory and possessed a long chancel and detached tower, all fitted on to a sharply angled corner plot (Figs 6.33 and 6.34). Its predecessor (of 1858) was a temporary wooden building, circular in plan, also by Truefitt. It cannot be coincidental that many of these unusual plan-forms were selected for awkward sites. Yet it also seems likely that architects were beginning to cast around for prototypes – from the earliest Christian shrines to contemporary foreign churches – which could serve the needs of congregational worship better than the linear and hierarchical layouts favoured by ecclesiologists.[151]

In 1859–60 an oval Congregational chapel was built in Bishop's Stortford, designed by W F Poulton of Reading (designer of the Winchester chapel), who was by then working jointly with W H Woodman.[152] The plan is not truly elliptical, since a section of each side wall is straight, but the curved ends dominate one's impression of the chapel and serve – like the elliptical churches and chapels of the 18th century – to shape the congregation into a united body of worshippers. As with the Presbyterian building of 1781–3 in Belfast, the pulpit is set on the long axis. Two tiers of galleries sweep around all but the pulpit end of the chapel, and even the ground-floor pews are curved in sympathy. A variant of this scheme was used by Poulton and Woodman at Lozells in Birmingham (1862–3; demolished after bomb damage in the Second World War), with the notable substitution of chairs for pews, and with a more classical front in which the curved wall of the auditorium was framed by a grand, pedimented portico.[153]

Then, in 1863–5, came the *magnum opus* of this group, Westminster Chapel. Twice the size of its forerunners (with 2,500 seats), even discounting its extensive lecture hall and ancillary rooms, Westminster Chapel was built for the eloquent Congregational minister Samuel Martin, whose preaching had attracted capacity attendances at the first chapel (of 1841) on this site in Buckingham Gate.[154] The façade, an essay in Lombardic Romanesque, accompanied by a corner tower and spire (the latter unfortunately scaled down before the Second World War) gives little away, and only a careful look down the side street betrays the chapel's curved shape. However, the interior that Poulton created for Samuel Martin is one of central London's hidden glories, a little-altered tribute to the princes of the Victorian pulpit and to the architectural skills which they fostered.

No other surviving building can match this amphitheatre of Nonconformity (Fig 6.35). The main gallery – a kind of dress circle – encircles

Fig 6.35
Interior of Westminster Chapel (Congregational, now independent evangelical), London, 1863–5 by W F Poulton. One of the great Nonconformist amphitheatres, the building is a testament to High Victorian preaching. [DP155982]

the entire space, while upper galleries are wrapped around each side of the chapel; all are designed to turn attention to the preacher's circular rostrum and the communion area in front. From the entrance the ground floor slopes gently down to the rostrum, with pews radiating like widening ripples on a pond. As at Spurgeon's Tabernacle the focus was essentially on the preacher, but after Martin's death the organ was moved from its eyrie above the entrance to fill the gallery behind the rostrum, creating what Nairn called an oratorio hall.[155] The high ceiling was said to have the second widest span in London (after that in the Royal Italian Opera House, Covent Garden), while the interior has a generosity of scale quite different from Poulton's preceding chapels – especially in the galleries. In addition, as with most chapels, this great place of worship accommodated a host of other social and educational facilities, including a lecture hall for 600, a school building (of 1843, part of Martin's first building campaign) and a suite of vestries and meeting rooms.

Despite Ian Nairn's generous judgement that Westminster Chapel represents 'the true reli-gious architecture of the nineteenth century', architectural history has largely ignored it.[156] Yet it was part of a movement which attracted even leading Ecclesiologists, including Street, who in 1864 seemed to advocate 'domical churches' and 'vast circular naves'.[157] Around the same time (and possibly under the influence of Beres-ford Hope), the talented young architect E W Godwin designed a 'modern cathedral' with an elliptical nave, but the Church of England failed to warm to such a proposal.[158] For the Noncon-formists there was George Bidlake's pattern-book design for a circular chapel, published in 1865.[159] Poulton's Westminster Chapel was more widely known, however – if only through its appear-ance in *The Builder* – and may have influenced the plan-forms of such American places of wor-ship as the large Fifth Avenue Presbyterian church, New York (1875, by Carl Pfeiffer) and the Methodist Episcopal church, Baltimore (1883–7, by McKim, Mead and White, known as the mother church of American Methodism), each of which has a nearly oval auditorium within a more conventional layout.[160]

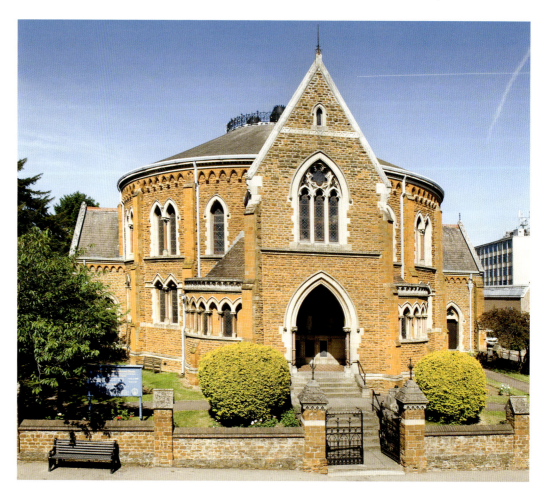

Fig 6.36
Congregational (now United Reformed) chapel, Wellingborough, Northamptonshire, 1874–5 by Edward Sharman and Caleb Archer. With its gabled Gothic porch, the exterior only hints at the nature of the interior space.
[DP081002]

Meanwhile Britain's most extraordinary oval chapel was built in High Street, Wellingborough for Congregationalists in 1874–5 (Figs 6.36 and 6.37).[161] Its egg-shaped plan, devised by Caleb Archer and adopted in all essentials by his senior fellow-architect Edward Sharman, could possibly be seen to symbolise the rebirth of the church following the healing of a rift between two congregations in 1873.[162] Regardless of this, however, the shape is ideal for congregational worship, with the organ, pulpit and communion area at the pointed end of the egg and the pews fanning out in the more rounded body of the chapel, below a serpentine gallery that follows the generous curve. Fold-out seating in the cross-gangways provides accommodation for extra worshippers (Fig 6.38). Aided by a sloping floor, sightlines are excellent, and the acoustics were also found to be faultless. Hermann Muthesius reproduced the plan of the Wellingborough building for his German readers in 1901, and in 1925 Ernest Drew called the layout 'probably the most original, daring, and – we can now confidently add – successful experiment in Free Church architecture in this country'.[163] In 1899 new choir stalls were installed (facing the congregation rather than at right angles, college-wise), along with a new pulpit, and about 14 years later small organ cases were installed each side of the main organ, further enriching

the area above the choir. Because one of the older chapels was retained nearby for Sunday-school purposes, the new chapel's only ancillary accommodation is a pair of vestries.

Caleb Archer's plan might take its place in a history of the baroque, but the chapel is largely Gothic in its details – a combination which works well enough inside, but creates some awkward moments externally. By contrast, the great oval building of King's Weigh House chapel (1888–93; now a Ukranian Catholic cathedral) in Duke Street, London, which Waterhouse designed for a distinguished Congregational church, has a commanding Romanesque exterior.[164] Inside, however, its rigidly linear ground-floor seating has always seemed to deny the logic of the plan. Despite this disparity, the King's Weigh House chapel also caught the imagination of Hermann

Fig 6.37
Interior of Congregational chapel, Wellingborough. Caleb Archer's plan produced a space unparalleled in British religious architecture, admired for both its originality and practicality. [DP081003]

Fig 6.38
Congregational chapel, Wellingborough. Fold-out seats in the cross-gangway were a useful feature, as chapels often attracted huge attendances for such special events as the Sunday-school anniversary. [DP080995]

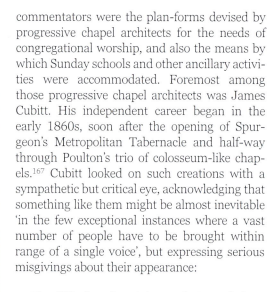

Muthesius, who published no fewer than five illustrations (including two plans) of it.[165]

By the end of the 19th century, the architecture of the English Nonconformist churches was of growing interest to foreign observers – people who had not been taught to regard the Nonconformists as being below the salt. As Karl Fritsch – editor of *Deutsche Bauzeitung* and secretary of the Union of Berlin Architects – reported in 1893, 'the church buildings of the sects offer even more stimulus to the architect than do the places of worship of the Anglican church'.[166] What principally interested such

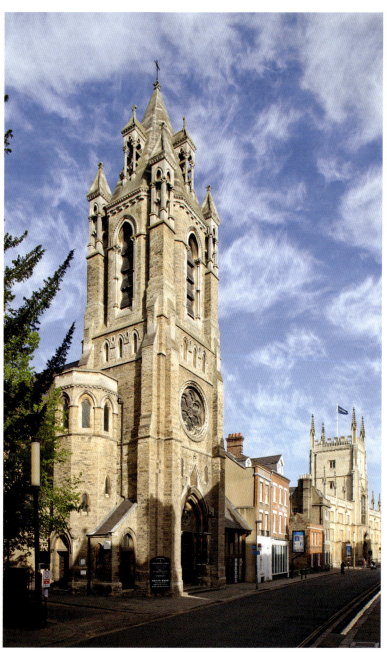

Fig 6.39
Emmanuel Congregational (now United Reformed) church, Cambridge, 1872–4 by James Cubitt. Although primarily concerned to create an interior with good sightlines, Cubitt was also determined that his building should have an impact on the city's skyline. [DP160132]

commentators were the plan-forms devised by progressive chapel architects for the needs of congregational worship, and also the means by which Sunday schools and other ancillary activities were accommodated. Foremost among those progressive chapel architects was James Cubitt. His independent career began in the early 1860s, soon after the opening of Spurgeon's Metropolitan Tabernacle and half-way through Poulton's trio of colosseum-like chapels.[167] Cubitt looked on such creations with a sympathetic but critical eye, acknowledging that something like them might be almost inevitable 'in the few exceptional instances where a vast number of people have to be brought within range of a single voice', but expressing serious misgivings about their appearance:

> The difficulty of retaining ecclesiastical character in such a type is evident enough. However convenient, it would be hard to make it beautiful, and even its convenience has certainly been overrated.[168]

As the reference to 'ecclesiastical character' might suggest, Cubitt wanted chapels that were dignified and strong, not ones that were (like so many theatres) all masonry outside and cast iron within. Conversely he had little time for the standard Anglican church, in which half of the aisle seats gave no view of the pulpit: 'No one designing at first hand a hall in which a few hundred people should listen to a speaker, would put two rows of columns down the middle of it.'[169] Writing first in the *Building News* and then in his book, *Church Design for Congregations* (1870), Cubitt argued that architectural decorousness was wholly compatible with the needs of Protestant worship.[170] He went on to provide a stimulatingly wide selection of potentially suitable historic plans, including Islamic, Byzantine, Romanesque and Gothic examples.

During the 1870s Cubitt designed a sequence of chapels, large and small, in which some of these ideas were worked through. Most challenging was the commission for a substantial Congregational chapel (of 1872–4; to be known as Emmanuel church) on a narrow site in Trumpington Street, Cambridge (Fig 6.39).[171] Here Cubitt could hardly avoid having a basilican arrangement. He therefore developed one of his 'plans with few columns', involving two large arches in the main arcade and so only one column to interrupt the view from either of the ungalleried side aisles. There is an apse for the communion table, and the pulpit stands to one side of what would otherwise be called the chancel arch; the organ and vestry transepts have little impact on the internal space. Externally the chapel makes its mark on Trumpington Street with a vigorous entrance tower.

The assured appearance of the new Emmanuel church – stylistically indebted to early French Gothic, especially Coutances Cathedral – seems almost calculated to deflect Matthew Arnold's forthright attack on the cultural deficiencies of Nonconformists and to celebrate the recent law which opened the university to non-Anglicans.[172] For the smaller Baptist chapel (of 1875–6) at Bourton-on-the-Water, Gloucestershire there was a site with more room for manoeuvre; here Cubitt's aisleless cruciform plan ensured that the commanding pulpit could be seen from every seat.[173] The only columns are set in the re-entrant angles, and the gallery spans the entrance end, leaving the central space more open. Both in Bourton and in Cambridge, the schoolrooms were built behind the chapel.

It was with the great Union Chapel, Islington (of 1875–7; Congregational, now United Reformed), however, that Cubitt was able to deploy his ideas about centralised spaces most fully (Figs 6.40 and 6.41).[174] An aerial view reveals that Union Chapel has a Greek-cross-and-octagon plan, not unlike that of Harecourt chapel (which stood only a few minutes' walk away), although Cubitt's declared inspiration was the small Byzantine church of Santa Fosca, Torcello.[175] However, the visitor is less likely to be conscious of such sources, and more likely to be taken by the originality of Cubitt's work. Union Chapel's memorable brick interior is created around a slightly elongated octagon of Bath stone columns, from which Gothic arches rise to

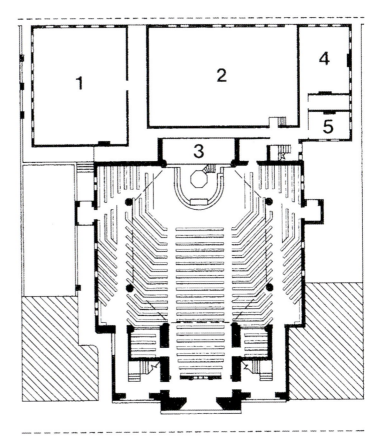

Fig 6.40 (below left)
Union Chapel (Congregational, now United Reformed), Islington, London, 1875–7 by James Cubitt. Behind the massive tower one can glimpse the octagonal roof of the main worship space.
[DP151710]

Fig 6.41 (below)
Union Chapel, Islington, London. This simplified plan of the interior shows the care taken to avoid placing seats behind columns, and also the importance of the school-rooms and lecture hall.
Key: 1 Lecture hall (first floor); 2 Sunday school; 3 Organ; 4 Classroom; 5 Vestry.
[Based on a plan published in The Builder, 29 March 1878, and additional measurements taken in 1991 by Survey of London]

Fig 6.42
Interior of Union Chapel,
Islington, London. It is a
tribute to Cubitt's design
that the chapel now
functions as effectively for
concerts as for services
(hence the temporary stage
over the communion area).
[DP151727]

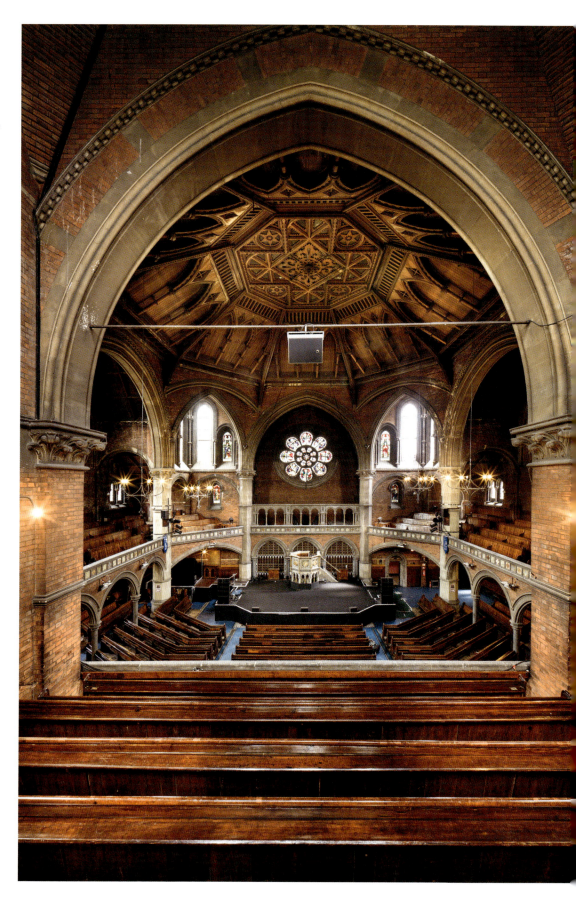

the roof (Fig 6.42). The pulpit and communion table stand in full view, facing the entrance and in front of one bay of the octagon. The almost square ground floor is filled with blocks of open-ended pews, angled and sloping gently to the pulpit, while raked galleries occupy seven bays of the octagon, not compromising the great central space. Everything possible is done to secure good views, and where necessary the gangways are arranged radially behind pillars so that no seat is obscured. It says much about Cubitt's careful planning that the chapel can now operate as a prime venue for concerts and stage productions, as well as maintaining its religious function. From the outset music filled a particularly important role in the worship here, but the minister (Henry Allon, who published several collections of hymns, psalms and anthems for Congregationalists) did not want the organ to be visually dominant.[176] As a result the Willis organ sits behind the pulpit, acoustically well placed but hidden from view by a wrought-iron screen.

The main space of Union Chapel is at once thrilling and dignified, and Cubitt was careful to avoid loading it with ornament. He allowed stained glass (of angel musicians by Frederick Drake of Exeter) in the east-facing rose window; marble is used sparingly for some subsidiary columns and for decorative panels on the gallery fronts as well as on the pulpit. Characteristically for large chapels of the time, there was an efficient system of heating (using large pipes in underfloor ducts) and ventilation (on the Tobin system). More notably, electric light was installed at the earliest opportunity (in 1881).[177] At the rear of the site, and with separate entrances from Compton Avenue, there is a full suite of accommodation for the many social and educational activities organised by the chapel. For the Sunday school Cubitt created a galleried hall, with curtained-off classrooms on the Akron principle that had been pioneered in America a decade earlier.[178] Union Chapel was one of the stars in Hermann Muthesius's survey of English church architecture in 1901; even the anti-Victorian writer Martin Briggs thought it a 'clever and original design'.[179] Though never as spectacular externally as some other major chapels of the time (its tower was eventually completed in 1889, without the full spire that had been first intended), Union Chapel is one of the buildings which helped to secure international attention for Nonconformist architecture.

By the late 1870s the revival of interest in central plans for churches began to gather momentum.[180] The Swedish architect Emil Viktor Langlet, who published a book on the subject in 1879, designed 12 such churches, including the Caroli Kyrka, Malmö (1879–80), which uses a variant of the octagon-and-Greek-cross formula.[181] Among German architects, too, there was growing enthusiasm for this kind of scheme. In the 1877–8 competition for the Peterskirche in Leipzig, elaborate octagonal designs were submitted by two entrants, and even the winner of the second prize incorporated an octagonal central space in his more linear scheme.[182] From the steady stream of subsequent examples, one might select the Dankeskirche in Weddingplatz, Berlin (1882–4, by August Orth) – another combination of the Greek cross and octagon – and the simpler octagonal church at Nietleben, near Halle (1884–6, by Otto Kilburger).[183]

Among the surviving British examples is Melbourne Hall (Fig 6.43) (1879–81, by Goddard and Paget) – a striking, red-brick lantern of a building erected as an evangelical power station in a working-class part of Leicester for the

Fig 6.43
Melbourne Hall (now Evangelical Free Church), Leicester, 1879–81 by Goddard and Paget. Built for F B Meyer, an important Baptist evangelist, the octagonal shape was designed to catch the eye at a busy road junction.
[© Geoff Brandwood]

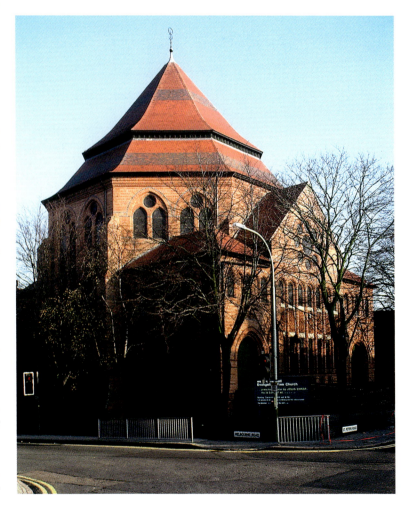

extraordinary F B Meyer, a gentlemanly Baptist preacher and social activist.[184] Its steep octagonal roof dominates the building's silhouette, although the internal arrangement only partly realises the potential of the shape. While the fenestration is nascent Gothic, the intention was clearly to avoid too ecclesiastical an appearance. The chapel itself is raised over a large lecture hall and classrooms, and at the rear are three floors of classrooms (erected in 1884), giving the whole building a considerable presence at a busy crossroads: 'On winter evenings, when lighted up, it would seem as though some giant, striding across the country had, for a moment, set down his huge lantern at the junction of four roads from one of which the building derives its name.'[185]

No less notable is Gustav Adolfs Kyrka (of 1883–4, by W D Caröe), the Swedish seamen's church in Liverpool (Fig 6.44), which has an octagonal pyramid roof and four short arms rising from a square plan.[186] The gallery and pew-plan here echoed the octagonal core of the chapel's shape, but the pulpit was set to one side of the communion apse, which occupied the central axis. Externally the use of distinctively Nordic details – most especially the neo-Viking finials, just then being revived in Oslo by Holm Munthe as part of a national 'Dragon style' – suggest that Caröe was in touch with contemporary developments in Scandinavia, but the plan may have owed as much to Cubitt as to Langlet.[187] Either way Gustav Adolfs Kyrka can be seen to mark a renewal of the long-established architectural link between continental Protestants (in this case Lutherans) and English Nonconformity.

Both Melbourne Hall and Gustav Adolfs Kyrka were intended to catch the eye by their very shape. Not all chapels of these years, however, were as radical in their outward form as in

Fig 6.44
Gustav Adolfs Kyrka (Lutheran), Liverpool, 1883–4 by W D Caröe. The design by the Anglo-Danish architect Caröe embodies the link between Nonconformity and continental Protestant church building. [AA040906]

their internal arrangements. A case in point is St James's Congregational (now United Reformed) church, Newcastle upon Tyne (1882–4, by T L Banks) – a building which might at first sight be taken for a stately Anglican church in an Early English style, complete with transepts, flying buttresses and crossing tower (Fig 6.45).[188] Indeed, on its opening in 1884 the church was described by the local paper as the 'Nonconformist Cathedral', implicitly grouping it with Pugin's St Mary's (the Roman Catholic cathedral since 1850) and the medieval St Nicholas (elevated to cathedral status as recently as 1882).[189] Once inside, however, there is no mistaking the Reformed nature of St James's. There is no chancel and no altar; instead attention is focused on the canopied wooden pulpit, before which stands the communion table. The plan is that of a modified Greek cross and the blocks of pews are angled towards the pulpit, with radial gangways occupying the blindspots behind the four widely spaced stone piers that carry the tower (Fig 6.46). Apart from a small gallery above the entrance, all the seating is on the (level) ground floor: further galleries were allowed for, but the need was never compelling.

Compared with the fully galleried, octagonal space of Union Chapel, the interior of St James's is hardly thrilling. Yet it is nonetheless an impressive product of what might be called the Cubitt school of thinking – being at once a plan with few columns and with a large central area,

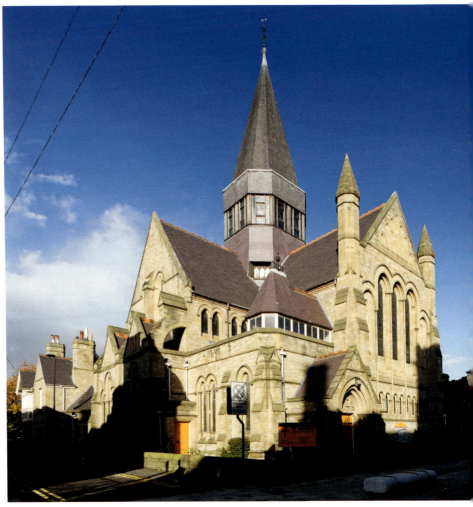

two of the basic concepts in Cubitt's analysis of Nonconformist needs.[190] And it was in turn to attract international interest. Illustrations of St James's appeared in at least three German publications, and are credibly thought to have inspired the plan of Lars Sonck's radical new Lutheran church (later cathedral) of St John, Tampere, Finland in 1900–7.[191] What Sonck seems to have found in Banks's work was a way of liberating church plans from the columned-nave-and-side-aisles formula that he had previously used, and a means of making the pulpit 'the fulcrum of the whole design' without sacrificing the appearance of strength and solidity: Cubitt's lesson, in fact.[192] One aspect that Sonck did not follow, however, was the treatment of ancillary accommodation. The Tampere church includes a basement hall and other rooms, whereas at St James's the vestries and parlour were constructed behind the chapel (in a robust but deliberately domestic style) alongside the extensive Sunday school, with 20

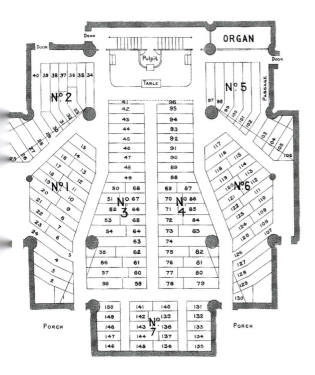

Fig 6.45 (above)
St James's Congregational (now United Reformed) church, Newcastle upon Tyne, 1882–4 by T L Banks. The lantern tower of this substantial building was originally of stone, with small flying buttresses to support the spire. At the rear of the church is an extensive suite of schoolrooms and domestic-looking vestries.
[DP156999]

Fig 6.46 (left)
St James's Congregational church, Newcastle upon Tyne. The compact plan was intended, like Cubitt's, to give everyone a clear view of the pulpit.

classrooms on the Akron principle. This desire to express all the chapel's functions – worship, educational and social – as distinct but closely connected parts of an architectural whole had long precedents in Nonconformity, and was again the preferred option for progressive designers such as Cubitt and Banks.

Another chapel whose plan reached an international audience is Abbey Congregational (now United Reformed) church, Romsey, Hants (Fig 6.47).[193] It dates from 1885–8 and was designed by Paull and Bonella, the architects of several distinguished Nonconformist works including the Queen Anne-style chapel in Upper Street, Islington (of 1887–8; *see* Fig 6.19). In replacing a late Georgian chapel in Romsey, Paull and Bonella grasped the opportunity to make something of the adjacent medieval gatehouse, and took on the formidable challenge of creating a building which could, in Pevsner's words, 'hold its own' against the town's venerable Norman abbey.[194] There was also the problem of a stream, which had undercut the foundations of the existing chapel. Paull and Bonella treated the stream as a moat, and the lower part of the chapel at this point is a battlemented wall with just a few small windows. Set well back from this is a tall clerestory, filled with Perpendicular tracery, while a giant, eight-light window in matching style illuminates the chapel from the street end. The gatehouse was incorporated fully into the composition and given a nicely calculated pepper pot

Fig 6.47 (above)
Abbey Congregational
(now United Reformed)
church, Romsey, Hampshire,
1885–8 by Paull and
Bonella. Sensitively
integrated into the medieval
gatehouse, the new building
overcame the challenges
of an awkward site.
[DP166285]

Fig 6.48 (right)
Interior of Abbey
Congregational church,
Romsey. Although the
central gangway and
recessed galleries are
departures from common
Nonconformist practice,
the central placing of
the pulpit reasserts the
Protestant tradition.
[DP166278]

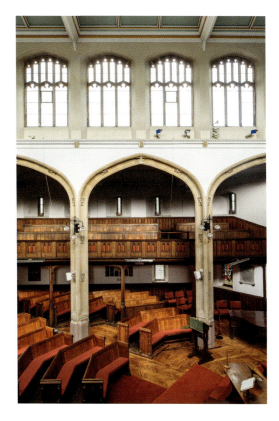

two shallowly chamfered corners (a response to the natural shape of the stream outside); the organ and pulpit occupy the apex of this space (Fig 6.48). Although the chapel is notionally divided into a nave and side aisles by twin arcades of stone pillars, the ground-floor pews cut across such logic by being arranged in a wide arc of concentric lines with the gangways radiating behind the pillars (Fig 6.49). Paull had first used curved pews in a Gothic chapel more than a decade before, but their appearance here is more unexpected.[197]

Fig 6.49
Interior of Abbey Congregational church, Romsey. The seating plan subtly cuts across the logic of nave and side aisles by angling the pews towards the pulpit.
[DP166282]

Conclusion

By the 1880s, largely unnoticed by the Anglican world, the most progressive of the architects who specialised in Nonconformist work were consistently producing designs of international significance. Nonconformity continued to encompass a very broad range of attitudes to faith and practice, however, and its buildings naturally reflected such pluralism. The tiny, astylar chapel of Zoar in Norwich was part of a Baptist continuum that also included Spurgeon's phenomenal Metropolitan Tabernacle, while the Wren-like Hinde Street chapel in London's West End was part of the same Wesleyan connexion as James Wilson's little Gothic building in Alton. These contrasts of scale, style and plan would seem natural in, say, Victorian railway stations, but can seem odd to someone expecting more consistent characteristics, such as the Church of England was then closer to achieving. Yet it was the overall absence of orthodoxy that kept refreshing Nonconformist architecture during the later Victorian years, and in many respects gave it an edge over Anglican developments.

turret. Everywhere the masonry is of local field flints with Bath stone dressings, and there are exposed timbers in the gables of the gatehouse and chapel.

It is a sensitive and yet creative design, avoiding competition with the neighbouring abbey in its materials, style and composition. Even Pevsner – not always noted for his generous treatment of Nonconformist buildings – thought it 'an outstandingly good job'.[195] What captured overseas attention at the time, however, was the plan.[196] The main space for worship is almost pentagonal, consisting of a wide rectangle with

7

The Nonconformist heyday?
1890–1914

The Nonconformist denominations entered the 20th century with the wind in their sails. Membership numbers were still increasing, almost across the board. Altogether the different strands of Methodism rose from 702,411 members in 1896 to 800,234 in 1906, and even the Quakers (whose small numbers had declined in the mid-Victorian era) grew from 16,102 in 1891 to 19,612 in 1911.[1] The Nonconformist conscience was a force to be reckoned with in political life, and a record number of Nonconformists entered parliament in the Liberal landslide of 1906.[2] Nonconformist influence was also to be seen in other areas of public life: the new national gallery of British art on Millbank (opened in 1897) became synonymous with its Unitarian donor Sir Henry Tate, while in the field of social reform the Cadburys and Rowntrees (both Quaker families) and the future Lord Leverhulme (a Congregationalist) were prominent.

Nonconformists were also becoming accustomed to the notion of their collective identity. During the 1890s hundreds of local Free Church councils had been established, and from 1896 there was a fully constituted National Council of Evangelical Free Churches.[3] The very name, Free Churches, gave a positive impression, in contrast to the negative associations of Dissent and Nonconformity. Throughout all this, chapel building continued at an impressive rate; the annual publications of the various denominations grew fat with illustrations of the latest chapels. A new generation of specialist architects emerged whose work was generally more enterprising than that of their Anglican counterparts, and, as the new century began, Hermann Muthesius was at the German embassy in London, studying the architecture of the Nonconformist churches.[4]

Not everything was plain sailing, however. Despite rising numbers of members, Nonconformists were failing to keep pace with the expanding population. The drift of wealthier people to the suburbs merely exacerbated the situation, depleting many urban congregations of vital skills and resources. As we shall see, the evangelical wing of Nonconformity responded imaginatively to the problems of the inner city in the Edwardian years. At best there was a rediscovery of the spirit that had characterised 18th-century Methodism, and the full-blown religious revival which swept across Wales in 1904 touched parts of England too. Many impressive buildings were erected as part of what Methodists called the Forward Movement, and the new century's first pattern book for chapel builders (Crouch and Butler's *Churches, Mission Halls and Schools for Nonconformists*, 1901) gave due prominence to these developments. Although city centres posed the major challenge, it was not necessarily easy to make headway in the suburbs – where much energy might be needed to generate a congregation – and many village chapels struggled in the face of rural depopulation.[5] Perhaps only in small towns had the circumstances of chapel building remained largely unchanged since the mid-Victorian years.

The period around 1900 was more of a time for banding together than for sectarianism. There was much talk of church unity, although the only immediate reorganisation of English denominations came in 1907, when the Methodist New Connexion amalgamated with the Bible Christians and the United Methodist Free Church to create the United Methodist Church. Locally, interdenominational co-operation (typically involving Baptists and Congregationalists) gave rise to places of worship which were designated Free Church chapels, but in most places the familiar denominational pattern continued. Of the recently established movements, the Salvation Army made a mark with its citadels, while the Christian Science Church was represented by a more select range of new premises. This was an era of many rather esoteric groups – ranging from Madame Blavatsky's Theosophical Society to the Spiritualists – but they tended not to commission new buildings, at least for the time being.[6] On the whole, the Nonconformists became more varied than ever in the architectural range of their places of worship, sharing quite fully in the stylistic repertoire and the structural innovations of early 20th-century architecture in Britain. Such heterogeneity was not so much an expression of denominational rivalry (although this undoubtedly survived into the era of Free Church collaboration), more a result of the desire to attract potential worshippers in an increasingly secular age.

The architectural cross-currents and shifting denominational sands of the years between 1890 and 1914 are not easily treated by a strictly chronological account, nor yet by firm stylistic categories. More than any of the earlier chapters, therefore, this one is organised around the implications of underlying demographic change: chiefly how Nonconformity responded to the loss of middle-class residents from the centres of towns and cities. It deals in turn with the pattern of chapel building in rural, urban and suburban locations, with the additional category of garden suburbs and garden cities. This allows at least some consideration to be given to the full spectrum of Nonconformist building types from these years, and also offers an opportunity to consider more conservative tendencies as well as new developments.

Village chapels

During the quarter-century preceding the First World War small country chapels were still built in significant numbers, although generally below the level of previous decades. After years of agricultural depression and rural depopulation, the resources for chapel building were stretched. The Norfolk village of Fulmodeston, whose population was shrinking steadily, can illustrate the point.[7] In 1902 its Primitive Methodist chapel, which in other circumstances might have been replaced, was extended and refitted by a local builder.[8] The new façade was unsophisticatedly Gothic, in that it had two pairs of lancet windows (in contrast to the older, almost rectangular, side windows) and a neatly arched doorway, all with Y-shaped glazing bars (Fig 7.1). By that date it was quite common for Primitive Methodists to adopt the Gothic style; any fear that it could lead to Catholicism had largely been overcome. The interior at Fulmodeston retains its turn-of-the-century atmosphere, with a set of wide pews and

a matchboard dado that rises behind the pulpit in a trio of pointed arches, as if evoking sedilia (Fig 7.2). Not that there was anything sacerdotal about worship here, for – in the Primitives' tradition – the chapel will have been served mostly by unpaid local preachers, while the harmonium that sits beside the pulpit is a reminder of the central role of hymns in Methodist services. The congregation would not have been composed entirely of the poorest class, but it must have included a good few farm labourers.[9] For people of such modest means, the decision to embark on the rebuilding of their chapel will have been an act of faith, given the village's decline.

In the decades around 1900 innumerable small country chapels were built or rebuilt in similar circumstances. Some were the outcome of even more limited means, such as the Baptist chapel at Bowerchalke, Wiltshire, constructed in 1897 (at a cost of £400) without architect or contractor, with much labour supplied by members of the congregation.[10] Yet small chapels were increasingly likely to be architect-designed. This was partly a matter of availability, since the architectural profession was expanding apace, and partly a matter of expectation.[11] Expectation on both sides, that is to say. Where villages were

Fig 7.1
Primitive Methodist chapel, Fulmodeston, Norfolk, 1902 (now without its Gothic glazing bars). Even into the 20th century, small chapels such as this were still sometimes built without the involvement of an architect.
[DP160453]

Fig 7.2
Interior of Primitive
Methodist chapel,
Fulmodeston. Even in small
country chapels tall,
narrow pulpits were
tending to give way to less
formal arrangements.
[DP160461]

prospering, perhaps because of suburbanisation or commuter travel, anyone commissioning a chapel was more likely to want well-designed new premises. Talented young architects were unlikely to feel any sense of stigma in undertaking small jobs, nor yet in working for Nonconformists. Characteristic of the mood at the turn of the century is the way in which Ford & Slater of Burslem in 1903 advertised their architectural services to Methodists with a pretty drawing of a recent village chapel in the Arts and Crafts fashion; as the caption explained, it seated 125 at a cost of £581, including fittings and furnishings.[12] The advertisement manages to imply that the architects brought even more verve to such small-scale schemes than to larger undertakings – not least the big, but unbuilt, Gothic church illustrated lower in the same advertisement.

More surprising than the contribution of Nonconformist specialists, such as Ford & Slater, is the involvement of major architects known chiefly for their secular work. In 1895, for instance, Norman Shaw, the doyen of the architectural world, provided a design from which the Congregationalist John Grover erected three small chapels amid the large houses and fir trees of Hindhead and the Surrey–Sussex border.[13] Although all three are interesting, they differ sufficiently in plan and elevation (the masonry exterior of the first was by Shaw's assistant,

Percy Ginham) for one to be uncertain about what Shaw designed.

There is no doubt, however, about Lutyens' authorship of the diminutive Wesleyan chapel of 1897–8 at Overstrand on the Norfolk coast.[14] Though less than 20 miles from Fulmodeston, Overstrand is in the heart of 'Poppyland', where the effects of the agricultural depression were masked by tourism and the building of smart villas. Like the fractionally larger chapel at Fulmodeston, the Overstrand building is of red brick and has a pantile roof (Fig 7.3).[15] There the similarities end, however, because Overstrand's chapel was built for Lord Battersea, who was in the throes of creating an extensive seaside mansion (the Pleasaunce) around two existing houses, and his architect was Edwin Lutyens, a rising star of English architecture. Lutyens' design – his first commission for a place of worship – was radical indeed. He devised what resembles a windowless brick box with a hipped roof, whose upper part seems to have sprung up like a jack-in-the-box to reveal a clerestory of lunette windows. Then, as if to prop the clerestory in its exposed position, three timber beams are pinned through the lower roof and continued outwards to rest on vertical buttresses that rise from the chapel's side walls. The building is part Norfolk cottage, part Roman baths and part French cathedral. Special care was taken with the entrance, where irregularly spaced courses of tile-bricks merge into the voussoirs of the receding brick arches that frame the round-headed doorway. Responding to praise of the design, Lutyens was self-deprecatingly dismissive: 'It is no use looking at the Overstrand chapel, it cost 2½d and is not Dutch or anything at all, just a brick wall and a skylight and a door and a stove.'[16] But it contained ideas that he was to develop in later buildings, secular as well as religious. The interior, relying completely on top-lighting, retains Lutyens' intended mood of self-containment, but many of the original fittings – not in any case altogether to Lutyens' design – have been altered.[17]

Like the country cottage and the terrace house, the wayside chapel was ripe for reinvention in the age of Arts and Crafts. One solution was to treat gable-end façades not with a symmetrical pair or group of windows, but with a single wide window. This was sometimes an opportunity for a display of licentious Gothic tracery, but the lunette window seems even more characteristic of the time, and could be fitted into the smallest façades. Norman Shaw – or was it Percy Ginham? – had used the lunette motif at Hindhead, and Harrison Townsend, architect of Whitechapel Art Gallery, did so for the tiny Congregational chapel (of 1901–2) at Blackheath, near Guildford.[18] Townsend's twist

was to use a shallow segmental shape with no fewer than seven mullions, thus nearly filling the gable end and charging the frontage with a mannerist energy. Complemented by roughcast walls and sloping buttresses in Voysey's manner, the Blackheath chapel was well calculated to hold its own among the other Townsend-designed buildings of the leafy hamlet.

It is not to be expected that Townsend's originality would often be matched, but younger architects were to employ similar themes in their country chapels. Reginald Longden is a good example. His first known commission, the little Wesleyan chapel of 1905 in Acton, a hamlet near Newcastle-under-Lyme, has a gable-end lunette under sheltering eaves, comparable to Townsend's design.[19] A classical flavour is imparted, however, first by the use of a Diocletian window and then by the pillar-like buttresses and broken-base pediment. Yet any sense of ponderousness is dispelled by the freehand lettering over the porch and the Art Nouveau glazing of the doors, bringing an echo of Mackintosh to rural Methodism. Three years later Longden reworked the Acton design for a Wesleyan chapel in the moorland settlement of Winkhill, Staffordshire, but already his domestic buildings were capturing national interest, and he seems to have designed no further places of worship after 1909.[20]

Fig 7.3
Wesleyan Methodist chapel, Overstrand, Norfolk, 1897–8 by Edwin Lutyens. Breaking through the conventions – and the normal budget – of rural chapel architecture, Lutyens gave free rein to his playful nature. [DP160449]

Longden exemplifies a generation of promising designers whose religious commissions coincided with a fecund era of Nonconformist architecture, but for whom secular commissions were to dominate their later careers. Another of that generation was Ethel Charles, the first female member of the RIBA. Her 1906 design for a Bible Christian chapel in the Cornish village of Mylor Bridge broke entirely from the tradition of gable-end façades.[21] In a piece of bad timing for Charles, the Bible Christians merged into the United Methodist Church in 1907 and her unusual design – in a rugged kind of early Georgian mode – was never built.

Fig 7.4
Albion Congregational (now United Reformed) church, Ashton-under-Lyne, Lancashire, 1890–5 by John Brooke. Built for a wealthy congregation, Albion was evidently intended to upstage the town's other churches and chapels.

Urban chapels

Although the leaching away of the middle classes to the suburbs slowly undermined the viability of many town centre chapels, there were still circumstances in this period when relatively well-heeled congregations did build urban chapels. It is to those chapels that we turn at this point.

The confident mood that characterised some Nonconformist causes at the end of the 19th century is wholly embodied in the chapel – or, rather, church – built for the Congregationalists of Ashton-under-Lyne in 1890–5 (Fig 7.4).[22] Although they had been prevented from building in the heart of the town, the Congregationalists here had the largest attendances and were the wealthiest denomination. In 1889 they decided to replace their existing Albion chapel – not because it was too small, but because they wanted something 'suitable in size, and for situation and architectural character, worthy of the standing and traditions of the Albion Church'.[23] So it was that they erected one of the most expensive chapels of the age, a grand cruciform building with a landmark spire and a full set of William Morris glass. Their architect was John Brooke of Manchester who adopted the late-Decorated-going-on-Perpendicular Gothic style that was returning to fashion, perhaps borrowing from Paley and Austin (the leading church specialists in north-west England) the squaring-off of details and the external use of blind tracery.[24]

Like the progressive Unitarian chapels of 40 years before, Albion was designed to steal a march on the local Anglicans – not only by its external form but also by its internal arrangement. The sole gallery is a small one above the vestibule, so that the congregation sits chiefly at ground level, and the long vista ends with a raised chancel for the choir, communion table and great 'east' window. Yet otherwise the plan, with its broad nave and transepts, and the side aisles reduced to mere passages, was one used by chapel builders since the 1850s – a design that ensured a clear view of the pulpit from every seat. Stained glass (Burne-Jones designs for Morris & Co) helps to reduce glare from the south-facing chancel, and acoustics were doubtless aided by the decision to span the 45 feet (13.7m) of the nave with a ceiled hammer-beam roof. The nearby parish church might still have had the best medieval glass in north-west England, but it also had an early Victorian layout in which a good many pews were behind the pulpit and others turned their backs on the chancel.

The Congregationalists must have thought such things unworthy. Although the new Albion was built without any ancillary accommodation save for vestries, the building committee was keen to stress that its 'educational and evangelistic work' would continue 'with undiminished vigour': the Sunday schools (with 2,300 scholars in 1889) and day schools (1,400) occupied purpose-built premises not far away, while the exceptionally full programme of activities and societies included a Band of Hope, Young Women's Guild, Working Mens' Class and the Dorcas Society; missions operated in poorer quarters of the town.[25] In practice, however, the lack of space for social events at the new Albion was a disadvantage, and a hall was built at the rear of the building in 1916.

Ashton-under-Lyne's Congregationalists had a confidence matured over three-quarters of a century. A rather different kind of confidence was to be found among Nonconformists in the new commuter districts. Sutton, the former Surrey village then becoming a sizeable town, provides a good example. The Wesleyans' first chapel here (of 1867) had been superseded by another in 1884, but that too proved inadequate, and in 1901 a large, central site was purchased for a place of worship and schools.[26] With little delay the commission to design the new buildings was awarded to the London architects Gordon & Gunton, who had already worked on 30 or more Wesleyan schemes.[27] Their successful design included an ungalleried Gothic church and detached school, as the trustees had specified, and added a formidable 140-foot (43m) tower with a crown spire, audaciously modelled on that of the cathedral in Newcastle (Fig 7.5).[28] The costs greatly exceeded the expected budget, however, with the result that construction was delayed until 1906–7.[29]

And so the Wesleyans built what is still the pre-eminent religious building in Sutton. (As Trinity church, it now serves a combined Methodist and United Reformed congregation.)

Fig 7.5
Wesleyan (now Trinity Methodist and United Reformed) church, Sutton, Surrey, 1906–7 by Gordon & Gunton. The noble Gothic church presides over an extensive suite of subsidiary buildings housing the congregation's busy social and educational activities. [DP160433]

Fig 7.6
Interior of Wesleyan
church, Sutton. The
adoption of a central
gangway was
accompanied by a
corresponding placing of
the pulpit to one side.
[DP160423]

Beyond the remarkable tower, Gordon & Gunton provided a noble, if unadventurous, church in 15th-century Gothic. Rather as at Ashton-under-Lyne, there is a wide clerestoried nave with a hammerbeam roof, transepts and shallow side aisles for access only (Fig 7.6). Instead of a full chancel, however, there is a polygonal apse for the communion table and choir, so as to retain just a little of the intimacy of older Methodist chapels. A modern touch was the choice of electric wall-lights, resembling Art Nouveau lilies of the valley. Among the most effective elements of the scheme is the grouping of the vestries, school and lecture hall; these face on to the adjoining streets and are an expression of the full range of activities sustained by large chapels.

In Long Street, Middleton (some six miles from Ashton-under-Lyne) an altogether more innovative Wesleyan building was erected in 1899–1901. It was to serve a growing congregation whose budget – a fraction of that spent on the Ashton or Sutton projects – also had to cover new schools and meeting rooms as well as a place of worship.[30] The chosen plot of land fronted a main street, but ground problems restricted its development. Fortunately the choice of architect fell on Edgar Wood, Manchester's foremost Arts and Crafts practitioner.[31] He filled one side of the site with the chapel, its gable facing the road, and alongside it created a small courtyard, the

ancillary buildings picturesquely ranged around two-and-a-bit of the remaining sides (Figs 7.7 and 7.8). It is in effect a kind of cloister, giving separate expression (and independent access) to each component of the congregation's life and work.

Compared with Wood's previous Noncon-formist schemes, the chapel itself is more medieval in its plan (of nave, side aisles and chancel), perhaps reflecting a liturgical tendency on the part of Middleton's Wesleyans, and was to be known as the church building. However, the architectural treatment is wholly free from Gothic rectitude. There is no tower or spire, and just a few blunt buttresses. Stone-flagged roofs and a mottled pattern of pale red bricks in header bond give a vernacular quality. The nave arcades have pointed arches without capitals, and the simply shaped windows of the aisles and clere-story have no mouldings: this is Gothic stripped of its ornament. By contrast, the end windows have inventive tracery, as free in its way as Mackintosh's detailing of Queen's Cross church, Glasgow. Like quite a few other large chapels of the time, it has no galleries, and the choir and organ chamber – as well as the communion table – are placed in the chancel. Yet even if the more concentrated atmosphere of some earlier chapels is missing, the nave is still the main arena for worship, the side aisles are not used for seating and the sturdy stone pulpit commands

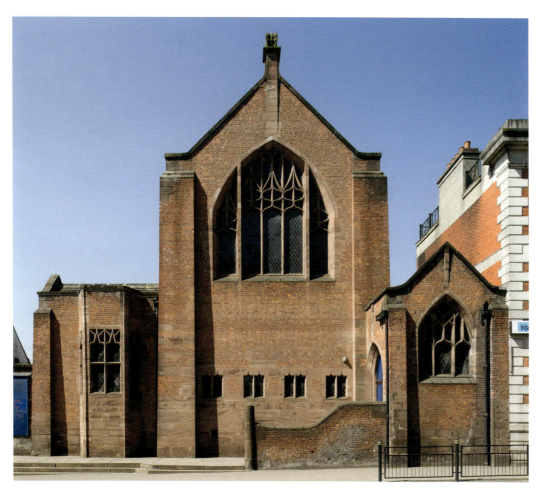

Fig 7.7
Wesleyan Methodist chapel, Middleton, Lancashire, 1899–1901 by Edgar Wood. Like Charles Rennie Mackintosh in Glasgow, Wood here combined inventive tracery with elegantly simplified blank masonry.
[DP143769]

Fig 7.8
Wesleyan Methodist chapel, Middleton. The long flank wall of the chapel overlooks the courtyard garden, around which are two ranges of schoolrooms, halls and parlour.
[DP143772]

*Fig 7.9 (right)
Baptist chapel, Rugby,
Warwickshire, 1905–6 by
George and R P Baines.
Packed with attractive
features, this kind of lively
composition won numerous
Nonconformist commissions
for the Baines practice.
[DP160638]*

*Fig 7.10 (below)
Baptist chapel, Rugby.
Many chapels of the
period had bricks or stones
engraved with the names
of the donors; here the
bricks in the school wall
record the initials of
children who collected for
the building fund.
[DP160641]*

the space. From the reverent atmosphere of this space for worship one can pass directly to the sequence of more domestically detailed accommodation – the lecture room, school hall, parlour and classrooms, which Edgar Wood planned with evident care. His drawing of the finished scheme gives full weight to each part of the ensemble, and includes a few embellishments, most notably a carved figure over the gateway to the courtyard, that were not realised.[32]

A few of the sandstone blocks at the base of the street front in Middleton are discreetly inscribed with initials in Art Nouveau lettering, a product of Edgar Wood's dislike for conventional memorial stones. No such inhibitions affected the architects of the new Baptist chapel that was built in Rugby in 1905–6 (Fig 7.9). Indeed, it has not only the memorial stone laid by the Reverend James Butlin (who had contributed £700 towards the cost of the site), but also dozens of inscribed bricks in the Sunday-school wall, recording the initials of each child who had collected a guinea for the building fund (Fig 7.10).[33] Fundraising, which had long been a chapel industry, developed new tactics in the years around 1900 and similar sets of initialled bricks may be found on many Nonconformist buildings of the time. Rugby's Baptists had to work hard to raise about £7,000 for their new chapel (here too referred to as the church) and school, but the round of bazaars and social events had the secondary effect of helping to consolidate a congregation that had been much depleted during the 1890s.[34] Under an energetic new minister numbers were again increasing, and the old chapel was outgrown. The Baptists' new premises, somewhat larger than those of Middleton's Wesleyans, were designed by George and Reginald Palmer Baines – one of the most successful specialist practices of the day, responsible for some 75 chapels in the period 1900–14.[35] For Rugby, the Baines partnership produced an eye-catching design in red brick and Bath stone, with generous amounts of Perpendicular tracery and a tapering corner tower topped by a nicely detailed flèche. It makes a lively contribution to the townscape, drawing on the so-called 'Free Gothic' approach pioneered by J D Sedding and Henry Wilson. This

is the style which Pevsner (writing about another Baines chapel) described as 'the much gayer and livelier, and in point of fact remarkably up-to-date, style which characterizes chapels about 1900 and is almost absent from churches'.[36]

The verve that the Baineses brought to the composition of exteriors must have gained them numerous clients, but at Rugby – as, doubtless, in many other places – the building committee was won over by the interior design.[37] It transforms one of the familiar Protestant plan-types, the T-shape, into a dynamic space. With its broad nave and short transepts, the plan brings the entire congregation within close reach of the preacher, and with some agility the modified hammerbeam roof enables the floor to be kept virtually free of columns.[38] As in many contemporary American churches, the pews are curved in a series of concentric arcs that further focus attention on the pulpit, communion and baptistery area, behind which the choir and organ form a backdrop (Fig 7.11). Everywhere there are reminders of the architects' progressive attitude to Arts and Crafts. Carved foliage scrolls adorn the pew ends, yet the pews have comfortably

Fig 7.11
Interior of Baptist chapel, Rugby. With its open vistas and curved pews that focus on the central pulpit, this is a powerful 20th-century reworking of the Protestant auditorium.
[DP160645]

convex backs and concave seats, thanks to the use of laminated oak. Meanwhile the stained glass has abstract, proto-Art Deco motifs rather than pictorial subjects. Alongside the main church, like a junior sibling, stands the school building; it houses a large, first-floor hall and a smaller hall below, as well as six classrooms and various meeting rooms and offices (Fig 7.12). If the arrangement is more conventional than Wood's scheme in Middleton, it nevertheless gives the school greater prominence – and more architectural presence – than many other Nonconformist projects. And while Edgar Wood's great talent was employed on six or seven new chapels, the Baineses created scores. Of all the specialist chapel designers at the start of the 20th century, it was the Baineses who did most to combine an advanced approach to church planning with a reinvigorated use of Gothic.

Gothic appealed to socially aspirational Nonconformists as well as some more radical souls, but it never came close to dominating chapel building in the way that it had monopolised Anglican efforts after about 1850. Many things sustained architectural pluralism among Nonconformists in the years around 1900. For instance, by then there was some reluctance to build a major Gothic place of worship unless one was prepared to dispense with side galleries. And so, where a full set of galleries was required, other styles were coming to be preferred. Perhaps this effect can explain the design of the large Bethesda chapel that was built for a Strict Baptist congregation in Ipswich in 1913 to replace a much-adapted Georgian building on an adjacent site.[39] It must be one of the last English chapels to have been built with a giant classical portico, and looks like a late-born offspring of Spurgeon's Tabernacle (*see* p 142). Yet neither the congregation nor their architect (Frederick G Faunch) can have been exclusive classicists, because the Sunday school he had created for them in 1906 was Gothic.[40] For the chapel, which seated 1,000, a galleried arrangement was probably most convenient, and the architect might well have felt more confident about handling that in a classical style. The granite columns of its Ionic portico certainly create an effective climax to the view up Northgate Street.

If Bethesda looked faintly old-fashioned for its time, no such criticism could be made of Darlington Street Wesleyan chapel, Wolverhampton (of 1899–1901, by Arthur Marshall), which deserves a place in the history of what later came to be called Edwardian baroque architecture (Fig 7.13).[41] Its central dome and twin-cupola façade are a clear homage to Wren's St Paul's, while the blocked columns and other details are more heavily indebted to Gibbs and Vanbrugh. The city churches of Wren and his successors had already influenced one cohort of chapel architects (*see* pp 152–4), but the Wolverhampton building is more full-blooded, all of a piece with the movement that produced the Old Bailey courts and Belfast's City Hall.

Any severity on the exterior is forgotten when one enters (Fig 7.14). It is a wonderful Methodist auditorium with galleries on each side, which is transformed by the central dome. The dome introduces a vertical emphasis, a generous source of top-light and also some rich decorative details: mosaic panels in the pendentives; plaster festoons around the drum; stained-glass ornament above. Directly below the dome, and at the

Fig 7.12
Baptist chapel, Rugby. Standing alongside the main chapel, the Sunday school is a worthy building in its own right. Its Perpendicular Gothic tracery is almost as elaborate as – though less extensive than – that of the chapel.
[DP160640]

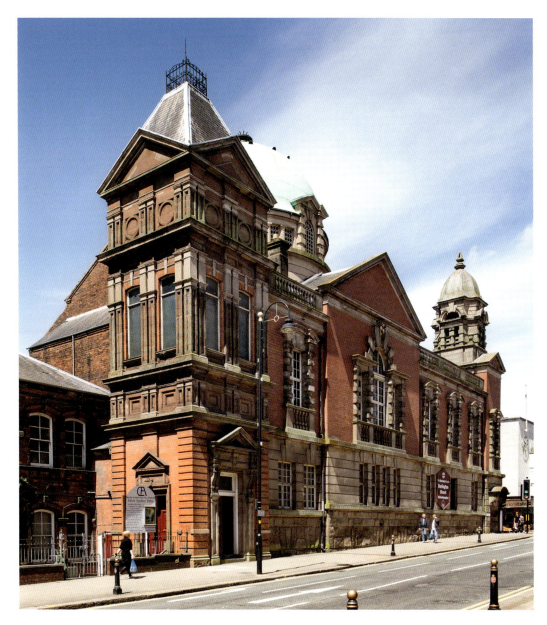

Fig 7.13
Wesleyan Methodist chapel,
Darlington Street,
Wolverhampton, 1899–
1901 by Arthur Marshall.
Beyond an earlier school
block and tower are the
baroque domes and
Gibbsian masonry of
the new chapel.
[DP166372]

heart of things, is a rostrum pulpit large enough to hold a whole team of preachers; behind is an apsidal gallery for the choir and organ, and before are the communion area and a broad block of pews. In an up-to-date spirit the galleries were supplied with tip-up seats from the outset (Fig 7.15). The arrangement is a world away from the long Gothic vistas and semi-detached choirs of many contemporary chapels. Instead it reaffirms some long-established habits of Methodist provision: the physical centrality of preaching, the emphasis on congregational singing, and the encircling gallery that binds everything together. Only the limited sightlines from the side pews (an unfortunate outcome of having major columns to support the dome and barrel vault)

mar the inclusive purpose. At the rear of the building is a comprehensive set of ancillary rooms which were retained when the earlier chapel was demolished c 1899 to make way for the present chapel.

In reporting on the opening of the Wolverhampton building, the *Wesleyan Chapel Committee Report* argued that its English Renaissance style was 'peculiarly fitted for Nonconformist places of worship, and very much in vogue at the time of the Wesleys'.[42] For any Nonconformists who still looked on medieval church architecture as an indelibly catholic creation, it must have been reassuring to be offered a model from the era when all English churches were Protestant. And for architects keen to show

*Fig 7.14 (above)
Interior of Wesleyan
Methodist chapel,
Wolverhampton. With its
splendid dome and ornate
electroliers, the uplifting
setting revitalised the
Methodist message in
the centre of this
industrial town.
[DP166377]*

*Fig 7.15 (right)
Wesleyan Methodist chapel,
Wolverhampton. The tip-up
seats in the gallery have
neat provision for stowing
caps and gloves.
[DP166384]*

that they were abreast of current fashions, it was a useful addition to the stylistic repertoire.

Take the example of the Primitive Methodist chapel (now Central Methodist church) of 1905 in High Street, Lincoln (Fig 7.16).[43] Its architects, Howdill and Son of Leeds, worked on more than 50 Primitive Methodist schemes and were proficient in a range of styles, including Gothic – to which the Primitive Methodists had not always been partial.[44] For the Lincoln commission the Howdills came up with an attractive Edwardian baroque façade bookended by a pair of towers, the taller of which has a domed turret. It is a lively composition, cheerfully mixing red brick and pale stone, and breathing fresh life into the so-called halo arch motif of 50 years before. Did Lincoln's Primitive Methodists want to distinguish themselves from the city's many Gothic churches and chapels (not to mention its cathedral), or were they keen to introduce a 20th-century note into this changing part of the High Street? Perhaps each factor played a part.

Fig 7.16
Primitive Methodist chapel
(now Central Methodist
church), Lincoln, 1905 by
Howdill and Son. The
stylish baroque frontage
was created by architects
who specialised in work for
the Primitive Methodists.
[DP165307]

The galleried interior is less innovative than that in Wolverhampton, though the stained-glass patterns are more stylish, and the rear hall is all part of the Howdills' scheme.

In the architectural melting pot of the Edwardian years, chapel architects were able to draw on a widening repertoire of forms and styles, with many congregations willing to consider quite novel proposals. Such was the case with Mary Baker Eddy's London followers, who employed the versatile R F Chisholm as architect for the First Church of Christ, Scientist (of 1905–8) in Sloane Terrace, Chelsea (Fig 7.17).[45] The building (now the Cadogan Hall) could be mistaken for a mosque, a piece of North Africa dropped into the red-brick streets of Chelsea. On sunny days the Portland stone is dazzlingly white, and the long façade – with a colonnaded loggia – culminates in a minaret-like tower. There is no attempt to imitate any of

Urban missions and central halls

The most systematic development of alternatives to the traditional types of chapel was to be found not in the places erected for affluent congregations, but in the buildings designed to attract members of the poorer classes. Small back-street missions were increasingly upstaged by efforts – and buildings – on a larger scale. The most obvious example is that of the Salvation Army, whose stock of new premises grew very significantly after the mid-1880s. Sheffield's major purpose-built citadel (of 1892–4, designed by William Gillbee Scott) illustrates the Army's approach quite clearly.[49] The façade, in Cross Burgess Street, is an elaboration on the fortress theme which E J Sherwood had established as the Army's house style in the 1880s. Battlemented turrets and parapets here crown a busy elevation, supplemented by machicolations, arrow slits and cross-slit openings – as if the forces of darkest England were to be kept at bay by buckets of boiling oil and a volley of arrows. The main hall had tiers of wooden benches, angled around three sides, and a similar canted gallery. All directed attention to the platform where the soldiers (uniformed members) sat, probably with the Army's band, framed by a proscenium arch.[50]

With no need for a communion area – Salvationists observe no sacraments – services would have been conducted from a rail at the front of the platform. At this focal point there would also have been a penitent-form or mercy seat, from which reformed sinners would dedicate their lives to Christ in front of audiences of up to 1,800. And Booth's followers had the knack of filling their halls. Of another new citadel from these years it was said that 'ventilation will be a special feature: nevertheless it will probably be magnificently warm on Sunday night, especially about 10 p.m.!'[51] Even in large numbers, the urban poor rarely had the means to pay for such buildings, however, and in Sheffield an adjoining range of shops and offices was erected by the Salvation Army in matching style. Shops had been incorporated into some citadel schemes since at least 1890, and were a useful source of rental income on expensive city centre sites. It was not an idea that originated with the Salvation Army, but was a welcome addition to Booth's ingenious fund-raising schemes.[52]

During the first years of the 20th century the Salvation Army gave fresh priority to its work with young people.[53] The Army's success in this

Fig 7.17
First Church of Christ, Scientist, Chelsea, London, 1905–8 by R F Chisholm. The heterodox façade helped to draw attention to the Christian Scientists as they established themselves in Britain. The building is now a concert hall.
[DP150844]

the Christian Science buildings from America. Elements of the design can be traced back to Chisholm's long career in India, from where he had recently returned, but the crucial choice of stone was apparently the client's.[46] The exterior certainly has presence, and its novelty must have been welcomed by the congregation as a distinctive sign of the new movement's presence in London.

Internally there were some minor Byzantine touches, but the main auditorium was more notable for its structure than its style: the great width of the steeply raked hall is spanned without columns and its galleries are cantilevered from the walls. Steel-framing was beginning to free architects from the constraints that had previously governed the construction of such large chapels. Worship was led from a pair of lecterns by two lay readers (there being no professional ministry, nor sacraments, in Christian Science) on a dais, with a large organ in the alcove behind.[47] Below the main hall were a Sunday school, a suite of meeting rooms and a reading room in which members of the public could consult religious literature or the *Christian Science Monitor*.[48] Many of the windows have interlace or geometric patterns with well-judged stained-glass highlights by Arild Rosenkrantz.

field (by 1905 the Portsmouth corps had no fewer than 43 companies of young people) helped to tackle what was increasingly recognised as a scandalous level of privation among children of the urban poor.[54] Architecturally the campaign was reflected by the new prominence given to young people's halls, placing them if possible side by side with the main hall, as can be seen in the coal-mining town of Royston, Yorkshire. This scheme (of 1911) with its Dutch gable and only vestigial battlements also illustrates the turn away from fortress imagery, a change associated with the years after 1906 when Oswald Archer became the Salvation Army's staff architect.[55] Characteristically, the reaching out to youth was taken far beyond the Army's own premises. One Sunday in 1912, for instance, Frank Matcham's glamorous Hackney Empire theatre was taken over for a young people's day attracting more than 2,000 – of whom about 750 came forward to seek guidance or to offer themselves as 'officers'.[56]

Mission halls were built by all of the major denominations, including the Church of England. It was to be expected that the Primitive Methodists, whose reputation was for success among the working classes, would make their mark in this field, and south London saw one of their most fruitful enterprises. In 1897 a 'disreputable drink shop' in Old Kent Road was acquired, and an impressive suite of buildings erected in its stead for the Primitive Methodists' Southwark mission, designed by Professor Banister Fletcher and his son.[57] It was paid for by an exceptional

campaign of nationwide fundraising. Called St George's Hall, the new buildings – which opened in 1899 – were in a rather beefy version of the latest baroque fashion. They consisted of a chapel for 650 (with galleries cantilevered on steel brackets) and behind it a large schoolroom that could be partitioned into classrooms or used as a gym. Vestries, kitchen, storerooms and caretaker's accommodation were also squeezed in. In addition to the regular services and Sunday school there were open-air services (complete with a brass band), meals for the destitute, unemployed clubs, an institute with billiards and bagatelle, women's own meetings, bible study classes, a band of hope and countless other activities.[58] Like the Salvation Army, the Primitive Methodists' initiative offered a wholesome alternative to the pub or the gin palace – appropriately, in view of the taproom it supplanted – and provided numerous schemes for social support as well as spiritual guidance. Architecturally, however, it was not so much 'blood and fire' as sweetness and light. It might have been taken for a Carnegie library, and the architects' drawing optimistically showed a row of pot plants on the sill of the staircase window.[59]

During the 1890s the Wesleyan Methodists were much exercised by the problem of the urban poor. John Wesley's early buildings – welfare centres as well as places of worship – provided a precedent, if any were needed. An interesting Wesleyan mission from these years survives in altered form in Lozells Street, amid the terrace houses of north Birmingham (Fig 7.18). The

Fig 7.18
Wesleyan Methodist mission, Lozells, Birmingham, 1893 by Crouch and Butler. Mission halls, thought Crouch and Butler, should have 'a general appearance of cheerfulness' and should avoid the 'Gothic Church type'. [From Crouch and Butler 1901, fig 30]

Fig 7.19
Westgate Wesleyan Methodist central hall (now Hillsong Church), Newcastle upon Tyne, 1901–2 by Crouch and Butler. Attracting attention with its strategically sited domed tower, Westgate Hall anticipated good rents from the shop units to support its mission to the urban poor.
[DP157035]

Lozells mission hall was begun in 1893 to the designs of Crouch and Butler; it consisted of a wide, ungalleried hall for about 1,250 people, with a tiered platform suitable for large choirs, bands of up to 30 musicians, and a complement of 10 speakers.[60] Instead of pews, the hall was supplied with 'comfortable and homely' Windsor chairs which could be rearranged for tea meetings – along with trestle tables that were stored under the rostrum.[61] Services were evidently of a rather informal character: no hint of the social hierarchy associated with pew rents. There was also a lecture hall which could be divided into classrooms by means of revolving shutters, as well as toilets, a small kitchen area and a pair of basement rooms for use as a gym. Except for some jaunty ventilation turrets and two pairs of finely worked iron gates, the exterior was quite restrained.[62] Some 10 years later the thriving mission gained a corner tower when a range of meeting rooms and hall was added, and in 1909 a further extension was constructed for the brand new boy scout movement.[63]

However, it was in city centre locations that the Wesleyans built their most conspicuous mission buildings. During the first years of the 20th century central halls – as they were called – began to be erected on prime locations across the country. Architecturally confident and sometimes lavish, they were designed to attract the kinds of people who might easily have been deterred from entering a conventional place of worship. Many central halls survive as landmarks, though often now serving incongruous purposes. Among the few early examples that remain in religious use is Westgate Hall (1901–2; now used by Hillsong Church), Newcastle upon Tyne, which coincidentally was also designed by Crouch and Butler (Fig 7.19).[64] Westgate Hall rises above the western approach to the city, with a corner clock-tower and pointed cupola heralding the presence of what at first glance seems to be a block of shops. These nine shop units were fundamental to the scheme; their position on a very busy street allowed the Wesleyans to charge good rents, thereby paying the mortgage and (it was hoped) support the costs of the mission.

Above the shops are four giant windows, evidence of the large hall within. Stylistically the block is a curious mixture of Tudor and baroque elements, in calculated contrast to the late Gothic of the nearby Anglican church of St Matthew: like virtually every central hall, the Westgate mission was designed on the principle that the probable audience would be deterred by buildings of 'a too distinctly ecclesiastical appearance'.[65] Along the side street, winged cherubs attractively preside over the entrances to the mission and its large, ground-floor schools. The main hall, upstairs, is a sumptuous affair, specifically designed to be just as attractive and comfortable as a modern concert hall or pub. Under a great oval dome the wide, galleried auditorium had 1,400 seats, and a grand proscenium arch – initially filled by a choir and organ, but now home to a modern band. It is thought that the recent chairs replace tip-up seats, with which many central halls were fitted in a bid to abandon the proprietorial and ecclesiastical associations of pews.

Central halls like this were an extraordinary phenomenon, at once places of worship and education as well as centres for entertainment and welfare. The example in Liverpool had a café, supper room, drill hall and lads' club, while its counterpart in Birmingham had a ragged school, along with a basement kitchen that could provide meals for the poor.[66] Moreover, by controlling the tenancies of the shops, the Wesleyans were able to influence the character of the neighbourhood. *The Builder* supposed that the 'arrangement of a church building with the ground floor let off for shops ... offers nothing objectionable to the Wesleyan mind', but such condescension did not deter the Methodists.[67]

Central halls were erected in almost every English city and many towns over the coming decades, often contributing significantly to the urban scene. On a pivotal site by Old Street roundabout in London, for instance, the Wesleyans' former Leysian mission (1901–4, by Bradshaw and Gass) has a bold front of shops and offices in an ebullient version of Waterhouse's terracotta style, topped by a copper cupola.[68] Birmingham's former central hall (1900–3, by Ewen and J Alfred Harper) makes an even finer show, also using terracotta, but with more composure (Fig 7.20). Its tower commands the sloping vista along the then new Corporation Street and answers Aston Webb's more picturesque law courts, opposite.[69] Civic improvements also provided the Wesleyans with the chance to acquire a crucial site when Tower Bridge Road was cut through the streets of south London. Here, at the junction with Bermondsey Street, an eye-catching central hall (of 1899–1900, by Charles Bell) was erected, with an entrance that Pevsner likened to a Tudor gatehouse.[70] In the fashion of a circus building, a pennant fluttered from the flagpole over its octagonal auditorium – at least in the architect's drawing.[71]

With several floors, multiple rooms and large numbers of users throughout the week, central halls presented architects with a challenge. Because many of the intended users came from slum conditions, a warm and dry environment with good toilets was an attraction. Yet ventilation was equally important. Fan-assisted systems of heating and ventilation were often employed, as at the central hall in Bermondsey.[72] Structurally it was common for steel to be used

so that large halls could be spanned with little fuss, and floor plans could be opened up a little. On occasion, more radical engineering was involved, the prime instance being the Wesleyan chapel (of 1902–5) in Sidwell Street, Exeter, which is fascinating for social as well as structural reasons.

During the 1880s the Wesleyans had a mission room in the working-class district of St Sidwell's, and in 1894 bought a site with shops (yielding £80 a year in rent) and space for a new

Fig 7.20
Wesleyan Methodist central hall, Birmingham, 1900–3 by Ewen and J A Harper. The main hall is marked by the tall windows with integral bays, above the seven shops nearest the camera. Following its closure as a Methodist building, the hall was used as a nightclub. [AA050468]

Fig 7.21
Wesleyan Methodist chapel,
Sidwell Street, Exeter,
1902–5 by F J Commin
and W H Coles. The
exterior presents a lively
example of Edwardian
baroque architecture. More
remarkable, however, is
the building's reliance on
Cottançin's reinforced
cement.
[DP158314]

Fig 7.22
Interior of Wesleyan
Methodist chapel, Exeter.
Cottançin's innovative
structural system –
adopted here because of its
potential to reduce costs –
allowed the gallery to be
erected entirely without
columns.
[DP166214]

building.[73] A large hall of Arts and Crafts character (designed by F J Commin of Exeter) was opened in 1897, to serve for the time being as a school and chapel. Five years later Commin's design for a grand Edwardian baroque chapel was selected to be built at the front of the site, next to the street (Fig 7.21). Roger Thorne has described it as a mission church, although he notes that the (largely working-class) casual attenders were expected to use the gallery, while pew-renters sat downstairs: in an age when wealthy congregations were building chapels without galleries, the body of the chapel was definitely the place to be.[74] It is clear that some middle-class families were involved from an early stage, but it seems also that the Sidwell Street mission was successful in encouraging a number of its working-class attenders into long-term membership.[75]

So far as building work was concerned, Commin's plan envisaged a brick and stone structure. This was unaffordable, however, and so the trustees adventurously gave Paul Cottançin the first major opportunity to use his patent system of reinforced brickwork and reinforced cement in Britain.[76] Only a close inspection reveals that the stonework – including all the seemingly carved details – is cast in cement, and the eye cannot detect the network of steel rods on to which the bricks have been threaded. Internally the structural daring is more evident, particularly in the apparently unsupported gallery which runs around five sides of the octagonal space: a counterpart of Wesley's 18th-century octagons without the inconvenience of columns. The interior functions well for worship (Fig 7.22). It receives a generous amount of light from the deep lantern of the dome (Fig 7.23), and everyone can see the oak rostrum, thanks

to a sloping ground floor and raked galleries. Gallery users are afforded the rare convenience of having stairs directly to the communion area. These stairs, another piece of virtuoso structural design, elegantly complement the set piece composition of rostrum, choir gallery and organ. Externally the chapel is a handsome sight, with plenty of decoration in Wren's Hampton Court mode and a bravura dome (its crowning tempietto housing the ventilator) which can be seen across the city. After 1907 the social and educational life of the mission continued in the original school-cum-chapel building (Fig 7.24), which still serves a multiplicity of uses, including the Boys' Brigade and Brownies, Sunday school and badminton.

In common with many other places of worship, Sidwell Street sometimes uses a projector in its current services. The roots of this habit can be traced back at least to the end of the 19th century, when 'magic lanterns' could be powered by electricity. Nonconformist missions were not slow to make use of the new technology for religious purposes, and in the 1890s the most commonly available sets of slides had moral themes, such as *Pilgrim's Progress*, temperance (or rather abstinence) and illustrated hymns.[77] The Baptist minister appointed to Poplar and Bromley tabernacle in the 1890s helped to revive the chapel's fortunes in that deprived neighbourhood by setting aside books in favour of the magic lantern at Sunday morning services. The texts of hymns, scripture readings and Lord's Prayer were projected on to a screen, and

Fig 7.23
Wesleyan Methodist chapel, Exeter. The octagonal dome helps to keep the chapel well lit and – thanks to the ventilator at its crown – well aired.
[DP166219]

Fig 7.24
Interior of Wesleyan Methodist chapel, Exeter. Shown here is the hall of 1897 which was designed by F J Commin. Until the main chapel was built, the hall temporarily served as the chapel as well as the Sunday school.
[DP166223]

Fig 7.25
Wesleyan Methodist central hall, Westminster, 1905–12 by Lanchester and Rickards. Although now the flagship of the whole Methodist movement, Westminster's central hall originally reflected the power of Wesleyanism. [DP150965]

sermons were illustrated by slides (for instance, of the life of Christ).[78] Cinema was also used: as early as 1903 the Salvation Army ventured into film-making as 'a novel method of influencing the unsaved', and many Nonconformist missions – including the Poplar and Bromley tabernacle – had introduced film-shows by about 1910.[79] Auditory chapels, designed to give every worshipper a full view of the pulpit, could be readily adapted for the showing of lantern slides or moving pictures, but this was hardly true for churches with wide side aisles, where many of the congregation would struggle to see.

By far the grandest Nonconformist building of the early 20th century is the Wesleyan central hall, Westminster, of 1905–12 (Fig 7.25).[80] In contrast to other central halls, the Westminster building was not so much a mission to the urban poor as 'a monumental connexional building' which would accommodate Wesleyan headquarters and could be used for conferences

as well as worship.[81] Like no other chapel, it embodies the confidence which buoyed up Nonconformity in the years around 1900. The site, with Westminster Abbey on one side and the Palace of Westminster across the square, clearly puts Methodism at the heart of church and state affairs. In Methodism's internal relations of the day, it was an emphatic reminder that the Wesleyans were the big players.[82]

Architecturally the Westminster central hall is one of the great buildings of the age, designed by Lanchester and Rickards in a lavish baroque style.[83] The architects argued that the design was based on a style 'belonging to the period when John Wesley began his life work', although the sources lay on the continent rather than in Georgian England.[84] Via a staircase that is grand enough for an opera house one reaches the main hall, a squarish space with deep, cantilevered galleries on three sides and a mighty organ on the fourth (Figs 7.26 and 7.27). Originally there were tip-up seats, which squeaked 'in unison' when the congregation rose to sing a hymn.[85] As a place of worship the hall is ideal for popular preaching and congregational singing – just like other central halls, in fact – but it was always intended to be used also for conferences, concerts and large public meetings, and so there is no fixed pulpit or communion area.

If the baroque vision came from Rickards, the efficient beaux-arts planning was Lanchester's. Behind the main hall are five floors of offices and committee rooms, while below it are a library, smaller halls and a basement tea room. The whole structure is supported by a mixture of modern technologies: Kahn's reinforced concrete, combined with partial steel framing, and a plenum system of pressurised ventilation.[86] From its opening in 1912, the new enterprise was served by ministers who were inspirational preachers, and crowds were drawn to its services. However, the building has also amply fulfilled its role as a venue for public events, including the inaugural

Fig 7.26
Interior of Wesleyan Methodist central hall, Westminster. The entrance hall and grand staircase evoke comparisons with baroque Vienna or Paris rather than early Georgian London.
[DP150989]

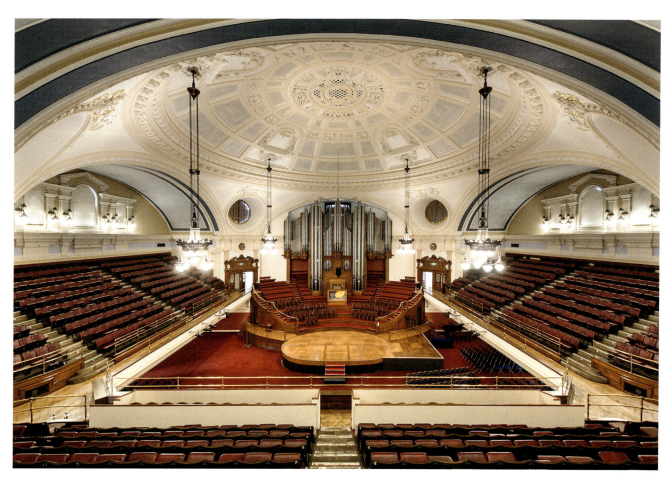

Fig 7.27
Wesleyan Methodist
central hall, Westminster.
Originally seating some
2,500, the great hall has
resounded to gifted
preaching and heartfelt
Methodist singing, as
well as hosting concerts,
political meetings
and conferences.
[DP150981]

meeting of the United Nations in 1946 and the Bloody Sunday inquiry of 2002–4. Westminster central hall has certainly created a role for itself in the affairs of the nation, and become a flagship for Methodism across the world.

Suburban chapels

The fresh thinking about architecture and worship which is embodied in central halls and other urban missions was a response to the accelerating decline of city centres as residential districts. A greater conservatism might therefore be expected of suburban chapel building. To an extent that was so, but shrewd planners understood the need to offer something special if people were to be lured from the gardens and relatively spacious houses that were the essential attraction of such neighbourhoods.

One 'new' feature of the period was the revival of octagons. As noted above, several central halls had octagonal auditoria, in conscious emulation of the Protestant preaching-house tradition. Octagons similarly appealed to the

builders of suburban chapels, particularly in less affluent places. For instance, the former Grange Congregational chapel (of 1891, by T C Hope) in Bradford looks like a 17th-century Dutch church dropped beside a busy road junction, where its octagonal shape tells to advantage.[87] Its two-storey school block resembles a board school, though with an idiosyncratic tower. At Gospel Oak in north London, Beresford Pite adopted an octagonal plan for an impressive (but now demolished) Wesleyan chapel of 1899–1900, involving one of his trademark Diocletian windows halfway up an Ionic portico.[88]

In the Sheffield suburb of Crookes – an area then being developed with terraces of workers' housing – two octagonal chapels were built to designs by W J Hale, a local architect. First came the Congregational chapel, built in 1906 on a steep, sharply angled corner site for which another architect had already planned a wedge-like chapel. Hale took over when the schoolroom and church parlour had been built across the widest part, leaving a kite-shaped plot; this he neatly filled with a fine Gothic octagon, its vestry extending to the apex of the site.[89] Externally the battered buttresses and central spirelet are nicely calculated for the hillside streetscape, while the galleried interior (now converted for office use) is an updated version of an 18th-century chapel. Following the success of this scheme, Hale created a second octagonal chapel, Wesley Hall (of 1906–8; now subdivided at gallery level), just a few streets away on another corner site.[90] Its exterior is less emphatically Gothic, and its interior employed many features of the Wesleyans' modern mission buildings. One local reporter enthused that it 'looks more like the Hippodrome than a place of worship' and the building was hailed as 'a triumph of modernity'.[91] The ventilation (including electric fans) and chairs (with underseat wire cages for hats) came in for praise, and there were good facilities for showing films. Whether congregational attention was focused on the pulpit or the screen, Nonconformists gave the octagon a new lease of life in the 20th century.

In wealthier suburbs, chapel building was not always so evangelical. A prime example is in Liverpool, where the Unitarians decided to abandon one of their city centre chapels. During the 1860s Charles Beard, a popular minister, had attracted large congregations, but as his powers waned the numbers fell away and in 1896 the 'residue of the old Unitarian families who had always supported the chapel' embarked on a new place of worship on Ullet Road in Sefton Park (Fig 7.28).[92] The 'residue' included a constellation of the city's leading families, for whom Sefton Park – with its grand villas and leafy views – was natural territory. Their new church (of 1896–9, by Thomas Worthington and Son) is of pressed red brick and sandstone, like many of the nearby villas (and indeed the Anglicans' neighbouring St Agnes, of 1883–5, by J L Pearson).[93] The Ullet Road chapel is a major Gothic work, set in its own grounds; high on its 'west' front is a replica of Thorvaldsen's statue of Christ. Though it might be taken for a parish church, the plan-form goes some way to reflect the needs of congregational worship: the side aisles are mere passages, the chancel is a shallow apse and the single transept is but

Fig 7.28
Ullet Road Unitarian church, Sefton Park, Liverpool, 1896–9 by Thomas Worthington and Son. Benefiting from its suburban site, the church borders a garden that is bounded on two other sides by a 'cloister' block and a hall of 1901–2, just visible on the right.
[AA040437]

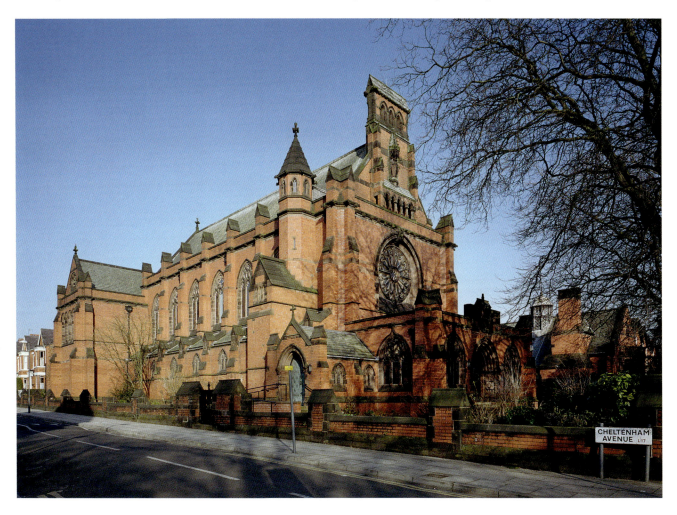

Fig 7.29
Interior of Ullet Road
Unitarian church, Sefton
Park, Liverpool. Overseen
by William Morris windows
and a canopied reredos of
the Last Supper, the
communion table enjoys a
particularly fine setting.
[AA040397]

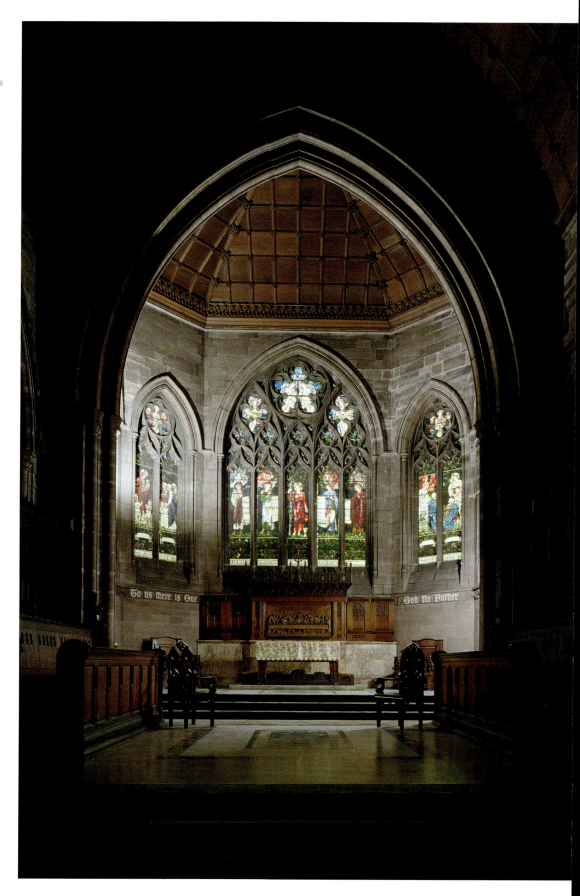

an organ chamber. There is an unusual deep narthex, entered through beautiful doors of beaten copper which feature a tree of life motif by R L B Rathbone, then teaching metalwork in the city's progressive new art school.[94]

The interior has a wealth of Arts and Crafts fittings (Fig 7.29), including stained glass (Burne-Jones designs for Morris & Co), embroidery (Royal School of Art Needlework), woodwork (Hatch of Lancaster and Martyn of Cheltenham) and electroliers (Artificers' Guild). Most unexpected are Gerald Moira's symbolist ceiling paintings in the vestry and library – although the central figure of Truth was originally *more* unexpected and had to be given draperies, to the artist's chagrin.[95] Sir John Brunner, the chemicals manufacturer, commissioned the paintings and, with Henry Tate junior, also paid for the 'cloister' and large hall that completed the building project in 1901–2.[96] The hall, for which Percy Worthington seems to have been chiefly responsible, provides a generous and handsomely detailed space for school and social events, and has independent access from the side street. Linking the parallel blocks of hall and church, the Gothic 'cloister' acts as a corridor which incorporates an impressive set of monuments from the city centre chapel.

In Sefton Park the Unitarians were one of the last denominations to build. Where a Nonconformist group could obtain the premier site, however, quite monumental buildings might result. Thus it was, for instance, in Four Oaks, an emerging suburb near Sutton Coldfield, where the Wesleyans acquired an outstanding piece of land at the junction of the Lichfield and Walsall roads, close to the railway station. Four Oaks attracted 'a large villa population, whose business interests [were] in many cases in the neighbouring city of Birmingham'.[97] Among the architects creating bespoke villas in this superior commuter-land were Crouch and Butler, and it was to their designs that the new Wesleyan church was built (in stages) between 1902 and 1909.[98] Discarding their central-hall baroque and restrained mission-hall modes, they produced a stately Gothic church of white limestone, fully cruciform and with a substantial crossing tower. There are Arts and Crafts touches and hints of the influence of Norman Shaw, but nothing daring. One might say that in this situation it was important for the church not to look *too* Methodist. Although the needs of congregational worship were acknowledged – especially in having side aisles as mere passageways – Crouch

later justified the provision of choir stalls on either side of the chancel because the creation of a choir gallery behind the preacher 'suggests a concert-room rather than a place of worship'.[99] Had he by then disowned his central halls and missions as places of worship? The Wesleyan church in Four Oaks makes an impressive sight, and its prominence is emphasised by a group of ancillary buildings – of school hall, manse and caretaker's house – which are laid out behind it.

Architecturally, the (former) First Church of Christ, Scientist in Victoria Park, Manchester is one of the most important new religious buildings – possibly *the* most important – of the Edwardian years (Figs 7.30 and 7.31). Victoria Park was not a new suburb, having been laid out in the 1830s, but open spaces had been preserved among the select villas, and in 1903

Fig 7.30
First Church of Christ, Scientist (now Victoria Park Christian Fellowship), Victoria Park, Manchester, 1903–8 by Edgar Wood. With reading room to the left and classroom to the right, the low wings balance the skyward thrust of the main building. [DP166642]

Fig 7.31
First Church of Christ,
Scientist, Manchester.
The curved parapet of the
shallow transept is to the
right of the porte cochère,
which provides level access
to the church.
[DP166641]

Britain's first purpose-built Christian Science church began to rise among the trees and greensward of Daisy Bank Road. The architect, Edgar Wood, whose previous work the Christian Scientists deemed 'most artistic and of a somewhat original character', entertained the idea of an octagonal chapel, either with an atrium for the ancillary buildings or two radial arms.[100]

However, the final design (erected, with modifications, in stages between 1903 and 1908) amply fulfilled Wood's reputation for originality and artistry.[101] His plan was Y-shaped, consisting of a long rectangular chapel and two short arms for the subsidiary accommodation. On paper it seems less than perfect, with awkward spaces at the junction, but in three dimensions it

Fig 7.32
Interior of First Church
of Christ, Scientist,
Manchester. Curtains now
conceal most of the figured
marble wall that forms a
reredos, although the
Christian Science church
would have had no
communion table.
[DP166644]

is spectacular. Dominating the composition is the tall and steep-gabled chapel, rather like a tithe barn, whose long roofs make an impressive display of rustic Westmorland slate and deep dormers. At the entrance the vernacular theme is augmented by borrowings from Mackintosh (a conically capped stair tower) and Lutyens (the receding arches of the doorway). Yet all of this is transformed by the proto-expressionist treatment of the whitewashed gable end – its verticality accentuated by a long stone strip that rises through the apex.[102] In contrast, the red-brick wings are earth-bound, and domestic in character. Their shape draws one towards the entrance. From the street a lych gate frames the view, its roof echoing the steep pitch of the chapel.

For the interior (Fig 7.32), Wood began with some familiar ideas: the floor slopes steadily down towards the rostrum, and the side aisles are only used for access. To separate the side aisles from the nave he introduced arcades of low, round arches (without mouldings), and allowed a grander effect only in the larger arches over the rostrum and the adjoining shallow transepts.[103] Above the whitewashed walls, the dark roof timbers are arrayed. The effect is neither that of a medieval church nor of an auditory chapel, but of a sophisticated barn. At a few points the simple materials act as a foil to richer effects. This is especially the case in the giant reredos, an almost secessionist essay in figured marble, and – for the organ gallery above the entrance – an elaborate screen that seems inspired by the wooden lattices of the Arab world (Fig 7.33). In 1956 Cecil Stewart described the dramatic interior as being 'furnished with long, rush-covered seats, with high tapered backs, in the manner of *art nouveau*'.[104] Sadly the furnishings have been lost, save for a lectern and two ceremonial chairs, all of walnut and carved with naturalistic decoration to Wood's design.[105] At the time of writing the building is again an active place of worship, now as a Pentecostal church, after more than 30 years of secular use.

Outstanding for quite different reasons is the Congregational (now United Reformed) church built in 1911–12 at Fairhaven, a recently developed suburb between Lytham and St Anne's (Fig 7.34).[106] It stands out first for its material: glazed white terracotta, which – it was argued – looked rather like marble, and would withstand the sea air better than stone.[107] The choice of colour has given the building its nickname, the 'White Church', and seems to put it in the popular imagination half outside the usually serious business of architecture.[108] It stands out also by height, with a corner tower that rises above the neighbouring houses, like a minaret or a coastal beacon.

Bentley's campanile at Westminster Cathedral was part of the inspiration, although in its compact plan the Fairhaven church is more directly Byzantine. Its shallow dome spans a centralised space that emphasises the congregational aspects of worship – very much the kind of arrangement that Cubitt had advocated more than 40 years before, and which was now being adopted by progressive church architects across Europe and America. At Fairhaven this was achieved with a hybrid structure, culminating in a concrete shell roof with permanent shuttering of metal laths, and steel beams on each side of the dome. The architects were Briggs, Wolstenholme and Thornely, who had recently completed the Mersey Docks and Harbour Board building (the first of Liverpool's 'Three Graces') using a steel frame, encased in concrete. In such ways, Nonconformist architecture continued to benefit

Fig 7.33
Interior of First Church of Christ, Scientist, Manchester. The organ screen at the entrance marks a turn to more exotic sources than the rustic Arts and Crafts themes of Edgar Wood's initial design.
[DP166645]

Fig 7.34
Fairhaven Congregational
(now United Reformed)
church, Lytham St Annes,
Lancashire, 1911–12 by
Briggs, Wolstenholme and
Thornely. Indebted to
Westminster Cathedral, the
building is transformed by
its white materials into
something vibrant.
[DP156969]

from its close relationship with the secular world. It might also be noted that there were parallels in the Jewish world. The innovative South Manchester synagogue of 1912–3 (by Joseph Sunlight), for instance, has a similar Greek-cross plan, with a dome and quietly Byzantine tower, and was constructed of reinforced concrete, faced with glazed terracotta.[109]

Those who know the White Church only from outside are often surprised by the quality of the interior (Fig 7.35). The furnishings are good, though the liturgical arrangements were modified in 1965, when the pulpit was moved from its central position to one side. The unexpected treasure, however, is the sequence of stained-glass windows (begun by 1904, to the designs of

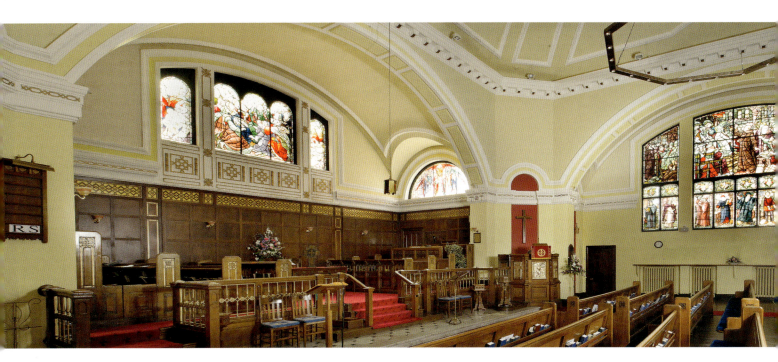

Charles Elliot, and made by Abbot and Co), which provide not only a source of glorious colour, but also an unusual iconography (Fig 7.36). Their subjects were conceived by a founding member of the congregation, Luke Slater Walmsley, a former art dealer who was keen to extend the usual selection of biblical scenes. So it is that two of the four large windows are devoted to Protestant topics, from the trial of Wyclif to the great ejection of Puritan ministers in 1662, and below them is a portrait gallery of 16 illustrious men, including Luther, Cromwell, Bunyan, Wesley and Livingstone.[110] Visually the windows are of great importance, but even greater is the new sense that Nonconformists felt able to celebrate their collective past, from a position of relative strength.

Fig 7.35
Interior of Fairhaven Congregational church, Lytham St Annes. The compressed cruciform plan creates a compact space for congregational worship.
[DP156961]

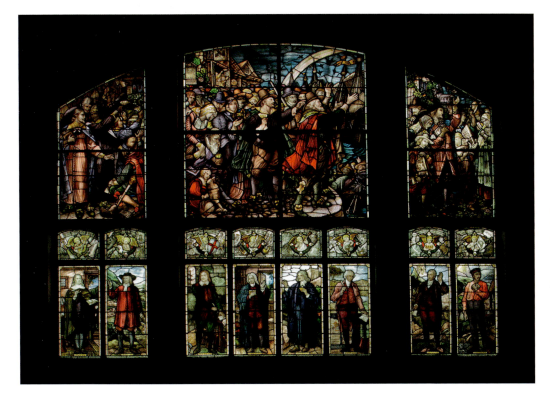

Fig 7.36
Stained-glass windows in Fairhaven Congregational church, Lytham St Annes. Above: the Pilgrim Fathers, flanked by the Westminster Assembly and the 1662 ejection of so many Puritan ministers from their livings. Below: Milton, Fox, Bunyan, Watts, Wesley, Carey, Williams and Livingstone.
[DP156986]

Stained glass

It is no surprise that stained glass seems not to have featured in the Nonconformists' early chapels and meeting houses. Even in the Church of England, there was relatively little demand for stained glass in the decades around 1700. With their emphasis on the reading of God's word, Protestants valued the light levels that came from clear glass, but generally did not object to the principle of coloured glass. The late Georgian rise of interest in stained glass affected Nonconformists as well as Anglicans, and during the early 19th century various types of painted and stained glass began to appear in chapels. Coloured margins, foliage patterns and geometric motifs were not uncommon, and fully figurative glass was installed in chapels by some denominations at least from the 1830s. Among the early subjects were Christ blessing the bread, Christ on the road to Calvary, and Christ walking on the water (these examples being in Wesleyan and Swedenborgian chapels).

During the 1840s designers such as Thomas Willement and William Warrington, who led the revival of medieval-style stained glass, created windows for Congregational and Unitarian chapels. Subsequently almost all of the major Victorian manufacturers (including Clayton and Bell, Hardman, Chance, William Morris and Heaton, Butler and Bayne) worked for Nonconformist clients. Burne-Jones's earliest design for Powell's, another stained-glass manufacturer, was a fetching portrayal of the Good Shepherd, dating from 1857. Originally in a window of 1861 or 1862 in a Congregational chapel, the work was said to have 'driven Ruskin wild with joy'. Some Nonconformists, such as the Quakers and Strict Baptists, would not have allowed such figurative glass. Those who did, however, were generally unremarkable in their choice of subjects. New Testament scenes predominated; faith, hope and charity were not unusual; and the Light of World became quite popular.

St George's German Lutheran church, London. Crucifixion window and relocated panels of stamped jewel work, by James Powell and Sons, 1855; the Crucifixion panel was designed by George Rees. [DP155961]

At the end of the 19th century the mainstream repertoire began to be augmented by distinctively Nonconformist imagery. In about 1889 Wesley's chapel in City Road, London gained a window of John Wesley preaching to the world, to be followed in 1924 by a depiction of the Wesleys' conversion. An ambitious portrait gallery of religious dissenters and their claimed predecessors (from Anselm and Bede via Zwingli and Cranmer to Cromwell and Milton, and then to Elizabeth Fry and Livingstone) fills the east and west windows of the chapel at the Congregationalists' Mansfield College, Oxford. The sequence, by Powell's, was given in 1906. In 1905 the first part of a comparable scheme (by Charles Elliott for Abbott and Co) for the future Congregational chapel at Fairhaven had been completed, later augmented by a lively set of narrative scenes – including Luther at the Diet of Worms and the departure of the Pilgrim Fathers. More limited groups of Puritans and Nonconformists were chosen for the apse windows (of 1905–6 by Henry Dearle for Morris and Co) at Emmanuel Congregational church, Cambridge and for the south transept window (1931, by Heaton, Butler and Bayne) at Christ Church, Port Sunlight. In Surrey *Pilgrim's Progress* provided the Baptists of Sutton with the theme for the main window (1934, by Christopher Webb) at their new chapel, and after the Second World War the work inspired a series of dramatic windows at Bunyan Meeting, Bedford. Of the great quantity of stained glass installed after war damage, the west window (of 1950) at Highbury Congregational chapel, Bristol is unusual for its Nonconformist flavour. In commemorating K L Parry, the chapel's hymn-writing minister, it features portraits of Martin Luther and Isaac Watts, along with the founders of Latin and Greek hymnody.

The subsequent turn towards non-figurative glass left little opportunity for explicitly Nonconformist themes. An example from the 1960s is the swirling design in *dalles de verre* (slabs of glass) at St Andrew's Methodist church, Worcester (1967–8 by Arthur Buss for Goddard and Gibbs); it symbolises the progress of the soul through fire, water and light. A more recent example is the chancel window (of 2002, by Rona Moody) at Psalter Lane Methodist (now Anglican and Methodist) church in Sheffield.

Here saturated yellow and blue serve to represent the act of creation and the light of Christ. In contrast to such abstraction – and such colour – two memorial windows (of 2001 and 2003) by Mark Cazalet at Wesley's chapel in City Road, London exemplify the current revival of interest in engraved and etched clear glass.†

Highbury Congregational chapel, Bristol (now Cotham Parish Church, see pp 126–7). Detail of the Parry memorial window of 1950. [DP166291]

Garden suburbs and garden cities

The role of chapel building in the garden city movement deserves special comment. Many leading Nonconformists – including W H Lever, George Cadbury and Joseph Rowntree – were involved in the movement, and the seminal publication *Garden Cities of Tomorrow* (1902; first published in 1898 as *Tomorrow: A Peaceful Path to Real Reform*) was the work of a Congregationalist, Ebenezer Howard. Such people naturally assumed that religion would have a place in the planned community, but what kind of a place?

At Port Sunlight the future Lord Leverhulme envisioned a sort of interdenominational parish church, a medieval complement to the old English atmosphere of the model village. The interdenominational element was of limited success, but architecturally Lever's hopes were fully realised: Christ Church (of 1902–4, by W and S Owen; now United Reformed) is a reposeful Gothic monument (Fig 7.37), with a peal of eight bells in its strong tower.[111] At Bournville, by contrast, space was allocated for Anglican as well as Quaker buildings, and the Cadburys ensured that the prominently sited Quaker meeting house (of 1905, by W A Harvey)

was all of a piece with the cottage-style architecture of the village (Fig 7.38).[112] Its Y-shaped plan and entrance composition were unmistakably borrowed from Edgar Wood's Christian Science church in Manchester (*see* Fig 7.30), but the proportions are tamer and the materials more rustic. The hall and parish church which the Anglicans built between 1912 and 1925 (also by W A Harvey) departed from this vernacular spirit, introducing an Early Christian style that was permitted – but not approved of – by Bournville's trustees.[113] At Letchworth, the first garden city, there was no proprietorial hand and many religious groups built places of worship. The first of these was the interdenominational Free Church (of 1905; by Parker and Unwin), a small whitewashed building with sloping buttresses as in some of the houses by the same architects.[114]

Even in Hampstead Garden Suburb, where the presiding figure was Henrietta Barnett – wife of the former vicar of Whitechapel – the first services (in a temporary hut) alternated between Anglican and Nonconformist formats.[115] In due course Henrietta Barnett allocated parallel sites for 'the Church and Chapel ... each at the end of one of the two great avenues' in the central square, and commissioned Edwin Lutyens to design the mighty twins that still dominate the

Fig 7.37
Christ Church (now United Reformed), Port Sunlight, Cheshire, 1902–4 by W and S Owen. This, the only place of worship in Lever's model community, was not intended to be identified with any one denomination. [DP143785]

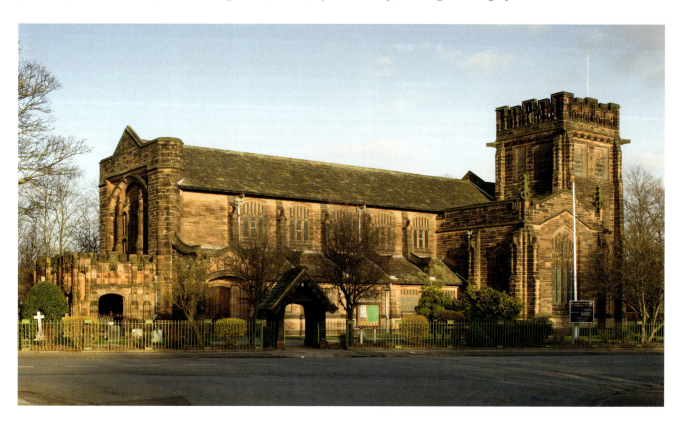

formal centrepiece of the suburb.[116] Rather like Lever at Port Sunlight, Barnett wanted the religious architecture to stand out from the domestic and public buildings. It was at her insistence that Lutyens reluctantly gave the Anglican church (St Jude's; begun 1910) a more or less Gothic spire, although for the Free Church building (begun in 1911) he was permitted to employ his own variations on the Byzantine style, mixed with quattrocento and early Georgian details (Figs 7.39 and 7.40). This pair of monumental churches represents a certain Edwardian view of English religion, in which the Nonconformists had collectively earned a place alongside the Church of England. 'God is larger than the creeds' was the legend inscribed (again, at Barnett's initiative) over the doorway of the Free Church: an ecumenical sentiment that it was not thought necessary, however, to repeat at the entrance of the Anglican church.

Beyond the headline story of the Free Churches' status in these planned communities, there was another significant development. Quakers, even if enthusiastic contributors to the Free Church movement, found it difficult to reconcile their style of worship with the sermons, prayers and hymns of other Nonconformists. Indeed, English Quakerism failed to capitalise on its otherwise successful home missions because 'the warm and friendly atmosphere' of the missions failed to prepare people for 'the formality and reserve' of Quakers' largely silent worship.[117] And so, in both Letchworth and

Fig 7.40
*Interior of Free Church,
Hampstead Garden
Suburb. Lutyens devised
an altogether more chaste
design for the Free Church
than for its Anglican
counterpart, which he also
designed and which had
been started a year earlier.*
[DP150932]

Hampstead Garden Suburb, the Quakers met separately from the Free Churches, and soon built their own premises. An early resident of Letchworth was Juliet Reckitt, daughter of the Humberside manufacturer, and for her in 1907 was erected a large house (architects, Bennett and Bidwell), complete with a hall for Quaker meetings.[118] Immediately the hall was given to the Society of Friends, and the rest of the house followed. Juliet Reckitt named the house Howgills, after the home of a 17th-century Quaker, and the wing intended for worship was closely modelled on the meeting house of 1675 at Brigflatts, near Sedbergh. The whitewashed render and stone-mullioned windows fit perfectly into the garden city aesthetic, while remaining true to the character of the original (Figs 7.41 and 7.42).

Such atavism was not unique. In 1913 the Quakers of Hampstead Garden Suburb built their meeting house (architect, Frederick Rowntree) to a design inspired by the 1688 meeting house at Jordans, Buckinghamshire.[119] The hipped roofs, warm red brick, lattice windows and painted wooden shutters are recognisably from that source, although the plan and the proportions are different. Henrietta Barnett's trustees had expected something much grander, and had to be persuaded to approve so simple a design.

This desire to replicate early meeting houses was quite new – all part of a fresh interest in the origin of Quakerism.[120] As their distinctive forms of dress and speech were gradually abandoned, so Quakers began to invest more meaning in the places and people of the movement's formative years. In 1912, for example, Swarthmoor Hall (the Lancashire home of Margaret Fell and George Fox) was purchased as a historic Quaker site, and in the same year Jordan's farm in Buckinghamshire (where William Penn and Isaac Penington had worshipped in the 1670s) was opened as a Quaker hostel for visitors. At Jordans meeting house, a short walk from the farm, weekly worship resumed – after an interval of more than a century.[121] Against all the complexities and challenges of the modern world, such little-altered country buildings seemed to offer a reassuring simplicity. They became places of pilgrimage (for American as well as British visitors) and oases of peace away from the noise of the city. In the era of Free Church unity Quakers were trying to distinguish themselves from other

Fig 7.41 (left)
Quaker meeting house, Letchworth, Hertfordshire, 1907 by Bennett and Bidwell. A quintessential piece of garden city architecture, yet derived from the 17th-century meeting house at Brigflatts (see Fig 1.9).
[DP088254]

Fig 7.42 (below)
Interior of Quaker meeting house, Letchworth, Hertfordshire. Although better lit and warmer than its north-country model, a little of the spirit of Brigflatts persists.
[DP088391]

Nonconformists, and were doing so – like the new open-air museums of vernacular buildings in each of the Scandinavian countries – by focusing on farmsteads rather than palaces. This search for identity was, of course, highly sophisticated. One's appreciation of the Jordans-inspired meeting house in Hampstead Garden Suburb is sharpened by the knowledge that its founder member was a Quaker stockbroker, John Braithwaite, the future chairman of the Stock Exchange.[122]

Taking stock

The buoyant mood with which many Non-conformists entered the 20th century can be sensed in their buildings. From the baroque grandeur of the Wesleyans' central hall in Westminster, holding its own alongside the citadels of church and state, to the Arts and Crafts radicalism of the Christian Science church in Manchester, Nonconformity contributed to the major architectural developments of the age. A similar confidence underpinned the Nonconformists' mission buildings, many of which vied with the era's best commercial architecture for splendour and practicality. In affluent areas, such as Four Oaks, there were congregations and architects quite capable of giving the Church of England a good run for its money when it came to conventional Gothic schemes. For the most part, chapel builders chose to do otherwise, however, working with

plan-forms that were more enterprising and more suitable for congregational worship – layouts that put Nonconformists in the mainstream of Protestant thinking in Europe and America. In external architecture too, chapel specialists such as George Baines were able to outdo their Anglican contemporaries, creating up-to-date designs that even Nikolaus Pevsner (not noted for his praise of chapels) could later admire.[123] More significantly, Nonconformist architecture began to be recognised by leading members of the Church of England at the time. The one major publication on modern church buildings in Britain was Nicholson and Spooner's *Recent Ecclesiastical Architecture*, published *c* 1911, and it included a number of Nonconformist schemes – not to mention a good sprinkling of Roman Catholic works – among its otherwise Anglican selection.[124] After decades, if not centuries, of being snubbed or patronised, this was a breakthrough.

Recognition came at a cost, however. A common explanation was that chapel architecture had improved. It was a narrative that many Nonconformists accepted, and promulgated. For instance, in 1897, the replacing of a Georgian Baptist chapel at Birchcliffe, Hebden Bridge was justified because of 'dry rot in the old chapel, *the growth of aestheticism* [my emphasis], and the inability to obtain seats'.[125] Attractive photographs of the new building were duly illustrated in *The Baptists of Yorkshire* (1912) along with unpromising views of the earlier meeting places, as if to demonstrate the aesthetic evolution of Nonconformity.[126] Confident in the knowledge that the latest chapels were architecturally impressive, Edwardian Nonconformists too often failed to appreciate the quality of what was being jettisoned. They were quicker to acknowledge the achievements of their forebears in gathering congregations than in designing places of worship.

A rare challenge to this state of mind appeared in 1910, when Joseph Crouch – of Crouch and Butler, architects – published *Puritanism and Art*, seeking to persuade Nonconformists that they were the inheritors of a positive aesthetic tradition. In one section of the wide-ranging book, Crouch wrote approvingly of early meeting houses, including that of 1699–1700 in Ipswich, which he knew from photographs and drawings. His emphasis was on the quality of its fittings, especially the 'beautiful' pulpit which 'might well have been designed by Wren himself', and which has carving 'that would not disgrace the reputation of Grinling Gibbons'.[127] Then, in 1914, Ronald P Jones's *Nonconformist Church Architecture* appeared, developing the evaluation of early chapels and continuing with an analysis of later examples. Again there were comparisons with Wren's church interiors, but in addition Jones had praise for chapel façades. He described the front of the early Georgian chapel at Underbank, Stannington, for instance, as 'a perfect piece of design and proportion'.[128]

As the first synoptic history of chapel building, *Nonconformist Church Architecture* marks a new seriousness in the study of the subject. It also quietly marked the end of an era. Jones was not exactly anti-Victorian, and indeed was generous in his account of the best Gothic chapels, but he believed that 'most of the talent and enthusiasm shown by the Gothic revivalists was futile and misdirected'.[129] He judged that Gothic required ample funds and a large, liturgically minded congregation 'if it is to be attempted at all'.[130] That final qualification was a kindly declaration that the Gothic revival had run its course, at least for ordinary situations. Of the possible alternatives, he noted – without enthusiasm – the attractions of 'some Byzantine treatment of brickwork' and 'what might be called the "Garden Suburb" style'.[131] In fact Jones's heart was with the age of Wren and the pre-Palladian phase of Georgian architecture. The Unitarians had inherited a particularly good selection of urban chapels from the years around 1700, and he (as a Unitarian) had been entrusted with the restoration of several of them.[132] The process informed Jones's later practice as a designer of new chapels, as will be seen in Chapter 8, but for the moment its importance lay in the implicit challenge to the view that Dissenters had been little more than worshippers in barns. Edwardian chapel building could be seen to have a fine aesthetic pedigree.

8

Chapels since 1914

Over the past hundred years there has been an overall general decline in chapel- and church-going. As early as 1909 Charles Masterman had noted a drift away from religion in general:

> The tide is ebbing within and without the Churches. The drift is towards a non-dogmatic affirmation of general kindliness and good fellowship, with an emphasis rather on the service of man than the fulfilment of the will of God.[1]

Even in those places where numbers have been sustained, the pattern of attendance has gradually changed. The routine of going to two or three services each Sunday grew weaker quite early in the 20th century, and the regular commitment to weekday events at chapel became less strong. These changing patterns of worship and social need have naturally influenced the planning of new premises, and the use of existing buildings. The general story is one of fewer, smaller places of worship. Within such long-term trends, however, the Second World War heralded a change of tone, a fact reflected in the separate introductions to the interwar and post-war sections of this chapter.

The interwar years

The quarter century which preceded the First World War was the last period of real prosperity so far as Nonconformist building activity was concerned. Membership numbers for the Methodist and Baptist denominations peaked before 1914, and at the same time the pace of chapel building seems to have slackened a little. Furthermore, there was a significant decrease in construction during the war years – in marked contrast to the boom in chapel building that had occurred during the Napoleonic Wars a century earlier – and the steep rise in building costs was a brake on many chapel projects for several years after 1918.[2] Tighter budgets and dwindling membership were also real challenges. Building, when it came, sometimes took the form of a dual purpose chapel-cum-Sunday school, an interim solution that did not always lead on to the erection of a full chapel. Nonconformists were adjusting to a situation in which growth was more limited and particular. During the 1920s and 1930s prosperous suburbs or commuter towns and villages were the most fertile territory for Nonconformist enterprise. Attention was still paid to the inner city, however, and some thought was given to the new working-class housing estates.

Underlying these changes, Nonconformity as a movement was becoming less of a force. The Liberal landslide of 1906 was subsequently judged to have brought few real gains for the Nonconformist denominations, and the rise of the Labour Party led to divided loyalties. And so, after a period at the heart of the nation's political culture, the Free Churches settled into a less adversarial role. Detailed discussions about church unity were held with the Church of England following an appeal from the Lambeth Conference in 1920.[3] The ecumenical spirit within Nonconformity led to the creation of the Methodist Church (formed by the union of the Wesleyan, Primitive and United Methodists) in 1932, and in 1939 the Presbyterians and Congregationalists drew up plans for the uniting of their congregations.[4] Individually and collectively, the Nonconformist denominations were seeking to redefine their position in the world. One leading figure expected that 'the struggle with Roman Catholicism will have to be re-fought' and that the Nonconformists would thereby 'recover their evangelical zeal and ancient power' – but it was not to be.[5] Irreligion remained the churches' greatest challenge, and the social needs of a population that had experienced first the First World War and then the Depression were urgent.

The 1920s were a comparatively conservative time for Nonconformist architecture, as for many other areas of British culture. Adventurous architects in Germany were devising expressionist or modern-movement churches of steel, concrete and glass, but for the time being Britain showed little appetite for that kind of thing. It was not merely a matter of architectural conservatism. Britain also responded cautiously to the liturgical changes which at that time inspired much of the new religious architecture on the continent. Paradoxically, just when round and polygonal plans were coming to play a greater part in European church design, Nonconformists became – at least temporarily – less likely to opt for such shapes. The tradition of central plans did continue in some of the post-1918 generation of central halls, but otherwise a characteristic chapel of the 1920s was likely to have a linear plan; it was also likely to be built of brick, perhaps in a quietly Gothic, Romanesque or Georgian style. At the same time it became increasingly common for new Nonconformist buildings to be known as churches rather than chapels, a tendency that had been gathering momentum among socially elite congregations since the 19th century.[6] During the 1930s liturgical and architectural thinking began to open up again in Britain, and a few Nonconformist places of worship embodied those fresh approaches.

Rural chapels

Given the overall downturn in Nonconformist membership figures, and the declining need for agricultural labour, it is no surprise that far fewer rural chapels were built between the wars. Two examples can give some idea of those that were erected, however. As was now normal, both chapels were architect-designed. At Ashton under Hill in Worcestershire the decent-looking Baptist chapel (of 1881) was deemed inadequate for the needs of the prosperous village, and so in 1923–4 it was replaced by a larger building (by F W Anderson) which – as a joint venture by local Methodists as well as Baptists – was to be called a Free Church (Fig 8.1).[7] The architecture of the conspicuous new chapel gives no sense of the wind having gone from the Nonconformist sails. Curvilinear tracery fills the main window towards the street and there is figurative stained glass in the pair of smaller south-facing (war-memorial) windows. These relatively sophisticated Gothic features were being used to signify a place of worship, but otherwise the architect's attitude to style was easy-going: classical motifs are mingled with the medieval, and the side windows are mostly domestic, wood-framed rectangles. It seems that neither denominational

Fig 8.1
Free Church, Ashton under Hill, Worcestershire, 1923–4 by F W Anderson. Elaborate Gothic tracery and frankly domestic details co-exist in this village chapel.

nor stylistic niceties were to stand in the way of Ashton's Nonconformists.

As a representative of the altogether simpler chapels that continued to be built, we can turn to an example from a decade later (1933–4): the Methodist chapel in Thursford, a small Norfolk village whose population had declined steadily for almost a century. Despite a tradition of Primitive Methodism, the village had previously been without a purpose-built place of Nonconformist worship.[8] In fulfilling an ambition to worship in their own chapel, however, Thursford's Methodists were careful not to overreach themselves. The graceful little building was designed by A F Scott and Son, whose reputation rested on well-detailed Gothic chapels, but by now there was a declining appetite for pointed windows, and the budget in this case (£417) did not run to carved tracery.[9] What might be called Gothic syntax remains – a steep roof, supported internally by corbelled arch-braces and externally by buttresses – yet the three slender windows in the gable end are round-headed and rectangular sash windows punctuate the side walls. Red brick and pantiles emphasise the building's local character. The chapel was fitted out with pews and a harmonium, and in the centre of the gangway was a small tortoise stove, its pipe rising directly to the roof. Victorian architecture might have been passing out of favour, but 19th-century apparatus was still normal in many rural districts.

The urban challenge

The sense that Nonconformists retained a place in the heart of the urban world was hardly diminished by the First World War. To illustrate the point one can turn to the Baptists' West Ham central mission, on Barking Road in Plaistow – a part of Essex that had long been industrialised and was to be absorbed into Greater London in 1965 (Fig 8.2). Barking Road tabernacle had begun a relief and welfare mission in 1900, in response to local unemployment, and planning soon began for new premises. Designs (by William Hayne) were ready in 1914, but, due to the intervening war, the building was erected only in

Fig 8.2
West Ham (Baptist) central mission, Plaistow, Essex, 1921–2 by William Hayne. The Byzantine building was the gateway to an extensive programme of social and educational activities as well as popular religious services.
[DP150886]

1921–2.[10] Its punchy façade, with two domed towers and an array of round-arched openings in red brick and stone-coloured terracotta, is a Byzantine landmark, conceived of as 'a great cathedral Church towering above the mean streets of West Ham'.[11] In one tower is a set of bells, bearing the names of 169 local men who had died in the war.

Cathedral-like or not, the building had a clear social purpose. The mission's hostel was immediately adjacent, and the old tabernacle was converted into a children's centre, with classes, clubs, kitchen and medical facilities. Internally the new building was fitted out with tip-up seats – rather than the pews originally intended – like many of the Methodist central halls. All 1,500 seats were regularly filled (the church had over 1,000 members in the 1930s, and many more attenders), but in the inflationary post-war years the capital costs were enormous. Baptist congregations from far and wide contributed to the fund, their names inscribed on stones around the building. The mission, with its team of ministers and deaconesses, was especially active through the hard years of the Depression; by 1936 it had built a rural home for poor mothers and babies as well as a home for old men – this latter overlooking the Queen's Gardens at the rear of the mission.[12] Then, right alongside the main building, it erected the Swift Hall for youth – looking like a theatre and containing not only a 450-seat auditorium, but also a library, study area, lecture hall and facilities for classes in health and fitness training.[13] In the years before the welfare state and wide access to secondary education, the mission was a remarkably comprehensive enterprise: part cathedral, part college, part leisure centre, and the entry point to a network of social services.

For the Baptist world, West Ham mission was an exceptional undertaking which attracted international support. Meanwhile the Methodists continued to build central halls quite widely.[14] A few examples must suffice. The central hall in Scarborough was built in 1919–23 (by G E Withers) as a successor to the Wesleyans' 80-year-old town centre chapel.[15] Like the West Ham mission it has a pair of domed Byzantine towers, avoiding the more ecclesiastical associations of Gothic. In Bristol a Wesleyan chapel and school were superseded in Old Market Street by a central hall (of 1922–5; architects, Gelder and Kitchen) with a great circular auditorium and an extensive suite of schoolrooms, all approached via a baroque frontage with shops and offices.[16] Something of the atmosphere of worship in these buildings can be conveyed by the account of a men's fellowship meeting in the 1920s at a (slightly larger) central hall in East Ham:

The thrill of it in those days and the difference on a Sunday afternoon, two thousand four hundred men there. They had a voluntary orchestra; they had a grand organ and a choir. At the first hymn, the organ, the orchestra and choir would all play and the gallery, well, you could feel it vibrating.[17]

With over 1,900 seats, Bristol's hall was capacious enough to offer a similar thrill, but it was almost the last of such big places. Ten years later, at Archway in north London, the Methodist central hall (built in 1933–4, just after Methodist union and so no longer specifically Wesleyan) accommodated just 1,200.[18] Archway was planned with all the facilities of a by-then traditional central hall, including shop units, offices, classrooms, a secondary hall and gym, and the main auditorium was equipped for use as a cinema or concert hall as well as place of worship. Stylistically, however, a different note was struck. The architects (G E and K G Withers) were by that date willing to allow the logic of steel-framed construction to influence the design, and included only a few classical references – in fact, much like a typical commercial block of its day.

It was generally in the largest towns and cities that newer religious bodies first gained a foothold. Such was the case with the Seventh-day Adventists. One of their first generation of congregations in England worshipped in a series of London venues before commissioning a bespoke building (of 1927–8 by Samuel A S Yeo) in Holloway Road (Fig 8.3), close to the tram stops at the Nag's Head junction, then local landmarks.[19] It was designed to hold its own against the showy frontage of Frank Matcham's Marlborough Theatre, which had become a cinema since the First World War.[20] The church's façade, composed with classical motifs and rhythms, is generously glazed, allowing ample daylight into the deep vestibule and the hall above. As a keenly proselytising body, the Adventists may also have wanted this transparency to signify their openness to the world. Beyond the vestibule and crush hall lies the main chamber, a two-storey space that is fitted with tip-up seats, although laid out a little more formally than in the Methodists' central halls. At the far end are the pulpit

Fig 8.3
Seventh-day Adventist church, Holloway Road, London, 1927–8 by A S Yeo. With its first-floor hall, the generously glazed entrance block stands in front of the slightly wider church building.
[DP151541]

and baptistery, set on a platform in front of stepped seats for the elders. The building was a milestone, not only in the history of the local congregation, but also in the development of the Adventist movement in Britain, and served as the home of the Adventists' national conference.

In thriving city centres the builders of offices, cinemas and shops looked enviously at some of the sites occupied by long-established chapels. Most congregations resisted the pressure to sell up, but a minority did take the money and moved to the suburbs. On occasion compromises were reached between commerce and religion. In central Birmingham, for instance, the Quakers allowed their Victorian meeting house to be demolished so that Lewis's could almost double the size of its department store, and in return were provided with a replacement meeting house 'at almost no cost'.[21] The new place of worship (of 1931–3), hidden behind the giant retail block in a courtyard off Bull Street, is a neat brick box, a marriage of Georgian propriety and 20th-century construction (Fig 8.4).

Its architect, Hubert Lidbetter, stepped back from the fuller classicism of Friends House (of 1924–7), the Quaker headquarters in London, with which he had made his name.[22] Some of the same planning principles are evident, however. At the core of the Birmingham building is the main space for worship, a squarish room that is largely top-lit and fitted out with Lidbetter's modern version of the traditional bench (Fig 8.5). Insulated (by a surrounding corridor and outer ancillary rooms) from the distractions of the world, it fosters the stillness and silence which are essential for Quaker worship. It is very different from the thrilling atmosphere of the Methodists' great central halls.

Yet Quakers too were keen to reach the urban poor, and from Bull Street they had established a pioneering network of adult schools and institutes in Birmingham. One of these, having been given a new entrance and staircase as recently as 1929, became in effect a wing of the new meeting house.[23] As part of the same complex, across the courtyard, there was another building (dating

Fig 8.4
Quaker meeting house, Bull Street, Birmingham, 1931–3 by Hubert Lidbetter. The proportions of Lidbetter's design were altered by the addition of an extra storey in the late 20th century. [DP143729]

Fig 8.5
Interior of Quaker meeting house, Birmingham. Since the 17th century, Quakerism has always had major urban meeting houses, as this 1930s contribution – with its central block of benches facing the stand – seems to remind us. [DP143731]

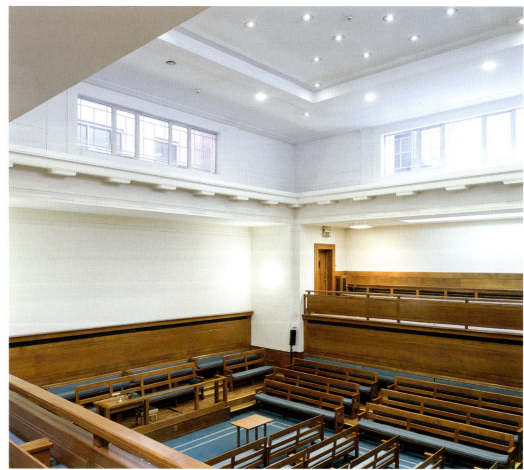

from 1880) where the Quakers had, besides a library, an office for the business of all their congregations in the district – business which had grown with the creation of more than a dozen suburban meeting houses in Birmingham.[24] The growth of these suburban congregations had paradoxically enabled Bull Street to create a new role for itself as a kind of headquarters for local Quakers.

In one important instance an 18th-century city chapel was rescued for its historic associations. John Wesley's New Room in Bristol (which, as Methodism's earliest purpose-built chapel, was discussed in Chapter 3, *see* pp 47–8) had been owned by a Welsh Calvinistic congregation since 1808. By 1928 it had fallen into a dilapidated condition, however, and the energetic minister in charge of the Wesleyans' central mission in Bristol suggested to a leading layman that the building should be saved.[25] That layman was Edmund Lamplough, a Lloyds' underwriter, who bought the New Room in 1929 and appointed the architect Sir George Oatley to use 'the very best means' to 'place this historic edifice in first rate order,

always bearing in mind its original form and characteristics'.[26] As a Gothic enthusiast, Oatley was not an instinctive neo-Georgian, but he undertook the restoration as a labour of love, removing most of the 19th-century work and re-creating a wide range of fittings, from the pews and upper pulpit to the candle sconces and door latches (Fig 8.6). In contrast to Wesley's chapel in City Road, London, which had become enriched with jasper columns, marble monuments and a good deal of stained glass, the New Room was prized for its uncluttered atmosphere. 'Is it not beautiful in its chaste simplicity?' asked Oatley at the reopening ceremony in 1930.[27] Although the restored building continued to be used for the Welsh congregation's Sunday services, ownership passed to the Wesleyans and the site became a kind of shrine for Methodists. Upstairs, the preachers' rooms were furnished as they might have been in Wesley's day, reminding visitors that the New Room had not been created solely as a place of worship. The restoration, coming at a time when the Methodists' programme of central-hall building was beginning to falter,

Fig 8.6
Wesley's New Room, Bristol, as restored 1929–30 by George Oatley. In re-Georgianising Wesley's first purpose-built premises, Oatley gave special dignity to the pulpits and communion area.
[DP166249]

*Fig 8.7 (below)
Unitarian church,
Cambridge, 1927–8 by
R P Jones. The well-
mannered building
incorporates motifs from
the 'age of toleration' but
possesses a gable-end
façade.
[DP160406]*

*Fig 8.8 (below right)
Interior of Unitarian
church, Cambridge. R P
Jones's admiration for the
architecture of Wren's era
helped to shape his designs
for the Unitarian church.
[DP160105]*

helped to emphasise the founder's vision of major urban chapels as bases for social and administrative as well as evangelical work.

Only rarely in the 1920s did one of the old Nonconformist denominations establish a new congregation in a historic town centre. One of those rare examples was in Cambridge, which gained its first chapel for Unitarians, in Emmanuel Road (the hall being erected in 1922–3 and the main building in 1927–8), to the designs of Ronald Potter Jones (Fig 8.7).[28] Jones, whom we met in Chapter 7 as the author of *Nonconformist Church Architecture*, injected into the familiar format of a gable-end-pediment chapel a little of his favourite 17th-century and early Georgian architecture. Above the door is an oval widow, similar to that in the Queen Anne meeting house in Bury St Edmunds (*see* Fig 2.7), while the flanking windows, though rectangular, have radiating glazing bars and wavy aprons. A small classical lantern sits on the roof ridge (just possibly a nod to Wren's chapel at Pembroke College).

The interior is quite unexpected (Fig 8.8): the walls are fully panelled in warm oak, in a way then popular with the builders of neo-Georgian houses. There are tall pilasters, a deep entablature and, as the climax, a colonnade around the raised communion apse. Pretty fanlights and festoons adorn the vestry entrances, while the pulpit and lectern are embellished with carving of a kind that Jones will have admired at the Ipswich meeting house. And the chandeliers are daintier equivalents of what he called the 'fine brass hanging candelabra of Dutch design' at Ipswich and Taunton.[29] With its long plan-form, high wall panels, congregational chairs and no more than an organ gallery, the Cambridge church building is far from recreating an early Dissenting interior. Yet Jones must have intended to give Unitarians a sense of continuity with the first great era of Nonconformist architecture, as well as turning away from the Gothic ideals which Unitarians especially had championed throughout the Victorian age.

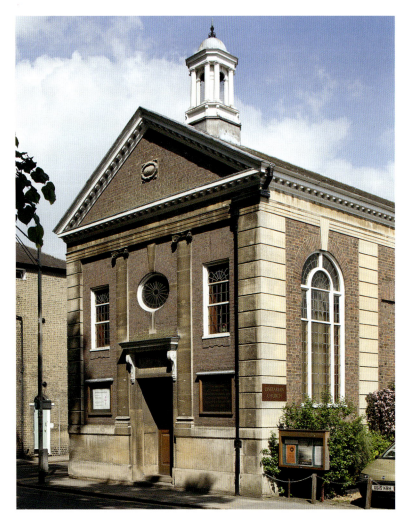

Gothic, old and new

For long after the First World War some Non-conformists – chapel-goers as well as architects – were attached to the Gothic ideal, and the leafy suburbs provided ample opportunity for pared-down versions of the medieval village church. At Psalter Lane in Sheffield, for instance, a United Methodist congregation erected a substantial new stone building in 1928–30 (by J A Teather), complete with transepts, chancel and narrow side aisles.[30] A flèche enlivens the roofline and stubby octagonal towers flank the broad west window, which has Perpendicular tracery. Characteristically for the 1920s, the Gothic details are generally restrained. The interior (greatly altered in 2001–2) was fully pewed. It had a central gangway leading to the chancel in which were choir stalls, an eastward communion table and reredos (Fig 8.9). Perhaps there was some appetite here for more sacramental forms of worship, which at least one Methodist theologian was then exploring.[31] For a congregation whose previous city centre chapel (a broad-fronted brick building, sold for development as a shop) celebrated its centenary in 1928, the shift to a suburban Gothic church must have been a great change, undertaken with a mixture of regret and adventure.[32] The architect produced a dignified and spacious structure, making a feature of the pulpit and a few other carefully designed fittings, but it would be difficult to argue that there was anything daring about the design. By 1930 the licentious Gothic that had characterised many Edwardian chapels seemed rather remote.

Gothic was still capable of inspiring young architects, however, as is demonstrated by one of the most adventurous Nonconformist

Fig 8.9
Interior of United Methodist (now St Andrew, Methodist and Anglican) church, Psalter Lane, Sheffield, 1928–30 by J A Teather. This worthy Gothic design was reordered for an ecumenical partnership in 2001–2.
[DP168478]

Fig 8.10
Baptist church, Sutton,
Surrey, 1934 by Welch,
Cachemaille-Day and
Lander. Turning away
from elaborate tracery and
spires, Cachemaille-Day
here showed his admiration
for Baltic brick Gothic and
the sheer brick walls of
Albi cathedral.
[DP160421]

Fig 8.11
Baptist church, Sutton,
Surrey. The understated
Gothic of the entrance front
offers barely a hint of the
extraordinary interior.
[DP160422]

projects of the 1930s: the Baptist church buildings on Cheam Road, Sutton, which opened in 1934 (Figs 8.10 and 8.11).[33] This was another case of a chapel being displaced from its High-Street location by a department store, even though in this instance the new, larger site was only a short distance away. The architects, Welch, Cachemaille-Day and Lander, were the rising stars of Anglican church architecture, and their excursion into the Nonconformist world at Sutton produced an exciting building. Externally the sheer brick walls and high windows reflect Cachemaille-Day's admiration for Albi Cathedral, interpreted (with cusp-like buttresses and herringbone tile-work) through an Arts and Crafts sensibility. Internally the debt to German expressionism is more explicit, and gives the building the edge over the architects' better-known Anglican churches. Primeval Gothic arches reach from floor to ceiling, their rustic brick mouldings standing out from the rough-plastered white walls (Fig 8.12). The final arches are angled inwards to focus attention on the chancel, which is steeply vaulted like Dominikus Böhm's Gothic-expressionist churches of the 1920s in the Rhineland. Against the end wall of the chancel – where Catholic churches would have the high altar – is the baptistery, on permanent view and having as its backdrop a kind of brick reredos, incorporating a stone slab carved with a baptismal scene (*see* p 228).[34] The stained glass (by Christopher Webb) above the baptistery is composed of scenes from the Nonconformist classic, Bunyan's *Pilgrim's Progress*: special effort was evidently taken to produce a Baptist iconography. Originally the communion table was placed at the front of the chancel, in full view of the congregation, and more recently it has been brought into the nave, with pews rearranged around it, an arrangement that recalls early meeting houses, and coincidentally was rediscovered in Germany in the early 20th

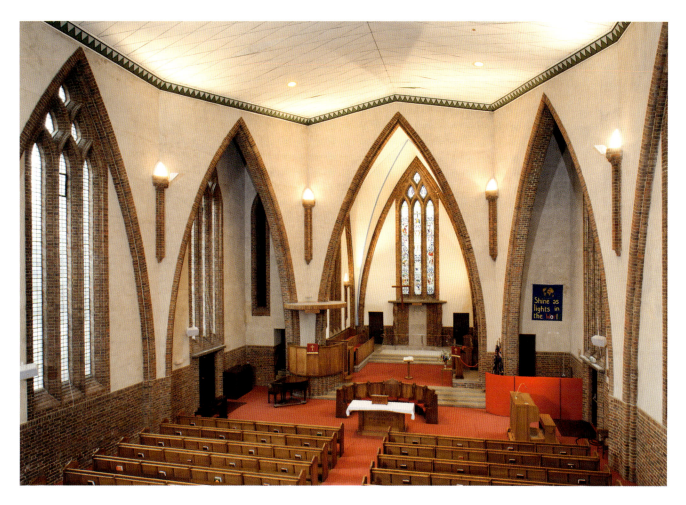

century.[35] A large pulpit with circular tester (again reminiscent of Böhm's work) clasps the chancel arch, clearly visible to all. Other things are hidden from view, however. The sound of the organ emerges only via brick grilles, and the electric lights are concealed in what look like medieval torches on the walls.

Although the effect is less overwhelming than in a fully expressionist church, this was clearly intended to be a spiritual space, even when not filled with worshippers, and from the outset it was open throughout the week 'for prayer and meditation'.[36] The idea of private devotion in a public place of worship, though not instinctively part of the Nonconformist tradition, had been attracting interest through the later 1920s.[37] If such an emphasis was new for Baptists, the familiar programme of social and educational activities was not neglected in Sutton. Adjoining the main entrance is a two-storey school block including kitchen and toilets, and then a church parlour and large hall, carefully detailed as an ensemble. There was room also for that new phenomenon, a car park.

Away from Gothic

The Baptist building in Sutton was exceptional in its radical paraphrase of Gothic forms, and was the work of an outstanding architectural practice. More characteristic was the work of Smee and Houchin, an experienced firm of Nonconformist specialists who worked a good deal in the London suburbs. In 1932 they created a group of Gothic buildings for the Congregationalists (now United Reformed Church) in Woodford Avenue, Ilford.[38] A lych gate gives access to the site, leading directly to the church porch at the base of an accomplished tower and spirelet, and at the far end a bold transept balances the composition. The details are not conventionally Gothic, however. The windows are quite deeply set, below angular heads, and are generally without tracery – a cutting to the bone of medieval architecture rather than a concern for its niceties. Complementing this stripped Gothicism, the interior is dominated by a deep vault that has a hint of German expressionism about it. Three years later, for the Free

Fig 8.12
Interior of Baptist church, Sutton, Surrey. Primeval arches and rustic brickwork invest the building with an expressionist power. The communion table and deacons' stalls were originally in the chancel, a little beyond the pulpit.
[DP160418]

Baptism

At the Reformation most Protestants continued the practice of infant baptism. Following Calvin's recommendation that the ceremony be held in full view of the congregation, and that immersion was unnecessary, Presbyterians and Congregationalists commonly used a bowl, which might be placed on the communion table when required or set in a bracket on the pulpit. A number of silver bowls survive, but examples in ceramic, pewter and other materials are known. In due course Moravians and Methodists also used such baptismal bowls (as indeed did many Anglicans). In the early Victorian years, under the influence of the Gothic revival, some Nonconformists began to use miniature pottery versions of medieval-style fonts in lieu of bowls. Freestanding fonts of wood or stone also started to appear in chapels at that time. These were generally placed near the pulpit or communion table and were permanently visible, a sign of the importance of baptism. A particularly elaborate example, of marble and polished limestone, was created for the Unitarian church at Todmorden in the 1860s. The liturgical movement of the 20th century further encouraged the tendency to provide a freestanding font close to the communion table and pulpit.

Some Protestants rejected infant baptism as unscriptural, however, and revived the New Testament practice of baptising only adults. Chief among these early groups were the Baptists, who normally baptised (by immersion) out of doors, often in streams or rivers. Outdoor baptisteries were created for some Baptist chapels in England during the 18th and 19th centuries, but over time indoor baptism became more usual. Baptismal pools were typically created beneath a chapel floor and covered by panels or floorboards when not in use. Tewkesbury Old Baptist Chapel has a good example. From the late 19th century some Baptist congregations commissioned chapels in which the baptismal pool was on constant show: examples may be seen at Umberslade, Warwickshire (1870s) and Sutton, Surrey (1930s). Among the other denominations who practise believers' baptism are the Open Brethren, Seventh-day Adventists, Church of Jesus Christ of Latter-day Saints (Mormons) and Jehovah's Witnesses.

There is a third strand of Protestantism, represented from the 17th century by the Quakers and later also by the Salvation Army and Christian Scientists, which sees no need for such external rites as baptism and communion. For this reason there are no fonts or baptisteries in Quaker meeting houses, Salvation Army citadels or Christian Science churches.[†]

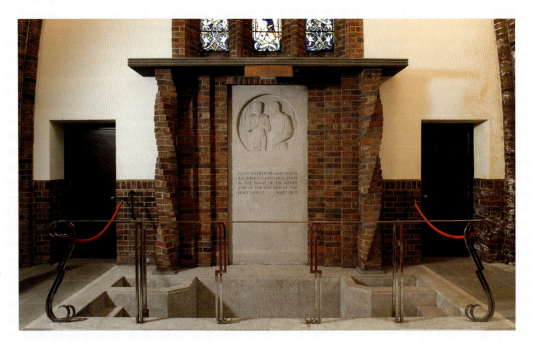

Baptist church, Sutton, Surrey, 1934. Here the carved roundel of a New Testament baptism, framed by Solomonic columns, overlooks the baptistery.
[DP160420]

Church (now United Reformed) at East Lane, Wembley Park, Houchin abandoned the Picturesque village church ideal, in favour of a tall and blocky design – one that might be called neo-Georgian were it not for the multiangled detail of the window heads.[39] It comes as a great surprise to discover that the interior – save for its axial entrance – is a twin of that at Woodford Avenue, not only in its plan, with shallow transepts and apse, but also in the low-sweeping white vault that is so clearly Gothic. Such stylistic disjunction between exterior and interior might appear transgressive, but in the age of Granada cinemas this cannot have seemed so great a violation.

More exotic treatments occasionally appeared. One instance is the Congregational chapel at Knowle, Warwickshire (of 1931–4, by John Wilson of Birmingham) in which the basic shape – a long, steep-roofed and buttressed building – is essentially Gothic, but there is not a pointed arch in sight.[40] Instead the façade has a collection of fancy curves, diaper masonry and late Renaissance metalwork, while russet pantiles complement the Snowcreted walls: part E S Prior and part Clough Williams-Ellis. There are echoes here of the national romantic eclecticism of Östberg or Tengbom, and perhaps more strongly (as Pevsner noted) of south-German architecture of the early 1920s, all injected with a Spanish flavour.[41] The interior is comparatively routine, but culminates in a proscenium arch of distilled rococo curves as a setting for the top-lit communion apse. It was hardly radical, but did reflect a desire for novelty.

Year by year fewer congregations were opting for Gothic designs, and younger architects were rarely inclined to advocate the style. Joseph Crouch was in his seventies when he wrote *The Planning and Designing of a Methodist Church* (1930), a book dedicated to the opinion 'that it is on the lines of the ancient Gothic style that the Methodist churches of today should be designed'.[42] Even Crouch was flexible, however. At one of his recent suburban commissions (Hall Green Wesleyan church, Birmingham, of 1923–4):

> Some of the promoters of the scheme objected to a purely Gothic design, and a compromise was effected by designing a church in which the general plan followed more or less the Gothic type while the details were classic in feeling. The result as a whole, especially the interior, has met with popular approval.[43]

In fact the interior is not so much classical as Romanesque, with a barrel vault and severe Tuscan columns. And Crouch employed a more richly detailed version of the same style in 1927–8, when it came to replacing the Wesleyans' town centre chapel in Stourbridge.[44] Crouch's near contemporary Sir George Oatley was another architect of Gothic inclinations who sometimes employed round arches in this period. A prime example is the Wesleyan church building of 1928–30 that presides over the central square of Sea Mills, Bristol's new garden suburb.[45] In contrast to the stone towers and tracery that he had used elsewhere, this is a brick basilica.[46] Oatley's transforming touch was to place the building across the site – contrary to what the master-plan envisaged – and so make a façade of one of the long sides. The broad, two-storey frontage with its hipped roof is an effective piece of townscape, and chimes with many of the features of the surrounding shops and council houses. It also resurrects the pattern of so many early meeting houses (something which Oatley as a Congregationalist must have realised), although the windows are more quattrocento than Queen Anne and the internal layout is at right angles, with a Romanesque barrel vault leading to the communion recess.

One younger Nonconformist architect who worked for many suburban and seaside congregations made a more systematic distillation of the Romanesque. He was Frederic W Lawrence, who first caught national attention in 1930 with a design for Immanuel Congregational church, near his home in Southbourne, 'a select and handsome suburb' of Bournemouth.[47] However, it was with the Congregational (now United Reformed) church building of 1934–5 in the commuter village of Oxted, Surrey that Lawrence got into his stride (Figs 8.13 and 8.14).[48] For Oxted he created a beautifully proportioned brick structure in which Romanesque rhythms are tempered by a neo-Georgian liking for plain parapets rather than pantiles and corbel tables. The plan, a Greek cross with a slightly lengthened nave and a square crossing tower, is essentially that of the so-called mausoleum of Galla Placidia in Ravenna – a building then widely enough admired for Osbert Lancaster to caricature a Christian Science version of it in 1936.[49]

It is a plan that can work well for congregational worship (*see*, for instance, St Saviourgate meeting house in York, Fig 2.1), and Lawrence emphasised this by making a strong feature of the crossing, allowing the four great arches to

Fig 8.13 (right)
Congregational (now
United Reformed) church,
Oxted, Surrey, 1934–5 by
Frederic W Lawrence.
Part Romanesque and part
Georgian in its sources,
such architecture achieved
tasteful effects with a
minimum of decoration.
[DP167377]

Fig 8.14 (below)
Interior of Congregational
(now United Reformed)
church, Oxted. The placing
of the communion table –
originally in front of the far
window – reflected a desire
to provide a more seemly
setting for the sacrament.
[DP167371]

spring almost from ground level in a Soanian fashion. Within the chancel, a further, narrower arch and matching window provided a dignified setting for the communion table. Lawrence gave much thought to the effects of light and colour, aiming to create a reverent and meditative atmosphere.[50] As with the recently opened Baptist building in Sutton, this was to be a spiritual space. In front of the entrance Lawrence set the scene with a fountain, lily-pond and bird bath – an ensemble that was to become a cliché for crematoria, but was as yet remarkable in a Nonconformist place of worship. Oxted's generally well-heeled Congregationalists took gracefully to these ideas, deciding to call the building 'The Church of the Peace of God', and – in the minister's words – praying that 'this chapel may long bear its silent witness in uniting men and women by its beauty and its sincerity to seek and worship the God of beauty and of truth'.[51]

Lawrence's achievement at Oxted brought him a stream of further commissions. It was seen as a model by writers who approved of the move from Victorian chapel design, and who recognised 'the new ceremonious regard for the communion table' as part of the liturgical movement spreading through progressive Catholic and Protestant churches in Europe.[52] But at that date neither Lawrence nor, it is thought, any other Nonconformist architect took the more radical step of placing the communion table in the centre of the congregation – an arrangement with ample precedent among Dissenters, and one which would have accorded with the introduction of central altars in a few Anglican and Catholic churches from the mid-1930s.[53] Thirty or forty years earlier Nonconformist architects such as Cubitt had helped inspire developments among church builders in Germany and beyond. Since then Germany had become the centre of a revolution in church architecture, and Britain was slow to catch up.

The shape of things to come?

Only very modest claims can be made for the influence of modern architecture on English chapel builders between the wars. Occasionally, for instance with the Baptist church in Sutton, the Arts and Crafts legacy metamorphosed into a kind of expressionism. More commonly, as in the secular world, there was a move into the Georgian revival, a move which was in places justified as a return to Nonconformist origins. The Georgian revival in this context was chiefly a matter of neat brickwork and sash windows rather than monumental classicism, for which most congregations had neither the budget nor the appetite. The Free Church of 1923 in Letchworth (architect, Barry Parker) (Fig 8.15) is described

Fig 8.15
Free Church, Letchworth, Hertfordshire, 1923 by Barry Parker. The Georgian Revival acquired a colonial inflection as Parker moved away from the roughcast and whitewashed walls of Letchworth's earlier architecture.
[DP088249]

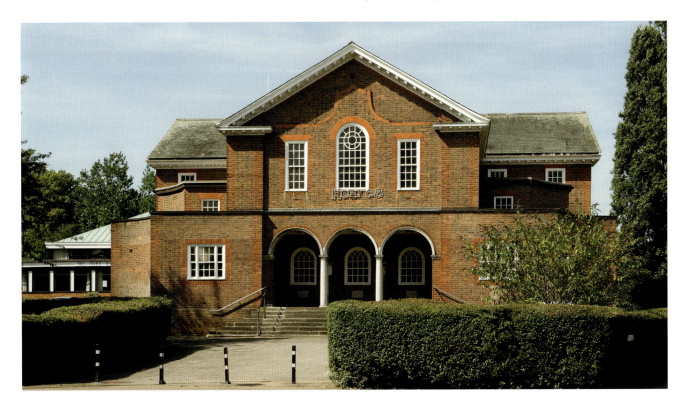

officially as illustrating the garden city's 'radical change in style and materials from the informal Arts and Crafts idiom to a more formal classicism', but this gives no hint of the refreshing lightness of touch that Parker brought to the design.[54] There is a faintly colonial air about the façade, from its arcaded porch to the unusual brick detail in its open pediment, and the airy interior is neither numinous nor monumental. It is a 20th-century equivalent of the meeting houses in which the rational gospel was expounded. By the mid-1920s Parker's Morrisian insistence on the superiority of handmade things had given way to an acceptance that 'the machine has come to stay', and his architecture had become less Picturesque, even if nowhere near as radical as the latest continental churches of concrete or steel.[55]

One British book took stock of modern church building from Europe and America: A L Drummond's *The Church Architecture of Protestantism*, which appeared in 1934. A Scottish Presbyterian minister, Drummond was interested in the theories that underpinned 20th-century religious architecture abroad, but had little sympathy for some of the physical results. He described Perret's widely acclaimed church of Notre Dame du Raincy, Paris (of 1922–3), as 'concrete, cold, and uninviting'.[56] German developments he found more stimulating, but even so:

It does not appear that, normally, the solution will be found in the building of either steel or reinforced concrete churches. It is not often that a church built on the analogy of a modern factory will distil a spiritual fragrance.[57]

Despite conceding that what he called 'modernistic pioneers' had a right to experiment with church architecture, Drummond thought that their principles were unlikely to be followed in Britain. Later he was to write that:

Radical modernist architecture, which was so widespread on the Continent between 1919 and 1939, is not likely to commend itself to many communities in Great Britain; they may use it for their shops, offices, and factories to an increasing extent, but are not prepared for 'machines to worship in'.[58]

Drummond's paraphrase of Le Corbusier's concept of the house as a *machine à habiter* was surely intended to reinforce the aesthetic conservatism which shaped so much religious architecture

in Britain between the wars. Yet, as he acknowledged, modern architecture was inspiring a growing number of secular buildings in this country, and it was to touch church building too.

Probably the first Nonconformist specialist to have worked with one of the big names of modern architecture was Edward Mills, a Methodist who began his professional apprenticeship with Smee and Houchin in 1930 – the year in which the practice was designing the stripped-Gothic Congregational church in Ilford (*see* p 227).[59] In 1934, attracted by socially committed modernism, Mills became assistant to Maxwell Fry, in whose office Walter Gropius (founding director of the Bauhaus) arrived later that year as an exile from Nazi Germany. Mills worked on the details of at least one of Gropius's English buildings before tackling as his first independent job a Methodist mission (of 1936–7) in Colliers Wood, south London. The Colliers Wood mission (at the time of writing used as a nursery) was thoroughly modern in its absence of historicist detail, its flat roof and horizontal lines.[60] Rather than the lychgate favoured by Smee and Houchin, a thin slab canopy on slender steel piers covered the main path from the street, and there were tubular metal gates and fencing, very much in the style of Fry and Gropius. Notwithstanding the use of a reinforced concrete frame, the facings are of brick. This was no doubt a disappointment for purists, but only a brave church committee would have accepted a 'white box' design at that date, and even Gropius had chosen brick for the village college at Impington in 1936.

Functionally the mission church had to be flexible, accommodating worship, Sunday school, young people's clubs and various other meetings. Mills followed the tried-and-tested Akron system, allowing classrooms to be formed with partitions along each side of the main space, but ensured (by using a minimum number of thin steel posts) that when the partitions were removed the whole space felt open and well lit – a prized quality among modernists. In addition, rather as in the latest schools, a line of glass double doors opened towards the large garden. There was no fixed furniture or dedicated communion area, but a liturgical focus was created by having a podium and lectern at one end of the space, below a mural of Christ washing the disciples' feet (the first of Hans Feibusch's many church paintings), with a small organ discreetly set at one side. These features were sufficient to signify that the building was a place of worship, even when not in use for services, but were not so visually powerful as to make activities such as a jumble sale seem sacrilegious. Many earlier chapels were effectively used like this as multi-purpose spaces, but here the understated character of the liturgical focus was rather new. For the chairs and tables Mills maintained his modernist principles, rejecting the usual ecclesiastical supplies in favour of bentwood and laminated pieces by Thonet and Aalto. The scheme was the promising first venture of a man who was to play an active role in English religious architecture after 1945, but for the moment it seems not to have been widely influential.

By the 1930s modern structural systems, such as that used by Mills at Colliers Wood, were routinely employed for central halls and other large Nonconformist buildings, though as a rule the stylistic treatment was – as we have seen – conservative. Such conservatism gradually eased, however, a prime example being the Unitarians' city centre Church of the Divine Unity in Newcastle upon Tyne, of 1939–40.[61] Needing to replace a pinnacled Gothic chapel, the thriving Unitarian congregation employed a local architectural practice (Cackett, Burns Dick and Mackellar) with a reputation for classical and baroque designs.[62] The set piece entrance – through a trabeated stone screen and a small courtyard to the framed doorway – is effectively classical, yet stripped of most historicist details. Otherwise the building belongs to the strand of English architecture that preferred Dudok to (on the one hand) Lutyens or (on the other) Le Corbusier: it is composed of long cuboid elements and a tall, off-centre tower, while its expanses of pale brick are interrupted by a row of tall windows. The interior, despite its traditional layout, is much less sedate. The steel and concrete frame allows the side aisles to be spanned without columns, and the cream décor gives way in the chancel to deep blue with a stepped Art Deco motif. Globe light-fittings, square-ended pews and cubic pulpit help to make this is one of England's most stylish places of worship from the 1930s (Fig 8.16). It was also, of course, one of the last cohort to have been built before the Second World War put an end to normal building activities.

Fig 8.16
Unitarian Church of the Divine Unity, Newcastle upon Tyne, 1939–40 by Cackett, Burns Dick and Mackellar. The building's Art Deco details and its wide open space make for a memorable interior.
[DP059763]

The Second World War years

As in 1914–18, chapel building all but ceased during the Second World War. More significant, however, were the effects of bombing. For instance, more than 2,600 Methodist church buildings were affected, and of these about 800 were destroyed.[63] Many important Nonconformist buildings were hit, and there is room here to mention only a few examples. In Manchester the Methodists' central hall in Oldham Street and the Unitarians' venerable chapel in Cross Street were among the casualties; in Bristol the Brethren lost their imposing Bethesda chapel and serious damage was inflicted on Butterfield's Highbury Congregational chapel. In London the Baptists' huge Metropolitan Tabernacle was gutted, and the Congregationalists suffered the loss of major chapels in Westminster Bridge Road (Christ Church), Holborn Viaduct (the City Temple) and Tottenham Court Road (Whitefield's). It was reported that over 400 of the 580 Methodist buildings in the capital were damaged, including all but three of the denomination's 118 London missions.[64]

From an early stage in the war, the threat – and then the reality – of bombing stimulated a quasi-official recognition that Nonconformist buildings were a significant part of the nation's heritage. Watercolours were made of a number of chapels as part of the Recording Britain scheme, and photographs were taken for the National Buildings Record. In 1940 John Betjeman published a very sympathetic essay on Nonconformist architecture, with lively illustrations by John Piper.[65] From within Nonconformity too, more attention was being given to the topic of historic places of worship. Hubert Lidbetter, the Quaker architect, began a systematic study of Quaker meeting houses (publishing articles on the subject in 1942 and 1946), and A L Drummond wrote an account of Victorian and 20th-century Congregational chapel building.[66] Martin S Briggs, a Congregationalist and an accomplished architectural writer, wrote *Puritan Architecture and Its Future*, the first book to provide an interdenominational history of chapel buildings from the Reformation to the 20th century.[67] Briggs gave his readers a good selection of plans and photographs, including some from the National Buildings Record.

In turning his readers' thoughts to post-war building, Briggs was keen to suggest that what he called the 'modest, retiring and domestic nature' of early meeting houses should be the model.[68] In so doing he seriously underplayed the architectural liveliness of such early designs as Norwich's Old Meeting, and disparaged the 'warm and cheerful atmosphere' of many Methodist chapels.[69] Where bomb-damaged chapels were to be brought back into use,

> destruction of carved and painted decorative features will permit of the elimination of all superfluous trappings, the design of an austere new colour-scheme, and – in general – the re-shaping of the church in the simple beauty that should be characteristic of our Puritan architecture in the 'Brave New World'.[70]

Like many of his generation, Briggs did not wholly regret the Luftwaffe's bombing of Victorian buildings. However, his argument that the so-called Puritan legacy should equip Nonconformists especially well for the task of creating post-war buildings was novel.

Wartime losses forced the hand of a number of dwindling urban congregations, with the result that some amalgamated and others dispersed. Yet many congregations remained, so that there was an enormous task of repair and rebuilding to be done, not to mention the development of new sites on housing estates. The Methodist Church prepared especially well for this, first creating a committee that worked on the subject during the war and then publishing *The Methodist Church Builds Again*, a book of guidance (written by the secretaries of the church's Department for Chapel Affairs) with illustrative plans.[71]

On 27 July 1945, the day that Attlee formed his new government, *The Architect and Building News* published a plan for a new kind of community church, a Methodist venture on a London County Council estate.[72] As well as the church and tower, the scheme incorporated a boys' hostel, communal restaurant, library, classrooms and shop; there were rooms for dances, meetings, youth work, games and social events, while an existing hall was to be used as a clinic, gym and venue for weekday classes. The architect of this project was Edward Mills, again keen to put his architectural skills to the service of Methodism. His vision was for a church that would meet the needs of what William Temple had lately described as a welfare state, and to do so with the spirit of modern architecture, including flat roofs and long sun-balconies. The church itself was inspired by the radical design of the Johanneskirche in Basel (of 1934–6, by Egender and Burckhardt), from its skeletal tower and fully glazed side wall to its asymmetric blocks of pews – the larger block facing the pulpit – and choir. In the event Mills did not get the opportunity to build this pioneering scheme, but it set the tone for what was to prove a more adventurous era.

Since 1945: downsizing and reaching out

As Britain emerged from the upheavals of the Second World War, there were signs that the gradual decline in faith was being reversed. Attendance at services generally increased, Sunday school enrolments grew and Billy Graham's evangelising crusades (starting in 1954) created an atmosphere in which it was possible to think that the nation might experience a sustained religious revival. Callum Brown has characterised the period between 1945 and 1958 as witnessing a return to piety.[73] The resurgence was not ultimately to last, however, and by the 1960s there were signs that attendance at chapel and church was again in decline. Against this background more moves towards church union emerged: Methodists and Anglicans talked about joining forces; in 1972 the United Reformed Church was created by the union of most Congregational churches and the Presbyterian Church of England; and across the country many individual chapels and churches came together in local ecumenical partnerships.[74] During the last decades of the century, as congregations recognised the likelihood of long-term decline, the number of redundant places of worship became a cause for concern.

If the traditional denominations were shrinking, however, some newer religious groups and movements were increasing. On the one hand, some of the proselytising American churches in Britain expanded very steadily; on the other, large numbers of people were drawn to more dynamic, charismatic forms of worship. Among the groups that more than doubled in size during the quarter century before 1995, for instance, were Jehovah's Witnesses, the Mormons (formally the Church of Jesus Christ of Latter-day Saints) and – most significantly – the Pentecostal churches.[75] Of these it was the Pentecostalists whose rate of expansion subsequently accelerated, and by 2013 they exceeded the combined total of Methodists and Baptists in Britain.[76] Another trend was for the creation of churches which appealed predominantly to one ethnic group, from the mostly black evangelical churches to the Chinese or Korean Protestants. Orthodox churches grew similarly. Of course the changing religious landscape was even more notable for the rise of other faiths in Britain, with Islam, Hinduism and Sikhism being the most prominent.

What have been the effects of these changes for Nonconformist buildings? After a very slow recovery from wartime conditions, building activity quickened appreciably during the 1950s for most Nonconformist denominations. At first the priorities were to replace damaged premises for existing congregations and to build places for fledgling congregations in housing estates and new towns. There was much talk of dual-purpose (that is, secular and religious) buildings and community churches, and of using modern materials. Rural chapel building dwindled even below its pre-war level, being generally required only in special circumstances. By the 1960s the emphasis gradually passed to well-heeled suburbs and commuter towns, although a number of older urban chapels were also replaced.

Demographic changes had led most central halls to lose their audiences, but in several towns the idea of worshipping 'over the shop' was revived when longer-established chapels on High-Street sites were rebuilt with commercial outlets at street level. Long before the word came into general use, downsizing was a necessity for many congregations. New liturgical and architectural attitudes came to play a larger part in Nonconformist thinking from the late 1950s, though the results were not as radical as in the Roman Catholic world. In succeeding decades the octagon was reclaimed by Nonconformists – perhaps emboldened by recent German examples, but certainly aware of Wesley's advocacy of the type – to such an extent that by the end of the century it became almost commonplace. Mormons have preferred to keep spires as a religious indicator. However, some of the rapidly growing denominations have worried less about distinctive architectural expression, with the result that externally their buildings can resemble smart retail warehouses, complete with generous car parks.

In recent decades traditional patterns of worship have often been augmented, and sometimes abandoned, by Nonconformists. Pulpits are rarely to be found in the latest chapels, as speakers generally prefer the informality of a lectern (and microphone), and in many places the Georgian tradition of a musicians' band has been reinvented, with space for a drum kit, guitar and electronic keyboard in full view of the congregation. A control desk for sound, lighting and projector is commonly tucked away behind the congregation. More varied services have led to flexible seating arrangements, an innovation as far-reaching as that which had transformed the layout of primary schools in post-war Britain. Rigid seating plans, sloping floors and fixed liturgical focal points have tended to yield to what architects have called 'loose-fit' spaces. The desire to provide facilities for wider community use – one of the strengths of Nonconformist provision – has if anything increased as society has become more secular.

The years of reconstruction

Hardly any places of worship were built in the five years after 1945.[77] Materials were in short supply, licences to build were not easily obtained, costs were rising very sharply and planning policies rarely gave priority to churches. To give a glimpse of the better world that lay ahead, a badly blitzed part of Poplar, in London's East End, was rebuilt as a 'live architecture'

exhibition, forming part of the 1951 Festival of Britain. Amid the new housing, schools and markets, two places of worship were erected, one Roman Catholic and one Nonconformist. The Catholic church (SS Mary and Joseph, by Adrian Gilbert Scott) was comparatively traditional in its monumental structure, but the Trinity Congregational (subsequently Methodist, now Calvary Charismatic Baptist) church by Cecil Handisyde and Douglas Stark seemed to embody the Festival spirit, attracting attention for its innovative construction, modern materials and extensive social accommodation (Fig 8.17).[78] One first perceives a slender brick campanile (its bell a relic from the church's bombed Victorian predecessor) that was apparently inspired by Stockholm Town Hall, although its tall aluminium crown owes as much to Moholy-Nagy as to Östberg. This is followed by the main church building, resembling a giant toast rack from whose concrete ribs the lightweight copper-clad walls are tilted in.[79] If the departure from traditional aesthetic values did not please everyone (the minister had been initially 'thunderstruck' on seeing the model), the result was praised by one writer as having 'a gaiety in its

Fig 8.17
Trinity Congregational (subsequently Methodist, now Calvary Charismatic Baptist) church, Poplar, London, 1951 by Cecil Handisyde and Douglas Stark. This star of the Festival of Britain marked a complete break from traditional materials and methods of construction. [BB93/20905]

outward appearance that is quite in keeping with a contemporary enlightened attitude towards religion'.[80] The airy interior (Fig 8.18) – carefully insulated against traffic noise – is well lit by strip windows and a battery of domed roof-lights, not to mention the pendant lamps with wiry satellites that so piquantly evoke the mood of 1951.[81]

Although the arrangement of chancel and pews was relatively conventional, the gallery treatment was less usual. Conscious of the changing pattern of attendance at services, the minister had asked for a layout in which a small congregation would not feel lost, but which could seat up to 400 worshippers on occasion.[82] The architects' very satisfactory solution to this 20th-century quandary was not the obvious expedient of movable partitions, but an intimately scaled ground-floor area, with galleries that barely impinge because they project outwards beyond the ground-floor walls. Important though this area for worship is, Trinity has always been just as notable for its extensive

social facilities. An elegant staircase hall gives access to a long, two-storey block of what were originally club rooms, along with a small hall and kitchen, while at the far end is a large hall and stage. These rooms, designed a little less self-consciously than the church, are laid out around a courtyard, with the club rooms offering views across the adjacent park. All this ancillary accommodation attracted widespread interest in 1951, not because such things were new to Nonconformity, but because the idea of a community church (sometimes called a church centre) seemed to have found its moment – even in the Church of England.[83]

Occasionally post-war reconstruction paid attention to the Victorian architecture which had so often suffered damage. In Exeter, for instance, the tower and spire of the bombed Southernhay Congregational chapel were retained, and the essential shape of John Tarring's 1868–70 building – including lofty nave, side aisles and transept – was re-created when the new place of

Fig 8.18
Trinity Congregational church, Poplar, London. Though now lacking its pews, the interior retains much of its innovative and even playful post-war atmosphere.
[DP166268]

worship rose from the ruins of the old in 1956–7 (Figs 8.19 and 8.20).[84] Despite the respect for the historic fabric, however, Gothic details were studiously avoided by the architects (R M Challice and Son) in the new work. A more peremptory approach was taken by Sir Edward Maufe when designing the replacement (of 1950–5) for the burned-out Scottish Presbyterian church of St Columba in Chelsea.[85] Maufe had little time for the Victorian ruin. Its red brick and lancet Gothic gave way to Portland stone and a curious blend of Georgian and Byzantine motifs in his big new church. Most Nonconformists, faced with the task of rebuilding even major chapels, had neither the ambition nor the budget for such monumental buildings. Congregations were generally smaller and architectural tastes were changing. For example, after wartime damage the Congregationalists retained only the tower and spire of the great Christ Church on Westminster Bridge Road; the site was redeveloped for a commercial office block, incorporating a new church (marked by a large screen wall with a Gaudí-like motif) on the ground floor.[86]

Smaller enterprises downsized in different ways. At Blackheath in south London, for instance, the shell of a war-damaged Congregational chapel (of 1854) was rehabilitated in 1957 for a congregation whose membership had fallen from 183 in 1939 to 100 in 1956.[87] In this case the architect, Trevor Dannatt, retained the outer walls at what had been the pulpit end of the 1854 building; he then constructed a new external wall across the width of the former nave, creating a

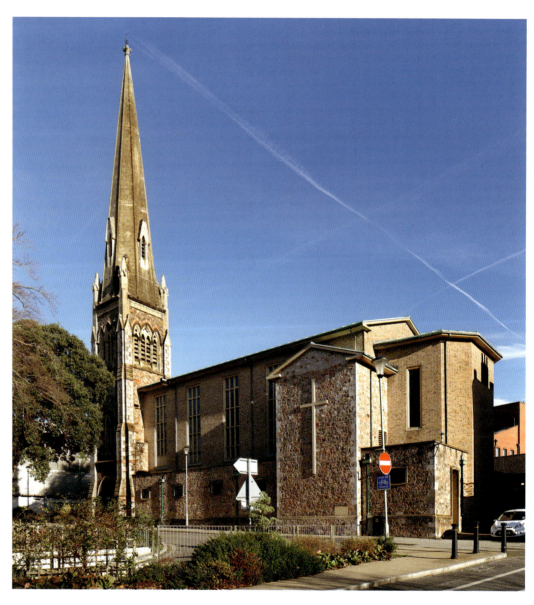

Fig 8.19
Southernhay
Congregational (now
United Reformed) church,
Exeter, 1956–7 by R M
Challice and Son. The new
building retains not only
the tower and spire, but
also the plan-form of its
predecessor, which suffered
bomb damage in the
Second World War.
[DP158307]

church in just half the area of the old.[88] A court-yard and garden were laid out in the remainder of the space, overlooked by the fully glazed new wall of the church. Dannatt seems to have drawn inspiration not from machine-age modernism, but rather from Le Corbusier's sophisticated peasant manner (as used for the house at Mathes), with rustic stone piers and deep eaves. Natural finishes were employed throughout, and the interior – now altered for secular use – had as its focus a low brick platform on which stood the font, communion table and straight-fronted wooden pulpit, set in front of the unadorned and blind end wall.[89] This artfully simple arrangement reflected the continentally inspired desire to restate the relationship between the word and the sacraments. Tellingly, the communion table, a freestanding brick pedestal supporting a polished slab, was more like an altar than a traditional wooden table.

Although the 1950s were on the whole a progressive period for Nonconformist architecture, many different kinds of building could then be described as 'modern'. At Stand, on the northern fringes of Manchester, for instance, the Georgian Revival was given a colonial American accent for the graceful Unitarian chapel that was built in 1952: 'GI-Georgian', it might be called.[90] The architect (J S A Young, of Young and Purves) appears to have taken his cue from the small bell tower and full-height, pedimented porch of its bombed predecessor, but turned to New England for the lantern spire and white painted woodwork that complement the neat brick walls of the replacement chapel.[91] Lit by round-headed windows – originally all with intersecting glazing bars – the interior of the new building has white walls, tasteful oak fittings and small brass chandeliers. Yet the liturgical arrangements are not those of the archetypal American meeting house. Pulpit and font stand to one side, in front of a high and classically detailed chancel screen which frames a view of the communion table and war memorial window.

Such a setting for the sacrament seems to reflect the continuing influence of R P Jones on

Fig 8.20
Interior of Southernhay Congregational (now United Reformed) church, Exeter. The cool palette and airy proportions of the new building create an air of tasteful reverence. The windows add to this effect, their stained glass being surrounded by generous amounts of clear glazing. [DP160714]

Unitarian practice. A more updated treatment of the colonial style was employed by Louis de Soissons for the Unitarian church of 1958 in Notte Street, Plymouth (Fig 8.21).[92] Its narrow central spire contributed a New World element to the post-war townscape of Plymouth, although the building's broad proportions and mannerist glazing gave a less historicist air to the design.

If anything, Nonconformists proved more willing than Anglicans to turn away from historical forms of architecture in the post-war years. Breaking from historicism was one thing, however; making a coherent architectural statement from the new aesthetic and material possibilities was another. The (now demolished) Punshon Memorial Methodist church,

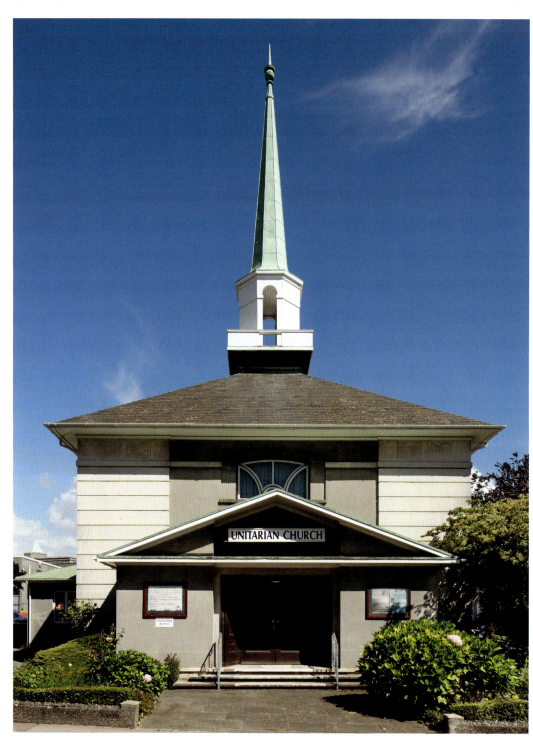

Fig 8.21
Unitarian church, Plymouth, 1958 by Louis de Soissons. Replacing a wide-fronted chapel of 1832, this square and sharply detailed church is topped by a spire that evokes New England meeting houses.
[DP159898]

Bournemouth, which finally opened in 1958, demonstrated the dilemma.[93] It was an ambitious scheme (by Ronald H Sims), replacing on a new site a late Victorian Gothic chapel that had suffered in an air-raid. It included innovative arrangements for parking and wheelchair access, a seemly space for worship and at least one eye-catching external feature (a needle spire). Rather like the contemporary cathedral at Coventry, however, it was opposed by those who wanted a traditional church and was susceptible to criticism from those who found that it fell short of proper modernism. One imagines that both camps would have expected the building's structural frame to have articulated the design (as with medieval Gothic, say, or one of Bartning's steel churches) rather than losing some of it to view behind 'a secondary ceiling ... made in idigbo wood, gold anodised aluminium and glass'.[94] Despite Sims's apparent admiration for Frank Lloyd Wright, the church was far from being a piece of organic architecture: perhaps too many ideas had shaped it.

A more resolved, and less controversial, design was that of 1954–6 for Trinity Presbyterian (now United Reformed) church, Norwich, another replacement for a blitzed church.[95] Here an expressionist mood is immediately established by the sharply angled roof with an acute gable facing the road. Internally that spirit continues in the timber-panelled facets of the deep ceiling, which rises from the almost-square space of the first-floor church, capturing a wedge of wall as a backdrop to the pulpit and communion area (Fig 8.22). The resurgence of church architecture in post-war Germany had turned the attention of many young designers towards such expressionism, and Frank Lloyd Wright's Unitarian church at Madison, Wisconsin had added to the currency of deep-folded roofs. But the architect in this case, Bernard Feilden, had drawn on other sources as well. The idea of a not-quite-detached campanile he borrowed from Ravenna, though his tower has an entasis and a crowning metal turret in homage to Stockholm.[96] Whatever his sources, Feilden felt that 'design must have unity'.[97] He synthesised the various elements, matching the copper of the great roof with that atop the tower, and introducing angularity not only to the arched openings of the church and tower, but also to the forecourt screen and paving. Similar care was taken over access. Cars were to drive through the base of the tower to park at the rear, rather than cluttering the forecourt. Inside the building

there was a modulated route via a lobby, vestibule and stairs (or the lift that was allowed for, but not installed until 1970) to the worship space itself.

By the later 1950s, as building activity quickened for almost every denomination, there was a corresponding growth in architectural options. Modern paraphrases of the age-old system of cruck-frame construction started to appear. Two early English examples were those of the Congregational (now United Reformed) church of

Fig 8.22
Trinity Presbyterian (now United Reformed) church, Norwich, 1954–6 by Bernard Feilden. The modern roof structure, which keeps the interior free from columns, focuses attention on the traditional ensemble of axial pulpit and communion table. [DP163635]

Digbeth-in-the-Field (Fig 8.23), at Yardley in outer Birmingham (1958–9, by Jackson and Edmonds), where the blades are of concrete, and the same denomination's church in Hoole Road, Chester (1957–8, by Paterson and Macaulay), where an A-frame of laminated timber was used.[98] With low side walls and steep roofs, such buildings seem to provide a link with the Arts and Crafts churches of Edgar Wood and W R Lethaby, although the sharp-angled dormers of Digbeth-in-the-Field give its exterior a more crystalline, expressionist character. A less dramatic approach was taken for the Salvation Army citadel in Hendon (of 1958, by C Wycliffe

Fig 8.23
Digbeth-in-the Field
Congregational (now
United Reformed) church,
Yardley, Birmingham,
1958–9 by Jackson and
Edmonds. With echoes of
Gothic naves or inverted
ship's hulls, the cruck-
framed church is lit largely
from dormers.

Noble and Partners), north London, which eschewed the Army's tradition of gable-end façades in favour of a low, square hall with plain brick walls and continuous clerestory lighting below a shallow roof.[99]

Different modernist traditions were evident in the new church buildings of the German and Scandinavian Lutherans in England. The Danish seamen's small church and social centre (now London City mission) of 1958–9 in Stepney, for instance, reflects a knowledge of Aalto's work at Säynätsalo in its combination of red brick walls, timber pergola and asymmetric monopitch roofs.[100] These elements continue inside the church, including the organ gallery and case. The architect here, Holger Jensen (working in association with Edward Armstrong and Frederick MacManus), has been praised for this 'invigorating Continental modernism'.[101] Scandinavian touches could be found even in such routine schemes as the wayside Methodist chapel of Bradshaw Brook, near Swan Green in Cheshire (1960, by Halliday and Agate), where the block of ancillary rooms has hallmarks of the Swedish-inspired New Humanism: square

openings and a shallow monopitch roof with definite eaves.[102]

More rarely, a motif from Le Corbusier appeared. A case in point is the new Methodist church (of 1960, by S W Milburn and Partners) at Fulwell, north of Sunderland. Here an unmistakably Corbusian long access ramp leads – alongside a grand flight of steps – to a big-boned, but far from Corbusian church with a concrete spire.[103] Though the justification for the ramp (that it was available for the elderly and invalids) might suggest an ageing congregation, the church was in fact built on the edge of a new housing estate, which presumably had a preponderance of young families. An extensive suite of classrooms, hall and kitchen was provided below the church; these were intended for a variety of community purposes, including youth activities.

One of the first Nonconformist projects to earn a place in the international surveys of postwar religious architecture was the group of Methodist buildings at Mitcham in Surrey. These were built in 1958–60 to replace a church that had been completely destroyed in the Second World War (Fig 8.24).[104] Mitcham provided

Fig 8.24
Methodist church, Mitcham, Surrey, 1958–60 by Edward Mills. Demonstrating Mills's deep knowledge of contemporary church architecture in Germany and beyond, the building is to be understood in an international context.
[© Elain Harwood]

Edward Mills with an opportunity to realise something like the community church that he had proposed in 1945: a church for 300, a hall for youth activities (with stage and dressing rooms), Sunday-school classrooms and a youth canteen, as well as the usual vestries and toilets. Mature trees were retained, and the site was large enough to allow Mills to group the buildings attractively around two gardens. Architecturally the hall and classroom blocks are of some quality, resembling the schools built by progressive local authorities in the 1950s, but it is the church itself that has always stood out – in character as well as height.

The articulating idea seems to have come from Rudolf Schwarz's church of St Joseph at Braunsfeld, near Cologne: a framework of tall, Y-shaped concrete posts carries a zigzag roof, with deep clerestory windows.[105] Mills made more lucid use of Schwarz's idea, however, simplifying the roofline and cumbersome exterior details, and opting for plain brickwork throughout. He also extended the roof along one flank to create an elegant colonnade beside the large garden. The airy interior too is finer than that at Braunsfeld. The wood cladding on the underside of the roof directs one's gaze to the blind end wall, where a plain cross hangs above the central communion table (Fig 8.25). In this, and the communion rail and lectern, there is something akin to the romantic minimalism of the much-admired Otaniemi chapel near Helsinki (built 1956–7).[106] Mills showed a similar sensitivity in designing the pews – which ingeniously incorporate a part-sunken organ console – and choir seats, ensuring that nothing would detract from the importance of the pulpit and communion area.

Edward Mills had become an influential figure. He was the author of *The Modern Church* (1956), the first British book to illustrate a good selection of European and American church designs of the period from the 1930s to the mid-1950s. It was widely used by architects across the denominations. In international surveys of modern church architecture, Mills's Mitcham scheme was commonly one of just two or three

Fig 8.25
Interior of Methodist church, Mitcham. The end wall of riven York stone and the cedar-boarded ceiling provide natural colour and texture to this important space. [© Elain Harwood]

English examples to be included. He designed the Anglican cathedral at Mbale, Uganda. Then, however, Mills came under attack. His book was dismissed as a 'general survey of an extremely superficial kind', with its chapter on planning criticised as being 'concerned far more with the exclusion of draughts and the provision of space for umbrellas and overcoats than with the relationship between word and sacrament'.[107] The author of this broadside was Peter Hammond, an Anglican priest; he shared Mills's enthusiasm for modern architecture, but believed that 'the design of the church must begin with the altar'.[108] After decades at the edge of English religious culture, liturgical renewal (emphasising the centrality of the eucharist for congregations) was now entering the mainstream. Hammond's New Churches Research Group was a think tank for the cause. On behalf of the Free Churches, Mills responded cautiously to the development, but he will have been aware that some of his fellow Methodists warmed to such ideas, as was subsequently to become clear in his own practice.[109]

The 1960s and 1970s

Once the task of post-war reconstruction was more or less complete, new priorities emerged. Recently established suburban congregations wanted their own buildings; replacements were required for some of the many chapels that became victims of new road schemes or town centre redevelopment; new premises were required for a few venerable chapels on which age had taken its toll, and occasionally a building was replaced because a congregation demanded something more contemporary. On the whole, indeed, Nonconformists seem to have expected modern designs. Mills's generation had prepared the ground.

The Quaker meeting house at Heswall, on the Wirral peninsula, provides an auspicious introduction to what we might call the *post*-post-war generation of Nonconformist buildings. Quakers had been worshipping in Heswall since 1938, meeting in a series of venues, and in 1958 commissioned the design for the meeting house that was finally built in 1961–3 (Fig 8.26).[110]

Fig 8.26
Quaker meeting house, Heswall, Wirral, 1961–3 by Dewi-Prys Thomas. The intriguing play of shapes is an important feature of the townscape and also works well inside the building. [DP143767]

Consciously rejecting the decent Arts and Crafts-cum-Georgian formula that was represented by Hubert Lidbetter's work, the small band of Quakers sought a more adventurous architect, and so chose Dewi-Prys Thomas of Liverpool. The outcome was an inspiring building, dramatising the site's rocky outcrop with the prow of the diagonally roofed, first-floor worship room, its height emphasised by a rank of slit windows. Answering this is the lower block of the warden's house, a similar sliced-off cube of silver-blue brick. If there are hints of Aalto or Jacobsen in the design, there is also a (now modified) Corbusian *promenade architecturale*, or what a local Quaker calls 'a spiritual journey through the heart of the Meeting house'.[111] Starting from the gentle entrance ramp, the route turns back across the vestibule to reach the 180-degree curve of the oriel that leads one upstairs to the 'soaring' main room of the meeting house.[112] Since they acknowledge neither sacraments nor priests, Quakers were above the fray in the controversy over liturgical renewal. However, the usual layout of this upper room, with chairs arranged around a central table (as had become standard practice among British Quakers in the 20th century) might have seemed newly fashionable in the age of central altars. Of course, it also enabled the room to be rearranged with ease for a busy programme of secular activities and social events.

The architectural vitality of the 1960s sometimes affected even those denominations that were reluctant to be seen as worldly. For instance,

the award-winning Octagon chapel (by Kenneth Steel, of Steel, Coleman, Davis; now an auction house), which opened in Taunton in 1965, was built for a Brethren congregation (Fig 8.27).[113] Passers-by will notice first the boldly lettered screen wall with cantilevered concrete canopy and then, beyond, the pale brick octagon of the chapel itself, topped by a flèche. The entrance is through a pair of doors, glazed with a fashionably dislocated pattern of panels. Internationally, octagonal plans were much favoured by church architects at that time, as a convenient shape for eucharistically centred worship. Taunton's Brethren may have been aware of those developments, and could even have been interested observers of the liturgical revival: the breaking of bread has long been an essential and distinctive feature of Brethren worship (often with seats arranged around the table). More immediately, however, their new building honoured the precedent of Wesley's 18th-century octagon nearby (*see* Fig 3.21), which they had only just vacated after more than a century of ownership.[114] Wesley, of course, had recommended octagons as being 'best for the voice', at a time when Methodist chapels were not expected to provide for communion. In the 1960s, however, it was the centrality of the sacrament as well as the word that made such central plans appropriate. One way and another, the octagon was back.[115]

Although Taunton's Octagon chapel was at once traditional and contemporary, many Nonconformists were happy to be seen as more

Fig 8.27
Octagon chapel, East Reach, Taunton, 1965 by Steel, Coleman, Davis. This building was designed for a congregation of the Brethren and was clearly inspired by the 18th-century Wesleyan octagon nearby.
[DP166295]

frankly modern. Thus, from the flurry of 1950s and 1960s church buildings of all denominations in the Leeds and Bradford area, one architectural writer has identified the Presbyterians' as the most radical.[116] The building in question is St Columba's church (now Headingley St Columba United Reformed church), erected in 1964–6 to the designs of W and J A Tocher to replace a Victorian chapel lost in the expansion of Leeds University.[117] It is radical initially because it uses the sloping site to provide parking at road level, attractively set beneath the arc of secondary rooms which project out from angled piers. At the higher level is the church itself – a dark brick rectangle with a deep, continuous clerestory, angular to match the folds of the oversailing roof. A jagged-stepped tower beside the entrance enhances the expressionist component of the design. Inside the potentially sombre effect of purplish brick is countered by much use of wood, from the parquet flooring to the timber-clad vaults of the pleated concrete roof. A slatted wooden canopy forms a backdrop to the dais on which are raised the elders' seats and communion table, with the pulpit set to one side. The table (now, at least) stands far forward, in acknowledgement of the influence of liturgical renewal among the Reformed churches.

Inner-urban redevelopment caused the Presbyterians of Leeds to seek a leafy suburban site; other churches maintained a presence, even if smaller, with modern premises in the city centre. Such was the case in Worcester, where the Meth-

odists' 700-seat Pump Street chapel was lost as part of the city's controversial Lychgate project. The replacement, St Andrew's Methodist church (of 1967–8, by Norman Webster of Shingler, Risdon Associates), is an octagonal building, providing a well-focused setting in which some 400 worshippers can gather.[118] Notably, however, the octagon is built above shops, and so its form – which is decently articulated on pilotis, with concrete beams and aggregate-faced panels – is barely noticed by pedestrians. To compensate for this, an eye-catching vertical feature is made of the entrance: a tall slab of dark brick with a white cross beside the staircase-hall that leads from the street to the top-floor church and its meeting rooms. The curtain wall of that three-storey hall is fully glazed with brightly coloured *dalles de verre* (thick pieces of glass) by Arthur Buss for Goddard and Gibbs in an expressive, abstract pattern, suggesting a spiritual progress through water, fire and light. The adoption of this stained-glass technique, which had spread from France to Britain in the post-war years and was taken up by John Piper, again shows the importance of recent continental practice as a source for English architects in the 1960s.

Modern glass and new architectural forms produced some striking designs in those years. Among these is Trinity Methodist church (of 1967–8, by Gordon A Ball) in Congleton, Cheshire, built when its much-repaired predecessor became unsafe (Fig 8.28).[119] The new building has a dramatic façade, dominated by

Fig 8.28
Trinity Methodist church, Congleton, Cheshire, 1967–8 by Gordon A Ball. With its expressionist windows, this eventful building brings drama to the street scene.

four diamond-shaped windows that reach from floor-level to roof ridge, resembling (as was said of another expressionist church of the time) a line of angels' wings. These west windows, filled with abstract glass, overlook the rear seats, while supplementary daylight is provided at the east end by a pair of what Corbusier called *canons à lumière* – although the form of these timber-clad, ceiling-piercing cylinders apparently owes something to the work of an Italian architect, Glauco Gresleri.[120] Another Corbusian touch are the shots of coloured light from irregular piercings of the building's concrete frame, surely inspired by Le Corbusier's renowned church at Ronchamp. After these fireworks the communion and pulpit area is more restrained, balanced by the asymmetric shape of the grille to the organ chamber.[121] The importance of hymns in the Methodist tradition, one is reminded, was not to be overwhelmed by the current emphasis on the eucharist.

There were plenty of observers, including admirers of Ronchamp, who yearned for something more disciplined than the revived expressionism which Congleton's Trinity Methodist church

exemplifies.[122] The most rigorous critics were those who found inspiration in the work of Mies van der Rohe, and it is his influence that one can see in the Baptist church at Waterlooville, Hampshire (of 1966–7), by Michael Manser Associates (Figs 8.29 and 8.30).[123] In essence this is a Miesian frame of black steel with a recessed glass wall, not quite immaculately detailed, but still of some quality. Breaking through the resolute flatness of the roof is a pale brick wall, almost half the width of the building and rising perhaps half as high again. Internally this wall defines the vestibule, screens the main worship space from public view and (on the other side) serves as the back wall of the wide dais on which the pulpit stands. More unexpectedly it funnels generous quantities of daylight on to the dais, so that the setting of the baptistery, pulpit and communion table gains a certain drama. The extended horizontal lines of the plain pulpit (little more than a wall) and table are in keeping with the building, in calculated contrast to the more baroque organ screen – fashioned from the pulpit of the former chapel – which projects from the opposite gallery. Times change, of course, and one corner of

Fig 8.29
Baptist church, Waterlooville, Hampshire, 1966–7 by Michael Manser Associates. Like other architects whose main work was secular, Michael Manser and his partner Peter Turnbull brought fresh ideas to the design of religious buildings.
[DP160445]

Fig 8.30
Interior of Baptist church, Waterlooville. The top-lit sanctuary, embraced on three sides by sheer brick walls, is a quite unexpected – but greatly admired – element in the steel and glass building.
[DP160444]

the dais now hosts the unminimalist lines of a drum-kit. Beyond the space for worship, the building continues with a full-height hall that was designed for badminton as well as the church's major social events (Fig 8.31); lower side wings house the meeting rooms and ancillary activities.

Steel and glass were not widely favoured for church schemes; even at the Illinois Institute of Technology, Mies van der Rohe used mostly brick for the walls of the chapel (1949–52). More characteristic of the time are the places of worship designed by the Midlands practice of Denys Hinton and Partners, generally combining restful brick exteriors with progressive liturgical arrangements. Hinton's 1968 replacement for a fire-damaged Methodist chapel at Cheadle Hulme, south of Manchester, is a dignified example, composed of four rectangular, flat-roofed elements (for worship, social events,

Fig 8.31
Baptist church, Waterlooville. The tall church hall backs on to the main worship space, with single-storey schoolrooms extending on each side.
[DP160442]

administration and utilities) of different heights (Fig 8. 32).[124] In fact the main part (for worship) subtly subverts the rectilinear order: its otherwise square plan has two curved corners, in one of which the brick walls overlap without touching, so leaving space for a narrow, full-height window. The logic of this becomes clear inside, for the opening illuminates the pulpit and communion area, augmented – rather as at Congleton and Waterlooville – by a roof light. Pulpit, table and font thus form a well-lit focal point, providing for the word and both sacraments, overseen by a large, free-standing cross behind and enclosed by a curved rail in front. With its sloping floor and segmental blocks of curved pews, arranged diagonally in the not-quite square plan, the layout owes much to Hermann Baur's church at Birsfelden in Switzerland.[125] The ancillary rooms, including a coffee bar and games room, open from a pleasant narthex, and were especially well used by youth clubs and young people's organisations.

In central Birmingham in 1968 the Hinton practice replaced the venerable Carrs Lane Congregational chapel with an octagonal building (housing a basement bookshop below the space for worship), connected by a glazed atrium to a block of meeting rooms and offices, and four floors of student flats.[126] Its architectural treatment is more angular, with toothing bricks at the junctions and parapets like broken gables. As in Cheadle Hulme, worship is focused on a top-lit area, in this case a dais with a broad table between two pulpit desks, but the seating is not fixed (Fig 8.33). Decoration is tasteful, from the angular boxing of the organ pipes and the pale glass of the slit windows to the graphic, nail-head depictions (by Edward Bawden, 1970) of the previous chapels. A third Hinton scheme, from 1967–8, was that of Highgate Baptist church centre in Birmingham.[127] In this case, it was the integration of religious and secular activities that attracted attention. A core worship space (with baptistery, communion table, reading desk and deacons' seats) was adjoined by a larger games hall, a lounge (where a day club for older people met) and a meeting room. Movable partitions enabled either the worship room or any of these other spaces to be enlarged. Highgate was seen as part of the movement for

Fig 8.32
Methodist church, Cheadle Hulme, Cheshire, 1968 by Denys Hinton and Partners. This calm and carefully composed building was designed by a modernist practice with a growing reputation for ecclesiastical work.

Fig 8.33
Interior of Carrs Lane
Congregational (now
United Reformed) church
centre, Birmingham, 1968
by Denys Hinton and
Partners. The building is
another instance of the
preference for top-lit
sanctuaries, a common
feature of the 1960s.

multipurpose churches, whose flagship was St Philip and St James, Hodge Hill, Birmingham (of 1963–8, by Martin Purdy).[128] Even a decade earlier Anglican authorities had strongly resisted the idea of allowing secular activities to be held in sight of the setting of a communion service, but for Nonconformists this was hardly new.[129]

Liturgical renewal continued as a strand of Nonconformist thinking for many years. For instance, the Methodists' new building at Banstead in Surrey (completed 1972; by Kenneth H Holgate and Associates) was clearly based on one of the continental churches most admired by the New Churches Research Group: Rainer Senn's St André, near Nice, of 1955–7.[130] Both are pyramidal and planned on a diagonal axis, with chairs in a ring around the free-standing table. In place of the timber principals, log walls and bitumen-paper roof-covering of Senn's church (built at a cost of £50 for a community of rag-pickers), Banstead's Methodists had a steel-framed structure, brick walls and a slate roof, but the liturgical concept was essentially the same. Indeed, Holgate embodied the idea of having a congregation 'gather at the table' by creating a circular communion rail and table, an unusual instance in Methodism.[131] It should be noted, however, that the matching pulpit emphasised the continuing importance of the word.

This balance between sacrament and word was nicely observed at Trinity-at-Bowes Methodist church (1973, by Edward Mills), on Bowes Road in north London, where the ministers believed that 'preaching, no less than other aspects of worship, is a joint exercise of pulpit and "pew"'.[132] The square plan, with an ambulatory, echoes that of Maguire and Murray's game-changing Anglican church at Bow Common, and had seats similarly arranged on three sides of a square communion area. Yet the presiding role here played by the pulpit (an item signally absent from Bow Common) shows that even liturgically progressive Methodists had no wish to diminish the role of preaching.[133] More radically, however, Mills ensured that the furnishings – communion table and rails, font, pulpit, dais and seating – could be reconfigured with ease to allow for experimental patterns of worship, perhaps encompassing drama, mime or visual aids, as well as traditional services. The building was thus prepared for some of the innovative features of late 20th-century worship, while embodying the principles of the liturgical movement.

Before leaving the topic of liturgical renewal, however, it should be noted that its emphasis on the eucharist (encapsulated in Hammond's observation that 'the design of the church must begin with the altar') was not the whole story. Fresh consideration was also given to the sacrament of baptism, as we have seen in the prominent fonts at Cheadle Hulme and Trinity-at-Bowes.[134] Such emphasis strengthened the resolve of some churches that practise baptism by immersion to make a central and permanent feature of their baptisteries, rather than covering them up when not in use. At the Baptist church in College Road,

Harrow (of 1982–4), for instance, one even finds an open baptistery by the entrance, an emphatic reminder of the crucial role of this rite in the journey to church membership.

At times the theological and liturgical debates of the 1960s focused on the gathered Christian community at the expense of taking the church's message out into the world. Likewise some architects envisioned their creations as sanctuaries from, or bulwarks against, the world. Trinity Congregational (now United Reformed) church at Hunter's Bar in Sheffield (of 1971, by John Mansell Jenkinson) has been described as 'uncompromising, a concrete blockhouse for God, repelling the invader more obviously than it welcomes the inquirer'.[135] The building, backing on to the rocky face of a former quarry, offers the citizens of Sheffield an almost windowless concrete frontage. Within this top-lit polygonal fort, the congregation 'gathers round the table on which the Bible lies open and behind which stands the plain stone pulpit whence the Word is expounded'.[136] Like Lasdun's National Theatre, the interior is more admired than the exterior. The architecture of *béton brut* (board-marked concrete) could easily be read as defensive in the context of declining attendances, and Trinity – as its name suggests – indeed resulted from the amalgamation of three separate congregations.

Another concrete bastion, though a more approachable one, is the Quaker meeting house (of 1971–2, by Trevor Dannatt) at Blackheath, south London (Figs 8.34 and 8.35).[137] Here the main space is a compact but airy octagon, in which meetings for worship are shaped by the grouping of chairs around a central (non-communion) table. With only one small window at eye level, the room fosters a suitably introspective mood, yet is uplifting because of the large lantern overhead, which gives ample daylight. As he had shown 15 years before in the design for the adjacent Congregational church, Trevor Dannatt was not a copybook modernist. For the Quakers he created an admirable building, part Vanbrughian castle and part Corbusian monastery; the intriguing shape attracts the eye and provides a rewarding sequence of internal spaces. By contrast the Thomas Cooper Memorial Baptist church (of 1973–4, by Frederick Gibberd and Partners) in High Street, Lincoln is a uniform brick block. Its three-bay front and hipped roof of pantiles might be a conscious reference to the buildings of early Dissent, though the restricted fenestration has an unrevealing character like that of Roman baths (Fig 8.36).[138] The contemporary influence seems to have been Louis Kahn's 'fortress-like closed buildings' at Ahmadabad, including the

Fig 8.34
Quaker meeting house, Blackheath, London, 1971–2 by Trevor Dannatt. The meeting house is approached as if over a drawbridge; it is raised on thick stilts with parking spaces below. [DP180137]

chamfered corners and void-like openings in the almost flawless brickwork.[139] As a space for worship, Gibberd's design has served the Baptists well, but the austerity of the exterior has been modified by lively signs. William Booth's citadels had a certain novelty, but Kahnian reticence was a less likely vehicle for the evangelical cause.

The influence of modern architectural forms and the reassessment of liturgy are the main themes of Nonconformist building in this period, set in the context of a general decline in membership and attendance. None of the mainstream denominations was able to consider a building programme like that of the Catholic Church in 1960s Britain. There was, however, a new initiative from an unexpected quarter. Following the expansion of its mission to this country, the Church of Jesus Christ of Latter-day Saints (the Mormons) recruited considerable numbers of followers: 6,357 British members in 1950 had grown tenfold to 67,849 in 1970 and rose further to 87,779 in 1980.[140] The Saints had a building campaign to match. Their second temple in Europe, built in 1955–8 near Lingfield, Surrey (architect, Edward Anderson of Utah; executed by T P Bennett and Son of London) was a statement of intent, with a sky-piercing spire and a budget of $1.25 million.[141]

Fig 8.35
Interior of Quaker meeting house, Blackheath, London. The main worship space (seen here uncharacteristically with little furniture) is octagonal and has just one window in its walls. [DP180131]

Fig 8.36
Thomas Cooper Memorial Baptist church, Lincoln, 1973–4 by Frederick Gibberd and Partners. In contrast to the arresting appearance of Gibberd's famous Roman Catholic cathedral in Liverpool, this Lincoln building is almost self-effacing. [DP165315]

Hundreds of Mormon meeting houses were built in the following decades, catering for British congregations who had previously met in rented accommodation. The example in Exhibition Road, South Kensington (of 1960–1, by T P Bennett and Son) might be taken for an office block with a hall – in fact, a 1,400-seat chapel – at street level, were it not for the set-back tower with its needle-like spire and *dalle de verre* stained glass.[142] More characteristic of the Mormons' American-inspired designs is the meeting house in Thirlestaine Road, Cheltenham (1963–4, by John Graham); it sits on an expanse of well-tended lawn and consists of a steep-roofed chapel and hall with a lower block at right angles, each with deep eaves.[143] The gable end has a *dalle de verre* window and to one side is a streamlined tower. No other denomination then employed spires and towers so regularly to signify a place of worship.

As an illustration of the expressive possibilities of Mormon architecture in those years, one might turn to the meeting house at Birchencliffe, Huddersfield (of 1963; now superseded). It had a similar plan to that at Cheltenham, but gained drama from its roof, which resembled a ski-jump.[144] The prow of the roof rose high above the dais end of the chapel, while at the other end of the building was the short, return slope of the hall. A semi-detached tower matched the building's angularity, and carried a delicate spike. When it came to the interior, however, Birchencliffe was representative of the Mormons' relatively conservative attitudes. Rows of fixed pews filled the long body of the chapel, with an axial lectern-pulpit in front of a raised block of choir stalls; a piano was set to one side.

The 1980s and after

For the mainstream Nonconformist denominations the problems of decline have loomed large in recent decades. A few statistics can illustrate the point. The stock of Methodist buildings in Britain (more than 14,000 in 1930) fell from 9,383 in 1970 to 6,825 in 1994 – a reduction of more than one-quarter in just 14 years.[145] Some of those buildings will have found new uses, but many will have gone altogether. In 2002 Alan Brooks lamented the fact that five out of seven important Nonconformist chapels in Gloucester had been demolished since the 1970s.[146] Not all towns and cities have permitted losses on such a scale, and denominations have not been equally affected, but almost everywhere urban congregations have struggled to survive.

One creative alternative to demolition has been downsizing. For example, a Methodist congregation in King's Road, Chelsea had its Edwardian building (over shops) adapted to create an intimate chapel (1984, by Bernard Lamb and Associates) alongside a pastoral centre with sheltered accommodation.[147] Nearly all of the furniture in the new chapel is movable, to allow for various styles of worship, and a simple mural – of stylised doves on a blue background with the chi-rho monogram – creates a suitably reverent atmosphere (Fig 8.37). At Bromley-by-Bow, in a less fashionable part of London, a formerly Congregational chapel was transformed by Gordon MacLaren into a flourishing community centre (beginning in 1985); a sail-like canopy at its heart helped to create a small space for ecumenical worship.[148] One of the more substantial schemes was at Lion Walk in Colchester. Here all but the tower and spire of an 800-seat Congregational (latterly United Reformed) chapel was demolished, to be replaced by shops at street level and a first-floor worship area with fewer than half as many seats, besides a hall and meeting rooms. The new worship area (of 1986, by David Roberts) is octagonal, echoing not the recently razed Victorian chapel but its Georgian predecessor. It is furnished with chairs below the pyramidal timber ceiling.[149]

Across the denominations, the revival of octagons gained momentum in the 1980s, bolstered – as at Colchester – by an awareness of 18th-century precedents and the realisation that the shape could signal a place of worship (or, at least, an auditorium) without reverting to towers and spires. Its functional advantages tended to be expressed not so much in liturgical as in congregational terms: one observer noted that 'the shape discourages the ranks of straight rows and means that members of the congregation begin to relate to each other simply by the way they are seated.'[150] For the Salvation Army, reducing the number of its corps and embarking on a programme to replace older premises, octagons have been a convenient way of distinguishing the main worship hall from secondary spaces and social facilities. An early example of this occurs in Hereford (of 1986, by Kevin Jefferson of ATP Group Partnership with the Army's chief architect, David Blackwell).[151] Here, backed by two subsidiary blocks, the octagon catches attention at a road junction, its lantern highlighted with chevrons of coloured glass. Quite similar designs were employed by

Salvationists for several schemes. These evolved into sleeker form for their Congress Hall in Brighton (2000, by chief architect David Greenwood), which has zinc canopies and a lantern roof in tune with the neighbouring early Victorian terrace.[152] This replaced a traditional battlemented Salvation Army citadel for 3,500 people, but only part of the site is occupied by the octagonal hall, thereby leaving room for parking, a café and several secondary blocks.

The same principle was useful to many kinds of downsizing congregations. In Reigate, for instance, the Quakers demolished their extensive meeting house in 1983, replacing it with a small octagonal building (by Barber, Bundy and Partners) and 20 flats for the elderly, including some facilities that were shared by residents and worshippers.[153] Similarly, at New Hampton Road in Wolverhampton, a large 19th-century Wesleyan chapel made way for a more compact but tallish octagonal building (Fig 8.38) (of 1991–2, by Ronald Baker, Humphreys and Goodchild).[154] Its Christian purpose is proclaimed by a cruciform window onto the road, while the rest of the site was given over to ancillary accommodation and sheltered housing.

Doubtless the general decline in churchgoing accelerated the ecumenical impulse among English churches in the final decades of the century. The process is evident not so much in top-level amalgamations, but rather where individual congregations have joined forces to form local ecumenical partnerships across denominational boundaries.[155] Some of the first purpose-built shared churches were in new centres of population. The newly created Essex town of South Woodham Ferrers provides an example. Close to the town's public library and schools, Holy Trinity church was built (in 1982, by Essex county architect's department) for the joint use of Anglicans, Roman Catholics and Methodists.[156] The hexagonal church can be opened on one side to the Anglicans' school hall, and on another to that of the Catholics. All three buildings use the palette of local materials and shapes recommended by the county council's influential design guide, but slates, not pantiles, appear on the necessarily complicated roof of the church.[157]

Another predictably named Trinity church of the 1980s was built amid the new housing of Lower Earley, Reading for Anglicans, Methodists and the United Reformed Church. This

Fig 8.37
Interior of Methodist chapel, King's Road, Chelsea, London, 1984 by Bernard Lamb and Associates. The intimate area for worship has been created within an older Methodist building and permits a variety of layouts.

Fig 8.38
Methodist church,
New Hampton Road,
Wolverhampton, 1991–2
by Ronald Baker,
Humphreys and Goodchild.
A rather heavily detailed
example of the octagonal
church buildings that
enjoyed a great revival
in the last decades of the
20th century.
[DP166367]

square building too is part of a suite of public facilities – including leisure centre, library and pub – all designed (by the Culpin Partnership, 1982–9) in a quasi-vernacular spirit.[158] A more imposing effect is achieved by Trinity church, Totton, near Southampton, which was built in 1992 for a combined Methodist and United Reformed congregation, and which adjoins the burgeoning town's shopping area and community facilities.[159] Here a tall, glazed entrance hall precedes the steep-roofed octagon of the main worship space, while shallow-roofed ancillary rooms project at an angle – almost paraphrasing (unconsciously, one presumes) Edgar Wood's preliminary scheme for the Christian Scientists of Manchester of 90 years before. Internally a folding glass screen separates the entrance hall from the yet taller worship area. On each side of the dais there are large windows, incorporating panels of contemporary stained glass by Barbara Rostill. The place is well used and its ecumenical role has been extended by agreement with the local Baptists, Anglicans and Roman Catholics.

It is possible that interdenominational agreements, both local and national, will lead to a world in which the concept of Nonconformist churches – not to mention a state church – will become defunct. Milton Keynes, with its exceptional number of ecumenical partnerships, has been a testing ground, and its city centre church is perhaps a vision of the future. Built for

no fewer than five denominations – Anglican, Baptist, Methodist, United Reformed and Roman Catholic – the domed church of Christ the Cornerstone (of 1988–91, by Iain Smith and Jon Muncaster of Planning Design Development Ltd) has architectural ambitions to do for central Milton Keynes what St Peter's does for Rome, though it is not clear in this case that the principle of ecumenical worship has produced as convincing a building.[160] Of course, such architectural uncertainty can be overcome; strong, distinctive designs will surely be created for congregations in which the divisions between the Established and the Free Churches, and even between Catholic and Protestant, are blurred if not dissolved. It may be premature to draft the obituary of Nonconformist church architecture, however. The signs of life must certainly be considered.

A little-noticed change in the religious scene has been the rise of Jehovah's Witnesses, whose membership in Britain doubled between 1970 and 1991.[161] By the 1960s, after a long period in which they had tended to meet in rented rooms or adapted premises, Witnesses embarked on a programme of bespoke kingdom halls: decorous structures, usually of brick and often with a windowless, gable-end façade. Since the early 1990s a series of standard designs has been employed, varied according to local conditions. Internally there is usually a large room with a dais and lectern – but no communion table or font – and a schoolroom or two, besides toilets and other ancillary accommodation. Of special note is the quick-build process, learned by British Witnesses from their American counterparts. It made its UK debut in 1983 with the kingdom hall at Weston Favell, near Northampton, a building which – to the astonishment of observers – was constructed, fitted out and decorated in less than four days by some 500 volunteers.[162]

Many kingdom halls were erected by a similar process. Even the Witnesses' 1,500-seat East Pennine assembly hall at Hellaby, near Rotherham (of 1985; design consultant, S Tingle) was rapidly completed by thousands of volunteers, once contractors had erected its steel frame, slate roof and concrete ground slab.[163] Such regional assembly halls are generally more architecturally enterprising and varied than the local kingdom halls. The Hellaby building, for instance, has a top-lit octagonal central space under a Maltese cross roof, with eight radiating arms. For the Bristol assembly hall at Almondsbury (of 1993–5, designed by Brendan Coffey), the challenges of the site, located on the edge of the village, stimulated a notable design (Fig 8.39). Voluntary labour again contributed to the scheme. Set amid well-tended grounds, the Bris-

tol assembly hall buildings are dominated by low-pitched roofs with deep eaves in the manner of Frank Lloyd Wright's prairie houses. Like the proverbial iceberg, however, the larger part is below the surface. Great quantities of rock were excavated to make space for a 1,200-seat auditorium, with matching catering facilities and teaching rooms. Excavation was necessary here because of planning restrictions on the building's height. The spoil was put to good use, helping to create a landscaped bund which shelters the site from the adjacent motorways. Jehovah's Witnesses have an advanced attitude to accessibility – a topic which has occupied many churches in recent decades. The Bristol assembly hall provides not only for wheelchair-users and the deaf, but its colour scheme also aids those with limited vision, while overlooking the auditorium is a sealed viewing area for people with environmental allergies. The fan-shaped auditorium, used chiefly for Saturday and Sunday assemblies, has tiered seating to provide unimpeded views of the broad dais, to one side of which is a baptismal pool.

Like Jehovah's Witnesses, the Mormons (properly the Church of Jesus Christ of Latter-day Saints) have built steadily in recent decades. For a while Prairie School influences were favoured, as can be seen in the crisply detailed

Fig 8.39
Jehovah's Witnesses'
Bristol assembly hall,
Almondsbury, Gloucester-
shire, 1993–5 by Brendan
Coffey. This carefully
designed hall is part of
a new generation of
buildings erected for –
and sometimes by –
Jehovah's Witnesses.

meeting house at Two Mile Ash in Milton Keynes (of 1985, by John Porter Associates).[164] Later, using standard plans for different sized meeting houses, more varied treatment was encouraged. The spreading meeting house at Lawley, Telford (of 2004–5, by McBains Cooper), for instance, looks like a post-modern paraphrase of a colonial meeting house. It catches the eye at one of the new town's many roundabouts with its mannerist motifs, neat aluminium spire and rendered, pale-coloured walls (Fig 8.40).[165] By contrast, its counterpart in Warwick (of 2005, by Fellows Burt Dalton and Associates) is an L-shaped structure of red brick, with blue-brick details and other Victorian touches; its white fibreglass spire sits on the two-storey ancillary wing rather than the lower roof of the chapel itself.[166] A common feature in this generation of Mormon meeting houses has been the provision of a baptismal area off the foyer, not – as in other denominations – within the main worship space. This indicates that baptism by immersion is of greater rather than lesser significance for the Latter-day Saints.

More spectacular than these new meeting houses is the second British temple, erected near Chorley, Lancashire (in 1996–8, by BDP – formerly Building Design Partnership – in association with Hanno Luschin of Utah) (Fig 8.41).[167] Heralding the temple's presence is a soaring granite spire, topped by a golden angel trumpeter, a motif previously used for the denomination's temples in Los Angeles and Washington, DC. Except for the spire, the exterior of the

Fig 8.40
Church of Jesus Christ of Latter-day Saints meeting house, Lawley, Telford, 2004–5 by McBains Cooper. A variety of architectural approaches is evident among recent Mormon meeting houses. [DP166328]

building is an essay in stripped classicism, rather like its 1955–8 forerunner in Surrey. Following the usual pattern for Mormon temples, the interior (only Saints are allowed entry) is divided into a number of comparatively small spaces, one of which contains the great baptismal font that is borne by 12 life-size oxen, carved in marble, akin to that created in 1845 for the seminal temple at Nauvoo, Illinois.[168] For the Latter-day Saints, whose first British mission had been to Preston in 1837, the building of a temple in Lancashire was concrete – or rather granite – evidence that the movement was here to stay.

A very different area of growth in the past quarter century has been among a spectrum of evangelical movements that include charismatic and Pentecostal groups, as well as various young churches that are reluctant to accept denominational labels. In Salisbury in 2006, for instance, Trevor Cooper found four 'so-called "New Churches" deliberately worshipping in hired premises' and a longer-established Pentecostal congregation in a former Primitive Methodist chapel.[169] In other places, former cinemas and warehouses have been fitted out for services. The tendency to use existing buildings has given these movements a lower profile than might otherwise have been expected, but continued expansion has recently led a number to commission purpose-built places.

One example is Huddersfield Christian Fellowship. It began as a house church in the 1980s, progressed to a 350-seat venue in the town centre and in 1999 adapted a former

Fig 8.41
Church of Jesus Christ of Latter-day Saints temple, near Chorley, Lancashire, 1996–8 by BDP with Hanno Luschin. This building, the second Mormon temple in Britain, spectacularly demonstrates the Church's strength at a time when many denominations are declining.
[DP143774]

electrical goods superstore to create an auditorium for 800 worshippers.[170] This in turn proved inadequate, and in 2006–9 a smart new building (by Aedas Architects) was erected, to seat 2,000.[171] Sited on the edge of Huddersfield town centre, it has parking for 250 cars, besides space for coaches, buses and an articulated outside-broadcast vehicle. Fronted by a fully glazed foyer between two stocky towers, the auditorium is a windowless rectangular hall, with a rear gallery and state-of-the-art facilities for lighting, sound and projection. There is a retractable baptistery (unseen except when in use), but otherwise the space has been designed to function as efficiently for concerts or conferences as for worship. Alongside the auditorium is a wedge-shaped concourse, with a bookshop and coffee shop, a crèche, a café and church offices. On the far side of this busy area is a three-storey block that contains rooms for teaching, seminars and youth work. Such a combination of social mission and evangelical purpose has a long pedigree in Nonconformity, and is here reinterpreted for the era of the retail park.

More unusual is a scheme for Nottingham Christian centre (previously known as Central Pentecostalist church). Here it is planned to replace the existing range of adapted buildings by a multistorey structure with a 65-foot (19.8m) spire, a 1,500-seat auditorium and many social facilities, combined with five levels of underground parking.[172] Providing for cars on a city centre site can be expensive, however, and at the time of writing the scheme has stalled for shortage of funds.

Among the newer groups to have grown significantly around the start of the present millennium, mention must also be made of the churches whose members are chiefly of African or Caribbean origin: what are now called black majority churches. Their strength contributed significantly to a 16 per cent rise in church-going among Londoners between 2005 and 2012.[173] The charismatic House on the Rock Church has a thriving – and largely Nigerian-British – congregation in north London (Fig 8.42). Since 2006 it has rescued, with great success, the former St George's church in Tufnell Park (see pp 168–9 and Figs 6.33 and 6.34); the building had served as a theatre since the 1970s, but had been more recently used by squatters. St George's was rehabilitated and its seating capacity increased through the installation of a glass-fronted gallery above the ambulatory that encircles the octagonal nave.[174] In this way

the centralised nature of the Victorian plan has been emphasised. Like the thrill-inducing services of the 1920s central halls, worship here is resonant and popular. Given the congregation's reputation for exuberant singing and music-making, particular measures (absorption pipes, secondary glazing and special upholstery) were necessary to reduce noise leaking from the building. The second element of the scheme (by Paul Davis and Partners), which was completed in 2010, involved a suite of new rooms for church and community use. These succeed in being entirely modern in spirit without competing with the strong forms and character of the original building.

During the same years, 2006–10, a congregation of the New Testament Church of God in an ethnically diverse part of Birmingham replaced its place of worship (the former Aston Villa Wesleyan chapel) with new premises in George Street by Paul Henry Architects.[175] Tall windows and block-like towers bring echoes of 1930s civic architecture to the latest structure, even if the result is not so gainly. Inside, rather than the long axis of the old chapel, a wide auditorium has been created, with tip-up seats for 1,000 worshippers. There is a very deep gallery, angled – like the sloping ground floor – to provide good views of the platform from which services are led. Royal blue upholstery creates a vibrant mood, and the windows use a sequence of blue and purple glass, coded to evoke the congregation's favourite hymn, 'Great is Thy Faithfulness'. Though the Pentecostal ministry would be unfamiliar to an 18th-century Methodist, the principles of designing for active congregational worship are little changed since Wesley's day.

Many people have been attracted to these large places of worship, no doubt in part because of the 'buzz' associated with growing enterprises, and perhaps also because the largest congregations can provide more support for young families, the elderly and the socially vulnerable. Something similar might be said of the great mid-Victorian chapels or their Georgian equivalents. As in those earlier periods, however, smaller places have accounted for the majority of new works, especially among the mainstream Nonconformist denominations. It is to these that we now turn.

Two contrasting schemes illustrate the different ways in which congregations responded to the continued pressure on High-Street sites in the decade around 2000. In Leamington Spa the Baptists sold their venerable, but much-altered

chapel to make way for a Waterstone's bookshop. In 1995–6 they erected a new building (by the Brown Matthews partnership) a few streets away, next to a social housing complex, as part of an urban redevelopment programme.[176] The front of the new building, fitting tightly into the street grid, does not immediately reveal its hand, but the clerestory and delicate rooftop spire are more indicative. Even these clues hardly prepare one for the character of the main worship space, however. It is a tall square hall, seating 300, and handsomely treated in a manner that evokes Schinkel by way of Otto Wagner or C R Mackintosh. First-floor galleries with *Quadratstil* balustrades are recessed behind square pillars, and the classical syntax is heightened by the

colour scheme of rich terracotta and white (Fig 8.43). The baptismal pool (again square) is on view in one corner, beside the dais. Elsewhere in the building there is a good range of community facilities, including crèche and youth club, a hall for badminton or drama, counselling rooms and kitchen.

Quite different from this scheme is one undertaken for the Methodists at Fulham Broadway, London (completed 2003, PMP Architects).[177] Although the starting point was the same – a developer wanting to acquire an existing chapel (in this case, dating only from 1971) for a shopping centre – the Fulham Methodists decided that the replacement should be a beacon, an invitation to passers-by to cross the threshold.

Fig 8.42
Interior of House on the Rock church, Tufnell Park, London, adapted 2006 by Paul Davis and Partners. The rescue of a mid-Victorian chapel by a charismatic church emphasises the links between congregational worship of the 19th and 21st centuries.
[DP151623]

Fig 8.43
Baptist church, Leamington
Spa, 1995–6 by the Brown
Matthews Partnership. In
giving new form to the
traditional functions of a
Nonconformist building, the
architects have created a
stylish auditorium and a
range of community
facilities.
[DP164511]

In a reversal of the usual approaches, the architects' solution was to provide an entrance wall of glass, allowing the simple worship space to be almost wholly visible from the street. The architectural precedent seems to be Mies van der Rohe's 1952 chapel at the Illinois Institute of Technology, but in 21st-century Britain there was a theological impulse, a desire to make the life of a church transparent to a sometimes ignorant world. On the street, a steel and timber screen provides a sort of proscenium arch, framing the glazed entrance to the small chapel (normally with just 50 seats) and boosting its visual strength alongside the new shopping development. Exploiting the return to fashion of urban living, three flats are provided above the chapel, each with a large balcony offering views across London, while a multipurpose hall is housed in the basement. Essentially the chapel's limited size has become its virtue, offering a calm and quiet space for prayer amid the clamour of the consumer society.

Nonconformists have long been adept at tailoring their buildings to different local circumstances. Yet the contrast between the examples from Leamington and Fulham is not entirely explained by such attitudes. Architectural pluralism, allied to the increasing likelihood that a new place of worship (as at Fulham, for instance) will have been designed by an architect who has not previously had such a commission, has encouraged diverse approaches to be taken.

Sometimes a Gothic spirit has survived as a signifier of religious architecture. One such case is the new building in Blackheath, south London, for the downsizing Sunfields Methodist church (2007–9, by BPTW Architects).[178] Steep pitched roofs cover what might be taken for a nave-and-chancel arrangement, and along the most visible flank is a series of deep, zinc-clad fins which rise like buttresses – although they house windows. The great gable end has etched and coloured glass (by Sarah Galloway) and the interior echoes the shape of a Gothic structure, with laminated timber beams on a portal frame.

More generally, however, different architectural models have found favour. Frank Lloyd Wright's influence can be detected in several new Nonconformist commissions, one of the most noteworthy examples being the Baptists' new building at Dawley Bank, Telford (of 2000–1, by Baart Harries Newall) (Fig 8.44).[179] Although it is of brick, one can immediately see the parallel with Wright's renowned Unity Temple, in particular the primary decision to treat the chapel proper and the church hall as visually discrete elements of one design, linked by a lower foyer.[180] This *dux et comes* ('leader and companion') arrangement dignifies the ancillary accommodation while acknowledging the leading role of the worship space. Chapel and hall are each essentially square, with shallow pyramidal roofs, inspired not by the flat concrete roofs of Unity

Fig 8.44
Baptist church, Dawley Bank, Telford, 2000–1 by Baart Harries Newall. Replacing a three-storey Victorian chapel, this more modestly scaled building sits comfortably alongside modern housing.
[DP166330]

Temple, but by Wright's prairie houses. The 120-seat chapel is the tallest element of the scheme, with deeply projecting eaves and a recessed clerestory – its chief source of light. In unequivocal homage to Wright (even if lacking his rigorous handling of details), each corner is marked by a flat-capped block, large enough to contain a vestry, although the function seems subservient to the form. Departing from the rectilinear discipline of Wright's early work, however, the lower walls of the worship space are curved, creating an agreeable external effect and hinting at the congregational character of the seating within.

Headington, in Oxford, provides a distinguished solution to the problem of designing for an architecturally sensitive location. Here the thriving Baptist congregation needed more room, but wanted to remain on its limited site in a conservation area. The resulting building (of 2006–7, by David Grindley) fronts Old High Street with what from one angle might be taken for a short row of houses, their Bath stone façades giving way to a timber-clad first floor without any sense of historical pastiche.[181] At the south end a tall glazed entrance reveals the building's public purpose and offers a view of the double-height foyer, an elegant modernist space. Beyond the foyer is the 200-seat worship space – a generous two and a half storeys high, which descends to a single level – and a similar but smaller hall, both of which are airy and amply lit. Sliding doors allow the two spaces to

be united for larger gatherings, and the platform and seating can be arranged to allow for an east–west or north–south axis. A gallery overlooks the worship space and also gives access to some of the meeting rooms along the front of the building. Everything is finished to a high standard, with much use of pale wood to complement the white décor. There is a kitchen and crèche on the ground floor, while a basement hall accommodates activities for children and young people. It is tempting to say that the church's many needs have been provided under one roof, but in fact there is a series of skilfully layered roofs, providing shallow clerestories and enabling the building to sit sensitively amid its neighbours. So thoughtful a response to context and function places Grindley's design in the tradition of what, almost a quarter of a century before, had been labelled romantic pragmatism.[182]

At Clevedon, Somerset a quite different type of design resulted from an ostensibly similar commission: the desire of a very active Baptist congregation to expand on an existing site in a conservation area. In this case the new building (of 2005–6, by Acanthus Ferguson Mann) was reoriented to face on to Clevedon's pedestrian square, amid shops.[183] The congregation did not want anything too reminiscent of a church in appearance, and so – rather like the central halls of a century before – it might be taken for a place of entertainment or a public building, in this case perhaps a cinema or library. Its curved front responds to the line of an adjacent Victorian

Fig 8.45
The entrance front of the Salvation Army corps hall, Chelmsford, 2009 by Hudson Architects. After erecting a number of octagonal halls in the late 20th century, the Salvation Army has taken a more varied approach in the design of its buildings over the past decade or so. [DP165295]

crescent, but the white walls and quasi-high-tech details are entirely contemporary. At street level there is a café and drop-in area, while upstairs (again as with central halls) is the main worship space – a broad and fan-shaped auditorium for 350, featuring a timber wall in Art Deco style behind the dais. This rich-coloured wood and the use of red upholstery give a sense of warmth and conviviality to the space, without impairing the more solemn aspects of worship.

It may be appropriate to conclude with something that invites comparison not with Edwardian chapel building, but with the heady atmosphere of 1951, when new ways of building opened up fresh possibilities for Nonconformists, for example, the Salvation Army citadel corps hall in Chelmsford (of 2009, by Hudson Architects) the rear elevation of which makes an arresting sight beside a dual carriageway, its bright, zinc-clad wall interrupted by the iridescent face of a 42-foot (12.8m) tower.[184] It is as great a break from the Salvation Army's recent octagonal buildings as it is from the fort-like brick citadels of the 1890s. The building is also a riposte to those groups who prefer to adapt retail hangars than to commission new places of their own in which to worship (Fig 8.45). Underneath the toughened zinc cladding (Fig 8.46) – which envelops the roof and two of the long frontages – the structure is a disarmingly simple system of what amounts to oversized panels of plywood.[185] These prefabricated panels, supplied with cut-to-order window and door spaces, allowed rapid construction and encouraged the architect to create an eventful roofscape whose varied slopes include six large dormer windows.

In keeping with the Salvation Army's founding ethos, facilities are provided for day-care of the elderly and preschool children, youth activities and other community events, not to mention worship. There is a foyer café, lounge, indoor sports hall and outdoor play area, as well as offices and meeting rooms. At the heart of all this is the 320-seat worship hall, in which the wooden panels of the roof and walls create an attractive setting. Allowing for the sound of brass bands and joyful singing, the lower sections of the side walls are insulated with acoustic panels in the Army's livery colours. If the external cladding has overtones of Frank Gehry, the internal spaces suggest parallels with the innovative genius of Hertfordshire's post-war schools (Fig 8.47). Within months of its opening, the building won a clutch of awards, recognising in equal measure its contributions to religious and

community architecture, as well as its spirit of ingenuity. In the multifarious world of Nonconformity, the Chelmsford corps hall is not a model that will be imitated by many. However, it is evidence that new solutions are continuing to be found for the changing needs of Christian worship, and that most Nonconformist denominations have had a head start in the current preoccupation with community facilities in places of worship.

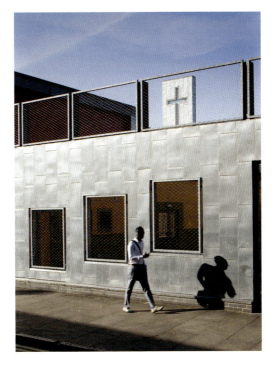

Fig 8.46
Salvation Army corps hall, Chelmsford. Zinc cladding and wire mesh lend a touch of Frank Gehry to this award-winning scheme. The rear of the iridescent tower appears above the roofline. [DP165288]

Fig 8.47
Interior of Salvation Army corps hall, Chelmsford. The worship hall is the heart of a complex – entirely constructed of prefabricated timber panels – in which an extensive programme of support for local people is undertaken. [DP165300]

Looking back and looking forward

Much has been made in this chapter of the contrast between the interwar years and the decades after 1945: the one era dominated by a range of quietly Gothic and Georgian styles and rather conservative plan-types, the other marked by an enthusiasm for new styles, materials and shapes. In other words a period of general insularity gave way to one in which Nonconformist architecture reasserted its role in an international movement. A contrary characterisation might draw attention to the well-crafted, and still much-loved, chapels of prosperous 1930s suburbs, as against the innovative post-war structures that sometimes failed the test of time in inner-city districts. Both accounts conceal the fact that almost all the traditional denominations have had to cope with reduced circumstances over the past hundred years, a fact which became more painfully apparent by the end of the 20th century. Downsizing or church-sharing have been the experience for many congregations, while extended community use of religious buildings – a matter in which Nonconformists have a long pedigree – has been the norm for even more. At times architects have risen to the challenge of designing for such circumstances by creating memorable buildings.

The growth of younger Christian movements has not outweighed the decline among long-established denominations, but it has certainly added to the variety of religious architecture in England. In a way that parallels some aspects of early Methodist chapel building, the Mormons and Jehovah's Witnesses have often used their own architects to adapt more-or-less standard designs for their numerous new places of worship. Both movements have also built a small number of large and headline-catching structures, some employing outside architects. The expansion of the charismatic and Pentecostal churches has been much more diffuse, generally without a coordinated approach to architecture: indeed, there has often been a preference for adapted premises rather than purpose-built accommodation. Whether the habit of fitting-out warehouses for worship will prove to be merely a phase – akin to William Booth's adaptation of redundant skating halls for worship or John Wesley's use of the former Moorfields foundry – is not yet clear. The recent examples of specially designed buildings for Huddersfield and Nottingham may point in that direction. Even so, for the moment it seems unlikely that the decentralised networks of new churches will choose to create buildings as denominationally distinctive as the Salvation Army's citadels or Whitefield's tabernacles.

For many observers, the most notable feature of this country's religious landscape in the past half century has been its increasing diversity. Understandably the construction of mosques – and to a lesser extent mandirs, gurdwaras, synagogues and pagodas – has attracted public interest. The Christian scene has also become more varied, however, as exemplified by the proliferation of warehouse churches, kingdom halls, black majority churches and Mormon meeting houses, to say nothing of the greatly expanded Orthodox churches and foreign-language Catholic congregations. In a society with a multiplicity of faiths, a widening range of Christian groups and a seriously reduced level of church-going, the concepts of Conformity and Nonconformity seem at best quaint. More than ever before, the story of English church architecture requires a perspective that does not regard one denomination as the norm.

Appendix:
Nonconformist groups

The following brief descriptions cover most of the groups and movements mentioned in the book. No claim can be made for the comprehensiveness of the selection, however. An exhaustive list of Nonconformist groups would require a volume in its own right.

Baptists

Baptists recognise only believers' (that is, adult) baptism. In the 17th century several English Baptist groups arose from contact with Dutch Protestants. Since that time there have been various English groupings of Baptists, although these divisions have been less apparent to outsiders than in the case of the different Methodist sects. The Particular Baptists held Calvin's view of predestination, whereas General Baptists believed in the universal possibility of salvation. Churches of both traditions were influenced by the Methodist Revival (an evangelical New Connexion of the General Baptists being formed in 1770), and in 1891 most came together in the Baptist Union – previously a Particular Baptist body. During the early 19th century, in reaction to the perceived theological liberalisation of these developments, some Particular Baptist churches banded together in Strict Baptist associations, with a renewed Calvinistic emphasis and a rule that only those who had been baptised by immersion as adults could be admitted to communion.

Bible Christians

The Bible Christians began in 1815 as an independent branch of Methodism in south-west England. They were especially successful in rural and mining communities. Their strength was always regional (Cornwall and Devon being the heartland), with hardly any chapels in most parts of the Midlands or northern England. In 1907 the Bible Christians combined with the Methodist New Connexion and United Methodist Free Church to form the United Methodist Church.

Brethren

Though founded in Dublin in 1827–8, the Brethren are sometimes referred to as the Plymouth Brethren, after the place where they established a congregation in 1830. They resist denominational identities and do not have paid ministers. Most emphasise the centrality of weekly communion – a ceremony referred to as the 'breaking of bread'. Since 1848 there have been two broad groupings. Open Brethren (sometimes

called Christian Brethren) are strongly evangelical, practise believers' baptism and co-operate with other like-minded congregations. Their buildings were often called gospel halls, though this is now less usual. Exclusive Brethren, whose buildings were sometimes known as 'The Room', are more wary of worldly involvement. They practise infant baptism.

Calvinistic Methodists

Several important figures who shared John Wesley's evangelical vision nonetheless differed from him theologically. Among those Methodists who favoured Calvin's position on the question of predestination were George Whitefield, Howel Harris and the Countess of Huntingdon. In England chapels were built for Whitefield and the Countess, and in Wales an extensive network of Calvinistic Methodist chapels (subsequently known also as the Presbyterian Church of Wales) was developed.

Catholic Apostolic Church

With roots in Edward Irving's heterodox Presbyterian ministry, the Catholic Apostolic Church was formed in the 1830s. It appointed 12 'apostles' and sought to establish a full order of prophets, evangelists and deacons (modelled on the early Church) that would survive until the imminent second coming of Christ. Priests wore vestments, and services involved much ritual, including elements from Roman and Greek liturgy. Since the death of the last 'apostle' in 1901, the church has become inactive.

Christian Science

The Church of Christ, Scientist was founded in Boston, MA by Mary Baker Eddy in 1879. Its special belief, that sickness – as well as sin – is the result of human error, underpins a holistic approach to spiritual and physical well-being. There are no paid ministers and no sacraments. Services consist of readings from the Bible and Mrs Eddy's writings, with hymns and (sometimes silent) prayer; there are also meetings at which testimony is given about healings. Healing practitioners are associated with many congregations. Public reading rooms, with Christian Science publications, are generally attached to the churches. In any place large enough to have more than one Christian Science church these are named sequentially: First Church of Christ, Scientist; Second Church of Christ, Scientist, and so forth.

Church of Jesus Christ of Latter-day Saints

The 1830 publication of *The Book of Mormon* in New York State helped to create what in 1838 became the Church of Jesus Christ of Latter-day Saints. This, its members believe, was the restoration of the true church that Christ had established in America. English converts tended to migrate to the USA – from 1846 to Utah – and only in the later 20th century was such emigration discouraged. Congregations worship in meeting houses, where the main worship space includes a raised area with a lectern and often choir seats. There are no paid ministers. Communion is celebrated each week, the bread and water (not wine) being passed around the congregation. Meeting houses usually have a baptismal pool, and some also possess a cultural hall that can be used for sport and social events. Special rituals, including the baptism of ancestors, are held in Mormon temples.

Congregationalism

Independent churches were founded on the principle that each congregation should be autonomous – appointing and employing its own minister, for instance. In the 17th century they were often called Separatist or Brownist churches after the Puritan preacher Robert Browne. Following the formation of the Congregational Union of England and Wales in 1832, most Independent churches came to be known as Congregational. In 1972 a large number of these churches became part of the United Reformed Church, while others joined together to form the Congregational Federation.

Countess of Huntingdon's Connexion

A patron of the evangelical revival of the 18th century, Selina, Countess of Huntingdon ultimately sided with the Calvinistic brand of Methodism rather than Wesley's movement. For many years the Countess was able to claim that the places of worship she built were her domestic chapels (private chapels did not need to be registered), but from 1782 she began to register them for public Nonconformist use and so her Connexion was born.

Free Church of England

Founded in 1844 in reaction to the rise of the Oxford Movement (with its High Church convictions and Catholic associations), the Free Church of England upholds what it sees as the historic – and Protestant – character of the Church of England. Worship is normally based on the *Book of Common Prayer*.

Huguenots

During the 1540s Calvin's ideas inspired a Protestant movement across France. French Calvinists, who came to be known as Huguenots, suffered widespread persecution. Through the 16th century many fled abroad, and after 1685 – when the 1589 Edict of Nantes was revoked – many thousands more went into exile. In Britain some émigré Huguenots ultimately conformed to the Church of England, but others maintained their Calvinist beliefs.

Independent churches *see* Congregationalism

Jehovah's Witnesses

This movement arose out of a Bible study group formed in Pennsylvania in 1872, which in 1896 became the Watch Tower Bible and Tract Society. Since 1932 its followers have been known as Jehovah's Witnesses. Local congregations hold services and scripture-based study in kingdom halls, and there are no paid ministers. Provision for the baptism of adults is now usually made at regional assembly halls. Once a year, on the eve of Passover, a memorial evening meal – or Lord's Supper – is observed.

Lutheranism

Martin Luther's teachings determined the character of Protestantism in Germany and Scandinavia, and through migration affected the USA. Accordingly the Lutheran churches that have been established in Britain since the 17th century have generally been for foreign settlers or visitors (characteristically traders and sailors). In the 1890s the small Evangelical Lutheran Church of England was formed as a native British body. Lutheran worship is liturgical, and congregational hymn singing has always been important.

Methodism

At Oxford in 1729 John Wesley established a group of earnest Christians who were nicknamed Methodists. Through close contact with the Moravian Brethren, Wesley became a committed evangelist and embarked on a lifelong itinerant campaign to win souls. Though he and his fellow ministers were ordained Anglicans, Wesley's campaign could not be contained by the Church of England.

At an early stage Methodism – as it had come to be known – divided on theological grounds, with George Whitefield and others of Calvinistic disposition separating from Wesley. Mainstream Methodism remained under Wesley's influence, however, and after his death in 1791 it became a denomination in its own right, with a network of chapels previously intended to supplement the system of parish churches. From 1797 until the second half of the 19th century a succession of groups broke from the original or Wesleyan body, invariably on matters of church government rather than doctrine. In 1932 all but a small number of these groups came together with the Wesleyans to form the Methodist Church of Great Britain.

Methodist worship has generally been based on the (pre-Tractarian) Anglican pattern, but with a greater use of extempore prayer and a central role for congregational singing of hymns. This latter reflects the influence of the Moravian Brethren, from whom Wesley also adopted the love feast, which became an occasion for Methodists to bear witness to their faith and experience. Methodist ministers are appointed to a circuit of chapels, not simply to one congregation, and regularly move to new circuits.

Methodist New Connexion

Those Methodists who found Wesleyan church government insufficiently responsive to the voice of the laity established the Methodist New Connexion at a meeting in Leeds in 1797. It was the first breakaway from the senior body since John Wesley's death. In 1907 the Methodist New Connexion was one of three groups that combined to form the United Methodist Church.

Moravian Church

Originating in 15th-century Bohemia as *Unitas Fratrum* (a unity of brethren), the Moravian Church resurfaced in the early 18th century and spread via Saxony to Britain and America. The Moravians' planned settlements (for example at Fulneck) might seem to suggest separation from the world, but the Church played a major role in the evangelical revival and greatly influenced John Wesley. Congregational singing has always figured prominently, and the love feast (sometimes held in preparation for communion) is another notable feature of Moravian worship.

Mormons *see* Church of Jesus Christ of Latter-day Saints

New Jerusalem Church *see* Swedenborgianism

New Testament Church of God

Established in 1953, the New Testament Church of God is one of the second generation of Pentecostal churches. It has grown rapidly in the past 20 years.

Pentecostalism

From its origins in America in the first years of the 20th century, Pentecostalism has spread to become one of the largest Christian movements. Inspired by the descent of the Holy Spirit on the apostles at Pentecost, services at a Pentecostal church characteristically involve much congregational participation – invariably song, clapping and dance, sometimes prophecy. Elim Pentecostal Church and the Assemblies of God are the most long-established Pentecostal groups in Britain, but there are numerous others, including some with a majority of black members. Through the charismatic movement Pentecostalism has also influenced mainstream Christianity – not only Nonconformist, but also Anglican, Roman Catholic and Orthodox churches.

Plymouth Brethren *see* Brethren

Presbyterians

Presbyterians take their name from a hierarchical (but not episcopal) system of church government involving elders and ministers. In their theology Presbyterian churches tend to hold to the Calvinist view of predestination. Presbyterians played a leading role in English church life in the 1640s and 1650s, but were suppressed at the Restoration. In Scotland the established church has been Presbyterian since 1690. During the later 18th century many English Presbyterians came to accept Unitarianism, and were able to do so more openly after legislation of 1813 and 1844. The Presbyterian Church of England (composed largely of Scottish migrants) was formed in 1876, and became part of the United Reformed Church in 1972.

Presbyterian Church of Wales *see* Calvinistic Methodists

Primitive Methodist Church

Primitive Methodism separated from the main (that is, Wesleyan) Methodist body in 1811. In part its origins were in the revivalist camp-meeting movement, and Primitive Methodism had a reputation for reaching poorer people, including farm workers and miners. It built a significant number of small rural chapels as well as larger urban buildings. In 1932 Primitive Methodists merged with the Wesleyan and United Methodists to form the Methodist Church of Great Britain.

Quakers

Quakerism emerged in mid-17th century England under the leadership of George Fox, whose followers identified themselves as 'friends of the truth' (hence, later, the Society of Friends). Quakers reject all sacraments and liturgy, and have no paid ministers. Their places of worship continue to be called meeting houses and meetings for worship are held in silence, interrupted only when someone is moved to speak. In older meeting houses there is generally a raised stand and often provision for the men's and women's business meetings to be held separately. There is no creed, although pacifism has been common among Quakers.

Salvation Army

Founded in London as a Christian mission by William Booth in 1865, and given its present name in 1878, the Salvation Army is an evangelical movement with a strong commitment to social work. The military metaphor runs through its organisation: its ministers are commissioned officers, its congregations are known as corps and its buildings have had such names as citadels and barracks. As they do not have sacraments, Salvationists have no need for fonts or communion tables, but a mercy seat or penitent form is normally provided as a locus for individual testimony. Characteristically music is supplied by a brass band.

Seventh-day Adventist Church

Combining a belief in the imminence of Christ's second coming with an emphasis on the importance of observing the Sabbath on Saturday, the Seventh-day Adventists originated in 19th-century America. The church is evangelical and its services tend to favour spontaneity rather than formal liturgy. The communion service (often celebrated quarterly) includes the ceremonial washing of feet. Like Baptists, the Church practises believers' baptism by immersion.

Society of Friends *see* **Quakers**

Strict Baptists *see* **Baptists**

Swedenborgianism

Following the death of Emanuel Swedenborg, the scientist and mystic, in 1772, his religious writings inspired a movement which led to the formation in England of the New (or New Jerusalem) Church in 1787. Swedenborg's followers acknowledge Christ as the one divinely human God and emphasise the significance of the spiritual world in everyday life.

Unitarians

Unitarians, who do not accept the doctrine of the Trinity, were specifically excluded from the provisions of the 1689 Act of Toleration and gained legal freedom to worship in Britain in 1813. During the later 18th century Unitarianism came to be seen as a rational faith, and in England many formerly Presbyterian congregations became Unitarian. As a result numerous important buildings from the early years of Dissent are now home to Unitarians. Increasingly Unitarian worship has drawn on elements from various faiths and philosophies, not only Christianity.

United Methodist Church

The United Methodist Church was formed in 1907 by the merger of the Bible Christians, Methodist New Connexion and United Methodist Free Church. In 1932 it amalgamated with the Primitive Methodists and Wesleyans to create the Methodist Church of Great Britain.

United Methodist Free Churches

Two groups of Methodists who had left the Wesleyan body came together in 1857 to create the United Methodist Free Churches. The groups were the Wesleyan Methodist Association and the Wesleyan Reformers, who had originated respectively in the 1830s and late 1840s as a reaction to the undemocratic exercise of authority by Wesleyan leaders. (Some Wesleyan Reformers remained separate in 1857, however, establishing the Wesleyan Reform Union, which continues to the present.) In 1907 the United Methodist Free Churches was one of three bodies that joined together to create the United Methodist Church.

United Reformed Church

The United Reformed Church was formed in 1972 by the amalgamation of the Presbyterian Church of England and most of the Congregational churches in England and Wales. The United Reformed Church's places of worship are generally buildings that were inherited from those older denominations.

Wesleyan Methodism *see also* Methodism

From the 1790s Methodism – that is, the tradition led by John Wesley – constituted what was a denomination in its own right, entirely separate from the Church of England. During the early 19th century, as various secessions occurred in Methodism, the Wesleyan connexion came to be distinguished from the newer groups by its social makeup (on average more middle class) and its conservative attitude to church government. Wesleyans were likely to have a high proportion of paid ministers, whereas Primitive Methodists and Bible Christians, for instance, generally relied more on (unpaid) local preachers. Such distinctions theoretically disappeared with Methodist union in 1932.

Wesleyan Methodist Association *see* **United Methodist Free Church**

Wesleyan Reformers *see* **United Methodist Free Church**

Notes

Abbreviations

BHB   *Baptist Handbook*
CYB   *Congregational Year Book*
ILN   *Illustrated London News*
ODNB   *Oxford Dictionary of National Biography*, 2004. Oxford: Oxford University Press
WCCR   *Wesleyan Chapel Committee Report*

Preface

1   The figures are drawn from Brierley 2014, table 1.3.1. Brierley's figures appear to omit non-Trinitarian congregations (for example Unitarians, Christian Scientists, Jehovah's Witnesses and Mormons).
2   Stell's four volumes are: *An Inventory of Nonconformist Chapels and Meeting-houses in Central England*, 1986; *An Inventory of Nonconformist Chapels and Meeting-houses in South-West England*, 1991; *An Inventory of Nonconformist Chapels and Meeting-houses in the North of England*, 1994; *An Inventory of Nonconformist Chapels and Meeting-houses in Eastern England*, 2002.
3   Butler 1999, 2 vols.
4   Early in the 17th century, a Nonconformist was someone who accepted Church of England doctrine, but did not follow all its practices (perhaps refusing to kneel for communion, for instance). Gradually the meaning of the word changed, and after the 1662 Act of Uniformity it was generally taken to mean someone belonging to a non-Anglican denomination.

1   Dissenters and places of worship before 1689

1   Brockett 1962, 11–14.
2   Spraggon 2003, 195–7; Clowes 1906, 28–9; Gillett and MacMahon 1980, 176–8.
3   Fairfax 1700, 18.
4   This account of Austin Friars draws on Young and Young 1956, 53–4 and 65–6; Lindenboom 1950; Yates 2008, 18–19. For Vincent van Gogh's drawing of the church *see* Bailey 1992, 8 and 122.
5   *See* Kirkpatrick 1845, 61–2; Sutermeister 1977, 12 and 24; Blomefield 1806, 342–3; *see also* Cobb 1942–3, 4–5.
6   Kirkpatrick 1845, 62.

7   Ridley 1968, 242–3; Brown 1895, **I**, 194–5. It has been suggested that Knox and the Scots showed a less conservative attitude to medieval buildings than did Calvin and the Swiss: for this *see* Drummond 1934, 20–1.
8   *The First Book of Discipline* 1621, 66.
9   Sprunger 1982, 30, 187.
10   Sprunger 1982, 91–3, 134, 162–3.
11   Wickham 1957, 34–5, 42.
12   Stell 1994a, 101–4.
13   Donnelly 1968, 10; Benes 2012, 2. For early occurrences of the term 'meeting house' *see Oxford English Dictionary*, 2 edn, IX, 1989, 564.
14   Watts 1978, 160 estimates that there were about 240 Baptist congregations in England and Wales by 1660.
15   Clowes 1906. For Bridge *see also* the *ODNB* entry.
16   Fincham and Tyacke 2007, 280–1, 333.
17   Browne 1877, 395, 402–3.
18   Pevsner 1967, 143–4; Stell 1994a, 239–41; Ricketts 2007, 120 and 229.
19   A stone font, dated 1673, stands towards the west end. It seems likely that a basin was originally used for baptisms at Bramhope, in keeping with the Calvinistic practice that predominated during the Commonwealth. Christopher Stell (1994a, 239) plausibly proposes that the introduction of a stone font – especially one at the west end – could indicate the appointment of a conforming minister by 1673.
20   Stell 1994a, 254–5; Ricketts 2007, 120–1, 254; Pace 1990, 233.
21   Swigchem, van *et al* 1984, 67, 110–11. Cf Yates 2000, 75–84; Upton 1986, 92–3; also Cromarty old church, before its 1730 changes.
22   *See* for example Watts 1978, 217–9; Dale 1907, 409–17. Presbyterian hopes that the revision of the Prayer Book would make significant concessions were almost wholly frustrated.
23   Watts 1978, 219.
24   Cameron 1979, 16–17; for details of Crosby Place *see* Schofield 1994, 161–3, etc.
25   *See* Butler 1999, **I**, 378–9, 382, 395–9; *see also* Schofield 1994, 163 and 202.
26   As Butler notes (Butler 1999, **I**, 395–400), the 1688 building was superseded by a larger meeting house in 1774, which

burned down in 1821 and was replaced by a new building in 1823.
27   Butler 1999, **II**, 515–9. Millerd's drawing, although imprecise, shows the meeting house with greater individuality than the nearby houses. John Rocque's 1742 survey of Bristol suggests that the meeting house measured about 100 feet by 45 feet (30.5m by 13.7m), Butler calculates.
28   Butler 1999, **II**, 517. Bristol was variously said to have had 'many more than 700' or even 'thousands' of Quakers in the 1650s (Braithwaite 1955, 253), and in the early 18th century there were 'about 2,000 and upwards' with a 'wealth not less than £500,000' (Dr John Evans's list, quoted in James 1867, 675–6).
29   Butler 1999, **I**, 256–8; Rowe 1970; Stell 2002, 136–8.
30   Watts 1978, 248; Dale 1907, 437–8.
31   *Calendar of State Papers, Domestic Series* 1672–3, 462 and 1673–5, 396–7.
32   Thoresby 1715, 4; Friedman 1997, 135–6.
33   Hewlings 2011; *see also* Hewlings 2012.
34   Two early depictions of the chapel are known: the first as item '6 A Meeting house' in William Lodge's 'The Prospects of the two most remarkable Towns', facing 160 in Thoresby 1715; the second on John Cossins's 1725 plan of Leeds.
35   Toulmin 1791, 29.
36   Swigchem, van *et al* 1984, 102–3; Hay 1957, 52–63; Gifford *et al* 1988, 172–5.
37   Butler 1999, **II**, 787–90; Stell 1994a, 305–7.
38   Matthew Hyde notes that Cumbrian churches were also whitewashed externally (Hyde and Pevsner 2010, 34–5).
39   Bunting 1994, 41–63 and 127. Basil Bunting actually died in Hexham; the *ODNB* states that he was cremated and his ashes scattered at Briggflats. According to his biographers (Caddel and Flowers 1977, 55), 'his ashes lie near a simple tombstone [sic] in the Quaker graveyard at Brigflatts'.
40   Dale 1862, 15–16, cited in Dale 1899, 170.

2   The age of toleration

1   This account of Henry Newcome and Cross Street chapel draws on the following sources: Urwick 1864, 217–22; Baker 1884, 13–15; Wade 1880, 28; Stell 1994a, 112–13.

2 Baker 1884, 13–15.

3 *See* Butler 1999, **II**, 616–18; Hutton 1783, 120–1 (from where the quotation derives); Upton 1993, 35–6; Foster 2005, 4, 103.

4 Ellerby and Pritchett 1993, 23 and 143; RCHME 1981, 55–6; Stell 1994a, 185–7.

5 *See* for example Swigchem, van *et al* 1984, 96–7 fig 1 and 58–9 fig 21; Hay 1957, fig 21 and plate 8b.

6 Probably coincidentally, a close match for the proportions (equal squares for the tower and two longitudinal arms, with shorter lateral arms) survives in the Dutch Reformed church at Oost-Vlieland in the Frisian Islands. Here a cruciform plan was created in 1647 when a pair of square arms was added to a plain rectangular church of 1605.

7 Blomefield 1806, 462–6; Stell 2002, 256–9.

8 Twin outer doorways were most convenient in wide-fronted buildings with corner staircases and a central block of seats. No evidence has emerged to associate them with segregated male and female seating in places of worship.

9 Among the Dutch precedents are the Amsterdam orphanage of 1634 by Jacob van Campen and Amsterdam's Sephardic synagogue of 1639.

10 Blomefield 1806, 478–9; Stell 2002, 259–60; Butler 1999, **I**, 454–5.

11 For example Briggs 1946, 24–7; but cf Ede *et al* 1994, 7.

12 Blomefield 1806, **IV**, 462–3.

13 Cf Kuyper 1980, 34.

14 Godfrey 1951; Stell 2002, 281–3.

15 Colvin 2008, 251–22; *see also* Rose 1951, 21–2, 55–8, plates I and II.

16 Colvin 2008, 25.

17 Stell 1994a, 16–20, 35–6.

18 Godfrey 1951; Stell 2002, 293–6; Hewett 1959; Reed [*c* 1992].

19 Fairfax 1700, 18.

20 Stell 1994a, 292–3.

21 Butler 1999, **I**, 182; Fitch [*c* 1963], 97–9.

22 Arnold 1960, 89–4, especially 103–4 and fig 9; Stell 1986, 98–100; [Tewkesbury Borough Council], 2001.

23 Stell 1991, 3.

24 Wren 1750, reprinted 1903, 195–6.

25 Butler 1999, **I**, 25–6; Stell 1986, 7–9.

26 Stell 1994a, 297–9; Ricketts 2007, 231.

27 Stell 1994a, 137–9; Higson 2007 (quotation on 104); Dobb 1978, 89–91.

28 *See* Dobb 1978.

29 Stell 1991, 32–4; Butler 1999, **I**, 59–61; Lake *et al* 2001, 86.

30 Moir and Letts 1999, 5.

31 Stell 1994, 10–14.

32 Jones 1996, 6–10; Scourfield and Haslam 2013, 372–3.

33 Stell 2002, 355–6; Butler 1999, **II**, 611–13.

34 Stell 2002, 307–9; Holmes and Rossi 1998.

35 The riots were associated with popular support for the zealously High Church Henry Sacheverell, who was successfully impeached by Parliament for his incendiary criticisms of 'false brethren in church and state': *see* for example Holmes 1973, 156–76; Watts 1978, 263–4; Dale 1907, 491–4.

36 Du Prey 2000, 49, 52, 155 note 6.

37 Wren 1750, reprinted 1903, 195–6.

38 Terry Friedman's statement (2011, 28) that the 1689 Toleration Act denied Nonconformists the right to erect steeples is incorrect, and the present author has not found evidence of any other legislation prohibiting Nonconformist steeples.

39 Jeffery 1996, 283–4.

40 For a summary of the churches built under the 1711 Act *see* Summerson 1970, 299–309.

41 The Act was repealed in 1719, along with the Occasional Conformity Act of 1711 (which had prevented Nonconformists from receiving communion in an Anglican church in order to hold a public office).

42 *See* Baker 1884, 22 and 76.

43 Matthews 1924, 104.

44 The Riot Act of 1715, which prescribed compensation from the public purse if churches or chapels were damaged or destroyed by rioters, was prompted by the attacks: *see* for example Dale 1907, 516.

45 Stell 1986, 248–9; May 1845, 205.

46 Among the contemporary parish churches with symmetrical entrance façades on the long south elevation (as well as at the west) are: Hawksmoor's St George-in-the-East, Wapping; Etty's Holy Trinity, Leeds; St Michael, Aynho, Northants; and St Peter, Gayhurst, Bucks. Hunslet Episcopal chapel, Leeds had twin entrances in the south front, none to the west (Friedman 1997, 106–9), and cf the later example of what became St Batholomew, Meltham, West Yorkshire (Royle 2011, 188–9). Single-storey buildings with long-wall entrances include St Margaret, Biddlesden, Bucks, though it forms one side of a stable block (Gomme 2000, 133–4, 461), and such almshouse chapels as Berkeley Hospital, Worcester, and what is now the Geffrye Museum, Shoreditch, East London. Later in the century several Anglican churches were erected in colonial Virginia with axial south entrances and north-wall pulpits (for which *see* Upton 1986, 33, 90–4).

47 Pevsner and Wilson 1997, 631–2 (and cf 407), plates 77–8; Stell 2002, 262–5.

48 Wright 1921 (17, quotation); Stell 1994a, 75–8; Dobb 1978, 106–7.

49 For chapels-of-ease *see* for example Dobb 1978, 62, 103; and Friedman 1997, 106–8.

50 Stell 1991, 193–6; Toulmin 1791, 29–32.

51 Toulmin 1791, 29–32.

52 Stell 1991 146–9. An interesting counterpoint to Ringwood is offered by Old South meeting house, Boston, MA. This was rebuilt in 1729 using a 'traditional' broad façade (to the south) and corresponding long-wall location for the pulpit, but giving increased status to the west-facing gable end by the addition of a tower and graceful spire. For the full shift from broad façades to longitudinal plans with gable-end entry in New England, *see* for example Andres 1980.

53 Arnold *et al* 1985, 26–9. Wren's views on St James's are in section 6 of his letter on the Commission for Building Fifty New Churches, printed in *Parentalia* (Wren 1750); *see also* Addleshaw and Etchells 1948, 55.

54 Butler 1999, **II**, 560–1, 890–1; Stell 1986, 218. Tantalisingly little is known about Edward Frith, a Quaker from Shenstone, whose name is given as the designer of the meeting house.

55 Butler 1999, **II**, 533–4; Stell 1991, 202–3.

3 Enthusiasm and enlightenment

1 Wesley's *Journal*, 28 Apr 1747 (where the quoted sentences occur); Stead 1998; Linstrum 1978, 243–4; Hutton 1909, 308–15; Stell 1994, 300–2; Friedman 2011, 30–1. As Stead notes, the central building was called Grace Hall until 1763, when it became the Congregation House, within which the chapel has always been the main space.

2 Friedman has observed that an opening originally at this point allowed simultaneous preaching to hearers in the chapel and outside on the terrace (1997, 129).

3 Cudworth nd, *Fulneck and Tong, Historical Account and Description*, 6 (here cited from Linstrum 1978, 243). Edward Graves of Newark was involved in several Moravian projects in England (personal communication from Hilary Smith); he was perhaps the man of that name who was a churchwarden of Newark parish church in 1757 (*see London Chronicle*, 27–29 Oct 1757). Cf the suggestion, on stylistic grounds, that George or John Platt of Rotherham might have been involved in the design (Friedman 2011, 31).

4 Hutton 1909, *passim*; Watts 1978, 308–13.

5 The similarity between the original plan of Fulneck's main building and that of Claverham must reflect a common source in secular architecture rather than a direct link.

6 Wesley's *Journal*, 17 Apr 1780; *see also* sources cited in note 1.

7 Wesley's *Journal*, 1 Aug 1738. Entries for the following days record Wesley's deep interest in the Moravians and their Herrnhut settlement.

8 Stell 1994b, 15–18.

9 For the Bristol building *see* Wesley's *Journal*, 9 May 1739 and 9 Feb 1748; Stell 1986, 66–8; Wilson 1968, 102–3; Richard Pedlar Architects 2002; Ison 1952, 61–2.

10 For the organ *see* Wilson 1968, 102–3. The restoration of 1929–30 is further discussed in Chapter 8.

11 Ison 1952, 61.

12 Butler 1999, **II**, 519–23; Ison 1952, 61–5; Gomme and Jenner 2011, 123–6.

13 Stamp 1863. The building was demolished to make way for a Wesleyan school in 1857; *see The Builder*, 30 May 1857, 310; *WCCR* 1858; Dolbey 1964, 43–5.

14 The quotation is from Whitefield 1771, 344 (here cited from Welch 1975, xiii). For the Moorfields tabernacle *see* Temple 1992, 126; Stell 2002, 95–6; Welch 1975, x–xv; Belden 1953, 192–206; Friedman 2011, 29–30.

15 Stell 2002, 77; Welch 1975, xiii–xv; Tyerman 1876–7, **2**, 372–4; O'Connell 2003, 151–2; *Survey of London*, **XXI**, 67–74 and plates 24–6; Belden 1953, 192–206; Walford 1878, 467–80; Timbs 1855, 177–8.

16 For the engraving (British Museum 1880-11-13-4733) *see* O'Connell 2003, 151–2; Tyerman 1876–7, **2**, 373–4.

17 Stell 1986, 85–6; Belden 1953, 192–206.

18 Gilbert 1976, 34.

19 Brandon and Johnson 1986; Stell 1994a, 133–6; Hartwell and Pevsner 2009, 563.

20 Stell 1994a, 234–6; Wood 1944.

21 Gwynn 2001, 131 and *passim*; Stell 2002, 116–17; Cherry *et al* 2005, 396; Kadish 2011, 138–41; *Survey of London*, **XXVII**, 221–5.

22 The quotation is from Young and Young 1956, 296.

23 *See* sources cited in notes 21 and 22 above, which are also relevant for this paragraph.

24 Stell 1991, 79–81; Brockett 1962, 132–7, 172–3; Meller 1989, 41–2. Little (1953, 69) has a photograph of the façade before street widening, suggestively juxtaposed with a view of Bartholomew Street Baptist chapel.

25 Stell 1994a, 327–8; Linstrum 1978, 99, 199; Friedman 2011, 462–5.

26 Downes 1969, 132–8.

27 Guillery 2004; Stell 2002, 118.

28 One Nonconformist instance was the late 17th-century meeting house at Kibworth, Leicestershire, 'where the Ten Commandments were lettered on the wall behind the pulpit' (Deacon 1980, 41–2).

29 Royal coats of arms were not unique to Anglican churches (*pace* Davies 1961, 40).

For instance Friar Gate Presbyterian chapel, Derby had a large canvas painted with the arms of William III (*see* Stell 1986, 45 and frontispiece), while the arms of Queen Anne hung above the communion table in St John's Square Presbyterian meeting house, Clerkenwell, London (*see* Holmes 1973, 174).

30 For Johnson *see* Colvin 2008, 577–8.

31 Stell 2002, 260–2; Taylor and Taylor 1848; Summerson 1970, 350, 563; Nierop-Reading 2002; Friedman 2003, 54–7; Hankinson 2007; Friedman 2011, 507–10. Friedman apparently confuses the origins of the Presbyterian congregation, which had been founded by John Collinge in the 1660s.

32 Wesley's *Journal*, 23 Nov 1757. To be precise, there are 17 sash windows at the upper level (the entrance face has three; all other faces have two).

33 Earlier octagonal churches in England include those at Moulton Chapel, Lincolnshire (of 1722), Ayot St Peter, Hertfordshire (of 1751) and Hartwell, Buckinghamshire (of 1753–5, by Henry Keene).

34 Nierop-Reading 2002.

35 Wesley's *Journal*, 23 Nov 1757.

36 Wesley's *Journal*, 8 Jul 1772.

37 Stell 1994a, 259–62; Linstrum 1978, 98, 200–1; Smithies 1988, especially 18–20; Onwin 1991; Sutcliffe 1996; Friedman 2011, 42–3, 493 and Doc 94.

38 The poem *Hhadash Hamishcan* (the extract given here is cited by Sutcliffe 1996, 23) was published anonymously, but the author's identity was an open secret, as Wesley indicated.

39 Wesley's *Journal*, 8 Jul 1772.

40 Stell 1986, 246–7; Anon 1978.

41 The Lutheran church in Wildbad (of 1746) and the French Reformed church in Königsberg (of 1733–5) are much larger counterparts of the plan of Bewdley's Presbyterian meeting house.

42 Brett 1967, 5–6 and plates 8–9; Larmour 1987, 2–3; Hague and Hague 1986, 60–1, 130–1. Among the German examples of elliptical plans are the long-axis church at Alten, near Dessau (1743), and the short-axis French Reformed church at Potsdam (1751–2, by G W von Knobelsdorff).

43 Wesley's *Journal*, 8 Jun, 1789.

44 For the Countess of Huntingdon *see* the *ODNB* entry, under Selina Hastings. For the Bath chapel *see* Stell 2002, 162–4; Seymour 1839, **I**, 466–8, 477–8; Wesley's *Journal*, 5 Oct 1766; Friedman 2011, 225–6. The chapel currently houses a permanent exhibition of the buildings of Bath.

45 The quotation, cited here from the *ODNB* entry, comes from Lady Llanover 1861, **2**, 28.

46 Seymour 1839, **I**, 466–8, 477–8.

47 For Trefecca *see* Scourfield and Haslam 2013, 579–82. Gothic featured significantly in a number of the Countess's chapels, as Schlenther notes (1997, 122). Cf Friedman's view that the Countess 'preferred plain classical forms' (2011, 29).

48 Dolbey 1964, 66–7, 99–115. *Minutes of Several Conversations between the Reverend Messieurs John and Charles Wesley and Others* [that is, minutes of the Methodist conference], 1770, 44–5.

49 Stell 1991 196–7; Toulmin 1791, 29–33. A 12-sided chapel was built in Canterbury and opened by Wesley in 1764: *see* Vickers 1961, 8–9. During the later 18th century quite a number of Nonconformist chapels and Anglican churches were built to octagonal plans, including *inter alia* the Octagon chapel, Liverpool (1763) and St Mary's church, Birmingham (1773–4).

50 Wesley's *Journal*, 27 Jul 1766; *Minutes of Several Conversations between the Reverend Messieurs John and Charles Wesley and Others* [that is, minutes of the Methodist conference], 1770, 44–5.

51 *Minutes of Several Conversations between the Reverend Messieurs John and Charles Wesley and Others* [that is, minutes of the Methodist conference], 1770, 44–5.

52 Temple 1992, 27–33; Stell 1994b, 18–29; Wesley's *Journal*, 1 Mar and 29 Nov 1776.

53 Bowmer 1951, 204. As Bowmer also notes (90, 99–102, 206–15) Wesley followed the Book of Common Prayer, adding only hymn singing and extempore prayer; from 1784 his revised version of the Prayer Book was published.

54 Wesley's *Journal*, 24 Dec 1787.

55 Wesley's *Journal*, 1 Nov 1778, 5 Dec 1785.

56 Wesley's *Journal*, 17 Dec 1777, 11 Mar 1779.

57 The resolutions from the 1790 Methodist conference are reprinted in Rack 2011, 736 and 738.

58 Wesley's *Journal*, 30 Mar 1781. For the Manchester chapel *see also* Dolbey 1964, 78–9 and plate 6; Aston 1816, reprinted 1969, 99–100; T Swindells 1907, 111–13; Anon 1981. I am grateful to E Alan Rose for information about the chapel.

59 The visitor's description is reprinted in Anon 1981.

60 Wesley's *Journal*, 18 Jun 1790; Stell 1994a, 224; Dolbey 1964, 90–1.

61 For Bedford and Ockbrook *see* Stell 2002, 3–4, and Stell 1986, 53–4.

62 Stell 1991, 213–4.

63 Stell 1994a, 92–3; Darley 1975, 78–80; Hartwell *et al* 2004, 203–6; Creese 1966, 6–9.

64 *See* the entry for La Trobe in *ODNB*; *see also* Colvin 2008, 635, and cf Mason and Torode 1997.

65 Summerson 1978, 212–13. It should be
noted that Wesley's chapel in City Road
did not gain a portico until the early
19th century.

4 The age of Methodism

1 The statistics cited in this paragraph are
drawn from Gilbert 1976, 30–9, including
tables 2.2, 2.3 and 2.4 and fig 2.1.

2 On the relative strengths of Nonconformity
in rural communities and medium-sized
towns, and its weaknesses in larger urban
areas, *see* Watts 1995, 126–9.

3 Estimates of the population before 1800
are especially problematic, but there were
perhaps fewer than 7 million people in
England in 1780 and around 13 million in
1831: *see* Darby 1976, 4, 166.

4 Cliff 1986; Laqueur 1976; Watts 1995,
284–303.

5 Butler 1999, **II**, 486.

6 Jewson 1957, 59–74. Grass 2012 lists an
additional four congregations that were
established in the same period, each of
which built a new chapel by 1822
(Framingham Pigot, Salhouse, Saxlingham
Thorpe and Wortwell).

7 Building dates for the chapels concerned
have been derived from several sources,
including Stell 2002.

8 Nightingale 1906, 18–50 (the quotation
being from 23–4). The Methodist concept
of a circuit was explicitly invoked as part of
the scheme: *see* Powicke 1907, 22. For a
wider account of the use of itinerant
preachers in these years *see* Watts 1995,
132–7.

9 Stell 1986, 70–3; Ison 1952, 81–4;
Gomme and Jenner 2011, 178–80 and
225; Foyle 2004, 142; Friedman 2011, 274
and doc 35.

10 For Blackburn *see ODNB* and Colvin 2008,
126–8.

11 Murch 1835, 116–24; for the schools that
were set up by Dr Lant Carpenter and his
daughter *see also ODNB* entries for Lant
Carpenter, Mary Carpenter and James
Martineau.

12 Stell 1994a, 144–5.

13 The Grundy family memorial, in front of
the chapel, records some of this story.
Grundy's firm advertised widely in the
Nonconformist press, announcing for
example in 1901 that its heating and
ventilating apparatus was 'specially
adapted to Methodist chapels' (*Minutes of
the One-Hundred-and-Fifth Annual
Conference of the Methodist New
Connexion*, 1901, facing page i).

14 Dobb 1978, 174.

15 For the comparative parish sizes in
different parts of England *see* Gilbert 1976,
98–105, 117–18.

16 Stell 2002, 251–2.

17 Wesley's *Journal*, 30 Oct 1781.

18 For the early financial and other records
see Norfolk Record Office mss FC 18/1, FC
18/14, FC 18/137.

19 Stell 1991, 72–4.

20 Anon, *Wesley's Methodist Chapel 1798*,
undated leaflet at Pentre Llifior chapel,
which includes information drawn from
the chapel accounts.

21 For an example of the effects of inflation
and the hazards of financing chapel
building *see* Telford 1886, 110–21.

22 The attempt to create a Congregational
Union in 1808–10 is summarised in Peel
1931, 32. For Thomas Wilson *see ODNB*
entry and Wilson 1846, *passim*.

23 For the new religious bodies *see* Appendix.
Strictly speaking the Bible Christians did
not secede, but were an independent
branch of Methodism.

24 Pocock 1834 included – and gave greater
currency to – a number of Nonconformist
plan-types that he would have known.

25 For individual architects *see* Colvin 2008;
for Rickman *see also ODNB*.

26 Dolbey 1964, 135–7; Wickham 1957,
55–8, 138–9; Stell 1994a, 310–11. An
engraved view of Carver Street chapel,
dated 1807 and ascribed to E Bennett, is
reproduced in Bostwick 1989, unpaginated.

27 For Jenkins *see* Dolbey 1964, 177–9;
Colvin 2008, 573–4; Lenton 2009, 178.

28 Willis 1964, 22–3. The engraving of New
Street chapel is reproduced in Hallett and
Rendall 2003, 77.

29 Stell 1994a, 6–7; Champness 2005, 87–8.

30 Dolbey 1964, 161–3 and plate 21; Vickers
1961, passim; Stell 2002, 166–7; Stell
1994a, 62–3; Colvin 2008, 573–4.

31 Ison 1948, 80 and plate 27; Stell 1991,
164–5; Forsyth 2003, 228; Jackson 1991,
48–9.

32 Stell 1991, 81; Dolbey 1964, 137–8 and
plate 13; Summerson 1978, 231–2 and
plate 41b.

33 Forsyth 2003, 228.

34 St Marylebone parish church, London
(1813–17 by Thomas Hardwick) had its
organ in a gallery behind the altar, with the
pulpit and lectern a little further forward:
see von Erffa and Staley 1986, 329–31 and
Clarke 1966, 125–6.

35 Stell 1994a, 170–1.

36 The quotation is from Watts 1995, 184–7.

37 The quotation is taken from a report in the
*Hampshire Telegraph and Sussex
Chronicle* of 1 Feb 1819.

38 Stell 1991, 98–9, 191; Stell 1994a, 170–1,
222.

39 Exterior photographs of St Mary's Baptist
chapel, Norwich are held in the Historic
England Archive (4334-154, previously
AA56/) and in the George Plunkett Archive

([3261] 1939-09-12); an interior
photograph is reproduced in Gould 1883,
facing page 117.

40 [Sheild] 1896, especially 11–13; Pocock
1824, 18–20, 27, and plates ix–xii, xli;
Home Missionary Magazine, 1 Jun 1832.
Neither the exterior nor the interior
conformed exactly to Pocock's published
design. Ranelagh chapel was transferred to
the English Presbyterian Church in 1845.

41 Ellerby and Pritchett 1993, 157–63; Stell
1994a, 187.

42 Stell 1986, 229; Leigh *et al* 2010; Trimen
1849, 137.

43 Queen Street Wesleyan chapel,
Huddersfield (1818–19), which was
slightly smaller than Bethesda, also had a
curved rear wall, although in this case
behind the pulpit, and its curved gallery
was set aside for Sunday-school pupils: *see*
Royle 1994.

44 Butler 1999, **I**, 382–8; Alexander 1820,
41–5 (the quoted phrase appearing on
page 41).

45 Staffordshire Record Office D1174/3/2/1;
Wakeling 1987.

46 Lascelles 1821, 237 and illustration
following 236; Dolbey 1964, 173 and plate
24; Sherwood and Pevsner 1974, 249.

47 Stell 1986, 22.

48 Temple 1992, 66–7.

49 Stell 1994a, 220.

50 Stell 1991, 156–7.

51 Little 1966, 45–6, 49 and plates 6a and 6c.
The comparison extends to the interiors.

52 Stell 1986, 223.

53 Knowles 1999; Stell 1986, 257–9;
Betjeman 1952, 97. Part of the description
of the Worcester chapel is based on notes
written by the present author for a visit by
the Society of Architectural Historians of
Great Britain in 2000.

54 Homan 1997; Stell 2002, 347–50; North,
[1996].

55 Stell 1986, 81.

56 Dutch examples of elongated octagonal
churches can be seen in Swigchem, van *et
al* 1984, for example 58 and 96. Among
other octagonal chapels of this period in
England were those in Liverpool
(Methodist New Connexion, 1801),
Hackney (Unitarian, 1809) and Swindon
(Wesleyan, 1813): *see* Picton 1875, 171;
Stell 2002, 85; Grinsell *et al* 1950, 142;
Pocock 1824, illustrated designs for two
octagonal chapels, one of elongated form.

57 Friedman 1997, 157–63.

58 Stell 1986, 46–7.

59 Stell 2002, 172–4.

60 Woodall *et al* 2009; Stell 1994a, 198;
Neave and Neave 1990, passim. The date
of 1812 is given by Woodall *et al* based
on recent research, but other sources give
1814.

61 *See* Neave and Neave 1990, 54; Woodall *et al* 2009, 3, 7.

62 Homan 1997; Stell 2002, 337–9; North, [1996], 14; Beevers *et al* 1989, 45. Variant arrangements for a singers' book-rest on communion tables were to be found in several Strict Baptist chapels in (at least) Sussex and Kent, but perhaps only at a later date.

63 Nairn and Pevsner 1965, 178.

64 Butler 1999, **I**, 141–2; Stell 1991, 72–6.

65 Daniel Henson was presumably related to Samuel Henson, who worked on several parish churches in the area in the following decade, for which *see* Cherry and Pevsner 2002, 686, and Colvin 2008, 513.

66 Butler 1999, **I**, 433–4 and **II**, 711–8.

67 Kendall nd, **I**, 110.

68 Alcock [1968], 51–5; Stephens 1970, 251–2; Kendall nd, **I**, 170–4; Stell 1986, 217. My thoughts on the Primitive Methodists' early buildings have greatly benefited from discussions with Dr Sandy (Alexander) Calder, whose research (*see* Calder 2012) has now been published (Calder 2016).

69 Butler 1999, **I**, 141–2.

70 Alcock [1968], 51–5.

71 Binfield 2007, especially 23–5.

72 Yates 2000, 116–7. In this context Yates is referring only to the use of three blocks of pews, without a central gangway, as the chapel fashion.

73 Port 2006, 98–100.

74 *See* Port 2006, 64.

75 Dale 1907, 582 (citing *Parliamentary Debates*, xviii, 710, 713).

76 Dale 1907, 583.

77 Wickham 1957, 71.

78 Watts 1995, 479.

5 Growth and renewal, 1820–50

1 Following the Lady Hewley case of 1833, Unitarian ownership of many older meeting houses became insecure. The Dissenters' Chapels Act of 1844 rectified the situation, securing the rights of any congregation that had worshipped in a building for the previous 25 years.

2 The strengths of the various strands of Nonconformity in these years are analysed in the second chapter of Gilbert 1976, especially 31–2 (table 2.2), 34 (table 2.3), 39 (fig 2.2) and 40–1 (table 2.5).

3 Among the exceptional instances of grander façades from the decades around 1800, Liverpool could boast two: Paradise Street Unitarian chapel (1791, by the builder–architect John Walmsley), an octagonal building whose pedimented entrance had four giant half-columns, and Brunswick Wesleyan chapel, Moss Street

(1811, designed by William Byrom), which had a full-height Ionic portico. *See* Austin *et al* 1832, 78, 97 and plates; and Picton 1875, **II**, 149, 423.

4 Stuart and Revett 1762–1830.

5 Rickman's *An Attempt to Distinguish the Styles of English Architecture from the Conquest to the Reformation* was first published in book form in 1817, and further editions continued to appear until the seventh in 1881.

6 Stell 2002, 333.

7 Colvin 2008, 1120; for Morell *see ODNB*.

8 ΜΟΝΩ θΕΩΑΙΑ ΙΗΣΟΥ ΕΡΙΣΤΟΥ ΑΟΕΑ, 'To God only wise, be glory through Jesus Christ' (Romans 16: 27).

9 An early illustration of Trinity chapel, showing its three-bay portico at the centre of a five-bay towered façade, is reproduced in Dale 1907, plate 10. The building subsequently became an Anglican church, and gained a Gothic frontage: *see* Antram and Morrice 2008, 77–8.

10 Stell 2002, 115. The Stamford Street chapel has generally been attributed to John Rennie (the future Sir John Rennie), but has also been ascribed to Charles Parker. *See* Colvin 2008, 850 note 1; Cherry and Pevsner 1983, 578; Young and Young 1956, 280.

11 Jones 1914, 28–30; Young and Young 1956, 280.

12 Wakeling 2001. An early, and radical, example of chapel seating on the model of classical theatre was Brunswick Wesleyan chapel, Liverpool, of 1811, for which *see* note 3 above. Cf also Pocock 1824, plates iii–v.

13 Wakeling 2001; Stell 2002, 332–3. A drawing in the RIBA collection (British Architectural Library, SD 68/4) shows the original layout, as well as the Ionic design first proposed for the Union Street façade.

14 Bingham 1991, 48, 53–4, 74. If Bingham is correct in identifying Busby as the author of the drawing in the RIBA collection, it seems possible that the chapel was designed by Busby, and that Wilds substituted a Doric order for the Union Street façade after Busby left the partnership.

15 Port 2006, 84.

16 Lee 1955, especially 37–8, 42, 95–6.

17 Port 1961, 61 and 142–3. The quotation is derived by Port from the Church Building Commission's minute book 21, 101.

18 Port 1961, 40.

19 Lake *et al* 2001, 50, 90; Colvin 2008, 894; Dolbey 1964, 146–7.

20 Sambell's proposal for 'a room nearly semi-circular, with one straight side; with the seats rising tier above tier to the extreme limits of the chapel, and with the minister lowest of all' appeared in his letter of 12 May 1841, published in the *Baptist Magazine* **XXXIII** 1841, 355.

21 Stell 1994a, 109; Austin *et al* 1832, 72.

22 Colvin 2008, 389–90 and 985.

23 For Smirke's design *see* Liscombe 1970. For St George, Regent Street (also known as Hanover chapel) *see* Watkin 1974, 136–45 and cf Middleton and Watkin 1980, 254.

24 Bindman and Riemann 1993, 178–9.

25 Elmes 1830, 169 and plate. Colvin's identification of this as William Brooks's design (Colvin 2008, 165–6) must be a very rare case of confusion on Colvin's part – the confusion being with the chapel in Finsbury Circus erected for the Revd Alexander Fletcher, for which *see* Elmes 1830, 163 and plate.

26 Butler 1999, **I**, 318–23; Stell 1994a, 114.

27 Stewart 1956b, 30. Homan (in *Quaker Studies*, **11**/1, Sep 2006, 124) uses the Manchester meeting house to illustrate his view that Quakers opted for classical motifs to express republican sympathies, but without supporting evidence.

28 The quotation, from *The British Friend*, 1845, 113–5, is cited in Butler 1999, **I**, 320.

29 Austin *et al* 1832, 61–2.

30 Austin *et al* 1832, 62. Quakers (who generally used open benches rather than enclosed pews) had a reputation as innovators in the field of heating places of worship. For American evidence *see* Nylander 1980, especially 87. The growing desire to heat places of worship did not always yield immediate results. In 1816, for instance, there was an unsuccessful attempt to heat the Quaker meeting house in Kendal by steam, followed in the same year by a method involving hot air, superseded in turn by a warm air system in 1825. *See* Butler 1999, **II**, 658.

31 Cunningham and Waterhouse 1992, 25, 30, 216.

32 The quotation is from Darbyshire 1897, 21, as cited in Colvin 2008, 628.

33 Butler 1999, **I**, 448–55; Stell 2002, 259.

34 Little 1966, 63; Colvin 2008, 787; Rossi 1998, 1–3.

35 The quotation is from Pevsner and Wilson 1997, 253; a similar phrase occurs on page 136. Patience's design for St Peter's Wesleyan chapel, Lady Lane, Norwich (of 1824) was different, involving a five-bay façade with Ionic porches in bays one and five (as shown by photograph NBR A43/1892 and others in the Historic England Archive (formerly National Monuments Record)).

36 Little 1966, 63; Rossi 1998, 1–3. In 1894–6 the building was adapted for use as a Catholic school, and after a period of disuse was converted for office use in 1991.

37 Two other examples were at Peckham (1826) and Stoke Newington (1828), for which *see* Butler 1999, **I**, 410–1, 419–21.

38   For Elmham Hall *see* for example Crook 1995, 125 and plate 141. Both Donthorn (sometimes spelt Donthorne) and Patience exhibited regularly at the Norwich Society of Artists.

39   Stell 1991, 161; Forsyth 2003, 222; Parker 1975. The chapel has also been known by the name of Ebenezer, but to avoid confusion in the present context, the more recent name has been used here.

40   Stell 1994a, 311–2; Harman and Minnis 2004, 168; Holland 1824, 155–6.

41   The quotation is from Stell 2000, 318 and plate 77.

42   Hair 1898; Elmes 1830, 151–2 and plate; Young and Young 1956, 263–4 and plate 61. The Bath stone frontage had late-Georgian terraces on each side (*see* for example the frontispiece to Hair 1898), and the brick flanks of the building with their substantial buttresses (visible in the Youngs' plate 61) were revealed only after war damage in 1945. As a result of that damage the building was demolished in the 1950s.

43   The west front of York Minster, although not a common model for 19th-century church builders, might have attracted special attention as a result of its restoration in 1801–16.

44   It might be noted, incidentally, that even York Minster's vaults are of wood, those in the nave being 1840s replacements for timberwork of 1354, and those in the choir being the work of Robert Smirke in 1829–32 (*see* Pevsner and Neave 1995, 140–1).

45   An illustration of the interior, predating changes of 1860, is reproduced in Hair 1898, facing page 132.

46   Hair 1898, 351.

47   Stell 1986, 208–9; Stell 1976, 18; Wright 1951, especially 16–17, 82–3, 95.

48   Matthews 1924, 196–7.

49   Stell 1986, 52.

50   Stell 1976, 19–20.

51   Thomas Bateman (1821–61), author of *Ten Years' Diggings in Celtic and Saxon Grave Hills*, 1861, was the grandson of Thomas Bateman (1760–1847), the man for whom the chapel was built. For the tomb and wall memorials *see* Stell 1986, 52, 58.

52   Foulston 1838, 52, 63–4, and plates 80, 95–8; Worth 1870, 65. The chapel was demolished in the early 20th century.

53   The diverse pattern of Nonconformist places of worship in Devonport is traced in two articles by Welch: 1962 and 1967.

54   Foulston 1838, 52, 63–4, and plate 95.

55   Stell 2002, 19–20; Welch 1996, 143.

56   The quotation, from the first edition of *The Velvet Cushion* (published anonymously, but known to be written by the evangelical Anglican minister John William Cunningham) 1814, 17, was omitted in subsequent editions, and was the subject of a robust critique in *The Evangelical Magazine*, May 1815, 187–9.

57   Gibbs 2008.

58   Serjeant 2011.

59   An early illustration of the interior is reproduced in Serjeant 2011, plate 8.6. Much of the interior survived a remodelling of 1896–1903, only to be sacrificed in 1979. *See* Powell 1980, unpaginated.

60   An illustration of the exterior is included in the *WCCR* 1899.

61   RCHME 1981, **5**, 52; Serjeant 2011; Stell 1994a, 188–9.

62   *See* Willis 1964, 27–33. Part way along St Saviourgate is the important Presbyterian chapel of 1692–3 (*see* pp 18–19).

63   For Brunswick, Leeds, *see* Linstrum 1978, 203; Stell 1994a, 287; and Serjeant 2011.

64   Kingston Wesleyan chapel, Witham, Hull (of 1840–1) was Simpson's only known variant of the Centenary design, complete with Ionic portico: *see VCH York ER*, **I**, 1969, 372, and *The Builder*, 2 Apr 1898, 322; *see also* Serjeant 2011.

65   Alger 1905.

66   To cite just one example, Pembroke Baptist chapel, Liverpool, of 1839, designed by Joseph Franklin. *See* Picton 1875, 442 and Whitley 1913, 342.

67   Both buildings are illustrated in the *CYB* 1847 and in Powell 1980. For Albion Street chapel, Hull, *see also VCH York ER*, **I**, 1969, 320.

68   *The Builder*, 2 Apr 1898, 318.

69   Stell 1986, 62–3; Gomme and Jenner 2011, 223–4; Foyle 2004, 103.

70   Little 1966, 75.

71   *ILN* 1843, **2**, 378; *VCH York ER*, **I**, 1969, 324; Neave 1991, 31.

72   Hitchcock 1954, **I**, 114. Note that Hitchcock misleadingly refers to it as an Independent chapel, a mistake which has subsequently been repeated by other authors.

73   Linstrum 1999, 7–8. Salmon has suggested that the chapel should be seen as an example of the revival of Roman forms (Salmon 2000, 243, note 50), while *The Builder* thought it was an 'imitation of Greek models' (*The Builder*, 2 Apr 1898, 320 and 327).

74   The function of each part of the building is summarised in *ILN* 1843, **2**, 378.

75   Curl 2000 provides a wide range of comparative and contextual material. Interestingly in the 1830s Thomas Allom, one of the architects of Great Thornton Street chapel, had drawn the illustrations for the unadopted Gothic buildings of Kensal Green Cemetery, and may have provided a watercolour of the final scheme, which incorporated chapels with prostyle porticoes and classical colonnades (Curl 2000, 48–59). Conversely the rise of Gothic can be gauged from the fact that in 1846 Cuthbert Brodrick, an assistant to Lockwood during the Great Thornton Street commission, designed the Gothic buildings of Hull's General Cemetery (Curl 2000, 134; Linstrum 1999, 10–11).

76   Intramural burials ceased following the Cemeteries Clauses Act of 1847, although Nonconformists had to wait until the Burials Act of 1880 for the right to conduct burial services in parish churchyards. Great Thornton Street chapel was largely replaced by a grand Wesleyan mission hall in 1908–9. The mission hall, along with the surviving fragments of the 1840s building, was destroyed by bombing in the Second World War.

77   Hitchcock 1971, 100.

78   Stell 1994a, 107–8; Thom 1854, 58–9; Hughes 1969, entry 37.

79   Stell 1986, 126; *ILN* 1845, **7**, 268. The chapel closed in 1939, and opened *c* 1950 as an adult education centre.

80   Seaborne 1971, 186–9 and plate 158. Hansom had just played a central role in the design of Birmingham Town Hall, which was based on the Roman Temple of Castor and Pollux (*see* Salmon 2000, 153–68).

81   *ILN* 1845, **7**, 268.

82   Hitchcock 1954, **I**, 134–5.

83   Stell 1986, 84; Butler 1999, **I**, 216–8.

84   For Daukes see Felstead *et al* 1993, 235; Verey 1973a and 1973b; Verey and Brooks 2002, 105.

85   Since 1902 the building has been extended for secular use. Stell 1986, 76–7; Butler 1999, **I**, 208–11; Verey and Brooks 2002, 240 (where Daukes is suggested as the architect).

86   Stell 1986, 217–18; Coad 1968, 66, 76–7; Rowdon 1967, 168, 176; Scammell 1887, 35–6; *VCH Staffs*, **VI**, 251–2.

87   For the Brethren's antipathy to using pulpits *see* Scammell 1887, 36. The internal fittings are said to have been replaced in 1930 (*see* Stell 1986, 217–8), but it was reported that the sloping floor, apparently modelled on the curving, tiered arrangement of the Brethren's Plymouth chapel, had been retained (Coad 1968, 66).

88   For Scott's work at St Mary's, Stafford *see* Fisher 1995, 32–64.

89   Stell 1994a, 34–5; [Cheshire County Council] 1988.

90   Stell 2002, 287–8; Grass 2012, 73–6.

91   Neither chapel has retained its original ground-floor arrangements: *see* Grass 2012, 73–6 and Evans *et al* 1979, 69–70.

92   Klaiber 1931, 79–80 (the quotation is from 80); Grass 2012, 67, 73–5. Earlier

hexagonal chapels are known (for example Grape Lane chapel, York, of 1781, for which *see* Ellerby and Pritchett 1993, 23–7, 145–7), but no immediate precedent for the Suffolk pair has been identified.

93 The quotation is from Barton 1975, 25.

94 Stell 1991, 117 and frontispiece.

95 A contemporary description of a characteristic American meeting house (including a gable-end belfry from which 'a slender spire shoots up, terminated with a gilt vane') appeared in the review article 'American Architecture' in *The North American Review*, **XLIII**, Oct 1836, 356–84. The article was extensively quoted in England by William Bardwell (1837, 164–8) and in *The Congregational Review*, 1847, 151–63 ('Remarks on Ecclesiastical Architecture as Applied to Nonconformist Chapels').

96 Densham and Ogle 1899, 135–6.

97 Densham and Ogle 1899, 135–6; cf Gillett 1993.

98 For example neither St James, Poole, as rebuilt in 1820, or St Peter, Bournemouth, as built in 1841–3, had a spire. Interestingly at least one Nonconformist defence of spires was to cite the American example: 'We are most partial to towers, turrets, and steeples, of moderate dimensions, and hail the day when every Nonconformist meeting-house will have its own belfry and its own bell. There is much of this in Scotland, and it is all but universal in America' (*The Christian Witness*, 1849, **VI**, 489).

99 Stell 1986, 231–2. Botham was the son of Joseph Botham, for whose Ebenezer Wesleyan chapel, Sheffield *see* note 40 and for whose Brunswick Wesleyan chapel, Leeds *see* note 63 (Colvin 2008, 145).

100 For the 1824 chapel in Graham Street, which was claimed to seat 2,500, *see* Langley 1939, 103–4 and facing 171; Little 1971, 22 and plate 43. *VCH Warwicks*, **VII**, 1964, 476. The 1848–9 chapel in Broad Street superseded the Presbyterians' first building on that site, of 1834.

101 One 18th-century precedent is the Presbyterian (latterly Unitarian) chapel at Frenchay, near Bristol, which has a prominent tower, provided with a bell by 1752. *See* Stell 1986, 102–4. A more recent instance was at Trinity Congregational chapel, Poplar, London (of 1840–1 by William Hosking, a pupil of William Jenkins), which was lost in the Second World War. *See* CYB 1847, 159; Timbs 1855, 176; *Companion to the Almanac*, 1842, 210–12. In reviewing Andrew Trimen's *Church and Chapel Architecture* in 1849, *The Christian Witness* (1849, **VI**, 486) told its Congregational readers that 'it were exceedingly desirable that every

Dissenting place of worship, both in town and country, had its bell'.

102 Foster 2005, 152–3 draws attention to Botham's borrowing of Ionic quadrants from St Thomas's, though these do not form part of the tower in the earlier church.

103 *ILN* 1849, **15**, 341; Stell 1986, 231–2. At the time of writing the former chapel functions as a bar and nightclub, for which use the virtual absence of windows seems to pose no disadvantage.

104 For the debate over town churches *see The Rambler*, Jan 1850, **V**, 11–18; Feb 1850, 124–6; Jun 1850, 525–6; and Street 1850. These references are from O'Donnell 2000, especially 118.

105 For the internal arrangements *see ILN* 1849, **15**, 341 (from which the quotation is derived); *The Builder,* 5 Aug 1848, 380; Pevsner and Wedgwood 1966, 139.

106 For Whitby *see* Wesley's *Journal*, 15 Jun 1788 and 18 Jun 1790.

107 *See* Allon 1863, 177–84; Stell 1986, 175; Stell 1991, 15, 18–20. At the time of writing Sherman chapels survive at Woodley (built about 1825), Caversham Hill (1827), Wargrave (1835) and Binfield Heath (1835).

108 More details of the financing of these chapels are to be found in Dearing 1993, 40–1, 45. Were any professional architects involved in the design of Sherman's chapels? He himself may have had some skill as a model-maker, having produced chessmen during his early apprenticeship to an ivory-turner (Dearing, 37), but 'obtained plans' for at least one chapel (Allon 1863, 179). Sherman perhaps knew the accomplished architect William Jay, who enlarged (in Gothic mode?) the Congregational chapel in Henley-on-Thames, just four miles from Binfield Heath, in 1829 (Dearing, 38; Colvin 2008, 570).

109 Dearing 1993, 37–9. For the Countess of Huntingdon's preference for Gothic, and in particular her chapel at Bath, *see* Chapter 3. For the Gothic character of the Bristol chapel *see* Gomme and Jenner 2011, 166–7.

110 Colvin 2008, 373–4.

111 Colvin 2008, 373; Bettley and Pevsner 2007, 53, 357.

112 The phrase, from the committee involved in the building of a new chapel for the Congregationalists of Harlow in 1838, is quoted in Colvin 1947, specifically 15.

113 Stell 2002, 198. For further comparisons in support of the attribution *see* note 115.

114 Stell 2002, 198. In 1764 the Baptists had built a chapel on the present site in High Street, its gable-end façade being distinguished by a large Venetian window (illustrated in Wright 1986, 54).

115 The earliest Gothic chapels currently documented as by Fenton are from 1836 (Independent chapel, Halesworth, Suffolk and Congregational chapel, Overton, Hants); two earlier Congregational chapels have also been attributed to him (Felsted, Essex, of *c* 1833, and March, Cambs, of 1836). *See* Stell 2002, 39, 54, 289–90; Stell 1991, 146. For the Congregational chapels at Billericay and Lincoln *see* Kaye 1999, 19 and Stell 2002, 48, 215.

116 Stell 1991, 10–12. Geoffrey Tyack and Simon Bradley have tentatively suggested that the chapel's builders, Job and Thomas Hanson, were the designers (Tyack *et al* 2010, 395).

117 The date of the side porches is given in Tyack *et al* 2010, 395.

118 The self-proclaimed purpose of *Tracts for the Times* is quoted in Cross and Livingstone 2005, 1645. The Tractarian's response to Newbury Wesleyan chapel was published in *British Critic*, 4 ser, 28, 1840, 478–9; quoted in Bradley 2000 (the cited observation appearing on 28).

119 Bradley 2000.

120 *British Critic*, 4 ser, 28, 1840, 478–9; quoted in Bradley 2000.

121 For Drummond *see ODNB*.

122 Stell 2002, 315–8; Colvin 2008, 164–5, 1122–5. Stell infers that Brookes played the subsidiary role until 1839, when he assumed sole responsibility following Wilkins's death.

123 The apostles, who included Drummond himself, were expected to live until the Second Coming, but the last survivor died in 1901.

124 *See* Atterbury and Wainwright 1994, 89; Hill 2007, especially 287, 300–1, 379–80, 501. As Hill notes (68–9), Pugin's mother had been a passionate follower of Edward Irving's preaching.

125 Stell 1994a, 105–7; Stell 2000 and plate 81 (which reproduces a lithograph of 1851, showing the grand design); Powell and de la Hey 1987, 50–9.

126 The building was demolished after an arson attack of 1986.

127 Stell 1994a, 115–6; Petford 2010, especially 13–19.

128 Extract from a letter of 2 Aug 1855, printed in Thom 1872, **II**, 33.

129 At least one local correspondent had been expecting a spire: *see Architectural Magazine*, **5**, Jan 1838, 46–8, quoted in Whiffen 1950, 14–15.

130 Hill 2007, 182–3, 511.

131 Petford 2010, 17.

132 Petford 2010, 18–9.

133 J J Tayler of Upper Brook Street was one of the editors (with James Martineau and others) of what became *The Prospective*

Review in 1845, the year in which R B Aspland of Dukinfield took over the editorship of *The Christian Reformer*. As Tayler wrote, these publications represented 'the two elements working amongst' Unitarians (Thom 1872, **I**, 212–4). *See also* the *ODNB* entry for R B Aspland.

134 The population statistics are cited from Doel 1994, 44; for the Anglican church *see* Port 2006, 331, and Hartwell *et al* 2011, 336–7. The chief sources of information for Old Chapel are Gordon 1896; Petford 2010, especially 19–24; and Stell 1994a, 8–10.

135 Petford 2010, 23.

136 Petford 2010, 24.

137 *See* Gordon 1896, 76–80, 90 and 95. The predecessor building had a clock, at least by the late 1830s (*see* a view signed by 'L. A.' and dated 1839, which is kept in the present chapel and is reproduced by Gordon 1896, facing 38).

138 A woodcut illustration of Tattersall's design, published in *The Civil Engineer and Architect's Journal*, **III**, Jan 1840 (and reproduced by Petford 2010, 21), may be compared with the temporary west front of 1840 (with a porch added in 1860), of which a photograph is reproduced by Gordon 1896, facing 85.

139 Stell 1994a, 276; Serjeant 2011.

140 The original arrangement still needs elucidation. I am grateful to Colin Dews for confirming that the transepts were originally used as a Sunday school and not as part of the chapel.

141 *See* Port 2006, 149. E B Lamb, whose Clerkenwell church – as Port notes – had iron columns, subsequently became an Aunt Sally for *The Ecclesiologist*, because of the overtly Protestant plans and unorthodox roofs of his later churches. R D Chantrell's iron columns at Christ Church, Leeds, which Simpson must have known, were designed to look like compound masonry piers, albeit slender (photograph in Port 2006, 143).

142 Stell 1994a, 131–3; Serjeant 2011; Powell 1980, unpaginated.

143 Stell 1986, 62; Crick 1975, 20 and plate 19; Gomme and Jenner 2011, 277; Foyle 2004, 231.

144 For Pope *see* Colvin 2008, 820–1; Gomme and Jenner 2011, 423–4.

145 Crossley Evans 1997, 2.

146 Crossley Evans 1997, 8; Wakeling 1998, especially 37. Until the 1860s legal restrictions prevented the holding of a Sunday school at this location. Gothic, two-storey places of worship of course had medieval precedents, most famously the Sainte-Chapelle in Paris, but hardly appealed to ecclesiologists in these years.

147 The quotations are from Latimer 1887, 303, and Little 1947, 129. Crick (1975, 20) echoes Little's praise, whereas Gomme and Jenner (2011, 277) take a more critical approach, as does Foyle (2004, 231).

148 On Butterfield's Nonconformist background and financial dependence on Wills *see* Thompson 1971, especially 8–26 and 42. As Thompson notes (16 and 24, note 11), Butterfield first had a letter published in *The Ecclesiologist* in Feb 1842, more than six months before the stone-laying ceremony for Highbury chapel, but only became a member of the Cambridge Camden (later Ecclesiological) Society in May 1844, 10 months after the chapel's opening (*see* Webster and Elliott 2000, 378).

149 Stell 1986, 64; Crick 1975, 20, 24 and plate 20; Ayres 1963, *passim*; Thompson 1971, especially 42, 134–5, 170–1; Gomme and Jenner 2011, 291–3. The following passage also draws on Wakeling 1984.

150 Thompson 1971, 134; cf Pugin 1841, 18, 45, and **II**.

151 Ayres 1963, 19.

152 The best account of these changes is still Ayres 1963, but *see also* Reid 1999, 137–8.

153 Ayres 1963, 11–15, 92.

154 *ILN* 1848, **12**, 235 names the architect as Redwick W Ordish, and describes the chapel as having been recently erected. Dates of *c* 1845 and 1844 appear respectively in Stell 1991, 18 and Tyack *et al* 2010, 589. R W Ordish is elsewhere known as Frederick Webster Ordish.

155 The quotation is from *The Builder*, 25 Apr 1857, 234.

156 *ILN* 1848, **12**, 235.

157 W J Butler, who became vicar of Wantage in 1846, was an active member of the Ecclesiological Society (*see* Webster and Elliot 2000, *passim*). For Butterfield's work at Charlton, and also his cemetery chapel of 1849 in Wantage, *see* Thompson 1971, especially 49, 147–8, 210, 217, 429. The Wesleyan chapel, seating 350, cost no more than £600; Butterfield's building at Charlton, seated about 90 and cost £200 (£80 more than his estimate).

158 Stell 1991, 5; Stell 2000, 321 and plate 79.

159 *The Builder*, 1 Nov 1851, 688; Tyack *et al* 2010, 179. Bourton House was classified as a seat in Bartholomew's *Gazetteer of the British Isles*, for example 9 edn, 1943, 84.

160 Pevsner 1969, 113; Hartwell and Pevsner 2009, 270.

161 The building was illustrated as frontispiece to the *CYB* for 1847. The remainder of this paragraph draws on Wakeling 1984, 137–8, and Wakeling 1998, 37–8. *See also* Stell 1994a, 90–1, and Nightingale 1891, **II**, 276–7.

162 *The Builder*, 27 Mar 1847, 151 and 8 Jul 1848, 329; *ILN* 1847, **10**, 181; Shaw 1894, **3**, 15–16.

163 *The Ecclesiologist*, **VII** (NS **IV**), 1847, 171–4 and **IX** (NS **VI**), 1848, 143–4.

164 Stell 1994a, 15–16. For the Dissenters' Chapels Act *see* note 1 above.

165 Petford 2010, 27. A woodcut illustration of St Oswald's, Liverpool was reproduced in *The Dublin Review* in 1841 and again in Pugin 1843: *see* Stanton 1971, 99.

166 On 7 Mar 1846 *The Builder*, announcing that the chapel was about to be built, named Weightman and Hadfield of Sheffield as the architects. Perhaps Matthew Hadfield, who was then working on St John's (RC), Salford (and had collaborated on what was to be published in 1846 under Henry Bowman's name as *Specimens of the Ecclesiastical Architecture of Great Britain from the Conquest to the Reformation*) had been involved initially? Henry Bowman was a member of the chapel in Upper Brook Street, Joseph Crowther had been articled to Richard Tattersall when the Dukinfield chapel was under way, and Bowman's pupil at the time was another young Unitarian, Thomas Worthington. *See* Petford 2010, 27, 30, 34; Felstead *et al* 1993, 224, 1023; and *The Builder*, 20 Nov 1909, 563.

167 *Christian Reformer*, **IV**, 1848, 504, as quoted in Petford 2010, 28–9, and 50, note 57.

168 For instance James Martineau studied in Berlin for several months in 1848–9 and John James Tayler had studied in Göttingen for more than six months in 1834–5.

169 The quotation, apparently originating in *The Christian Reformer*, **IV**, 1848, 185 ff, appears in Petford 2010, 29. A photograph (reproduced in Middleton 1908, facing 43) suggests that the font may at first have been positioned in front of the chancel arch.

170 A list of the original stained glass and other items is to be found in Middleton 1908, 46–51.

171 The reference is to the 1844 Dissenters' Chapels Act (*see* note 1, above), of which the Unitarians were the chief beneficiaries.

172 Stell 1991, 32, 38; Colvin 2008, 894; Lake *et al* 2001, 94, 97.

173 Hope 1835.

174 Colvin 2008, 1115–8; *The Builder*, 14 Oct 1848, 499; *CYB* 1848, 202. *See also* Reid 2000.

175 For Ramsgate's places of worship *see* Homan 1984, 82–3 and Newman 1976, 416–23; cf also Stell 2002, 183-4, and Kadish 2011, 35–9.

176 Stell 2002, 183; Stell 2000, 320. Can one exclude the possibility that Romanesque was chosen partly in homage to the architecture of St Lawrence's church, some distance inland?

177 *See* Bullen 2004, especially 154–5 and note 85.

178 *The Builder*, 15 Apr 1848, 186–7, including illustration; Stell 2002, 74–5. Gibson proved to be a very capable designer of Gothic places of worship, as well as his better known role as architect to the National Provincial Bank.

179 *ILN* 1848, **13**, 356, where will also be found a view of the Baptist chapel with its French Protestant neighbour (of 1846 by Ambrose Poynter). An illustration of the three chapels together is reproduced in Bowers 1999, 17.

180 For Hope's nomenclature *see* Hope 1835, **I**, 230–1. San Zeno is illustrated in **II**, plate VI.

181 Peto, who had joined the Baptists following his second marriage (of 1843), was the chief building contractor for the new Palace of Westminster; in this capacity he is presumed to have met John Gibson, who was Charles Barry's assistant until 1844. For Peto's role in persuading William Brock to become pastor of the Bloomsbury chapel *see* Jewson 1957, 100. The apocryphal story of the spires, as retold in the official schedule adding the chapel to the list of historic buildings, is that 'when Peto sought to lease the land, the First Commissioner of Woods & Forests told him that nonconformist chapels were too dull: he liked a church with a spire. "A spire?" exclaimed Peto. "My Lord, we shall have two!"'

182 The most convenient account of St John, Islington is in Temple 1992, 57–60. For the likely American progeny of Gibson's design *see* Bowers 1999, 30.

183 For the changes of 1913 *see* *BHB* 1914, 511 and unnumbered plate. Since 1929 the chapel's immediate neighbour has been Britannia House, which matches the chapel's towers in height, as does the more recent office building across Bucknall Street to the north.

184 *See* Davies 1873, 81–4, and Bowers 1999, passim.

185 *BHB* 1914.

186 Stell 2002, 198; *The Builder*, 8 Nov 1850, 535; Wright 1986, 48–9.

187 The spire of the Independent chapel rose to 110 feet (33.5m), less than half the 272 feet (83m) of the Stump. Of Boston's new Anglican churches, neither the chapel-of-ease (the future St Aidan's, of 1821–2 or *c* 1828, by Jeptha Pacey) nor Holy Trinity (1846–8, by George Gilbert Scott) had a spire.

188 Stephen Lewin's *Lincolnshire Churches* had been published in 1843. For his Anglican church designs *see* for example Pevsner and Harris 1995, 192, 263, 396, 618, 737.

189 The general effect had some early medieval precedents, including the largely 12th-century cathedral at Trani in Southern Italy, which has a lower and an upper chapel as well as an asymmetrically placed tower.

190 *See The Builder*, 8 Nov 1850, 535. Such laminated timber arches had been used by Paxton – not for the first time – at the great conservatory, Chatsworth (of 1836–40). As Hitchcock has observed (Hitchcock 1954, **I**, 156), they were about to be used more publicly at both the Crystal Palace and King's Cross Station.

191 Stell 1994, 44–5; Thomas and Porteus 1936. A similar use of the style was to be seen in the Crescent chapel (Congregational) schools, Liverpool, of 1846, as illustrated in *The Builder*, 14 Nov 1846, 546 and *CYB* for 1847.

192 For the United Presbyterian Church, Renfield Street, Glasgow (1848, by James Brown) *see* Wordsall 1981, 85 and Binney and Burman 1977 (where a photograph of the interior, wrongly identified as Renfield Free Church, is included among the unnumbered plates between 146 and 147).

193 'Remarks on Ecclesiastical Architecture as Applied to Nonconformist Chapels', in *CYB* 1847, 150–63. The article has commonly, but not universally, been attributed to John Blackburn, editor of the *CYB* for its first two years.

6 The age of pluralism, 1850–90

1 For example, it has been estimated that 155 Nonconformist places of worship were built in Sussex in the years 1851–90, compared with 132 Anglican and 34 Catholic churches (Elleray 1981, 42), and that during the years 1852–91 in Kent 425 Nonconformist, 219 Anglican and 29 Roman Catholic places of worship were built (Homan 1984, 12).

2 A convenient summary of the membership figures is to be found in Gilbert 1976, 38–9, figs 2.1 and 2.2. It seems possible that chapel attendance reached a peak before 1890, however: *see* Gill, 2003.

3 To give but one example: St James's Congregational chapel, Newcastle upon Tyne (a building of 1826 by John Dobson) was replaced by a new building in 1858, a chief requirement being to provide for a large Sunday school on the same site as the chapel (Stewart 1984, 15).

4 The phrase appears in Kendall nd, **II**, 455–6. Kendall records that in 1847 the movement had 1,421 chapels and 3,340 rented rooms or premises, but that by 1868 there were 3,235 chapels and 3,034 rented places.

5 Presbyterians in England trebled between 1851 and 1876, from about 15,000 to more than 46,000 (Gilbert 1976, 41–2), largely because of Scottish, Welsh and Irish migration.

6 Parliamentary Papers, 1852–3, **LXXXXIX** (*Report of the Census of Religious Worship, 1851*). One of very many recent interpretations of the statistics is to be found in Watts 1995, especially 671–5, 682–717, 789–870.

7 A version of this account previously appeared in Wakeling 1995, 89 and 97, notes 15–17.

8 The census returns show that the 1823 chapel, at Higherland, had seats for 280, but an evening attendance of 351 and over 300 Sunday-school children. *See VCH Staffs*, **VIII**, 1963, 61–2.

9 The original building (of 1799, as enlarged in 1822–3) in Marsh Street was reported as having 550 seats in 1851, with an evening attendance of 400 on census day and up to 480 scholars in the adjacent school hall (also of 1822–3). *See VCH Staffs*, **VIII**, 1963, 61, and C[ooper] 1950. The 1857–8 building is now in secular use.

10 *Staffordshire Times*, 3 Sep 1859, 10 Sep 1859; *VCH Staffs*, **VIII**, 1963, 58.

11 *Staffordshire Advertiser*, 23 Mar 1861, 30 Mar 1861; *VCH Staffs*, **VIII**, 1963, 59–60. The Wesleyans' former chapel, on which a debt of £775 was outstanding in 1857 (*see* Staffordshire Record Office D 3155/2) was sold to the United Methodist Free Church in 1863. The 1860–1 building does not survive.

12 For Sir George Gilbert Scott's 1873–6 rebuilding of St Giles's church, *see VCH Staffs*, **VIII**, 1963, 20–1.

13 *See* Ambler 1979, 122.

14 The chapel bears the date 1859 and a century later recorded a seating capacity of 90. It cost £140, and was paid for by Mr John Adams. *See* the Methodist Church Department for Chapel Affairs, 1963, 125; *Newcastle Courant*, 17 Aug 1860.

15 *See* Pevsner and Harris 1989, 2 edn (revised by N Antram) 1995, 795, and *ODNB* entry for T W Mossman.

16 Although the date on the United Methodist Free Church chapel (now in secular use) is badly weathered, local sources suggest that it was also built in 1859. The village's Wesleyan and United Free Methodist (sic) chapels are noted in White 1872, 510–11, while Morris and Co 1863, 515, confusedly notes that the 'Free Methodists and Reformers have each chapels here'. For the Louth Methodists *see* Beckerlegge 1957, 71.

17 A summary of chapel-aid funds and the like can be found in Wakeling 1984, 26–32 (but note on 27 the misprinted date of 1884 instead of the correct 1824 for the creation of the London Baptist Building Fund). For the English Congregational Chapel-Building Society *see* Peel 1931, 203–7.

18 The *CYB* was illustrated fitfully from 1846 to 1850 and annually from 1855; the *WCCR* carried illustrations each year from 1855, and the *BHB* was occasionally illustrated in the 1860s and annually from 1869.

19 *CYB* 1862; Hughes 2003.

20 *CYB* 1864 and 1868. Bidlake was in practice with W H Spaull of Oswestry when contracts were issued for the Abbey Foregate chapel (*see The Builder*, 4 Apr 1863, 248 and 18 Apr 1863, 286).

21 *The Builder*, 19 Feb 1870, 153.

22 Cox 1997, 64–5.

23 *The Builder*, 4 Oct 1879, 1119; *WCCR* 1878. The building was converted to residential use in 2007.

24 Cox 1997, 59. For Deakin *see* Newman and Pevsner 2006, passim. The Baptist chapel erected behind other premises in Wyle Cop in 1863 was by H Weatherby of unknown location (*see The Builder*, 5 Sep 1863, 643). Of the town's four or five further chapels for which designers have not been identified, it is possible that at least some were erected without the services of a professional architect.

25 Nidderdale Chase Heritage Group, 2012. The chapel's seating capacity was estimated at 80 in 1960 (Methodist Church Department for Chapel Affairs 1963, 116).

26 Lake *et al* 2001, 65–9.

27 *See* for example Benes 2012, fig 1.2 (a lithographic interior view of East Church, Salem, MA, dated *c* 1847); and Mallary 1985, for example 112–6. Some surviving English examples (such as at Puddletown church, Dorset and Middleton, Lancashire) seem to have been balustraded super-structures on squires' pews.

28 For other examples *see* Stell 1991, 42–5, 51–2.

29 Anon 1948.

30 The General Baptists' building, known as St Mary's Baptist chapel, was built in 1811–2 and replaced in 1951–2 after damage in the Second World War.

31 Jewson 1957, 94–5; *see also* Binfield 2003, specifically 162–3 and 182.

32 For a neutral account of the controversies *see* Kruppa 1982, 404–44.

33 *CYB* 1847, 162–3.

34 The study of a rural area of Norfolk indicates that 14 of the 15 chapels built between 1850 and 1890 had capacities below 150, compared with 6 out of 14 chapels built in the preceding half century and 4 out of 5 in the following 25 years. A comparative study of the town of Derby produced less reliable data, and fewer small chapels at any period, but even here the largest proportion of small chapels seems to have been built between 1850 and 1890 (Wakeling 1984, appendices 1 and 2).

35 *See* for example *The Builder*, 3 Dec 1853, 733.

36 Temple 1992, 117.

37 The builder's contract was for £2,436, and the final cost was reportedly £3,000. The galleried chapel seated 800 adults and 200 children, while the basement school was designed for about 560 (*The Builder*, 5 Oct 1850, 478; *CYB* 1851, 258).

38 The contractor's tender was for £4,979, and the total cost was reportedly £7,600, including land (*The Builder*, 20 May 1854, 272; *CYB* 1856, 261). The *Survey of London* (**XLII**, 391–2) cites a total cost of £8,748, including acquisition of the site.

39 *The Builder*, 23 Jan 1869, 75; *Survey of London*, **XLII**, 391–2.

40 *CYB* 1862, between 320 and 321 (which includes a view of the chapel, not quite as executed); Stell 1991, 126–7.

41 Committee of the English Congregational Chapel-Building Society, 1862. The Shaftesbury chapel appears as the second illustration of the illustrated appendix, 1863. Clapham 1878 (the quoted phrase appears on 207).

42 Stell 1994a, 312.

43 It is 'the only aesthetically successful building at Saltaire', wrote Pevsner, soon after mentioning the 'hideous' portal of the Institute, the 'monotony of the housing' and the 'feeble Italianate trimmings' of the mill. Pevsner 1967, 427–8.

44 Lockwood and Mawson's Lister Hills Independent chapel of 1853–4, in nearby Bradford, was a cruciform Gothic building; *see The Builder*, 19 Nov 1853, 704.

45 Linstrum 1978, 334–9; Linstrum 1999, 16. For Lockwood's classical chapels of the 1840s in Hull *see also* pp 108–9.

46 Lockwood and Mawson might well have taken special interest in Leeds Town Hall (of 1853–8): they were placed second in the competition for its design and the successful architect, Cuthbert Brodrick, had been articled to Lockwood in Hull 1837–43.

47 For a view of the interior in 1859, showing the original pulpit, organ and (more elaborate) light fittings *see ILN* 1859, **35**, 627–8.

48 *The Builder*, 10 Apr 1875, 333 and 3 Jun 1876, 535.

49 The system pioneered at Akron, Ohio in the 1860s allowed for children to be taught in graded classes, but still under the observation of a single superintendent. *See* Pond 2007 and Cliff 1986, 178–81. For the suggestion that the Saltaire Sunday school could have been the first British example *see Building News*, 2 May 1884, 672. Cf Union Chapel, Islington later in this chapter.

50 For Spurgeon a basic source is still Spurgeon 1897–1900 (autobiography).

Of the many biographies Kruppa 1982 may be mentioned.

51 *The Builder*, 12 Feb 1859, 105; Spurgeon 1897–1900, **II**, 327–8. The competition proved controversial, featuring in every issue of *The Builder* from 12 Feb to 23 Apr 1859, and occasionally in later months.

52 When the Metropolitan Tabernacle first opened its seating capacity was stated to be 4,404, including 200 flap-seats, with standing room for an additional large number (*The Builder*, 4 May 1861, 302–3); later sources estimated a total capacity of about 6,000, including standing spaces. During Spurgeon's lifetime the building was regularly filled to capacity.

53 The interior of the tabernacle was illustrated in *The Builder*, 4 May 1861, 302–3; photographs may be found in, for example, *The Survey of London*, **XXV**, plate 81 and Spurgeon 1897–1900, **II**, 354–5. For the interior of the Surrey Gardens Music Hall *see ILN* 1856, **29**, 91. Pocock's design featured towers and a domed roof (*see The Builder*, 26 Mar 1859, 219–21 and Spurgeon 1897–1900, **II**, 320), but the towers were omitted on Spurgeon's insistence, as being for mere show (*see* Spurgeon 1897–1900, **II**, 321 and 336).

54 Stell 2002, 114.

55 The rebuilt Tottenham Court Road chapel was illustrated and described in the *CYB* for 1865 (295–6 and unnumbered plate); it also appeared in *ILN* 1864, **46**, 161. For the Surrey tabernacle *see The Builder*, 17 Sep 1864, 694; Powell and de la Hey 1987, 115; Davies 1873, 119 (from which the quotation is derived); and Pevsner 1952, 399. Neither building has survived. As evidence of the tabernacle's international influence, one can point to the iron-galleried interior of Blasieholm church, Stockholm (of 1864, by Gustaf Sjöberg; demolished 1977); *see* Andersson and Bedoire 1988, 15.

56 *BHB* 1886, 341–2 and plate; Stell 1991, 238–9.

57 *BHB* 1882, 381 and unnumbered plate.

58 Of Newtown's other chapels, only the Wesleyan building in Severn Place (replaced in 1987) was classical. George Morgan's first classical chapel (for English Baptists in Carmarthen, 1870) had a narrower frontage, while that in Swansea (Mount Pleasant Baptist, of 1874–6) is more of a precedent for Zion in Newtown.

59 Jobson 1850, 43.

60 Ibid.

61 Serjeant, 2011, 147–9, 157–8; Stell 1994a, 293–4; cf also *The Builder*, 8 Oct 1859, 670.

62 Linstrum 1978, 384.

63 For the Fly-Sheet controversy *see* Watts 1995, especially 614–25. For Wesleyan membership losses in Market Rasen *see*

Obelkevich 1976, 196–7. White 1856 and 1872. A historic photograph of the Methodist Free Church chapel of 1861 is reproduced in Ambler 2000, 32. The chapel was closed in the 1960s, and for some time served as a tyre depot.

64 *The Builder*, 18 Jul 1863, 518; Stell 2002, 218. *See also* Morris and Co 1863, 492.

65 *The Builder*, 8 Jun 1861, 396; 15 Jun 1861, 415; and 15 Nov 1862, 825; Stell 1994a, 265; Hitchen and Dawson 1962.

66 *The Builder*, 1 Sep 1860, 564 and 6 Sep 1862, 642; *ILN* 1863, **42**, 145; *CYB* 1863, 299–302; Stell 1994a, 265.

67 *The Builder*, 15 Jun 1861, 415 and 15 Nov 1862, 825; *ILN* 1863, **42**, 145; *CYB* 1863.

68 *The Builder*, 24 Aug 1861, 585; 9 Nov 1861, 776; and 6 Dec 1862, 879; *Building News*, 23 Aug 1861, 703; 27 Sep 1861, 794; and 1 Nov 1861, 880; Stell 1994a, 315.

69 *The Builder*, 14 Sep 1867, 688ix; *see also* Elleray 1981, plate 136, and Hague and Hague 1986, 83–4.

70 *The Builder*, 10 Feb 1866, 108 and 14 Apr 1866, 276. The chapel appears to have been closed before 1963.

71 *CYB* 1857, 253–4; *The Builder*, 27 Jan 1855, 41; 20 Oct 1855, 500; 30 Aug 1856, 472; and 20 Sep 1856, 516. The building survives, but has been converted for residential use.

72 For the Truro chapel *see* Colvin 2008, 894; Stell 1991, 53.

73 *See The Builder*, 19 Nov 1853, 705 and 3 Dec 1853, 733. Oliver's design was also included in the illustrated appendix to the Committee of the English Congregational Chapel-Building Society's *Practical Hints on Chapel-Building* in 1863. One version was built in 1855 as Zion Congregational chapel, Whitstable (for which *see CYB* 1856, 269; Homan 1984, 100 and plate 75).

74 For the Middlesbrough chapel *see also The Builder*, 5 Apr 1856, 187–8 and 24 Jan 1857, 52–3; and Lillie 1968, 84–5.

75 Hughes 2003, 119.

76 For Salem chapel, Porthmadog *see CYB* 1861, 269.

77 Jones 1984, 57–8 (and 1996, 62–6).

78 The motif of an arch rising into a pediment is of Roman origin (*see* for example the peristyle of Diocletian's palace at Split). It later appeared, for instance, in Wren's great model for St Paul's and Hawksmoor's St Alfege, Greenwich.

79 Craster 1907, **VIII**, 374–5; *The Newcastle Courant*, 8 Jan 1858; Colvin 2008, 321, 759; Stell 1994a, 173.

80 *The Builder*, 1 Nov 1856, 596 and 9 Jan 1858, 28; *Newcastle Courant*, 8 Jan 1858.

81 Stell 1991, 246–7.

82 *ILN* 1863, **42**, 97; Temple 1992, 123; *The Builder*, 30 Aug 1862, 623.

83 Pevsner 1952, 230.

84 For the 1860 Union of Benefices Act, a list of the demolished churches and proposals for many more demolitions *see* Jeffery 1996, 165–9.

85 Stell 2002, 69–70.

86 *The Builder*, 26 Oct 1872, 855; 23 May 1874, 650; and 21 Sep 1878, 986–7; *ILN* 1875, **66**, 129; Dawson 1901, 94–5.

87 'Seats are provided for 2,500 people, and some hundreds more can be accommodated by the use of camp stools in the aisles, and the steps of the gallery gangways' (Dawson 1901, 95). 'The City Temple … is regularly filled with a congregation of well over two thousand' (Harris and Bryant [*c* 1913], 286).

88 Stell 2002, 125; *Building News*, 4 Nov 1887, 682 and illustration; *ILN* 1887, **91**, 450.

89 *The Builder*, 27 Feb 1886, 356; *ILN* 1888, **93**, 432.

90 Temple 1992, 72–3; *Building News*, 20 Dec 1889; Stell 2002, 96–7.

91 'Sweetness and light', a phrase used by Swift (in *The Battle of the Books*, 1704), was taken up by Matthew Arnold (in *Culture and Anarchy*, 1869) and subsequently in Mark Girouard's important work, *Sweetness and Light*, 1977.

92 Blackwell 1959, 30–5.

93 Sandall 1950, **2** , especially 87, 216, 377; Blackwell 1959, 31; Oakley 2011, especially 25–7 and 43–5. Oakley reproduces Sherwood's drawing of the façade (25).

94 Oakley records that in 1883, the year of the opening of the York barracks, 34 buildings were erected or purchased by the Salvation Army, seating a total of 46,900 at an overall cost of £22,000 (Oakley 2011, 26).

95 Hall and Hall 1973, 104; Neave and Neave 1990, 14 and 46. The building closely followed the standard design by Sherwood, illustrated in Oakley 2011, 26.

96 Stell 2002, 120–1; Matthews 1989, especially 1–9. The street was formerly Castle Street East, and older sources refer simply to Castle Street Welsh Baptist chapel.

97 Nairn 1966, 95.

98 The original, smaller organ was replaced in 1909 (*see* Matthews 1989, 29–30).

99 *The Builder*, 11 Dec 1858, 837; *CYB* 1860, 257–8; Stell 2002, 147.

100 *The Builder*, 6 Aug 1859, 519; *Building News*, 20 Sep 1861, 771.

101 *The Builder*, 14 Jul 1866, 530; Pearson 1967; Stell 1991, 133. Foster and Wood are named as the architects in each of these sources, but on page 21 of the centenary booklet it is said that 'there is every reason to believe that' James Wilson of Bath 'produced the design … for the firm of Foster and Wood'. For the building erected since the 2002 fire *see* 'New Weymouth Methodist church rises from the ashes' in *Church Building*, **121**, Jan–Feb 2010, 28–31.

102 Pearson 1967, 22–5, 50.

103 In Norfolk, with a significant number of small or medium-sized chapels, the incidence of Gothic-detailed chapels appears to have declined in the early Victorian period and recovered very gradually thereafter. Only in the 1890s, however, did it exceed 20 per cent of new chapels (Virgoe and Williamson 1993, 65–8 and fig 5).

104 *The Builder*, 26 Oct 1867, 781. The scheme was for the Wesleyan chapel in Prince of Wales Road, off Haverstock Hill. As finally built (in 1872, by the same architect), however, the chapel was emphatically classical.

105 Jobson 1850. An account of the book's genesis – including the Wesleyan conference's support – appears on vii–x.

106 *See* Gregory 1884; also the entry on Jobson in *ODNB*.

107 Jobson 1850, 40.

108 In addition to the Portwood and Islington chapels, which Jobson identified as being by Wilson, the Poplar and Clerkenwell chapels had been designed by him (*The Builder*, 4 Sep 1847, 424; 12 Feb 1848, 82; and 3 Nov 1849, 521; *ILN* 1848, **13**, 176). None of the chapels described by Jobson has survived.

109 For the Fly-Sheet controversy *see* Watts 1995, especially 614–25.

110 An indicative chronology of Wilson's Nonconformist work is included in Wakeling 1984, appendix 3. For the Haslingden chapel *see The Builder*, 23 Jun 1855; 13 Oct 1855, 485; and 7 Mar 1857, 136; *WCCR* 1856. It is possible that Haslingden's Wesleyans were prompted to replace their Georgian chapel by the local Independents' decision in 1854 to build a Gothic place of worship (for which *see The Builder*, 15 Apr 1854, 204 and 29 Jul 1854, 402; *see also CYB* 1856, 260–1).

111 The chapel was extended and radically altered internally in 1884–5 to the designs of William Waddington and Sons. A photograph of the interior prior to the alterations is included in Hatch 1957.

112 *Staffordshire Advertiser*, 31 Oct 1857, 5; *The Builder*, 7 Nov 1857, 645. The chapel is reported to have closed in 1959, and has since been in secular use.

113 Stell 1991, 61.

114 Buffard 1961; Ikin 1997; *BHB* 1861, frontispiece; *The Builder*, 28 Apr 1860, 272.

115 Stell 1986, 256; *The Builder*, 13 Jun 1863, 432; 15 Aug 1863, 588; and 6 Aug 1864, 590. An earlier version of the design, built

in Darlington in 1861–2, was included in the illustrated appendix to the Committee of the English Congregational Chapel-Building Society's *Practical Hints on Chapel-Building* in 1863.

116 *The Builder*, 15 Feb 1868, 123.

117 For the St Ives chapel *see The Builder*, 7 Nov 1863, 797 and 24 Sep 1864, 709; *CYB* 1866, 319 and plate; Stell 2002, 157; Wagner 1982; Carter 2005. For Lady Margaret Road chapel *see The Builder*, 29 Aug 1863, 628; Stell 2002, 78.

118 *The Builder*, 12 Feb 1859, 118 and 17 Sep 1859, 620–1.

119 On the potential for galleries in these chapels *see The Builder*, 15 Aug 1863, 588; *CYB* 1866, 319, and the illustrated appendix to the Committee of the English Congregational Chapel-Building Society's *Practical Hints on Chapel-Building* 1863.

120 Mate and Riddle 1910, 249–50.

121 Mornement and Holloway 2007, 98–9. The Shrubland Road chapel, which has been used by the Sight of Eternal Life Church since 1976, was offered for sale in 2012.

122 *See* Bailey 1992, especially 12, 66–7, 143–4.

123 Kaye 1999, 24, 59.

124 *CYB* 1856, 259.

125 For Christ Church *see The Builder*, 21 May 1864, 378; the Baptist magazine *The Church*, 1 Jun 1865, 166; Hickman 1970, 34; Betteridge 2010, 454. For S S Teulon's work at St Mary, Ealing *see* Saunders 1982, 21–2.

126 The judgement appeared in *The Church*, 1 Jun 1865, 166.

127 *The Builder*, 21 May 1864, 378; Dishon 2000, 204.

128 Robertson 1975, 82; Jackson 1991, 162–4; Stell 1991, 161.

129 Stell 2002, 77; *The Builder*, 18 Jun 1859, 409; Stamp and Amery 1980, 40–1; Hitchcock 1954, **I**, 157–8.

130 An account of the services in Gordon Square can be found in Davies 1873, 146–55.

131 Stell 1994a, 324–6; *ILN* 1869, **55**, 433; *The Builder*, 3 Feb 1866, 90; 17 Apr 1869, 311; 24 Apr 1869, 331; and 17 Jul 1869, 569; Fox 1924.

132 Christ Church, Todmorden cost £3,913 (*see* Port 2006, 246, 335). For the final cost of the Unitarian chapel *see ILN* 1869, **55**, 433, and cf *The Builder*, 3 Feb 1866, 60 and 17 Apr 1869, 311. For Fielden *see* Weaver 1987. The Unitarian chapel has been vested in the Historic Chapels Trust since 1994.

133 For details of the materials and contractors *see ILN* 1869, **55**, 433 and Kershaw 1969.

134 The quotation is from Fox 1924, 60. The paraphrase of Gaskell's comments is based

on the summary in Historic Chapels Trust 2000.

135 Stell 1994a, 116–7; *The Builder*, 30 Dec 1871, 1034. For Worthington more generally *see* Pass 1988.

136 *See* Hartwell *et al* 2004, 370–1, 373–4.

137 The paintings, by J Milner Allen, date from 1886 (*see The Builder*, 18 Sep 1886, 436).

138 *The Builder*, 16 Aug 1873, 645; 23 Aug 1873, 663; and 31 Aug 1874, 916; Stell 1986, 163–4; Hague and Hague 1986, 98. Since its closure in 1983 the building has served as a heritage centre for the lace industry and, more recently, as a bar and restaurant; further details in Harwood 2008, 98.

139 *The Builder*, 10 Jan 1857, 22 and 24 Jan 1857, 50–1; *see also* 27 Sep 1856, 532. The building in question, Trinity Presbyterian church, Southgate Road, Kingsland, was designed by T E Knightley. For its subsequent history *see* Temple 1992, 62.

140 Stell 1994a, 258–62; *CYB* 1858, 264–6 and plate; *The Builder*, 21 Apr 1855, 189; 5 May 1855, 214; 22 Aug 1857, 482; and 27 Jun 1863, 461–2.

141 Hubbuck's comments are quoted in Pevsner 1967, 627; *see also* Royle 2011, 200. There was no need for a schoolroom since the adjacent 18th-century chapel was retained for that purpose.

142 *The Builder*, 27 Jun 1863, 461–2.

143 *The Builder*, 25 Jan 1851, 62; 11 Jun 1851, 377; and 19 Nov 1853, 698; *CYB* 1855, 262–3; Stell 1991, 152–3.

144 *See* 'The United Church, Jewry Street, Winchester' in *Church Building* **27**, 1994, 35–7.

145 *The Builder*, 27 May 1854, 281 and 17 Nov 1855, 554–5; *CYB* 1856, 256–7 and frontispiece; Lemprière 1980, 102.

146 *The Builder*, 17 Feb 1855, 74–5 and 14 Jul 1855, 333; *CYB* 1855, 259–60 and 1876, 438 and plate. The interior has lost many of its original fittings.

147 *CYB* 1866, 323 and plate; Cunningham and Waterhouse 1992, 28, 53, 216 and plate 29. Most unfortunately the chapel was demolished in 1866 to make way for a railway.

148 *The Builder*, 5 May 1855, 210–11. The Diorama was a spectacular light show, in which large translucent paintings were viewed by a rotated audience.

149 For Harecourt chapel (demolished after a fire in the 1980s and replaced in 1991) *see The Builder*, 3 Nov 1855, 522–3 and Temple 1992, 129–30 (cf also the Anglican church of St Matthew, Cambridge, built in 1866 to a similar plan). For the Carlisle chapel *see The Builder*, 12 May 1860, 301 and *CYB* 1862, 324.

150 The congregation of the 1858 building seceded from the Established Church in

1860 (*see* for example *The Essex Standard*, 1 Apr 1860). By 1867, however, sufficient rapprochement was achieved for the new building to be consecrated under the authority of the Anglican bishop (*see The Standard*, 30 Sep 1867, 7). Cf Cherry and Pevsner 1998, 655 and Clarke 1966, 96. More recent changes to the building are discussed in Chapter 8.

151 For a comparison between Harecourt Congregational chapel and the (Lutheran) Trinity church, Oslo *see* Cherry 2007, 55–6.

152 *The Builder*, 25 Jun 1859, 430 and 5 May 1860, 284; *CYB* 1861, 275–7; Stell 2002, 130–1. For recent changes to the building *see* 'Water Lane United Reformed Church, Bishop's Stortford' in *Church Building* **72**, Nov–Dec 2001, 29–30.

153 *The Builder*, 22 Mar 1862, 214; 29 Mar 1862, 230; and 14 Mar 1863, 193; *CYB* 1862, 293–6 and 1864, 288; The Committee of the English Congregational Chapel-Building Society, 1862 (Illustrated Appendix, 1863), illus 11–13, 63–4; Stell 1986, 231.

154 *The Builder*, 14 Feb 1863, 113; 12 Mar 1864, 196; and 1 Oct 1864, 722–3; *CYB* 1866, 325–6 and plate; *ILN* 1865, **47**, 335, 341; Stell 2002, 122–3. For Samuel Martin *see* Peel 1948, 187–8.

155 Nairn 1966, 62. Interestingly a similarly shaped Venetian church, built by Sansovino for the Ospedale degli Incurabili, may have been designed to provide a favourable acoustic for choral music: *see* Howard 1980, 159–60.

156 Nairn 1966, 62.

157 *See* Muthesius 1972, 146–7 (from where the quotation is derived) and note 79.

158 Godwin's design, illustrated in Howell 1968, 20–1, is in the RIBA drawings collection (Ran 7/A/1) and is mentioned in the context of Godwin's interest in central planning by Reid 1999, 138–9. For Hope's ideas *see* Beresford Hope 1861 and Muthesius 1972.

159 Bidlake 1865, plates 8 and 9.

160 For these examples *see* Fritsch 1893, 518 (fig 992) and 525 (figs 1019–20); *see also* Roth 1983, 100–3, and Kilde 2002, passim, but especially 118–21 and fig 5.6.

161 *The Builder*, 14 Aug 1875, 737 and 1 Jan 1876; *CYB* 1876, 448–9 and plate; Stell 1986, 150–1; Drew 1925, especially 30–3; *Wellingborough News*, 11 Dec 1875.

162 Archer's draft plan, in pencil, is kept at the chapel. For Archer's role *see* Drew 1925, 30–3. Archer worked as Sharman's assistant and later became his partner; *see Northampton Independent*, 3 Mar 1923.

163 Muthesius 1901, 126 (fig 86) and 129; Drew 1925, 30. Ernest Drew had been the minister in Wellingborough since 1912

(*Who's Who in Congregationalism*, [*c* 1933], 47).

164 *Survey of London*, **XL**, 87–9; Stell 2002, 123–5; *The Builder*, 18 Jan 1890, 44 and 9 May 1891, 372; Cunningham and Waterhouse 1992, 264; Drummond 1942, especially 321–2.

165 Muthesius 1901, 140–1 (figs 105–8 and plate xxvii) and 149.

166 Fritsch 1893, 513 (translation by the present author).

167 For Cubitt's career *see* Binfield 2001.

168 Cubitt 1870, 86–7.

169 Cubitt 1870, 3.

170 Cubitt's articles and illustrations 'Churches for Congregations' in *Building News*, in 1869 appeared on: 30 Jul, 83–4, 91; 6 Aug, 108, 110; 27 Aug, 161, 173; 3 Sep, 185–6, 193; 24 Sep, 234–5, 241; 22 Oct, 299–301, 307; and 29 Oct, 318–9, 325.

171 *The Builder*, 5 Apr 1873, 264, 267 and 18 Jul 1874, 615; *CYB* 1873, 424–6 and 1874, 414; Stell 2002, 30–1.

172 *See* for example Arnold 1869, 26–31. (In 1865 Cubitt had already criticised 'the class to which Dissenters for the most part belong' by quoting Matthew Arnold: *see* Cubitt 1865, 163.) The University Tests Act of 1871 finally gave non-Anglicans full access – as students, fellows or staff – to Oxford, Cambridge and Durham. Only divinity courses were excluded from this provision.

173 Cubitt 1892, 35; Binfield 2001, 13–16, 39–40; Stell 1986, 61–2.

174 *The Builder*, 28 Nov 1874, 994; 5 Dec 1874, 1004; 3 Apr 1875, 292–4; 10 Apr 1875, 333; 17 Apr 1875, 356; and 3 Jun 1876, 546; *CYB* 1876, 447–8; Cherry 2007, passim; Temple 1992, 47–51; Binfield 2001, 45–64; Stell 2002, 97–8.

175 An aerial view, drawn by Anthony Richardson, is reproduced in Cherry 2007, 11; cf also the drawing in Muthesius 1901, 139, fig 104. For Cubitt and Torcello *see* *The Builder*, 3 Apr 1875, 292–4; *see also* Binfield 2001, 52–5, and Wakeling 2007, especially 62–5.

176 For Allon *see* *ODNB*. Allon's notes for architects who were to submit designs for the chapel are reproduced in *The Builder*, 5 Dec 1874, 1004.

177 *See* Richardson 2007, especially 15–16, and Binfield 2001, 60.

178 For the Akron system *see* Saltaire Sunday school of 1875–6, *see* p 142.

179 Muthesius 1901, 137–9 (figs 102–4) and 148; Briggs 1946, 41–3.

180 This paragraph is based on material first published in Wakeling 2007, especially 64–7.

181 Langlet 1879; Fritsch 1893, 447–9.

182 Fritsch 1893, 291–2 (and figs 476–8).

183 Fritsch 1893, 372–4, 400–1 (figs 682–3, 746–7).

184 *BHB* 1881, 399–400 and unnumbered plate; *The Builder*, 5 Jun 1897, 503–4; Kendall 1955, 30–7; Brandwood and Cherry 1990, 75–6; Muthesius 1901, 148–50 (figs 122–4) and 154. For Meyer *see* Fullerton [*c* 1929]; Street 1902.

185 Kendall 1955, 33.

186 Freeman 1990, 25, 43–4; Lee, R [*c* 2009]; Brown and Figueiredo 2008, 68–70.

187 For the Dragon style *see* Tschudi-Madsen 1981–3, especially 67–74. Freeman (1990) notes that the construction of the Baltic spire was paid for by Caröe's father, the Danish consul in Liverpool, so that the building should make a 'worthy appearance before foreigners'.

188 *The Builder*, 29 Sep 1883; *CYB* 1883, 391–2 and plates; Binfield 1982; Boag and Boag 1927; Binfield 2010; Stell 1994a, 168–70.

189 *Newcastle Daily Chronicle*, 12 Feb 1884, quoted in Binfield 1982, note 61.

190 Plates II–VII of *Church Design for Congregations* (Cubitt 1870) are categorised as 'plans with few columns' and VIII–IX are 'plans with large central area'. Clyde Binfield has suggested (1982, 172) that the plan of St James's might have been influenced by H H Richardson's Trinity church, Boston, MA (of 1872–7). The possibility that Richardson's plan had been influenced by Cubitt – either through *Church Design for Congregations* or the earlier articles in *Building News* – should also be considered.

191 Plans and drawings of St James's were reproduced in March 1892, figs 36–7; Fritsch 1893, 521–2 (figs 1007–8); Muthesius 1901, 124–5 (figs 84–5) and 129. For Sonck's possible debt to the plan of St James's *see* Kivinen *et al* 1981, 34–55.

192 The quoted phrase, by Kivinen, is from Kivinen *et al* 1981, 46–7.

193 *CYB* 1886, 225–6 and plate; *Building News*, 6 Nov 1885, 728, 744 and 4 May 1885, 654; Stirling 1988; Stell 1991, 150.

194 Pevsner and Lloyd 1967, 486–7.

195 Ibid.

196 March 1892, fig 40; Fritsch 1893, 521–2 (fig 1006).

197 H J Paull's 1874 design for the T-shaped Congregational chapel at Cleckheaton, employing such seating, was illustrated in the *CYB* for 1875 (437–8 and plate), and also *Building News*, from where it later appeared in Muthesius 1901, 123 (figs 81–3).

7   The Nonconformist heyday? 1890–1914

1 *See* Gilbert 1976, 32–3 (table 2.2) and 40 (table 2.5).

2 *See* Bebbington 1982.

3 Jordan 1956; Bebbington 1982, chapter 4.

4 Muthesius's book, *Die neuere kirchliche Baukunst in England* (1901), has been mentioned in Chapter 6. Less well known is the fact that his doctoral dissertation ('Der Kirchenbau der englischen Secten', 1902) was on the subject of Nonconformist places of worship.

5 For contemporary assessments of the decline of rural Nonconformity *see Minutes of the Primitive Methodist Conference*, 1896, 183–4, and *BHB* 1894, 77 (both cited in Thompson 1972, 238–9).

6 The Theosophical Society did embark on a major headquarters in Tavistock Square, London, designed by Lutyens, but the buildings were eventually completed as headquarters for the British Medical Association. And Clare Hartwell notes a purpose-built Spiritualist church of 1896 in Blackpool (*see* Hartwell and Pevsner 2009, 139).

7 The population of Fulmodeston had reached 400 in 1861, but fell to 339 by 1901 and in 1911 was only 300.

8 One of the memorial stones, laid on 16 Apr 1902, names W Towler as the builder.

9 Local sources suggest that the chapel was closely associated with the agricultural workers' union.

10 *BHB* 1898, 324 and plate.

11 Alastair Service notes that 7,800 people identified themselves as architects in 1891, a number which rose to 10,700 in 1901 (Service 1977, 7).

12 *Minutes of the One-Hundred-and-Seventh Annual Conference of the Methodist New Connexion*, 1903, vii. For the chapel itself (Sandy Lane, Brown Edge; now demolished) *see WCCR* 1901 and 1903, and Lawton 1998, 26, 43 and 50.

13 Saint 1976, 434, 458; *CYB* 1905, 130–1 and plates; Stell 2002, 325, 352; Cleal 1908, 435–7.

14 *The Builder*, 20 Aug 1898, 176; Stell 2002, 264; Richardson 1991; Skidmore 2012.

15 In 1960 the Fulmodeston chapel was reckoned to seat 100, compared with 90 at Overstrand (*see* the Methodist Church Department for Chapel Affairs 1963, 103–4).

16 A letter written to his wife, 7 Aug 1899, and quoted in Ridley 2002, 130. *See also* Percy and Ridley 1985.

17 The letter cited in note 16 above continues: 'The inside spoilt – as its one salvation was simplicity – by a d—d moulding and horrid E light fittings. So long as they can make a noise in it, no one else cares for aught else.'

18 For the Blackheath chapel *see* Service 1975, 164–7 (where it is dated *c* 1893); Service 1977, 32–3; Cleal 1908, 398 and facing illustration; Reason [*c* 1962], 22 and unnumbered plate.

19 *WCCR* 1906. The chapel is no longer in use for worship.

20 For the Winkhill chapel *see The Builder*, 9 May 1908, 551; Wardle 1943, 15.

21 Walker 2011, specifically 133–4.

22 *The Builder*, 10 Sep 1892, 204 ff; *CYB* 1897, 168 and plate; Binfield 1988; Rose 1974; Stell 1994a, 75.

23 Quoted in Binfield 1988, 178.

24 The extensive blind tracery on the north (entrance) elevation of Albion church does not feature in the drawings published in 1890 (*Ashton-under-Lyne Reporter*, 20 Sep 1890, supplement) for at that stage three large windows were envisaged. Cf Herbert Austin's use of blind tracery at St George, Stockport (designed from 1891, erected from 1893).

25 Appeal leaflet issued on behalf of the building committee, Aug 1890 (photocopy in author's collection); Rose 1974, 70–2; *The Builder*, 26 Apr 1862, 298.

26 Howard 2009.

27 A list of more than 70 Nonconformist commissions by Gordon and Gunton (or Gordon, Lowther and Gunton) between 1892 and 1914 can be found in Wakeling 1984, appendix 3.

28 *WCCR* 1902; Howard 2009, 16–20.

29 *WCCR* 1907; Howard 2009, 16–23; Stell 2002, 116. As Colin Howard records (17 and 24), the total costs recorded by 1909 were £18,743, as compared with an anticipated maximum sum of £8,000 in 1901.

30 *The Builder*, 31 Dec 1904, 697; *WCCR* 1901 and 1902; Archer 1963–4, 170–1 and figs 32–4; Middleton Local Studies Group, 1950; Nicholson and Spooner [*c* 1911], 156–7; Stell 1994a, 117–9. The project in Long Street, Middleton cost about £9,500, roughly half the cost of the Sutton scheme. Albion church is generally believed to have cost about £50,000 (and is known to have cost at least £40,000).

31 For Edgar Wood the fullest account is still Archer 1964; but *see also* [Manchester City Art Gallery] 1975.

32 The drawing was reproduced in the *WCCR* for 1901 and then (with the addition of a plan) in *The Builder*, 31 Dec 1904, 697. A further drawing, illustrated in the *WCCR Report* for 1902, shows other unexecuted details, including a rather Secessionist gateway at street level, leading to the right-hand porch.

33 Dougherty 2003, 12–17.

34 The building contract was £5,881 8s 3d (*The Builder*, 18 Mar 1905, 303). For the cost of the site (£1,200) and an account of the congregation's development *see* Dougherty 2003, 11–17.

35 *BHB* 1904 (394 and plate) and 1905 (374–5 and plate); *The Builder*, 18 Mar 1905, 303; *Rugby Advertiser*, 18 Mar 1905, 2–3, and 17 Feb 1906, 3. George Baines (1852–1934) practised under his own name until 1900. Reginald Palmer Baines added his name to that of his father between 1900 and 1905, and thereafter the firm was styled George Baines and Son. They worked a good deal – but by no means exclusively – for Baptist congregations. For a list of Baines commissions up to 1914 *see* Wakeling 1984, appendix 3.

36 Pevsner 1974, 355.

37 Rugby Baptist church building fund committee minutes of 19 May and 14 Jul 1903. Thanks are due to Mr Peter Pugh of Rugby Baptist church for sharing a transcription of these minutes.

38 The Baines practice had already worked with the steelwork specialists Dawnay and Sons to create a sophisticated – but concealed – roof structure for the Presbyterian church in Muswell Hill (*see* Middleton [*c* 1906], **IV**, 132–3).

39 Smith 1963; Grass 2012, 90–1; Stell 2002, 296.

40 *The Builder*, 31 Mar 1906, 355 and 14 Jul 1906, 54.

41 *The Builder*, 4 Feb 1899, 122 and 19 Aug 1899, 181; *WCCR* 1899 and 1901; Stell 1986, 223. A photograph of the preceding chapel building is reproduced in Williams 2006, 119.

42 *WCCR* 1901.

43 *The Builder*, 3 Jun 1905, 604; Stell 2002, 216. The preceding chapel, purchased for railway development, is illustrated in Kendall nd, **I**, 467–9.

44 For the Howdills *see The Builder*, 8 Nov 1918, 294 and 15 Aug 1941, 150; Dews 2011; Wakeling 1983, appendix 3.

45 *The Builder*, 25 Jul 1908, 105–6.

46 The Rundbogen motif of subdivided windows over an arcade resembles Chisholm's 1860s Presidency College, Madras (Chennai), while the tower is more akin to his later Indo-Saracenic style. His Ruskinian taste for polychromy is notably absent here, however. For a summary of Chisholm's work in India *see* Lang *et al* 1997, 77, 101–2.

47 For a description of a service in the Chelsea church *see* Hillson 1940, 105–8. I am grateful to John Dearing for this reference.

48 The *Christian Science Monitor* began publication in Nov 1908, coincidentally the year in which the Chelsea premises were completed. *See* Beasley 1952, 471–80.

49 Wiggins 1964, 232–5; Harman and Minnis 2004, 97. William Gillbee Scott appears to have acted as the Salvation Army's architect for a time before the appointment of Alexander Gordon as head of the architect's department in 1893 (*see* Blackwell 1959, 30–3 and Oakley 2011, 26–9).

50 A late 20th-century plan of the Sheffield citadel, reproduced in Oakley 2011, 51 perhaps dates from the 1957–8 alterations when the hall was subdivided horizontally and lost its ground floor. The building is no longer used by the Salvation Army and at the time of writing is semiderelict.

51 Blackwell 1959, 32–3. In 1881 the Salvation Army had an average attendance of 1,314 at its main service in 28 large towns, almost double the next highest denomination (the Roman Catholics) in the survey: *see* Gill 2003, 229–32.

52 Among the precedents for incorporating shops, one can mention Sion chapel in the East End of London (*see CYB* 1867, 363–4 and plate) and a Wesleyan chapel of 1886 in central Birmingham (*see The Builder*, 31 Jul 1886, 182–3; 18 Dec 1886, 874, 881). For the financing of Salvation Army buildings *see* Blackwell 1959, 32; Wiggins 1964, 232–5.

53 Wiggins 1964, 350–2; Wiggins 1968, 267–72.

54 The Portsmouth example is given in Wiggins 1968, 286. Wiggins also recounts the story of 26,000 pairs of boots being supplied by the Salvation Army for needy children in 1905 (294). Among many contemporary reports to highlight concerns about the plight of the young were Charles Booth's *Life and Labour of the People of London* (1889–1903) and Seebohm Rowntree's *Poverty: A Study of Town Life* (1901); the issue had also featured prominently in General William Booth's *In Darkest England and the Way Out* (1890).

55 Blackwell 1959, 33–4; Oakley 2011, 28.

56 Wiggins 1968, 267.

57 Kendall nd, **II**, 513–6 (the cited phrase being on 514); *The Builder,* 10 Jul 1897, 29–31; 12 Aug 1899, 159; and 13 Jan 1900, 43; Muthesius 1901, 155. Banister Fletcher was professor of architecture at King's College, London; his son, Banister Flight Fletcher, wrote the famous *A History of Architecture on the Comparative Method*, first published in 1896.

58 An impressive account is to be found in Harris and Bryant [*c* 1913], 348–64; *see also* Kendall nd, **II**, 514–6.

59 The drawing was reproduced in *The Builder*, 10 Jul 1897, 31.

60 *The Builder*, 16 Dec 1893, 456; Crouch and Butler 1901, 39–42 and figs 28–31.

61 The quotation is from Crouch and Butler 1901, 40.

62 Could the gates be by the Bromsgrove Guild, which had a full-page advertisement on 202 of Crouch and Butler's *Churches, Mission Halls and Schools for Nonconformists*?

63 For the first extension *see WCCR* 1903 and Crouch and Butler 1901, 41–2 and fig 32.

64 *WCCR* 1901 and 1902; Crouch and Butler 1901, 42–3 and figs 33–7 (figs 33–5 show

65 Crouch and Butler 1901, 38.
66 *See The Builder*, 3 Oct 1903, 340 and 30 Apr 1904, 473; Middleton [*c* 1906], **VI**, 1–6.
67 *The Builder*, 27 Nov 1897, 437. The comments were directed at the chapel in Corporation Street, Birmingham (of 1886 by Osborn and Reading), which became King's Hall once the central hall (of 1901–3) was built further along the street (*see* Abbott 2009, 278–9).
68 *WCCR* 1901; Temple 1992, 33–6.
69 *The Builder*, 27 Jul 1901, 85 and 3 Oct 1903, 340; *WCCR* 1900 and 1903.
70 *WCCR* 1898; *The Builder*, 5 Aug 1899, 131 and 13 Oct 1900, 324; Cherry and Pevsner 1983, 601.
71 *WCCR* 1898.
72 *The Builder*, 13 Oct 1900, 324.
73 Thorne 2011.
74 Ibid.
75 Among the members was the paper manufacturer W H Reed, who is commemorated by a stained-glass window and the Reed Hall (of 1924–5).
76 *The Builder*, 16 Aug 1902, 154; 6 Dec 1902, 534; 13 May 1905, 521; and 20 May 1905, 549; Howard 1977; Thorne 2011; Stell 1991, 83; 'Sidwell Street Methodist, Exeter' in *Church Building* **98**, Mar–Apr 2006, 40–3. For the earlier use of Cottançin's system at St Jean-de-Montmartre *see* Collins 1959, 113–7 and plates 31–3.
77 *See* for example Cook 1963, 91–6.
78 Harris and Bryant [*c* 1913], 7–8.
79 Wiggins 1964, 394 (*see also* 1968, 293–4); Harris and Bryant [*c* 1913], 8; cf also Farr 1991, 25.
80 Stell 2002, 125.
81 Goodall 1962; Turner *et al*, 2005.
82 The Wesleyans were not only the largest Methodist body, but also the largest Nonconformist body. R W Perks MP, who had masterminded the fundraising, the purchase of the site and the architectural competition for the hall (*see* Goodall 1962 and Turner *et al* 2005), was also the man who engineered a 'deliberate attempt to prevent the union' between three other branches of Methodism. The union took place in 1907 (*see* Beckerlegge 1957, 101).
83 The competition for the design attracted much attention (*see The Builder*, 24 Jun 1905, 667–9; 1 Jul 1905, 14; 8 Jul 1905, 42; 15 Jul 1905, 70; 22 Jul 1905, 96; 29 Jul 1905, 126; and 5 Aug 1905, 156). For the prize-winning design and subsequent details of the building *see The Builder*, 17 Jun 1905, 657; 24 Jun 1905, 667, 682–3; 11 Oct 1912, 410–6, 452–3; and 1 Nov

1912, 522–3; *see also WCCR* 1912. For Rickards's design for the first round of the competition and other drawings *see* Service 1975, 344–5.
84 *The Builder*, 24 Jun 1905, 682–3. A planned pair of towers, which might have invited comparisons with St Paul's, was not constructed because of difficulty over a neighbouring building's right to light (*see WCCR* 1912; *see also* Clunn 1936b, 217).
85 Harris 1935, 112–5.
86 Many of the technical details are given in *The Builder*, 11 Oct 1912, 410–16, 452–3.
87 *CYB* 1891, 212–3 and plate. The building stands at the junction of Great Horton Road and All Saints' Road – it is possibly not a coincidence that it is not far from the site of one of Wesley's octagonal chapels.
88 *See The Builder*, 10 Jun 1899, 573; 16 Jun 1900, 593; and 24 Aug 1907, 223; *see also* Service 1975, 399–400.
89 For the earlier proposal (by Hemsoll and Paterson) and the limits of what was built, *see CYB* 1899, unnumbered plates. For Hale's chapel *see The Builder*, 15 Dec 1905, 699 and *CYB* 1906, 192–3 and plate; *see also* Wilson 1998.
90 *WCCR* 1906; *The Builder*, 4 May 1907, 543.
91 The first quotation, from the *Sheffield Daily Telegraph*, is cited in Harman and Minnis 2004, 277. The second quotation and details in the following sentence are cited in Wilson 1998, 59 and note 30 – which refers to the *Sheffield Daily Telegraph*, 19 Jun 1908, 27.
92 Jones 1958; the quotation is from 78. The minister, Charles Beard, died in 1888.
93 *The Builder*, 1 Jul 1899, 19; *Essex Hall Year Book*, 1900; Jones 1914, 56–7 and plate 12; Jones 1958; Stell 1994a, 109–10; Mooney 1996.
94 For Rathbone and the doors *see* [Walker Art Gallery] 1981, unpaginated, cat items 158–74 (and preceding text) and 269–77. The Rathbones were prominent members of the congregation.
95 R P Jones describes (in 1958, 81) the changes that Moira was required to make.
96 *Essex Hall Year Book*, 1903.
97 Crouch 1930, 28.
98 *WCCR* 1902 and 1909; *The Builder*, 15 Nov 1902, 453; Nicholson and Spooner [*c* 1911], 177–81; Crouch 1930, 27–30 and figs 1–2. C E Bateman subsequently designed Anglican churches for two nearby sites (published in Middleton [*c* 1906], **V**, 1–3 and *The Builder*, 26 May 1906, 560), but neither was built as such (*see* Herbert and Shackley 2009, 443). For villas in Four Oaks *see* Crawford 1984, 41–60 *passim* and 155–6.
99 Crouch 1930, 22.
100 The quotation is from Tatham Woodhead 1934, 33. Wood's octagonal schemes are illustrated as figs 5 and 9 in Hill 2010.

101 *The Builder*, 3 Dec 1904, 578; Nicholson and Spooner [*c* 1911], 246; Archer 1964, 173–4, 180; [Manchester City Art Gallery] 1975, 40–6; Richardson 1983, 122–5; Stell 1994a, 113–4; Hill 2010.
102 Both the contract drawings of 1903 and the presentation drawing of 1904 (*see* Richardson 1983, 125 and *The Builder*, 3 Dec 1904, 578) show that a figure sculpture was intended for this location. Paradoxically its omission may have added to the building's reputation as a harbinger of modernism.
103 The transepts are part of a change of plan between 1903 and 1908: compare the contract drawings (reproduced by Richardson 1983) with the final scheme (plan reproduced by Nicholson and Spooner [*c* 1911]).
104 Stewart 1956a, 38; a similar phrase is found in Stewart 1956b, 133.
105 For the furniture, now in the Whitworth Art Gallery, *see* [Manchester City Art Gallery] 1975, 41–2.
106 *CYB* 1906, 185 and 1912, 130–1 and plate; *The Builder*, 9 Jun 1911, 725 and 1 Nov 1912, 507–9; Binfield 1992; *see also* Stell 1994a, 111–2.
107 The use of ceramo from Leeds was justified in the *CYB* for 1912 and also in *The Builder*, 1 Nov 1912, 507–9.
108 This section incorporates material written by the present author and first published in the conference notes of the Society of Architectural Historians of Great Britain, 2004.
109 *See* Kadish 2011, 180–2.
110 A full account of the windows can be found in Walmsley 1912, while a shorter version is available in Dawson 1956 and more recent editions. The first windows were ready by 1904, and the complete set was installed in 1912.
111 For Christ Church *see The Builder*, 13 Sep 1902, 230; 11 Oct 1902, 326; and 25 Jun 1904, 696; *see also* Powicke 1907, 266–7; Nicholson and Spooner [*c* 1911], 104–8; Hubbard and Shippobottom 1988, 38–42, 57; Stell 1994a, 3–5.
112 For the Bournville meeting house *see* Butler 1999, **II**, 623–4; Gardiner 1923, 151–2, 191–5; Foster 2005, 258–9; Stell 1986, 231; Harrison 2009.
113 Harrison 2009, 542–4.
114 Miller 1989, 94–6. Thomas Adams, who masterminded the project, was a Presbyterian who aimed to make the congregation 'the most alive body on the estate' (Simpson 1985, 33 and note 65). The foundation stones, which survive in a later hall, were laid by Ebenezer Howard and the Baptist F B Meyer, and the first minister was a Congregationalist.
115 Miller and Gray 1992, 114.

116 Miller and Gray 1992, 77–86, 89 and 114–7; Anon 1960; *see also The Builder*, 17 Feb 1911, 219 and 30 Aug 1912, 251–2, 258.

117 Punshon 1986, 192–4. It is notable that George Cadbury introduced the practice of hymn singing, followed by a scripture reading, at the start of meetings for worship in Bournville, and that he and his wife gave the meeting house an organ (*see* Gardiner 1923, 192–4; Stell 1986, 231), but these were exceptional and did not influence the general pattern of Quaker worship.

118 Butler 1999, **I**, 262; Miller 1989, 96; and cf Pietrusiak 2004. A beaten copper plaque records the gift of the meeting house in 1907.

119 Butler 1999, **I**, 395; Robson 2014, 48. Note that the meeting is officially known as Golders Green Meeting, thus avoiding confusion with the Hampstead meeting house – which Frederick Rowntree had also designed. *See also* Miller and Gray 1992, 117, although this identifies the source as a Pennsylvania building that the present author has been unable to trace.

120 A convenient account of the renaissance of Quaker history can be found in Punshon 1986, 221–6.

121 Christopher Stell (in 1986, 7) and others give 1910 as the date when weekly meetings resumed, while David Butler (in 1999, **I**, 25–6) gives the date as 1926 – although noting that Jordans resumed membership of a network of local Quaker congregations ('monthly meeting') in 1911.

122 On Braithwaite *see* Miller and Gray 1992, 117, 132.

123 For comments about the relative strength of Nonconformist architecture around 1900 *see* for example Pevsner 1954, 186, and Pevsner 1974, 355.

124 Nicholson and Spooner [*c* 1911]. The authors are not always explicit about the denominations represented, and unwary readers might assume by default that some buildings (for example Christ Church, Port Sunlight or Holy Rood, Watford) are Anglican.

125 Robinson *et al* 1912, 217.

126 Robinson *et al* 1912, 67; see also *BHB* 1898, 322–4; *The Builder*, 15 Jan 1898, 64 and 11 Nov 1899, 447; Stell 1994a, 267–8.

127 Crouch 1910, 222.

128 Jones 1914, 23. Underbank chapel is illustrated at fig 3.8.

129 Jones 1914, 39–40.

130 Jones 1914, 58.

131 Jones 1914, 59.

132 In 1900, for instance, Jones had renovated the Ipswich meeting house (which Crouch was to admire in *Puritanism and Art*, 1910, 222). *See* Hewett 1959, 13–14; Godfrey 1951.

8 Chapels since 1914

1 Masterman, C F G 1909 *The Condition of England*, 207–8, quoted in Thompson 1972, 228.

2 A useful assessment of the changing costs of church building from 1908 to 1955 is to be found in Mills 1956, 116.

3 *See* Jordan 1956, 168–79.

4 Accounts of the Methodist union of 1932 are to be found in almost every subsequent history of Methodism. For the proposed Presbyterian and Congregationalist scheme *see* for example *CYB* 1940, 240–1.

5 The author was Albert Peel, writing in the additional chapter for Horne 1926 edition, 450. For Peel *see* Taylor and Binfield 2007, 176–7.

6 Among the first denominations to formalise this change were the Congregationalists, whose Chapel-Building Society was renamed the Church Building and Extension Committee in the 1930s.

7 Cox 1982, 6; Pevsner and Brooks 2007, 113. The composition of the building, with a porch at the angle of two arms of the building, recalls the scheme for a village chapel in Crouch and Butler 1901, 36–7 and figs 24–5.

8 For the 1851 religious census the Primitive Methodists of Thursford recorded attendances of 14 in the afternoon and 50 for the evening service, perhaps held in a cottage or farm building: *see* The National Archives HO 129/243. The 1934 building was sometimes referred to as the Primitive Methodist chapel, although the Primitive Methodist Church formally ceased to exist with Methodist unification in 1932.

9 Norfolk Record Office mss FC 18/15. Among the many Gothic designs by the practice is Castle Street Primitive Methodist chapel, Cambridge, of 1914.

10 *BHB* 1915 (484 and plates) and 1923 (298); *VCH Essex*, **VI**, 1973, 123–41.

11 The quotation is reproduced in an unpublished report by Matthew Lloyd Architects 2010, 4.

12 For 'Child Haven' and the Angas Home for Aged Men *see BHB* 1936, 362. The lych gate entrance to Queen's Gardens had been created in 1931 (*BHB* 1932, 336).

13 *BHB* 1936, 363.

14 At least 23 were built in the period 1915–29, and at least 13 in 1930–45 (Connelly 2013, especially 86).

15 Pevsner 1966, 324; for the preceding chapel *see* Serjeant 2011, specifically 157.

16 A plan and exterior photograph of the Bristol building are reproduced as figs 1 and 3 in Connelly 2013, 78 and 82.

17 The extract from an interview with Jack Hart (b 1912), part of Paul Thomson's 'The Edwardians', is quoted here from Connelly 2013, 85. It refers to the Wesleyan mission in East Ham, built in 1905–6 to the designs of Gordon and Gunton.

18 Temple 1992, 104–6; Connelly 2013, 86 and 90.

19 *The Builder*, 30 Mar 1928, 534–5, 538; Temple 1992, 39; Clunn 1936b, 303.

20 For the Marlborough Theatre (demolished in 1962) *see The Builder*, 10 Oct 1903, 369 and Howard 1970, 149.

21 Butler 1999, **II**, 615–22 (the quotation being on 621). Asa Briggs misleadingly gives the date of 1928 (rather than 1931–2) for the completion of Lewis's 'new "island" bloc' (Briggs 1956, 105–6), and describes the extension without mention of the meeting house.

22 Gawne 1998; Clark 2006.

23 Butler 1999, **II**, 615–22; Gardiner 1923, 39–56. The analogy with central halls extended even to the inclusion of rented shops into the frontage on Upper Priory.

24 Strictly speaking, not all of these suburban buildings were always known as meeting houses. For the full list of Quaker places of worship in Birmingham *see* Butler 1999, **II**, 614–31 and cf 646 and 692–3.

25 For the New Room in general *see* Stell 1986, 66–8. A relatively full account of the 1929–30 restoration is given in Little and Cook 1986.

26 The quotations are from Little and Cook 1986, 3. For Lamplough *see also Who's Who in Methodism* 1933, 352. For Oatley the chief source now is Whittingham 2011.

27 Oatley 1930 (copy in the New Room archive).

28 Hague and Hague 1986, 102–5; *Who's Who in Architecture*, 1923.

29 Jones 1914, 20.

30 Harman and Minnis 2004, 232–4. A plan of the building and its internal arrangements was made by the architects Peter Wright and Martyn Phelps in 1999, prior to their scheme of reordering.

31 Charles Ryder Smith, soon to become Principal of the Wesleyan theological college at Richmond, published *The Sacramental Society* in 1927.

32 The previous building, South Street Methodist New Connexion chapel, in The Moor, is illustrated in Packer nd, 65; *see also Methodist New Connexion Magazine*, 1905, 399. The chapel is reported to have made way for a Marks and Spencer shop (www.remotegoat.com, accessed 16 Aug 2013).

33 *BHB* 1935, 335; 'New Baptist Church, Sutton' in *Architect and Building News*, 5 Oct 1934, 8–11; Pettman and Kingsford 1969; Anon 1934. For the 1883 chapel in High Street *see also BHB* 1883, 351 and unnumbered plate.

34 The carving was by Julian Phelps Allan (previously Eva Dorothy Allan). It shows a

scene from the Acts of the Apostles (8: 25–39) in which an Ethiopian eunuch is baptised by Philip the Deacon.

35 A comparison between the architects' plans and the photographs of the completed building (in *Architect and Building News*, 5 Oct 1934, 8–11) suggests that the location of the communion table and the lectern were determined at a late stage. One of Cachemaille-Day's Anglican churches (St Alban, Southampton, of 1933) had a central altar.

36 *BHB* 1935, 335. Cf Otto Bartning's desire to create Protestant churches that would be sacred spaces (described in Bartning 1919).

37 *See* for example Drummond 1934, 165–7, 188–9, 217–9.

38 *CYB* 1931, 216; 1932, 211–2; and 1933, 217. Smee and Houchin are named in 1931, henceforth Houchin alone, though the exterior view illustrated in 1932 bears both names. The Pevsner Guide gives the design to Percy Brand, however (Cherry *et al* 2005, 329).

39 *CYB* 1935, 260, and 1936, 685. For the preceding building of 1930, then known as North Wembley Free Church, *see CYB* 1931, 213.

40 *CYB* 1934, 243-4. The photographs published here show that the original external lanterns were closely modelled on Italian Renaissance protoypes.

41 Pevsner and Wedgwood 1966, 330.

42 Crouch 1930, 21.

43 Crouch 1930, 35 and figs 12–14. Formally the designs should be attributed to Crouch, Butler and Savage.

44 Crouch 1930, 31–2 and figs 6–8; Williams 2006, 66.

45 Bristol City Council 2011, especially 13, 18, 19, 28 and 41; Whittingham 2011, 257; *Architectural Review*, Mar 1930, 138, fig 30. Oatley's partner was his brother-in-law George Lawrence.

46 Apart from Oatley's most famous Gothic work, the Wills Memorial building at Bristol University, there was for example Avonmouth Congregational church (1900–2) and the cruciform Anglican church of St Edyth, which Oatley and Lawrence had begun in 1926 at one end of the Sea Mills estate.

47 The quotation is from Clunn 1936a, 469. For Lawrence *see* Binfield 1984; for Immanuel *see* 'Congregational Church, Southbourne, Hants' in *Architects' Journal*, 27 Aug 1930, 297–9 and *CYB* 1932, 209–10.

48 *CYB* 1934, 244–5, and 1936, 682; Pritchard 1975; Binfield 1984; Briggs 1946, 88 (fig 20) and plate XX.

49 Lancaster 1936, 32–3.

50 Since 2000 the building has been altered, providing a new entrance concourse and reducing the area of the main worship space, where chairs have replaced pews.

51 Pritchard 1975, 17.

52 The quotation is from Routley 1961, 132–3. Among other writers to mention Oxted were Briggs 1946, 51–2, 88 and plate XX and Drummond 1942, 327.

53 *See* Harwood 1998, especially 52–3 and 56–7.

54 The description is part of the official schedule adding the chapel to the list of historic buildings. The first Free Church building (of 1905, by Parker and Unwin, *see* p 212), although twice extended, had been outgrown.

55 The quotation, from Parker's Oct 1925 lecture 'Art and industry' at Balliol College, Oxford, is here cited from Davey 1980, 180 and 182 (n 18).

56 Drummond 1934, 136.

57 Ibid.

58 Drummond 1942 (the quotation being from 326).

59 This account draws partly on the obituaries of Mills by Andrew Saint (*The Guardian*, 11 Feb 1998) and Alan Powers (*The Independent*, 2 Mar 1998).

60 'Colliers Wood Methodist Mission: Designed by Edward D Mills' in *Architects' Journal*, 9 Sep 1937, 402–4 and 'Methodist Mission, Colliers Wood' in *Architects' Journal*, 9 Sep 1937, 420; Mills 1956, 175.

61 Hague and Hague 1986, 110.

62 The Unitarians' previous chapel (of 1853–4, by John Dobson) stood in New Bridge Street. Their 1939–40 building is a few minutes' walk away in Ellison Place, on a site previously occupied by one of Dobson's Anglican churches (St Peter, of 1840–3), a Gothic landmark amid classical terraces. Both buildings are illustrated in Faulkner and Greg 1987, 59.

63 Perkins and Hearn 1946, 26–7. The figures appear to refer to the whole of Britain rather than to England alone: if so, about one in six Methodist buildings suffered air-raid damage.

64 Davey 1955, 175.

65 Betjeman 1940 (subsequently reprinted in Betjeman's *First and Last Loves*, 1952).

66 Lidbetter 1946, 99–116; Drummond 1942.

67 Although published in 1946, *Puritan Architecture and its Future* was written during the war, as its foreword bears the date March 1945.

68 Briggs 1946, 24.

69 Briggs 1946, 73.

70 Briggs 1946, 84.

71 Perkins and Hearn 1946.

72 Mills 1945. A summary of the scheme (for the St Helier estate in Morden) was later published in Mills 1956, 98.

73 Brown 2001, 170–5. For a different view, *see* for example Wickham 1957, chapter 5, especially 210–13. On Sunday schools *see* Cliff 1986, 272–3.

74 In 1989 at least 1,138 local ecumenical partnerships existed in England, the majority of which involved the uniting of two or more congregations (of different denominations) to create a new entity. *See* Brierley 1991, 13–15.

75 Brierley and Wraight 1995, 237–84.

76 Peter Brierley 2014 (unpaginated), tables 1.2.6, 1.3.2 and 1.3.5. The Pentecostal total was 432,687, compared with 231,357 for the Methodists and 189,152 for the Baptists.

77 A rare, and interesting, exception is the church of the Christian Community, Glenilla Road, London, designed by Kenneth Bayes in 1948. Despite the restricted availability of materials, Bayes was able to create the flowing lines that are so characteristic of Rudolf Steiner's vision, especially evident in the door, side windows and pulpit. (*See* notes by Andrew Worth for a Chapels Society visit to Hampstead, 2012.)

78 *The Builder*, 16 Jun 1950, 800–12; *Architectural Design*, May 1950, 113 and Jun 1950, 155; *The Architects' Journal*, 6 Sep 1951, 274, 284–6; Mills 1956, 94–5; Banham and Hillier 1976, 138–43; Harwood 2001, especially 152–3.

79 Le Corbusier's 1931 project for the Palace of the Soviets is likely to have been the ultimate source for the idea of suspending the roof from an external frame of concrete ribs.

80 Harwood 2001, 153; *The Architects' Journal*, 6 Sep 1951, 274.

81 Cecil Handisyde was a specialist in insulation and contributed a chapter on that subject to de Maré 1948, and revised edition 1951.

82 The bombed Victorian chapel had 1,500 seats. In 1939 there were 170 members and 300 Sunday scholars (*CYB* 1940, 375). At the new premises in 1956 there were 80 members and 100 Sunday scholars (*CYB* 1957, 199).

83 In the foreword to *Sixty Post-War Churches* [Incorporated Church Building Society] in 1956, Hugh Gurney observed that 'the establishment of what have been termed "Church Centres" appears to have been generally successful, and evidence exists that this form of plan has often integrated religious and secular activities in a way which is beneficial to the Church generally'. Among the examples of this type illustrated in the book (86–7) is St Nicholas and All Hallows, Poplar, built in 1955 barely a mile from the Congregationalists' Trinity.

84 For the Victorian chapel *see The Builder*, 21 Mar 1868, 220; *CYB* 1870, 337 and plate; Brockett 1962, 203.

85 For the 1883–4 church *see* Cameron 1979, 148–56. Illustrations of that building, and an account of the new one, are contained in the booklet, *St Columba's 'Out of the Ashes'*, 2005.

86 For the 19th-century Christ Church *see* for example Stell 2002, 106–7. A summary of the post-war building (1958–60 and 1972–6, by Peter J Darvall) is given in Cherry and Pevsner 1983, 339–40. Was the screen directly inspired by that in the Maria-Lourdes-Kirche, Vienna (as illustrated, for example in Weyres and Bartning 1959, 180)?

87 The membership figures are as reported in *CYB* 1940, 366, and 1957, 196.

88 *CYB* 1855, 265; Dannatt 1959, 192–3; [Dannatt] 1972, 21–3.

89 The building closed for worship in 1974: *see* Weatherhead 1983, and Rhind 1976, 132–3. I am indebted to Dr David Knight for these references.

90 Hague and Hague 1986, 112–13. Drummond (in *The Church Architecture of Protestantism*, 1934, 263) had noted a revival of interest in colonial meeting-house architecture almost 20 years earlier.

91 The 1818 building was also approximately the same shape as its successor. *See* Herford 1893 (photograph facing 51) and Thackray 1922 (photograph facing 6). It had two-storey fenestration, however, reflecting the galleried arrangement.

92 Hague and Hague 1986, 101, 110.

93 [Methodist Church's Department for Chapel Affairs] 1961, unpaginated. For a full account of the struggle to gain approval for the building of the Punshon Memorial church *see* Binfield 1999.

94 The quotation is taken from [Methodist Church Department for Chapel Affairs] 1961.

95 Binfield 2003, especially 143–60.

96 Feilden wrote that the tower was an allusion 'to the early Christian Church of St Appolinari in Nuovo [sic] near Ravenna, which I had seen during the war' (quoted in Binfield 2003, 155–6). This might mean either Sant'Apollinare in Classe or Sant'Apollinare Nuovo, but both have round towers, unlike the square tower Feilden designed for Trinity. Norwich already had one Stockholm-inspired tower, that of its city hall.

97 The quotation comes from Feilden's own statement in Emanuel 1980, 248.

98 For Digbeth-in-the-Field, Yardley *see* Lloyd 1988 (*see also* Routley 1961, facing 133); personal communication from Mr J Butcher. For Hoole Road, Chester *see* Hartwell *et al* 2011, 278.

99 Dannatt 1959, 205–6; Oakley 2011, 68–9.

100 'Lutheran Church in Stepney for Danish seamen', in *Churchbuilding* **9**, Apr 1963, 15–22.

101 Cherry *et al* 2005, 96.

102 [Methodist Church Department for Chapel Affairs] 1961; Dickinson and Hodgson 1986, 33; *see also* inscription and datestone of the previous (Wesleyan) chapel in front of the present building.

103 [Methodist Church Department for Chapel Affairs] 1961.

104 A summary of successive proposals by Mills for the Mitcham building can be found in *Architecture and Building*, Jan 1960, 24. A modified version of the original scheme was published in 'Proposed new Methodist Church at Mitcham, Surrey' in *Architect and Building News*, 31 Mar 1950, 332–5 and 'Proposed Methodist Church, Mitcham' in *Architectural Design*, Mar 1950, 60–2. A reorganised design is illustrated in Mills 1956, 27 and 140, and in Weyres and Bartning 1959, 354. For the final building *see* 'Methodist Church at Mitcham' in *Architect and Building News*, 13 Jul 1960, 53–8; 'Church' in *Architecture and Building*, Jan 1960, 24–8; 'Methodist Church, Mitcham' in *Architectural Review*, Dec 1959, 324–6; [Methodist Church Department for Chapel Affairs] 1961; Smith 1961, 52–3; Smith 1964, 34–7.

105 For the Braunsfeld church (nicknamed 'the holy zigzag') *see* for example Weyres 1957, 116 and plates 98 and 109; *see also* Biedrzynski 1958, 54–7 and plates 22–4.

106 For the Otaniemi chapel (by Kaija and Heikki Sirén, following a 1954 competition), *see* for example Smith 1964, 60–7. As Smith noted, the communion table at Mitcham came from the old church, but the other furnishings were designed by Mills.

107 Hammond 1960, 180 and 105.

108 Hammond 1960, 39.

109 Mills 1964, 70–7; Billington 1969, especially 140–80.

110 Noble 2013; Butler 1999, **I**, 49.

111 Cragg 2013.

112 Ibid. For the architect's original plan and a description of subsequent changes *see* Noble 2013, 24 and 29–40.

113 Personal communication from Peter C Davis; White 1991.

114 Wesley's Octagon, off Middle Street, is mentioned in Chapter 3.

115 The publication of George Dolbey's *The Architectural Expression of Methodism* in 1964 must also have raised awareness of Wesley's Octagon chapels.

116 The writer is Charles O'Brien, in Leach and Pevsner 2009, 77.

117 Leach and Pevsner 2009, 495 and (for the preceding chapel) 469: *Architectural Review*, Jan 1974, 19.

118 Information about the Worcester building and its predecessor has been gathered from the Methodist Property Office (courtesy of Ian Serjeant); The Methodist Church Department for Chapel Affairs 1963, 37; and Bridges and Leech 2002.

119 Alcock [1968], 46–50; [Methodist Church Division of Property] 1974, 10–11.

120 Gresleri's church of the Blessed Immaculate Virgin, Bologna (of 1961) had been illustrated in Smith 1964, 198–202.

121 Could the relationship between organ grille, choir, communion table and pulpit have been influenced by the Johanneskirche, Basel of 1936, by Burckhardt and Egender (which had been illustrated, for example, in Mills 1956, 42)?

122 *See* for example Lockett 1964, 76 and caption to plate 30; Hammond 1960, 80.

123 'Church, Waterlooville' in *Architect and Building News*, 30 Aug 1967, 359–66. The new building, in its suburban site, was built to succeed a Victorian chapel in the High Street.

124 [Methodist Church Division of Property] 1974, 22–3; Sharp 1969, 101–2. The lead architect was Charles Brown.

125 The Bruderklausen Kirche, Birsfelden (which is of bare concrete, and stylistically quite different) had been praised in Hammond 1960, 90–1, 136, and featured in Smith 1964, 270–3.

126 Foster 2005, 90.

127 Betteridge 2010, 421, 447–8; Davies 1968, 245 and plate XVI.

128 Harwood 1998, 74; Davies 1968, 243–5.

129 For Anglican scruples *see* [Incorporated Church Building Society] 1956, 6–14.

130 [Methodist Church Division of Property] 1974, 18–19. For Senn's church *see* Hammond 1960, 89, 158, 164 and plate 48; Hammond 1962, 161; Senn 1963; Maguire and Murray 1965, 102–4.

131 The phrase is that of the local Methodist minister, quoted in [Methodist Church Division of Property] 1974, 19.

132 [Methodist Church Division of Property] 1974, 20–1.

133 A full account of St Paul, Bow Common can be found in 'Anglican Church in Stepney', in *Churchbuilding* **7**, Oct 1962, 14–24 (with the question of preaching mentioned on 17 and 23).

134 The key publication in this respect was Davies 1962; for a Methodist response *see* Billington 1969, especially 142–6.

135 Binfield 2003, specifically 135–6. I am grateful also to Andrew Shepherd, architect

136 Binfield 2003, 136.

137 'Meeting House, Blackheath, London' in *Architectural Review*, Apr 1973, 265–9; Stonehouse 2008, 198–201; Butler 1999, **I**, 375–6.

138 Pevsner and Harris 1989, 502.

139 The quotation is from Lampugnani 1986, 186.

140 Cowan 1990, 193–204 (the statistics being on 195).

141 Cowan 1990, 197–200; [Church of Jesus Christ of Latter-day Saints] 1992, 596–7; Nairn and Pevsner 1971, 381–2.

142 Cowan 1990, 203–4; Cherry and Pevsner 1991, 466. Properly speaking, Mormons distinguish between the meeting house (the whole building) and the chapel, which is the main space for services. In practice this distinction is not always observed.

143 Verey and Brooks 2002, 240.

144 Bielby 1978, 102–3; *see also* Bailey 1984, 66–7. Following a fire in 1992, the 1963 building was soon replaced (www.ckcricketheritage.org.uk, accessed Jan 2014), using a less spectacular design – for which *see* Giles 1996.

145 Brierley and Wraight 1995, 259; Calvert 1994, 3.

146 Verey and Brooks 2002, 459.

147 Cherry and Pevsner 1991, 561; Calvert 1994, 57, 61; *WCCR* 1902. The Edwardian buildings had been damaged by bombing in 1941.

148 MacLaren 1992 and Mawson 1992; [Methodist Church Property Division] 1990, 63.

149 Stell 2002, 51–2; Kaye 1999, 12, 42, 59.

150 Calvert 1994, 10.

151 Oakley 2011, 30–1, 76, 91; Brooks and Pevsner 2012, 314.

152 For Brighton's 1883 Congress Hall (the name perhaps chosen to avoid the controversy of a Salvation Army citadel in a residential area) and its 2000 successor *see* Oakley 2011, 33, 54–5, 76–7, 94; Elleray 1981, 53; Antram and Morrice 2008, 184. *See also* Greenwood 1996 and Spears 2001.

153 Butler 1999, **II**, 593–5.

154 The building, often known as Cranmer Methodist church, bears an inscription which names the architects. A photograph of the preceding chapel is reproduced in Williams 2006, 120.

155 The creation of local ecumenical partnerships was simplified by the Sharing of Church Buildings Act of 1969. A snapshot of the extent of those partnerships (LEPs) is found in Brierley 1991, 13–15. Methodists were the most active participants in LEPs, followed by Anglicans and the United Reformed Church. Baptists and Catholics were also recorded in significant numbers.

156 Calvert 1994, 15; Bettley and Pevsner 2007, 726.

157 Essex County Council 1973 (on page 72 of which: 'Welsh slates are … acceptable provided they do not dominate the scene').

158 Tyack *et al* 2010, 485.

159 Trinity, Totton was commissioned from the Stocks Group of Leeds, using the 'design and build' system, no architect being named in the contract. Calvert 1994, 40; personal communication from Mr Steve Irish and the Revd Anthony Parkinson.

160 Dees 1991a. On Christ the Cornerstone *see* Pevsner and Williamson 1994, 489–92; Dees 1991b and 1993. For the architects' account *see* Smith and Muncaster 1992.

161 61,913 UK members in 1970, rising to 125,836 in 1991 (Brierley and Wraight 1995, 278). In 2010 the total stood at 133,000 (*Whitaker's Almanack* 2011, 489).

162 This account of Jehovah's Witnesses' buildings has benefited greatly from conversations with Andrew Morgan, and Chris and Lilian Harris. For the kingdom hall at Weston Favell *see Building Design*, 660, 7 Oct 1983, 8–9, and [Watchtower Bible and Tract Society] 1993, 324.

163 *See The Structural Engineer*, Sep 1986, **64A**/9, A3 and cover illustration.

164 Gradidge 1988; cf Pevsner and Williamson 1994, 558.

165 *See* 'The Church of the Latter-day Saints' in *Church Building* **92**, Mar–Apr 2005, 54–6 (which also outlines the Mormons' building programme for Western Europe).

166 *See* 'Jesus Christ of the Latter-day Saints' in *Church Building* **95**, Sep–Oct 2005, 70–1.

167 Hartwell and Pevsner 2009, 218–9.

168 For the Nauvoo temple and the functions of these buildings *see* Andrew 1978, especially chapters 3 and 4.

169 Cooper 2007, especially 18, 20, 29–31, 42 note 65 and 43 note 69.

170 'Huddersfield Christian Fellowship' in *Church Building* **95**, Sep–Oct 2005, 50–2, supplemented by personal communication.

171 'Huddersfield Christian Fellowship' in *Church Building* **95**, Sep–Oct 2005, 50–2; 'Huddersfield Christian Fellowship' in *Church Building* **121**, Jan–Feb 2010, 16–19.

172 Planning permission for the scheme (by Benoy, Handley) was sought in 2008, and permission was granted in 2011, after various changes. *See* Nottingham City Council application 08/00578/PFUL3.

173 Brierley 2014 (unpaginated), sections 12.1 and 12.11; Brierley 2013.

174 'St George's Church, Tufnell Park, London by Paul Davis + Partners' in *Architects' Journal*, 25 Feb 2011 (www.architectsjournal.co.uk/buildings/specification/st-georges-church-tufnell-park-london-by-paul-davis-partners/8611816.article, accessed Jan 2017); 'St George's Church, Tufnell Park, London' in *Church Building* **126**, Nov–Dec 2010, 4–11. For St George's *see* pp 168–9.

175 'New Testament Church of God, Lozells, Birmingham' in *Church Building* **122**, Mar–Apr 2010, 44–7. For the preceding chapel *see ILN* 1865, **47**, 73; *The Builder*, 20 Jun 1863, 446 and 1 Jul 1865, 473.

176 Betteridge 2010, 453–4; 'Leamington Spa Baptist Church' in *Church Building* **40**, Jul–Aug 1996, 96–7. Charles Brown, architect of the Leamington building, had been lead architect at Denys Hinton's practice for the Methodist chapel, Cheadle Hulme and for Carr's Lane Congregational chapel, Birmingham (*see* pp 249–51) in the 1960s.

177 Price 2004.

178 Kunna 2004; Wright 2009.

179 Betteridge 2010, 454–5; 'Dawley Baptist Church, Dawley, Telford' in *Church Building* **68**, nd [but 2001], 45–8. For the preceding chapel *see* Stell 1986, 193–4.

180 As a Unitarian place of worship, Unity Temple might have been thought an especially appropriate model for a Nonconformist commission. It has featured in almost all of the long list of books on Wright, but particularly worthy of mention is Robert McCarter's thorough monograph on the building, which appeared in 1997 as part of Phaidon's 'Architecture in Detail' series.

181 Grindley 2007; 'Headington Baptist Church' in *Church Building* **108**, Nov–Dec 2007, 12–13. For the preceding buildings *see* Stell 1986, 179.

182 *Architectural Review* devoted its Sep 1983 issue to what it termed 'romantic pragmatism'. Perhaps coincidentally the featured new building was from Oxford, the Sainsbury Building at Worcester College by MacCormac Jamieson Prichard.

183 Burne 2008.

184 Oakley 2011, 79–80; 'Salvation Army Citadel Corps, Chelmsford, Essex' in *Church Building* **119**, Sep–Oct 2009, 52–5.

185 The system of cross-laminated wooden panels was created by KLH of Austria.

Boxed essays

1 Graveyards and memorials

†   Butler 1999, **II**, 902–6; Darley 2013.

2 Meeting houses, temples, tabernacles and synagogues

†   Du Prey 2000, especially 40, 47–8, 155 note 1; [Thoresby] 1832, **1**, 109–111; Krinsky 1996; Rosenau 1941; Kadish 2001.

3 Communion

†   Wordsworth 2012, especially 103 and 115; Stell 1997, specifically 169; Spufford 1968, specifically 83–4; Anon 1896, 10; Winter 1960; Bowmer 1951.

4 Music

†   Buckley 1928; Pottle 1950, 259; Brandon and Johnson 1986; Lovell 2013, 21–2. Useful general accounts of musical traditions in various denominations are to be found in Sadie 2001 (**2**, 672–80 on Baptist music; **5**, 824–6 on Christian Science and the Church of Jesus Christ of Latter-day Saints; **6**, 295–300 on Congregationalism; **16**, 521–9 on Methodism; **7**, 969 on Moravianism; **19**, 317–9 on Pentecostalism; **21**, 78–86 on Reformed and Presbyterian churches; **22**, 183–5 on the Salvation Army; **26**, 74–6 on Unitarianism). The well-documented account of 17th- and 18th-century music among Nonconformists in New England (in Benes 2012, 40–8) offers many close parallels with the English experience.

5 What's in a name?

†   *See* Chambers 1963, 40–1; *see also* Rose 2009.

6 Seating

†   The Chapels Society 2013.

7 Stained glass

†   McMurray 1988; Walmsley 1912; Kaye 1996, 77–81; Smith 2002.

8 Baptism

†   Davies 1972, 44–64.

Bibliography

Abbott, D 2009. 'Frank Barlow Osborn' in Ballard, P (ed), *Birmingham's Victorian and Edwardian Architects*. Wetherby: Oblong for the Birmingham and West Midlands Group of the Victorian Society, 275–91

Addleshaw, G W O and Etchells, F 1948. *The Architectural Setting of Anglican Worship*. London: Faber

Alcock, J P [1968]. *Methodism in Congleton*. Congleton: Dean Crest Publicity

Alexander, W 1820. *Observations on the Construction and Fitting up of Meeting Houses &c for public worship*. York: W Alexander

Alger, B A M 1901. *History of the Derby and District Affiliated Free Churches*. Derby: Bacon and Hudson

Alger, B A M 1905. *King Street Wesleyan Chapel, Derby 1805–1905*. Derby: J F Hill & Co

Allon, H 1863. *Memoir of the Life of the Rev. James Sherman, Including an Unfinished Autobiography*, 2 edn. London: James Nisbet & Co

Ambler, R W (ed) 1979. *Lincolnshire Returns of the Census of Religious Worship 1851*. Lincoln: Lincoln Record Society (**72**)

Ambler, R W 2000. *Churches, Chapels and the Parish Communities of Lincolnshire 1660–1900*. (History of Lincolnshire ser **9**). Lincoln: History of Lincolnshire Committee for the Society for Lincolnshire History and Archaeology

Anderson, J H 2009. 'Primitive Methodism and the Gothic Revival'. *Chapels Society Newsletter*, **41**, May 2009, 11–13

Andersson, H O and Bedoire, F 1988. *Stockholm Architecture and Townscape*. Stockholm: Bokförlaget Prisma

Andres, G M 1980. 'Lavius Fillmore and the federal style meeting house' in Benes, P and Benes, J M (eds) 1980. *New England Meeting House and Church: 1630–1850. The Dublin Seminar for New England Folklife Annual Proceedings 1979*. Boston, MA: Boston University, 30–42

Andrew, L B 1978. *The Early Temples of the Mormons*. Albany: State University of New York Press

Anon 1896. *A History of Northampton Castle Hill Church, Now Doddridge, and its Pastorate, 1674–1895*. Northampton: Taylor & Son; London: Congregational Union of England and Wales

Anon 1934. *Sutton Baptist Church – Glimpses of the Past – 1884–1934*. [Sutton, Surrey: np]

Anon 1948. *"Thou Shalt Remember...": A Short History of the Strict and Particular Baptist Church Meeting at Zoar, St Mary's Plain, Norwich*. [np]

Anon 1960. *God is Larger Than the Creeds: Fifty Years of Witness, Hampstead Garden Suburb Free Church 1910–1960*. [London: the church]

Anon 1978. *The Church of the Holy Family, Bewdley 1778–1953–1978*. [Bewdley: the church]

Anon 1981. *Tell it How it Was: The Story of 200 Years in Oldham Street*. Manchester: Manchester and Salford Methodist Mission

Antram, N and Morrice, R 2008. *Brighton and Hove*. New Haven and London: Yale University Press

Archer, J H G 1964. 'Edgar Wood: A notable Manchester architect'. *Transactions of the Lancashire and Cheshire Antiquarian Society*, **73–4**, (1963–4), 153–87

Arnold, H G 1960. 'Early meeting houses'. *Transactions of the Ancient Monuments Society*, new ser **8**, 89–139

Arnold, H G et al 1985. *Hallelujah! Recording Chapels and Meeting Houses*. London: Council for British Archaeology

Arnold, M 1869. *Culture and Anarchy*. London: Smith, Elder & Co

Aston, J 1816. *A Picture of Manchester* (facsim edn 1969 Manchester: Morten)

Atterbury, P and Wainwright, C (eds) 1994. *Pugin: A Gothic Passion*. New Haven and London: Yale University Press in association with The Victoria and Albert Museum

Austin, S et al 1832. *Lancashire Illustrated*. London: H Fisher, R Fisher, and P Jackson

Ayres, W F 1963. *The Highbury Story: Highbury Chapel, Bristol*. London: Independent Press

Bailey, J R 1984. *Religious Buildings and Festivals*. Huddersfield: Schofield & Sims

Bailey, M 1992. *Van Gogh in England*. London: Barbican Art Gallery

Baker, T 1884. *Memorials of a Dissenting Chapel, its Foundation and Worthies: Being a Sketch of the Rise of Nonconformity in Manchester and of the Erection of the Chapel in Cross Street, with Notices of its Ministers and Trustees*. London: Simpkin, Marshall & Co

Ballard, P (ed) 2009. *Birmingham's Victorian and Edwardian Architects*. Wetherby: Oblong for the Birmingham and West Midlands Group of the Victorian Society

Banham, M and Hillier, B (eds) 1976. *A Tonic to the Nation: The Festival of Britain, 1951*. London: Thames & Hudson

Bardwell, W 1837. *Temples, Ancient and Modern*. London: printed for the author

Bartning, O 1919. *Vom neuen Kirchbau*. Berlin: Bruno Cassirer

Barton, D A 1975. *Discovering Chapels and Meeting Houses*. Aylesbury: Shire Publications

Bateman, T 1861. *Ten Years' Diggings in Celtic and Saxon Grave Hills*. London: J R Smith and Derby: W Bemrose & Sons

Beasley, N 1952. *The Cross and the Crown: The History of Christian Science*. New York: Duell, Sloan & Pearce

Bebbington, D W 1982. *The Nonconformist Conscience: Chapel and Politics, 1870–1914*. London: G Allen & Unwin

Beckerlegge, O A 1957. *The United Methodist Free Churches: A Study in Freedom*. London: Epworth Press

Beeskow, A 2005. *Die Ausstattung in den Kirchen des Berliner Kirchenbauvereins (1890–1904)*. Berlin: Gebr Mann Verlag

Beevers, D et al 1989. *Sussex Churches and Chapels*. Brighton: Royal Pavilion, Art Gallery & Museums

Belden, A D 1953. *George Whitefield, the Awakener*, 2 edn. London: Rockcliff

Benes, P and Benes, J M (eds) 1980. *New England Meeting House and Church: 1630–1850. The Dublin Seminar for New England Folklife Annual Proceedings 1979*. Boston, MA: Boston University

Benes, P 2012. *Meetinghouses of Early New England*. Amherst: University of Massachusetts Press

Beresford Hope, A J B 1861. *The English Cathedral of the Nineteenth Century*. London: Murray

Betjeman, J 1940. 'Nonconformist architecture'. *Architectural Review* **88**, Dec 1940, 160–74

Betjeman, J 1952. 'Nonconformist architecture' *in* Betjeman, J *First and Last Loves*. London: John Murray, 90–119

Betteridge, A 2010. *Deep Roots, Living Branches: A History of Baptists in the English Western Midlands*. Leicester: Matador

Bettley, J and Pevsner, N 2007. *Essex*. New Haven and London: Yale University Press

Bidlake, G 1865. *Sketches of Churches designed for the Use of Nonconformists*. Birmingham: S Birbeck

Biedrzynski, R 1958. *Kirchen unserer Zeit*. Munich: Hirmer

Bielby, A R 1978. *Churches and Chapels of Kirklees*. Huddersfield: Kirklees Metropolitan Council, Libraries and Museums Service

Billington, R J 1969. *The Liturgical Movement and Methodism*. London: Epworth Press

Bindman, D and Riemann, G (eds) 1993. *Karl Friedrich Schinkel: 'The English Journey', Journal of a Visit to France and Britain in 1826*. New Haven and London: Published for the Paul Mellon Centre for Studies in British Art by Yale University Press

Binfield, C 1982. 'The building of a town centre church: St James's Congregational Church, Newcastle upon Tyne'. *Northern History* **18**, 155–81

Binfield, C 1984. 'Art and spirituality in chapel architecture: F W Lawrence (1882–1948) and his churches', *in* Loades, D (ed) *The End of Strife*. Edinburgh: T & T Clark, 200–226

Binfield, C 1988. 'The dynamic of grandeur: Albion Church, Ashton-under-Lyne'. *Transactions of the Lancashire and Cheshire Antiquarian Society* **85**, 173–92

Binfield, C 1992. 'The White Church, Fairhaven: An artist trader's Protestant Byzantium'. *Transactions of the Historic Society of Lancashire and Cheshire* **142**, 155–77

Binfield, C 1999. 'Victims of success: Twentieth-century Free Church architecture', *in* Shaw, J and Kreider, A (eds) *Culture and the Nonconformist Tradition*. Cardiff: University of Wales Press, 142–81

Binfield, C 2001. *The Contexting of a Chapel Architect: James Cubitt, 1836–1912* (The Chapels Society Occ Pubs Ser **2**). London: The Chapels Society

Binfield, C 2003. 'Strangers and dissenters: The architectural legacy of twentieth-century English Nonconformity – context, case study and connexion', *in* Sell, A and Cross, A (eds) *Protestant Nonconformity in the Twentieth Century*. Carlisle: Paternoster Press, 132–83

Binfield, C 2007. '"The most vital bonds of union": Union Chapel and congregationalism', *in* Cherry, B (ed) *Dissent and the Gothic Revival* (The Chapels Society Occ Pubs Ser **3**). London: The Chapels Society, 19–38

Binfield, C 2010. 'The prime of T Lewis Banks', *in* Skidmore, C (ed) *Chapels and Chapel People: Miscellany 2* (The Chapels Society Occ Pubs Ser **5**). London: The Chapels Society, 73–103

Bingham, N 1991. *C A Busby: The Regency Architect of Brighton and Hove*. London: RIBA Heinz Gallery

Binney, M and Burman, P 1977. *Chapels & Churches: Who Cares*. London: British Tourist Authority in association with Country Life

[Blackburn, J] 1847. 'Remarks on ecclesiastical architecture as applied to Nonconformist chapels', *Congregational Year Book*, 1847, 150–63

Blackwell, D R 1959. 'Evolution of corps architecture in the United Kingdom', *Salvation Army Yearbook*, 1959, 30–5

Blake, S T 1979. *Cheltenham's Churches and Chapels, AD 773–1883*. Cheltenham: Cheltenham Borough Council Art Gallery and Museum Service

Blomefield, F 1806. *An Essay towards a Topographical History of the County of Norfolk, Vol IV*. London: Printed for W Miller by W Bulmer & Co

Boag, L and Boag, H (eds) 1927. *St James's Past and Present*. Newcastle-upon-Tyne: A Reid

Booth, C 1889–1903. *Life and Labour of the People in London*. London: Macmillan

Booth, W 1890. *In Darkest England and The Way Out*. London: International Headquarters of the Salvation Army

Bostwick, D 1989. *The Great Sheffield Picture Show*. Sheffield: RLP

Bowers, F 1999. *A Bold Experiment: The Story of Bloomsbury Chapel and Bloomsbury Central Baptist Church 1848–1999*. London: Bloomsbury Central Baptist Church

Bowmer, J C 1951. *The Sacrament of the Lord's Supper in Early Methodism*. London: Dacre Press

Bradley, S 2000. 'The roots of ecclesiology: Late Hanoverian attitudes to Medieval churches', *in* Webster, C and Elliott, J (eds) *'A Church as it Should be': The Cambridge Camden Society and its Influence*. Stamford, Lincs: Shaun Tyas, 22–44

Bradshaw, Paul (ed) 2002. *The New SCM Dictionary of Liturgy and Worship*. London: SCM Press

Braithwaite, W C 1955. *The Beginnings of Quakerism*, 2 edn, revised by Henry J Cadbury. Cambridge: Cambridge University Press

Brandon, V and Johnson, S 1986. 'The Old Baptist Chapel, Goodshaw Chapel, Rawtenstall, Lancs'. *Antiquaries Journal* **66**/2, 330–57

Brandwood, G and Cherry, M 1990. *Men of Property: The Goddards and Six Generations of Architecture*. Leicester: Leicestershire Museums, Arts and Records Service

Brett, C E B 1967. *Buildings of Belfast, 1700–1914*. London: Weidenfeld & Nicolson

Bridges, T and Leech, A 2002. *The Churches and Chapels of the City of Worcester: A Brief Guide*. [Worcester: Worcestershire and Dudley Historic Churches Trust]

Brierley, P 1991. *Prospects for the Nineties, All England: Trends and Tables from the English Church Census, with Denominations and Churchmanships*. London: MARC Europe

Brierley, P and Wraight, H (eds) 1995. *UK Christian Handbook 1996/97*. London: Evangelical Alliance

Brierley, P 2013. *Capital Growth: What the 2012 London Church Census Reveals*. Tonbridge: ADBC Publishers

Brierley, P (ed) 2014. *UK Church Statistics 2: 2010–2012*. Tonbridge: ADBC Publishers

Briggs, A 1956. *Friends of the People: The Centenary History of Lewis's*. London: Batsford

Briggs, J and Sellers, I (eds) 1973. *Victorian Nonconformity*. London: Edward Arnold

Briggs, M S 1946. *Puritan Architecture and its Future*. London: Lutterworth Press

Bristol City Council, 2011. *Sea Mills Character Appraisal and Management Proposals*. (www.bristol.gov.uk/documents/20182/33832/sea-mills-character-appraisal.pdf accessed 31 May 2016)

Brockett, A 1962. *Nonconformity in Exeter 1650–1875*. Manchester: Manchester University Press for the University of Exeter

Brooks, A and Pevsner, N 2012. *Herefordshire*. New Haven and London: Yale University Press

Brown, C G 2001. *The Death of Christian Britain*. Abingdon: Routledge

Brown, P H 1895. *John Knox. A Biography*, 2 vols. London: A & C Black

Brown, S and Figueiredo, P de 2008. *Religion and Place: Liverpool's Historic Places of Worship*. Swindon: English Heritage

Browne, J 1877. *History of Congregationalism and Memorials of the Churches in Norfolk and Suffolk*. London: Jarrold

Buckley, A 1928. 'The "Deighn Layrocks"'. *Baptist Quarterly* **IV** (1928–9), 43–8

Buffard, F 1961. *Heath Street Baptist Church, Hampstead 1861–1961*. [London: np]

Bullen, J B 2004. 'The Romanesque revival in Britain, 1800–1840: William Gunn, William Whewell, and Edmund Sharpe'. *Architectural History* **47**, 139–58

Bunting, B 1994. *The Complete Poems* (assoc ed Caddel, R). Oxford: Oxford University Press

Burne, D 2008. 'Clevedon Baptist Church'. *Church Building* **111**, May–Jun 2008, 48–51

Butler, D M 1978. *Quaker Meeting Houses of the Lake Counties*. London: Friends Historical Society

Butler, D M 1999. *The Quaker Meeting Houses of Britain*, 2 vols. London: Friends Historical Society

Butler, D M 2004. *The Quaker Meeting Houses of Ireland*. Dublin: Irish Friends Historical Committee

Butler, D M 2013. 'Seating in the Quaker meeting house'. *Chapels Society Journal* **1**: *Sitting in Chapel*, 28–38

Caddel, R and Flowers, A 1977. *Basil Bunting: A Northern Life*. Newcastle upon Tyne: Newcastle Libraries and Information Service in association with the Basil Bunting Poetry Centre, Durham

Calder, A J 2012. 'The Primitive Methodist connexion – tackling the myth'. Unpublished PhD thesis, Open University

Calder, S 2016. *The Origins of Primitive Methodism*. Woodbridge: The Boydell Press

Calvert, D 1994. *Building in Progress: New Methodist Chapels 1980–1993*. Manchester: Methodist Church Property Division

Cameron, G C 1979. *The Scots Kirk in London*. Oxford: Becket Publications

Carter, Mary 2005. *A Remarkable Journey: The History of the Free Church in St Ives*. Huntingdon: Westmeare Publications

Chambers, R F 1952. *The Strict Baptist Chapels of England I: The Chapels of Surrey and Hampshire*. Privately published for the Strict Baptist Historical Society

Chambers, R F 1954. *The Strict Baptist Chapels of England II: The Chapels of Sussex*. Privately published for the Strict Baptist Historical Society

Chambers, R F 1956. *The Strict Baptist Chapels of England III: The Chapels of Kent*. Privately published for the Strict Baptist Historical Society

Chambers, R F 1963. *The Strict Baptist Chapels of England IV: The Chapels of the Industrial Midlands*. London: Published for the Strict Baptist Historical Society, by the Fauconberg Press

Champness, J 2005. *Thomas Harrison, Georgian Architect of Chester and Lancaster 1744–1829*. Lancaster: Centre for North-West Regional Studies, University of Lancaster

Chapels Society 2013. *Chapels Society Journal* **1**: *Sitting in Chapel*

Cherry, B (ed) 2007. *Dissent and the Gothic Revival* (The Chapels Society Occ Pubs Ser **3**). London: The Chapels Society

Cherry, B and Pevsner, N 1983. *London 2: South*. Harmondsworth: Penguin Books

Cherry, B and Pevsner, N 1991. *London 3: North West*. Harmondsworth: Penguin Books

Cherry, B and Pevsner, N 1998. *London 4: North*. Harmondsworth: Penguin Books

Cherry, B and Pevsner, N 2002. *Devon*. New Haven and London: Yale University Press

Cherry, B *et al* 2005. *London 5: East*. New Haven and London: Yale University Press

[Cheshire County Council] 1988. *Faith in Action: The Story of Primitive Methodism in Cheshire with a Guide to Englesea Brook Chapel and Museum*. [Chester: Cheshire County Council]

Child, S M 2014. *A History of the Non-Conformist Churches in Burnley*, 2 vols. Burnley: Burnley Historical Society

[Church of Jesus Christ of Latter-day Saints] 1992. *Church History in the Fulness of Times: The History of The Church of Jesus Christ of Latter-day Saints*, revised edn. Salt Lake City: Church of Jesus Christ of Latter-day Saints

Clapham, J A 1878. 'Gothic Congregational Churches'. *The Congregationalist* **VII**, 202–7

Clark, J 2006. *Eminently Quakerly: The Building of Friends House*. London: Quaker Books

Clarke, B F L 1966. *Parish Churches of London*. London: Batsford

Cleal, E E, assisted by Crippen, T G 1908. *The Story of Congregationalism in Surrey*. London: James Clark & Co

Cliff, P B 1986. *The Rise and Development of the Sunday School Movement in England 1780–1980*. Redhill, Surrey: National Christian Education Council

Clowes, J E 1906. *Chronicles of the Old Congregational Church at Great Yarmouth, 1642 to 1858*. Great Yarmouth: [np]

Clunn, H 1936a. *The Face of the Home Counties*. London: Simpkin Marshall

Clunn, H 1936b. *The Face of London*, 6 edn. London: Simpkin Marshall

Coad, F R 1968. *A History of the Brethren Movement*. Exeter: Paternoster Press

Cobb, G 1942–3. *The Old Churches of London*, 2 edn. London: Batsford

Collins, P 1959. *Concrete, the Vision of a New Architecture*. London: Faber & Faber

Colvin, H M 1947. 'The architectural history of Marlow and its neighbourhood'. *Records of Buckinghamshire* **XV**, 5–19

Colvin, H 2008. *A Biographical Dictionary of British Architects 1600–1840*, 4 edn. New Haven and London: Yale University Press

Committee of the English Congregational Chapel-Building Society 1862. *Practical Hints on Chapel-Building* (2 edn, 1 edn pub 1855, the *Illustrated Appendix* is dated 1863). London: John Snow

Connelly, A 2010. 'Methodist central halls as public sacred space', unpublished PhD thesis, University of Manchester

Connelly, A 2013. 'Wesleyan alhambras: Tip-up seats in the central halls'. *Chapels Society Journal* **1**: *Sitting in Chapel*, 77–92

Cook, Olive 1963. *Movement in Two Dimensions*. London: Hutchinson

C[ooper] E W 1950. *Ebenezer Methodist Church, Newcastle, Staffs, 150th Anniversary 1800–1950*. [Newcastle, Staffs: np]

Cooper, T 2007. ' "Worthy of the age in which we live": Churches and chapels in Salisbury'. *Ecclesiology Today* **37**, 5–44

Cowan, R O 1990. 'The Church comes of age in Britain', *in* Cannon, D Q (ed) *Regional Studies in Latter-day Saint Church History: British Isles*. Provo, Utah: Department of Church History and Doctrine, Brigham Young University

Cox, B G 1982. *Chapels and Meeting Houses in the Vale of Evesham*. Gloucester: Alan Sutton for the Vale of Evesham Historical Society

Cox, J V 1997. ' "Simplicity without meanness, commodiousness without extravagance": The Non-conformist chapels and meeting-houses in Shrewsbury in the nineteenth century'. *Transactions of the Shropshire Archaeological and Historical Society* **LXXII**, 52–97

Cragg, S 2013. 'A soaring space'. *The Friend*, 14 Jun 2013, 10–11

Craster, H H E 1907. *A History of Northumberland VIII: The Parish of Tynemouth*. Newcastle and London: Andrew Reid & Co; Simpkin, Marshall, Hamilton, Kent & Co

Crawford, A (ed) 1984. *By Hammer and Hand: The Arts and Crafts Movement in Birmingham*. Birmingham: Birmingham Museums and Art Gallery

Creese, W L 1966. *The Search for Environment*. New Haven and London: Yale University Press

Crick, C 1975. *Victorian Buildings in Bristol*. Bristol: Bristol & West Building Society in conjunction with the City Art Gallery, Bristol

Crook, J M 1995. *The Greek Revival*, 2 edn. London: John Murray

Cross, F L and Livingstone, E A (eds) 2005. *The Oxford Dictionary of the Christian Church*, 3 edn, revised. Oxford: Oxford University Press

Crossley Evans, M J 1997. *By God's Grace and To God's Glory: An Account of the Life and Times of Buckingham Chapel, Clifton, Bristol, 1847–1947*. Bristol: Buckingham Chapel

Crouch, J 1910. *Puritanism and Art*. London: Cassell & Co

Crouch, J 1930. *The Planning and Designing of a Methodist Church*. Birmingham: Silk & Terry

Crouch, J and Butler, E 1901. *Churches, Mission Halls and Schools for Nonconformists*. Birmingham: Buckler & Webb

Cubitt, J 1865. 'Chapel architecture in 1864'. *Building News*, 10 Mar 1865, 163–5

Cubitt, J 1870. *Church Design for Congregations: Its Development and Possibilities*. London: Smith, Elder & Co

Cubitt, J 1892. *A Popular Handbook of Nonconformist Church Building*. London: James Clarke & Co

Cunningham, C and Waterhouse, P 1992. *Alfred Waterhouse 1830–1905: Biography of a Practice*. Oxford: Clarendon Press

[Cunningham, J W] 1814. *The Velvet Cushion*. London: T Cadell & W Davies

Curl, J S 2000. *The Victorian Celebration of Death*. Stroud: Sutton

Dale, A 1967. *Fashionable Brighton 1820–1860*, 2 edn. Newcastle upon Tyne: Oriel Press

Dale, A W W 1899. *The Life of R W Dale of Birmingham, by his Son*. London: Hodder & Stoughton

Dale, R W 1862. *Churchmen and Dissenters: Their Mutual Relations as Affected by the Celebration of the Bicentenary of St Bartholomew's Day, 1662*. Birmingham: Walter J Sackett

Dale, R W 1907. *History of English Congregationalism*. London: Hodder & Stoughton

Dannatt, T 1959. *Modern Architecture in Britain*. London: Batsford

[Dannatt] 1972. *Trevor Dannatt: Buildings and Interiors 1951/72* (introduction by Theo Crosby). London: Lund Humphries

Darby, H C (ed) 1976. *A New Historical Geography of England After 1600*. Cambridge: Cambridge University Press

Darbyshire, A 1897. *An Architect's Experiences*. Manchester: J E Cornish

Darley, G 1975. *Villages of Vision*. London: Architectural Press

Darley, G 2013. 'Equal in death: The Moravian burial ground'. *Chapels Society Newsletter* 53, May 2013, 9–14

Davey, C J 1955. *The Methodist Story*. London: Epworth Press

Davey, P 1980. *Arts and Crafts Architecture*. London: Architectural Press

Davies, C M 1873. *Unorthodox London: Or Phases of Religious Life in the Metropolis*. London: Tinsley Brothers

Davies, H 1961. *Worship and Theology in England: From Watts and Wesley to Maurice, 1690–1850*. Princeton, NJ: Princeton University Press

Davies, H 1975. *Worship and Theology in England: From Andrewes to Baxter and Fox, 1603–1690*. Princeton, NJ: Princeton University Press

Davies, J G 1962. *The Architectural Setting of Baptism*. London: Barrie & Rockliff

Davies, J G 1968. *The Secular Use of Church Buildings*. London: SCM Press

Davies, J G (ed) 1972. *A Dictionary of Liturgy and Worship*. London: SCM Press

Dawson, A 1901. *Joseph Parker, DD, His Life and Ministry*. London: S W Partridge & Co

Dawson, A E 1956. *The Story of the Stained Glass Windows in the Fairhaven Congregational Church*. [Lytham St Annes, Lancs: the church]

Deacon, M 1980. *Philip Doddridge of Northampton 1702–51*. Northampton: Northamptonshire Libraries

Dearing, J 1993. *The Church That Would Not Die: A New History of St Mary's Castle Street, Reading*. Reading: Baron Birch

Dees, N 1991a. 'The ecumenical sharing of churches'. *Church Building* **19**, Autumn 1991, 12–14

Dees, N 1991b. 'The shared Church of Christ the Cornerstone, Milton Keynes: An appraisal by Nigel Dees – Part One'. *Church Building* **19**, Autumn 1991, 14–16

Dees, N 1993. 'The shared Church of Christ the Cornerstone, Milton Keynes: Nigel Dees completes his appraisal'. *Church Building* **24**, Winter/Spring 1993, 33–4

de Maré, E (ed) 1948. *New Ways of Building*. London: Architectural Press (and revised edn 1951)

Densham, W and Ogle, J 1899. *The Story of the Congregational Churches of Dorset*. Bournemouth: W Mate & Sons

Dews, D C 2011. 'Thomas Howdill (1840–1918) & Charles Barker Howdill (1863–1940)', *in* Webster, C (ed) *Building a Great Victorian City: Leeds Architects and Architecture 1790–1914*. Huddersfield: Northern Heritage Publications in association with the Victorian Society, West Yorkshire Group, 279–92

Dickinson, P and Hodgson, J 1986. *Now and Then: An Illustrated Regional Survey of Aspects of the Architectural Heritage of the Methodist Church*. Chorley: Countryside Publications

Dishon, D 2000. 'Three men in a gondola: Ruskin, Webb and Street', *in* Webster, C and Elliott, J (eds) *'A Church as it Should be': The Cambridge Camden Society and its Influence*. Stamford, Lincs: Shaun Tyas, 190–210

Dobb, A J 1978. *Like a Mighty Tortoise: A History of the Diocese of Manchester*. Littleborough, Lancs: distributed by Upjohn and Bottomley Printers

Doel, D C 1994. *Old Chapel and the Unitarian Story*. London: Lindsey

Dolbey, G W 1964. *The Architectural Expression of Methodism: The First Hundred Years*. London: Epworth Press

Donnelly, M C 1968. *The New England Meeting Houses of the Seventeenth Century*. Middletown, CT: Wesleyan University Press

Dougherty, B 2003. *Rugby Baptist Church Bicentenary: A History of 200 Years of Baptist Worship in Rugby*. [Rugby: the church]

Downes, K 1969. *Hawksmoor*. London: Thames & Hudson

Drew, E M 1925. *Then and Now: A Brief History of the United Congregational Church, Wellingborough*. [Wellingborough: the church]

Drummond, A L 1934. *The Church Architecture of Protestantism: An Historical and Constructive Study*. Edinburgh: T & T Clark

Drummond, A L 1938. 'The architectural interest of the English meeting house'. *RIBA Journal*, 15 Aug 1938, 909–17

Drummond, A L 1942. 'A century of chapel architecture, 1840–1940'. *Congregational Quarterly* **XX**/4, Oct 1942, 318–28

Duckworth, D 1998. *A Branching Tree: A Narrative History of the General Conference of the New Church*. London: General Conference of the New Church

Du Prey, P de la Ruffinière 2000. *Hawksmoor's London Churches: Architecture and Theology*. Chicago and London: University of Chicago Press

Ede, J *et al* 1994. *Halls of Zion: Chapels and Meeting-Houses in Norfolk*. Norwich: Centre of East Anglian Studies

Elleray, D R 1981. *The Victorian Churches of Sussex*. London: Phillimore

Ellerby, W and Pritchett, J P 1993. *A History of the Nonconformist Churches of York* (Borthwick Texts and Calendars 18, Royle, E (ed)). York: University of York, Borthwick Institute of Historical Research

Elmes, J 1830. *Metropolitan Improvements or London in the Nineteenth Century ... original drawings ... by Thos H Shepherd*. London: Jones & Co

Emanuel, M (ed) 1980. *Contemporary Architects*. London and Basingstoke: Macmillan

Erffa, H von, and Staley, A 1986. *The Paintings of Benjamin West*. New Haven and London: Yale University Press

Essex County Council 1973. *A Design Guide for Residential Areas*. [Chelmsford]: Essex County Council

Evans, N *et al* 1979. *Looking Back at Fressingfield*. Fressingfield, Suffolk: Fressingfield WEA

Fairfax, J 1700. *Primitiæ Synagogæ, a Sermon Preached at Ipswich, April 26 1700, at the Opening of a New Erected Meeting-House*. London: printed for Tho Parkhurst in Cheapside, and sold by Henry Truelove at Ipswich

Farr, N 1991. *At the Heart of the City: A Methodist Mission in the Twentieth Century*. Sheffield: Victoria Hall Methodist Church

Faulkner, T and Greg, A 1987. *John Dobson, Newcastle Architect 1787–1865*. Newcastle upon Tyne: Tyne and Wear Museums Service

Felstead, A *et al* 1993. *Directory of British Architects 1834–1900*. London and New York: Mansell

Fenwick, J 2004. *The Free Church of England: Introduction to an Anglican Tradition*. London: T & T Clark

Fincham, K and Tyacke, N 2007. *Altars Restored: The Changing Face of English Religious Worship, 1547–c 1700*. Oxford: Oxford University Press

The First Book of Discipline (1560) as printed in *The First and Second Book of Discipline*, 1621. Amsterdam: [G Thorp]

Fisher, M 1995. *A Vision of Splendour: Gothic Revival in Staffordshire 1840–90*. Stafford: M Fisher

Fitch, S H G [c 1963] *Colchester Quakers*. Colchester: Stanley G Johnson

Forsaith, P 2013. 'Material and cultural aspects of Methodism: Architecture, artefacts and art', *in* Gibson, W *et al* (eds) *The Ashgate Research Companion to World Methodism*. Farnham, Surrey, and Burlington, VT: Ashgate, 387–406

Forsyth, M 2003. *Bath*. New Haven and London: Yale University Press

Foster, A 2005. *Birmingham*. New Haven and London: Yale University Press

Foulston, J 1838. *The Public Buildings Erected in the West of England as Designed by John Foulston*. London: J Williams, Library of Arts

Fowler, G H 1873. *A Manual on Chapel Architecture for the Use of Methodist Churches*. [London]: Primitive Methodist Book Room.

Fox, A W 1924. *Annals of the Todmorden Unitarian Church: A Centennial Sketch*. Todmorden: Waddington & Sons

Foyle, A 2004. *Bristol*. New Haven and London: Yale University Press

Freeman, J M 1990. *W D Caröe RStO, FSA: His architectural achievement*. Manchester and New York: Manchester University Press

Friedman, T 1997. *Church Architecture in Leeds 1700–1799* (Thoresby Society 2 ser **7**). Leeds: Thoresby Society

Friedman, T 2003. 'The Octagon Chapel, Norwich'. *The Georgian Group Journal* **XIII**, 54–77

Friedman, T 2011. *The Eighteenth-Century Church in Britain*. New Haven and London: Yale University Press

Fritsch, K E O 1893. *Der Kirchenbau des Protestantismus*. Berlin: [np]

Fullerton, W Y [c 1929] *F. B. Meyer: A Biography*. London and Edinburgh: Marshall, Morgan and Scott

Gardiner, A G 1923. *Life of George Cadbury*. London: Cassell

Gawne, E 1998. 'Buildings of endearing simplicity: The Friends meeting houses of Hubert Lidbetter'. *Twentieth Century Journal* **3**: *The Twentieth Century Church*, 85–92

Gay, J D 1971. *The Geography of Religion in England*. London: Duckworth

Gibbs, S 2008. *Mr Metcalfe's Congregational Chapel at Roxton*. Roxton, Beds: Guilden

Gifford, J *et al* 1988. *Edinburgh*. Harmondsworth: Penguin

Gilbert, A D 1976. *Religion and Society in Industrial England: Church, Chapel and Social Change 1740–1914*. London: Longmans

Giles, R 1996. 'A review: The new Church of Jesus Christ of the Latter-day Saints'. *Church Building* **40**, Jul–Aug 1996, 67

Gill, R 2003. *The 'Empty' Church Revisited*. Aldershot: Ashgate

Gillett, E and MacMahon, K A 1980. *History of Hull*. Oxford: Oxford University Press

Gillett, M 1993. *Talbot Village: A Unique Village in Dorset 1850–1993*, new edn. Bournemouth: Bournemouth Local Studies Publications

Girouard, M 1977. *Sweetness and Light: The 'Queen Anne' Movement 1860–1900*. Oxford: Clarendon Press

Godfrey, W H 1951. 'The Unitarian chapels of Ipswich and Bury St Edmunds'. *Archaeological Journal* **108**, 121–7

Gomme, A 2000. *Smith of Warwick: Francis Smith, Architect and Master-Builder*. Stamford, Lincs: Shaun Tyas

Gomme, A and Jenner, M 2011. *An Architectural History of Bristol*. Wetherby: Oblong

Goodall, T 1962. *Westminster Central Hall: The First Fifty Years, 1912–1962*. London: Westminster Central Hall

Gordon, A 1896. *Historical Account of Dukinfield Chapel and its School*. Manchester: Cartwright and Rattray Ltd

Gould, G P 1883. *Sermons and Addresses by the Late George Gould ... with a Memoir by His Son*. London: Jarrold & Sons

Gradidge, R 1988. 'Weathervane of Taste'. *Country Life* **182**, 16 June 1988, 174–5

Grass, T 2012. *'There my friends and kindred dwell': The Strict Baptist Chapels of Suffolk and Norfolk*. Ramsey, Isle of Man: Thornhill Media

Greenwood, D 1996. 'Salvation Army halls'. *Church Building* **41**, Sep–Oct 1996, 33

Gregory, B 1884. *The Life of F J Jobson*. London: T Woolmer

Grindley, D 2007. 'Headington Baptist'. *Church Building* **105**, May–Jun 2007, 54–7

Grinsell, L V *et al* 1950. *Studies in the History of Swindon*. Swindon: Swindon Borough Council

Guillery, P 2004. *St George's German Lutheran Church*. London: Historic Chapels Trust

Gwynn, R 2001. *Huguenot Heritage: The History and Contribution of the Huguenots in Britain*, 2 edn. Brighton: Sussex Academic Press

Hague, G and Hague, J 1986. *The Unitarian Heritage: An Architectural Survey of Chapels and Churches in the Unitarian Tradition in the British Isles*. Sheffield: PB Godfrey [distributor]

Hair, J 1898. *Regent Square: Eighty Years of a London Congregation*. London: James Nisbet & Co

Hall, I and Hall, E 1973. *Historic Beverley*. York: William Sessions

Hallett, M and Rendall, J (eds) 2003. *Eighteenth-Century York: Culture, Space and Society*. York: University of York, Borthwick Institute of Historical Research

Hamberg, P G 2002. *Temples for Protestants: Studies in the Architectural Milieu of the Early Reformed Church and of the Lutheran Church* (first pub in Swedish in 1955). Gothenburg: Acta Universitatis Gothoburgensis

Hammond, P 1960. *Liturgy and Architecture*. London: Barrie & Rockliff

Hammond, P (ed) 1962. *Towards a Church Architecture*. London: Architectural Press

Hankinson, S 2007. *The Octagon Unitarian Chapel, Norwich*. Norwich: Octagon Unitarian Chapel

Harman, R and Minnis, J 2004. *Sheffield*. New Haven and London: Yale University Press

Harris, H W and Bryant, M [*c* 1913]. *The Churches and London*. [London]: Daily News and Leader

Harris, M 1935. *Pulpits and Preachers*. London: Methuen & Co

Harrison, M 2009. 'William Alexander Harvey', *in* Ballard, P (ed) *Birmingham's Victorian and Edwardian Architects*. Wetherby: Oblong Creative for the Birmingham and West Midlands Group of the Victorian Society, 527–53

Hartwell, C and Pevsner, N 2009. *Lancashire: North*. New Haven and London: Yale University Press

Hartwell, C *et al* 2004. *Lancashire: Manchester and the South-East*. New Haven and London: Yale University Press

Hartwell, C *et al* 2011. *Cheshire*. New Haven and London: Yale University Press

Hartwell, C *et al* 2016. *Derbyshire*. New Haven and London: Yale University Press

Harwood, E 1998. 'Liturgy and architecture: The development of the centralised eucharistic space'. *Twentieth Century Journal* **3**: *The Twentieth Century Church*, 51–74

Harwood, E 2001. 'Lansbury'. *Twentieth Century Journal* **5**: *Festival of Britain*, 141–54

Harwood, E 2008. *Nottingham*. New Haven and London: Yale University Press

Hatch, H 1957. *Manchester Road Methodist Church, Centenary 1857–1957*. [np]

Hay, G 1957. *The Architecture of Scottish Post-Reformation Churches, 1560–1843*. Oxford: Clarendon Press

Herbert, R and Shackley, B 2009. 'Crouch and Butler' *in* Ballard, P (ed) *Birmingham's Victorian and Edwardian Architects*. Wetherby: Oblong for the Birmingham and West Midlands Group of the Victorian Society, 451–78

Herford, R T 1893. *Memorials of Stand Chapel*. Prestwich: H Allen

Hewett, A P 1959. *The Story of an Old Meeting House: A Short History of St Nicholas Old Meeting House, Now Called the Unitarian Meeting House, Friars Street, Ipswich*, 2 edn. Ipswich: Unitarian Press

Hewlings, R 2011. 'A lost architect revealed: Weston Park, Staffordshire'. *Country Life* **250**, 3 Aug 2011, 34–9

Hewlings, R 2012. 'The architect of Weston Park'. *Georgian Group Journal* **XX**, 22–32

Hickman, D 1970. *Birmingham*. London: Studio Vista

Higson, P J W 1965. 'Some leading promoters of Non-conformity and their association with Lancashire chapelries following the revolution of 1688. *Transactions of the Lancashire and Cheshire Antiquarian Society* **75** & **76**, (1965–6), 123–63

Higson, P J W 1972. 'A dissenting northern family: The Lancashire branch of the Willoughbys of Parham, 1640–1756'. *Northern History* **VII**, 31–53

Higson, P J W 2007. *The singular Lords Willoughby*. Newcastle-under-Lyme: Friarswood

Hill, R 2007. *God's Architect: Pugin and the Building of Romantic Britain*. London: Allen Lane

Hill, S 2010. 'The cross and the crown: The First Church of Christ, Scientist, Manchester, by Edgar Wood', *in* Skidmore, C (ed) *Chapels and Chapel People: Miscellany 2* (The Chapels Society Occ Pubs Ser **5**). London: The Chapels Society, 52–72

Hillson, N 1940. *Inquiring Christian in England*. London: Methuen

Historic Chapels Trust 2000. *Todmorden Unitarian Church*. London: Historic Chapels Trust

Hitchcock, H-R 1954. *Early Victorian Architecture in Britain*, 2 vols. New Haven: Yale University Press; London: Architectural Press

Hitchcock, H-R 1971. *Architecture: Nineteenth and Twentieth Centuries*, 1st paperback edn. Harmondsworth: Penguin

Hitchen, H S and Dawson, T E 1962. *Wesley Chapel, Harrogate 1862–1962*. [Harrogate: the church]

Holland, J 1824. *The Picture of Sheffield*. Sheffield: George Ridge

Holmes, D and Rossi, A 1998. *Walpole Old Chapel*, 2 edn. Laxfield, Woodbridge: Walpole Friends of the Historic Chapels Trust

Holmes, G 1973. *The Trial of Doctor Sacheverell*. London: Eyre Methuen

Holt, A 1938. *Walking Together: A Study in Liverpool Nonconformity 1688–1938*. London: G Allen & Unwin

Homan, R 1984. *The Victorian Churches of Kent*. Chichester: Phillimore

Homan, R 1997. 'Mission and fission'. *Sussex Archaeological Collections* **135**, 265–82

Homan, R 2006. 'The aesthetics of Friends' meeting houses'. *Quaker Studies* **11**/1, 115–28

Hope, T 1835. *An Historical Essay on Architecture by the Late Thomas Hope. Illustrated from Drawings made by him in Italy and Germany*, 2 edn, 2 vols. London: John Murray

Horne, C S 1926. *A Popular History of the Free Churches* (1926 edn with additional chapter by Albert Peel). London: Congregational Union of England and Wales

Howard, C 2009. *A History of Trinity Church, Sutton 1907–2007*. [Sutton: the church]

Howard, D 1970. *London Theatres and Music Halls 1850–1950*. London: Library Association

Howard, D 1980. *The Architectural History of Venice*. London: Batsford

Howard, M 1977. 'Cottancin and an Exeter church'. *Concrete*, Jan 1977, 24–7

Howell, P 1968. *Victorian Churches*. Feltham: Country Life Books

Hubbard, E and Shippobottom, M 1988. *A Guide to Port Sunlight Village*. Liverpool: Liverpool University Press

Hughes, J Q 1969. *Liverpool*. London: Studio Vista

Hughes, S 2003. 'Thomas Thomas, 1817–88: The first national architect of Wales'. *Archaeologia Cambrensis* **152**, 69–166

Hutton, J E 1909. *A History of the Moravian Church*. London: Moravian Publication Office

Hutton, W 1783. *An History of Birmingham*, 2 edn. Birmingham: [np]

Hyde, M and Pevsner, N 2010. *Cumbria: Cumberland, Westmorland and Furness*. New Haven and London: Yale University Press

Ikin, C W 1997. *A Guide to Heath Street Chapel, Hampstead*. [London: np]

[Incorporated Church Building Society] 1956. *Sixty Post-War Churches*. London: Incorporated Church Building Society

Ison, W 1948. *The Georgian Buildings of Bath*. London: Faber & Faber

Ison, W 1952. *The Georgian Buildings of Bristol*. London: Faber & Faber

Jackson, N 1991. *Nineteenth Century Bath: Architects and Architecture*. Bath: Ashgrove

James, T S 1867. *The History of Litigation and Legislation Respecting Presbyterian Chapels and Charities in England and Ireland Between 1816 and 1849*. London and Birmingham: Hamilton, Adams & Co

Jeffery, P 1996. *The City Churches of Sir Christopher Wren*. London: Hambledon Press

Jewson, C B 1957. *The Baptists in Norfolk*. London: Carey Kingsgate Press

Jobson, F J 1850. *Chapel and School Architecture as Appropriate to the Buildings of Nonconformists, Particularly to those of the Wesleyan Methodists: with Practical Directions for the Erection of Chapels and School-Houses*. London: Hamilton, Adams, & Co

Jones, A 1962. *Thesis and Survey of the Nonconformist Chapel Architecture in Merthyr Tydfil*. Merthyr Tydfil: Merthyr Libraries

Jones, A 1984. *Welsh Chapels*. Cardiff: National Museum of Wales

Jones, A 1996. *Welsh Chapels* (2 edn, expanded and revised). Stroud: Sutton

Jones, L (ed) 2005. *Encyclopedia of Religion*, 2 edn. Farmington Hills, MI: Macmillan Reference USA

Jones, P 1980. *Capeli Cymru*. Talybont: Y Lolfa

Jones, R P 1914. *Nonconformist Church Architecture: An Essay*. London: Lindsey Press

Jones, R P 1958. 'Memories of the origin and building of Ullet Road Church, Liverpool (1896–1899)'. *Transactions of the Unitarian Historical Society* **XI**/3 (1955–8), 77–82

Jordan, E K H 1956. *Free Church Unity: History of the Free Church Council Movement 1896–1941*. London: Lutterworth Press

Kadish, S 2001. *Bevis Marks Synagogue*. Swindon: English Heritage

Kadish, S 2011. *The Synagogues of Britain and Ireland*. New Haven and London: Yale University Press

Kaye, E 1996. *Mansfield College, Oxford: Its Origin, History and Significance*. Oxford: Oxford University Press

Kaye, R 1999. *Chapels in Essex*. [Colchester]: Chellow Dean

Kendall, E E 1955. *Doing and Daring: The Story of Melbourne Evangelical Free Church, Leicester*. Rushden, Northants: SL Hunt

Kendall, H B nd. *The Origin and History of the Primitive Methodist Church*, 2 vols. London: Edwin Dalton

Kershaw, H (ed) 1969. *1869–1969, The Centenary of the Todmorden Unitarian Church*. [Todmorden: the church]

Kilde, J H 2002. *When Church Became Theatre: The Transformation of Evangelical Architecture and Worship in Nineteenth-Century America*. Oxford: Oxford University Press

King, C and Sayer, D 2011. *The Archaeology of Post-Medieval Religion*. Woodbridge: The Boydell Press

Kirkpatrick, J 1845. *History of the Religious Orders and Communities of Norwich, Written About the Year 1725*. London and Norwich: Edwards and Hughes

Kivinen, P et al 1981. *Lars Sonck 1870–1956, Arkkitehti*. Helsinki: Museum of Finnish Architecture

Klaiber, A J 1931. *The Story of the Suffolk Baptists*. London: Kingsgate Press

Knowles, J M 1999. *Huntingdon Hall: Chapel to Concert Hall*. Worcester: Huntingdon Friends

Krinsky, C H 1996. *Synagogues of Europe*, 2 edn. New York: Dover

Kruppa, P S 1982. *Charles Haddon Spurgeon: A Preacher's Progress*. New York and London: Garland

Kunna, F 2004. 'Sunfields Methodist, Blackheath'. *Church Building* **90**, Nov–Dec 2004, 70–1

Kuyper, W 1980. *Dutch Classicist Architecture*. Delft: Delft University Press

Lake, J et al 2001. *Diversity and Vitality: The Methodist and Nonconformist Chapels of Cornwall*. Truro: Cornwall County Council, Archaeological Unit

Lake, J 2013. 'The survival of seating in Cornwall's Methodist and Nonconformist chapels'. *Chapels Society Journal* **1**: *Sitting in Chapel*, 59–76

Lampugnani, V M 1986. *The Thames and Hudson Encyclopaedia of 20th Century Architecture*. London and New York: Thames and Hudson

Lancaster, O 1936. *Progress at Pelvis Bay*. London: John Murray

Lang, J et al 1997. *Architecture and Independence: The Search for Identity – India 1880–1980*. Delhi, Oxford: Oxford University Press

Langlet, E V 1879. *Protestantiska Kyrkobyggnader enligt Centralsystemet*. Stockholm: Samson & Wallin

Langley, A S 1939. *Birmingham Baptists Past and Present*. London: Kingsgate Press

Laqueur, T W 1976. *Religion and Respectability: Sunday Schools and Working Class Culture 1780–1850*. New Haven and London: Yale University Press

Larmour, P 1987. *Belfast: An Illustrated Architectural Guide*. Belfast: Friar's Bush Press

Lascelles, R 1821. *The University and City of Oxford Displayed*. London: Sherwood, Neely and Jones

Latimer, J 1887. *Annals of Bristol in the Nineteenth Century*. Bristol: W & F Morgan

Lawton, E (ed) 1998. *Alan Pointon's History of Brown Edge*. Leek: Churnet Valley Books

Leach, P and Pevsner, N 2009. *Yorkshire West Riding: Leeds, Bradford and the North*. New Haven and London: Yale University Press

Lee, C E 1955. *St Pancras Church and Parish*. London: St Pancras Parochial Church Council

Lee, R [c 2009]. *The Scandinavian Seamen's Church in Liverpool*. Liverpool: A Wood & Co

Leigh, J et al 2010. *Bethesda Methodist Chapel, Hanley, Stoke-on-Trent: A History and Guide*. London: Historic Chapels Trust

Lemprière, R 1980. *Buildings and Memorials of the Channel Islands*. London: Hale

Lenton, J 2009. *John Wesley's Preachers*. Milton Keynes: Paternoster

Lessiter, S 2015. 'Architecture of the Church of the Christian Science'. *Acta Comparanda, Subsidia* **II**, 67–85

Lewin, S 1843. *Lincolnshire Churches*. Boston, Lincs: [np]

Lidbetter, H 1946. 'Quaker meeting houses, 1670–1850'. *Architectural Review*, Apr 1946, 99–116

Lidbetter, H 1979. *The Friends Meeting House*, 2 edn. York: Sessions

Lillie, W 1968. *The History of Middlesbrough*. Middlesbrough: The Mayor Alderman and Burgesses of the County Borough of Middlesbrough

Lindenboom, J 1950. *Austin Friars: History of the Dutch Reformed Church in London 1550–1950*. The Hague: Martinus Nijhoff

Lindley, K 1969. *Chapels and Meeting Houses*. London: John Baker

Linstrum, D 1978. *West Yorkshire Architects and Architecture*. London: Lund Humphries

Linstrum, D 1999. *Towers and Colonnades: The Architecture of Cuthbert Brodrick*. Leeds: Leeds Philosophical and Literary Society

Liscombe, R 1970. 'Economy, character and durability: specimen designs for the Church Commissioners, 1818'. *Architectural History* **13**, 43–57

Little, B 1947. *The Buildings of Bath, 47–1947*. London: Collins

Little, B 1953. *Exeter*. London: Batsford

Little, B 1966. *Catholic Churches Since 1623*. London: Hale

Little, B 1971. *Birmingham Buildings*. Newton Abbot: David and Charles

Little, W J and Cook, J D G 1986. *John Wesley's Chapel (The New Room 1739), A Short History of the Period 1929–1980*. Bristol: New Room booklet **6** (revised reprint of a 1980 pamphlet)

Llanover, Lady A W H (ed) 1861. *The Autobiography and Correspondence of Mary Granville, Mrs Delaney*. London: Richard Bentley

Lloyd, M 1988. *Digbeth-in-the-Field, 1938–1988*. [Digbeth: the church]

Lockett, W (ed) 1964. *The Modern Architectural Setting of the Liturgy*. London: SPCK

Lovell, J 2013. *Wattisham Baptist Church 1763–2013, 250 Years All of Grace*. Stowmarket: Polstead Press

MacLaren, G 1992. 'Bromley by Bow church and centre: Architect's report'. *Church Building* **23**, Autumn 1992, 48–50

McMurray, N 1988. *The Stained Glass of Wesley's Chapel*. London: Friends of Wesley's Chapel

Maguire, R and Murray, K 1965. *Modern Churches of the World*. London: Studio Vista

Mallary, P T 1985. *New England Churches and Meetinghouses*. New York: Vendome Press

[Manchester City Art Gallery] 1975. *Partnership in Style: Edgar Wood and J Henry Sellers*. Manchester: Cultural Services Department

March, O 1892. 'Ueber evangelischen Kirchenbau in England'. *Deutsche Bauzeitung* **XXVI**/59, 23 July 1892 , 351–4 and **XXVI**/61, 30 July 1892, 361–3

Mason, J and Torode, L 1997. *Three Generations of the La Trobe Family in the Moravian Church*. Newtownabbey: Moravian History Magazine

Mason, R 2015. 'The design of nineteenth-century Wesleyan space: Re-reading F J Jobson's *Chapel and school architecture*'. *Wesley and Methodist Studies* **7**/1, 78–99

Mate, C H and Riddle, C 1910. *Bournemouth 1810–1910*. Bournemouth: W Mate & Sons

Matthews, A G 1924. *The Congregational Churches of Staffordshire*. London: Congregational Union of England and Wales

Matthews, D H 1989. *Castle Street Meeting House – a History 1889–1989*. [London: D H Matthews]

Matthew Lloyd Architects, 2010. *Memorial Community Church [West Ham] ... Statement of Significance and Justification* (Unpublished)

Mawson, A 1992. 'Bromley by Bow: A theological perspective'. *Church Building* **23**, Autumn 1992, 51

May, G 1845. *A Descriptive History of the Town of Evesham*. Evesham and London: G May

Meller, H 1989. *Exeter Architecture*. Chichester: Phillimore

[Methodist Church Department for Chapel Affairs] 1961. *New Methodist Churches*. Manchester: Methodist Church Department for Chapel Affairs

Methodist Church Department for Chapel Affairs 1963. *Report for 1963, Statistical Returns made 1st December 1960*. Manchester: Methodist Church Department for Chapel Affairs

[Methodist Church Division of Property] 1974. *Plans and People*, *Division of Property Annual Report*. Manchester: Methodist Church Division of Property

[Methodist Church Property Division] 1990. *Everything's Possible: Renewal through buildings in rural Methodism*. Manchester: Methodist Church Property Division

[Methodist Church Property Division] 1994. David Calvert, *Building in Progress: New Methodist Chapels 1980–1993*. Manchester: Methodist Church Property Division

Middleton, G A T [c 1906]. *Modern Buildings, Their Planning, Construction and Equipment*, 6 vols. London: Caxton Publishing Co

Middleton Local Studies Group, 1950. *There is Holy Ground: A History of Methodism in Middleton 1760–1950*. Middleton: Middleton Local Studies Group

Middleton, R and Watkin, D 1980. *Neoclassical and 19th Century Architecture*. New York: Harry N Abrams

Middleton, T 1908. *A History of Hyde Chapel*. Manchester: Cartwright & Rattray

Miller, M 1989. *Letchworth: The First Garden City*. Chichester: Phillimore

Miller, M and Gray, A S 1992. *Hampstead Garden Suburb*. Chichester: Phillimore

Mills, E D 1945. 'The community church of the future'. *Architect and Building News*, 27 July 1945, 58–62

Mills, E D 1956. *The Modern Church*. London: Architectural Press

Mills, E D 1964. 'New churches for Nonconformists', *in* Lockett, W (ed) *The Modern Architectural Setting of the Liturgy*. London: SPCK, 70–7

Minnis, J with Mitchell, T 2007. *Religion and Place in Leeds*. Swindon: English Heritage

Moir, J and Letts, J 1999. *Thatch: Thatching in England 1790–1940* (English Heritage Research Transactions 5). London: James & James

Mooney, L 1996. *A Guide to Ullet Road Unitarian Church*. Liverpool: Ullet Road Unitarian Church

Mornement, A and Holloway, S 2007. *Corrugated Iron: Building on the Frontier*. London: Frances Lincoln

Morris and Co 1863. *Commercial Directory and Gazetteer of Lincolnshire*. Nottingham: Morris and Co

Murch, J 1835. *A History of the Presbyterian and General Baptist Churches in the West of England*. London: R Hunter

Muthesius, H 1901. *Die neuere Kirchliche Baukunst in England*. Berlin: W Ernst & Sohn

Muthesius, H 1902. *Der Kirchenbau der englischen Secten*, Königlich Sächsischen Technischen Hochschule zu Dresden. Halle: Buchdruckerei des Waisenhauses

Muthesius, S 1972. *The High Victorian Movement in Architecture 1850–1870*. London: Routledge and Kegan Paul

Nairn, I 1966. *Nairn's London*. Harmondsworth: Penguin

Nairn, I and Pevsner, N 1965. *Sussex*. Harmondsworth: Penguin

Nairn, I and Pevsner, N 1971. *Surrey*, (2 edn, revised by Cherry, B). Harmondsworth: Penguin

Neave, D (comp) 1991. *Lost Churches and Chapels of Hull*. Hull: Hull City Museums & Art Galleries

Neave, D and Neave, S 1990. *East Riding Chapels and Meeting Houses*. Beverley: East Yorkshire Local History Society

Newman, J 1976. *North East and East Kent*, 2 edn. Harmondsworth: Penguin

Newman, J and Pevsner, N 2006. *Shropshire*. New Haven and London: Yale University Press

Nicholson, C and Spooner, C [c 1911]. *Recent English Ecclesiastical Architecture*. London: Technical Journal

Nidderdale Chase Heritage Group 2012. *A History of Wath Chapel*. [Nidderdale]: Nidderdale Chase Heritage Group

Nierop-Reading, V 2002. 'Two Classical Nonconformist chapels in Norwich'. Unpublished MPhil thesis, University of Bath

Nightingale, B 1891. *Lancashire Nonconformity, Vol II*. Manchester: J Heywood

Nightingale, B 1906. *The Story of the Lancashire Congregational Union 1806–1906*. Manchester and London: J Heywood

Noble, J 2013. *Heswall Quakers: The Story of the First Seventy-Five Years of a Quaker Meeting*. Heswall: Society of Friends

North, J E [1996]. *A History of Jireh Chapel, Lewes*. Windmill Hill, Sussex: Huntingtonian Press

Nylander, J C 1980. 'Toward comfort and uniformity in New England meeting houses, 1750–1850', *in* Benes, P and Benes, J (eds) *New England Meeting House and Church: 1630–1850*. Boston, MA: Boston University, 86–100

Oakley, R 2011. *To the Glory of God: A History of the Development of the Salvation Army in the British Isles as Expressed, Illustrated and Symbolised Through its Buildings and Some Paintings*. Leamington Spa: R Oakley

Oatley, G 1930. 'On Wesley's New Room: An Address at the Re-opening of John Wesley's "New Room" in the Horsefair, Bristol, Feb 14, 1930'. (Copy in the New Room archive)

Obelkevich, J 1976. *Religion and Rural Society: South Lindsey 1825–1875*. Oxford: Clarendon Press

O'Connell, S 2003. *London 1753*. London: British Museum Press

O'Donnell, R 2000. ' "… blink [him] by silence?" The Cambridge Camden Society and A W N Pugin', *in* Webster, C and Elliott, J (eds) *'A Church as it Should be': The Cambridge Camden Society and Its Influence*. Stamford, Lincs: Shaun Tyas, 98–120

Oliver, R W 1968. *The Strict Baptist Chapels of England V: The Chapels of Wiltshire and the West*. London: Fauconberg Press for the Strict Baptist Historical Society

Onwin, G 1991. *As Above So Below*. Leeds: Henry Moore Sculpture Trust

Orbach, J 2011. 'Welsh chapels 1859–1914', *in* Sladen, T and Saint, A (eds) *Churches 1870–1914* (Victorian Society Studies in Victorian Architecture and Design **3**). London: Victorian Society, 44–61

Owen, D H 2012. *The Chapels of Wales*. Bridgend: Seren

Pace, P G 1990. *The Architecture of George Pace*. London: Batsford

Packer, G (ed) nd. *The Centenary of the Methodist New Connexion 1797–1897*, 2 edn. London: George Burroughs

Parker, G 1975. *Widcombe Baptist Church, Bath: The First 150 Years*. [Bath: np]

Parkinson, A J 2003. 'Chapel architecture', *in* Lionel Madden (ed) *Methodism in Wales: A Short History of the Wesley Tradition*. Llandudno: Conference Arrangements Committee, Methodist Conference, 39–60

Pass, A J 1988. *Thomas Worthington: Victorian Architecture and Social Purpose*. Manchester: Manchester Literary and Philosophical Publications

Payne, E A 1944. *The Free Church Tradition in the Life of England*. London: SCM Press

Pearson, E M 1967. *Maiden Street Methodist Church – Weymouth, 1867–1967*. Weymouth: Maiden Street Methodist Church

Peel, A 1931. *These Hundred Years: A History of the Congregational Union of England and Wales, 1831–1931*. London: Congregational Union of England and Wales

Peel, A 1948. *The Congregational Two Hundred 1530–1948*. London: Independent Press

Percy, C and Ridley, J (eds) 1985. *The Letters of Edwin Lutyens to his Wife Lady Emily*. London: Collins

Perkins, E B and Hearn, A 1946. *The Methodist Church Builds Again: A Consideration of the Purpose, Principles, and Plans for Methodist Church Building*. London: Epworth Press

Petford, A 2010. '*Horribile dictu*: Unitarians and ecclesiology in Northern England', *in* Skidmore, C (ed) *Chapels and Chapel People:*

Miscellany 2 (The Chapels Society Occ Pubs Ser **5**). London: The Chapels Society, 13–51

Pettman, K and Kingsford, H 1969. *Sutton Baptist Church 1869–1969*. [Sutton, Surrey: the church]

Pevsner, N 1952. *London except the Cities of London and Westminster*. Harmondsworth: Penguin

Pevsner, N 1954. *Cambridgeshire*. Harmondsworth: Penguin

Pevsner, N 1966. *Yorkshire: The North Riding*. Harmondsworth: Penguin

Pevsner, N 1967. *Yorkshire: The West Riding* (2 edn, revised by Radcliffe, E). Harmondsworth: Penguin

Pevsner, N 1969. *Lancashire 2: The Rural North*. Harmondsworth: Penguin

Pevsner, N 1974. *Suffolk* (2 edn, revised by Radcliffe, E). Harmondsworth: Penguin

Pevsner, N and Brooks, A 2007. *Worcestershire*. New Haven and London: Yale University Press

Pevsner, N and Harris, J 1989. *Lincolnshire* (2 edn, revised by Antram, N 1995). Harmondsworth: Penguin

Pevsner, N and Lloyd, D 1967. *Hampshire and the Isle of Wight*. Harmondsworth: Penguin

Pevsner, N and Neave, D 1995. *Yorkshire: York and the East Riding*. Harmondsworth: Penguin

Pevsner, N and Wedgwood, A 1966. *Warwickshire*. Harmondsworth: Penguin

Pevsner, N and Williamson, E 1994. *Buckinghamshire* (2 edn). Harmondsworth: Penguin

Pevsner, N and Wilson, B 1997. *Norfolk 1: Norwich and North-East*. Harmondsworth: Penguin

Phillips, H 1964. *Mid-Georgian London*. London: Collins

Picton, J A 1875. *Memorials of Liverpool*, 2 vols. London: Longmans, Green

Pietrusiak, J 2004. 'The local philanthropy of the Reckitt family, with particular reference to Hull Garden Village'. *Quaker Studies* **8**/2, Mar 2004, 141–71

Pocock, W F 1824. *Designs for Churches and Chapels*, new edn. London: J Taylor (copy in Princeton University Library)

Pond, C C 2007. 'The Sunday school and the life and design of the chapel', *in* Cherry, B (ed) *Dissent and the Gothic Revival* (The Chapels Society Occ Pubs Ser **3**). London: The Chapels Society, 72–83

Port, M H 1961. *Six Hundred New Churches: A Study of the Church Building Commission 1818–56*. London: SPCK

Port, M H 2006. *Six Hundred New Churches: The Church Building Commission 1818–1856*, 2 edn. Reading: Spire Books

Pottle, F A (ed) 1950. *Boswell's London Journal 1762–1763*. London: Heinemann

Powell, K 1980. *The Fall of Zion: Northern chapel architecture and its future*. London: SAVE Britain's Heritage

Powell, K and de la Hey, C 1987. *Churches – A Question of Conversion*. London: SAVE Britain's Heritage

Powicke, F J 1907. *A History of the Cheshire County Union of Congregational Churches*. Manchester: Griffiths

Price, D 2004. 'Two centuries of worship: New Methodist Church at Fulham Broadway'. *Church Building* **86**, Mar–Apr 2004, 28–31

Pritchard, Charles 1975. *"The Church Is People": A History of the Congregational Church in Oxted 1900–1975*. Tunbridge Wells: Flo-Print

Pugin, A W 1836. *Contrasts: or, a Parallel between the Noble Edifices of the Fourteenth and Fifteenth Centuries, and Similar Buildings of the Present Day; Shewing the Present Decay of Taste* (also revised 2 edn, 1841). London: A W Pugin

Pugin, A W 1841. *True Principles of Pointed or Christian Architecture*. London: John Weale

Pugin, A W 1843. *The Present State of Ecclesiastical Architecture in England*. London: Charles Dolman

Punshon, John 1986. *Portrait in Grey: A Short History of the Quakers*, revised edn. London: Society of Friends

Rack, H D (ed) 2011. *The Works of John Wesley, Vol 10*. Nashville: Abingdon Press

Reason, J [c 1962]. *A Fellowship of Churches, 1662–1962*. [Guildford: np]

Reed, C [c 1992]. *A Suffolk Tabernacle: The Ipswich Unitarian Meeting House*. Ipswich: William Lea

Rees, W B 1903. *Chapel Building: Hints and Suggestions*. Cardiff: Cardiff Printing Works

Reid, A 1999. 'The architectural career of E W Godwin' *in* Soros, S W (ed) *E W Godwin: Aesthetic Movement Architect and Designer*. New Haven and London: Yale University Press, 127–84

Reid, R 2000. 'George Wightwick: A thorn in the side of the ecclesiologists', *in* Webster, C and Elliott, J (eds) *'A Church as it Should be': The Cambridge Camden Society and Its Influence*. Stamford, Lincs: Shaun Tyas, 239–56

Rhind, N 1976. *Blackheath Village and Environs 1790–1970: Vol 1, The Village and Blackheath Vale*. Blackheath: Bookshop Blackheath

Richard Pedlar Architects 2002. *Conservation Plan for John Wesley's New Room*. (Unpublished)

Richardson, A 2007. 'The building of Union Chapel', *in* Cherry, B (ed) *Dissent and the Gothic Revival* (The Chapels Society Occ Pubs Ser **3**). London: The Chapels Society, 5–18

Richardson, M 1983. *Architects of the Arts and Crafts Movement*. London: Trefoil

Richardson, M 1991. 'Overstrand Methodist Chapel', *Society of Architectural Historians of Great Britain, Annual Conference notes*, 49–50

Ricketts, A 2007. *The English Country House Chapel: Building a Protestant Tradition*. Reading: Spire Books

Rickman, T 1817. *An Attempt to Discriminate the Styles of English Architecture from the Conquest to the Reformation*. London: Longmans

Ridley, J 1968. *John Knox*. Oxford: Clarendon Press

Ridley, J 2002. *The Architect and his Wife: A Life of Edwin Lutyens*. London: Chatto & Windus

Robertson, C 1975. *Bath: An Architectural Guide*. London: Faber

Robinson, H W *et al* 1912. *The Baptists of Yorkshire: Being the Centenary Memorial Volume of the Yorkshire Baptist Association*. Bradford: William Byles and Sons; London: Kingsgate Press

Robson, P 2014. *Fred Rowntree, Architect*. York: Newby Books

Rose, E 2009. 'What is the name of this house?' *Chapels Society Newsletter*, 41, May 2009, 8–11

Rose, E A 1974. 'Ashton churches and chapels', *in* Harrop, S A and Rose, E A (eds) *Victorian Ashton*. Ashton-under-Lyne: Tameside Libraries and Arts Committee, 60–75

Rose, M 1951. *The East End of London*. London: Cresset Press

Rosenau, H 1941. 'The synagogue and protestant church architecture'. *Journal of the Warburg and Courtauld Institutes* IV (1940–1), 80–4

Rossi, A 1998. 'Norwich Roman Catholic Cathedral', in *Miscellany 1* (The Chapels Society Occ Pubs Ser **1**). London: The Chapels Society, 1–34

Roth, L M 1983. *McKim, Mead & White, Architects*. New York: Harper & Row

Routley, E 1961. *The Story of Congregationalism*. London: Independent Press

Rowdon, H H 1967. *The Origins of the Brethren 1825–50*. London: Pickering & Inglis

Rowe, V A 1970. *The First Hertford Quakers*. Hertford: Religious Society of Friends

Rowntree, B S 1901. *Poverty: A Study of Town Life*. London: Macmillan & Co

RCHME 1981. *An Inventory of the Historical Monuments in the City of York, V: The Central Area*. London: HMSO

Royle, E 1994. *Queen Street Chapel and Mission, Huddersfield*. Huddersfield: Huddersfield Local History Society

Royle, E 2011. 'From Philistines to Goths: Nonconformist chapel styles in England', *in* Christopher Dyer *et al* (eds) *New Directions in Local History Since Hoskins*. Hatfield: University of Hertfordshire Press, 186–215

Rudolph, H 1938. *Herrnhuter Baukunst und Raumgestaltung: Der bürgerliche Barock der Brüdergemeine Herrnhut*. Herrnhut: [np]

Sadie, S (ed) 2001. *The New Grove Dictionary of Music and Musicians*, 2 edn. Oxford: Oxford University Press

Saint, A 1976. *Richard Norman Shaw*. New Haven and London: Yale University Press

Salmon, F 2000. *Building on Ruins: The Rediscovery of Rome and English Architecture*. Aldershot: Ashgate

Sandall, R 1950. *The History of the Salvation Army, Vol 2*. London: Nelson

Saunders, M 1982. *The Churches of S S Teulon*. London: Ecclesiological Society

Scammell, S D 1887. *Jubilee and Bicentenary Memorial of the Old Stafford Meeting House*. Stafford: Halden and Son

Schlenther, B S 1997. *Queen of the Methodists: The Countess of Huntingdon and the Eighteenth-century Crisis of Faith and Society*. Bishop Auckland: Durham Academic Press

Schnell, H 1973. *Der Kirchenbau des 20. Jahrhunderts in Deutschland*. Munich and Zürich: Verlag Schnell & Steiner

Schofield, J 1994. *Medieval London Houses*. New Haven and London: Yale University Press

Scourfield, R and Haslam, R 2013. *Powys*. New Haven and London: Yale University Press

Seaborne, M 1971. *The English School: Its Architecture and Organization, 1370–1870*. London: Routledge and Kegan Paul

Senn, R 1963. 'The Spirit of Poverty'. *Churchbuilding* **9**, Apr 1963, 23

Serjeant, I 2011. 'James Simpson (1791–1864)', *in* Webster, C (ed) *Building a Great Victorian City: Leeds Architects and Architecture 1790–1914*. Huddersfield: Northern Heritage Publications in association with the Victorian Society, West Yorkshire Group, 135–58

Serjeant, I 2013. 'From joiner to architect: James Simpson and the design of pews'. *Chapels Society Journal* **1**: *Sitting in Chapel*, 39–58

Service, A (ed) 1975. *Edwardian Architecture and its Origins*. London: Architectural Press

Service, A 1977. *Edwardian Architecture: A Handbook to Building Design in Britain 1890–1914*. London: Thames and Hudson

Seymour, A C H 1839. *The Life and Times of Selina, Countess of Huntingdon*, 2 vols. London: W E Painter

Sharp, D (ed) 1969. *Manchester*. London: Studio Vista

Shaw, W A 1894. *Manchester Old and New*, 3 vols. London: Cassell

[Sheild, G W C] 1896. *Jubilee of Belgrave Presbyterian Church, West Halkin Street: An Historical Sketch of the Congregation, Schools and Mission from 1845 to 1895*. London: GWC Shield

Sherwood, J and Pevsner, N 1974. *Oxfordshire*. Harmondsworth: Penguin

Simpson, M 1985. *Thomas Adams and the Modern Planning Movement*. London: Mansell

Sinclair, J B and Fenn, R W D 1990. *Marching to Zion: Radnorshire Chapels*. Kington, Herefordshire: Cadoc Books

Skidmore, C 2012. 'Chapel beginnings of a secular architect: The case of Edwin Lutyens'. *Chapels Society Newsletter*, 50, May 2012, 10–12

Sladen, T and Saint, A (eds) 2011. *Churches 1870–1914* (Victorian Society Studies in Victorian Architecture and Design **3**). London: Victorian Society

Smith, A A (revised by Phillips, A) 2002. *Emmanuel United Reformed Church, Cambridge: The Bond Memorial Windows*. [Cambridge: the church]

Smith, F G 1963. *The Bethesda Story*. [Ipswich: np]

Smith, G E Kidder 1961. *The New Architecture of Europe*. Harmondsworth: Penguin

Smith, G E Kidder 1964. *The New Churches of Europe*. London: Architectural Press

Smith, I 2004. *Tin Tabernacles: Corrugated Iron Mission Halls, Churches and Chapels of Britain*. Pembroke: Camrose Organisation

Smith, I and Muncaster, J 1992. 'The Church of Christ the Cornerstone, Milton Keynes, architects' account'. *Church Building* **22**, Summer 1992, 52–3

Smithies, P 1988. *The Architecture of the Halifax Piece Hall 1775–1779*. Halifax: [P Smithies]

Southall, K H 1974. *Our Quaker Heritage: Early Meeting Houses built prior to 1720 and in use today*. London: Friends Home Service Committee

Spears, P 2001. 'Salvation Army redevelopment, Park Crescent Terrace, Brighton'. *Church Building* **72**, Nov–Dec 2001, 10–13

Spicer, A (ed) 2012. *Lutheran Churches in Early Modern Europe*. Farnham: Ashgate

Spraggon, J 2003. *Puritan Iconoclasm during the English Civil War*. Woodbridge: Boydell Press

Sprunger, K L 1982. *Dutch Puritanism: A History of English and Scottish Churches of the Netherlands in the Sixteenth and Seventeenth Centuries*. Leiden: Brill

Spufford, M 1968. 'The dissenting churches in Cambridgeshire from 1660 to 1700'. *Proceedings of the Cambridge Antiquarian Society* **61**, 67–95

Spurgeon, C H 1897–1900. *C H Spurgeon's Autobiography, compiled from his diary, letters and records*, 4 vols. London: Passmore and Alabaster

Stamp, G and Amery, C 1980. *Victorian Buildings of London, 1837–87*. London: Architectural Press

Stamp, W W 1863. *The Orphan House of Wesley*. London: J Mason

Stanley-Morgan 1955. 'Some Victorian chapel-builders: An analysis of 19th century congregational architecture in England'. *Congregational Quarterly* **XXXIII**/3, July 1955, 236–46

Stanton, P 1971. *Pugin*. London: Thames and Hudson

Stead, G 1998. *The Moravian Settlement at Fulneck 1742–1790* (Thoresby Society 2 Ser, **9**). Leeds: Thoresby Society

Stell, C 1976. *Architects of Dissent: Some Nonconformist Patrons and their Architects*. London: Dr Williams's Trust

Stell, C 1986. *An Inventory of Nonconformist Chapels and Meeting-houses in Central England*, RCHME. London: HMSO

Stell, C 1991. *An Inventory of Nonconformist Chapels and Meeting-houses in South-West England*, RCHME. London: HMSO

Stell, C 1994a. *An Inventory of Nonconformist Chapels and Meeting-houses in the North of England*, RCHME. London: HMSO

Stell, C 1994b. 'Wesley's Chapel, City Road, Islington'. *Transactions of the Ancient Monuments Society* **38**, 15–29

Stell, C 1997. 'Nonconformist chapels and meeting-houses', *in* Hicks, C (ed) *Cambridgeshire Churches*. Stamford, Lincs: Paul Watkins, 168–79

Stell, C 1998. 'Great meeting houses', in *Miscellany 1* (The Chapels Society Occ Pubs Ser **1**). London: The Chapels Society, 34–49

Stell, C 1999. 'Puritan and Nonconformist meetinghouses in England', *in* Finney, P C (ed) *Seeing beyond the Word: Visual Arts and the Calvinist Tradition*. Grand Rapids, MI and Cambridge, UK: Eerdmans, 49–51

Stell, C 2000. 'Nonconformist architecture and the Cambridge Camden Society' *in* Webster, C and Elliott, J (eds) *'A Church as it Should Be': The Cambridge Camden Society and Its Influence*. Stamford, Lincs: Shaun Tyas, 317–30

Stell, C 2002. *An Inventory of Nonconformist Chapels and Meeting-houses in Eastern England*. Swindon: English Heritage

Stell, C 2008. *Nonconformist Communion Plate and Other Vessels* (The Chapels Society Occ Pubs Ser **4**). London: The Chapels Society

Stephens, W B (ed) 1970. *History of Congleton*. Manchester: published for the Congleton History Society by Manchester University Press

Stewart, C 1956a. *The Architecture of Manchester: An Index to the Principal Buildings and their Architects 1800–1900*. Manchester: Libraries Committee

Stewart, C 1956b. *The Stones of Manchester*. London: Edward Arnold

Stewart, M 1984. *300 Years – The Story of St James's*. Newcastle upon Tyne: [St James's United Reformed Church]

Stirling, I 1988. *'The Church by the Arch': An Historical Outline of the Abbey United Reformed Church, Romsey, 1662–1988*. [Romsey: the church]

Stonehouse, R 2008. *Trevor Dannatt, Works and Words*. London: Black Dog

Street, G E 1850. 'On the proper characteristics of a town church'. *The Ecclesiologist* **11**, 227–33

Street, M J 1902. *F B Meyer, His Life and Work*. London: Partridge

Stuart, J and Revett, N 1762. *The Antiquities of Athens*, first published in parts between 1762 and 1830 and reissued regularly until 1858. London: various

Summerson, J 1970. *Architecture in Britain 1530–1830,* 1st integrated edn. Harmondsworth: Penguin

Summerson, J 1978. *Georgian London*, revised edn. Harmondsworth: Penguin

Survey of London 1949. **XXI** *Parish of St Pancras, Part 3: Tottenham Court Road and Neighbourhood*. London CC: London

Survey of London 1955. **XXV** *St George's Fields*. London CC: London

Survey of London 1957. **XXVII** *Spitalfields and Mile End New Town*. London CC: London

Survey of London 1980. **XL** Grosvenor Estate in Mayfair, Part 2 (The Buildings). London CC: London

Survey of London 1986. **XLII** *Kensington Square to Earl's Court*. London CC: London

Sutcliffe, J 1996. *The History and Architecture of Square Chapel, Halifax*. Hebden Bridge: J Sutcliffe

Sutermeister, H 1977. *The Norwich Blackfriars*. Norwich: City of Norwich, Norwich Survey

Swigchem, van, C A *et al* 1984. *Een Huis voor het Woord: Het Protestantse Kerkinterieur in Nederland tot 1900*. The Hague: Staatsuitgeverij

Swindells, T 1907. *Manchester Streets and Manchester Men*. Manchester: Cornish

Tabor, J A 1863. *Nonconformist Protest Against the Popery of Modern Dissent, as Displayed in Architectural Imitations of Roman Catholic Churches*. Colchester: [np]

Taylor, J and Binfield, C (eds) 2007. *Who They Were in the Reformed Churches of England and Wales, 1901–2000*. Donington: Shaun Tyas for the United Reformed Church History Society

Taylor, J and Taylor, E 1848. *History of the Octagon Chapel, Norwich*. London: Charles Green

Telford, J 1886. *Two West End Chapels*. London: Wesleyan Methodist Book Room

Temple, P 1992. *Islington Chapels*. London: RCHME

[Tewkesbury Borough Council] 2001, *Old Baptist Chapel Court and Burial Ground, Tewkesbury*. Tewkesbury: Tewkesbury Borough Council

Thackray, E 1922. *Stand Chapel and School 1672–1922: 250th Anniversary of the Royal Licensing of the Congregation*. Whitefield: H Bingham

Thom, D 1854. *Liverpool Churches and Chapels*. Liverpool: E Howell

Thom, J H (ed) 1872. *Letters, Embracing his Life, of John James Tayler*, 2 vols. London and Edinburgh: Williams and Norgate

Thomas, J A 1976. 'Liturgy and architecture 1932–60: Methodist influences and ideas'. *Proceedings of the Wesley Historical Society* **XL**/4, 106–13

Thomas, J and Porteus, C A 1936. *Memorials of Lowther Street Congregational Church, Carlisle 1786–1936*. Carlisle: Charles Thurnam & Sons

Thompson, D M 1972. *Nonconformity in the Nineteenth Century*. London: Routledge & Kegan Paul

Thompson, P 1971. *William Butterfield*. London: Routledge & Kegan Paul

Thoresby, R 1715. *Ducatus Leodiensis*. London: printed for Maurice Atkins

[Thoresby] 1832. *Letters of Eminent Men Addressed to Ralph Thoresby, FRS*, 2 vols. London: Henry Colburn and Richard Bentley

Thorne, R 2011. *The Methodist Church, Sidwell Street, Exeter: A Visitor's Guide*, revised reprint. Exeter: Sidwell Street Methodist Church

Timbs, J 1855. *Curiosities of London*. London: Bogue

Toulmin, J 1791. *The History of the Town of Taunton*. London: J Johnson

Trimen, A 1849. *Church and Chapel Architecture*. London: Longman, Brown, Green and Longmans

Tschudi-Madsen, S 1981–3. 'Veien hjem. Norsk arkitektur 1870–1914' *in* Berg, K (ed) *Norges kunsthistorie Vol 5*. Oslo: Glydenhal, 7–108

Turner, Revd M *et al* 2005. *Methodist Central Hall, Westminster*. Norwich: Jarrold

Tyack, G *et al* 2010. *Berkshire*. New Haven and London: Yale University Press

Tyerman, L 1876–7. *The Life of the Rev George Whitefield*, 2 vols. London: Hodder and Stoughton

Upton, C 1993. *A History of Birmingham*. Chichester: Phillimore

Upton, D 1986. *Holy Things and Profane: Anglican Parish Churches in Colonial Virginia*. New York: Architectural History Foundation; Cambridge, MA: and London: MIT Press

Urwick, W (ed) 1864. *Historical Sketches of Nonconformity in the County Palatine of Cheshire*. London and Manchester: Kent & Co and Septimus Fletcher

VCH Essex VI 1973. Powell, V (ed) *A History of the County of Essex, Vol VI*. Oxford: Oxford University Press

VCH Staffs VI 1979. Greenslade, M and Johnson, D (eds) *A History of the County of Stafford, Vol VI*. Oxford: Oxford University Press

VCH Staffs VIII 1963. Jenkins, J (ed) *A History of the County of Stafford, Vol VIII*. Oxford: Oxford University Press

VCH Warwicks VII 1964. Stephens, W (ed) *A History of the County of Warwick, Vol VII, the City of Birmingham*. Oxford: Oxford University Press

VCH York East Riding I 1969. Allison, K (ed) *A History of the County of York East Riding, Vol 1, the City of Kingston upon Hull*. Oxford: Oxford University Press

Verey, D 1973a. 'Architecture of great assurance: Samuel Whitfield Daukes I'. *Country Life* **154**, 6 Dec 1973, 1914–16

Verey, D 1973b. 'A Victorian eclectic at work: Samuel Whitfield Daukes II'. *Country Life* **154**, 13 Dec 1973, 2016–18

Verey, D and Brooks, A 2002. *Gloucestershire 2: The Vale and the Forest of Dean*. New Haven and London: Yale University Press

Vickers, J A 1961. *The Story of Canterbury Methodism*. Canterbury: St Peter's Methodist Church

Virgoe, N and Williamson, T (eds) 1993. *Religious Dissent in East Anglia*. Norfolk: Norfolk Archaeological and Historical Research Group and the Centre of East Anglian Studies, University of East Anglia

Wade, R 1880. *The Rise of Nonconformity in Manchester with a Brief Sketch of the History of Cross Street Chapel*. Manchester and London: 'Unitarian Herald' Office

Wagner, M 1982. *Not an Easy Church*. St Ives, Cambridgeshire: Free Church URC St Ives

Wakeling, C 1984. 'The architecture of the Nonconformist churches during the Victorian and Edwardian years'. Unpublished PhD thesis, University of East Anglia

Wakeling, C 1987. 'Methodist architecture in north Staffordshire: The first seventy-five years', *in* Morgan, P (ed) *Staffordshire Studies: Essays Presented to Denis Stuart*. Keele: University of Keele, 155–67

Wakeling, C 1995. 'The Nonconformist traditions: Chapels, change and continuity', *in* Brooks, C and Saint, A (eds) *The Victorian Church*. Manchester: Manchester University Press, 82–97

Wakeling, C 1998. 'Rolling in the aisles: Nonconformist perspectives on the Gothic', *in* Salmon, F (ed) *Gothic and the Gothic Revival*. Manchester (University of Manchester Faculty of Arts): Society of Architectural Historians of Great Britain, 37–44

Wakeling, C 2001. 'A room nearly semi-circular'. *Architectural History* **44**, 265–74

Wakeling, C 2007. 'Nonconformity and Victorian Architecture', *in* Cherry, B (ed) *Dissent and the Gothic Revival* (The Chapels Society Occ Pubs Ser **3**). London: The Chapels Society, 39–71

Wakeling, C 2013. 'Sitting around: Some nonconformist shapes of worship'. *Chapels Society Journal* **1**: Sitting in Chapel, 3–27

Walford, E 1878. *Old and New London, Vol 4*. London: Cassell

[Walker Art Gallery] 1981. *The Art Sheds 1894–1905*. Liverpool: Walker Art Gallery

Walker, L 2011. 'Women and church art', *in* Sladen, T and Saint, A (eds) *Churches 1870–1914* (Victorian Society Studies in Victorian Architecture and Design **3**). London: Victorian Society, 121–43

Walmsley, L S 1912. *Fighters and Martyrs for the Freedom of Faith*. London: James Clarke

Ward, W R 1966. 'The cost of establishment: Some reflections on church building in Manchester' *in* Cuming, G J (ed) *Studies in Church History Vol 111*. Leiden: Brill, 277–89

Wardle, J W 1943. *Sketches of Methodist History in Leek and the Moorlands 1753 to 1943*. [np]

[Watchtower Bible and Tract Society] 1993. *Jehovah's Witnesses: Proclaimers of God's Kingdom*. New York: Watchtower Bible and Tract Society

Watkin, D 1974. *The Life and Work of C R Cockerell, RA*. London: Zwemmer

Watts, M R 1978. *The Dissenters I: From the Reformation to the French Revolution*. Oxford: Clarendon Press

Watts, M R 1995. *The Dissenters II: The Expansion of Evangelical Nonconformity*. Oxford: Clarendon Press

Watts, M R 2015. *The Dissenters III: The Crisis and Conscience of Nonconformity*. Oxford: Oxford University Press

Weatherhead, P 1983. 'Working for the Church', in *Building Refurbishment and Maintenance*, **3**/8, Dec 1983, 48–9

Weaver, S A 1987. *John Fielden and the Politics of Popular Radicalism 1832–1847*. Oxford: Clarendon Press

Webster, C (ed) 2011. *Building a Great Victorian City: Leeds Architects and Architecture 1790–1914*. Huddersfield: Northern Heritage Publications in association with the Victorian Society, West Yorkshire Group

Webster, C and Elliott, J (eds) 2000. *'A Church as it Should be': The Cambridge Camden Society and Its Influence*. Stamford, Lincs: Shaun Tyas

Welch, E 1962. 'Dissenters' meeting houses in Plymouth to 1852'. *Report and Transactions of the Devonshire Association for the Advancement of Science, Literature and Art* **94**, 579–612

Welch, E 1967. 'Dissenters' meeting houses in Plymouth 1852–1939'. *Report and Transactions of the Devonshire Association for the Advancement of Science, Literature and Art* **99**, 181–212

Welch, E 1995. *Spiritual Pilgrim: A Reassessment of the Life of the Countess of Huntingdon*. Cardiff: University of Wales Press

Welch, E (ed) 1975. *Two Calvinistic Methodist Chapels 1743–1811: The London Tabernacle and Spa Fields Chapel*. London: London Record Society

Welch, E (ed) 1996. *Bedfordshire Chapels and Meeting Houses: Official Registration 1672–1901*. Bedford: Bedfordshire Historical Record Society

Wesley, J. *The Journal of the Rev John Wesley*. Various printed versions; the standard or bicentenary edn (Curnock, N ed) was published in London in 1938 by Epworth Press

Westfall, W and Thurlby, M 1990. 'Church architecture and urban space: The development of ecclesiastical forms in nineteenth-century Ontario', in Keane, D and Read, C (eds) *Old Ontario: Essays in Honour of J M S Careless*. Toronto, Oxford: Dundurn Press, 118–147

Weyres, W 1957. *Neue Kirchen im Erzbistum Köln 1945–1956*. Düsseldorf: [np]

Weyres, W and Bartning, O 1959. *Kirchen: Handbuch für den Kirchenbau*. Munich: Callwey

Whiffen, M 1950. *The Architecture of Sir Charles Barry in Manchester and Neighbourhood*. Manchester: Royal Manchester Institution

White 1856 and 1872. *History, Gazetteer and Directory of Lincolnshire*, 2 edn 1856, 3 edn 1872. Sheffield: White

White, H W 1991. *Taunton's Historic Chapels, A Visitor's Guide* (leaflet)

Whitefield G 1771. *A Select Collection of Letters of George Whitefield, Vol I*. London: printed for Edward and Charles Dilly

Whitley, W T 1913. *Baptists of North-West England*. London: Kingsgate Press

Whittingham, S 2011. *Sir George Oatley: Architect of Bristol*. Bristol: Redcliffe Press

Who's Who in Architecture 1923. London: The Architectural Press

Who's Who in Congregationalism [c 1933]. London: Shaw Publishing Co with the Independent Press

Who's Who in Methodism 1933. London: The Methodist Times and Leader (Methodist Publications Ltd)

Wickham, E R 1957. *Church and People in an Industrial City*. London: Lutterworth Press

Wiggins, A R 1964. *The History of the Salvation Army, Vol IV, 1886–1904*. London: Nelson

Wiggins, A R 1968. *The History of the Salvation Army, Vol V, 1904–1914*. London: Nelson

Williams, N 2004. *Black Country Chapels*. Stroud: Sutton Publishing

Williams, N 2006. *More Black Country Chapels*. Stroud: Sutton Publishing

Williams, N 2008. *Black Country Chapels: A Third Selection*. Stroud: Sutton Publishing

Willis, R 1964. *Nonconformist Chapels of York 1693–1840*. York: York Georgian Society

Wills, J [c 1884] *Hints to Trustees of Chapel Property and Chapel Keepers' Manual*, 3 edn. (Reprinted 1993 with introduction by David Barton. Woodbridge: The Chapels Society)

Wilson, J 1846. *A Memoir of the Life and Character of Thomas Wilson*. London: John Snow

Wilson, M 1968. *The English Chamber Organ*. Oxford: Cassirer

Wilson, N D 1998. ' "Sane, if unheroic": The work of William John Hale (1862–1929)', in *Miscellany 1* (The Chapels Society Occ Pubs Ser **1**). London: The Chapels Society, 51–73

Winter, E P 1960. 'The administration of the Lord's Supper among Baptists of the seventeenth century'. *Baptist Quarterly* **XVIII**, 196–204

Wood, F T 1944. *A History of Underbank Chapel, Stannington*. Sheffield: JW Northend

Woodall, D *et al* 2009. *Newport Wesleyans and their Chapel 1789–2009*. [Newport, East Yorks: np]

Woodhead, B T 1934. *An Historical Sketch of the Beginnings of Christian Science in Lancashire and the North of England, and the Early Days of First Church of Christ, Scientist, Manchester*. Manchester: John Taylor

Wordsall, F 1981. *The City that Disappeared*. Glasgow: The Molendinar Press

Wordsworth, R B (ed) 2012. *The Cockermouth Congregational Church Book (1651–c 1765)*, Cumberland and Westmorland Antiquarian and Archaeological Society, Record Ser **XXI**. [Carlisle]: Cumberland and Westmorland Antiquarian and Archaeological Society

Worth, R N 1870. *History of the Town and Borough of Devonport*. Plymouth: Brendan

Wren, C 1750. *Life and Works of Sir Christopher Wren. From the Parentalia or Memoirs by his Son Christopher*, reprinted 1903. Campden, Glos: Essex House Press

Wright, N R 1986. *The Book of Boston*. Buckingham: Barracuda

Wright, J J 1921. *The Story of Chowbent Chapel*. Manchester: H Rawson

Wright, W G 1951. *Notes for a History of Armitage*. Lichfield: AC Lomax's Successors

Wright, P 2009. 'Sunfields Methodist Church – architect's account'. *Church Building* **119**, Sep–Oct 2009, 8–11

Wykes, D L 1991. 'James II's religious indulgence of 1687 and the early organization of dissent: The building of the first Nonconformist meeting-house in Birmingham'. *Midlands History*, 86–102

Yates, N 2000. *Buildings, Faith and Worship: The Liturgical Arrangement of Anglican Churches 1600–1900*, revised edn. Oxford: Oxford University Press

Yates, N 2008. *Liturgical Space: Christian Worship and Church Buildings in Western Europe 1500–2000*. Aldershot: Ashgate

Young, E and Young, W 1956. *Old London Churches*. London: Faber

Index